Bilingual Course of Athletic Training

运动防护学双语教程

张恩铭　主编

北京体育大学出版社

策划编辑 佟 晖
责任编辑 佟 晖
责任校对 潘海英
版式设计 联众恒创

图书在版编目（CIP）数据

运动防护学双语教程 = Bilingual Course of
Athletic Training：汉、英 / 张恩铭主编 . -- 北京：
北京体育大学出版社 , 2024.12
ISBN 978-7-5644-4101-2

Ⅰ . ①运… Ⅱ . ①张… Ⅲ . ①运动保护－双语教学－
高等学校－教材－汉、英 Ⅳ . ① G819

中国国家版本馆 CIP 数据核字 (2024) 第 107105 号

运动防护学双语教程
YUNDONG FANGHUXUE SHUANGYU JIAOCHENG
                                            张恩铭　主编

出版发行：北京体育大学出版社
地　　址：北京市海淀区农大南路 1 号院 2 号楼 2 层办公 B-212
邮　　编：100084
网　　址：http://cbs.bsu.edu.cn
发 行 部：010-62989320
邮 购 部：北京体育大学出版社读者服务部 010-62989432
印　　刷：北京科信印刷有限公司
开　　本：787mm×1092mm　1/16
成品尺寸：185mm×260mm
印　　张：28.75
字　　数：733 千字
版　　次：2024 年 12 月第 1 版
印　　次：2024 年 12 月第 1 次印刷
定　　价：120.00 元

编委会

Preface

With the rapid development of national fitness programs in China, it is widely recognized and accepted by society that exercise can help prevent disease and enhance health. More and more people are participating in sports nowadays. In the field of national fitness, the demand for knowledge and services of scientific sports is increasing. In the field of competitive sports, athletes' requirements for preventing and rehabilitating of sports injuries are gradually increasing due to the higher level of competition and training. The cooperation and integrated development of multiple disciplines are necessary to meet the different needs of various groups of people who participate in sports because of complicated factors leading to sports injuries and multiple disciplines involved. Sports medicine is an all-encompassing interdisciplinary subject, and its professionals can provide targeted guidance and services. Athletic training is an important branch of sports medicine, specializing in research and service of preventing and managing sports injuries and diseases.

Different countries and regions have different developmental histories and experiences to prevent and manage sports injuries. Around the 2008 Beijing Olympic Games, Beijing Sport University established the undergraduate major of Sports Rehabilitation by combining the educational system of athletic training education in North America with the Chinese characteristics in athletic training. For over a decade, sports rehabilitation in China has made great progress, with a larger scale and a higher number of talented personnel; the concept and method of athletic training have been widely spread and applied; more and more professional athletes and fitness enthusiasts have benefited from it. However, in China, textbooks on athletic training remain relatively rare in the process of cultivating professionals. Having integrated Western theories and methods and Chinese experience and characteristics in athletic training, this textbook introduces modern athletic training theories and methods systematically, as well as demonstrates how traditional Chinese medicine is widely used in the prevention and treatment of injuries. This textbook aims to provide more options for the cultivation of athletic training professionals and more various professional reading materials for fitness enthusiasts. Additionally, in the background of the Belt and Road Initiative, we hope this bilingual athletic training textbook with Chinese characteristics can contribute to cultivating more professionals majoring in sports rehabilitation in developing countries.

This book is divided into four parts. The first part concerns basic concept of athletic training, mainly introducing the history of athletic training, and its status and importance in sports medicine. This part also takes Chengdu Sport University as an example to introduce how athletic training is conducted with the integration of traditional medicine in competitive sports. The responsibilities of foreign athletic trainers are elucidated in the end. The second part, "Sports Risk Management", gives an overview of strength and conditioning training, nutrition and environment. Additionally, this part also includes the details of on-the-field and off-the-field injury assessment and management. The third part discusses the common musculoskeletal injuries according to different body parts, including prevention, assessment, and identification and management. The fourth part covers theories and techniques of athletic training in traditional Chinese medicine, including common therapeutic techniques utilized in Chinese sports teams, such as *cupping*, *Guasha*, *Tuina*, and *Daoyin* in traditional rehabilitation.

Many thanks to Dr. Catherine Ortega, former president of the World Federation of Athletic Training & Therapy (WFATT), for her guidance and advice on this textbook. Thanks for the efforts of all of our editors. We took references from professional books in sports medicine, athletic training, sports medical supervision and traditional Chinese medicine, and endeavored to realize the original intention of compiling the textbook. Due to the limitations of time and the length of the textbook, we welcome criticism and correction of the shortcomings in order to make it better-conceived in the second edition. We also hope students majoring in Athletic Training and fitness enthusiasts can benefit from this book.

Zhang Enming
October, 2024

前言

　　随着我国全民健身事业的快速发展，运动对疾病预防和促进健康的作用已得到社会的广泛认同和接纳，同时参与运动的人数也在不断增加。在全民健身领域，人们对科学运动的知识和服务需求也日益增多；在竞技体育领域，随着比赛和训练水平的不断提升，运动员对相关运动伤病的预防和康复的要求也逐渐提高。由于运动伤病的影响因素较为复杂，涉及的学科领域也较多，这就需要多学科的协作和融合发展，以满足各类人群参与运动的不同需求。运动医学作为一门包罗万象的交叉学科，其分支领域的各类专业人才可以为科学运动提供有针对性的指导和服务。其中，运动防护（Athletic Training）正是专门针对运动伤病的预防和管理进行研究和开展服务工作的一个重要分支。

　　针对运动伤病预防和管理，不同的国家和地区都有着不同的发展历史和经验成果。为迎接 2008 年北京奥运会，北京体育大学借鉴北美地区运动防护专业的教育体系，并结合我国在运动防护方面的自身特色，创设了运动康复本科专业。十多年来，国内运动康复专业的办学规模得到较大扩张，培养的人才数量有了较大增长，运动防护的理念和方法进而得到广泛的传播和应用，越来越多的专业运动员和运动健身爱好者也从中受益。然而，在运动康复人才的培养中，目前国内运动防护课程相关专业教材的选择还较少。本教材将西方运动防护方面的理论和方法与我国运动防护工作的经验和特色相融合，在系统介绍现代运动防护理论和方法的同时，也介绍了中国传统医学治疗理论和技术在预防和治疗伤病中的广泛应用，为我国运动康复人才的培养提供了更多的教材选择，也为广大运动爱好者提供了更丰富的专业读物。此外，在"一带一路"倡议的背景下，这本具有中国特色的运动防护双语教材将为帮助发展中国家进行运动康复人才的培养工作贡献力量。

　　本教材分为四部分。第一部分"运动防护概论"主要介绍运动防护在国内外的发展历史，以及运动防护在运动医学中的位置和角色。这部分还特别以成都体育学院为例，介绍国内竞技体育领域中，结合传统医学的理论方法开展运动防护工作的相关情况；最后详细介绍了国外运动防护师的职责范围。第二部分"运动风险管理"主要围绕体能因素、营养因素及环境因素在运动伤病预防中的重要作用进行介绍。此外，这部分内容还分别对运动防护师在场地和场外对损伤的评估和处理进行了详细的介绍。第三部分"常见肌肉骨骼损伤"按照身体不同部位进行分章论述，各章均包括了常见损伤的预防、评估以及识别和处理三部分内容。第四部分"中医运动防护"特别介绍了我国传统医学中运动防护的理论基础和技术；在技术部分主要介绍了国内运动队广泛使用的拔罐、刮痧及推拿等治疗技术以及在传统康复养生中经典的导引技术。

　　感谢世界运动防护联合会（WFATT）前主席 Catherine Ortega 博士对本教材的指导和

建议，感谢编写组各位同仁的辛勤付出。在教材的编写中，编写组参考了国内外运动医学、运动防护、运动医务监督及中医学方面的专业书籍，力求实现编撰本教材的初心。鉴于编写时间和教材篇幅的限制，不足之处在所难免，欢迎读者批评指正，以期再版时能更加完善。我们希望运动防护相关专业的学生和广大运动健身爱好者能从本教材中受益。

张恩铭

2024 年 10 月

ONTENTS

PART IV Athletic Training in Traditional Chinese Medicine

目录

PART Ⅰ The Basic Concept of Athletic Training

第一部分　运动防护概论

1 History of Athletic Training

Athletic training (AT) is a new professional field that integrates multiple subjects such as sports training, medicine, physical therapy and physical education. The athletic trainers specialize in first aid, preventing, diagnosing and treating sports injuries and diseases. In clinics, educational institutions (such as colleges, universities and secondary schools), professional sports teams and other healthcare institutions, the athletic trainers cooperate with physicians, other medical personnel, administrators, coaches and parents to form a complete healthcare team for people participating in various physical activities. Although the concept of modern athletic training is relatively new and has not been introduced in China for a long time, the related work of athletic training has a long history nationwide and internationally.

一、运动防护的发展历史

运动防护是融合了运动训练、医学、物理治疗学和体育教育等多个学科知识结构的新专业领域。运动防护师是专门从事现场急救，运动伤病的预防、诊断和康复的专业人士。在诊所、中学、大学、职业运动队以及其他运动医疗机构中，运动防护师与医生、其他医疗人员、管理人员、教练、监护人合作，组成一个完整的医疗保障团队，为参与各种类型体力活动的人员提供服务。虽然现代运动防护概念形成和引入我国的时间不长，但是关于运动防护的相关工作在国内外都有着悠久的历史。

2 Sports Medicine and Athletic Training

The term "sports medicine" generically refers to a broad field of health care related to physical activity and sport. The American College of Sports Medicine (ACSM) defines sports medicine as "a multidisciplinary discipline that includes physiological, biomechanical, psychology and pathology related to exercise, whose application can maintain and improve an individual's function in physical activity, physical exercise and training." The field of sports medicine may be divided into performance promotion and injury prevention/management. The professional fields of performance promotion include exercise physiology, biomechanics, sport psychology, sports nutrition and physical training. The professional fields of sports injury prevention and treatment include clinical medicine, athletic training, physical therapy, sports massage, sports dentistry, osteopethy, orthopedics/prosthetics, chiropractic, pedopathy and emergency medical technology.

The field of athletic training mainly encompasses the prevention, first-aid, on-the-field treatment, and rehabilitation of athletic injuries and diseases. Specifically, three main distinctions between the AT scope of practice and other professions include: ① on-the-field emergency care; ② injury prevention; ③ end-stage functional rehabilitation. Research on the prevention of sports injuries has become a new medical field. Thus, a number of academic conferences in sports medicine, orthopedic medicine and trauma medicine have focused on injury prevention, which has enabled a platform for the AT profession to present this area of expertise.

二、运动医学与运动防护的关系

"运动医学"通常是指与体力活动和体育运动相关的广泛医学领域。美国运动医学学会（American College of Sports Medicine，ACSM）将运动医学定义为包括与运动有关的生理学、生物力学、心理学和病理学等多学科交叉的学科，这些学科的应用可以维持和改善个人的体力活动、体育锻炼和运动训练的功能能力。运动医学领域涵盖的内容可以分为运动表现促进和运动损伤的预防及处理两大部分。运动表现促进的专业领域主要包括运动生理学、生物力学、运动心理学、运动营养学、体能训练学等；运动损伤的预防及处理的专业领域包括临床医学、运动防护、物理治疗、运动按摩、运动牙科、整骨医学、矫形/假肢、整脊、足病和急诊医学技术等。

运动防护领域主要包括运动伤病的预防、急救、现场处置与康复训练等。特别是现场救护、损伤预防和后期功能康复三个方面工作，是运动防护区别于其他医学专业的主要内容。关于运动伤病预防方面的研究已经成为一个新的医学领域。大量的运动医学、骨科医学、创伤医学方面的学术会议把焦点放在伤病预防问题上，这为运动防护专业人士提供了一个展示这一领域专业知识的平台。

3 Athletic Training in Traditional Medicine

The theory and method of Traditional Chinese Medicine (TCM) are widely used in China's competitive sports. Chengdu Sport University (CDSU) is the paradigm that applies the theory and method of traditional medicine to the prevention and management of sports injuries. With the academic system of TCM running through multi-level training, CDSU has trained a large number of excellent sports medicine practitioners. CDSU has come to be known as the "Cradle of the Team Doctor" due to its sustained and excellent contribution to China's competitive sports healthcare.

Professor Zheng Huaixian is a famous sports medicine expert, martial artist and educator, founder of TCM sports medicine and pioneer of "Zheng's TCM Sports Medicine." He is recognized for utilizing various manipulations, skills and traditional Chinese herbs to treat acute and chronic sports injuries and diseases. In 1948, Mr. Zheng started teaching at the Sichuan

Provincial Physical Education College (the predecessor of CDSU) and engaged in martial arts education. After the foundation of the People's Republic of China, Mr. Zheng devoted himself to sports medicine and martial arts. In 1958, under the instruction of Marshal He Long that "a sports hospital must be set up," Mr. Zheng established China's first sport hospital–Affiliated Sport Hospital of CDSU. He also established the training courses of orthopedics and traumatology to train which would be China's first professional athletic trainers for The First National Games of the People's Republic of China. In 1960, the Ministry of Education and the National Sports Commission approved the establishment of the Sports and Health Department of CDSU, with Mr. Zheng appointed as the dean of the department. Then, he dedicated himself to teaching, research and clinical work related to sports injuries.

The clinical system of "Zheng's TCM Sports Medicine" is particularly famous for preventing and treating sports injuries through Chinese medicine, domestically and internationally. Professor Zheng initiated 11 types of osteopathy methods, 13 kinds of *Tuina* methods, 12 methods of meridians and acupoints for the treatment of sports injuries, pioneered the system of sports massage, summed up 55 Zheng's experiential acupuncture points, and more than 100 of Zheng's unique herbal prescription, and worked out a well-established method of functional exercise for sports injuries. All these methods originated from both Professor Zheng's work experience as well as TCM books. Mr. Zheng's successors introduced modern rehabilitation medicine, biomechanics, sports anatomy, pathophysiology and formed an injury prevention system which integrated medicine and sports and was based on the combination of TCM and Western medicine. This system has been widely used in the preparation for previous Olympic Games and major events nationwide and abroad.

三、传统医学中的运动防护

中国传统医学的理论和方法在国内竞技体育领域的应用非常广泛，其中最有代表性的是成都体育学院将传统医学中运动防护的理论和方法应用于损伤预防和康复中，将中医运动医学理论知识和专业技能贯穿于多层次人才培养体系中，培养了大批运动医学人才，为我国竞技体育事业做出了卓越贡献，被誉为"队医的摇篮"。

郑怀贤教授是我国著名的运动医学专家、武术家、教育家，是我国中医运动医学学科的奠基人，"郑氏中医运动医学"流派的开创者。他擅长运用手法、功法及中药治疗各种急慢性运动创伤及运动性疾病。1948年郑怀贤教授开始任教于四川省立体育专科学校（成都体育学院前身），从事武术教育工作。新中国成立后，郑怀贤教授全身心投入到运动医学和武术事业当中。1958年，在贺龙元帅"一定要把体育医院办起来"的指示下，郑怀贤教授开创了中国第一家体育医院——成都体育学院附属体育医院，并开始招收"骨伤科训练班"学员，旨在为新中国第一届全运会培养运动创伤防治的专业人才。1960年，教育部、国家体育运动委员会批准创建成都体育学院运动保健系，郑怀贤任系主任。由此，他全身心投入到运动创伤的教学、科研、临床中。

在"郑氏中医运动医学"临床体系中，尤以中医药手段防治运动创伤而蜚声国内外。郑怀贤教授开创了用于治疗运动创伤的正骨 11 法、推拿 13 法以及经穴 12 法，首创了运动按摩体系，总结出 55 个郑氏经验穴以及郑氏特色方剂 100 余个，并摸索出完善的运动创伤功能锻炼方法。究其源流，一方面源自于郑怀贤教授习武行医的人生经历，另一方面来源于中医传统典籍。其后，他的学生又在郑怀贤教授的理论基础上，将现代康复医学、生物力学、运动解剖学、病理生理学等理论引入，形成了"医体融合、衷中参西"的中西医结合防治运动创伤学术体系，被广泛运用到历届奥运会及国内外重大比赛的备战工作中。

4 Responsibilities of the Certified Athletic Trainer

Athletic Trainers Certified (ATC) are professionals who have received higher education in athletic training and specialize in this field. In the US, a certified athletic trainer must have a bachelor's or entry-level master's degree from a university or college that has an athletic training program accredited by the Commission on Accreditation of Athletic Training Education (CAATE) and have passed the Board of Certification (BOC) examination. The athletic training curriculum includes formal instruction in areas such as injury/illness prevention, first-aid and emergency care, assessment of injury/illness, human anatomy, physiology, physiotherapy, psychology and nutrition. Classroom learning is enhanced through clinical practice. Certified athletic trainers must complete a certain number of continuing education units (CEUs) to maintain and continue to expand their knowledge and skills as long as they continue to practice as athletic trainers.

The modern athletic training system in China has been established most recently, relatively late, and the relevant certification and responsibility norms are being gradually constructed and formed.

Athletic Training Domains
Athletic training mainly involves the following five areas abroad:
- Injury/disease prevention and wellness promotion.
- Injury examination, assessment and diagnosis.
- Emergency aid.
- Therapeutic intervention for sports injuries.
- Medical management and professional responsibility.

4.1 Injury/Disease Prevention and Wellness Promotion

Prevention is the best way to reduce the occurrence of sports injuries. The athletic trainer need to minimize the possibility and severity of sports injuries by paying attention to and monitoring the athlete's body, sports environment and potential risk factors during activities. Prevention can be carried out from: ① pre-participation physical exam; ② proper training and conditioning; ③ monitoring environmental conditions; ④ selection, installation, and maintenance of protective equipment; ⑤ proper diet and lifestyle; ⑥ appropriate medication use.

4.1.1　Pre-participation Physical Exam

The athletic trainer obtains a medical history and conducts physical examinations of the athletes before participation. The physical exam includes the measurement of height, weight, blood pressure and body composition. The medical exam should concentrate on cardiovascular, respiratory, abdominal, genital, skin, ear, nose, throat systems, and may include blood test and urinalysis. A brief orthopedic evaluation would include joint range of motion, muscle strength and functional tests.

4.1.2　Proper Training

It is essential that the athletes maintain a consistently high level of fitness during the preseason, the competitive season and the off-season. The stable physical fitness level is not only beneficial for improving athletic performance, but also plays a crucial role in preventing injuries and secondary injuries. The athletic trainer works to ensure safe body conditioning for peak performance by recovery during training periodization.

4.1.3　Monitoring the Environment

In order to maximize the performance of athletes and avoid sports injuries caused by the environment. The athletic trainer need to ensure a safe environment for competition (e.g., removing hurdles or gymnastics equipment from the perimeter of the practice area), and be familiar with the potential dangers associated with practicing or competing under inclement weather conditions to assist with adjustment of training or competition schedules as needed.

4.1.4　Protective Equipment

The athletic trainer shall select the protective equipment together with the coach and equipment managers, and be responsible for maintaining its state and safety. The design, manufacture and installation of specific protective orthopedic devices are also the responsibility of the athletic trainer.

4.1.5　Healthy Diet and Lifestyle

The athletic trainer understands the basic principles of nutrition and is aware of unhealthy lifestyle habits such as alcohol, tobacco and drug abuse. The athletic trainer encourages and educates athletes to make healthy lifestyle choices.

4.1.6　Using Medications Appropriately

Athletic trainers need to have certain knowledge of drug use, based on their understanding of the indications for drugs and the possible side effects that athletes may experience, to assist doctors in making reasonable decisions on the appropriate use of drugs. Additionally, athletic trainers should educate athletes to properly use medicine as prescribed and strategies to avoid drug abuse.

4.2 Examination, Assessment and Diagnosis

The athletic trainer is skilled in recognizing the nature and extent of an injury and provides the appropriate first aid, then transfers the appropriate first aid and then transfer the patient to appropriate medical personnel.

The off-the-field examination includes a brief medical history of what happened according to the athlete, observation, palpation and special tests (tests for range of motion, muscle strength, joint stability and brief neurological examinations). The athletic trainer shall record initial examination information. Once the athlete is transferred, the athletic trainer will hand it over to the physician, who is responsible for providing the final medical diagnosis of the injury. The initial clinical diagnosis can usually provide the basis and reference for the final medical diagnosis.

4.3 Emergency Aid

Due to the high risk of injury during training, team doctors cannot attend every training session. Therefore, athletic trainers must identify potential and serious injuries or illnesses on site and be able to promptly and correctly handle acute injuries.

4.4 Therapeutic Intervention

An athletic trainer is part of the sports medicine team and works in cooperation and under the guidance of the team physician. The athletic trainer will design rehabilitation protocols by selecting the appropriate therapeutic exercise, treatment equipment, manual therapy techniques and therapeutic exercises.

4.4.1 Designing and Supervising Rehabilitation Programs

Rehabilitation should start immediately after diagnosis of an injury or disease. The athletic trainer is responsible for designing, implementing and supervising the rehabilitation program from the time of initial injury until complete recovery. Therefore, sports protection professionals need to have a sufficient understanding of various rehabilitation training techniques and how these techniques can be most effectively integrated into rehabilitation plans. The athletic trainer establishes both short-term and long-term goals for the rehabilitation process and then will consistently reassess the condition of the athlete in order to modify and promote the treatment plan with precision.

4.4.2 Offering Psychosocial Intervention

Injury and illness produce a wide range of psychological disorders and trauma, which are critical yet often neglected in the rehabilitation process. The athletic trainers are educated to understand the behavior of athletes after injury, distinguish various symptoms of injury or disease caused by emotional problems, and help athletes complete rehabilitation tasks after a serious injury. If necessary, the athletic trainer will refer the athlete to a physician in timely manner to decrease the progression of a psychological issue that could impact the athlete's health or performance.

4.5 Health Management and Professional Responsibility

The athletic trainer is responsible for managing the health and injury records of patients, ordering and managing the inventory of sports protection supplies and equipment of his institution, and establishing daily regulations for sports protection.

4.5.1 Record Keeping

The athletic trainer should keep healthy records very carefully, including medical histories, pre-participation examinations, injury reports, treatment records and rehabilitation programs. Accurate documentation and records can help resolve medical disputes.

4.5.2 Ordering Equipment and Supplies

The athletic trainer should carry a variety of protective equipment to deal with any situation that may arise. The athletic trainer should plan the purchase of equipment and supplies based on past experience and prioritization of needs when working with stringent budgets.

4.5.3 Supervising the Assistants and Students

High quality and efficient athletic training assistants and students are important. It is the responsibility of the head athletic trainer to provide an environment in which assistants and athletic training students can continually learn and develop professionally.

4.5.4 Establishing Rules and Regulations for Daily Athletic Training Work

Athletic trainers should develop emergency management regulations for injuries and use appropriate channels for referral after receiving emergency treatment for injuries. In addition, effective preventive measures must be taken to reduce the occurrence and spread of contact-transmitted infectious diseases. Besides, effective preventive measures must be adopted to reduce the occurrence and spread of contagious diseases.

Scenario: Job of an athletic trainer

The athletic trainer works for professional and collegiate sports teams, secondary schools, sports medicine clinics, hospital ER and rehab clinics, military/government/law enforcement, and so on. The athletic trainer plays different roles when working in different agencies. Here are the responsibilities of an athletic trainer working in a secondary school in the US:

① Prevention of athletic injuries, including assessment of an athlete's physical status to participate.

② Management of athletic injuries.

③ Minimize the risk of re-injury and ensure the athlete's return to sport.

④ Health care administration, including keeping medical records, documentation and reporting of injuries, writing regulations and procedures, budgeting and transferring the injured athletes to appropriate health care professionals when indicated.

⑤ Education and counseling of coaches, parents, student athletic trainers and athletes.

⑥ Risk management and injury prevention, including: assisting in the arrangement of pre-participation examinations; assisting in the proper selection and fitting of protective equipment, including the application of bandages, braces, tape and pads; assisting in the inspection of fields and playing surfaces for safety;advising on weather-related conditions and paying attention to the protection of weather related injuries or diseases; advising on designing and implementation of fitness and physical conditioning programs for athletes; advising athletes on the achieving and maintaining optimal body weight and physical condition to prevent and avoid athletic injuries; advising the athletes on avoiding drug abuse.

⑦ Management of athletic injuries, including: recognizing the various types of musculoskeletal and nervous system injuries that may occur in athletes; understanding the various phases of healing and promoting an environment that assists in the healing process; and, after the initial management of the injury, referring the athlete for further assessment and accurate diagnosis.

⑧ Emergency aid of athletic injuries and physical conditions, including responsibilities for: assessment of acute injuries; correct first aid and emergency treatment for injured athletes, and using an automatic external defibrillator if necessary; the recognition and evaluation of potentially serious, life threatening injuries.

⑨ Treatment and reconditioning of athletic injuries, including: under the supervision of a physician, designing reconditioning programs that make use of appropriate therapeutic exercise, reconditioning equipment or therapeutic modalities in relation to athletic injuries; supervising the rehabilitation process and making the athletes completely return to exercise; designing and supervising an athletic injury reconditioning program and modifying that program based on the healing process; using appropriate therapeutic exercise techniques; designing a series of sport related activities that allow the athletes to gradually progress to complete functional ability; providing help in the social support of injured athletes, including compliance, competitiveness and adaptability after injury.

⑩ Organization and administration, including: responsibility for athletic training room maintenance;maintaining detailed injury reports, treatment records, and reconditioning programs; organizing equipment and materials; establishing rules and policies for the daily operation of the athletic training room; educating students majoring in athletic training by providing a high-quality environment that meets all rules and regulations, enabling them to achieve professional development.

⑪ Professional development and responsibilities, including: attending continuing education programs offered at state, district or national meetings; providing consultation and review for professional journals and textbooks; educating the community health care professionals in the role of certified athletic trainer; informing parents, coaches and athletes of the importance of high-quality health care for physical activities.

四、执业运动防护师的职责

执业运动防护师（Athletic Trainer Certified，ATC）是指接受过运动防护专业的高等教育并专门从事该领域工作的专业人员。在美国，成为一名执业运动防护师必须取得运动防护教育认证委员会（Commission on Accreditation of Athletic Training Education，CAATE）认可的大学或学院所开设的运动防护项目的学士学位或达硕士水平，完成相关课程及临床实践，毕业后通过运动防护师认证委员会（Board of Certification，BOC）的认证考试。运动防护专业的课程主要包括运动伤病预防、急救和紧急护理、损伤和疾病评估、人体解剖学和生理学、理疗学、心理学和营养学等。运动防护专业的学生通过临床实践进一步强化课堂学习。执业运动防护师必须在认证期内完成一定数量的继续教育单元的课程学习，以保持和不断拓展其作为运动防护师的专业知识和技能。

我国现代运动防护体系的建立时间较晚，相关的认证和责任规范正在逐步构建和形成中。

运动防护的工作领域

在国外，执业运动防护师的工作职责主要涉及以下五个领域：

● 运动伤病的预防和健康促进。

● 运动伤病的检查、评估和诊断。

● 现场紧急处理。

● 运动伤病的治疗干预。

● 医疗管理和专业责任。

（一）运动伤病的预防和健康促进

预防是减少运动损伤发生的最好手段。运动防护师需要关注并监控运动员身体、运动环境以及活动进行过程中可能出现的危险因素，尽可能降低运动伤病发生的可能性与严重性。可从以下几个方面进行预防：①赛前体检；②合理的防护和训练计划；③监测环境；④选择、正确安装和保养防护装备；⑤合理的饮食和生活方式；⑥合理使用药物。

1. 赛前体检

运动防护师应了解运动员的病史，并在运动员参与运动之前对其进行体检。检查的内容应包括身高、体重、血压和身体成分的测量。医学检查应集中于心血管、呼吸、腹部、生殖器、皮肤，以及耳、鼻和咽喉系统，还可以进行血液检测和尿分析。简单的评估包括关节活动度、肌肉力量和功能测试。

2. 合理的训练

运动员在赛季前、赛季中、赛季后都要保持一贯的高水平状态，这种稳定的体能水平不仅能够提高竞技表现，而且对于防止损伤和二次损伤的出现起到至关重要的作用。运动防护师的工作就是要让运动员在周期训练中通过运动后的恢复确保安全的身体条件，以达到最佳运动表现。

3. 监测环境

为了让运动员得到最好的发挥，避免因环境而造成运动损伤，运动防护师要确保运动环境的安全性。例如：清理练习区域周边障碍物、训练器材，熟悉恶劣天气的影响等，以帮助调整训练或比赛的安排。

4. 防护装备

运动防护师应与教练及设备管理人员一起选择防护设备，并负责保持其状态、维护其安全。特定保护矫形装置的设计、制作和安装也是运动防护师的职责。

5. 健康饮食和生活方式

运动防护师应对营养学有基本的了解，还应该了解不健康的生活习惯，如酒精、烟草和药物滥用等问题，鼓励和教育运动员选择健康的生活方式。

6. 合理使用药物

运动防护师要具备一定的药物使用知识，基于对药物的适应症以及运动员可能会出现的副作用的认识，协助医生对药物的恰当使用做出合理的决定。此外，运动防护师还应教育运动员恰当地按照处方使用药物，避免药物滥用。

（二）运动伤病的检查、评估和诊断

运动防护师必须熟练地识别伤病的性质和程度，并给予正确的现场急救处理，然后将患者转诊给相应的医务人员。

现场检查应包括：运动员的简短病史、观察、触诊、特殊实验（关节活动度、肌肉力量、关节稳定性的测试以及简单的神经学检查）。在初次检查中获得的信息应由运动防护师来记录，一旦运动员被转诊，运动防护师便应将其交予医生，医生负责提供损伤的最终医学诊断。初始临床诊断通常可以为最终的医学诊断提供基础的参考。

（三）现场紧急处理

由于训练过程中极其容易发生损伤，但是队医不可能出席每次训练过程，因此运动防护师必须要做到在现场就识别出潜在的、严重的损伤或疾病，而且要能及时正确处理急性损伤。

（四）运动伤病的治疗干预

运动防护师是运动医学团队的一部分，在队医的指导下合作开展相关工作。运动防护师通过选用恰当的治疗方法、康复设备、手法或运动疗法，设计出合适的康复方案。

1. 制订康复计划并监督执行

损伤或疾病的评估和诊断结束后，应立即进入康复阶段。运动防护师负责设计、实施和监督从最初损伤到完全恢复身体活动的康复计划。因此，运动防护师对康复训练的各种技术以及这些技术如何能够最有效地并入康复计划中要有足够的了解。运动防护师应该为运动员建立短期和长期的康复目标，并通过阶段性再评估来判断运动员的康复进展，合理准确地修改和推进康复计划。

2. 给予心理支持

损伤和疾病往往会带来一定的情绪反应和心理创伤，心理创伤的治疗是康复过程的一个至关重要但经常被忽视的方面。运动防护师需要解读运动员受伤后的行为，区分由情绪问题导致的损伤或疾病的各种症状，帮助运动员在受到严重损伤后完成康复任务，并在有需要时及时转诊，减少可能影响运动员健康和运动表现的心理问题。

（五）医疗管理和专业责任

运动防护师应该对运动员的健康和损伤记录进行管理，对所在机构的运动防护用品和设备进行订购和库存管理，以及制订日常运动防护工作规章。

1. 做好治疗记录

运动防护师要准确而详细地保持记录，包括病历、预先检查、损伤报告、治疗记录和康复计划。这些记录能够让运动防护师避免与运动员产生医疗纠纷。

2. 订购设备和用品

运动防护师应随身携带各种防护用品，以便处理任何可能出现的情况。在预算经费紧张时，运动防护师要基于过去的经验和需求的优先次序对设备和用品的购买做出规划。

3. 指导助理和运动防护学生

在进行运动防护的过程中，助理和运动防护学生的工作质量和效率是至关重要的。首席运动防护师有责任为助理和运动防护学生提供一个可以持续学习和发展专业能力的环境。

4. 制订日常运动防护工作规章

运动防护师应制订损伤的应急管理规章，在损伤得到紧急治疗后应使用恰当的渠道进行转诊。另外，必须采用有效的预防措施来减少接触性传染病的发生和传播。

示例：

运动防护师的工作机构包括职业／大学运动队、中学、运动医学诊所、医院急诊室和康复诊所、军队／政府／执法部门等。运动防护师在不同的机构开展工作时，在工作责任上也会有所不同，以下以美国某中学运动防护师的工作职责为例进行介绍。

①预防运动损伤，包括评估运动员参加运动前的身体准备情况。

②处理运动损伤。

③尽可能将再损伤风险最小化并确保运动员重返运动。

④医疗管理，负责病史记录、损伤记录和报告的保管，制订规范和流程，以及在必要时编制预算并将受伤的运动员转诊给合适的医疗人员。

⑤为教练、家长、运动防护专业的学生和运动员提供咨询和教育。

⑥损伤风险管理和预防，包括：协助运动前查体的安排；协助防护装备的合理选择和佩戴，包括绷带、支具、贴扎、衬垫的使用；协助检查场地安全；对天气相关状况提出建议，并注意与天气相关损伤或疾病的防护；对设计和实施运动员健身和训练项目提出建议；为运动员达到并保持最佳体重及身体条件以预防运动损伤提供建议；建议运动员避免滥用药物。

⑦运动损伤的处理，包括：识别可能发生在运动员身上的不同类型的肌肉骨骼和神经系统损伤；理解组织愈合的不同阶段，为损伤的康复提供更好的条件；在损伤的初步处理后，让运动员接受进一步的评估和准确的诊断。

⑧运动伤病的现场处理，包括：对急性损伤进行初级评估；对损伤运动员进行正确的急救和紧急处理，必要时使用自动体外除颤仪；识别并评估潜在的、危及生命的损伤。

⑨运动损伤的治疗和康复，包括：在医生的监督下，设计康复项目，包括利用与运动损伤相关的、合理的运动疗法、康复设备或其他治疗方法；监督康复过程，并使运动员完全地重返运动；设计和监督运动损伤康复项目，并基于康复过程调整项目；使用合理的运动治疗技术；设计一系列的与运动项目有关的活动，以使运动员能够渐进地恢复受伤部位的功能能力；在受伤运动员的社会支持上提供帮助，包括依从性、竞争性以及受伤后的适应能力。

⑩其他组织和管理工作，包括：负责维护运动防护室设施；及时记录详细的损伤报告、治疗记录、恢复计划；负责整理设备和物资；建立运动防护室日常操作的规则和政策；通过提供优质的、符合所有规则和规定的环境来教育运动防护专业的学生，使其得到专业的发展。

⑪专业的发展和责任，包括：参加国家、地区或国际性会议所提供的继续教育项目；对专业期刊、教材提供咨询、评审；以执业运动防护师的角色对社区医疗专业人员进行教育；告知监护人、教练和运动员高质量的健康管理对体育运动的重要性。

Summary

1. With the popular trend of sports and the need for care of athletes, the profession of athletic training was established and developed in the US, Canada and Japan. The coordination between martial arts and medicine has provided a foundation and reference for modern athletic training in China.

2. The field of sports medicine may be divided into performance promotion and injury prevention/management. The field of athletic training mainly encompasses the prevention, first aid, treatment and rehabilitation of athletic injuries and diseases as well as functional rehabilitation. Athletic training is a part of the field of sports medicine.

3. The theory and methods of traditional medicine are widely used in China's competitive sports injury management.

4. Athletic training mainly involves the following areas: Injury/disease prevention and wellness promotion; Examination, assessment and diagnosis; Emergency aid; Therapeutic intervention; Medical management and professional responsibility.

O Reviews

1. Please briefly describe the development of athletic training in the world and in China.
2. Please briefly describe the relations between sports medicine and athletic training.
3. Please briefly describe the responsibilities of ATC.

小结

1. 随着体育运动的流行以及运动员对医疗的需求，运动防护在美国、加拿大、日本等国家逐步发展起来。中国武医结合的模式为现代运动防护提供了重要参考。

2. 运动医学领域主要包括运动表现增强及损伤的预防和处理，而运动防护领域主要包括运动伤病的预防、急救、现场处置、康复训练。运动防护是运动医学领域的一部分。

3. 中国传统医学的理论和方法在国内竞技体育领域运动损伤的预防和康复中应用非常广泛。

4. 执业运动防护师的职责主要包括以下几个领域：运动伤病的预防和健康促进；运动伤病的检查、评估和诊断；现场紧急处理；运动伤病的治疗干预；医疗管理和专业责任。

O 复习题

1. 请简述运动防护在国内外的发展历史。
2. 请简述运动医学与运动防护的关系。
3. 请简述执业运动防护师的职责。

PART Ⅱ Sports Risk Management

第二部分　运动风险管理

Chapter 1 Strength and Conditioning Considerations
第一章　体能因素

⭕ Main Contents

1. Basic principles of strength and conditioning training.
2. Principles and methods of cardiorespiratory endurance training.
3. Principles and methods of muscle strength training.
4. Principles and methods of flexibility training.
5. Principles and methods of progressive functional training.

⭕ 主要内容

1. 体能训练的基本原则。
2. 心肺耐力训练的原则和方法。
3. 肌肉力量训练的原则和方法。
4. 柔韧性训练的原则和方法。
5. 渐进性功能训练的原则和方法。

1 Basic Principles of Strength and Conditioning Training

To minimize the risk of injury, the following principles should be applied in all training programs:

1.1 Safety

Ensure the safety of training. It is important that the trainers should teach the correct technique from the beginning; the athletes need to know whether they can keep the intensity based on their physical state. Athletes need regular sports injury screening to decrease the risk of sports injuries. The trainers need to record the outcomes of assessments and sports testing level so that they can establish the appropriate goals for athletes.

1.2 Overload

Overload refers to the load of training programs beyond the intensity that athletes have adapted. The SAID (specific adaptation to imposed demands) principle states that the body will gradually adapt to and overcome the stresses and overloads of varying intensity. Without overload stimulation, even the best plan will be limited in improving athletic performance. The purpose of the overload principle is to emphasize the higher training pressure on the body than before; however, the change of load must be controlled to avoid overtraining and sports injuries.

1.3 Consistency

The improvement in all aspects of the body achieved through training is temporary so that when the training load is inadequate or completely removed, the previous adaptations in physical and athletic performance will be partially or completely lost. Therefore, the athletes must engage in a consistent and regular training program to ensure effectiveness and improvement.

1.4 Progression

The intensity should be increased gradually within the individual's ability.

1.5 Specificity

The athletes are trained in a specific way to produce specific adaptations so as to obtain training benefits. In specific training, the participating muscles, movement patterns, and the way of muscle working (such as near and far fixation, movement speed, etc.) are similar to the actual sports skills of the athletes. Moreover, the arrangement of specific training is closely related to the seasonal cycle of the athletes. As the athletes enter the season stage, all forms of training should gradually transition from general training to specific training.

1.6 Individuality

Some people can handle high volumes of training while others may respond better to high intensities. The coaches should personalize and optimize the program for the individuals based on their differences.

1.7 Periodization Training

Physical fitness training may contain several cycles. Periodization refers to the period from the start to the end of one cycle. The goal of periodization is to keep the optimal performance and reduce the risk of injuries or overtraining. This can be achieved by following the principles:

● The training plan should be designed according to the main goals of performance in the season.

● Training loads should be increased gradually and periodically.

● Each training stage should follow a certain logical sequence.

● The training process should have a structured plan with scientific monitoring.

● Recovery or regeneration techniques should be contained in the program.

● Skill development and maintenance should be emphasized throughout the program.

● Each training program should be based on the previous one.

The cycles in sports training are generally divided into multi-year cycles, major cycles, medium cycles, and minor cycles. The duration of the multi-year cycle is generally more than 4 years; the major cycle usually lasts for no more than 1 year; the medium cycle lasts for 3~4 weeks; the minor cycle lasts for 1 week. In seasonal sports, the major cycle can be divided into pre-season, in-season and off-season. A medium cycle is further divided into transition, preparatory and competition periods. In the process of a major cycle, the training intensity, training quantity, and training characteristics change constantly, so that athletes can keep the best physical condition for the competition. As the competition approaches, the training program changes from high-volume, low-intensity, and non-sport-specific training to low-volume, high-intensity, and sport-specific training.

一、体能训练的基本原则

为减少损伤的风险，所有训练都应该遵循以下原则。

（一）安全性原则

确保训练环境安全；指导运动员正确的技术动作，让他们知道训练时应有的感觉以及运动强度是否适宜；运动员需要定期进行运动损伤筛查，降低运动损伤风险；运动防护师应该对运动员进行建档，记录运动员各种损伤评估的结果以及运动测试水平，以建立适合运动员的训练目标。

（二）超负荷原则

超负荷是指训练方案的负荷强度设定应超过运动员已经适应的负荷强度。SAID（Specific Adaptation to Imposed Demands）原则指出，当身体承受不同强度的压力和超负荷时，它会逐渐地适应并克服施加的负荷。如果没有超负荷的刺激，即使是再好的训练计划，也会在提升运动员的能力方面受到限制。超负荷原则的目的在于强调对身体施加比以往更高的训练压力，但是调节训练负荷一定要谨慎，不可为追求负荷强度而引起训练过度及运动损伤。

（三）持续性原则

通过训练获得的身体各方面素质的强化是暂时的，所以当训练负荷不足或者完全停止时，之前在身体和运动表现上所获得的适应，就会部分或者完全丢失。为了保证训练的有效性，运动员必须进行持续的、有规律的训练从而达到持续的进步。

（四）渐进性原则

逐步增加训练强度，确保个人能力能够适应增加的负荷。

（五）专项性原则

以专项的方式训练运动员以产生专项适应从而获得训练效益。在专项性训练中，参与的肌肉、动作模式以及肌肉的工作方式（如近远固定、动作速度等）都与运动员的实际运动技术相似。此外，专项性运动的安排与运动员的赛季周期密切相关，随着运动员进入赛季阶段，所有训练形式都应该逐渐从一般性训练向专项性训练过渡。

（六）个体化原则

有的运动员能够适应大训练量，而有的运动员能够适应高强度。因此，教练应该能够判断出个体差异并调整或改变训练计划，使其对每一名运动员来说都是最合适的。

（七）周期训练原则

体能训练以周而复始的方式进行，每一个循环的开始到结束就是一个周期。遵循周期训练能够为运动员带来最佳表现，同时减少出现运动损伤和过度训练的风险。现代周期训练理论的主要原则如下：
- 训练计划要根据赛季的主要目标设计。
- 训练负荷的增加要循序渐进且呈周期性。
- 各训练阶段要遵循一定的逻辑顺序。

- 训练过程要有科学监测计划。
- 训练计划中要安排促进恢复技术的应用。
- 训练计划中要重视专项技能发展及维持。
- 训练计划的每个阶段都应建立在前一阶段的基础之上。

运动训练过程中的周期一般分为多年周期、大周期、中周期和小周期。多年周期持续时间一般在 4 年以上，大周期持续时间一般小于 1 年，中周期一般持续 3 ~ 4 周，小周期一般持续 1 周。在赛季型运动中，大周期可分为赛季前、赛季中、赛季后阶段。中周期又可以进一步分为过渡期、准备期和比赛期。在大周期的过程中，训练的强度、训练量及训练特征都在不断变化，这样运动员就可以为比赛准备好最佳的体能水平。当比赛临近时，训练逐渐从大训练量、低强度、非专项训练向低训练量、高强度、专项训练转变。

2 Principles and Methods of Cardiorespiratory Endurance Training

Cardiorespiratory endurance is the ability to keep the whole body and large muscles active for a long time. Oxygen is supplied to tissues by the cardiorespiratory system. Cardiorespiratory endurance is critical for exercise performance and for preventing overfatigue for individuals who participate in sports. Cardiorespiratory endurance tests monitor the performance of the heart, lungs, and muscles during moderate to high-intensity exercise. Increasing cardiorespiratory endurance can improve oxygen intake and prolong the duration of exercise. Cardiorespiratory endurance may be improved through several methods, depending largely on individual's initial levels of cardiorespiratory endurance.

When exercising consistently, adaptation is formed in the cardiorespiratory system and the body can will be more healthy and utilize and produce energy more efficiently. Cellular metabolism will also be enhanced. The improvement in heart function is as follows: the heart's contractions are strengthened; the oxygen and blood flow of the heart itself are increased; the heart can pump more blood per beat; the heart's cavity size may increase in young adults; more blood is pumped through the circulatory system from the heart during each contraction. The improvement of cellular metabolism is as follows: increased muscle capillaries improve the capacity of oxygen supply and metabolic waste excretion; muscles can maximize the use of energy and oxygen, so they can work more efficiently; the number and size of the mitochondria increase; fats and lactic acids can be better utilized by muscles; the cells can be protected from chemical damage caused by free radicals.

2.1 Principles of Cardiorespiratory Endurance Training

Key factors in cardiorespiratory endurance training programs involve four considerations (FITT): Frequency, Intensity, Type, and Time.

2.2.1 Frequency

It is important to determine the appropriate training frequency based on the interaction between the intensity and the duration of the training, the training condition of the athlete, and the particular season. Excessive training will elevate the risk of injury, illness, and overtraining. On the contrary, low training frequency is difficult to promote body performance and adaptation.

2.1.2 Intensity

The intensity of training is the most critical factor, particularly in the early stages of training, when the body is forced to adjust to the increased load demand. The most accurate way to regulate the intensity of training is to monitor the oxygen consumption during exercise to determine the percentage of VO$_2$max. And the blood lactate concentration should be measured periodically to determine its relationship with VO$_2$max. If VO$_2$max testing is not available, we usually use heart rate (HR) or rating of perceived exertion (RPE) to monitor the intensity of the exercise. Heart rate is probably the most commonly used method to measure the intensity of aerobic training because it is closely related to oxygen consumption (Table 1-1). The exact measurement of maximal heart rate (HRmax) involves exercising at a maximal level and monitoring HR using an electrocardiogram, which is difficult to perform outside the laboratory. When laboratory testing is unavailable, age-predicted maximal heart rate (APHRmax) can be used as the basis for determining exercise intensity.

Table 1-1 Maximal oxygen uptake, heart rate reserve and maximal heart rate

%VO$_2$max	%HRR	%HRmax
50	50	66
55	55	70
60	60	74
65	65	77
70	70	81
75	75	85
80	80	88
85	85	92
90	90	96
95	95	98
100	100	100

The latest estimation of HRmax in adults would be HRmax = 206.9–(0.67×Age), according to *ACSM Guidelines for Exercise Testing and Prescription* (8*th ed*). Heart rate reserve (HRR) is used to determine exercise intensity: HRR = HRmax–HRrest. The larger the heart rate reserve is, the greater the range of potential training heart rate intensities. The Karvonen equation can also calculate exercise heart rate at a given percentage of target intensity: Exercise HR = % of target intensity × (HRmax–HRrest) + HRrest.

2.1.3 Type

The exercise to improve cardiorespiratory endurance is mainly aerobic exercise. Aerobic exercise indicates the activities that elevate and maintain the heart rate for an extended time, generally involving prolonged, repetitive, large-muscle movements, such as running, walking, cycling, swimming, jumping rope, climbing stairs, cross-country skiing, and so on. However, athletes should choose a training mode close to the competition situation as much as possible, to make a positive adaptation to the physiological system. Athletes who participate in more than one aerobic endurance exercise or individuals interested in general aerobic endurance training programs can adopt cross-training or compound aerobic endurance exercise.

2.1.4 Time

At least 20 minutes of continuous activity is needed to achieve minimal improvement in cardiorespiratory endurance. However, recent evidence suggests that 12 minutes may be sufficient. Generally, the longer the duration of the workout, the greater the improvement can be achieved.

二、心肺耐力训练的原则和方法

心肺耐力是维持全身及大肌肉长时间活动的能力。氧气可以依靠心肺系统供应到身体的不同组织。对于参加运动的人来说，心肺耐力在运动表现及预防过度疲劳方面很重要。心肺耐力测试就是监测心、肺、肌肉在中、高强度运动中的表现，良好的心肺耐力水平能提高个体心肺的氧气摄入，延长运动时间。提高心肺耐力的方法很多，但提高的水平很大程度上取决于个体的初始心肺耐力水平。

在进行持续性运动时，身体心肺系统会产生适应，身体会变得更健康，也能更高效地利用和产生能量，细胞代谢也会增强。心脏功能的改善体现在以下几个方面：心脏收缩加强；心脏自身的供氧和血流量增加；当心肌功能提高时，心脏的每搏输出量增加；年轻成人的心腔会增大；由于血容量增加，心脏每次收缩会泵出更多的血液流经循环系统等。细胞代谢的改善如下：肌肉毛细血管的数量增加，这会增加身体的供氧量，使代谢废物排出得更快；肌肉能够最大化利用能量和氧气，因此能更高效地工作；线粒体的数量和大小增加；肌肉利用脂肪和乳酸的能力提升；能够保护细胞免于自由基造成的化学损害。

（一）心肺耐力训练的原则

心肺耐力训练的关键因素主要包括四个方面（FITT 原则）：频率（frequency）、强度（intensity）、类型（type）、时间（time）。

1. 频率

训练频率由训练的强度和持续时间、运动员的训练状态以及特定的赛季等因素相互作用决定。适当的训练频率非常重要，过多的训练会导致受伤、疾病及过度训练的风险，相反，太低的训练频率很难使身体产生积极的适应。

2. 强度

训练强度是最重要的因素，尤其是在训练早期。这时身体正在被迫对增加的负荷需求做出调整。调控有氧运动训练强度最准确的方法是监控运动中的摄氧量，以确定最大摄氧量百分比（%VO$_2$max），并定期测量血乳酸浓度，以确定其与最大摄氧量的关系。如果无法进行最大摄氧量测试，通常我们使用心率或者自觉疲劳程度量表（rating of perceived exertion，RPE）等指标来监控训练强度。而心率可能是测定有氧训练强度的最常用方法，因为心率与摄氧量有着密切的关系。最大心率（maximal heart rate，HRmax）的精确测量需要让一个人在最大强度下运动并用心电图监测心率，但是这个过程很难在实验室外进行。当无法进行实验室测试时，可以通过最大心率年龄预测法（age-predicteol maximal hert rate，APHRmax）为运动强度提供参考。

根据《ACSM 运动测试与运动处方指南》（第 8 版），最大心率 = 206.9 –（0.67 × 年龄）。运动强度可以由储备心率（heart rate reserve，HRR）确定。心率储备是安静心率与最大心率的差值：心率储备 = 最大心率 – 安静心率。差值越大，心率储备越大，运动时心率强度范围也越大。在给出目标运动强度百分比时，可以用 Karvonen 公式来计算运动时心率：运动时心率 = 目标运动强度百分比 ×（最大心率 – 安静心率）+ 安静心率。

3. 类型

提高心肺耐力的运动主要是有氧运动。有氧运动是指增加心率并长时间保持这一水平的运动，通常包括长时间的、重复的、全身的大肌肉运动，比如跑步、步行、骑行、游泳、跳绳、爬楼梯、越野滑雪等。但对于运动员来说，应尽可能选择接近比赛情况的练习模式来训练，从而引起生理系统的积极适应。参与多个有氧耐力运动的运动员或对一般性有氧耐力训练计划感兴趣的个体，可以采用交叉训练或者复合型的有氧耐力运动。

4. 时间

至少 20 分钟的连续运动才能达到使心肺耐力提高的水平。但是也有研究表明，12 分钟的运动也能提高心肺耐力。总的来说，运动的持续时间越长，心肺耐力提高得越多。

2.2 Methods of Cardiorespiratory Endurance Training

2.2.1 Slow Long-Distance Training

In slow long-distance training, the heart rate is usually 70% of the maximum heart rate, and the duration is from 30 minutes to 2 hours. For athletes, the training distance should be longer than the race distance. The athletes should be able to talk without breathing difficulties at this intensity and duration. The physiological benefits of this type of training program mainly include the enhancement of cardiovascular and the thermoregulatory functions, the enhancement of mitochondrial oxidative capacity and fat utilization in skeletal muscle, and the enhancement of the body's ability to use fat, to remove lactic acid, and to raise the lactate threshold.

2.2.2 Interval Training

Interval training consists of alternating periods of relatively intense workouts and active recovery. The high-intensity periods are typically at or close to anaerobic exercise, while the recovery periods involve low-intensity activities. Most interval training is anaerobic. This type of training should only be used if athletes have a solid foundation of cardiorespiratory endurance training. The main physiological benefits of interval training are the increased VO$_2$max and anaerobic metabolism level.

（二）心肺耐力训练的方法

1. 长距离慢速训练

在长距离慢速训练中，心率常为最大心率的 70%，持续时间应该为 30 分钟至 2 小时。对于运动员来说，训练距离应该大于比赛距离。运动员在这种强度和时间下的训练中应该能够进行无呼吸困难的交谈。此种类型的训练计划带来的生理益处主要包括增强心血管和体温调节功能，提升骨骼肌中线粒体的氧化能力和脂肪利用率，从而达到增强身体对脂肪利用以及对乳酸清除的能力而使乳酸阈提高。

2. 间歇性训练

间歇性训练是指一系列相对高强度的训练和主动恢复的交替训练。高强度阶段通常处于或接近无氧运动，而恢复期涉及较低强度的主动恢复运动。该运动方式的大多数运动是在无氧状态下进行的。只有在具有很好的心肺耐力训练基础后，才可以使用此类训练方法。间歇性训练带来的主要生理益处包括增加最大摄氧量和提高无氧代谢水平。

3 Principles and Methods of Muscle Strength Training

Muscular strength is the force of a muscle during a single contraction. Muscular endurance is the ability of the muscle to contract repetitively against resistance for a long time. Muscular power is the ability to generate force instantly. There are three types of contraction: the isometric contraction, the concentric contraction, and the eccentric contraction. The isometric contraction means increased tension without changing the muscle length; the concentric contraction means shortened muscle length as contracting; the eccentric contraction means lengthened muscle length during muscle contracting as the resistance is greater than the muscular strength.

3.1 Principles of Strength Training

Strength training can also be designed and arranged according to the FITT principles. In addition, the following training principles should be noted.

3.1.1 Overload

Increasing the load gradually and then achieving overload is the basic principle to develop strength.

3.1.2 Loads Sequence

Major muscle groups should be trained first before minor muscle groups, and the same muscle groups should avoid being activated in two consecutive exercises.

3.1.3 Specificity

Muscles have specific adaptations to the load. Training methods including joint angle, weight, and movement speed can affect muscle strength; thus, strength training for athletes must be combined with their specific sports.

3.1.4 Appropriate Training Interval

Muscle strength gained by resistance exercises is reversible, so the body must be continually stimulated to maintain the fruits of training, while leaving enough time to recover from fatigue is also necessary.

3.1.5 Comprehensiveness

Strength of both major and minor muscle groups should be developed. Balance between strength of the agonist mucle and antagonistic muscle, as well as balance between the concentric and the eccentric strength of the same muscle group, should also be emphasized.

3.1.6 Recurring Principle

Because of the reversibility of strength training, if the strength training is terminated in a short time, the strength will be lost very soon. The principle of recurring is very important for improving muscle quality and preventing delayed onset muscle soreness.

3.1.7 Separation of Strength Training and Endurance Training

The body has specific adaptability to strength training and endurance training. Doing these training at the same time will lead to the conflict of body adaptation and reduce the training effect.

3.1.8 Overall Control of the Training Load

Strength training is an integral part of overall training rather than an additional part. The relationship between specific sports training and strength training, and the relationship between strength training and endurance training should be carefully managed to avoid overtraining injuries.

3.2 Design of Strength Training Program

The process of designing strength training is complex and requires understanding and addressing seven key factors: requirement analysis, training selection, training frequency, training sequence, training load and repetitions, training volume, and rest time.

3.2.1 Requirement Analysis

Before designating a strength training plan, a requirement analysis should be carried out to assess the requirements and characteristics of the sport as well as the athlete's condition. For example: ①torso and limb motion patterns and involved muscles (motion analysis); ②muscle strength, power, priority of muscle hypertrophy and muscular endurance (physiological analysis); ③common joint and muscle injury sites, and the factors leading to injury (injury analysis); ④athletes' training status, training background, skills and experience; ⑤athletes' physical fitness test and evaluation. The main objectives of the strength training plan are determined by the physical fitness test results, the analysis results of sports events, and the training priority of competition season.

3.2.2 Training Selection

In order to make the right selection of training, the athletic trainers should be familiar with the various types of strength training movements and methods, and choose the safest, the most effective, and the most practical method of training. The closer the training activity is to the actual sport, the greater the possibility of positive transfer to the sport will happen. The following are common strength training methods:

(1) Functional Strength Training

The body can move in three planes of motion, so isolated training on one plane does little to improve functional ability. Functional strength training occurs in three planes and applies integrated exercises to increase strength and improve neuromuscular control, stabilization, and dynamic flexibility. In functional training, muscles contract concentrically, eccentrically, or isometrically to remain stable. It utilizes training variables to force constant neural adaptations instead of merely focusing on morphological changes. Training variables involve plane of motion, body position, the base of support, upper-extremity symmetry, lower-extremity symmetry, balance, and external resistance. In order to understand functional strength training, the athletic trainers must understand the concept of the kinetic chain. They must understand that the kinetic chain is an overall functional unit, which is not only composed of muscles, tendons, fascia, and ligaments, but also includes joints and the nervous system. These systems, as a whole unit, play the role of structure and function at the same time. The failure of any system results in adaptation and compensation from other systems, which can further lead to overload, decreased performance and injuries.

(2) Core Stability Training

Muscles located in the lumbar spine, in the abdomen, and around the hips and pelvis are collectively called "the core." The core area is where the center of gravity is located, and it is also where all movements started. There are 29 muscles connected to this area. The completion of an action is usually the result of a coordinated effort by kinetic chain. The core has three main functions in sports: generating strength, transmitting strength, and controlling strength. A weak core can lead to inefficient movements and even injuries. Strong muscles in the extremities and weak muscles in the core are not enough for efficient movements. Core stability training can help individuals gain strength, neuromuscular control, power and muscular endurance of the core muscles, and it is an important component of strengthening programs. Core stability training can improve the control ability of the human body in an unstable state, enhance the balance ability, activate deep minor muscle groups, coordinate the strength output of major and minor muscle groups, enhance sports function, and prevent sports injury.

(3) Body Weight Training

Body weight training refers to training with one's own weight, such as push-ups, pull-ups, squats, aerobics, yoga, and gymnastics. Body weight training is mostly a compound exercise with high requirements on the core muscle group and is a kind of low-input and high-return training method. However, body weight training tends to increase relative strength only, because the lack of weight progress makes it impossible to improve absolute strength significantly.

(4) Variable Resistance Exercise

In traditional training, the external load is constant, but the force exerted by the muscles varies according to the mechanical efficiency of the joint during the exercise. In modern physical fitness training, iron chains and elastic bands are often used to provide resistance. With the change in movement amplitude, the load exerted by the iron chain and elastic band changes. For example, when squatting behind the neck with the barbell, the elastic band is tied to both ends of the barbell. With the changing of the range of motion, the maximum load is at the top of the squat and the minimum load is at the bottom of the squat.

(5) Circuit Training

Circuit training indicates a series of exercise stations arranged in a specific sequence, where participants complete the prescribed exercises and meet the requirements at each stations. These stations encom pass weight training, flexibility training, and aerobic exercises. The individual finishes all exercises at one station within a specified time. A typical circuit consists of 8 to 12 stations, and the entire circuit is repeated three times. Muscular strength and endurance can be improved through circuit training.

(6) Unilateral Training

In physical training, unilateral training is often used, such as Bulgarian split squats, single-leg squats, step training, and single-hand snatches. Unilateral training is often used in rehabilitation training to reduce the excessive development of bilateral imbalance.

(7) Plyometric Exercise

In plyometric exercise, a rapid eccentric contraction of a muscle is followed by a rapid muscle concentric contraction, which can develop a forceful and explosive movement over a short period. Muscle gains potential energy after eccentric contraction. It will generate additional force, but this energy disappears very quickly, so the interval time between eccentric and concentric contraction must be very short. The process is also called the stretch-shortening cycle and is the underlying mechanism of plyometric training. Plyometric exercises emphasize the speed of the eccentric phase more than the magnitude. The development of eccentric control is the highlight of plyometric exercises, which involve hops, bounds, and depth jumping for the lower extremities and using medicine balls and other types of weighted equipment for the upper extremities.

(8) Eccentric Strength Training

In eccentric strength training, the muscle fibers are stretched while contracting. Most non-contact acute muscle injuries occur in the eccentric contraction stage, so strong eccentric strength training can reduce stress and prevent injuries. Eccentric strength training can help increase muscle mass and improve power. Regular training can improve or maintain the ability of rapid force of the neuromuscular system. It is also required for many sports. For example, during baseball pitching, the involved muscle groups must provide decelerative contractions to preserve the joints from injury. Additionally, in the landing stage of jumping, lower limb muscles must be strong enough to absorb the stress of landing; otherwise, the stress will strike the joints, and increase the injury risks.

① Training classification. According to the purpose of training, eccentric strength training can be divided into two categories: protective eccentric training and eccentric training to develop maximum strength. In protective eccentric strength training, the applied load should not be more than the maximum load that the individual can lift. For example, in the process of a dumb-bell curl, slowly lowering the dumb-bell down is the protective eccentric strength training of the biceps brachii. This eccentric strength training refers to ordinary strength training, but it emphasizes the eccentric contraction part and increases the time to put down the weight. In order to achieve the goal of eccentric strength training, it takes at least 5 seconds to put down the weight; otherwise, the trainer will have no real resistance in the process of putting up the weight. In eccentric strength training to develop maximum strength, the applied load should be more than the maximum load in concentric training that the individual can take. The following two conditions should be met for the eccentric strength training to develop maximum strength: The applied weight in eccentric training should not be less than maximum load in concentric training; The eccentric strength training should take twice as long to complete as the concentric training. In this kind of training, an assistant is needed to assist the individual, and then the individual should slowly put down the load under control. For example, the eccentric contraction training is highly effective in bench press and leg flexion.

② Training tips. The following points should be paid attention to in eccentric strength training: It can easily lead to delayed onset muscle soreness after the first eccentric strength training; The training should be progressive; In the eccentric strength training to develop maximum strength, the load is so great that it is impossible to complete by the athletes, so the assistance and protection are necessary; Athletes should only begin eccentric strength training after achieving a solid base in strength training. Starting without any basic strength training can induce connective tissue and muscle injuries.

3.2.3 Training Frequency

The training frequency can be determined after the analysis of training status, season stage and target requirements. In the traditional sense, athletes were advised to train no more than three days a week, so as to ensure sufficient rest time between two training sessions. However, with the adaptation to training and the change of season stage, the training frequency can be increased to four days or even six days a week. In order to guarantee the same muscle group recovery under this condition, different muscle groups are trained on different training days.

3.2.4 Training Sequence

A training course contains different training sections, and how to carry out these sections needs to be scientifically arranged and planned. The basic principle is that the sequence arrangement can enable the athletes to complete the training of each section with the correct technique and maximum strength. Common training sequences start with explosive training before other major exercises, or alternating upper and lower body exercises with push and pull exercises.

3.2.5 Training Load and Repetitions

The number of repetitions that can be performed in sports training is inversely proportional to the load. The heavier the load, the fewer the repetitions. First of all, the athletic trainer should understand the relationship between the number of repetitions and the percentage of 1RM (Table 1-2).

Table 1-2 The relationship between the number of repetitions and the percentage of 1RM

%1RM	Repetition
100	1
95	2
93	3
90	4
87	5
85	6
83	7
80	8
77	9

%1RM	Repetition
75	10
70	11
67	12
65	15

In requirement analysis, according to the training goal, analysis of sports and sports season phase changes can specify the motion load and repetition plan by RM. If the goals are muscular strength and muscular power, a relatively high load of low repetition is needed. If the goal of training is muscular endurance, a relatively greater number of repetitions of the fewer load is needed. According to the principle of progressive resistance and overload, athletes need to increase their training load as they adapt to the training stimulation.

3.2.6 Training Volume

Training volume is the total load of the training. The training volume can only represent the total work done in each training course, but can not reflect the real load intensity of training. Due to differences in training targets, load, repetition, and set variables, the same volume does not necessarily get the same training effects (Table 1-3).

Table 1-3 Training objectives and training volume

Training Goal	Repetition of Goal	Set
Strength	≤ 6	2–6
Power Single Contract Multiple Contract	 1–2 3–5	 3–5 3–5
Muscular Hypertrophy	6–12	3–6
Muscular Endurance	≥ 12	2–3

3.2.7 Rest Time

The rest time between two groups is closely related to the training target, weight load, and the training status of the athletes. The heavier the load is, the longer the rest time is needed (Table 1-4).

Table 1-4 Training objectives and intervals

Training Goal	Rest Time
Strength	2–5 min
Power	2–5 min
Muscular Hypertrophy	30 s–1.5 min
Muscular Endurance	≤ 30 s

3.3 Strength Training for Females

Strength training is essential for women. Female muscle volume depends on testosterone levels. Women with high testosterone levels tend to have more masculine characteristics, and their muscle volume often has the potential to increase. Due to the increase in neuromuscular efficiency, both men and women initially experience rapid strength growth, but women's muscle strength growth often enters a plateau period after 3-4 weeks. The strength-to-weight ratio is the most important difference in physical activity ability between males and females. Due to the higher body fat ratio in females, their strength-to-weight ratio is lower. Strength training can reduce body fat content while increasing lean body weight to improve strength-to-weight ratio.

3.4 Strength Training in Prepubescent Children and Adolescents

The principles of resistance training discussed previously may be applied to younger individuals. If properly supervised, prepubescent children and adolescents can improve strength, power, endurance, balance, and proprioception; can develop a positive body shape; can improve sports performance and prevent injuries. Close supervision, proper instruction, appropriate modification of progression and intensity based on the degree of physical development of each individual can ensure effective exercises.

三、肌肉力量训练的原则和方法

肌肉力量指肌肉在收缩时所产生的力量；肌肉耐力指肌肉在长时间内抵抗一定阻力而反复收缩的能力；肌肉爆发力指肌肉在最短时间收缩时所能产生的最大张力。骨骼肌的收缩类型有三种：等长收缩、向心收缩、离心收缩。等长收缩是指肌肉收缩使张力增加但是肌肉长度并不改变；向心收缩是指肌肉收缩抗阻时肌肉长度缩短；离心收缩是指当施加的阻力比肌肉产生的力大时，肌肉继续收缩时长度变长。

（一）力量训练的原则

力量训练的设计和安排同样可按照 FITT 原则进行。除此之外，在力量训练中要注意以下训练原则：

1. 超负荷原则

发展肌肉力量最基本的原则就是训练的负荷应不断超过已适应的负荷。

2. 负荷顺序

训练时要先进行大肌群练习再进行小肌群练习，前后相邻的运动避免使用同一肌群。

3. 特异性原则

肌肉对施加的负荷有专一的适应性。训练方式如关节角度、负荷重量、动作速度等因素都会对肌肉用力方式产生影响，因此运动员的力量训练必须结合其专项特点。

4. 合理的训练间隔

因为通过抗阻练习获得的肌肉力量是可逆的，所以必须不断地给机体适宜的刺激，但是也要有足够的时间使机体恢复。

5. 全面性原则

力量训练不仅要发展大肌群的力量，也要发展小肌群的力量，还要注意主动肌与拮抗肌之间的力量平衡、同一肌群向心力量与离心力量的平衡等。

6. 经常性原则

由于力量训练的可逆性，如果在较短时间内终止力量训练，其结果将会很快消失。经常性原则对于提高肌肉质量和预防延迟性肌肉酸痛非常重要。

7. 力量训练与耐力训练分离

机体对力量训练和耐力训练有专一的适应性，如果同时安排力量训练和耐力训练，必然会导致身体适应的冲突，降低训练的效果。

8. 整体控制训练负荷

力量训练是运动员整体训练的组成部分，而不是额外部分，因此要处理好专项训练与力量训练、力量训练与耐力训练的关系等，避免运动员因过度训练而导致损伤。

（二）力量训练计划设计

设计力量训练的过程相当复杂，需要了解并处理7个关键要素：需求分析、训练选择、训练频率、训练顺序、训练负荷与重复次数、训练量和休息时间。

1. 需求分析

在确定力量训练计划之前，首先需要进行需求分析，评估运动项目的需求和特征以及运动员的自身状态。例如：①躯干与肢体的动作模式以及参与的肌肉（动作分析）；②肌肉力量、爆发力、肌肉肥大与肌肉耐力的优先顺序（生理分析）；③常见的关节与肌肉的损伤部位，以及导致损伤的因素（损伤分析）；④运动员的训练状态、训练背景、技术和经验；⑤运动员的体能测试与评估。力量训练计划的主要目标由运动员的体能测试结果、运动项目的分析结果以及运动赛季的训练优先性决定。

2. 训练选择

为了做出正确的训练选择，运动防护师应该熟悉各种类型的力量训练动作和方式，选择安全、有效、符合实际的训练方法。训练活动与运动员的实际运动项目越贴近，该项运动正向迁移的可能性就越大。以下是常用的力量训练方式：

（1）功能性力量训练

身体是在三个运动平面上运动的，因此某一个运动平面上孤立的训练无法提高功能能力。功能性力量训练发生在三个平面内，应用综合方法来增强肌肉力量、神经肌肉控制能力、稳定性及动态柔韧性。在进行功能性力量训练时，部分肌肉向心收缩产生运动；部分肌肉离心收缩；部分肌肉等长收缩，为功能性运动创造稳定的基础。功能性力量训练的一个主要原则是利用训练变量来产生持续的神经性适应，而非仅仅关注形态改变。训练变量包括运动平面、身体姿势、支撑面、上下肢对称、平衡、外界阻力。为了理解功能性力量训练，运动防护师必须理解运动链的概念，必须理解运动链是一个整体功能单位，不仅由肌肉、肌腱、筋膜、韧带组成，还包括关节和神经系统，这些系统作为一个整体单位同时发挥结构和功能的作用。如果运动链的任何一个系统工作失效，其他系统就不得不产生适应和代偿，进而导致组织过度负荷、运动表现下降以及相关的损伤。

（2）核心稳定性训练

腰椎、腹部、髋和骨盆周围的肌肉总称为"核心"。核心区域是重心所在的区域，也是所有动作发出的位置，有 29 块肌肉与该区域相连接。一个动作的完成通常是一个运动链协同工作的结果。身体核心部位在运动中有三个主要功能：产生力量、传递力量和控制力量。核心力量差是导致无法高效运动的主要因素，进而会导致损伤，如果四肢的肌肉强壮但核心肌肉弱，人体将无法提供高效运动所需的力。核心稳定性训练能够增加核心区肌肉的力量、神经肌肉的控制力、爆发力和耐力，是力量训练中的重要组成部分。核心稳定性训练还能够提高人体在非稳定状态下的控制能力，增强平衡能力，激活深层小肌群，协调大小肌群的力量输出，增强运动机能，预防运动损伤。

（3）自重训练

自重训练即以自身重量提供训练的负重，例如俯卧撑、引体向上、深蹲，以及健美操、瑜伽和体操等。自重训练多为复合运动且对核心肌肉群的要求较高，是一种低投入、高回报的训练方法，但是自重训练往往只能增加相对力量，因为缺乏负重的增长，所以无法显著提高绝对力量。

（4）变阻训练

传统训练中，外部的负荷是恒定不变的，但是肌肉施加的力会随着运动中所设计的关节机械效率的变化而改变。现代体能训练中，常使用铁链和弹力带进行变阻训练。随着运动幅度的变化，铁链和弹力带施加给肌肉的负重也会发生变化。例如在做杠铃颈后深蹲时，在杠铃两端绑上弹力带，随着运动幅度的变化，在深蹲的最顶端负荷最大，深蹲的最底端负荷最小。

（5）循环训练

循环训练是指应用一系列训练站，按照一定的顺序，依次完成每站所规定的练习内容和要求的训练方法。这些训练站由力量训练、柔韧性练习、有氧训练等构成。训练者在特定时间内完成所在训练站的训练内容。通常一次循环训练包括 8 ~ 12 个训练站，整个循环训练需要重复 3 次。循环训练能够提高肌肉的力量和耐力。

（6）单侧训练

在体能训练中，往往会采用单侧训练，例如保加利亚分腿蹲、单腿深蹲、台阶训练、单手抓举等。单侧训练往往被用于康复训练中以减少双侧不平衡现象的过度发展。

（7）快速伸缩复合训练

快速伸缩复合训练是一种先进行快速的肌肉离心拉伸，紧接着进行快速的肌肉向心收缩的方法，可以在短时间内形成有力的、爆发性的运动。离心收缩后肌肉获得潜在的能量会产生额外的力量，但这种能量消失地特别快，所以向心和离心收缩之间的时间必须非常短。这一过程也经常被称为"牵伸—缩短"循环，这也是快速伸缩复合训练的根本机制。快速伸缩复合训练强调离心阶段的速度，牵伸的速度比牵伸的程度更重要。快速伸缩复合训练的优势在于它能够提高动态运动中的离心控制能力。快速伸缩复合训练的下肢训练包括单足跳、向前跳、跳深，上肢训练包括药球及其他力量器械辅助下的训练。

（8）离心力量训练

离心力量是指肌肉收缩时肌纤维并未缩短反而拉长时产生的张力。多数非接触性急性肌肉损伤发生在离心收缩阶段，所以离心力量强可以缓冲压力，减少损伤的发生。离心力量训练可以增大肌肉体积，提高爆发力，定期训练可以提高或保持神经肌肉系统快速发力的能力。离心力量也是很多运动专项所需的，比如，在棒球投球后，相应肌群必须收缩来减速以保护关节。此外，在跳跃落地阶段，如果下肢肌肉足够强大，就能吸收地面反作用力，否则这种作用力会被关节吸收，导致损伤风险增加。

①训练分类。按照训练目的可将离心力量训练分为两类：保护性离心训练和发展最大力量的离心训练。保护性离心训练是指负荷小于训练者的最大负荷的离心性力量练习。比如，在举哑铃屈臂过程中，缓慢将哑铃放下的过程，就是肱二头肌的保护性离心力量训练。这种离心训练是指普通的力量训练但是强调离心收缩部分，即增加放下重量的时间。为了实现离心力量训练的目标，放下重量的时间至少需要5秒，否则在放下重量的过程中训练者将无法有效抗阻。发展最大力量的离心训练是指训练时的负荷超过训练者最大向心负荷的一类练习。发展最大力量的离心练习应满足以下两个条件：一是离心力量练习的重量≥向心力量练习的最大负荷；二是完成离心力量练习的时间应该是向心力量练习的一倍。在这类训练中，需要一名助手辅助训练者，然后训练者要有控制地将负荷缓慢放下。卧推和屈腿等训练中用这种离心收缩训练效果非常好。

②训练提示。离心力量训练应注意以下几点：运动员在初次进行离心力量训练后，极易引起延迟性肌肉酸痛；训练要遵循循序渐进的原则；发展最大力量的离心训练的负荷极大，运动员自己不可能完成，要有同伴在场，做好必要的帮助和保护；运动员必须在有良好的力量训练基础上再开始进行离心训练，过早开始离心训练可能会导致结缔组织和肌肉损伤。

3. 训练频率

当在需求分析中了解到运动员的训练状态、赛季阶段以及目标要求后，就可以据此来确定训练频率。传统意义上，建议运动员每周训练不超过3天，这样才能保证在两次训练课之间有充足的休息时间，但随着对训练的适应以及赛季阶段的变化，训练频率可以增长至一周4天乃至6天。这时为了保证同一肌群的休息恢复，常采用分化训练的方法，即在不同的训练日训练不同的肌群。

4. 训练顺序

一节训练课中包含不同的训练动作，如何安排这些动作的顺序也需要进行科学的计划，训练顺序安排的基本原则在于能使运动员以正确的技术、用最大的力量完成每个动作的训练。常见的训练顺序安排包括先进行爆发力训练，再进行其他主要练习，或者上肢与下肢的交替练习、推与拉的交替练习。

5.训练负荷与重复次数

运动训练中所能执行的重复次数与负荷成反比关系即负荷越重，重复次数越少。运动防护师应首先了解重复次数与1RM百分比的关系。

在需求分析中，根据运动员的目标、运动项目的分析以及运动赛季阶段的变化可以制订出运动负荷和重复次数的计划。如果训练的是肌肉力量和爆发力，需要采用相对较重、重复次数少的负荷；如果训练的是肌肉耐力，则需要采用相对较轻、重复次数多的负荷。根据渐进性抗阻和超负荷原则，当运动员适应训练刺激后就需要增加训练负荷。

6.训练量

训练量是指训练课中完成的重量总数，也是一次训练的总负荷量。训练量只能代表每次训练课的总做功量，无法反映运动员训练的真实负荷强度。由于训练目标不同，训练计划的负荷、次数、组数均存在差异，相同的训练量不一定获得同样的训练效果。

7.休息时间

两组训练之间用于恢复的时间与训练目标、重量负荷以及运动员的训练状态密切相关，运动员完成的负荷越重，需要的休息时间就越长。

（三）女性力量训练

力量训练对女性来说是非常重要的。女性肌肉体积取决于睾酮水平。睾酮水平高的女性往往更具有男性特征，她们的肌肉体积也往往更有增大的潜力。由于神经肌肉效能的增加，男性和女性最初力量增长得都很快，但是女性的肌肉力量增长在3～4周后往往会进入平台期。男性和女性之间身体活动能力最重要的差异就是力量—体重比，由于女性体脂比例高，所以女性力量—体重比低。可通过力量训练来减少体脂含量，同时增加去脂体重来提高力量—体重比。

（四）青春期前儿童及青少年的力量训练

上述讨论的抗阻训练原则也适用于年轻训练者。如果适当监控，青春期前儿童及青少年可以通过力量训练来提高力量、爆发力、耐力、平衡和本体感觉等，改善体形，提高运动表现和预防损伤的能力。为达到抗阻训练的有效性，需要给予训练者密切的监控和合适的指导，并基于训练者的身体发育程度适当地调整训练进度和强度。

4 Principles and Methods of Flexibility Training

4.1 Principles of Flexibility Training

① Before high-intensity stretching, warm up by jogging to prevent muscle strain.

② Stretch to the point where tightness or resistance occurs, or perhaps some discomfort.

③ Stretching should not be painful. Pain indicates that something is wrong and should not be ignored.

④ Avoiding overstretching the ligaments and capsules that surround joints.

⑤ Be caution when the low back and neck are stretched. Exercises that compress the vertebrae and their discs can cause injury.

⑥ Be sure of normal breathing constantly during a stretch. Do not hold your breath.

⑦ Static stretching and PNF (proprioceptive neuromuscular facilitation, PNF) stretching techniques are often recommended for individuals who want to improve their ROM.

⑧ Dynamic stretching should be done only by those who are already flexible or accustomed to stretching and should be done only after static stretching.

4.2 Methods of Improving Flexibility

4.2.1 Ballistic Stretching

Ballistic stretching involves a bouncing movement in which repetitive contractions of the agonist muscle are used to produce quick stretches of the antagonist muscle. Although ballistic stretching can significantly improve joint mobility, it has been controversial in the past. The improvement of joint mobility is achieved by rapid stretching of antagonistic muscles. If the force generated by rapid stretching is greater than the flexibility of the tissue, the muscle may get injured. In addition, rapid stretching triggers stretch reflexes, which produce protective muscle contractions, and passive rapid stretching during contraction is also easy to injury.

4.2.2 Dynamic Stretching

Dynamic stretching prepares the body for active movements through a series of ordinary and special tensile actions. Dynamic stretching is controllable, relatively slow, no rebounding so as to avoid the negative effect of ballistic stretching. The advantage of dynamic stretching is that it helps improve dynamic flexibility and develop specific motion patterns and range of motion.

4.2.3 Static Stretching

Static stretching involves passively stretching a given antagonistic muscle by placing it in a maximal range of motion and holding it there for 30 to 60 seconds, repeating it three or four times. Static stretching is less likely to cause hyperextension and does not cause a stretch reflex of the stretched muscle. Compared with the first two types of stretching, static stretching can improve the range of motion better. Thus, it is commonly used in rehabilitation of painful or strained muscles.

4.2.4 PNF Stretching Techniques

PNF stretching techniques include slow-reversal-hold-relax, contract-relax, and hold-relax techniques. All the techniques include alternating contraction and relaxation of both agonist and antagonistic muscles. PNF stretching is divided into three stages. No matter which technique is used, the first stage is 10 s passive stretching. From the second stage, the three types of techniques are different. When the stretched muscle (antagonistic muscle) finishes isometric contraction, which is the maintenance stage, then it does concentric movement, which is the contraction stage. At this time, it can obtain the effect of autogenic inhibition. The process of concentric movement of agonist muscle is called agonist muscle contraction, aiming to obtain the effect of reciprocal inhibition.

四、柔韧性训练的原则和方法

柔韧性是指单个或多个关节平滑且轻松地全范围活动的能力。全范围、不受限的关节活动度是日常活动的基本要素，一些体育运动的优异表现需要更好的柔韧性，如体操和芭蕾。

柔韧性可分为静态柔韧性和动态柔韧性。静态柔韧性也称为被动活动度，关节可以被动地移动到当前活动度末端的程度；动态柔韧性也称为主动活动度，是关节在运动过程中能达到的最大幅度。

（一）柔韧性训练的原则

在柔韧性训练中应遵循以下原则：

①在进行大强度拉伸之前，先通过慢跑进行热身，预防肌肉拉伤。

②应拉伸到感到有些紧绷或者有阻力产生，或有些不适感的程度。

③拉伸时不应该感到疼痛。疼痛往往代表可能有损伤的问题，因此不应被忽视。

④避免过度拉伸关节周围的韧带和关节囊。

⑤拉伸腰部和颈部时要小心。压缩椎骨及椎间盘的运动可能会造成损伤。

⑥被拉伸者在拉伸时应正常呼吸，不能屏气。

⑦静态拉伸和本体感受神经肌肉促进技术是改善关节活动度的首选。

⑧动态拉伸适用于已经有一定柔韧性或已经习惯拉伸的人群，并且只能在适当的静态拉伸之后进行。

（二）柔韧性训练的方法

1. 弹震式拉伸

弹震式拉伸是指在弹震式动作中主动肌重复收缩引起的拮抗肌的快速拉伸。弹震式拉伸虽然能显著提高关节活动度，但是在过去饱受争议。该方法是通过对拮抗肌的快速拉伸来提高关节活动度的，如果快速拉伸产生的力比组织的延展性更大，肌肉就可能会受伤。此外，因为快速拉伸会引发牵张反射，牵张反射会产生保护性的肌肉收缩，在收缩时被动快速拉长也易造成损伤。

2. 动态拉伸

动态拉伸是指关节和肌肉在全关节活动范围内的主动运动。动态拉伸是一种功能性拉伸，可以通过一系列普通及专项拉伸动作使身体为运动做好准备。动态拉伸全程具备可控性，速度相对缓慢，避免了弹震式的运动，从而避免了弹震式拉伸的负面作用。动态拉伸的优势就在于它有助于改善动态柔韧性，发展专项所需的动作模式以及关节活动度。

3. 静态拉伸

静态拉伸是指被动拉伸特定的拮抗肌，即把特定的拮抗肌摆放在能拉伸到的最大位置并保持一段时间。保持在拉伸体位的最佳时间为 30～60 秒，每个肌肉的静态拉伸应重复 3～4 次。静态拉伸时关节过伸的风险更低，并且不会引起被拉伸肌肉的牵张反射。相比于前两种拉伸方法，静态拉伸对关节活动度的改善效果更好，所以静态拉伸通常应用在疼痛或紧张的肌肉损伤康复中。

4. PNF 拉伸技术

PNF 拉伸技术包括慢反转—保持—放松、收缩—放松和保持—放松三种技术，这三种技术包括主动肌和拮抗肌交替收缩和放松。PNF 拉伸分为三个阶段，无论是哪种技术，第一阶段均为 10 秒的被动拉伸，从第二阶段开始三种技术类型各有不同。当被拉伸的肌肉（拮抗肌）做等长收缩时为保持阶段，做向心运动时为收缩阶段，此时肌肉获得自身抑制的效果。主动肌向心运动的过程被称为主动肌收缩，肌肉可获得交互抑制的效果。

5 Principles and Methods of Progressive Functional Training

Progressive functional training involves a series of basic sport-specific movements and upgrades according to the difficulty of the skills and the athlete's performance. The target is to ensure athletes return to play. In this process, various systems of the body adapt to the gradual overload and can afford a higher level of physiological pressure, and the corresponding body will respond to the load by achieving specific functional adaptations. Progressive functional training is based on the principle of SAID, which means that the body has specific adaptability to the load requirements. A progressive functional training program should be designed based on the SAID principle that is relevant to specific sports and includes their main movements. Because a specific action may require speed and flexibility in one sport, but may place more emphasis on strength in another sport.

According to the SAID principle, the body will change because it adapts to specific needs. In progressive functional training, by gradually increasing the difficulty of practice, muscles will gradually and adaptively become stronger, develop a higher level of strength and endurance, and achieve stronger neuromuscular control, coordination and functional ability. In different types of training, we can increase the load by properly controlling the variables such as frequency, intensity, duration, and/or training mode.

The grading principle of progressive functional training is as follows:

Level 1: muscle independent training;

Level 2: muscle independent resistance training;

Level 3: functional training;

Level 4: increasing functional challenge and resistance;

Level 5: increasing resistance to multiple muscle groups and challenging core stability;

Level 6: adding balance training to increase the functional challenge, speed, and/or rotation.

5.1 Indicators to Start

Progressive functional training is an activity that makes a bridge between clinical rehabilitation and motor function. Athletes start from traditional rehabilitation to progressive functional training only when they meet specific clinical goals, including tissue healing, swelling, pain, joint mobility, and strength. The indicators to start progressive functional training are as follows.

Firstly, the healing tissue should not be stressed beyond its tolerance during any phase of rehabilitation. Many factors affect the reaction of injured body parts, including immobilization, the natural recovery process after the surgical or non-surgical intervention, the condition of the injured tissue, the overall general conditioning before the injury, and the age of the athlete. Therefore, sports protection professionals must consider these factors and develop, monitor, and adjust progressive functional training plans accordingly.

Secondly, at the beginning of progressive functional training, the swelling caused by joint injury should have basically disappeared. If there is still swelling in the joint, exercise that does not increase swelling should be performed. Therapeutic modalities such as high-volt galvanic stimulation, intermittent or constant compression, and cryotherapy can be applied to reduce swelling.

Thirdly, pain is a decisive factor in determining whether rehabilitation activities are too intense. During the advanced process, athletes should feel mild pain, even painless. If pain occurs during a certain exercise, it should be avoided, or the amount of training should be reduced. Before starting progressive functional training, painkillers, electrotherapy, or cold therapy can be used for treatment.

Fourthly, before starting progressive functional training, the ROM of the injured side should be the same as that of the uninjured side. In addition, joint activity should be normal and there should be normal terminal sensation. If the joint range of motion is insufficient, it should not focus on progressive functional training, but on active, active auxiliary, or passive joint range of motion training. When the range of motion of the joint is enough to complete the simplest progressive functional training without obstacles, formal progressive functional training can be started.

Fifthly, muscle strength needs to reach a foundational level to engage in progressive functional training. A sufficient strength base is necessary for any sport. For the rehabilitation of lower limb injury, the strength of both lower limbs should be symmetrical. However, the rehabilitation of upper limb strength needs to be combined with specific characteristics. For example, in throwing sports, the strength of the hand should be 10%–15% greater than the other one.

5.2 Guideline Principles

The athlete should always be evaluated and reevaluated throughout the training process. If the evaluation results meet the standards, the athlete can gradually move on to the next step. If there are any problems, the athlete should remain at that stage until the symptoms disappear.

Guidelines for advancement during functional progression are as follows. Firstly, the accuracy of the movement should be emphasized at the beginning; then the speed can be increased when the motion is performed correctly. Secondly, athletes should progress from simple rehabilitative exercises to sport-specific skills. Therefore, the athletic trainer needs to have a clear understanding of the movement characteristics of each specialized sport. Thirdly, athletes should progress from short distances to long distances. Without adequate anaerobic or aerobic endurance, the risk can be high in long-duration activity. Fourthly, athletes should progress from unloaded activities to loaded activities under supervision.

5.3 Key Components

The progressive functional training is based on individual and should be adjusted according to the personal key components.

5.3.1 Monitoring Symptoms and Signs

The continued monitoring of the symptoms and signs of the patient during the functional progression is critical. Symptoms and signs include swelling, joint pain, significant muscular fatigue or loss of control, and decreased joint motion. The presence of any of these slows down the functional progression.

5.3.2 Establishing Continuous Progression

Adjusting and progressing regularly can optimize effects in strength, motion, and function. Frequent, periodic reevaluations of function and consistent monitoring of performance assure continuous progression since the beginning of the program.

5.3.3 Basic Progressions Combined with Sport-Specific Progressions

The balance between specific training and the basic progressions ensures the development of strength and athletic skills. Additionally, core stability and hip strengthening progressions during the return program are fundamental to functionally specific programs.

5.3.4 Objective Examination and Functional Tests Guiding Progression

Objective examination can be combined with functional tests to guide the progression. For example, a patient with a knee injury who tested positive for Trendelenburg suggests the need for more specific and basic exercises to increase core and gluteus medius strength. Additionally, the kinetic chain principle is an important concept in evaluation. Athletic trainers often pay too much attention to the injured joint during assessment and other parts of the kinetic chain are ignored, resulting in inadequate attention in rehabilitation treatment and progressive functional training programs.

五、渐进性功能训练的原则和方法

渐进性功能训练是利用一系列基本的运动专项动作模式，根据动作的难易程度以及运动员的完成程度来进阶的训练方法，其最终目标是使运动员能够及时安全地重返赛场。在这一过程中，机体的各个系统逐渐地超负荷，使机体逐渐承受更高水平的生理压力，相应的机体会通过达到特定的机能适应对负荷做出反应。渐进性功能训练遵循 SAID（specific adaption to imposeal demanols）原则，即机体对施加的负荷要求有专项的适应性。应该基于 SAID 原则设计与特定运动项目相关的并且包含其主要动作的渐进性功能训练方案。因为某一特定动作在一项运动中可能需要速度和灵活性，但是在另一项运动中可能更注重力量。

根据 SAID 原则，机体会因为适应专项的需求而发生改变。在渐进性功能训练中，渐进性增加练习的难度，肌肉会逐渐地、适应性地变得更强壮，从而发展到更高的力量和耐力水平，获得更强的神经肌肉控制、协调和功能能力。在不同类型的训练中，可以通过恰当地控制频率、强度、持续时间和 / 或训练模式等变量来实现机体负荷的增加。

渐进性功能训练的分级原则如下：

第一级：肌肉独立训练；

第二级：肌肉独立抗阻训练；

第三级：加入功能训练；

第四级：功能和阻力的联合增加；

第五级：对多个肌群增加阻力，挑战核心稳定性；

第六级：加入平衡训练，增加功能性挑战、速度和 / 或旋转运动。

（一）开始进行渐进性功能训练的指征

渐进性功能训练在临床康复与运动功能之间起到桥梁的作用。当运动员满足特定的临床指征时才能从传统康复进阶到渐进性功能训练，这些临床指征包括组织愈合、肿胀、疼痛、关节活动度以及肌肉力量。

渐进性功能训练的指征如下：

①在康复的任何阶段，愈合组织的受力都不要超过其耐受能力。很多因素直接影响运

动损伤后身体部位的反应，如损伤后制动的影响、手术或非手术干预后的自然恢复的进程、损伤组织的状况、损伤前个人的整体健康状况、运动员的年龄。因此，运动防护师必须考虑这些因素并据此制定、监测以及调整渐进性功能训练计划。

②渐进性功能训练开始时，关节损伤引起的肿胀应当基本消失。如果关节依然存在肿胀，应进行不会增加肿胀的运动。此外，可以使用高频电刺激、间歇或持续加压及冷疗等理疗方法进行减轻肿胀。

③疼痛是判断康复活动是否过于剧烈的决定性因素。在进阶过程中运动员应该感受到轻微的疼痛，甚至无痛。如果在某一运动中出现疼痛，则应该避免进行这一特定的运动或减小训练量。在渐进性功能训练开始前，可以使用镇痛药、电疗或者冷疗进行处理。

④在开始渐进性功能训练之前，受伤侧关节活动度应该与未受伤侧关节活动度相同。此外，关节活动应该正常，且有正常的终末感觉。如果关节活动度不足，不应以渐进性功能训练为主，而应该强调主动、主动辅助或被动关节活动度训练。当关节活动度足够顺利完成最简单的渐进性功能训练时，就可以开始进行正式的渐进性功能训练了。

⑤肌肉力量需达到一定水平才能进行渐进性功能训练。足够的力量基础对于任何体育运动来说都是必需的。此外，对于下肢损伤的康复，双侧下肢的力量应该是对称的。但上肢力量的康复需要结合专项特征，比如在投掷型运动中，运动员的利手力量应该比非利手的力量大 10% ～ 15%。

（二）渐进性功能训练的指导原则

在整个渐进性功能训练过程中，运动员应该分阶段对运动员进行评估和再评估。如果评估结果达标，则可以渐进到下一步；如果评估结果不达标，运动员则应该保持在这一阶段的训练而不进阶或退阶，直到症状消失。

渐进性功能训练的进阶指导如下：

首先，在训练初期应该保持慢速，强调训练动作的正确性。一旦动作可以正确地进行，就可以加速。其次，运动防护师应该要求运动员从简单的康复训练进阶到其专项所需的难度更高的动作训练。因此，运动防护师需要清楚各专项运动的动作特点。再次，运动员应该从短距离运动进阶到长距离运动。没有足够的无氧耐力和有氧耐力，进行长时间的活动风险可能很高。最后，运动员应该从无负重运动进阶到负重运动。在进阶到负重运动时，应该对运动员进行更多的监督和管理。

（三）渐进性功能训练的关键要素

渐进性功能训练的设计必须因人而异，应该根据以下关键要素进行调整。

1. 监测症状和体征

在渐进性功能训练中，持续监测运动员的症状和体征是非常重要的。通常包括：肿胀、关节疼痛、明显的肌肉疲劳或失控，以及关节活动度下降。这些症状和体征单独或同时出现时，都会减慢渐进性功能训练的进程。

2. 持续性进阶

要使力量、活动度及功能达到最佳化，就需要持续地调整并进阶训练项目，进行经常性、周期性的功能再评估以及持续的运动表现监测。

3. 基本进阶训练结合专项训练进阶

专项训练与其所需的基本进阶训练之间的平衡是非常重要的，只有这样才能确保基础力量增长和专攻技能发展的平衡。此外，在重返赛场阶段的训练中，核心稳定性和臀部力量的进阶不可忽视，因为这些训练是专项功能训练的基础。

4. 应用客观检查和功能检查来指导进阶训练

客观检查可以与功能检查相结合来指导训练的进阶。比如，当膝部损伤的运动员特伦德伦堡检查呈阳性，说明在进行更高阶的训练之前需要进行针对性的基础体能训练来增加核心及臀中肌的力量。此外，运动链原则是评估技术中的重要理念。运动防护师在评估时经常过于关注运动员受伤的部位，以至于运动链中的其他部分被忽视，导致其在康复治疗和渐进性功能训练中没有得到适当的重视。

Summary

1. Proper physical training can improve performance and help prevent injuries. Training should follow its basic principles and the theory of periodic training.

2. Improving cardiovascular endurance can enhance athletic performance, prevent injuries, and delay fatigue. Continuous training and interval training help improve cardiorespiratory endurance.

3. Seven factors need to be paid attention to in the process of designing strength training: requirement analysis, training selection, training frequency, training sequence, training load and repetitions, training volume, and rest time.

4. Flexibility plays a key role in many sports. The methods of increasing flexibility include ballistic stretching, dynamic stretching, static stretching, and the PNF technique.

5. Progressive functional training is crucial for an injured athlete to return to play. Clinical indicators should be closely observed and the principles should be strictly followed in the progression.

⭕ Review Questions

1. What are the general principles of strength and conditioning training?

2. What are the periodization principles of strength and conditioning training?

3. What are the common methods of aerobic training?

4. How to design a strength training plan?

5. How is progressive functional training graded?

小结

1. 适当的体能训练可以帮助运动员提高运动表现，预防运动损伤。训练应该遵循其基本原则以及周期训练理论。

2. 提高心肺耐力可以提高运动表现，预防损伤，延缓疲劳。长距离慢速训练和间歇性训练都能够提高心肺耐力。

3. 力量训练方案设计需要注意 7 个关键要素：需求分析、训练选择、训练频率、训练顺序、训练负荷与重复次数、训练量和休息时间。

4. 很多运动需要良好的柔韧性，提高柔韧性的方法包括弹震式拉伸、动态拉伸、静态拉伸、PNF 拉伸技术等。

5. 渐进性功能训练是运动员受伤后重返赛场的重要环节，应密切观察其临床指征，严格遵循训练进阶原则和标准。

复习题

1. 在进行体能训练时，要遵循的基本原则是什么？

2. 体能训练的周期训练原则是什么？

3. 常用的心肺耐力训练方法有哪些？

4. 如何设计一个力量训练计划？

5. 渐进性功能训练如何分级？

Chapter 2 Nutrition Considerations
第二章　营养因素

○ Main Contents

1. Nutrition and nutrients.
2. Common nutrition supplements and recommendations.
3. Sports nutrition during competition.
4. Body composition and weight control.
5. Common eating disorders.

○ 主要内容

1. 营养和营养素。
2. 常见营养补充剂及使用建议。
3. 比赛期间的营养。
4. 体成分和体重控制。
5. 常见的饮食紊乱。

1 Nutrition and Nutrients

Nutrition plays an important role in physical exercise. The appropriate combination of nutrition and training can improve body development, health, and athletic performance. In competitive sports, the combination of correct athlete talent selection, scientific training, and appropriate nutrition leads the athletes to success. The appropriate nutrition can help athletes replenish energy, regulate organ function, improve athletic ability, and promote physical recovery. In the recreational fitness field, appropriate nutrition can prevent and treat diseases, promote growth and development, and improve metabolism, body composition, post-exercise organ function, mental state, etc.

Nutrients are substances required for human metabolism, which include carbohydrates, dietary fiber, fat, proteins, water, vitamins, and minerals. Macronutrients include carbohydrates, proteins, and fats, which are the absorbable components in food and the source of energy. When the body needs energy, the metabolism of the macronutrients follows this sequence: carbohydrates, fats, and proteins. Micronutrients include vitamins and minerals, which can not provide energy but are necessary for macronutrients to metabolize. Some of the nutrients can be synthesized in the body. However, the essential nutrients must be supplied by the diet. There is no single natural food that contains all the nutrients needed for health. Thus, a balanced diet is very important.

1.1 Carbohydrates

Carbohydrates are the main source of energy, including monosaccharides, disaccharides, oligosaccharides, and polysaccharides. Monosaccharides and disaccharides are classified as simple carbohydrates. Monosaccharides are the basic units of carbohydrates, including glucose, fructose, and galactose. Most monosaccharides are found in fruits, syrups, and honey. Disaccharides are composed of two monosaccharide molecules, including sucrose, maltose, and lactose. Oligosaccharides are composed of 3–10 monosaccharides, most of which cannot or can only be partially absorbed. However, they can be utilized by gut probiotics to promote the growth and reproduction of the microbiota. Their fermentation products also play a protective and promotive role in the intestines. Polysaccharides are composed of over 10 monosaccharides, including glycogen, starch, and dietary fiber.

Some people believe that restricting carbohydrate intake is a way to lose weight. However, most body weight loss is caused by body fluid loss. Additionally, many high-carbohydrate foods have high nutritional value, and reducing the intake of these foods can cause health problems. Reducing the intake of carbohydrates can increase protein and fat intake, which can raise cholesterol levels.

1.2 Dietary Fibers

Dietary fiber refers to non-starch polysaccharides and non-polysaccharide lignin that human digestive enzymes cannot absorb. Dietary fibers are divided into soluble fiber (gum, pectin) and insoluble fiber (cellulose). The food sources of soluble fiber are oats, beans, etc. While the food sources of insoluble fiber are whole wheat bread, coarse grain, etc.

The major functions of dietary fiber include: (1) Bacterial fermentation. The short-chain fatty acids produced by the digestion of dietary fiber provide energy for intestinal nuclear bacteria. (2) Water absorption. The powerful water absorption capacity of dietary fiber increases the volume of feces in the intestine and accelerates its transport. (3) Viscosity effect. The viscous properties allow it to form a mucinous solution. (4) Combining organic compounds. Dietary fiber can combine cholic acid and cholesterol, and reduce cholesterol levels. (5) Cation exchange. Dietary fiber can combine with inorganic salts so as to affect absorption.

1.3 Fats

Fat is one of the primary sources of energy and is essential for growth and development. Fat also plays a key role in maintaining cell function, metabolism of some vitamins, and maintaining normal body shape. Fat is divided into saturated fat and unsaturated fat. Saturated fat can be found in animal products such as meat and milk, while unsaturated fat can be found in plant products such as soybeans and nuts. Excessive intake of saturated fat can increase cholesterol levels in the body, and prolonged accumulation of cholesterol on blood vessel walls can block blood vessels and cause cardiovascular disease. Obesity, high blood pressure, and diabetes can also be caused by overconsumption of saturated fat. Trans fat, a kind of saturated fat, is created when hydrogen is added to vegetable oil. Trans fat can be found in cookies, dairy products, meat, etc. Intakes of trans fat can increase bad cholesterol (low-density) levels and decrease good cholesterol (high-density) levels, as well as increase risks of type 2 diabetes. Even intake of a small amount of trans fat is unhealthy.

Cholesterol is a waxy fat-like substance, which is an important structural and functional component of all cell membranes, but a high level of cholesterol induces atherosclerosis. Low-density lipoprotein (LDL), also known as bad cholesterol, is a kind of lipoprotein particle that carries cholesterol into peripheral tissue cells. Excess LDL can also lead to cardiovascular disease. High-density lipoprotein (HDL), which is known as good cholesterol, is an anti-atherosclerotic lipoprotein that transports cholesterol from peripheral tissue to the liver, and then the cholesterol is transformed into bile and excreted.

1.4 Proteins

Proteins, the body's major structural components, play an essential role in growth, maintenance, and repair of all body tissues, and the formation of enzymes, hormones, and antibodies. Proteins can be found in meat, beans, dairy products, fish, eggs, etc. Amino acids are the basic unit of protein, and most of them can be produced by the human body. The amino acids that the human body cannot produce must be obtained from food and are called essential amino acids.

Athletes spend more energy than the average people and need more nutrients to recover from the intense training. Protein can repair and strengthen muscle tissue, but protein intake also has a limit. The protein requirements for athletes are determined by their overall eating pattern. Adequate consumption of carbohydrates and fat means less need for protein to provide energy; thus, it is also important for athletes to meet carbohydrates and fat requirements. Duration and intensity of training also affect protein needs.

The American College of Sports Medicine recommends 1.2 to 2.0 grams of protein per kilogram of body weight per day for athletes. Most athletes can get the recommended amount of proteins through food without additional protein supplements. Adolescents require extra proteins because they are at a stage of rapid growth. Protein intake at 0.11 g/kg/h after exercise is enough in the condition of sufficient energy supply. Consuming excessive protein is not beneficial, particularly using protein supplements. The body will convert excessive protein to fat and during this conversion, excessive water is removed from cells, inducing dehydration and possible damage to the kidneys or liver. Moreover, protein intake should be distributed in each meal and after competitions, and high-quality protein consumption within two hours after exercise enhances muscle repair and growth.

1.5 Vitamins

Vitamins help the body perform specific functions by regulating metabolic processes. The requirement for vitamins is very small, and all foods contain vitamins. A balanced diet can provide the vitamins needed for the body. If the diet can not provide enough vitamins, vitamin supplements should be taken.

Vitamins are classified into fat-soluble and water-soluble vitamins. Fat-soluble vitamins include vitamin A, vitamin D, vitamin E, and vitamin K. Water-soluble vitamins include vitamin B6, vitamin B12, vitamin C, thiamin, riboflavin, niacin, folate, biotin, and pantothenic acid. Fat-soluble vitamins are dissolved in fat and stored in the liver. Thus, excessive fat-soluble vitamins can lead to vitamin poisoning. Water-soluble vitamins are dissolved in watery solutions and the excess water-soluble vitamins are urinated out of the body. Thus, they should be supplied in the daily diet. Vitamin C, vitamin E, and beta-carotene can prevent health problems like premature aging, cancers, and heart disease. They are called antioxidants. But excessive intake of vitamins C and E may cause diarrhea or vitamin toxicity.

1.6 Minerals

Minerals are chemical elements that are needed for building bones and muscles, conducting nerve impulses, maintaining metabolism and heart function. Each mineral has different functions, and has an important impact on body functions. Therefore, a variety of food intake is the best way to obtain an appropriate amount of minerals.

Calcium helps maintain the health of bones, teeth, and the function of the heart. The lack of calcium intake leads to osteoporosis. Dairy products are rich in calcium, such as milk and cheese. Vitamin D facilitates the absorption of calcium from food. On the other hand, smoking, excessive intake of caffeine and salt can cause the loss of calcium from the body. Teenagers need calcium every day to build the skeleton. Additionally, as bone loss accelerates with age, men over 70 years old and women after menopause require extra calcium to maintain their bone mass.

Iodine can ensure normal thyroid gland functions. Iodine is mainly from marine food such as seaweed and seafood, dairy products, and eggs. Mild iodine deficiency affects hearing, intelligence, and mental capability. Severe iodine deficiency results in goiter and hypothyroidism. Pregnant women need more iodine for their babies' development.

Iron plays an important role in hemoglobin production, which carries oxygen around the body and also ensures the normal function of the immune system. Iron deficiency induces paleness, tiredness, lethargy, disability of concentrating, and weak immunity. Taking unnecessary iron supplements, a high alcohol intake, hepatitis or hemochromatosis may lead to excessive iron in the blood. Babies, children, and teenagers need more iron because of growing rapidly; Women need more iron due to the menstrual cycle; Pregnant women need enough iron for themselves and their growing fetus; Athletes, especially in endurance sports, need more iron. There are two types of iron in food: heme and non-heme iron. Heme iron, which is found in red meat, chicken, and fish, can be easily absorbed. Non-heme iron, which is found in plant foods, is hard to absorb. The intake of foods rich in Vitamin C and the combination of heme foods and non-heme foods help increase iron absorption, while tea reduces iron absorption.

Selenium, which is a kind of antioxidant, can regulate blood pressure and maintain immune system function. It exists in cereals, meat, fish, eggs, and nuts. But excessive consumption of selenium leads to selenium toxicity.

Sodium, which exists as salt, is important to maintain fluids' osmotic pressure and electrolytes stable, especially when sweating during exercise. Most sodium in diets comes from processed and manufactured food. Excessive intake of sodium can increase the risk of high blood pressure, calcium losses in the urine, and the risk of osteoporosis. Thus, the low-salt diet is recommended.

Zinc is a trace mineral with important functions. Zinc is mainly found in seafood, lean red meat, chicken, and wholegrain cereals. Zinc deficiency causes loss of appetite, poor growth, loss of hair, a poorly functioning immune system, poor wound healing, and changes in taste sensation. Teenagers need more zinc to support growth and development. Since vegetarians eat more beans and whole grains, which contain phytates that reduce the absorption of zinc, vegetarians' zinc absorption is lower than others. Additionally, they lack meat, a source of zinc; thus, vegetarians need to intake more zinc.

1.7 Water

Water is the most important nutrient for athletes. Athletes need to pay special attention to their hydration status. When fluid loss exceeds fluid intake for a long time, the body will be in a state of dehydration, showing the increasing core temperature, decreasing plasma volume, increasing heart rate, and increasing fatigue. Hydration status can be assessed by monitoring urine specific gravity, weight change before and after the athlete's exercise, urine color, etc. The athlete's thirst level cannot indicate whether they need to drink water or not. Most athletes do not drink enough water during competitions. Sweating results in water loss and electrolyte loss, which leads to muscle cramping and heat intolerance. Thus, athletes should drink water before, during and after exercise. Failure to resupply fluids in time can lead to dehydration. Symptoms and signs of dehydration include headache, dizziness, fatigue, and thirst. Mild dehydration occurs when the water loss is over 2% of body weight and can impair performance.

一、营养和营养素

营养在体育运动中起到重要作用。营养与运动科学配合能够促进生长发育，提高运动员的健康水平和运动成绩。在竞技体育中，正确选材、科学训练与合理营养相结合才能使运动员取得优异成绩。合理的营养能够帮助运动员补充能量，调节器官功能，提高运动能力，促进体力恢复。在全民健身领域，合理的营养也能够防治疾病，促进生长发育，改善代谢和身体成分，提高运动器官的工作能力，改善心理状态等等。

营养素是指人体新陈代谢所需的物质，包括碳水化合物、膳食纤维、脂肪、蛋白质、维生素、矿物质、水。碳水化合物、蛋白质、脂肪统称为宏量营养素，为食物中可吸收的成分，也是能量的来源。机体需要能量时，代谢顺序依次是：碳水化合物、脂肪、蛋白质。维生素和矿物质统称为微量营养素，虽然不提供能量，但是如果没有足够的微量营养素，来自宏量营养素的能量就无法被利用。身体虽然可以产生一些营养素，但人体必需的营养素主要从食物中获得，没有某一种天然食物包含人类健康所需的所有营养素，所以均衡的膳食摄入非常重要。

（一）碳水化合物

碳水化合物是人体最主要的能量来源，可分为单糖、二糖、寡糖和多糖。单糖和二糖又被称为简单碳水化合物。单糖是碳水化合物的基本单位，包括葡萄糖、果糖和半乳糖，多存在于水果、糖浆和蜂蜜中。由 2 个单糖分子组成的糖类代合物称为二糖，包括蔗糖、麦芽糖和乳糖。寡糖是由 3 ~ 10 个单糖分子组成，多数寡糖不能被吸收或只能被部分吸收，但是可被肠道益生菌利用，促进菌群生长和繁殖，其发酵产物也会对肠道起到保护、促进作用。多糖是由 10 个以上的单糖组成的大分子糖，包括糖原、淀粉和膳食纤维。

有人通过限制摄入碳水化合物的方式来减体重，但是这种方式引起的体重下降往往来源于体液的丢失。此外，很多高碳水化合物食物有极高的营养价值，减少此类食物的摄入会引起健康问题。若减少碳水化合物摄入的同时增加蛋白质和脂肪的摄入，会提高人体胆固醇水平。

（二）膳食纤维

膳食纤维是指不能被人体消化酶所吸收的非淀粉多糖以及非多糖类的木质素，可分为水溶性纤维（树胶、果胶）和非水溶性纤维（纤维素）。水溶性纤维的食物来源为燕麦、豆类等，非水溶性纤维的食物来源为全麦面包、粗粮等。

膳食纤维的主要功能包括：①细菌发酵作用。膳食纤维在肠道内被细菌酵解后产生的短链脂肪酸可作为肠道细胞核细菌的能量来源。②吸水作用。膳食纤维强大的吸水作用可增大肠道中粪便的体积，加快其转运速度。③黏滞作用。膳食纤维的黏滞性能使其形成黏液型溶液。④结合有机化合物。膳食纤维可结合胆酸和胆固醇，降低体内胆固醇水平。⑤阳离子交换作用。膳食纤维可在胃肠内结合无机盐，影响吸收。

（三）脂肪

脂肪是能量的主要来源之一，是身体正常生长发育所必需的，在维持细胞功能和某些维生素的新陈代谢、保持正常体型等方面也发挥着重要作用。脂肪可分为饱和脂肪和不饱和脂肪。饱和脂肪常存在于肉、奶等动物产品中；不饱和脂肪常存在于大豆、坚果等植物产品中。摄入过多的饱和脂肪会增加体内的胆固醇水平，胆固醇长时间在血管壁上堆积会堵塞血管，引起心血管疾病。此外，肥胖、高血压、糖尿病等也都与摄入过量脂肪有关。反式脂肪是植物油氢化时产生的脂肪，也是一种饱和脂肪，常存在于曲奇饼干、奶制品、肉等食品中。摄入过多含有反式脂肪的食物会增加体内有害胆固醇（即低密度脂蛋白）水平，同时也会降低体内有益胆固醇（即高密度脂蛋白）水平，增加患 2 型糖尿病的风险，即使摄入微量的反式脂肪也是不安全的。

胆固醇是一种蜡状的类似脂肪的物质，是所有细胞膜的重要结构和功能成分，但体内胆固醇含量过高会导致动脉粥样硬化。低密度脂蛋白（low-density lipoprotein，LDL）又被称为有害胆固醇，是一种运载胆固醇进入外周组织细胞的脂蛋白颗粒。LDL 摄入过量会导致胆固醇积存于动脉壁上引发心血管疾病。高密度脂蛋白（high-density lipoprotein, HDL）又被称为有益胆固醇，是一种抗动脉粥样硬化的脂蛋白，可将胆固醇从肝外组织转运到肝脏进行代谢，由胆汁排出体外。

（四）蛋白质

蛋白质是构成人体的主要结构成分，参与身体组织的生长、维持和修复，也参与酶、激素、抗体的组成。蛋白质的食物来源包括肉、豆类、乳制品、鱼、蛋等。氨基酸是蛋白质的基本组成单位，大部分氨基酸能够由人体产生，人体不能产生的氨基酸必须从食物中获得，因此称为必需氨基酸。

由于运动员比普通人消耗更多的能量，他们的身体也需要额外的营养素来使其从剧烈的训练中恢复。因为蛋白质有助于修复、加强肌肉组织，所以在运动员的饮食计划中，蛋白质起到很重要的作用，但这并不意味着摄入越多的蛋白质就越好。运动员的蛋白质需求量取决于其整体饮食模式，如果摄入了足够的碳水化合物和脂肪，就需要更少的蛋白质来供能，那其摄入的蛋白质就可以用来增加和维持体重而非供能。因此，运动员不仅要满足蛋白质需求，还必须要满足碳水化合物和脂肪的需求。训练时间和强度都会影响蛋白质需求量。

美国运动医学学会建议运动员根据其训练每天摄入 1.2 ~ 2.0 克 / 千克体重的蛋白质，大多数运动员仅从食物中就能够获取建议的蛋白质摄入量，不需要补充剂。但青少年处于生长发育最快的阶段，需要额外的蛋白质。假设青少年已摄入足够的能量，那么在运动后恢复期每小时应摄入 0.11 克 / 千克体重的蛋白质补充，以补充运动引起的氨基酸消耗，满足其正常生长发育的需要。摄入过量的蛋白质是无益的，尤其是以补充剂的形式。如果摄入的蛋白质多于需求量，过量的蛋白质则会被转换为脂肪储存，转换过程会从细胞中吸收过量的水，导致脱水，进而损害肾脏或肝脏。此外，蛋白质的摄入应该分散到全天及赛后，运动后 2 小时内摄入高质量蛋白质能够促进肌肉修复和生长。

（五）维生素

维生素可以通过调节新陈代谢来帮助机体执行具体功能。维生素的需要量很小，且所有食物中均含有维生素，均衡膳食即可获得人体所需的维生素。但是若膳食无法满足需求，也可通过服用维生素补充剂来获取。

维生素可分为脂溶性维生素和水溶性维生素。脂溶性维生素包括维生素 A、D、E、K；水溶性维生素包括维生素 B_6、B_{12}、C、硫胺素、核黄素、烟酸、叶酸、生物素和泛酸。脂溶性维生素在脂肪中溶解，多余的维生素储存在肝脏内，因此，脂溶性维生素过量会导致维生素中毒。水溶性维生素在水溶液中溶解，多余的维生素通过尿液排出体外，因此水溶性维生素每天都需摄入。维生素 C、E 以及 β - 胡萝卜素等能够预防衰老、癌症、心脏疾病等，这些营养素被称为抗氧化物质。但是需要注意的是，维生素 C 和维生素 E 摄入过量可能造成腹泻或中毒。

（六）矿物质

矿物质是形成骨骼和肌肉、传导神经冲动、维持代谢和心脏功能所需的无机化学元素。每一种矿物质都有着不同的功能且都对身体功能有重要的影响。多种类的食物摄入是获得适量矿物质的最佳途径。

钙对于骨骼、牙齿健康以及心脏的正常功能来说是必不可少的，钙的摄入量过低会导致骨质疏松症。乳制品中钙含量最丰富，包括牛奶、奶酪等。维生素 D 有助于食物中钙的吸收，而吸烟以及摄入过量咖啡因和盐会造成体内钙的流失。青少年需要每天摄入钙来强健骨骼。此外，由于随着年龄增长，骨质流失加快，超过 70 岁的男性以及绝经期后的女性需要补充额外的钙来维持骨量。

碘是饮食中必不可少的，可以确保人体正常的甲状腺功能。碘的主要来源是海洋食物，比如海藻、海鲜，以及乳制品和蛋类。轻度缺碘会影响听力、智力以及心理能力；重度缺碘会导致甲状腺肿和甲状腺功能衰退。怀孕的女性需要补充碘来确保胎儿的发育。

铁有助于产生血红蛋白，血红蛋白能将氧气输送到身体各处，免疫系统的正常工作也需要铁。血液中铁含量过低会导致脸色苍白、疲劳和昏睡，精神涣散以及抵抗力下降。但是若在不必要时服用铁补充剂、酒精摄入量过高，以及患有肝炎或血色病都会导致血液中铁过量。婴儿、儿童以及青少年由于生长速度快，需要更多的铁；女性由于生理周期，也需要更多的铁；怀孕的女性需要为自己和发育的胎儿提供足够的铁；运动员需要更多的铁，尤其是耐力性运动员。食物中富含两种类型的铁：血红素铁和非血红素铁。血红素铁多存在于红肉、鸡肉和鱼肉中，易吸收；非血红素铁多存在于植物性食物中，不易吸收。摄入富含维生素 C 的食物能够帮助增加铁吸收，将含血红素铁食物和含非血红素铁食物结合摄入也有助于增加铁的吸收，但是茶会降低铁吸收量。

硒作为一种抗氧化剂可以保护机体免受伤害，也可以调节血压，保持免疫系统的健康。硒常存在于谷物、肉、鱼、蛋和坚果中。但是摄入过量的硒是有害的，会导致硒中毒。

钠主要以盐的形式出现在食物中，机体需要少量的盐来维持体液和电解质平衡，当运动时由于出汗而导致体内钠流失时这一点尤其重要。膳食中的大多数钠都来自加工食品，摄入过量的盐会增加患高血压的风险，加快尿液中的钙流失，增高骨质疏松症的风险。最好通过选用低盐饮食等方式来减少钠的摄入。

锌在人体中是一种微量矿物质，但是有着重要的功能。锌存在于海鲜、瘦红肉、鸡肉以及全谷物等中。缺锌会导致食欲不振、生长不良、脱发、免疫系统功能低下、伤口愈合不良和味觉变化。青少年需要更多的锌来促进其生长发育。因为素食主义者会吃更多的豆类和全谷物，其中含有的植酸会减少对锌的吸收，所以素食主义者对锌的吸收较低，而且其还缺少肉类这一锌的来源，因此，素食主义者需要补充更多的锌。

（七）水

水对运动员来说是最重要的营养素。运动员需要特别观察自己的水合状态。当长时间处于超过液体摄入量的汗液流失状态下，身体将进入脱水状态，伴随着核心温度升高、血浆容量减少，心率上升和疲劳感增加等表现。可通过监测尿比重、运动员运动前后的体重变化、尿液颜色等来评估水合状态。需要注意的是，不能根据运动员的口渴程度判断是否需要补水，大多数运动员在比赛时摄入的水分都不足以补充其出汗等生理过程所流失的水分。出汗会导致身体中水和电解质丢失，电解质不足会造成肌肉痉挛及热不耐受，因此运动员在活动前、中、后都要补水。如果运动员没有及时补水，会导致脱水，其症状和体征包括头痛、头晕、疲劳、口渴。失水量超过体重的 2% 就会出现轻度脱水，影响运动表现。

2 Common Nutrition Supplements and Recommendations

2.1 Vitamin Supplements

Athletes can get enough vitamins by eating a balanced diet; thus, supplements are unnecessary. Excessive vitamin consumption is harmful to the body. For instance, excessive vitamin C intake can cause diarrhea and kidney stones. If a balanced diet is unavailable, athletes can take vitamin supplements once each day.

2.2 Mineral Supplements

All foods are rich in minerals. Athletes need mineral supplements only when they have an unbalanced diet. Calcium and iron intake may be low for those who do not consume dairy products, red meats, bread, and cereals. Less calcium intake than needed can lead to osteoporosis; iron deficiency can lead to iron-deficiency anemia and further impair performance. In such circumstances, mineral supplements should be taken.

2.3 Protein Supplements

It is still controversial as to whether athletes need protein or amino acid supplements. On the one hand, athletes do not require additional protein or amino acid supplements. Athletes in strength training who require additional protein supplementation can be satisfied by consuming protein-rich foods. 30 g of meat can provide 7000 mg of high-quality amino acids, but a typical amino acid supplement can provide only 500 to 1000 mg of amino acids. On the other hand, although a balanced diet can meet protein intake requirements, protein supplements have the advantages of being economical, easy to absorb, of higher protein purity, and easy to carry and use. Therefore, protein supplements have the advantage of being recommended for those athletes who need extra protein or have poor digestion or absorption function.

2.4 Creatine Supplements

Creatine is a natural organic compound synthesized by the kidneys, liver, and pancreas. Creatine level is quite high right after exercise. Creatine can be obtained from meat and fish. Athletes taking creatine supplements for strength training seem to improve their short-term and high-intensity exercise ability, but the long-term effect is not clear. Therefore, one should be careful when taking creatine supplements.

2.5 Glucose Supplements

Consuming large quantities of glucose immediately before exercise can improve performance. But athletes who are sensitive to high-carbohydrate food or intolerant to fructose may have some issues when consuming such food. Therefore, athletes should test themselves with various high-carbohydrate foods in advance.

二、常见营养补充剂及使用建议

（一）维生素补充剂

运动员在训练时摄入均衡膳食即可获得所需维生素，因此不需要维生素补充剂。摄入过量维生素对人体有害，如摄入过量的维生素 C 可能会造成腹泻、肾结石等病症。但是如果运动员的膳食不合理，则可以每天服用一次维生素补充剂。

（二）矿物质补充剂

所有食物中都富含矿物质，除非膳食不均衡，否则运动员不需要摄入矿物质补充剂。如果饮食中不含乳制品、红肉、面包和谷物，则钙、铁的摄入量会很低。缺钙会导致骨质疏松症，缺铁会导致缺铁性贫血，影响运动表现。在这种情况下，可适当补充相应的矿物质补充剂。

（三）蛋白质补充剂

运动员是否需要蛋白质或氨基酸补充剂还存在争议。一种观点认为，运动员不需要额外的蛋白质或氨基酸补充剂。力量训练中的运动员如需额外补充蛋白质，可通过食用富含蛋白质的食物满足。30 克红肉中可提供 7000 毫克的优质氨基酸，但是一种典型的氨基酸补剂仅能提供 500 ~ 1000 毫克氨基酸。另一种观点认为，虽然均衡的饮食能够满足蛋白质摄入需求，但是蛋白质补充剂具有经济效益高、吸收效率快、蛋白质纯度更高以及方便携带和使用的优点，所以针对蛋白质需求无法满足或者消化吸收功能较差的运动员来说，蛋白质补充剂是比较推荐的。

（四）肌酸补充剂

肌酸是一种由肾、肝、胰腺合成的自然有机化合物。运动后人体的肌酸水平非常高。肌酸可以从肉、鱼中获得。进行力量训练的运动员服用肌酸补充剂后，短时间、高强度的运动能力似乎有所提升，但是目前其长期效果尚未明确。因此，摄入肌酸补充剂时应慎重。

（五）葡萄糖补充剂

在运动前立即摄入大量葡萄糖有助于提高运动表现。但是对高碳水化合物敏感或对果糖不耐受的运动员可能会出现一些问题。因此，运动员应该提前测试自己对高碳水化合物的反应。

3 Sport Nutrition During Competition

3.1 Pre-Event Meals

The pre-competition diet should fully consider the factors such as sports events, time arrangement, dietary and liquid composition, and athletes' personal preferences, so as to maintain the blood glucose and glycogen reserves as well as the hydration status of the body to the greatest extent.

The glycemic index (GI) indicates the effects of different types of carbohydrates on blood glucose levels. Foods with a low to medium GI before an event are recommended, because the small fluctuations in blood glucose and insulin levels ensure a slower release of energy. The nutrients consumed over several days before competition are much more important than what is eaten several hours before an event.

The nutrition requirements before the competition are as follows: ① the nutrition should be able to maintain an appropriate weight and body fat; ② the diet should be diversified, delicious and balanced; ③ reducing the intake of protein and fat to promote gastrointestinal emptiness and reduce gastrointestinal burden; ④ eating more vegetables and fruits; ⑤ consuming an appropriate amount of vitamins; ⑥ supplementing with sugar increase glycogen reserve; ⑦ increasing the activity of antioxidant enzymes; ⑧ ensuring adequate water; ⑨ adjusting the meal time according to the requirements of the competition.

The nutrition requirements for the day before the competition are as follows: ① small size, light and easy to digest, providing 500–1000 kcal energy; ② eating 3–4 hours before the event; ③ choose the food which the athletes used to eat; ④ when participating in long time high-intensity competition or under high-temperature environment, 500–700ml fluid should be replenished before the competition; ⑤ avoiding high fat, high protein and alcohol;

⑥ carbohydrate supplementation should be carried out before the competition in endurance sports. The best timing of carbohydrate supplementation is 2 h or 15–30 min before the event. The amount of carbohydrate intake should not exceed 50 g/h or 1 g/kg weight.

3.2 During-Event Meals

For aerobic endurance competitions that last more than 45 minutes and intermittent sports or multiple competitions in a day, maintaining hydration status during the competition helps prevent overheating, dehydration and heatstroke. Appropriate supplementation of sugar and amino acids can maintain energy supply and reduce muscle damage. The best sports drink should contain 460 to 690 mg of sodium, 78 to 195 mg of potassium and a carbohydrate concentration of 5 to 10 percent per liter.

Athletes who participate in a full-day event have to eat less per meal and have more meals during the day. The foods should contain a small amount of proteins and fats, and a lot of complex carbohydrates and fluids. The food should be taken early to ensure food is fully digested before the start of competition.

3.3 Post-Event Meals

It is the best time to replenish energy stores after the event. Besides the fluids resupply, the complex carbohydrates combination food is the good option for athletes. High-GI foods are recommended. The addition of protein can enhance performance in endurance sports. At least 10 g of protein should be consumed within 3 h after endurance sports and 20–25 g of high-quality protein with a high leucine should be supplemented after high-intensity strength training.

三、比赛期间的营养

（一）赛前餐

赛前饮食应充分考虑赛事或运动项目、时间安排、膳食和液体成分及运动员的个人偏好等因素，从而最大限度地维持血糖和糖原储备量以及身体的水合状态。

血糖指数（glycemic index，GI）是衡量不同碳水化合物对血糖水平影响程度的指标。赛前建议摄入低、中 GI 的食物，因为这种食物不会引起血糖和胰岛素水平的大幅波动，能够长时间、缓慢地释放能量。赛前几天摄入的营养比赛前一天摄入的营养要重要得多。

赛前几天的营养要求如下：①能够保持适宜的体重和体脂；②饮食多样化、色香味美、营养平衡；③减少蛋白质和脂肪的摄入，促进胃肠排空，减少胃肠负担；④多吃蔬菜和水果；⑤摄入适量维生素；⑥补糖，增加糖原储备；⑦增加抗氧化酶活力；⑧摄入充足的水；⑨根据比赛需求调整进餐时间。

赛前一天的营养要求如下：①食物体积小、重量轻、易消化，提供 500 ~ 1000 千卡能量；②在比赛开始前 3 ~ 4 小时进食；③不宜换新的食物；④参加大量出汗的比赛项目及在高温环境下比赛时，应在赛前补液 500 ~ 700 毫升；⑤避免摄入高脂、高蛋白食物以及酒精；⑥耐力项目应进行赛前补糖，补糖时间在赛前 2 小时或 15 ~ 30 分钟为宜，补糖量不超过 50 克 / 时，或 1 克 / 千克体重。

（二）赛中餐

对于持续时间超过 45 分钟的有氧耐力比赛、间歇运动或一天内有多场比赛的情况，赛中保持水合状态有助于预防过热、脱水和中暑，适当补充糖分和氨基酸能保持能量供给，减少肌肉损伤。最佳的运动饮料每升应包含 460 ~ 690 毫克的钠、78 ~ 195 毫克的钾且碳水化合物浓度为 5% ~ 10%。

参加全天比赛的运动员应少食多餐，食物应含有少量蛋白质和脂肪及大量复合碳水化合物和液体。进餐时间一定要提前，在开始运动前使食物得以充分消化。

（三）赛后餐

赛后是补充体内能量储备的最佳时机，除注意补液外，运动员应吃复合碳水化合物，推荐食用高 GI 的食物。在碳水化合物补充剂中加入蛋白质能够增强有氧耐力表现，应当在耐力运动后 3 小时内摄入至少 10 克蛋白质，在大负荷力量训练后应补充 20 ~ 25 克高质量、高亮氨酸含量的蛋白质。

4 Body Composition and Weight Control

4.1 Introduction of Body Composition

Body weight is often divided into fat weight (body fat) and fat-free weight (lean body mass) by the different physiological functions. Lean body mass includes muscles, skin, bones, organs, fluids, and other non-fat tissues. Body composition is usually expressed as body fat percentage. The body fat percentage should be more than 3 percent in males and 12 percent in females; otherwise, the internal organs are prone to be injured without the protection of fat.

4.2 Body Composition Assessing Methods

4.2.1 Body Mass Index

Body mass index (BMI) indicates body composition. BMI = weight (kg) /height (m)^2. The overweight value of BMI is 25 to 30 kg/m²; if the BMI is over 30 kg/m², that indicates obesity.

4.2.2 Measurement of Skinfold Thickness

The skinfold thickness measurement method refers to using a skinfold caliper to measure the thickness of the subcutaneous fat layer at several points in the human body, and then calculating the percentage of body fat by substituting it into the formula. It is more accurate than BMI but still has a significant margin of error. However, it is time-effective and easy to operate.

The commonly used calculation formula in China is as follows:

Body fat % (male) = (457/body density)–414.2

Body fat % (female) = (495/body density)–450

Body Density (male) = 1.0913–0.00116X

Body Density (female) = 1.0897–0.00133X

X = Skinfold Thickness in Subscapularis + Skinfold Thickness in Triceps

4.2.3 Hydrostatic Weighing

In hydrostatic weighing, the subject is placed in a specially designed underwater tank to determine body density. The subject is required to dive into the water in a swimsuit, remain still, and exhale air from the lungs almost completely. This technique is very accurate if done properly, but it is time-consuming and expensive.

4.2.4 Bioelectrical Impedance

Bioelectrical impedance technology is to measure the resistance of the body through selected points. The disadvantage of this method is that the percent of body fat can be overestimated if the body is dehydrated. The equipment is also expensive.

4.3 Weight Control

A positive caloric balance, in which more calories are consumed than expended, leads to weight gain; conversely, a negative caloric balance causes weight loss. Weight control includes weight loss and weight gain.

The first step of body weight control is understanding calorie balance and estimating calorie demands. The daily calorie consumption mainly includes basal metabolism, physical activity consumption, and the thermal effect of food. The daily calorie requirement is affected by many factors, such as genetics, training plan, age, etc. Many athletes' weight and body composition are within the normal range, but in order to improve their competitive ability, some sports, such as weightlifting and wrestling, require athletes to lose weight quickly before the competition; some sports, such as gymnastics and diving, require athletes to keep their weight and body fat low in the long term. Dieting, exercise, or a combination of both are commonly utilized to lose weight. Diet weight loss will reduce 35%–45% of non-adipose tissue, while exercise weight loss has almost no reduction of non-adipose tissue. It is very difficult to lose weight only through diet or exercise, and the combination of the two is the most efficient way. 150 to 250 minutes per week of moderate-intensity physical activity can contribute to weight loss; meanwhile, calorie intake should be limited to a moderate level. Weight loss of 0.68 to 0.91 kg per week is ideal, weight loss of more than 1.81 to 2.27 kg per week may be caused by dehydration. A weight-gaining program should aim at increasing lean body mass. Strength training should be performed along with a slight increase in calorie consumption. More protein should be taken with increased strength training intensity. The weight gain is recommended to be 0.45 to 0.91 kg per week.

四、体成分和体重控制

（一）体成分

根据生理功能不同，常把体重分为脂肪重（体脂重）和去脂体重（瘦体重）。去脂体重包括肌肉、皮肤、骨骼、器官、体液及其他非脂肪组织。体成分通常用体脂百分数来表示。男性体脂百分比不应低于 3%，女性不应低于 12%。若低于上述比例，内部器官可能会因缺乏脂肪的保护而容易受到损伤。

（二）体成分测量方法

1. 体质指数（BMI）

体质指数（body mass index，BMI）可以用来表示体成分，BMI = 实际体重（千克）/ 身高（米）^{2}。BMI 为 25 ~ 30 为超重，BMI ≥ 30 为肥胖。

2. 皮褶厚度测量法

皮褶厚度测量法是指用皮褶卡尺测量人体几个位点的皮下脂肪层的厚度，代入公式后计算体脂百分比。此方法相比于 BMI 估算更准确，但依然存在较大误差。优点在于此方法省时，且测量方法易掌握。

国内常用计算公式为：

体脂 %（男）=（457 / 身体密度）- 414.2

体脂 %（女）=（495 / 身体密度）- 450

身体密度（男）= 1.0913 - 0.00116X

身体密度（女）= 1.0897 - 0.00133X

式中，X = 肩胛下角处皮褶厚度 + 肱三头肌处皮褶厚度。

3. 水下称重法

水下称重法是指将运动员置于专门设计的水下槽中来测量身体密度。要求运动员着泳装潜入水中并保持静止，需要尽力将肺中的空气完全排出。如果操作正确，这种技术测量非常准确，但是很耗时，且设备昂贵。

4. 生物电阻抗技术

生物电阻抗技术是通过测量身体选定点间的电阻来计算体成分的。缺点在于如果身体脱水，体脂百分比的测量结果往往会偏高。这种测量方法使用设备的价格也相对较高。

（三）体重控制

摄入的热量大于消耗的热量时为正能量平衡，体重增加；反之，体重减轻。体重控制包括减体重和增体重。

控制体重首先要了解热量平衡，估算热量需求。人体每天的热量消耗主要分为基础代谢、体力活动消耗、食物的热效应，而每天所需的热量受多种因素影响，例如遗传、训练计划、年龄等。很多运动员的体重和体成分在正常范围内，但是为了提高竞技能力，有的项目的运动员需要在比赛前快速减轻体重，如举重、摔跤等；有的项目的运动员需要长期将体重和体脂控制在较低水平，如体操、跳水等。常用的减体重的方法为节食、锻炼或二者结合。节食减重会有 35% ~ 45% 的非脂肪组织的减少，而锻炼减重几乎没有非脂肪组织的减少。仅通过节食或锻炼来减重非常困难，二者结合才最高效。每周进行 150 ~ 250 分钟的中等至高强度运动才能使体重下降，同时，热量摄入也应限制在中等水平。每周减重应为 0.68 ~ 0.91 千克，若每周减重超过 1.81 ~ 2.27 千克，则可能是由脱水导致的。增体重的目标应为增加肌肉重量，应进行力量训练，同时略微增加热量的摄入。随着力量训练强度的提高，应增加膳食中蛋白质的摄入。增重速率应为 0.45 ~ 0.91 千克 / 周。

5 Common Eating Disorder

Eating disorder is a spectrum of abnormal eating behaviors, including food preferences, anorexia nervosa as well as bingeing and purging. Eating disorder can be caused by social, familial, physiological, and psychological factors. Athletes are more susceptible to eating disorders because they need to enhance their performance and control weight at the same time. Anorexia nervosa, exercise anorexia and female athlete triad syndrome are the common eating disorders in athletes.

Anorexia nervosa is a self-obsessive hunger syndrome. Female gymnasts, dancers, etc, have a higher risk. These people pay too much attention to their weight and they always believe they are overweight based the incorrect calculations, and lose weight by dieting. It may cause musculoskeletal, neurological, and cardiovascular disorders.

Exercise anorexia is similar to anorexia nervosa but is specific to athletes. The symptoms and signs include gastrointestinal complaints, primary amenorrhea, menstrual dysfunction, excessive fear of being obese, bingeing or purging, compulsive eating, and/or restriction of caloric intake.

Female athlete triad syndrome is an important problem that involves eating disorders (overeating or anorexia), amenorrhea, and osteoporosis (decreased bone density). Female athlete triad syndrome commonly occurs in adolescent or highly competitive female athletes. The skeletal immaturity of adolescent athletes makes them more susceptible to female athlete triad syndrome. All-female athletes should be screened for the female athlete triad every year. Early signs include weight changes, and repeated fractures; long-term symptoms include low peak bone mineral density, osteoporosis, even suicide tendency, as well as kidney and liver dysfunction.

Female athlete triad syndrome needs to be solved by an interdisciplinary team. First, nutrition should solve the problem of energy imbalance, which is the main cause of the triad. Second, psychological factors often lead to eating disorder or overtraining. Athletes with long-term eating disorder have a higher risk of suicide. Therefore, it is necessary for psychologists to help athletes adjust their mental health. Third, the athletic trainers should offer pharmaceutical management and regular physical check-ups.

五、常见的饮食紊乱

饮食紊乱是指一系列异常的饮食行为，包括偏食症、厌食症和暴饮暴食症等。社会、家庭、生理和心理因素等都会导致饮食紊乱。而运动员为了提高运动表现需要控制体重或体成分，饮食紊乱的发生率明显高于一般人群。主要的饮食紊乱包括神经性厌食、运动性厌食和女运动员三联征。

神经性厌食是一种自我强迫性饥饿综合症，常见于女子体操运动员、舞蹈演员等。这部分人群过度注意体重，错误地认为自己过胖，往往通过控制饮食的方式来减体重。这可能会造成肌肉骨骼、神经以及心血管功能的紊乱。

运动性厌食症是运动员特有的情况，特征与神经性厌食症相似。主要表现为：胃肠不适、原发性闭经、月经紊乱、体重减轻、过度害怕变胖、暴食或排空、强制性饮食和/或限制热量摄入。

女运动员三联征也是一个重要问题。三联征包括饮食失调（暴食或厌食）、闭经、骨质疏松症（骨密度降低）。女运动员三联征常见于青少年或高竞技水平的女性运动员。青少年运动员中最常见，主要是因为她们骨骼不成熟，骨密度低，更容易受到身体和代谢刺激的影响。所有的女运动员每年都应该进行三联征筛查。早期症状包括体重变化、反复骨折；长期症状包括出现低峰值骨密度、骨质疏松症，甚至产生自杀倾向以及肝肾功能障碍。

跨学科的团队对于女运动员三联征的管理是必要的。首先，营养学家应该解决能量失衡的问题，这是导致三联征的主要原因。其次，心理因素往往导致饮食失调或过度训练，长期饮食失调的运动员的自杀风险更高。因此，心理学家有必要帮助运动员恢复心理健康。最后，运动防护师可以帮助管理三联征运动员的药物，并对其进行定期体检。

Summary

1. Nutrients include carbohydrates, dietary fibers, fats, proteins, vitamins, minerals and water. Carbohydrates, fats, and proteins provide energy. Vitamins regulate body processes,

minerals regulate physiological functions and water is the most essential nutrient.

2. Supplements are not necessary when sufficient nutrition can be provided by daily diet; the excessive supplements are harmful.

3. Nutrition supplements during the competition are important. Before the event, foods with a low to medium GI are recommended to ensure the slower release of energy; after the event, foods with a higher GI are recommended to restore glycogen.

4. Methods of assessing body composition include skinfold thickness, hydrostatic weighing, bioelectrical impedance, and body mass index. The body weight control plan is determined by body composition assessment.

5. Eating disorders are common problems for athletes. The problem should be detected and treated as early as possible.

O Reviews

1. Please briefly describe the varieties of nutrients and their functions.

2. Please briefly describe the usage advice of common nutrition supplements.

3. Please briefly describe the nutritious recommendations during the competition.

4. Please briefly describe the measuring methods of body composition and methods of weight control.

5. Please briefly describe the types and performances of eating disorder.

小结

1. 营养物质包括碳水化合物、膳食纤维、脂肪、蛋白质、维生素、矿物质和水。碳水化合物、脂肪和蛋白质提供能量，维生素调节身体活动，矿物质调节生理功能，水是最基本的营养素。

2. 若通过饮食能够获得充足的营养则不需要服用补充剂，过量的补充剂会对身体有害。

3. 比赛期间的营养补充非常重要。赛前应服用低、中 GI 的食物，因其可在长时间内缓慢释放能量；赛后建议服用高 GI 的食物，促进糖原的恢复。

4. 测量体成分的方法包括皮褶厚度测量法、水下称重法、生物电阻抗技术和体质指数。通过体成分可以判断运动员是否为肥胖，进而决定控体重的计划。

5. 饮食紊乱是运动员常见的问题，应该及时发现并加以治疗。

○ 复习题

1. 请简要描述营养素的种类及其主要功能。
2. 请简要描述常见营养补充剂的使用建议。
3. 请简要描述比赛期间的营养补充建议。
4. 请简要描述体成分的测量方法及控制体重的方法。
5. 请简要描述饮食紊乱的种类及表现。

Chapter 3 Environmental Considerations
第三章　环境因素

O Main Contents

1. Treatment and prevention of hyperthermia.
2. Treatment and prevention of hypothermia.
3. Treatment of high altitude sickness.
4. Other environmental considerations.

O 主要内容

1. 高体温症的处理及预防。
2. 低体温症的处理及预防。
3. 高原疾病的处理。
4. 其他环境因素。

1 Treatment and Prevention of Hyperthermia

Training, extreme heat, infection, and abnormal thermoregulatory systems can result in high body temperature and a series of symptoms, which is referred to as hyperthermia. Hyperthermia often happens when the athletes train in hot, humid, and stuffy weather. Besides, if the athletes are dehydrated or cannot dissipate heat in exercise, they also have a high risk of suffering from hyperthermia, even in a cold environment.

1.1 Treatment of Hyperthermia

Hyperthermia includes heat cramps, heat syncope, heat exhaustion, and heatstroke.

Heat cramps are dehydration and sodium loss caused by excessive sweating, resulting in increased muscle excitability and involuntary contractions. The symptoms include involuntary contraction of abdominal and calf muscles, with clear consciousness and normal body temperature. Treatment includes drinking water, stretching spasms in muscles, and ice treatment.

Heat syncope refers to temporary fainting and dizziness in high temperatures. The treatment is to transfer the patients to a cool place and drink water.

Heat exhaustion refers to severe dehydration caused by prolonged exercise in a hot and humid environment. The symptoms include dizziness, headache, nausea, vomiting, fatigue, muscle cramps, oppression in the chest, shortness of breath, strabismus, sweating, decreased blood pressure, normal body temperature, etc. Treatment includes transferring to a cool place, ice therapy, and sipping water. Call medical assistance if the patient loses consciousness.

Heatstroke refers to an acute disease mainly manifested by the central nervous system and/or cardiovascular dysfunction due to thermoregulation center dysfunction or sweat gland failure as well as excessive loss of water and electrolytes in a stuffy environment with high temperature or humidity. It is quite dangerous. Heatstroke is characterized by core body temperature over 40℃ and multiple organ dysfunction, always associated with central nervous system changes. Symptoms and signs include loss of consciousness, shortness of breath, no sweat/little sweat, red and dry skin, fast pulse, high temperature, and decreased blood pressure. Treatment includes: removing the athlete's clothing; the whole body except head immersing in ice water at 2 to 15℃; placing a cold wet towel at the neck, armpit, groin, and feet; raising lower limbs. It is recommended to initiate cooling within 10 min and to keep it until the core body temperature is 39℃, measuring rectal temperature every 5–10 minutes.

1.2 Prevention of Hyperthermia

1.2.1 Training Schedule

When the weather is hot, training time should be arranged reasonably to avoid training during the hottest time of the day. Ensure adequate sleep and medical supervision.

1.2.2 Appropriate Uniforms

Wear light-colored clothing and hats. Avoid wearing rubberized suits.

1.2.3 Appropriate Hydration

The athletes should take sufficient fluids throughout the 24-hour period before the competition, in the way of small quantities several times. Hydration status can be assessed by measuring body weight changes, urine color, urine specific gravity (USG), or urine volume. Eating foods rich in liquid components, such as fruits and vegetables, can also help replenish body fluids. Eating salty foods can help retain liquids. Drinking sports drinks to replenish lost bodily fluids is more effective than simply drinking water.

1.2.4 Nutrition Supplement

Pay attention to the supply of protein, vitamins B1, B2, and C in food.

1.2.5 Gradual Heat Acclimatization

Gradual acclimatization should be started 1 to 2 weeks before the competition. On the basis of conducting 2-hour training in the morning and afternoon respectively in the first week, 80% of environmental adaptation should be achieved. Each practice period should include a 20-minute workout and a 20-minute rest.

1.2.6 Identification of Heat Susceptible Individuals

Before the competition, the athletes who are susceptible to hyperthermia or have a related history should be screened comprehensively, including those who suffer from viral infections, have a fever, or have a skin rash; the obese; the young; the elderly; and those with poor fitness levels.

1.2.7 Guidelines for Athletes' Weight Losing

Athletes who dehydrate themselves to lose weight are more susceptible to hyperthermia. Weight loss should be achieved by reducing body fat rather than dehydration, and it can take several weeks or even months to achieve the weight loss goal.

1.2.8 Weight Records

Weights should be measured before and after exercise for at least the first 2 weeks. Weight loss indicates dehydration, and weight gain indicates overdrinking.

1.2.9 Heat Index Monitoring

The Heat Index is a measurement of how hot it feels when relative humidity is factored in with the actual air temperature. In a hot, humid, and light-adequate environment, special attention should be paid to the monitoring of the heat index (Figure 3-1). When the temperature is constant, the higher the humidity is, the higher the thermal index is. When the humidity is constant, the higher the temperature is, the higher the thermal index is. As an example, if the air temperature is 96°F (about 35.6℃)and the relative humidity is 65%, the heat index—how hot it feels—is 121°F(about 39.5℃).

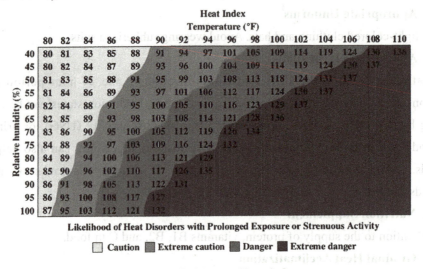

Figure 3-1 Reference of heat index

A preseason heat acclimatization plan should be based on the type of activity and the wet bulb globe temperature index (WBGT), including training periods, rest periods and fluid replacement. Athletes should stay in shady or cool areas, replenish fluids and remove equipment.

一、高体温症的处理及预防

运动、环境温度过高、感染、体温调节系统异常等情况都可能造成体温升高而出现一系列症状，被称为高体温症。运动员在高温、高湿、通风不良的环境中运动时极易发生高体温症。同时，如果运动员脱水或热量无法散发，即使在寒冷环境下运动，运动员也容易患高体温症。

（一）高体温症的处理方法

高体温症包括热痉挛、热晕厥、热衰竭、热射病。

热痉挛是指大量出汗引起脱水和钠流失，导致肌肉兴奋性升高，发生非自主性收缩的现象。症状和体征为：腹部和小腿肌肉非自主性收缩，但意识清楚、体温正常。处理措施包括：补水、拉伸痉挛的肌肉、冰敷。

热晕厥是指因暴露在高温环境下而出现短暂的晕厥和头晕。处理措施包括：将运动员转移至阴凉处、补水。

热衰竭是指长时间在炎热潮湿环境中运动导致身体严重脱水。症状和体征为：头晕、头痛、恶心、呕吐、疲惫、肌肉痉挛、胸闷、呼吸短促、斜视、多汗、血压下降、体温正常等。处理措施包括：将患者转移至阴凉处、冰敷、小口喝水。若运动员失去意识，则应尽快寻求医生的帮助。

热射病是指在温度或湿度较高、不透风的环境下，因出现体温调节中枢功能障碍或汗腺功能衰竭，以及水、电解质丢失过多等情况，从而发生的以中枢神经和／或心血管功能障碍为主要表现的急性疾病，危险性较高。热射病特征是核心体温超过40℃及以上，导致器官功能障碍，常与中枢神经系统改变有关。症状和体征为：无意识，呼吸短促，无汗／少汗，皮肤发红、干燥，脉搏快，体温高，血压低。处理措施包括：去除运动员的衣物；将运动员浸泡在 2 ~ 15℃ 的冰水中，浸没颈部；用湿冷毛巾冷敷颈部、腋窝、腹股沟、脚；抬高下肢。建议在 10 分钟内就开始冷疗，可每 5 ~ 10 分钟测量一次直肠温度来监控核心体温，直到核心体温降到 39℃ 以下。

（二）高体温症的预防

1. 训练时间

天气炎热时，应合理安排训练时间，避免在一天中最热的时间段训练。保证充足睡眠，加强医务监督。

2. 适当的服装

穿浅色衣服，戴遮阳帽，避免穿橡胶质的衣服。

3. 适当补液

赛前 24 小时内运动员应该少量多次摄入充足的液体。可通过测量赛前和赛后体重变化、监测尿液颜色、尿比重、尿量来评估水合状态。食用富含液体成分的食物（如水果、蔬菜）也有助于补充体液。食用咸味的食物有助于液体滞留。饮用运动饮料补充丢失的体液比单纯喝水更有效。

4. 营养补充

注意食物中的蛋白质，维生素 B_1、B_2、C 的供给。

5. 逐渐适应环境

在赛季前 1 ~ 2 周进行渐进性环境适应。第一周在上午、下午分别进行 2 小时训练的基础上，应该实现 80% 的环境适应。可以选择 20 分钟热环境下训练和 20 分钟阴凉处休息交替的周期进行。

6. 不耐热人群的识别

赛季开始之前进行全面的医学筛查，辨别易感高体温症及有相关病史的运动员，如：患有病毒性感染、发烧或严重皮疹的人群，超重人群，年轻人，老人，体适能水平较低的人群。

7. 减重运动员的指导

通过脱水来减重的运动员更容易患高体温症。减体重应该通过降低体脂而非脱水来实现，并且需花费几周甚至几个月的时间来实现减重目标。

8. 体重记录

在运动前后测量体重，至少持续 2 周。体重减轻提示运动员缺水，体重增加提示饮水过量。

9. 热指数监测

热指数是将相对湿度与实际空气温度结合在一起来体现人体真实热感知的指标。在炎热、潮湿且光照充足的环境下，要格外注意热指数的监测。温度一定，湿度越大，热指数越高；湿度一定，温度越高，热指数也越高。举个例子，如果空气温度是 96°F（约 35.6°C），相对湿度是 65%，那么热指数是 121°F（39.5°C）。

赛前高温适应方案应该基于活动类型和湿球黑球温度指数（wet bulb temperature index，WBGT）制订，包括训练时间、休息时间、补液的相关建议。运动员应尽量待在阴凉或凉爽的地方，补充水分，并撤除装备。

2 Treatment and Prevention of Hypothermia

Hypothermia occurs when body temperature falls below 35°C. When heat loss exceeds heat production, the athletes, especially those with low energy supplies, are susceptible to hypothermia.

2.1 Treatment of Hypothermia

Symptoms and signs of mild hypothermia include headache, dizziness, feeling cold, shivering, numbness, increased blood pressure, subtle movement skill impairment, lethargy, apathy, and mild amnesia. Symptoms and signs of moderate and severe hypothermia include cessation of shivering, low body temperature, lisp, unconsciousness, gross movement skill impairment, and arrhythmia.

The treatment of hypothermia is as follows: ① Transfer the patient to a warm and dry place. ② Remove wet clothing. ③ Wrap the patient with a blanket to raise body temperature. ④ Apply heat only to the torso and heat-exchange body parts, including armpits, chest wall, and groin. Massaging the limbs at the same time will cause the cold blood of the limbs to flow into the core area, which in turn lowers the temperature of the core area. ⑤ Have warm, alcohol-free liquid and food containing 6 to 8 percent carbohydrates. ⑥ If the symptoms are serious, the patient may need CPR and should be sent to the hospital.

2.2 Prevention of Hypothermia

2.2.1 Wearing Appropriate Clothes

Suitable clothing is required when engaging in outdoor activities. The material of clothing should be suitable for sweating and dissipating body heat, or sweat and heat will remain on the clothing, causing people to feel cold when exercise stops.

2.2.2 Putting On and Taking Off Clothes in Time

It is best to wear multiple layers of thin clothing to adjust the amount of clothing with temperature changes and avoid wearing wet clothes. Attention should be paid to keeping warm before, after, and during rest. Additionally, wearing a hat, gloves, a scarf, and a windproof mask can also help avoid heat loss.

2.2.3 Hydrate

Dehydration can reduce blood volume, resulting in energy loss. It is necessary to drink in time when training in a cold environment.

2.2.4 Warm-Up

Athletes are prone to hypothermia if they cannot warm up sufficiently or are inactive during training. Therefore, athletes should warm up adequately before exercise.

2.2.5 Wind Speed Monitoring

Wind can increase the incidence of hypothermia in cold weather. As shown in Figure 3-2, compared with the temperature in calm weather, the temperature will decrease with the increase of wind speed (Figure 3-2). For example, when there is no wind, the temperature is 40°F (about 4°C). When the wind speed is 5 mph (about 8 kilometers per hour), the temperature drops to 36°F (about 2°C). When the wind speed is 30 mph (about 48 kilometers per hour), the temperature drops to 28°F (about −2°C). Additionally, dampness can also increase the risk of hypothermia. Thus, in cold, windy, and humid weather, extra attention should be paid to the safety of outdoor sports.

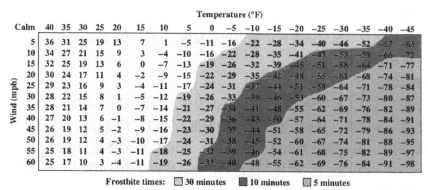

Figure 3-2 Wind's impact on the temperature

二、低体温症的处理及预防

核心体温降低到 35℃ 称为低体温症。运动员在寒冷天气中进行运动时，当身体流失的热量超过产生的热量，则易出现低体温症，尤其是能量供应较低的运动员。

（一）低体温症的处理

轻度低体温症的症状和体征包括：头痛、头晕、感觉发冷、寒颤、麻木、血压升高、精细运动技能障碍、嗜睡、冷漠、轻度健忘；中重度低体温症的症状和体征包括：寒颤停止、低体温、口齿不清、意识丧失、粗大运动技能障碍、心率不齐。

低体温症的主要处理方法如下：①将运动员转移到温暖、干燥的环境中。②脱去潮湿的衣物。③包裹毯子以回升体温。④仅在躯干和热量交换的部位予以热量，包括腋窝、胸壁、腹股沟。若同时揉搓四肢会使四肢低温的血液流入核心区，进而使核心区温度降低。⑤进食温热、无酒精的液体以及含 6% ~ 8% 碳水化合物的食物。⑥若症状较为严重，可能需要进行心肺复苏，并且送医治疗。

（二）低体温症的预防

1. 穿着合适的服装

在进行户外运动时需要穿着合适的服装。衣服的材质应该适宜排汗和散发体热，否则，汗液和热量留在衣服上，运动停止时会使人感到寒冷。

2. 及时增减衣物

最好穿多层薄衣服，以便随着温度的变化而增减衣物，避免穿着湿衣服。运动前、后及休息时都应注意保暖。此外，戴帽子、手套、围巾、防风面罩等也可以减少热量流失。

3. 及时补液

脱水会造成血容量降低，从而导致身体热量减少，所以在寒冷环境中运动时应该注意补液。

4. 充分热身

如果运动员热身不充分或者在运动中相对怠惰，则易发生低体温症，因此，运动员在运动前应进行充分热身。

5. 风速监测

在寒冷的天气中，刮风会增加低体温症的发生。与无风时的温度相比，随着风速的增大，温度会进一步降低。比如，在无风时的温度为 40°F（约 4°C），当风力为 5 英里 / 时（约 8 千米 / 时），温度则降为 36°F（约 2°C）；当风力为 30 英里 / 时（约 48 千米 / 时），温度则降为 28°F（约 -2°C）。此外，潮湿的环境也使得运动员更易发生低体温症。因此，在寒冷、刮风、潮湿的天气中，要格外注意户外运动的安全。

3 Treatment of High Altitude Sickness

High altitude regions can be divided into high altitude (1500–3500 m) regions, very high altitude (3500–5500 m) regions, and extreme altitude above 5500 m regions. Humans face two major challenges in high-altitude environments: climate and low air pressure. First of all, the temperature differs largely between day and night in high altitude, with high temperature and abundant sunshine during the day and low temperature at night. Strong wind and low humidity at high altitudes can lead to rapid dehydration. Additionally, the air pressure at high altitudes is low. In high altitudes, the circulating red blood cells become less saturated and the tissues are deprived of oxygen.

Acute mountain sickness is the most common high altitude sickness, but it is usually benign and self-limited. High altitude pulmonary edema and high altitude cerebral edema occur rather rarely but are life-threatening.

3.1 Acute Mountain Sickness

Acute mountain sickness (AMS) includes various pathological reactions after short-term exposure to a hypoxic environment, which usually appear at an altitude of over 3000 meters. Symptoms include headache, insomnia, nausea, vomiting, loss of appetite, fatigue, dyspnea, etc. For individuals who suffer from headaches and only moderate acute mountain sickness, staying at the current altitude for adaptation is recommended. They should also do no exercise or only slight exercises, drink appropriate fluid, and if necessary, take pain killers and/or antiemetics. Moving or transferring to higher altitudes before symptoms have disappeared is not allowed. If the symptoms persist or worsen, it is necessary to transfer to low-altitude areas. For patients with severe symptoms, they should be transferred to low-altitude areas and given low-flow oxygen (2-4 L/minute) or high-pressure oxygen bags. Pharmacological treatment includes acetazolamide and/or dexamethasone.

3.2 High Altitude Pulmonary Edema

High altitude pulmonary edema (HAPE) often appears on initial entry or re-entry to the plateau above 3000 meters. Symptoms include headache, dyspnea, inability to lie supine, pale, etc. If left untreated, the mortality rate can reach 50%. Athletes should be transferred to lower altitudes and given oxygen (2–4 L/min) or a hyperbaric bag as soon as possible. Take the nifedipine for medical treatment.

3.3 High Altitude Cerebral Edema

Severe acute mountain sickness can develop into high altitude cerebral edema (HACE). HACE refers to severe dysfunction of the central nervous system caused by acute hypoxia, which can lead to coma and death and is usually associated with HAPE. Symptoms include severe headache, vomiting, lethargy, irritability, ataxia, coma, etc. HACE can be fatal if it is not treated within 24 hours. Early diagnosis and treatment are crucial. Once diagnosed with HACE, patients should be transferred to lower altitudes and given oxygen (2–4 L/min) or a hyperbaric bag. Take the dexamethasone for medical treatment.

3.4 Sickle Cell Trait Reaction

Sickle cell anemia is an autosomal dominant inherited hemoglobin disorder. Some people with sickle cell trait (SCT) might experience complications of sickle cell disease (SCD), but most of them do not have any symptoms of SCD. In extreme conditions, the following conditions could be harmful to people with SCT: increased pressure in the atmosphere, low oxygen levels in the air, dehydration, and high altitudes. Some people with SCT have been shown to be more likely than those without SCT to suffer from heatstroke when doing intense exercise under unfavorable temperatures or conditions. These problems can be reduced by avoiding dehydration and overheating during training.

三、高原疾病的处理

高原通常分为高海拔（1500 ~ 3500 米）地区、超高（3500 ~ 5500 米）地区以及极端海拔（5500 米以上）地区。人类在高原环境下面临两大挑战：气候和低气压。首先，高原地区昼夜温差大，白天高温、日照充足，晚上寒冷。高原地区风大、湿度低，易引起快速脱水。此外，高原地区的气压相对较低，在高原环境下，参与循环的红细胞饱和度下降，使组织处于缺氧状态。

急性高原病是常见的高原疾病，但通常都是良性、自限性的。高原肺水肿和高原脑水肿较为少见，但会危及生命。

（一）急性高原病

急性高原病指人体短期暴露于低氧环境后产生的各种病理反应，常在进入海拔 3000 米以上地区时出现。症状为：头痛、失眠、恶心、呕吐、食欲减退、疲倦、呼吸困难等。只有头痛或急性高原病症状仅为中度的患者可以待在原海拔地区，同时停止运动或仅做非常轻量的运动，摄入适量的液体，如果必要，可以服用镇痛药和 / 或止吐药。在不适症状消失之前不要向更高海拔地区转移。如果症状持续或加重，则需要转移至低海拔地区。对于症状严重的患者，应将患者转移到低海拔地区，给予低流量氧气（2 ~ 4 升 / 分）或使用高压氧袋。药物治疗包括利尿剂和 / 或地塞米松。

（二）高原肺水肿

高原肺水肿常在初次进入或重返高原时出现，尤其是当海拔超过 3000 米时。症状为：头痛、呼吸困难、不能平卧、面色土灰等。如果不及时治疗，死亡率可达 50%。此时应尽快将患者转移到低海拔地区并给予氧气（2 ~ 4 升 / 分）或高压氧袋。药物治疗可选择硝苯地平。

（三）高原脑水肿

严重的急性高原病会发展为高原脑水肿。高原脑水肿是由急性缺氧引起的中枢神经系统功能严重障碍，会导致昏迷和死亡，通常会与高原肺水肿并发。症状为：剧烈头痛、呕吐、嗜睡、烦躁、共济失调及昏迷等。高原脑水肿如果在 24 小时内未得到治疗，则会危及生命。因此，早期诊断及治疗非常重要。一旦诊断出高原脑水肿，应尽快将患者转移到低海拔地区，给予氧气（2 ～ 4 升 / 分）或高压氧袋。药物治疗可选择地塞米松。

（四）镰状细胞特征反应

镰状细胞贫血是一种常染色体显性遗传血红蛋白病。虽然有些具有镰状细胞特征（sickle cell trait，SCT）的人可能会有镰状细胞病的并发症，但是大多数人并无症状。在极端条件下，以下情况对 SCT 人群有害：大气压力增加，空气中含氧量低，脱水以及高海拔。与健康人相比，一些 SCT 人群在不适宜的温度或条件下进行剧烈运动时，更容易出现中暑。可以通过避免脱水及避免出现训练中过热来减少这些现象的发生。

4 Other Environmental Considerations

4.1 Circadian Dysrhythmia

Athletes may experience abnormal circadian rhythms due to circadian dysrhythmia during competitions or training, which typically manifests as fatigue, headaches, digestive system disorders, and changes in blood pressure, heart rate, and endocrine function. Any change can have a negative impact on an athlete's performance.

The methods to minimize the effect of jet lag are as follows: ① Adjust the circadian rhythm in advance. For example, when it comes to participating in a competition in a Western country, every time a time zone is crossed, sleeping and waking up are postponed by one hour. ② Drink plenty of water to avoid dehydration caused by dry cabin air, high altitude, and low humidity. ③ When participating in competitions in Western countries, it is advisable to consume moderate amounts of caffeine, while when participating in competitions in Eastern countries, caffeine intake should be avoided. ④ Avoid drinking alcohol before, during, and after traveling. ⑤ Before participating in competitions in Western countries, adjust the exercise or training time later. ⑥ When participating in competitions in Western countries, try to expose yourself to sunlight as much as possible upon arrival. ⑦ After arriving, adapt to the local training, diet, and sleep schedule as soon as possible.

4.2 Overexposure to Sun

Athletes who are excessively exposed to ultraviolet (UV) radiation during outdoor activities can suffer from skin sunburn. The symptoms of sunburn include reddish skin, pain, swelling, fatigue, and increased skin temperatures; severe symptoms include rash, nausea, fever, dizziness, even blistering, dehydration, edema, and fainting. In areas with strong ultraviolet radiation, direct exposure to sunlight for 15 minutes can cause sunburn. Sunburn not only occurs in summer, but prolonged exposure to strong ultraviolet radiation on snowy or cloudy days can also lead to sunburn. Long-term excessive exposure to sunlight may lead to premature aging of the skin and increase the risk of skin cancer.

Sunscreens can prevent UV radiation. Sun protection factor (SPF) indicates a sunscreen's effectiveness in absorbing ultraviolet radiation. For example, an SPF of 6 means that before the skin starts to turn red, athletes who apply this sunscreen can be exposed to ultraviolet radiation for six times longer than those who do not use sunscreen. Although clothes and hats can provide some sun protection, they cannot replace sunscreen. People who often go outdoors should apply sunscreen regularly, and it is recommended to use it 15-30 minutes before going out, especially from 10 AM to 4 PM.

4.3 Wind Speed

Wind speed is an intervening factor in some sports, such as running and cycling and outdoor ball games. It can affect athletes' regular technical performance. In the sailing competition, the performance will be affected by the wind, especially when it is in a different direction from that in training. The athletes who adapt to strong wind will be affected by the breeze. On the contrary, the sailing athletes who adapt to the breeze will be affected by the strong wind.

4.4 Rain

Rain, which often occurs with wind or other inclement weather, can affect the tactics and results of outdoor sports. Overcoming the influence of rain requires both psychological and physical training. A proper pair of shoes for the wet floor is necessary. If the temperature is cold on rainy days, the athletes also need to prepare appropriate clothing and equipment.

4.5 Thunder and Lightning Safety

A comprehensive emergency action plan (EAP) for all outdoor venues should be established. Firstly, the EAP should include a decision-making system during lightning storms. The athletic trainer should help athletes, coaches, and spectators transfer to a safe place. Secondly, the athletic trainer should closely monitor local weather. Thirdly, the place where lightning can be avoided shall be near the playground. Fourthly, specific criteria and guidelines should be developed for suspending and resuming activity. For example, training may continue if there is no lightning or thunder within 30 minutes after the last thunder or lightning. Fifthly, the athletic trainer should perform cardiopulmonary resuscitation (CPR) if a lightning strike occurs. Finally, lightning safety slogans and education should be promoted to raise safety awareness. In a sudden storm, the following principles should be followed: go indoors; stay away from metal products; avoid using electronic devices; avoid showering; avoid standing near trees/poles; avoid standing on the summit.

4.6 Air Pollution

The athletes who train outside are more susceptible to air pollution. To avoid pollution-related problems, the athlete must stop or decrease physical activities during periods of high pollution.

4.7 Crowd Noise

When the game is held in a large indoor or outdoor stadium, the team will not be able to hear its own signal due to the interference of crowd noise. Professional teams usually use a large sound system to play very loud noise to their players during training to prepare them for the game in this case.

4.8 Hilly or Rugged Topography

For runners and cyclists, especially those who adapt to flat training, special training is needed to adapt to multi-slopes or rugged landforms. Hill training is often accomplished through interval training or stationary exercise machines that permit the athlete to adjust the level and resistance of the training.

四、其他环境因素

（一）时差反应

运动员因为参赛或训练需要，可能因为时差反应而导致昼夜节律异常，一般表现为疲劳，头痛，消化系统紊乱，血压、心率和内分泌改变等问题。任何一种变化都可能对运动员的发挥产生负面影响。减小时差反应的方法如下：①提前调整昼夜节律。比如，当需要去西方国家参加比赛时，每跨越1个时区，就推迟1小时睡觉和起床。②多喝水，避免因机舱空气干燥、高海拔、低湿度而脱水。③去西方国家参加比赛时，可摄入适量的咖啡因，去东方国家参加比赛时则应避免摄入咖啡因。④在旅行前、中、后都要避免饮酒。⑤去西方参加比赛前，将运动或训练时间调晚。⑥去西方参加比赛时，到达后要尽可能多接触阳光。⑦到达后，尽快适应当地的训练、饮食和睡眠时间等。

（二）过度暴晒

运动员在户外运动中，过度暴露在紫外线下会导致皮肤晒伤。晒伤的症状包括：皮肤发红、疼痛、肿胀、疲劳、皮温升高。严重时症状包括：皮疹、恶心、发烧、头晕，甚至出现水疱、脱水、水肿和昏厥。在紫外线较强的地方，身体直接暴露在阳光下 15 分钟就会晒伤。晒伤不仅仅会发生在夏季，在雪天或阴天时长时间暴露在紫外线较强的地方也有可能导致晒伤。长期的过度暴晒可能会导致皮肤提前衰老并增加患皮肤癌的风险。

涂抹防晒霜可预防紫外线辐射。防晒系数（Sun Protection Factor，SPF）可以表示防晒霜吸收紫外线辐射的效果。比如，SPF 为 6 表示在皮肤开始变红之前，运动员涂抹此防晒霜后可以暴露在紫外线下的时间是不涂防晒霜时的 6 倍。虽然衣服和帽子能够起到一定的防晒作用，但是无法代替防晒霜。经常在户外的人群应该有规律地涂防晒霜，建议出门前15 ~ 30 分钟涂抹，尤其是上午 10 点到下午 4 点。

（三）风速

在跑步、自行车以及在开放场地进行的球类运动等比赛中，风速会成为一个干扰因素，影响运动员的常规技术表现。虽然在帆船等比赛中风是推动力的基本要素，但是如果风与日常训练时显著不同，运动员的表现也可能受到影响。适应强风的帆船运动员在微风时的方法和战术会受到影响；反之，适应微风的帆船运动员在强风时也会受到影响。

（四）下雨

下雨通常伴随着刮风或其他恶劣天气，对几乎所有户外运动的战术和比赛结果都有严重影响。克服下雨这一因素的影响既需要运动员进行心理训练，又需要进行身体训练。若下雨时场地湿滑，要准备好合适的鞋子；若下雨时天气寒冷，还需要准备好合适的服装。

（五）雷电安全

所有室外场所都应具有一个全面的紧急行动计划（emergency action plan，EAP）。第一，EAP 应该包括在雷暴期间的决策指挥系统，运动防护师需负责将运动员、教练、观众等转移到安全地带。第二，运动防护师应密切关注当地天气情况。第三，应在运动场附近确定可躲避雷电的地方。第四，应该制订暂停和恢复比赛的特定标准和指导方针。比如，最后一次雷声或闪电过后 30 分钟之内无闪电或雷声，则可继续比赛。第五，如果运动员受到雷击，若有需要，运动防护师应实施心肺复苏。第六，可通过闪电安全标语和教育来提高人们的安全意识。在突遇暴雨时，应遵循以下原则：户外活动应转到室内；远离金属制品；不要使用电子设备；不要洗澡；不要站在树/电线杆附近；不要站在高地/山顶等。

（六）空气污染

长时间在室外训练的运动员通常更容易受到空气污染的影响。为了规避空气污染的影响，运动员必须在高污染时期停止或减少体育训练。

（七）人群噪声

当比赛在大型室内或室外体育场举办时，由于人群噪声干扰，运动员将无法听到队内的信号。专业运动员通常使用大型音响系统，在训练中对队员播放高分贝的噪声，以此来应对比赛中的类似情况。

（八）山地地形

对于跑步及自行车运动员来说，尤其是适应平地训练的运动员，他们需要特殊训练来适应多坡或崎岖的地形。一般通过结合间歇性训练或使用可调节训练难度和阻力的固定训练设备来完成山地训练。

Summary

1. The athletes need to take measures to prevent hyperthermia when training in an environment with high temperatures and humidity. They should replenish water, adapt to the environment early, wear proper clothing, record their weight and monitor the heat index.

2. The athletes need to protect themselves from cold injuries when training in a cold, windy and damp environment. They should wear the apparel correctly and replenish fluids in time.

3. When the athletes go from a low to a high altitude, they need to get trained before the competition. The problems caused by the high altitude need to be treated as soon as possible; otherwise, it can be life-threatening.

4. Circadian dysrhythmia can negatively affect performance; thus, jet lag needs to be adjusted when athletes travel through time zones.

5. There are many other problems in training or competition, including weather conditions like overexposure to the sun, wind, rain, lightning; interruptive factors like air pollution and noise; and the impacts of fields like hilly topography. The athletes need to be prepared for adaptation, prevent some problems and react to emergencies.

◯ Review

1. Please briefly describe the types and prevention of hyperthermia.
2. Please briefly describe the treatment and prevention of hypothermia.
3. Please briefly describe the common illnesses and treatments at high altitudes.
4. Please briefly describe ways to minimize the effect of jet lag.

小结

1.在高温潮湿环境下训练时，运动员需要采取一些措施防止高体温症，比如及时补液、提前适应环境、适当着装，以及及时监测体重和热指数。

2.在寒冷、大风、潮湿的环境下训练时，运动员应该注意预防低体温症，合理着装，及时补液。

3.从低海拔到高海拔时，运动员在赛前需要进行适应性训练。若出现高海拔引起的相关疾病，应及时治疗，否则可能会危及生命。

4.昼夜节律失常会对运动员的运动表现产生负面影响，当跨时区移动时应注意调整。

5.运动员在训练或比赛时还会遇到很多其他问题，包括过度暴晒、刮风、下雨、雷电等恶劣天气，空气污染、噪声等外界干扰因素，山地地形等场地影响。运动员应采取相应的措施以提前适应、预防和应急。

○ 复习题

1.请简要描述高体温症的分类和预防。

2.请简要描述低体温症的处理和预防。

3.请简要描述高原地区常见的疾病及处理方法。

4.请简要描述减小时差反应的方法。

Chapter 4 Techniques of Athletic Training
第四章 运动防护技术

○ Main Contents

1. On-the-field injury assessment and management.
2. Off-the-field injury assessment and management.

○ 主要内容

1. 场地评估及处理。
2. 场外评估及处理。

1 On-the-Field Injury Assessment and Management

1.1 Principles and Methods of On-the-Field Injury Assessment and Management

1.1.1 Injury Assessment of On-the-Field

The on-site first aid assessment helps determine the nature and extent of the injury and provides guidance for the decision-making of emergency rescue. On-the-field assessment can be divided into primary assessment and secondary assessment.

1.1.2 Primary Assessment

The primary assessment aims to find out the existence of potentially life-threatening situations, including the level of consciousness, airway, breathing, circulation, severe bleeding and shock. These aspects take precedence over all other aspects of the assessment of the injured. Patients whose lives are in danger should be treated as soon as possible and transported to medical first aid institutions. Patients with clear consciousness and stable condition do not need a primary assessment, but unconscious patients should be monitored for life-threatening problems. Glasgow Coma Scale (GSC) can be used to assess athletes' consciousness.

When the primary assessment excludes the possibility of life-threatening injury or disease, the secondary assessment is to observe the injury situation carefully, collect the specific information about the patient's injury in detail, and systematically assess the vital signs and symptoms.

1.1.3 Secondary Assessment

(1) Pulse, Breath and Blood Pressure and Other Vital Signs

① Pulse is a palpable arterial throb on the body surface. A normal person's pulse coincides with the heart rate. The frequency of pulse is affected by age and gender. The frequency of pulse of the athletes is lower than that of normal adults.

In normal adults, the pulse should be 60–100 beats per minute, and the average pluse is around 72 beats per minute. The pulse of the fetus is 110–160 beats per minute. The pulse of the infant is 120–140 beats per minute, and the school-age child's pulse is 80–90 beats per minute. Older people's pulse is slower, usually 55–60 beats per minute.

The change of pulse can indicate the existence of pathological conditions. For example, a fast but weak pulse may represent shock, bleeding, diabetic coma or heat exhaustion; a fast and strong pulse may represent heat stroke or severe shock; a strong but slow pulse may indicate a skull fracture or stroke; and no pulse means cardiac arrest or death.

② Breathing refers to the process of gas exchange between the body and the external environment. The respiratory rate is 12–20 breaths per minute in normal adults and 15–30 breaths per minute in children.

The athletic trainer should pay attention to the patient's frequency and manner of breathing during the assessment. For example, coughing up foamy blood may be caused by a rib fracture, resulting in hemopneumothorax and other problems.

③ Blood pressure refers to the peripheral pressure of blood acting on the blood vessel wall per unit area when it flows in the blood vessel. It is the force that promotes blood flow in the blood vessels. Generally, blood pressure refers to the arterial blood pressure of the systemic circulation. The normal adult blood pressure range: systolic blood pressure is 90–139 mmHg, diastolic blood pressure is 60–89 mmHg.

The decrease in blood pressure can indicate hemorrhage, shock, heart attack or visceral organ damage, while the increase in blood pressure can indicate heatstroke, etc.

④ Other signs. Reddening or itching of the skin may indicate sunburn or allergic reaction; pale skin may indicate shock or bleeding; jaundice indicates liver disease or dysfunction.

Pupils can reflect the condition of the nervous system accurately. Dilation of one or two pupils may indicate head injury, heatstroke or bleeding. If the pupil has no light reflex, that may indicate alcohol or drug poisoning. In the evaluation, the pupillary light reflex is more important than the pupillary size.

The change of body temperature can be reflected on the skin. For example, hot and relatively dry skin may indicate infection or heatstroke; cold and sticky skin may reflect shock or trauma; cold and dry skin may be the result of overexposure to a cold environment.

(2) Musculoskeletal Assessment: Observation, Palpation, Movement, Measurement and Special Test

① Observation: gait posture, colour of the skin, swelling, deformity and blood stasis, muscle atrophy, scar, wound secretion, wound shape and depth, local bandaging and fixation, etc.

② Palpation: bony marks, tenderness, a sense of bone friction, skin temperature, muscle tension, etc. If the pain is very sensitive, palpation can be carried out at the last step.

③ Movement: joint range of motion for active and passive movements, muscle strength, etc.

④ Measurement: limb length measurement, limb and joint circumference measurement, limb axis measurement, etc.

⑤ Special tests: Different injuries have its special tests and different methods also have different specificity and sensitivity. The appropriate test methods should be chosen based on both experience and symptom.

Principles of musculoskeletal assessment:

• Examination sequence (healthy side first and active movement first; the affected side second, and the passive movement second).

• Full exposure, contrast on both sides.

• Combining objective examinations with subjective symptoms.

● Combination of global and local examinations.

● Standard and gentle assessment technique to avoid aggravating injury.

(3) Injury Management of On-the-Field

Due to the limited time of on-the-field management, after the completion of life safety assessment and treatment, the above musculoskeletal injury examinations can be quickly carried out for further treatment decisions. A more detailed inspection should be taken during off-the-field assessments. All the assessment results should be recorded. After completing the first aid assessment on site, the athletic trainer should make correct treatment decisions: the type and severity of the injury; choosing the necessary field first aid methods; deciding whether it is necessary to immediately transfer to the doctor for further evaluation; choosing the transfer mode from the field to the off-field, clinic or hospital.

Management of unconscious injured patients:

① The athletic trainer should immediately pay attention to the position of the injured and confirm the consciousness and reaction status.

② Neck injury should be considered when analyzing the cause of coma.

③ If the injured can not breathe autonomously or his/her breathing is weakened, the injured should be placed in a supine position carefully and immediately. Cardiopulmonary resuscitation (CPR) and artificial chest compression need to be started as soon as possible to establish artificial circulation; if the injured is still breathing, the athletic trainer should monitor the injured carefully until consciousness is restored.

④ If the athlete wears a helmet, it should not be removed until the neck and spine injuries are clearly excluded. The mask must be removed before cardiopulmonary resuscitation (CPR).

⑤ Life support for patients in coma should be maintained until emergency medical personnel arrive.

⑥ Once the patient's condition is stabilized, the athletic trainer should start a secondary assessment.

For bleeding, fracture and other injuries, hemostasis and fracture fixation should be performed immediately for subsequent transport. In closed soft tissue injuries, reducing swelling and inflammation can shorten rehabilitation, which is the primary goal of on-the-field injury management. The basic treatment of acute closed soft tissue injury followed the "POLICE" principle.

P (Protect): Protect the injured part from secondary damage.

OL (Optimal Loading): Give appropriate sports load and avoid absolute braking.

I (Ice): Ice can inhibit inflammatory reaction and reduce pain and swelling. In the early stage, an ice bag can be used for 20 to 30 minutes every 2 hours.

C (Compression): Compress and suppress swelling.

E (Elevation): Raise the affected limb, promote blood flow and reduce swelling.

1.2 Emergency Medical Services and Emergency Action Plan

Emergency medical services refer to the actions that should be taken as quickly as possible to minimize the harm to the injured in an emergency. The main purpose of emergency services is to maintain cardiovascular function and central nervous system function of the patients. Any kind of damage in these systems can cause death. In some cases, these emergency rescues can not only save the current life but also determine the degree of disability of the injured.

The key to emergency assistance is the preliminary assessment of the injured. It is necessary to evaluate quickly and accurately for the athletic trainer so as to provide the right first aid at the first time.

The perfect emergency plan can provide an effective guarantee for emergency rescue. Each sports ground or gymnasium should have a special emergency plan. Common emergency plans shall include the following aspects:

① Define the responsibilities of the first aid personnel during training or competition, and revise and rehearse regularly (for example, the division of work among the athletic trainers, doctors and rescue teams should be clear). In the event of an emergency, everyone can perform their duties and enhance cooperation. At the same time, it is recommended that emergency personnel regularly practice the use and operation of emergency equipment, such as stretchers and automatic external defibrillators (AED).

② Formulate specific operation procedures for removing protective equipment, especially helmets and shoulder pads.

③ Ensure that communication devices such as telephones are available and ready to be used to access the emergency medical system at any time. In China, the emergency call is 120 or 999. The person making the emergency call must provide the following information: types of emergency and suspected injury; the condition of the athletes; the current medical support (such as CPR); the exact location of the emergency; any restrictions around the building (whether the ambulance can reach the scene easily).

④ Make sure that the exit way is clear, and the elevator can accommodate the stretcher.

⑤ Assign a specialized person to accompany the injured athlete to the hospital.

⑥ Carry the contact information of all the athletes, coaches and other personnel at any time. For minors, their guardians should also provide medical consent.

1.3 Cardiopulmonary Resuscitation and Heimlich Maneuver

1.3.1 Definition of CPR

Cardiopulmonary resuscitation (CPR) is a life-saving technique for cardiac and respiratory arrest. The purpose is to restore the patient's spontaneous breathing and circulation. In 2010, the American Heart Association's (AHA) Guidelines for CPR rearranged the order of CPR steps. Today, instead of the A-B-C subsequence, which stands for airway and breathing first, followed by chest compressions, the AHA teaches rescuers to practice the C-A-B subsequence: chest compressions first, then airway and breathing. This change highlights the importance of chest compressions in creating circulation. In 2015, the American Heart Association revised the technical details of the rescue to make on-site emergency treatment more effective.

1.3.2 Procedure of CPR

- Confirm that the field environment is safe.
- Examine the consciousness level, breath and pulse of the injured. If there is no response, call 120 or 999.
- If an automatic external defibrillator (AED) is available, provide one shock immediately and initiate CPR as early as possible.
- Before CPR, place the injured person in the supine position, remove the coat, overlap the hands, align the palmar root with the midpoint of the line between the two nipples, and perform chest compressions 30 times at a compression rate of no more than 120 times/min.
- Open the airway and clear the mouth, and then give mouth-to-mouth breathing twice (each ventilation lasts for about one second until the chest rises).
- A compression-ventilation ratio of 30:2 and at least provide five cycles of CPR with the same compression-ventilation ratio.
- If the patient has no response after five cycles, use AED for a shock.
- Continue to use CPR until the patient recovers consciousness and self-breathing, or medical help arrives.

1.3.3 Precautions of CPR

The high-quality CPR procedure includes fast (compressions at a rate of 100–120/min), forceful pressing (a depth of 5–6 cm for an average adult), chest full rebound, minimizing press interruption and avoiding excessive ventilation. For professional first-aid personnel, it is recommended to implement CPR in the form of team as the basic principle to ensure the implementation of high-quality CPR to the maximum extent.

CPR standards for children (age one to adolescence) and infants (postnatal to one-year-old): In the process of CPR implementation, compared with adults, more attention should be paid to the importance of artificial ventilation in the recovery of children and infants, and it is not recommended to only implement the recovery strategy of chest compression for children. In addition, for young patients, including children and infants, the time of CPR should be prolonged and not terminate CPR easily. The procedure of CPR standard for children is similar to that for adults.The main difference is the depth of chest compression, which should be controlled at about 5 cm for children, and the ratio of compression-ventilation should be 15:2 (30:2 for adults) when there are two or more professional first-aid personnel on the scene.When CPR is carried out for infants, patting the baby's foot makes sure whether the baby has consciousness. When carrying out external chest compression, use two fingers for vertical pressing (single person) or double thumb encircling (double person). The pressing depth is about 4 cm, and the compression-ventilation ratio is the same as that of children.

1.3.4 Heimlich Maneuver

Heimlich Maneuver, or abdominal thrusts, is a very effective first-aid technique for asphyxia caused by obstruction of the airway, and also suitable for drowning asphyxia. The possible causes of asphyxia in sports are: athletes block the airway due to masks, mouthguards, tooth fragments, chewing gum, etc.; comatose patients may block the airway when their tongue falls down to the throat. When such an emergency occurs, it should be identified and dealt with as soon as possible.

The adult Heimlich emergency should be performed as follows: Firstly, the athletic trainer should stand behind the patient, stretch the arms forward from both armpits and let the patient's body lean forward slightly. Then, the athletic trainer should make a fist with one of his/her hands and place it just above the patient's navel and below the rib cage, with the thumb side against the abdomen, then grasp his/her fist with the other hand to form an "encirclement" . Then, the athletic trainer pulls his/her hands forcefully toward himself/herself, into the patient's abdomen and slightly upward with a quick thrust. In this way, due to abdominal depression, the content of the abdominal cavity moves up, forcing the diaphragm to rise and squeezing the lung and bronchus, so that each shock can rapidly increase the intrathoracic pressure, acting as an artificial cough that can help dislodge the foreign body. After the pressure is applied, release the arm immediately, and then repeat the operation until the foreign body is discharged.

For patients with unconsciousness, the athletic trainer can first make the patient in the supine position, then ride on the patient's thighs or both sides of the patient, place both hands and palms above the patient's navel, and suddenly press forward and down with the root of the palm, and repeat. If the patient is completely unresponsive and has lost heartbeat and breathing, cardiopulmonary resuscitation should be given immediately.

1.4 Management of Hemorrhage

Blood loss from the heart and vascular cavity is called hemorrhage. Hemorrhage can happen in arteries, veins and capillaries, externally or internally. The color of venous blood is dark, and the flow is characterized by surging; the color of capillary bleeding is between bright red and dark red, and the flow is characterized by oozing; the color of arterial blood is bright red, and the flow is characterized by spurt. All severe bleeding will eventually lead to shock. Even if the patient does not show any indication of shock, they should keep quiet and maintain the body heat at a proper body temperature.

Hemorrhage may come from skin wounds such as abrasions, cuts, lacerations, stabs and open fractures. The treatment of external bleeding includes pressure bandaging, elevation, finger pressure directly and tourniquet hemostasis.

Perform appropriate pressure directly on a sterile gauze pad by hand during pressure bandaging. Athletic trainers should use disposable latex gloves every time they contact with blood or other body fluids to prevent blood-borne pathogens and other diseases. During pressing, the bleeding area should be elevated to an anti-gravity level to reduce the venous blood pressure, promote the venous and lymphatic return, and thus slow down bleeding. When the pressure bandaging combined with elevation fails to effectively control the external bleeding, the finger pressure hemostasis can be performed. The thumb presses the upper part (near the heart) of the bleeding blood vessel to stop bleeding. Operation essentials are as follows:

① Hemostasis by compression of temporal artery: For overhead and temporal artery bleeding, the method is to use the thumb or index finger to press the mandibular joint in front of the ear.

② Hemostasis by compression of external maxillary artery: For rib and facial bleeding, press the artery on the mandible with the thumb or index finger about 1 cm in front of the mandibular angle.

③ Hemostasis by compression of carotid artery: It is often used when the head and neck are bleeding and other hemostasis methods are ineffective. The injured carotid artery should be compressed in front of the deep sternocleidomastoid muscle, on the outside of the trachea towards the fifth cervical vertebra. However, it is forbidden to press both sides at the same time.

④ Hemostasis by compression of subclavian artery: For bleeding in the axillary fossa, shoulders and upper limbs, the method is to touch the pulsation of the artery with the thumb in the supraclavicular recess, and press the thumb downward and inward towards the first rib.

⑤ Brachial artery compression hemostasis: For bleeding in the hand, forearm and lower part of the upper arm, the brachial artery is compressed against the medial aspect of the humerus.

The tourniquet is used to stop bleeding in large arteries of the extremities. The tourniquet is usually placed on the upper third of the upper arm and the upper third of the lower limb. The tourniquet should be properly tightened to prevent bleeding from the wound, but it should not be too tight, which is easy to cause skin, nerve and muscle damage at the tourniquet area, or even necrosis of the distal limb. The time of a tourniquet should be marked. No strict consensus exists on ideal tourniquet time. The existing literature recommends 1 to 3 hours as a safe limit for the tourniquet. In order to prevent limb ischemia and necrosis, the tourniquet should be loosened every 30 to 60 minutes for 2 to 3 minutes. The tourniquets should be loosened slowly. At the same time, the finger pressure hemostasis should be applied to reduce the bleeding.

Internal bleeding is invisible and usually needs to be identified by image or other diagnostic techniques. If internal bleeding is suspected, blood pressure should be monitored frequently. Internal bleeding can occur in subcutaneous (bruise or contusion), intramuscular, intraarticular and body cavity. Bleeding in the body cavity (such as skull, chest or abdominal cavity) is life-threatening and requires special attention. Therefore, the medical staff needs to carry out a comprehensive examination of the patients with internal injuries and suggest hospitalization observation to determine the status of the injury.

1.5 Management of Shock

Shock is a syndrome of severe ischemia and hypoxia of vital organs (brain, heart, lung, kidney and liver) caused by acute decrease of effective blood circulation volume and disturbance of microcirculation. Its typical symptoms are pale face, cold and humid limbs, low blood pressure, weak pulse and vague mind. The main causes of shock are the decrease of blood volume, the decrease of cardiac output and the increase of peripheral blood vessel volume, which lead to the sharp decrease of effective blood circulation volume and the disturbance of microcirculation. These lead to tissue ischemia, hypoxia, metabolic disorders, and serious even irreversible damage to vital organs. Extreme fatigue, extreme dehydration, electrolyte loss, overheated or supercooled external environment and diseases are common causes of shock in athletes.

Other common types of shock are as follows:

① Hemorrhagic shock results from blood loss. There is not enough blood in the circulatory system to provide sufficient oxygen to organs.

② Pulmonary shock occurs when the lung cannot provide enough oxygen to the circulating blood, such as pneumothorax.

③ Neurotic shock is usually called syncope. It is caused by a temporary dilation of blood vessels, which reduces the normal blood volume in the brain.

④ Cardiogenic shock refers to a condition in which the heart pump function is impaired or the cardiac blood flow outlet is damaged, causing a rapid decrease in cardiac output and compensatory rapid vasoconstriction, resulting in insufficient effective circulating blood volume, low perfusion, and low blood pressure. Cardiogenic shock includes the shock caused by pathlological changes in the heart itself, cardiac compression or abstruction.

⑤ Septic shock usually comes from bacterial infection. The toxin released by bacteria leads to the expansion of small blood vessels in the body.

⑥ Anaphylactic shock is the result of severe allergic reactions caused by food, insect bites, drugs, dust, pollen, or other substances. Adrenaline should be used for allergic reactions.

⑦ The causes of metabolic shock are diabetes and other serious diseases, and the rapid loss of body fluids (such as urination, vomiting or diarrhea).

1.5.1 Symptoms and Signs of Shock

Moist, pale, clammy skin; weak and rapid pulse; increased and shallow respiratory rate; decreased blood pressure. Systolic blood pressure is usually less than 90 mmHg. In severe situations, there may be urinary retention and fecal incontinence. If the patient is conscious, he/she may show indifference, irritability, restlessness or excitement to their surroundings or show extreme thirst.

1.5.2 Treatment and Prevention of Shock

According to the causes of shock, the following emergency care should be given:

① The position after shock depends on the type of injury. For neck injury, the athletes should be fixed and stabilized; For head injury, the head and shoulder should be raised; For leg fractures, the leg should be kept horizontal, or raised after fixation. In the case of vomiting, the patient's head should be turned to one side.

② Shock can also be caused by the psychological reaction of the athletes after receiving stimulation, such as fear or sudden recognition of a serious situation. The athletic trainer should help them gain confidence patiently.

③ The key intervention of shock is prevention. The athletes should be trained scientifically and have regular physical examinations. The athletic trainer should master the basic principles and methods of dealing with shock. Especially for the athletes who have been in shock, extra attention should be paid.

④ Avoiding long-term training and competition under high temperature, high humidity and no wind conditions. Sugar, salt and water should be supplemented in time for long-distance exercise. Don't stand still immediately after sprinting. Don't stand up suddenly after squatting for a long time. Don't swim long distances while breath-holding.

1.6 Moving and Transporting the Patient

According to the severity of the injury and the transportation distance, different moving techniques and transport facilities can be applied.

In general, handed transfer is used for the wounded in a mild condition without fractures in a short distance. Stretcher transport should be used for the injured with serious illness in a long distance. All patients with suspected fractures should be fixed with a splint before moving. Unconscious patients should be treated as if they had a cervical fracture. A spine board should be used to avoid head and neck movement. In the process of transferring the injured, secondary injury should be avoided.

1.6.1 Transfer of the Patient with Limb Fracture

The patients who are suspected of limb fracture shall be temporarily fixed with a splint. In the process of carrying, move gently to avoid vibration and shear force on the fracture and reduce pain.

Note for temporary fixation:

① Not moving. Do not move the injured limb without reason during fracture fixation.

② Do not reset. Do not attempt to restore when fixed.

③ Not returning. Open fracture, with the fracture end exposed but not retracted.

④ Fix the upper and lower joints. The length of the splint used for fixation must exceed the upper and lower joints of the fracture site.

⑤ The elasticity is suitable. The fixed tightness should be appropriate and secure.

1.6.2 Transfer of the Patient with Spinal Injury

When using the hard board stretcher for transportation, the on-site rescue personnel shall stand on the head, back, hips and lower limbs of the injured side. If necessary, the patient's head and neck must be fixed by a neck bracket or hands. All persons should squat down together, lift the wounded horizontally with both hands, stand up and lift the wounded synchronously to ensure that the spine is always in the neutral position. Put the wounded on the transport vehicle.

When transferring on a stretcher, keep the patient's head back and feet forward, in a horizontal state, and observe the patient's changes at all times; generally, the wounded usually take a supine position; when there is a coma, the head should be tilted to one side. When there is cerebrospinal fluid otorrhea, the head should be raised by 30° to prevent cerebrospinal fluid reflux and asphyxia. In the process of transfer, the movement should be gentle, agile, and coordinated. It is strictly prohibited for the patient to sit up, stand or be carried by two persons lifting the shoulders and legs.

1.6.3 Transfer of the Comatose Patient

Make the patient lie on the stretcher on his/her side or prone, with the head leaning to one side to facilitate the drainage of respiratory secretion.

1.6.4 Transfer of the Patient with Pelvic Injury

Bandage the pelvis in a ring with a triangular towel or a large piece of wound bandaging material. When transferring, let the wounded lie on his/her back on a hard stretcher, with slightly bent knees and padded lower knees.

1.6.5 Transfer of the Patient with Intracranial Hemorrhage

Patients suspected of having an intracranial hemorrhage should be transported lying flat, keeping warm, turning their heads to the side, keeping their respiratory tract clear, and being transferred to the hospital as soon as possible. During the transfer, the patient shall not eat or drink water.

1.6.6 Swimming Pool Rescue

Athletic trainers should master the common performance of different drowning people (conscious or unconscious, injured or not), the basic techniques of life-saving swimming (treading water, diving and towing), the release techniques after being caught and the use of life-saving equipment (lifebuoys, life-saving poles and life-saving floats). Pool rescue should follow the principle that equipment rescue is preferable to the unarmed rescue, shore rescue is preferable to in-water rescue. When the injured swimmer is rescued from the swimming pool, the athletic trainer shall make every effort to reduce the movement of head and neck as much as possible, and place the swimmer on the first aid board in the water.

1.7 Bandaging and Taping

1.7.1 Bandaging

Commonly used bandages include elastic bandages and gauze bandages. The elastic bandages are divided into non-viscous elastic bandages and self-adhesive elastic bandages. An elastic bandage is frequently applied in sports injuries due to its conformity to the body parts. The width and length of the elastic bandage are determined by the body part to be wrapped. Wrinkles should be avoided when applying bandages to avoid skin irritation. The self-adhesive elastic bandage can hold itself in place without the need for metal clips or adhesive tape.

The bandage roll should be held in the preferred hand, which controls the tension and direction but not too tight. The effect of elastic bandages winding should be firm, but not too tight. It is necessary to ensure smooth lymphatic circulation. Excessive pressure will hinder the normal blood flow of limbs. Therefore, patients' fingers and toes should be checked regularly to observe for signs of circulatory disorders. Moreover, the elastic bandage should be applied beginning from the distal to the proximal end of the limb. The elastic bandage can be removed by unwrapping or by cutting with scissors. Herringbone bandages are suitable for the hip and shoulder joints; figure of eight bandages are usually placed over the ankle, knee, elbow, wrist and hand joints.

Wrapping can apply compression and fix the ice pack to reduce swelling and shorten recovery time. Moreover, gauze bandages can also hold a dressing in place over an open wound, providing support or limiting range of motion for an injured area.

1.7.2 Taping

Taping is a non-invasive treatment that applies adhesive tape to the skin to enhance or protect the musculoskeletal system. Taping can provide additional support, stability and compression for the affected body part, and prevent second injuries. Its purpose also includes achieving painless functional movement and protected movement, reducing pain, and providing support for body repair and rehabilitation.

Tapes can be classified into nonelastic adhesive tape and elastic adhesive tape, both of which are usually used together. Nonelastic adhesive tape is widely used for its uniform quality, good adhesion, light weight and supporting strength. Support level, quality of adhesive mass, and winding tension should be considered when buying tapes. The ability to contract and expand allows elastic adhesive tape to be used in soft tissue and areas requiring greater range of motion; the conformability and strength allow it to be applied in small, angular body parts such as feet, wrists, hands and fingers. Tapes should be placed in cool environment to avoid damage to their flexibility and adhesion.

(1) The Use of Nonelastic Adhesive Tape

① Preparation for taping. Perspiration, oil and dirt should be removed before taping; otherwise, they will affect the adhesion of the tape. The preparation steps for taping are as follows. Firstly, skin surface should be cleaned with soap and water; hair should be shaved. Secondly, a quick-drying tape adherent spray can be used. Thirdly, applying foam pads with a small amount of lubricant can help prevent blisters. Fourthly, skin membranes can protect the skin from irritation.

② Rules for tape application. Here are several important rules for taping:

● The tape should be applied in a stable place in the joints; the contraction and relaxation should be allowed in musculature parts.

● Overlap the tape at least half the width of the tape below.

● Avoid continuous taping with nonelastic adhesive tape.

● Keep the tape roll in the hand whenever possible.

● Smooth the tape as it is laid on the skin.

● The tape should adapt to the natural contour of the skin. Otherwise, there will be wrinkles and gaps, which can irritate the skin.

● Start taping with an anchor piece and finish taping with a lock strip.

● Avoid applying tape if the skin is hot or cold after a therapeutic treatment.

● Follow the rules of applying tape in a particular sport.

The tapes can be removed by hand, tape scissors, tape cutters, or chemical solvents. When removing tapes by hand, the tape should be pulled in a direct line with the hairs to avoid tearing or irritating the skin. One hand gently removes the tape while the other hand pressures the skin.

(2) Kinesio Taping

Kinesio tape can be stretched to 140%–150% of its original length, providing a constant tension force to the skin. However, the elasticity will be damaged if the tension exceeds 50% to 70% of its maximum tension. This mechanism produces signals that alter pain pathways and promote blood and lymphatic circulation. Kinesio tape is air permeable and water resistant and can be worn continuously for 3 to 4 days.

① Mechanism and physiological effect. Kinesio tape can improve circulation of blood and lymph by reducing fluid or bleeding beneath the skin, correct muscle function by strengthening weakened muscles, reduce pain through neurological suppression, reset subluxated joints by relieving abnormal muscle tension, and enhance proprioception by applying pressure and pulling on the skin.

The physiological effects of kinesio tapes are as follows.

● Relieving pain: the pain is relieved by increasing input of the tactile nerve and inhibiting input of the pain nerve, and it is also related to gate control theory.

● Improving space of hypodermis: the effect of the tape retracting to the center can improve the space of hypodermis and its permeability, further promoting blood circulation and metabolism. The tension of tape is 15%–25% of its maximum. Multilayer taping like a star or taping with a hole in the middle is the most common technique used for this purpose.

● Relieving edema: the tension of tape should be 0–20% of its maximum. The taping should be umbrella-like and overlap each other. When applying tape, the limb should be in an extension position.

● Promoting muscle performance: the tension should be 15%–35% of its maximum. The shape of the tape is like a "Y", matching the direction of the muscle, from the starting point to the end point of the muscle. The limb is in an extension position.

● Relaxing muscles: the tension should be 15%–35% of its maximum. The tape should be applied from insertion to origin.

● Protecting and supporting ligaments and tendons: the tension should be 50%–70% of its maximum.

● Mechanical fixation: the tension should be 50%–75% of its maximum.

② Applying principles. The tape should be applied from one end of a muscle to the other, with little to no stretch. It can support the muscle if applied from origin to insertion; and it can relax the muscle if applied from insertion to origin. Stretching the tape to 10% of its original length means gentle functional stretch.

Contraindications of kinesiology taping include open wounds, deep vein thrombosis, cancer, lymph node removal, diabetes, allergy, and fragile skin.

Summary

1. In order to more accurately determine the nature and severity of the injury, in addition to the primary assessment on the field, the athletic trainer should fulfill the second assessment on the sideline.

2. Emergency is an accident requiring emergency medical rescue. The main focus is to maintain cardiovascular function and central nervous system function.

3. The contents of high-quality CPR include: fast (compressions at a rate of 100–120/min), forceful pressing (a depth of 5–6 cm for an average adult), chest full rebound, minimizing press interruption and avoiding excessive ventilation. The compression–ventilation ratio is 30 : 2. One

AED shock after 5 circulations.

4. Heimlich Maneuver is a very effective first aid for suffocation caused by airway foreign body.

5. Bleeding can occur externally and internally. The treatment of external bleeding includes pressure bandaging, elevation, finger pressure hemostasis and tourniquet hemostasis. Internal bleeding can occur subcutaneously, intramuscularly or in the body cavity. Therefore, monitoring blood pressure is very important.

6. There are many causes of shock, which may be hemorrhagic, pulmonary, neurogenic, cardiogenic, allergic or metabolic. The common symptoms are pale skin, low blood pressure, weak pulse and vague mind.

7. Patients suspected of fracture should be fixed with a splint before moving. Unconscious patients must be treated as having cervical fractures and treated with spinal plates to prevent head and neck movement.

8. Bandages include elastic bandages and gauze bandages. They can provide compression and support, and hold the dressing or pad in the injured area.

9. Tapes are classified as nonelastic adhesive tapes and elastic adhesive tapes. The correct materials must be chosen, the patient must be in an appropriate position, and the proper procedures must be followed.

10. Kinesio taping can relieve pain and edema, improve circulation and muscle performance; it can support or relax muscles depending on the way of its application.

◯ Review Questions

1. Briefly describe the principles of on-field assessment and treatment.

2. On the football field, a player fell down suddenly and cannot stand up again. What should you do as an athletic trainer at this time?

3. In a short track speed skating competition, one of the skaters fell down and the other was also brought down. His thigh was cut by the ice skate and bleeding. What should you do as an athletic trainer at this time?

4. A basketball player stepped on another player's foot and fell down and sprained his ankle with a painful face. What should you do at this time?

一、场地评估及处理

（一）场地评估及处理的原则及方法

1. 现场损伤急救评估

现场损伤急救评估有助于确定患者受伤的性质和程度，为紧急救护的决策提供指导。场地评估可以分为初级评估和次级评估。

2. 初级评估

初级评估是为了发现潜在的危及生命情况的存在，包括意识水平、气道、呼吸、循环、严重出血和休克等问题。这些问题的评估优先于患者所有其他方面的评估。有生命危险的患者应尽快处理并运送到医疗急救机构。意识清醒和情况稳定的患者不需要进行初级评估，但对无意识的患者要时刻监控是否有危及生命的问题。判断运动员意识状态可使用格拉斯哥昏迷量表（Glasgow coma scale，GSC）。

当初级评估排除了存在危及生命的伤害或疾病，次级评估会仔细观察受伤情况，详细收集患者损伤的具体信息，系统地评估生命体征和症状。

3. 次级评估

（1）评估脉搏、呼吸和血压以及其他生命体征

①脉搏为人体表可触摸到的动脉搏动。正常人的脉搏和心跳是一致的。脉搏的频率受年龄和性别的影响，运动员的脉搏通常比普通人更慢。

正常成人的脉搏为 60 ~ 100 次 / 分，平均约 72 次 / 分；胎儿脉搏为 110 ~ 160 次 / 分；婴儿脉搏为 120 ~ 140 次 / 分；幼儿脉搏为 90 ~ 100 次 / 分；学龄期儿童脉搏为 80 ~ 90 次 / 分；老年人脉搏较慢，通常为 55 ~ 60 次 / 分。

脉搏的改变可以提示病理状况的存在。例如，快但弱的脉搏可能意味着休克、出血、糖尿病昏迷或热衰竭；快且强的脉搏可能意味着中暑或严重的惊吓；强但慢的脉搏可能指示颅骨骨折或中风；没有脉搏意味着心脏停搏或死亡。

②呼吸是指机体与外界环境之间气体交换的过程。正常成人安静时的呼吸频率为每分钟 12 ~ 20 次，儿童为每分钟 15 ~ 30 次。

运动防护师在评估时应注意观察呼吸频率和方式，例如咳嗽出泡沫血液可能是肋骨骨折导致血气胸等问题。

③血压是指血液在血管内流动时作用于单位面积血管壁的侧压力，它是推动血液在血管内流动的动力。通常所说的血压是指体循环的动脉血压。成人安静状态下的血压正常范围是：收缩压 90 ~ 139 毫米汞柱，舒张压 60 ~ 89 毫米汞柱。

血压降低可以提示出血、休克、心脏病发作或内脏器官损伤；而血压升高提示可能中暑等。

④其他体征。皮肤变红或瘙痒可能提示晒伤或过敏反应；皮肤苍白可能是休克或出血；

黄疸提示肝脏疾病或功能障碍。

瞳孔能敏锐反映神经系统的情况，一个或两个瞳孔扩大，可提示头部损伤、中暑或出血；如果瞳孔无对光反射，提示可能有酒精或药物中毒。在评估中，瞳孔的对光反射比瞳孔大小更重要。

体温的变化可以反映在皮肤上。例如，热且相对干燥的皮肤可能提示感染或中暑；凉且黏湿的皮肤可以反映休克或创伤；凉且干燥的皮肤可能是过度暴露于寒冷环境的结果。

（2）肌肉骨骼评估：视诊、触诊、动诊、量诊和特殊试验检查

①视诊：步态姿势、局部皮肤有无发红、有无肿胀畸形和瘀血、有无肌肉萎缩、有无包块瘢痕、创面分泌物情况、伤口形状与深度、局部包扎和固定情况等。

②触诊：骨性标志有无异常、有无压痛、有无骨擦感、皮温、肌张力等。如疼痛激惹度很高，可最后一步进行触诊。

③动诊：主被动运动的关节活动度、肌肉力量等。

④量诊：肢体长度测量、肢体和关节周径测量、肢体轴线测定等。

⑤特殊试验检查：不同的损伤有不同的特殊试验检查方法，不同的方法也有不同的特异性和敏感性，检查者应将经验和循证相结合，选择合适的检查方法进行检查。

检查原则：检查顺序按照先健侧、先主动，后患侧、后被动；充分暴露，两侧对比；客观检查与主观症状相结合；系统检查与局部检查相结合；手法规范轻柔，避免加重损伤。

（3）现场损伤急救的处理

由于现场处理的时间有限，在完成确保生命安全的评估和处理后，可快速地对肌骨损伤进行上述检查，为进行下一步治疗决策提供依据，而更详细的检查应该在场外的评估中进行。所有的检查都应做好记录。在完成现场急救评估后，运动防护师应正确做出以下决策：判断损伤的性质和严重程度；选择必要的现场急救方法；是否需要立即转诊给医生进行进一步评估；选择从现场转移到场外、防护室或医院的方式。

对无意识患者的处理方法：

①运动防护师应立即注意患者体位并确定意识和反应的水平。

②分析患者昏迷原因时，应考虑颈部损伤的可能。

③如果患者无自主呼吸或呼吸减弱，应立即小心地将其放置仰卧位，并且开始心肺复苏的评估和操作，尽快对患者进行人工胸外按压以建立人工循环；如果患者仍有呼吸，应密切监视，直到恢复意识。

④如果患者佩戴了头盔，应该在明确排除颈部等脊柱损伤后再妥善移除，在进行心肺复苏前必须去除面罩。

⑤应保持对昏迷患者的生命支持，直到紧急医疗人员到达。

⑥一旦患者稳定（不再表现出危及生命的状况），运动防护师应开始次级评估。

对于现场发生的出血、骨折等损伤应在现场进行止血和骨折固定，以便后续的转运。对于一般性的闭合性软组织损伤，减少肿胀和减轻炎症反应，可减少后期康复所需时间，也是现场救护的主要目标。一般急性闭合性软组织损伤的治疗遵循 POLICE 原则，即：

P（Protect）保护受伤部位不受二次伤害。

OL（Optimal Loading）适当运动负荷，避免绝对制动。

I（Ice）冰敷抑制炎症反应，降低疼痛，减少肿胀。在急性损伤早期，每 2 小时用冰袋冰敷 20 ～ 30 分钟。

C（Compression）加压，抑制肿胀。

E（Elevation）抬高患肢，促进血液回流，减少肿胀。

（二）紧急医疗救助和紧急预案

紧急医疗救助指在对待突发事件时，应尽可能地迅速采取医疗措施应对，将患者的伤害降到最低的行动。紧急医疗救助的主要关注点是维持心血管功能和中枢神经系统功能。这些系统中的任一种的伤害都可能导致死亡。在某些情况下，紧急医疗救助不仅能挽救生命，而且能决定患者残疾的程度。

紧急医疗救助的关键是对受伤患者的初步评估。运动防护师必须迅速而准确地进行评估，以便能够在第一时间提供正确的急救。

制订完善的紧急预案可为紧急医疗救助提供有效保障，每个运动场或体育馆都应制订专门的紧急预案。常见的紧急预案应包括以下几个方面：

①明确训练或比赛期间各急救人员职责并定期修订、排练（如，运动防护师、医生和救援队分工明确）。一旦紧急情况发生，每个人能各司其职并加强合作。同时，建议急救人员定期练习应急设备的使用和操作，例如担架和自动体外除颤器等。

②制订关于拆除防护装备（特别是头盔和肩垫）的具体操作流程。

③确保电话等通讯设备畅通，随时可用于接入紧急医疗救援系统。在我国，可以通过拨打 120 或 999 来寻求紧急救护支援。拨打紧急电话的人应该提供以下信息：紧急情况的类型，可能存在的伤害类型，患者的现状，当前的处理情况（如，心肺复苏术），发生紧急情况的确切位置，建筑物周围的任何限制（如，救护车是否能顺利到达现场）。

④确保通道畅通，电梯可以容纳担架。

⑤指派专人陪同患者前往医院。

⑥随时携带所有运动员、教练员和其他人员的联系方式，对于未成年人，还应获取其监护人签属的医疗同意书。

（三）心肺复苏和海姆立克急救法

1. 心肺复苏的概念

心肺复苏术（cardiopulmonary resuscitation，CPR）是针对心脏和呼吸的骤停采取的急救技术。目的是恢复患者的自主呼吸和自主循环。2010 年，美国心脏协会将 CPR 流程进行了修改，将 CPR 流程 ABC（airway, breathing, compression）的缩写改为 CAB——建立人工循环，清理通畅气道，进行人工呼吸。这一变化强调了胸外按压在创造自主循环中的重要性。2015 年美国心脏协会又对抢救的技术细节进行了修订，以便更有效地进行现场急救。

2. 心肺复苏的流程

- 确认现场环境安全，可以介入。
- 判断患者意识水平、呼吸和脉搏，确定无应答后呼叫 120 或 999。
- 如果自动体外除颤器（AED）马上可用，则立即提供 1 次冲击，并尽早开始 CPR。
- 进行 CPR 前摆放患者到仰卧位，除去患者外衣，急救人员两手交叠并将掌根对准其两乳头连线中点，以不超过 120 次 / 分的频率进行 30 次胸部按压。
- 开放气道并清除口腔异物，然后给予两次口对口呼吸（每次通气 1 秒左右至胸部上升）。
- 继续施以 30 次按压：2 次呼吸为一个循环，进行至少 5 个循环。
- 经过 5 个循环后，如果患者还没有反应，应使用 AED 施加一次冲击。
- 继续 CPR，直至患者恢复意识和自主呼吸或医疗急救人员到达。

3. 心肺复苏的注意事项

高质量 CPR 的内容包括：快速（按压速率 100 ~ 120 次 / 分）、用力按压（成人按压深度 5 ~ 6 厘米），胸廓充分回弹，尽量减少按压中断和避免过度通气。对于专业的急救人员，建议以团队形式实施 CPR 作为基本原则，以最大限度保证高质量 CPR 的实施。

儿童（年龄在 1 周岁至青春期）和婴儿（出生后至年满 1 周岁）的 CPR 标准：在 CPR 实施过程中，相对于成年人，对儿童和婴儿的复苏应该更加重视人工通气的重要性，不建议对儿童实施单纯胸外按压的复苏策略。此外，对年轻患者，包括儿童和婴儿，应该延长 CPR 的时间，不轻易终止 CPR。儿童 CPR 标准的操作流程与成人大致相同，主要的差别是胸外按压的深度，儿童应控制在 5 厘米左右，在实施双人儿童 CPR 时，按压 / 通气比例应该为 15 : 2（成人为 30 : 2）。为婴儿实施 CPR 时，判断患儿意识采用拍打足底的方法，胸外按压时采用二指垂直按压（单人）或双拇指环抱法（双人），按压深度约为 4 厘米，按压 / 通气比与儿童一致。

4. 海姆立克急救法

海姆立克急救法，又称腹部冲击法，是针对气道被异物阻塞引起窒息的急救技术，也适用于溺水窒息。在体育运动中出现窒息的原因可能有：患者因口罩、护齿、牙齿碎片、口香糖等阻塞气道；昏迷的患者可能因舌后坠而阻塞气道。当这些紧急情况出现时，应尽早识别并及时处理。

成人的海姆立克急救法具体操作为：运动防护师首先站在患者身后，并让其身体略前倾，然后将双臂分别从患者两腋下前伸并环抱患者。一手握拳，虎口贴在患者胸部下方、肚脐上方的上腹部中央，另一手从前方握住握拳手，形成"合围"之势，然后突然用力收紧双臂，向患者上腹部内上方猛烈施压，迫使其上腹部下陷。这样由于腹部下陷，腹腔内容上移，迫使膈肌上升而挤压肺及支气管，这样每次冲击可以迅速增大胸内压，从而像人为的咳嗽一样将异物冲出。施压完毕后立即放松手臂，然后再重复操作，直到异物被排出。

对于意识不清的患者，运动防护师可以先使患者成为仰卧位，然后骑跨在患者大腿上或在患者两边，双手两掌重叠置于患者肚脐上方，用掌根向前、下方突然施压，反复进行。

如果患者完全无反应，已经失去心跳呼吸，则应该立即给予心肺复苏。

（四）出血的处理

血液自心、血管腔流出称为出血。出血可以分为静脉出血，毛细血管出血或动脉出血，或者可以分为外部或内部出血。静脉血的颜色暗沉，流动的特征是涌；毛细血管出血颜色介于鲜红色与暗红之间，流动特征是渗；动脉血颜色鲜红，流动特征是喷。所有严重出血最终都会导致休克，即使患者没有外在表现出休克，也应该使患者保持安静，保存身体的热量，将体温稳定在正常的温度。

外出血源自开放性皮肤伤口，例如擦伤、切伤、裂伤和刺伤，也可能来自开放性骨折。外出血的处理包括加压包扎、抬高、指压止血法和止血带止血法。

加压包扎时可用手在无菌纱布垫上直接施加适当压力。运动防护师应在每次与血液或其他体液接触时使用一次性乳胶手套，以预防血源性病原体感染和其他疾病。按压的同时抬高出血部位，可抵抗重力降低静脉血压，促进静脉血和淋巴回流，从而减缓出血。当加压包扎结合抬高未能有效控制外出血时，可选择指压止血法，用拇指压住出血的血管上方（近心端），使血管被压关闭，中断血液。操作要领如下：

①颞动脉压迫止血法：用于头顶及颞部动脉出血。方法是用拇指或食指在耳前正对下颌关节处用力压迫。

②颌外动脉压迫止血法：用于肋部及颜面部的出血。用拇指或食指在下颌角前约1cm外，将动脉血管压于下颌骨上。

③颈总动脉压迫止血法：常在头、颈部大出血且采用其他止血方法无效时使用。方法是在气管外侧、胸锁乳突肌前缘，将伤侧颈动脉向后压于第五颈椎上。但禁止双侧同时压迫。

④锁骨下动脉压迫止血法：用于腋窝、肩部及上肢出血。方法是用拇指在锁骨上凹摸到动脉跳动处，以拇指向下、向内压向第一肋骨。

⑤肱动脉压迫止血法：用于手、前臂及上臂下部的出血。方法是在患者上臂的前面或后面，用拇指或四指压迫上臂内侧动脉血管。

止血带用于四肢大动脉出血时进行止血。捆扎止血带的部位在上肢常选用上臂上 1/3 处，在下肢常选用大腿上 1/3 处。捆止血带要松紧适中，以伤口不出血为度，但也不能过紧，这样容易造成止血带处的皮肤、神经和肌肉的损伤，甚至引起肢体远端的坏死。要标注好止血带使用时间。对于理想的止血带时间并没有严格的共识，现有文献推荐止血带使用时间 1~3 小时为安全限度。为防止肢体的缺血坏死，每隔 30 ~ 60 分钟应放松止血带 2 ~ 3 分钟，松止血带时动作要缓慢，放气也要缓慢，同时用指压止血以减少出血。

内出血是肉眼不可见的，一般不易诊断，通常需要结合影像或其他诊断技术识别。如果怀疑出现内出血，应密切监测血压。内出血可发生在皮下（瘀伤或挫伤）、肌肉内、关节内和体腔内。体腔内（如颅骨、胸腔或腹腔）的出血是危及生命的，需格外注意。因此，医务人员需对疑似内出血的患者进行全面检查并建议其住院观察，以确定受伤的性质和程度。

（五）休克的处理

休克是一种由于有效循环血量锐减、全身微循环障碍引起重要生命器官（脑、心、肺、肾、肝）严重缺血、缺氧的综合征。其典型表现是面色苍白、四肢湿冷、血压降低、脉搏微弱、神志模糊。引发休克的原因主要是血量减少，心输出量减少及外周血管容量增加等，引起有效循环血量剧减、微循环障碍，导致组织缺血、缺氧，代谢紊乱，重要生命器官遭受严重的乃至不可逆的损害。极度疲劳、极度脱水、电解质丢失、过热或过冷的外部环境和疾病，是运动员休克的常见原因。

其他常见的休克类型有以下几种：

①失血性休克大多来自于有失血的创伤，循环系统中没有足够的血液，不能为器官供应足够的氧气。

②肺源性休克发生在肺不能向循环血液提供足够的氧气时，例如气胸。

③神经性休克通常称为晕厥。它是由血管的暂时扩张引起的大脑中正常的血液量减少而导致的。

④心源性休克是指心脏泵功能受损或心脏血流排出道受损，引起心排出量快速下降而引发代偿性血管快速收缩，导致的有效循环血量不足、低灌注和低血压状态。心源性休克包括心脏本身病变、心脏压迫或梗阻引起的休克。

⑤脓毒性休克通常来自细菌的感染，细菌释放的毒素导致身体中的毛细血管扩张。

⑥过敏性休克是由食物、昆虫叮咬、药物、粉尘、花粉或其他物质引起的严重过敏反应的结果。应使用肾上腺素对过敏反应进行治疗。

⑦代谢性休克的原因一是糖尿病等疾病，二是体液快速丢失（如排尿、呕吐或腹泻）。

1. 休克的表现

皮肤潮湿、苍白、湿冷；脉搏微弱而急促；呼吸频率增加且呼吸浅；血压下降（收缩压通常低于90毫米汞柱）。在严重的情况下，还会出现尿潴留和大便失禁。如果患者有意识，可能表现出对周围环境不感兴趣、易怒、不安或兴奋，也可能表现出极度口渴。

2. 休克的治疗和预防措施

根据休克的原因，应给予以下紧急处理：

①休克后的体位因受伤类型而异。对于颈部损伤，患者应该固定不动；对于头部损伤，患者头部和肩部应抬高；对于腿部骨折，患者腿部应保持水平，或在固定后抬高。如有呕吐时应将患者的头部偏向一侧。

②休克还可以是患者遭受刺激后产生的心理反应，例如恐惧，或突然意识到发生严重情况。在对待受伤后有明显情绪波动的患者时，运动防护师应耐心地给予患者信心。

③休克重在预防。运动员应科学训练，定期体检。运动防护师应掌握休克的基本处理原则和方法，特别是对于曾经休克过的运动员，应格外注意。

④避免在高温、高湿度或无风条件下进行长时间训练和比赛；进行长距离运动时要及时补充糖、盐和水分；疾跑后不要立即站立不动；久蹲后不要骤然起立；不在闭气下作长

距离游泳。

（六）患者转移和搬运技术

根据患者病情严重程度和转移路程远近，可以采用不同的转移技术和设备。

徒手转移法通常用于路程较近、病情较轻无骨折的患者；对于路程较长、病情较重的伤者应采用担架搬运法。所有疑似骨折的伤者在移动前应用夹板固定。无意识的患者应该被当作有颈椎骨折的情况处理，使用脊柱固定板固定以避免头颈部运动。在转移伤者的过程中应最大程度地避免对其造成二次损伤。

1. 肢体骨折患者的转移

怀疑有肢体骨折的患者，需先用夹板临时固定，使用担架运送患者。运送过程中动作要轻，避免患者震荡，以减少患者疼痛，避免骨折处受到剪切力。

临时固定需要注意：

①不移动。骨折固定时不要无故移动伤肢。

②不复位。固定时不要试图整复。

③不回纳。开放性骨折，断端外露时不回纳。

④固定上下关节。固定所用夹板的长度必须超过骨折部位上、下两个关节。

⑤松紧适宜。固定的松紧要合适、牢靠。

2. 脊柱损伤患者的转移

使用硬板担架进行搬运脊柱有损伤的患者时，现场救护人员分别站立在患者同侧的头部、背部、臀部和下肢旁边，必要时专人用颈托或手固定其头颈部。救护人员一起蹲下，双手平抬患者，同时站立抬起患者，确保脊柱始终处于中立位。同步将患者放于运输工具上。

用担架转移时，患者头部向后、足部向前。要随时观察患者变化，使患者保持水平状态。一般情况下患者多采取仰卧位，有昏迷时头部应偏向一侧，有脑脊液耳漏时头部应抬高至与水平面成30°角，防止脑脊液逆流和窒息。转移过程中，动作要轻巧敏捷，协调一致，寻找合适的交通工具进行转送。严禁患者坐起、站立，严禁救护人员两人抬肩抱腿搬运。

3. 昏迷患者的转运

使患者侧卧或俯卧于担架上，头偏向一侧，以利于呼吸道分泌物引流。

4. 骨盆损伤患者的转运

将骨盆用三角巾或大块包伤材料做环形包扎，转运时让患者仰卧于门板或硬担架上，微屈膝，膝下部加垫。

5. 颅内出血患者的转运

对怀疑存在颅内出血的患者，转运时应让其平躺，注意保暖，头转向侧面，保持呼吸道畅通，尽快转送到医院，期间禁食、禁水。

6. 泳池救援

运动防护师应掌握不同溺水者的常见表现（清醒还是昏迷、是否受伤）、游泳救生的基本技术（踩水、潜泳和拖带）、被抓后的解脱技术和救生器材（救生圈、救生竿和救生浮漂）的使用方法。泳池救援应遵循器材救生优于徒手救生、岸上救生优于水中救生的原则，充分发挥集体的力量和智慧。当从游泳池中救出受伤的患者时，运动防护师应尽一切努力尽量减少其头部和颈椎的运动，同时将患者放置在水中的急救板上。

（七）绷带包扎和贴扎技术

1. 绷带包扎

常用的绷带包括弹性绷带和纱布绷带，弹性绷带又分为无黏性弹性绷带和自黏性弹性绷带。因为在包扎时弹性绷带较易贴合不同的身体部位，所以弹性绷带在运动损伤处理中最常用。弹性绷带的宽度和长度的选择都取决于要包扎的身体部位，弹性绷带使用时应避免褶皱以防对皮肤产生刺激。自黏绷带可以不额外使用金属夹或贴布固定。

使用弹性绷带时，用利手持绷带卷轴，并在缠绕时控制绷带的拉力及方向。弹性绷带缠绕效果应该牢固但不能过紧，要保证淋巴循环通畅，过度的压力也会阻碍患者肢体正常的血液流动。因此，应该经常检查患者的手指和脚趾，观察是否有循环障碍的体征。此外，使用弹性绷带时应该从患者肢体远端向近端缠绕。拆除弹性绷带时可以直接解开缠绕的绷带或用剪刀剪开。人字形绷带通常用于髋关节和肩关节，8字形绷带通常用于踝、膝、肘、腕、手关节。

包扎时既可以提供合适的压力，也可以将冰袋固定于伤处，以减轻关节肿胀，进而缩短受伤部位的恢复时间。此外，也可以用纱布绷带也可以将敷料固定在开放伤口上，可以将加压板或保护板固定在患者的受伤部位，为受伤部位提供支撑或限制其关节活动度。

2. 贴扎技术

贴扎是一种将贴布贴于皮肤以达到增进或保护肌肉骨骼系统的非侵入性治疗。其主要目的是为受影响的身体部位提供额外的支撑、稳定、加压，尤其是防止之前受伤过的关节或肌肉再次受伤。其目的还包括实现无痛的功能性运动及保护下的运动，减轻疼痛，为身体的修复和康复提供支持。

贴布主要分为非弹性贴布和弹性贴布，二者通常结合使用。非弹性贴布黏接质量均匀、黏着性好、重量轻、支撑材料的相对强度大，因此其应用范围广。购买非弹性贴布时，支撑等级、黏着能力、缠绕张力等因素都应该被考虑在内。弹性贴布可以伸缩，通常用于需要更大活动度的部位，也用于缠绕软组织或肌群。弹性贴布也有服帖性和支撑性，可用于小的、有棱角的部位，比如脚、腕、手和手指。贴布应该放置在阴凉处，以免太阳光直射损坏贴布织物的柔韧性或影响黏接质量。

（1）非弹性贴布的使用

①准备工作。汗水、油、灰尘都会影响贴布的黏着能力，故贴扎前应对皮肤进行清理。准备步骤如下：第一，用肥皂和水清洁皮肤表面，去除灰尘和油；此外，应剔除汗毛，防止移除贴布时产生皮肤疼痛。第二，使用速干助黏喷雾帮助贴布附着于皮肤上。第三，额外使用泡沫垫及少量的润滑剂可以减少水泡的发生。第四，可以使用皮肤膜保护皮肤免受刺激。

②贴扎使用法则。在贴扎时应遵循以下法则：

● 当贴扎部位为关节时，要将贴布放于稳定的位置。当贴扎部位为肌肉时，要确保肌肉的正常收缩和舒张。

● 贴布至少覆盖上一层贴布的一半。

● 非弹性贴布使用时要避免连续缠绕。

● 尽可能将贴布卷拿在手里。

● 将贴布缠绕于皮肤后，抚平贴布。

● 贴布应该适应皮肤的自然轮廓，否则就会有褶皱和缝隙，进而刺激皮肤。

● 开始贴扎时先用锚点固定，结束时"锁住"。

● 如果在治疗后皮肤过冷或过热，暂时不要使用贴布。

● 贴扎的使用必须遵循专项运动的贴扎使用规定。

贴布的去除通常有以下几种方法：手动撕除、使用贴布剪、鲨鱼剪或使用化学溶剂。用手撕除贴布时，应顺着汗毛的方向，不要撕扯或刺激皮肤。一只手轻轻向一个方向撕拉贴布，另一只手轻轻按压住皮肤。

（2）肌内效贴

肌内效贴布有很好的弹性，可以拉长到原长度的140%～150%，因此可以为其作用部位的皮肤提供持续的张力。但是如果拉力超过其最大拉力的50%～70%，肌内效贴布的弹性就会遭到破坏。将肌内效贴应用于身体上后，贴布会稍稍回弹，并轻轻提起皮肤，这会在皮肤和皮下组织之间形成一个极小的空间，这一机制会产生改变疼痛通路的信号以及促进血液和淋巴液循环的效应。肌内效贴布透气且防水，贴布一次可以持续使用3～4天。

①工作原理及生理效应。肌内效贴布通过改善血液循环和淋巴循环减少皮下组织液渗出或出血；通过增强薄弱肌肉的力量来纠正肌肉功能；通过神经抑制来减轻疼痛；通过缓解异常肌肉张力来使半脱位关节复位；通过对皮肤施加压力及牵拉来增强本体感觉。

肌内效贴的生理效应包括以下几点：

● 缓解疼痛：通过增加触觉神经输入、抑制痛觉神经输入来缓解疼痛，这与闸门控制学说有关。

● 改善皮下组织间隙：四周贴布向中间回缩可以改善皮下组织间隙，进而改善皮下组织通透性，并促进血液循环及代谢。此时贴布的拉力为15%～25%；常使用星形多层贴扎或中洞形贴扎方式。

● 减轻水肿：此时贴布的拉力为0～20%，肌内效贴的形状为伞形重叠交叉；肢体位于伸展体位。

● 促进肌肉表现：此时贴布的拉力为15%～35%，肌内效贴的形状为Y形，配合肌肉走向，由肌肉起点至止点；肢体位于伸展体位。

● 放松肌肉：此时贴布的拉力为15%～35%，贴布走向为由肌肉止点至起点。

● 保护支持韧带/肌腱：此时贴布的拉力为50%～70%。

● 机械性固定矫正：此时贴布的拉力为50%～75%。

②使用原则。使用贴布时应从肌肉的一端开始到肌肉的另一端终止，小幅度拉长或不拉长贴布。如果贴布始于肌肉起点，止于肌肉止点，则会对肌肉起到助力支持的作用；如果贴布起于肌肉止点，止于肌肉起点，则会起到康复放松的作用。如果贴布应用时被拉长到原长度的 10% 左右，则会对肌肉产生轻微的功能性牵拉作用。

此外，要注意肌内效贴的禁忌征：开放伤口、深静脉血栓、癌症、淋巴结切除、糖尿病、过敏、皮肤脆弱。

小结

1. 为更准确地确定损伤的性质和严重程度，运动防护师除了在场上进行初步评估外，应在场边对其进行进一步的损伤评估。

2. 紧急情况是需要紧急医疗救援的意外事件，主要关注点是维持心血管功能和中枢神经系统功能。

3. 成人高质量 CPR 的内容包括：快速（按压速率 100～120 次 / 分）、用力按压（成人按压深度 5～6 厘米），胸廓充分回弹，尽量减少按压中断和避免过度通气。胸外按压和人工呼吸的比例为 30∶2，完成 5 个循环后用 AED 电击 1 次。

4. 海姆立克急救法是对气道异物阻塞引起窒息非常有效的急救技术。

5. 出血可以发生在外部和内部。外出血的处理包括加压包扎、抬高、指压止血法和止血带止血法。内出血可以在皮下、肌肉内或体腔内发生，通常不易察觉，因此，对血压的监控非常重要。

6. 休克的原因有很多，可能有失血性、肺源性、神经源性、心源性、过敏性或代谢性的原因。症状常见皮肤苍白、血压降低、脉搏微弱和神志模糊。

7. 疑似骨折的患者在移动前应用夹板固定。无意识的患者必须被当作有颈椎骨折的情况处理，使用脊柱板固定以避免头颈部运动。

8. 绷带包括弹性绷带和纱布绷带，可以起到加压和支持、固定辅料或夹板的作用。

9. 贴布主要包括非弹性贴布和弹性贴布。帖扎时应选用合适的材料，让患者处于合适的体位，遵循正确的操作步骤。

10. 肌内效贴可以起到减轻疼痛和水肿、促进循环、增强肌肉运动表现的作用，根据其使用方法的不同，可以起到支持或放松肌肉的作用。

◯ 复习题

1. 简要阐述场地评估和处理的原则。

2. 足球赛场上，一名球员突然倒地不起。作为运动防护师你应该怎么做？

3. 短道速滑赛上，一名选手不慎摔倒，另一名选手也被带倒，还被其冰刀割伤大腿，当即血流不止。作为运动防护师你应该怎么做？

4.一名篮球运动员在落地时，踩到了另一名球员的脚，从而扭到脚踝，立刻倒地，面色痛苦。作为运动防护师你应该怎么做？

2 Off-the-Field Injury Assessment and Management

2.1 Principles and Methods of Off-the-Field Injury Assessment and Management

After the patient has been transported away from the field, the evaluation to assess/diagnose the current injury or illness for the athlete needs to be organized by the athletic trainer in the athletic training room or the physician's office.

2.1.1 Off-the-Field Assessment Process

Off-site injury assessment is divided into four parts: history, observation, palpation and special examinations, also known as HOPS protocol. The athletic trainers should obtain accurate information related to the injury, and make plans for further examination and follow-up treatment.

(1) History

The collection of medical history includes the patient's chief complaint, present injury, past medical history, clinical treatment process and complications, which can help the athletic trainer understand the patient's physical condition, injury process and severity of injury, and plays an important role in injury assessment.

① Chief complaint: the patient's age, gender and other basic information and the main concerns bothering the patient.

② Present injury: including the occurrence of the patient's injury/illness and the following process. The athletic trainer should record the time, irritation, location, nature, severity, and the factors that relieve or aggravate the pain.

③ Past medical history: help sports protection professionals understand whether patients have experienced similar problems in the past, how they were treated, and whether there are other issues related to medical history.

④ Clinical treatment process: what kinds of treatment have been implemented before this visit, and what is the curative effect?

⑤ Complications: besides the main symptoms, there may be other symptoms. The common symptoms associated with pain in musculoskeletal system injuries include limited joint motion, difficulty in posture change, pale complexion, cold sweat, dizziness, vomiting, etc.

(2) Observation

Observation is usually conducted while inquiring about medical history, and the degree of functional impairment, functional level, posture and force line, balance and weight-bearing ability, and walking ability can all be observed through the examination. The key body surface markers should be exposed as much as possible.

(3) Palpation

The abnormalities of skin, soft tissue and bone can be assessed by palpation.

① Skin: check the temperature and humidity of the affected skin.

② Soft tissue: check tenderness, flexibility and stiffness, spasms, muscle guarding and nodules of the muscles, fascia, ligaments and tendons. During palpation, pain should be reduced as much as possible.

③ Bone: check alignment and tenderness by palpating the bony prominences.

The athletic trainer should also check the arterial pulsation of the injured area to determine whether there is a vascular injury. Acute injury and chronic injury can be distinguished by palpation. In acute injury, the skin is moist, the skin temperature is increased, the ligament tenderness is severe, and the swelling and tension of different muscle layers are increased. In chronic injury, the skin becomes cold, tight or hollow, the ligament is thickened, and the muscular layer becomes hard or fibrosis.

(4) Special Examinations

Special examinations are usually used to confirm the conclusions obtained by inquiring about history, observation and palpation, including active and passive movement examination, joint range of motion measurement, manual muscle strength test, nerve function test and functional screen test. The athletic trainer should pay attention to the comparison between the affected side and the unaffected side through standardized operation. If necessary, the athletic trainer should also check the patient's body posture, limb length and circumference.

① Active movement examination: the active movement is checked by letting the patient take the initiative to do flexion and extension, adduction and abduction, and internal and external rotation. In the process of patients' motion, the athletic trainer should pay attention to observing the range of movement, symmetry and speed, whether there is pain and where the pain appears, and whether the patients are willing to do or are afraid of activities. Through active movement, we can roughly determine the location of pain, the exact location of pain within the range of motion, the impact of exercise on the degree of pain, whether the movement mode is normal or not, the patient's existing motor function level, and the patient's subjective desire for movement.

② Passive movement examination: including physiological movement examination and accessory movement examination. Passive examination is used to determine whether the main disease or symptom of the patient is caused by non-contractile components or tissues. Physiological movement examination is used to examine the state of non-contractile tissue. In addition to determining the degree of joint movement limitation and pain, passive movement examination can also determine the nature of end feeling and identify whether joint movement restriction is caused by joint cystic lesions or injuries. The accessory movement examination mainly checks the mobility of the joint, and the information of joint laxation can be obtained by the accessory movement examination.

The combination of active and passive movement examinations can further find out the types of injured tissue, such as: active and passive are limited, and pain appears in the same direction, indicating joint capsule and joint injury; active and passive movement are limited, and pain appears in the opposite direction, indicating contractile tissue damage, which needs further anti-resistance examination to clarify.

③ Joint range of motion measurement: including active joint range of motion measurement and passive joint range of motion measurement. The measurement of active joint range of motion is used to examine the influence of muscle contraction strength on joint range of motion. Passive range of motion (PROM) is used to measure the limitation of the patient's joint movement, to judge the nature of the end feeling of joint movement, and to determine whether there are abnormal structural changes in limiting joint movement.

④ Manual muscle test: utilized in checking contractile tissue, i.e., muscle and its accessory structures. By exerting manual resistance, the athletic trainer can separate the contraction tissue as the source of pain. Lovett divided muscle strength into six grades: normal, good, fair, poor, weak and no contraction.

Normal (Grade 5): able to complete the range of motion of the whole joint under the condition of anti-gravity and maximum resistance.

Good (Grade 4): able to complete the full range of motion of the joint while resisting gravity and exerting partial resistance.

Fair (Grade 3): in the case of anti-gravity, without any resistance, can complete the range of motion of the whole joint.

Poor (Grade 2): can complete the full range of motion of the joint without gravity.

Weak (Grade 1): only muscle contraction phenomenon, no joint movement without gravity.

No contraction (Grade 0): no muscle contraction through palpation.

⑤ Nerve function examination: including muscle strength, deep reflection, nerve root mobility, sensation and brain function examination, which can help the athletic trainer determine whether the patient's symptoms are related to nerve injury.

● Muscle strength: the level of nerve injury can be determined by muscle strength and joint motion tests associated with specific spinal cord levels.

● Deep reflection: the interruption of any part of the reflection arc can cause the deep reflection to weaken or disappear.

● Mobility test of nerve root: the compression symptoms of nerve root exhibited in the nerve traction test indicate that nerve root is compressed.

• Sensation function examination: screen with light touch to determine the presence and disappearance of skin sensation, and associate the results with skin segments or peripheral nerve innervation. If the patient has an obvious nerve defect, more detailed sensory examinations should be carried out, such as temperature sensation, proprioception, etc.

• Cerebral function examination: generally includes checking on the level of consciousness, intellectual performance, emotional state, thinking content, sensory response (visual, tactile, auditory) and language expression ability.

⑥ Functional screen

• Functional movement screen

Functional movement screen (FMS) is a tool used to identify functional movement defects caused by body asymmetry. FMS evaluates the risk of injury by testing its flexibility and stability in 7 basic motion modes. The movements include squats, hurdle steps, straight-line lunge squats, shoulder flexibility, active straight leg lifts, trunk stability push-ups, and rotational stability.

• Upper limb injury risk screen

The closed kinetic chain upper extremity stability test (CKCUEST) is used to determine the stability of the upper limb shoulder straps, and the test performance depends on muscle strength level, balance, and coordination. The upper limb Y-balance test can comprehensively observe the stability of the arm, scapula, and torso on the supporting side of the upper limb, as well as the flexibility of the arm, scapula, and torso on the moving side.

• Lower limb injury risk screen

The lower limb Y-balance test is a single-leg dynamic test involving strength, flexibility, core control and proprioception.

In addition, in order to comprehensively understand the patient's injury condition, special examinations should also include imaging and laboratory tests such as CT, MRI, ultrasound, electrocardiogram, electroencephalogram, blood tests, and arthroscopy.

2.1.2 SOAP Recording Mode

(1) Purpose of Recording

The record of injury assessment is a systematic record of the characteristics, development, change, diagnosis and treatment of the patient's disorder. It not only records the situation of the dysfunction, but also records the analysis, judgment, diagnosis, treatment process and prognosis estimation of the athletic trainer, which is also important evidence for medical disputes and lawsuits.

(2) Basic Requirements of Records

① The content is authentic and reliable. ② Refine the description and highlight the key points. ③ The format is standardized and systematic. ④ Record in time. ⑤ Be continuous.

(3) SOAP Recording Mode

SOAP recording mode (subjective examination, objective examination, assessment, plan) is the standard recording mode for on-site, off-site and clinical injury assessment, which is composed of information provided by the patients and evaluation results of the therapists.

During the whole process of rehabilitation treatment, the athletic trainer should record the progress of each treatment regularly. The record of the rehabilitation process can be a supplementary explanation of the treatment process or a weekly treatment summary, and SOAP recording mode can also be used. However, the record of the rehabilitation process focuses on the type of treatment received by the patient and the patient's feedback on the treatment, the progress of medium and short-term rehabilitation goals, the change of goals and the subsequent treatment plans.

- S (subjective): Subjective examination. It includes the subjective description from the patient and his/her family members of the injury history (including the location, time and mechanism of injury). In addition, the degree and nature of pain and the degree of disability of the patient also need to be recorded.

- O (objective): Objective examination. It is the result of observation, palpation, active movement examination, passive movement examination, resistance test and special examinations. Therefore, the objective examination record will include the results of posture assessment, examination of deformity and swelling, determination of the location of tenderness points, limitation of active movement, pain appearance or pain disappearance during passive and resistance movements, and joint stability.

- A (assessment): Assessment. The injury assessment is a professional judgment of the appearance and nature of injury by the athletic trainers, including the professional analysis and judgment of subjective and objective data.

- P (plan): Treatment Plan. The treatment plan includes an overall treatment plan and a specific treatment plan, as well as short-term and long-term goals. For example, the short-term goal is to move from walking with two crutches to walking with a single crutch, while the long-term goal is to stop limping and walk with a normal gait.

Injury assessment can find and determine the location, scope, nature and degree of the injury, as well as the causes and prognosis of the disorder, so as to provide evidence for prevention and development of goals and plans or rehabilitation treatment. Therefore, the athletic trainer should have anatomy, physiology, pathology and other related basic professional knowledge. The athletic trainer should pay attention to the sequence of examination, avoid abusing the examination, pay attention to communication skills, and integrate assessment into the whole process of rehabilitation treatment.

2.1.3 Principles and Methods of Off-the-Field Injury Management

Most musculoskeletal injuries are treated conservatively first, including correction of abnormal activity patterns, rehabilitation training and the use of orthotics. Surgical treatment should be considered if conservative treatment fails or fractures or tendon ruptures are present.

Rehabilitation treatment can be divided into three stages: acute stage (1 to 3 weeks after injuries or surgery), recovery stage (3 to 6 weeks after injuries or surgery) and functional stage (6 to 12 weeks after injuries or surgery). The specific objectives and basic measures for each stage are as follows:

Acute stage: reduce inflammation, relieve pain, maintain the range of motion in the painless range, exercise in static muscle contraction, and prevent muscular atrophy and the formation of deep vein thrombosis. Interventions include the use of non-steroidal anti-inflammatory drugs and analgesics, physiotherapy, electrical stimulation, static muscle contraction exercises and full-body training.

Recovery stage: correct the patient's dysfunction, such as flexibility, muscle strength, range of motion, balance and proprioception. This includes physiotherapy, joint mobilization, static and dynamic contraction exercises, proprioception exercises, balance exercises and specific motor exercises.

Function stage: mainly carry out specific sports training to help the athletes return to the field as soon as possible. Increase muscle explosive power, muscle endurance, neuromuscular control and other training methods, including muscle strengthening training, multi-plane neuromuscular control exercises.

2.2 Common Therapeutic Modalities

The development and implementation of therapeutic modalities must be based on an understanding of how tissues respond physiologically to injury and at what stage the tissue healing process is. The athletic trainer can only decide when and how to treat patients with physical therapy after understanding their symptoms and signs, as well as the stage of injury healing they are in.

The therapeutic modalities frequently used by athletic trainers include thermotherapy, cryotherapy, electrical stimulation, shortwave diathermy, low-level laser therapy, ultrasound, phonophoresis, traction and massage. The forms of energy related to physical modalities include thermal conductive energy, electrical energy, electromagnetic energy, sound energy and mechanical energy. The essence of thermotherapy and cryotherapy is the transfer of thermal energy. The electrical stimulating currents utilize electrical energy. Short-wave and low-power lasers use electromagnetic energy. Sound energy is used in ultrasound. Mechanical energy is utilized in traction, intermittent compression, and massage.

2.2.1 Thermotherapy

The type, intensity of heat energy and its duration of application, as well as thermosensitive reaction, can impact the body's response to it. Thermotherapy can increase the extensibility of collagen tissue, relieve joint stiffness, alleviate pain and muscle spasms, have anti-inflammatory and edema-reducing effects on tissues during the healing period, and increase blood circulation. Common methods are as follows:

① Hydrocollator packs. Hydrocollator packs contain silicate gel in a cotton pad, which is immersed in thermostatically controlled hot water at a temperature of 160°F (71.1°C) to 170°F (76.7°C). Hydrocollator packs can be mainly used to improve the cycle of Pain–Spasm–Ischemia–Hypoxia–Pain, but they cannot act on deeper tissues, including muscle tissue.

② Whirlpool baths. Whirlpool therapy is a combination of massage and water immersion. The whirlpool provides both heat conduction and convection, respectively achieved by skin contact with the higher water temperature and with the water swirls. Whirlpool can reduce swelling, spasms, and pain. The buoyancy of water can also facilitate active movements.

③ Paraffin baths. Paraffin baths apply heat to distal extremities. The temperature is controlled between 52°C to 54°C. Paraffin baths are particularly effective in treating chronic injuries occurring in multiple body areas such as hands, wrists, ankles, and feet. Attention: paraffin baths should be avoided in body areas with open wounds or poor circulation.

2.2.2 Cryotherapy

Cryotherapy can reduce swelling in an acute inflammatory response by lowering the metabolic rate and facilitating vasoconstriction. Declined metabolism leads to decreased muscle guarding thereby reducing the metabolic waste generated by muscle spasms. Cryotherapy can also slow down nerve impulses and make nerve endings less sensitive, reduce muscle fatigue as well as increase or maintain muscular contraction. Common methods are as follows:

① Ice massage. Ice massage is a cryotherapy method applied to a small body part. Stretching or exercising can be done when the patient feels less or no pain.

② Cold water immersion. Cold water immersion is preferred when cold treatment is needed in and around a certain area of your body. Mix water and crushed ice together at a temperature of 10°C to 15°C. The patient immerses the body part in the water for 10 to 15 minutes, and then removes it from water and starts regular movement when he/she feels no pain. Immerse in the water again when pain reappears, and this process can be repeated three times.

③ Ice packs. Ice packs are easier to apply to various parts of the body. Wet ice packs provide the best cooling effects compared to other types. An ice pack can be made by crushed ice in a wet towel or in a plastic bag. The patient will experience four phases, including cold, aching, burning and numbness. The treatment should be stopped immediately when the patient has any sign of allergy or abnormal reaction like numbness.

④ Vapocoolant spray. The most popular vapocoolant is fluoromethane, which is nonflammable and nontoxic. A vapocoolant spray can help reduce muscle guarding and increase range of

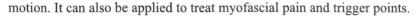

motion. It can also be applied to treat myofascial pain and trigger points.

2.2.3 Electrical Energy Modalities

Electricity can reduce pain by depolarizing sensory nerves; stimulate muscle contraction by depolarizing motor nerve fibers; excite biological tissues or facilitate the healing process at the cellular level by creating an electrical field; and create an electrical field on the skin surface to transport beneficial ions into deeper target tissues. Common methods are as follows:

① Iontophoresis. Iontophoresis is a therapy that directly introduces ions into human tissue through direct current. It is commonly used in clinical practice to treat inflammatory diseases of the musculoskeletal system. This therapy can be used for pain relief, scar repair, and promoting wound healing, eliminating swelling, calcium deposition, and edema. Athletic trainers should be able to choose appropriate ionic liquids to treat patients when facing specific injury situations. The most common problem in iontophoresis therapy is chemical burns, which are usually caused by improper current intensity settings and are unrelated to the ion solution used.

② Interferential current. Interferential current combines the characteristics of mid-frequency and low-frequency electrotherapy and can be used to treat pain, joint pain accompanied by swelling, neuritis, post-fracture healing, and restricted movement.

③ Low-intensity stimulators. Low-intensity stimulators refers to the use of very low current frequency and intensity to electrically stimulate the body, promote the healing process of bones and soft tissues, relieve pain, and promote the healing of wounds and fractured tissues, Achilles tendons, and ligaments.

2.2.4 Electromagnetic Energy Modalities

① Shortwave diathermy. Shortwave diathermy can emit electromagnetic energy to deeper tissues to increase partial temperature. Tissues with high water content, such as muscles, selectively absorb the heat transferred by shortwave diathermy. It can be applied to treat bursitis, capsulitis, osteoarthritis, and muscle strains.

② Low-level laser therapy. Laser therapy can accelerate collagen synthesis, decrease microorganisms, facilitate vascularization, and reduce pain and inflammation; it can also treat painful triggers or acupuncture points. Contraindications include cancerous tissue, direct contact with the eyes, and the first trimester of pregnancy.

2.2.5 Sound Energy Modalities

① Therapeutic ultrasound. Ultrasound machines use sound energy. High-frequency sound waves are inaudible to the human body, and they can produce both thermal and non-thermal effects. Continuous ultrasonic waves can produce thermal effects. The effect of pulsed ultrasound or low-intensity continuous ultrasound is to produce a non-thermal effect and mechanical effect, promoting soft tissue healing. The dose of ultrasound therapy is determined by the depth of the tissue being treated and the state of injury (such as subacute or chronic disease). In clinical application, ultrasonic therapy is divided into three zones, namely 0.1–0.3 W/cm^2 being low intensity, 0.4–1.5 W/cm^2 being moderate intensity, and 1.5–3 W/cm^2 being high intensity. Ultrasound should not be used to treat areas of the body with abundant blood flow, such as the eyes, ears, testicles, brain, spinal cord and heart, and pregnant women should not be treated with ultrasound. In the acute stage of injury, non-thermal ultrasound can be used for treatment, and thermography sonography is contraindicant. Epiphysis areas in pediatric patients cannot be treated with ultrasound.

② Phonophoresis. Phonophoresis can transport medications through the skin by the mechanical vibrations produced by an ultrasound generator. This method has been proposed for treating trigger points, tendinitis and bursitis.

2.2.6 Mechanical Energy Modalities

① Traction.Traction is a method of treating disease by applying tension to the body, mostly used in the cervical and lumbar regions. It is most commonly used to treat compression of the spinal cord and nerve roots, reduce muscle guarding, and treat muscle strain or spinal ligament sprain and discomfort caused by spinal compression.

Traction involves manual traction and mechanical traction. The force, direction, duration, and patient position applied during manual traction can be adjusted in real-time, making it more flexible and adaptable to the body. Traction can also be divided into sustained traction and intermittent traction. Sustained traction is preferred in the treatment of lumbar disk problems; while intermittent traction is used for controlling or decreasing swelling after acute injuries or for pitting edema.

② Massage. Massage is the systematic manual therapy of soft tissues. The athletic trainer applies manipulations like push, compression, stretch, percussion, and vibration on the patient's body. From the mechanical perspective, massage can promote venous and lymphatic drainage and mildly stretch superficial and scar tissue. From a physiological perspective, massage can facilitate circulation, and thus increasing metabolism and removing metabolites; it can also decrease venostasis and edema by promoting circulation and assisting in blood return. From a psychological perspective, massage can help build trust between the athletic trainer and the patient.

2.3 Common Manual Therapies

2.3.1 Joint Mobilization

Joint mobilization aims at improving joint movement disorder by passive movement of bare hands, using large amplitude and low-speed techniques. Joint mobilization can promote the flow of joint fluid, increase the nutrition of the blood-free area of articular cartilage disc, reduce pain, stretch and lengthen the periarticular tissue, especially the joint capsule and ligament tissue, improve muscle tension or stretch reflex, and improve proprioception.

When applied, physiological or accessory movements of the joint can be selected as treatment methods. It can be divided into swing, rolling, sliding, rotation, traction and extrusion.

① Swing. The bone moving like a lever is called a swing. The swing of joint includes flexion, extension, adduction, abduction and rotation, which is commonly known as physiological movement. When swinging, the proximal end of the joint should be fixed and the distal end of the joint should be moved back and forth. The swing can only be applied when the range of motion of the joint reaches 60% of the normal. For example, the swing manipulation of shoulder flexion should be applied at least when the shoulder flexion reaches 100 degrees. If it does not reach this range, it should be improved by means of accessory movement.

② Rolling. When a bone rolls on another bone, the surface shape of the two bones must be inconsistent, and the contact point changes at the same time, and the movement occurs in angular motion. Regardless of the concave and convex degree of the joint surface, the rolling direction is always toward the direction of the angular bone movement. When the joint function is normal, rolling does not occur alone, and is generally accompanied by joint sliding and rotation.

③ Sliding. When a bone slides on another bone, if it is simply sliding, the surface shape of the two bones must be the same, either flat or curved. If it is a curved surface, the concave and convex degrees of the two bone surfaces must be equal. When sliding, the same point on the surface of one bone contacts different points on the opposite bone surface throughout the slide. The sliding direction depends on the concave-convex shape of the joint surface of the moving bone.

Concavity and convexity rule: When the concave articular surface is fixed, and the convex surface is moving, the gliding movement in the joint occurs in a direction opposite to the bone movement. Conversely, if the convex articular surface is fixed while the concave surface is mobile, the gliding occurs in the same direction as the bone movement.

The relationship between rolling and sliding: The closer the shape of the joint surfaces, the more sliding of one bone on the surface of another bone during movement. The more inconsistent the shape is, the more rolling there will be. In clinical application, because sliding can relieve pain, sliding combined with traction can release joint capsule, making joint relaxed and improving. However, rolling squeezes joints, which is easy to cause injury and is less used alone.

④ Rotation.The moving bone rotates around the rotating axis on the stationary bone surface. When rotating, move the same point on the bone surface to make a circular motion. Rotation often occurs simultaneously with sliding and rolling, rarely acting alone.

Different joints have different positions of rotation axes. For example, the rotation axis of the glenohumeral joint passes through the center of the humeral head and is perpendicular to the glenoid. The rotation of physiological movement is the rotation of the humerus around its long axis. The rotation of the hip joint is the rotation of the femoral head around the rotation axis passing through the center of the femoral head and perpendicular to the acetabulum. The rotation of the forearm joint is the same as that in physiological movement, in which the radius rotates around the ulna.

⑤ Traction. When the external force makes the two bone surfaces of the joint separate at right angles, it is called separation or intra-articular traction; when the external force acts on the long axis of bone to shift the distal end of the joint, it is called traction or long axis traction. The difference between separation and traction: When separating, the external force should be perpendicular to the articular surface, and at the same time, the joint surface of the two bones must be separated; when tracting, the external force must be parallel to the long axis of the bone, and the articular surface may not be separated. For example, when the humeral joint is tracted, the external force is parallel to the long axis of the humerus, and the articular surface slides; when the glenohumeral joint is separated, the external force is perpendicular to the glenoid, and the articular surface is separated from each other.

⑥ Extrusion. Reduce the space between the bones in the joint cavity. Muscle contraction produces a certain amount of pressure, which can improve the stability of the joint. However, when rotating toward other bone directions, it can cause compression in the angular movement direction of the bone. When the pressure is abnormally increased, the articular cartilage will be deformed and damaged. Therefore, extrusion technology is rarely used.

Maitland classified mobilization into four levels as follows:

Level Ⅰ: At the beginning of the joint range of motion, the joint is mobilized back and forth in a small range rhythmically.

Level Ⅱ: Within the allowable range of motion, mobilize the joint in a wide range and rhythmically back and forth, but do not contact the beginning and end of joint motion.

Level Ⅲ: Mobilize the joint in a wide range and rhythmically back and forth within the allowed range of motion, and contact the end of joint motion.

Level Ⅳ: At the end of the joint motion, mobilize the joint in a small range and rhythmically back and forth to contact the end of joint motion.

In the Maitland grading system, level Ⅰ and Ⅱ mobilization manipulations are used to treat limited joint motion due to pain; Level Ⅲ mobilization is used to treat pain with limited movement; Level Ⅳ mobilization is used to treat limited joint movement caused by adhesion and contracture of surrounding tissues.

2.3.2 Myofascial Release

Myofascial release is a group of techniques used to relieve soft tissue from the abnormal grip of tight fascia. The Fascia is a kind of special connective tissue layer that covers muscles, bones and joints to provide protection and support for the body. It is mainly composed of collagen and elastic fibers. It was generally believed in the past that the role of the fascia in the body is passive, which could transmit the mechanical tension caused by muscle activity and external force. However, some recent studies have shown that the fascia can actively contract like muscles, which has an impact on musculoskeletal dynamics. The fascia is continuous from head to foot and is connected with many sheaths and flat surfaces. Therefore, the fascia must be free to extend and move in the activity.

Myofascial release belongs to soft tissue mobilization, although from the technical level, joint mobilization and soft tissue mobilization both involve soft tissue, and have a strong correlation. However, the key point of joint mobilization is to restore joint activity and act on specific joints. According to the different directions and joint surface shapes, the direction and application principles are also different. However, myofascial mobilization mainly focuses on the local treatment and relies on the subjective feelings and experience of the operator. Once the myofascial limitation is located, the release position should be fixed at this position, from the shallower to the deep. Once the limitation of soft tissue is released and eliminated, the effect of joint mobilization will be better.

The common myofascial release methods include non-invasive manipulation, the use of foam roller and fascial knife release, as well as the release by puncture needle, little needle knife or radio frequency needle under B mode ultrasound.

2.3.3 Proprioceptive Neuromuscular Facilitation

Proprioceptive neuromuscular facilitation advocates a new therapeutic concept that utilizes stretching, joint compression, traction, and resistance to improve and promote muscle function by stimulating proprioceptors and applying spiral diagonal motion patterns. The principles and techniques of PNF are mainly based on neurophysiology, anatomy and auxanology. It is characterized by the normal exercise mode and development of sports as the basic technology, emphasizing the overall rather than single muscle activity. It is characterized by active, passive and resistant spiral diagonal movement of limbs and trunk, which is similar to functional activities in daily life. It advocates influencing the movement mode through hand contact, language command and visual guidance. It can improve muscle strength, endurance and control ability, effectively mobilize the potential function of human body coordination, establish the balance between stability and activity, and improve the ability of activities of daily living.

The ten basic elements of PNF are manual contact, command and communication, stretching, traction and squeezing, resistance, posture and body mechanics, diffusion and reinforcement, sequence, visual stimulation, and movement mode.

PNF training mode consists of three groups of movements: flexion and extension, adduction and abduction, and internal rotation and external rotation.

Upper limb D1: flexion–adduction–external rotation; extension–abduction–internal rotation

(grab safety belt; buckle safety belt)

Upper limb D2: flexion–abduction–external rotation; extension–adduction–internal rotation (draw a sword; insert a sword)

Lower extremity D1: flexion–adduction–external rotation; extension–abduction–internal rotation (kick a ball; toe off)

Lower limb D2: flexion–abduction–internal rotation; extension–adduction–external rotation (martial arts kick; Ballet position)

PNF technology is usually used to improve strength and range of motion. Among them, PNF strength enhancement technology includes rhythmic initiation, repetitive contraction, slow reversal, slow reversal–hold and rhythmic stabilization. PNF stretching techniques include contract–relax, hold–relax, and slow–reverse–hold–relax.

① Repetitive contraction. Repeated contractions of a single muscle or muscle group can be used to solve the problem of insufficient strength of the whole body muscles or some muscles. The patient's isokinetic contraction works against the maximum resistance of the athletic trainer until the patient feels tired. Once fatigue develops, stretch is applied to the muscle at that point in the range to facilitate greater strength production. All resistance should be adjusted according to the patient's condition. Because the patient is required to use the maximum force to work, it should be avoided for some injuries.

② Rhythmic initiation. Rhythmic initiation includes a whole set of progressive programs. First is passive activity, then the active assisted movement, and then the active movement is carried out through the contraction of agonistic muscle. It can be applied from the day of the patient's injury, and gradually increase the intensity and scope within the patient's tolerance in the next few days and weeks. This technique can help patients with limited mobility gradually increase their strength and improve their range of motion.

③ Stable reversals. The objective of this technique is to increase the patient's stability and balance, increase muscle strength and coordination between the agonistic and antagonistic muscles. Apply resistance on both agonistic and antagonistic muscles to help them contract smoothly and rhythmically.

④ Slow reversal–hold. In this technique, the patient completes isotonic contraction with the agonistic muscle, and then does isometric contraction. The patient is told to hold the position at the end of each isotonic contraction. The main purpose of this is to increase muscle strength at some point in the range of motion.

⑤ Rhythmic stabilization technique. Rhythmic stabilization technique utilizes isometric contraction of the agonistic muscle, followed by isometric contraction of the antagonistic muscle. The maximum strength can be achieved by repeated contraction.

⑥ Contract–relax. Passively move body parts until resistance is felt. The patient is then told to contract the antagonistic muscles isometrically. The athletic trainer maintains this movement for 10 seconds, or until the patient feels tired. Patients rest for 10 seconds. The athletic trainer will pull in the other direction or repeat it three times in the same direction.

⑦ Hold–relax. The hold–relax technique is similar to the contract–relax technique, both utilizing isometric contraction. The patient actively moves his body until he feels resistance and maintains the position. Athletic trainers hold 10 seconds against the patient's isometric contraction. Patients rest for 10 seconds, and then passively or actively move to a new range of motion. Repeat the technique three times.

⑧ Slow reverse–hold–relax. The patient moves his body until he feels resistance and holds the position.

2.3.4 Muscle Energy Technology

Muscle energy technology (MET) is a manual stretching technique that involves neurophysiology to relax over activated muscles and/or stretch chronically shortened muscles. It can be used to treat complex dysfunction of the kinetic chain. It is a branch of PNF contract–relax and hold–relax techniques. MET is a method for patients to contract actively against the resistance of different intensities at the distal extremities exerted by athletic trainers.

The following five points should be noticed when using MET:

① Patients should actively contract.

② Muscle contraction should be in a specific direction.

③ Patients should have certain control of contraction.

④ The athletic trainer controls the joint position.

⑤ The athletic trainer should provide appropriate resistance.

The manipulation of MET is to stretch a tight muscle to the end of joint mobility, which is called resistance barrier point. Starting from the resistance barrier point, the patient contracts the antagonistic muscle (the muscle to be elongated) for 10 seconds. At this point, the patient needs to completely relax, and then the athletic trainer moves the body to the next resistance barrier point. This step should be repeated 3–5 times until the range of motion does not change.

2.4 Common Therapeutic Exercises

2.4.1 Muscle Strength Training

Muscle strength, endurance, or power can be measured by manual muscle test, progressive resistance test or isometric contraction test. Isometric contraction tests usually provide the most reliable objective indicator of force change.

Muscle strength training is a kind of training that can recover or enhance the muscle strength of patients by using different muscle contraction forms through active or passive movement. Strength training increases the relative strength of the human body and improves the contraction speed and power of muscles. Muscle strength training is of great significance in preventing and managing various muscle atrophy, promoting the recovery of muscle strength after nervous system damage, correcting joint deformity, and maintaining joint stability. It is also the foundation of preventing sports injuries. The commonly used muscle strength training methods include assisted active movement, active movement, resisted active movement, isometric contraction, and so on.

(1) The Main Way of Movement

According to the source of strength of human movement, human movement can be divided into passive movement and active movement.

Active movement is the movement that the human body completes by actively contracting muscles. According to the force, it can be divided into assisted active movement, active movement and resisted active movement.

Passive movement relies on the external force to move the human body. External forces include manipulative therapy by therapists, movement under instruments, and the human body's own driving (gravity and healthy side limb driving affected side limb movement), etc. Passive movement is usually used by patients with limb paralysis and muscle strength below level 2 who can not perform active movement. It is used to maintain the range of motion, prevent muscle adhesion and joint contracture, maintain muscle tension and elasticity, and prepare for active movement.

(2) The Form of Muscle Contraction

According to the changes in muscle length and tension, muscle contraction can be divided into three types. According to different purposes of rehabilitation treatment and muscle strength of patients, different forms of muscle contraction should be selected for exercise.

① Isometric contraction. Isometric contraction refers to muscle contraction, which is only produced in the static state; although the muscle contracts and the muscle tension increases significantly, muscle length basically does not change and does not produce joint movement. Isometric contraction is caused by an external force that makes the muscle lengthen equal to the maximum tension produced by the muscle itself. Isometric contraction training is often used in the early stage of rehabilitation after a period of joint immobilization. Isometric training can increase static muscle strength and reduce atrophy, improve the weakness of strength in any direction, and form a muscle pump effect to eliminate effusion and edema, thus reducing swelling.

② Isotonic contraction. Isotonic contraction refers to the process of muscle contraction, in which muscle tension is basically unchanged, but muscle length changes, resulting in joint movement. According to the direction of movement of the starting and ending parts of the muscle, it can be divided into two types: concentric contraction and eccentric contraction.

Concentric contraction refers to when muscles contract, the starting and ending points of muscles getting closer to each other, and the muscle is shortened, which is also known as shortening contraction and restraint contraction; eccentric contraction refers to when muscles contract, both starting and ending points of muscles are getting far away from each other, making the muscle longer. Concentric contraction often acts on the joint to make the joint move, while eccentric contraction is often produced by antagonistic muscles against joint movement. The effect of eccentric contraction is opposite to the direction of joint movement, and is used to stabilize the joint, and control the movement of limbs or the speed of limbs falling.

Isotonic contraction can be used in a wide range of joint motions. The ratio of torsion force, average strength, total work and rotation force to body weight can be calculated by an isotonic contractile instrument, and each of these indexes can be used as a diagnostic index by athletic trainers. The value of isotonic contraction is usually used as an indicator of whether athletes can return to functional training after injury.

③ Isokinetic Contraction. Isokinetic contraction refers to the movement mode in which the speed of muscle contraction remains constant within the whole joint range of motion under the guidance of specified equipment. In isokinetic exercise, the length of muscle changes in the process of contraction, while the speed of muscle contraction remains unchanged. It is a highly effective method to improve muscle strength, only with muscle strength condition of level 3 or above is it suitable to perform.

In theory, the resistance provided by isokinetic training equipment is the maximum resistance in the process of movement. In the whole range of motion (at all angles of joint movement), the muscle produces the maximum tension, so it can achieve better training effects.

(3) Classification of Common Exercise Forms

① Open kinetic chain (OKC). Open kinetic chain movement refers to the movement in which the proximal side of the limb is fixed while the distal joint is active, such as the swing phase when walking. Open chain movement is characterized by a single joint. For example, when performing dumbbell curls, the elbow is fixed and the dumbbell is held in the hand for elbow flexion and extension exercises.

In sports training, open kinetic chain exercise can train a certain muscle of the body in isolation, so open kinetic chain exercise is often used for strength training of a muscle; during open kinetic chain exercise, the range of motion of the distal side is larger than that of the proximal side, and the speed is also faster than that of the proximal, so open kinetic chain exercise is often used to train muscle power.

In the early stage of muscle strength rehabilitation training, because the shear force produced by open kinetic chain exercise is greater than that of closed kinetic chain exercise, open kinetic chain exercise should not be selected to restore function, so as to avoid increasing the load of the injury part. In the later stage of rehabilitation, when the function and proprioception of the joint are strengthened by closed kinetic chain movement, open kinetic chain exercise can be used to train the muscle groups near the joint.

② Closed kinetic chain (CKC). Closed kinetic chain movement refers to the movement in which the distal side of the limb (palm or sole of the foot) is fixed and the proximal side is active, such as the supporting phase in walking. Closed chain movement features multiple joint coordination. For example, when using a barbell for weight-bearing squat training, the feet are fixed, and the hip, knee and ankle joint complete the movement in coordination.

In sports training, the closed kinetic chain exercise involves more muscles and joints, which needs to be completed by multi–joint coordination, and is closer to real sports movements, being the preferred sports training mode for professional athletes.

In muscle strength rehabilitation training, closed kinetic chain movement is a multi–joint cooperative movement without increasing joint shear force, which can stimulate joint proprioceptive receptors and generate limb motions and protective reflex arc, and fully improve the overall coordination of the joint and promote the functional recovery of the joint proprioception, so as to promote the stability of the joint and functional rehabilitation, so the closed kinetic chain exercise should be selected in the early stage of rehabilitation.

2.4.2 Core Stability Training

Core stability training can improve the control of human body, enhance balance ability, activate deep small muscle groups, coordinate the strength output of large and small muscle groups, enhance motor function, and prevent injury.

During core stability training, patients must strictly control the body posture, emphasize the participation of the nervous system, focus on the quality of exercise completed, not the number. Athletic trainers should guide the participants to maintain rhythmic breathing, make the breathing cooperate with the movement, and gradually increase the difficulty of training with the improvement of the ability.

The common core stability training includes abdominal bridge, side bridge, glutes bridge and "dead bug" training, which can be combined with a Swiss ball, resistance band and balance foam pad to increase difficulty.

2.4.3 Progressive Functional Training

This is described in chapter 1 "Strength and Conditioning Considerations" of Part Ⅱ.

2.4.4 Balance and Coordination Training

Balance refers to a stable state of the human body and the ability to automatically adjust and maintain posture regardless of position, movement or external forces. Balance function can directly or indirectly affect the patient's body control and self-care ability in the future. The coordination function is the ability of the human body to adjust itself and complete smooth, accurate and controlled random movement. The quality of coordination function determines the fluency and accuracy of the patient's movement, and directly affects the patient's daily movement. Balance and coordination are fundamental to human movement. Good balance and coordination function can guarantee the human body maintains stable posture and complete movement accurately.

The balance of the human body can be maintained under various changes of its own and external environment, which depends on the participation, interaction and integration of sensory system and motor system under the control of central nervous system. Somatosensory, visual and vestibular sensory systems play different roles in maintaining balance. The factors that maintain coordination function include reflex, regulation of the superior center, basal ganglia, cerebral cortex, sensory afferent and cerebellum's regulation of motor.

(1) Basic Principles of Balance Training

① The support area changes from large to small.

② From static balance to dynamic balance.

③ Progressive change of body center of gravity from low to high.

④ From maintaining balance to maintaining posture when losing balance.

⑤ From maintaining balance under attention to maintaining balance under inattention.

⑥ Visual shielding.

⑦ Destroy the balance of vestibular organs to train them to keep balance.

(2) Order of Balance Training

① According to the functional postural system, balance from sitting position to hand-knee position and both knees kneeling position, and finally restore standing position balance.

② From easy to difficult, gradually increase the difficulty, from the most stable position to the most unstable position, from large support surface to small support surface, center of gravity from low to high, from static balance training to dynamic balance training, from eye-opening training to eye closing training, from no head and neck involvement movement to adding head and neck involvement movement.

(3) Key Points of Coordination Training

① Be sure to complete specific practice tasks.

② Before the coherent movement, complete the single action first.

③ Do related exercise training.

2.4.5 Hydrotherapy

Water is considered to be an auxiliary, supportive and resistance medium. Hydrotherapy mainly uses the buoyancy and resistance of water to increase range of motion, reconstruct correct motion patterns, improve strength, explosive power and muscle endurance.

Water buoyancy can improve the patient's range of motion and control. While the patient's body sinking into the water, the limbs can be lifted by the buoyancy of the water. The patient can actively increase the range of motion by buoyancy.

Resistance is another application of hydrotherapy. The affected part should resist the upward force of water and go down. The maximum resistance occurs when the limb is at the right angle to the horizontal plane. Resistant technology can also be advanced by using different devices. For additional resistance, the patient can push or pull the floater into the water.

In addition to using special exercises, patients can practice their exercise skills by utilizing the buoyancy and resistance of water in the most suitable way for them. For example, they can practice moving or throwing techniques to restore normal movement patterns. Swimming pools can be very good places to restore functional ability and cardiopulmonary endurance.

2.4.6 Neuromuscular Control Training

After an injury, rest and immobilization lead the nervous system to "forget" how to integrate the impulses transmitted by the muscle and joint mechanoreceptors with the sensation from skin, vision and vestibular system. Neuromuscular control is our conscious perception of a particular movement in our body. Repeating a particular movement pattern can gradually make it easier and more comfortable, and ultimately automated.

Strength training, especially functional strength training, is crucial for the recovery of neuromuscular control. For athletic trainers, reconstructing the sense of position and motion of proprioception should be the primary focus. Position perception is the ability to determine joint position, while motion perception is the ability to detect motion continuously. Our ability to sense the position of joints is a mixture of mechanical stimulus receptors in muscles and joints, as well as skin sensation, vision, and vestibular sensation. Neuromuscular control relies on the central nervous system to translate and integrate positional and motor senses and control muscles and joints to coordinate movements.

Restoring neuromuscular control means regaining the established sensory patterns. The central nervous system compares the intention and result of a certain action with the previously stored information, and gradually modifies the action until it is completely correct. The four major factors in the restoration of neuromuscular control are: proprioception; dynamic stability; feedforward and muscular regulation according to feedback; conscious and subconscious functional movement mode.

Summary

1. Off-the-field assessment methods mainly include medical history, observation, palpation, and special tests. The record should follow the SOAP model, which is the abbreviation of subjective, objective, assessment and plan.

2. Thermotherapy mainly includes hydrocollator packs, whirlpool baths and paraffin baths. Cryotherapy includes ice massage, cold water immersion, ice pack and vapocoolant sprays.

Electrical energy modalities involve iontophoresis, interference currents and low-intensity stimulators. Electromagnetic energy modalities involve shortwave diathermy and low-level laser therapy. Common sound energy modalities are therapeutic ultrasound and phonophoresis. Mechanical energy modalities mainly include traction and massage.

3. In the Maitland grading system, level I and II mobilization manipulations are used to treat limited joint motion due to pain; Level III mobilization is used to treat pain with limited movement; Level IV mobilization is used to treat limited joint movement caused by adhesion and contracture of surrounding tissues.

4. Soft tissue mobilization is able to eliminate scar tissue/adhesions. Myofascial release belongs to soft tissue mobilization. The common myofascial release methods include non-invasive manipulation and fascial knife release.

5. PNF technology is usually used in rehabilitation to improve strength and range of motion.

6. According to the form of muscle contraction, muscle strength training can be divided into isometric contraction, isotonic contraction, and isokinetic contraction. According to the way of limb fixation, muscle strength training can be divided into open kinetic chain (OKC) and closed kinetic chain (CKC).

7. The core part of the body has three main functions in sports: generating strength, transmitting strength and controlling strength; thus, core stability training is very important. Core stability training mainly includes abdominal bridge, side bridge and glute bridge.

8. Balance and coordination function is one of the basis of human movement. Good balance and coordination function can make the human body maintain a stable posture and complete movement accurately.

9. Hydrotherapy can provide either buoyancy or resistance. It can be utilized to assist the patient to exercise.

10. The four major factors in the restoration of neuromuscular control include proprioception; dynamic stability; feedforward and muscular regulation according to feedback; conscious and subconscious functional movement mode.

O Review Questions

1. What's the content of off-field injury evaluation and methods of recording the athlete's injuries?

2. What are the principles of thermotherapy? What are the methods of thermotherapy?

3. What is Muscle Energy Technology?

4. What are the therapeutic exercises commonly used by the athletic trainer?

二、场外评估及处理

（一）场外评估及处理的原则和方法

患者被转移离开场地后，运动防护师需要在运动防护室、医务室等地方对患者当前的损伤或疾病进行评估或诊断。

1. 场外评定流程

场外评定分为四部分：病史、视诊、触诊和特殊检查，也称 HOPS（history, observation, palpation, special examinations）方案。运动防护师应全面地获取与损伤有关的准确信息，并为进一步的检查和后续的治疗制订计划。

（1）病史

病史的采集包括患者的主诉、现病史、既往史、临床治疗过程及并发症等，可帮助运动防护师了解患者身体状况、损伤过程和受伤程度，在损伤评定中占有重要的地位。

①主诉：包括患者年龄、性别等基本信息和困扰患者的主要问题。

②现病史：包括患者出现伤病及之后的全过程。运动防护师应记录患者疼痛发生的时间和诱因、疼痛的部位、疼痛的性质、疼痛的程度、缓解或加剧疼痛的因素。

③既往史：帮助运动防护师了解患者以往是否发生过同样的问题、是怎样治疗的、是否有其他与既往病史相关的问题。

④临床治疗过程：本次就诊前实施过何种治疗、疗效如何。

⑤并发症：在主要症状的基础上可能伴随有其他症状，肌肉骨骼系统损伤中与疼痛伴随的常见症状有关节活动受限、体位变化困难、面色苍白、出冷汗、眩晕、呕吐等。

（2）视诊

视诊通常在询问病史的同时进行，有关功能障碍的程度、功能水平、姿势及力线、平衡负重能力以及行走能力都可以通过视诊观察到。视诊时患者应尽量暴露关键的体表标志点。

（3）触诊

触诊检查用于发现皮肤、软组织和骨的异常。

①皮肤：检查受伤皮肤的温度与湿度。

②软组织：检查肌肉、筋膜、韧带和肌腱有无压痛，同时还应注意柔韧性和硬度的变化，注意有无疼挛、肌卫和结节。触诊时手法应尽量减少患者痛苦。

③骨：通过触诊骨性突起部位，检查关节对位对线、压痛。

运动防护师还应检查受伤部位的动脉搏动以确定是否存在血管的损害。通过触诊可鉴别急性损伤和慢性损伤。急性损伤时皮肤潮湿、皮温增高、韧带压痛剧烈、不同肌层肿胀和张力增加；慢性损伤时皮肤发凉、发紧或凹陷，韧带增厚，肌层变硬或纤维化。

（4）特殊检查

特殊检查通常用来证实通过询问病史、视诊、触诊得到的结论，包括主动和被动运动检查、关节活动度测量、徒手肌力检查、神经功能检查及功能性筛查等。运动防护师在做特殊检查时应注意健患两侧的对比和操作的规范性，必要时还应检查患者的身体姿态、肢体长度和围度。

①主动运动检查：通过让患者主动做屈伸、内收外展、内外旋等各方向的动作来检查主动运动。在患者运动过程中，运动防护师应注意观察运动的范围、对称性、速度、是否出现疼痛以及疼痛出现在运动过程中的何部位、患者是否愿意活动或恐动等。通过主动运动，可以大体确定疼痛的部位、疼痛发生在关节活动范围内的确切位置、运动对疼痛程度的影响、运动模式正常与否、患者现有的运动功能水平、患者对于运动的主观愿望。

②被动运动检查：包括生理运动检查和附属运动检查，通过被动检查来确定患者的主要疾病或症状是否由非收缩成分或组织引起。生理运动检查用于检查非收缩组织的状态，除了确定关节运动受限的程度以及疼痛外，通过被动运动检查，还可以确定终末感性质，以及鉴别关节活动受限是否由于关节囊性病变或损伤所致。附属运动检查中，主要检查关节的可动性，通过附属运动检查可获得关节松弛程度的信息。

主动和被动运动检查相结合，可以进一步确认损伤组织的类型，如：主动和被动均受限，并且在相同方向上出现疼痛，提示关节囊和关节损伤；主动和被动运动均受限，疼痛出现在相反方向，提示收缩组织损伤，需要进一步做抗阻力运动检查加以明确。

③关节活动度测量：包括主动关节活动度测量和被动关节活动度测量。主动关节活动度的测量用于检查患者肌肉收缩力量对关节活动度的影响。被动关节活动度的检查用于测量患者的关节活动受限程度，来判断关节运动终末感的性质，从而确定是否在限制关节运动的异常结构变化。

④徒手肌力检查：用于检查收缩组织即肌肉及其附属结构。运动防护师通过施加徒手阻力，可将收缩组织作为疼痛产生的来源分离出来。

Lovett 将肌肉力量分为正常、良好、尚可、差、微弱和无收缩六个等级：

正常（5级）：在抗重力并施予最大阻力的情况下，能够完成全关节活动范围的运动。

良好（4级）：在抗重力并施加部分阻力时，能够完成全关节活动范围的运动。

尚可（3级）：在抗重力的情况下，不施加任何阻力，能够完成全关节活动范围的运动。

差（2级）：在去除重力的情况下，能够完成全关节活动范围的运动。

微弱（1级）：在去除重力的情况下，仅有肌肉收缩现象，没有产生关节的运动。

无收缩（0级）：未触及肌肉的收缩。

⑤神经功能检查：包括肌力、深反射、神经根的可动性，感觉和脑功能检查，可帮助运动防护师确定患者的症状是否与神经损伤有关。

●肌力：通过与特定脊髓水平相关的肌力和关节运动检查，可以确定神经损伤水平。

●深反射：反射弧任何部位的中断均可导致深反射减弱或消失。

●神经根的活动性检查：神经牵拉试验所表现出的压迫症提示神经根受压。

●感觉检查：采用轻触觉进行筛查，以确定皮肤感觉的存在与消失情况，并将所查结果与皮肤节段或周围神经支配相联系。若患者出现明显的神经功能障碍，应进行更详细的感觉检查，如温度感觉、本体感觉等。

● 脑功能检查：一般包括意识水平、智力表现、情绪状态、思维内容、感官反应（视觉、触觉、听觉）和语言表达能力方面的检查。

⑥功能性筛查：

● 功能性动作筛查。功能性动作筛查（functional movement screen，FMS）是一种用来识别由身体的不对称导致的功能性运动缺陷的工具。FMS通过测试在7种基本运动模式下的灵活性和稳定性来评价损伤风险。动作包括：深蹲、跨栏步、直线弓步蹲、肩部灵活性、主动直腿上抬、躯干稳定俯卧撑、旋转稳定性。

● 上肢损伤风险筛查测试。上肢闭链稳定性测试用于测定上肢肩带的稳定性，测试表现取决于肌肉力量水平、平衡以及协调性。上肢Y-平衡测试能综合观察上肢支撑侧手臂、肩胛带、躯干的稳定性，以及移动侧的手臂、肩胛带及躯干的灵活性。

● 下肢损伤风险筛查测试。下肢Y-平衡测试是一项力量、柔韧、核心控制和本体感觉共同参与的一种单腿动态稳定性测试。

此外，为了全面地了解患者的损伤状况，特殊检查中还应该包括CT、MRI、超声、心电图、脑电图、血液检查和关节镜检查等影像学和实验室检查。

2. 损伤评定的记录——SOAP记录模式

（1）记录的目的

损伤评定的记录是关于患者功能障碍的特征、发展变化、诊疗情况的系统记录。它不仅记录功能障碍的情况，同时也记录运动防护师对功能障碍的分析、判断、诊断、治疗过程以及对预后的估计，也是相关医疗纠纷及诉讼的重要依据。

（2）记录的基本要求

①内容真实可靠。

②描述精炼，重点突出。

③格式规范、系统。

④及时。

⑤具有连续性。

（3）SOAP记录模式

SOAP记录模式（主观检查、客观检查、评定、治疗计划）为现场、场外以及临床损伤评估的标准记录模式，该记录模式由患者提供的信息和运动防护师的评估结果组成。

运动防护师应在整个康复治疗过程对患者每次的进展进行定期记录。康复进程的记录可以是对治疗过程的补充说明或是每周的治疗总结，同样可以采用SOAP记录模式。但康复进程的记录侧重于患者接受的治疗类型和患者对于治疗的反馈、短期康复目标的进展、目标的变化以及接下来的治疗计划。

● S（subjective）：主观检查，包括患者及其家属的主观描述和患者对其损伤史（包括损伤的部位、时间以及损伤机制）的说明。另外，疼痛的程度和性质以及患者的残疾程度也需要进行记录。

● O（objective）：客观检查，包括视诊、触诊、主动活动检查、被动活动检查、抗阻测试以及特殊试验检查的结果。因此，客观检查的记录会包含姿势评估、畸形和肿胀的检查和确定压痛点的位置、主动活动的受限情况以及被动运动和抗阻运动中出现疼痛或疼痛消失的情况、关节稳定性等结果。

● A（assessment）：评定，损伤的评定是运动防护师对损伤的表象和性质的专业判定，包括对主观和客观资料的专业分析判断。

● P（plan）：治疗计划，治疗计划包括总体治疗计划和具体治疗方案，以及短期目标和长期目标。例如：短期目标是从需要双拐行走到能够单拐负重行走，长期目标是患者不再跛行，能够用正常步态行走。

通过损伤评定能发现和确定损伤部位、范围、性质、程度以及障碍发生的原因、预后，为预防和制订明确的康复目标和康复治疗计划提供依据。为此，运动防护师应具有解剖学、生理学、病理学等相关基础专业知识。运动防护师应注意检查顺序，避免滥用检查，重视沟通技巧，将评定贯穿于康复治疗的全过程。

3. 场外处理的原则和方法

大多数肌肉骨骼损伤会首先使用非手术治疗，包括纠正异常活动模式、康复训练以及矫形器的应用。若保守治疗失败或存在有骨折、肌腱断裂等情况，则应考虑手术治疗。

康复治疗可分为三个阶段进行：急性期（通常是损伤或术后1～3周）、恢复期（通常是损伤或术后3～6周）和功能期（通常是损伤或术后6～12周）。每个阶段的具体目标和基本措施如下：

急性期：减轻炎症，缓解疼痛，保持无痛范围内的关节活动度，肌肉静力性收缩练习，防止肌肉萎缩和深静脉血栓的形成。干预措施包括非甾体抗炎药和镇痛药的使用、理疗、电刺激、肌肉静力性收缩练习以及全身训练等。

恢复期：纠正患者的功能障碍，如柔韧性、肌力、关节活动度、平衡和本体感觉等。具体措施包括理疗，关节松动术，静力性和动力性收缩练习，本体感觉练习，平衡练习，以及专项运动练习。

功能期：主要进行专项运动练习，帮助患者尽早返回赛场。增加肌肉爆发力、肌耐力、神经肌肉控制等训练，方法包括肌肉增强训练，多平面内的神经肌肉控制练习等。

（二）常用的物理因子治疗技术

物理因子治疗方案的制订和实施必须在理解组织对于损伤的生理反应如何以及组织的愈合过程处于什么阶段的基础之上。运动防护师在了解清楚患者的症状和体征以及患者处于损伤愈合的哪一阶段后才能决定何时以及如何用物理疗法对患者进行治疗。

运动防护师常用的一些物理因子治疗技术包括：热疗法、冷疗法、电刺激疗法、短波治疗法、低强度激光疗法、超声波和超声透入疗法、牵引疗法以及按摩等。与物理疗法相关的能量形式包括：热传导能、电能、电磁能、声能以及机械能。热疗和冷疗的本质是热能的相互传导；电刺激是电能的使用；短波、低强度激光疗法的本质是电磁波疗法；超声波是声能的应用；牵引、间歇性加压以及按摩使用的是机械能。

1. 热疗

人体对热能的生理反应取决于所施加的热能的类型、强度、持续时间，以及人体的热敏反应。热疗能够增加胶原组织的伸展性，缓解关节僵硬，减轻疼痛及缓解肌肉痉挛，在组织愈合期对组织有消炎和消除水肿，以及增加血液循环的效果。常用方法如下：

①水凝胶包：水凝胶包是将棉衬垫中包裹的硅酸盐凝胶浸在温度为 160 ℉（约 71.1℃）至 170 ℉（约 76.7℃）的恒温热水中。水凝胶包主要用于改善"疼痛—痉挛—局部缺血—局部缺氧—疼痛"这一循环过程，但是无法作用于包括肌肉组织在内的较深的组织。

②漩涡浴：漩涡浴疗法是将肢体浸入水中进行按摩的一种疗法。漩涡浴实现了热传导和对流，皮肤与较高水温的水接触是热的传导过程，水在皮肤周围旋转形成热对流。漩涡浴能够减少治疗部位的肿胀、肌肉痉挛以及疼痛。水的浮力还能够促进肢体的主动活动。

③石蜡浴：石蜡浴常用于对四肢远端进行热疗。石蜡浴温度恒定在 52℃ 至 54℃。石蜡浴对于治疗发生在身体多部位的慢性损伤特别有效，例如手、手腕、脚和脚踝等处的损伤。需要注意的是，石蜡浴不能用于治疗身体有开放性伤口或循环不好的部位。

2. 冷疗

冷疗能够降低组织的代谢率并且使血管收缩，所以它会降低组织在急性炎症反应期中的肿胀程度；组织的代谢率降低也可以减少肌卫现象，也因此能减少肌肉痉挛所生成的代谢废物。冷疗也能够减慢神经冲动的传导，降低神经末梢的敏感性；缓解肌肉疲劳，保持或增加肌肉的收缩能力。常用方法如下：

①冰按摩：冰按摩法是用于治疗身体小范围区域的冷疗法。当患者疼痛减轻时，再进行拉伸和锻炼。

②冷水浴：在身体某一部位及周围都需要进行冰敷时可选择使用冷水浴。将水和碎冰混合在一起使冰水混合物的温度到达 10℃ 至 15℃。患者将身体的一部分浸入冰水中，持续 10 至 15 分钟。当疼痛消失时，将肢体从冰水中移出，开始进行正常的运动模式。当身体再次感觉到疼痛时，再浸入冰水中，可如此重复三次。

③冰袋：冰袋更容易应用于身体各部位。在各种类型的冰袋中，湿冰袋冷却效果最佳。湿冰袋可通过用湿毛巾包裹着片状的碎冰块或将碎冰放在密封塑料袋中制成。患者会经历冷反应的四个阶段：寒冷感、疼痛、灼热和麻木。在治疗过程中，只要患者出现麻木等不良反应和过敏现象，应立即停止治疗。

④冷冻喷雾剂：目前最常用的一种冷冻喷雾剂是氟甲烷喷雾剂，它是一种无毒、不可燃的物质。主要用于减少肌卫现象，增加运动范围。它还可以用于治疗肌筋膜和扳机点处的疼痛。

3. 电疗法

电疗能够使感觉神经纤维去极化以缓解疼痛；使运动神经纤维去极化刺激肌肉的收缩；产生电场刺激生物组织或促进细胞水平的愈合进程；在皮肤表面产生电场将有助于愈合的

离子运输到更深层的靶组织中。常用方法如下：

①离子导入疗法：离子导入疗法是一种通过直流电将离子直接导入人体组织的疗法。在临床上常用于治疗炎症性的骨骼肌肉系统的疾病。该疗法可以用于镇痛，修复疤痕和促进伤口愈合，消除肿胀、钙沉积和水肿。运动防护师在面对具体损伤情况时要能够选择合适的离子液来治疗患者。离子导入疗法中最常见的问题就是化学性烧伤，它通常由设置的电流强度不当造成，与使用的离子溶液无关。

②干扰电疗法：干扰电疗法兼有中频和低频电疗的特点，可用于治疗疼痛、关节疼痛伴随肿胀、神经炎、骨折后愈合以及运动受限等。

③低强度电刺激仪：低强度电刺激仪是指用非常低的电流频率和电流强度来对机体进行电刺激，促进骨和软组织的愈合过程，用于缓解疼痛和促进伤口、骨折后组织、跟腱和韧带的愈合。

4. 磁疗法

①短波热透疗法：短波透热疗法能够向深层的组织传递电磁能，使组织温度升高。具有较高含水量的组织（如肌肉）会选择性地吸收由短波透热所传递的热量。短波透热疗法常用于治疗滑囊炎、关节囊炎、骨关节炎以及肌肉劳损。

②低能级激光疗法：激光的治疗效果包括加速胶原组织合成、消灭微生物、促进血管生成以及减少炎症和疼痛。激光也可以治疗扳机点和穴位的疼痛。激光疗法不适用于癌性组织，不能直接照射眼睛，不能在妊娠的前 3 个月进行治疗。

5. 声疗

①超声波疗法：超声波仪使用的是声能，是人体听不见的、高频率的声波，能够产生热效应和非热效应。连续超声波可产生热效应。而脉冲超声或低强度的连续超声的作用效果是产生非热效应和机械效应，有促进软组织愈合的作用。超声波治疗的剂量由治疗组织的深度和损伤状态（如亚急性期或慢性疾病）决定。临床应用中，超声波治疗分为三个强度，即 0.1 ~ 0.3 瓦 / 厘米 ^{2} 的低强度；0.4 ~ 1.5 瓦 / 厘米 ^{2} 的中等强度；1.5 ~ 3 瓦 / 厘米 ^{2} 的高强度。超声波疗法不能用来治疗身体中的血流丰富的区域，如眼睛、耳朵、睾丸、脑、脊髓和心脏，并且孕妇也不可进行超声波治疗。在损伤急性期可使用非热超声进行治疗，禁忌使用热超声。儿童的骨骺区域不能用大剂量的超声波进行治疗。

②超声透入疗法：超声透入疗法是使用超声波产生的机械振动将药物导入至皮下组织的方法。超声透入疗法常用于治疗肌肉扳机点、肌腱炎和滑囊炎。

6. 机械力疗法

①牵引：牵引是通过对身体施加张力来治疗疾病的一种方法，常用于脊柱的颈部和腰部区域。牵引最常用于治疗脊髓、神经根的受压，还可以用于缓解肌肉紧张，治疗肌肉或脊柱韧带的扭伤，并且能够治疗脊柱压迫引起的不适。

牵引包括手法牵引和机械牵引。进行手法牵引时施加的力、力的方向、持续时间和患者体位可以即时调整，因此更有灵活性并且能够更加适应身体。牵引也可分为持续牵引和间歇牵引。持续牵引是椎间盘相关问题的较优选项，而间歇性加压装置用于控制、减轻急性损伤后的肿胀或指压性水肿。

②按摩：按摩是指针对机体软组织的有体系的手法治疗。运动防护师综合推、按压、牵拉、点按、振动等手法作用于患者的机体进行治疗。从力学角度，按摩能促进血液和淋巴液流动，以及轻度拉伸浅表和瘢痕组织。从生理学角度，按摩可以促进体液循环，增强肌肉组织的代谢以及有助于消除代谢产物；也可以通过促进损伤部位周围循环、辅助正常的血液回流的方式来消除局部静脉瘀滞和水肿。从心理学角度，按摩将有助于建立防护师和患者之间的信任。

（三）常用的手法治疗技术

1. 关节松动术

关节松动术是通过徒手的被动运动，利用较大振幅、低速的手法，改善关节运动障碍的治疗方法。关节松动术可以促进关节液的流动，增加关节软骨、关节盘无血区的营养，减少疼痛，拉伸和拉长关节旁组织，尤其是关节囊和韧带组织，改善肌张力或牵张反射，提高本体感觉。

在应用时可选择关节的生理运动或附属运动作为治疗手段，通常可分为摆动、滚动、滑动、旋转、牵引和挤压。

①摆动：骨的杠杆样运动叫摆动。关节的摆动包括屈曲、伸展、内收、外展、旋转，即通常所说的生理运动。摆动时要固定关节近端，关节远端做往返运动。摆动必须在关节活动范围达到正常的 60% 时才可应用。例如，肩关节前屈的摆动手法，至少要在肩前屈达到 100° 角时才能应用。如果没有达到这一范围，应先用附属运动的手法来改善。

②滚动：当一块骨在另一块骨表面发生滚动时，两块骨的表面形状必然不一致，接触点同时变化，所发生的运动为成角运动。不论关节表面凹凸程度如何，滚动的方向总是朝向成角骨运动的方向。关节功能正常时，滚动并不单独发生，一般都伴随着关节的滑动和旋转。

③滑动：当一块骨在另一块骨上滑动时，如为单纯滑动，则两骨表面形状必须一致，或是平面，或是曲面。如果是曲面，那么两骨表面的凹凸程度必须相等。滑动时，一侧骨表面的同一个点接触对侧骨表面的不同点。滑动方向取决于运动骨关节面的凹凸形状。

凹凸法则：运动骨关节面凸出，滑动方向与成角骨运动方向相反；运动骨关节面凹陷，滑动方向与成角骨的运动方向相同。

滚动与滑动的关系：关节表面形状越接近，运动时，一块骨在另一块骨表面的滑动就越多；相反，关节表面形状越不一致，滚动就越多。临床应用时，由于滑动可以缓解疼痛，合并牵拉可以松解关节囊，使关节放松，改善关节活动范围，因此使用较多。而滚动手法可以挤压关节，容易引起损伤，单独使用较少。

④旋转：移动骨在静止骨表面绕旋转轴转动。旋转时，移动骨表面的同一点作圆周运动。旋转常与滑动和滚动同时发生，很少单独作用。

不同关节，旋转轴的位置不同。如盂肱关节的旋转轴经肱骨头中心并垂直于关节盂。

而生理运动的旋转是肱骨围绕自身长轴转动。髋关节的旋转是股骨头绕着经过股骨头中心，并垂直于髋臼的旋转轴转动。前臂联合关节的旋转与生理运动中的旋转相同，都是桡骨围绕尺骨转动。

⑤牵引：当外力作用使构成关节的两骨表面呈直角相互分开时，被称为分离或关节内牵引；当外力作用于骨长轴使关节远端移位时，被称为牵拉或长轴牵引。分离和牵拉的区别如下：分离时外力要与关节面垂直，同时两骨关节面必须分开；牵拉时外力必须与骨的长轴平行，关节面可以不分开。如盂肱关节牵拉时，外力与肱骨长轴平行，关节面发生滑动；而盂肱关节分离时，外力与关节盂垂直，关节面相互分开。

⑥挤压：使关节腔内骨与骨之间的间隙变小。肌肉收缩产生一定压力，可以提高关节的稳定性。但是，在向其他骨方向转动时，会对骨的角运动方向引起压迫。当压迫力异常增高时，会产生关节软骨的变形和损伤。因此，挤压技术较少应用。

Maitland 将松动术分为 4 级：

Ⅰ级：在关节活动的起始端，小范围、节律性地来回松动关节。

Ⅱ级：在关节活动允许范围内，大范围、节律性地来回松动关节，但不接触关节活动的起始端和终末端。

Ⅲ级：在关节活动允许范围内，大范围、节律性地来回松动关节，接触关节活动的终末端。

Ⅳ级：在关节活动的终末端，小范围、节律性地来回松动关节，接触关节活动的终末端。

在 Maitland 分级系统中，Ⅰ、Ⅱ级松动手法用于治疗因疼痛引起的关节活动受限；Ⅲ级松动手法用于治疗疼痛并伴有活动受限；Ⅳ级松动手法用于治疗关节周围组织粘连、挛缩而引起的关节活动受限。

2. 肌筋膜松解术

肌筋膜松解术是一系列从紧张筋膜的异常牵扯中松解软组织的技术。筋膜是一种包裹着肌肉、骨骼和关节，为身体提供保护和支撑的特殊结缔组织层，主要由胶原和弹性纤维构成。过去认为筋膜在身体中的作用是被动的，能够传递肌肉活动和外力带来的机械拉力。最近研究表明，筋膜能够像肌肉一样主动收缩，对肌肉骨骼动力学产生影响。筋膜从头到脚是连续的并与很多鞘和平面相连接，因此，在活动中筋膜需要一定的伸展和活动度。

肌筋膜松解术属于软组织松动术，尽管从技术层面来讲，关节松动术和软组织松动术都涉及软组织，有很强的相关性。但关节松动术的侧重点是恢复关节活动，作用于特定的关节，并且根据运动方向的不同和关节面形状不同，其作用方向和应用原则也是不同的。而肌筋膜松动手法主要关注治疗的局部，并依赖于操作者的主观感觉和经验。一旦肌筋膜受限位置确定，松解位置就应固定在该位置上，从表面到深部进阶。肌筋膜松解后就可以实施关节松动术，一旦软组织的受限被松解和消除，关节松动术的效果会更好。

常见的肌筋膜松解术有非侵入性的手法、泡沫轴的使用和筋膜刀松解，也有通过穿刺针、小针刀或者射频针在 B 超下进行的松解。

3. 本体感觉神经肌肉易化技术

本体感觉神经肌肉易化技术（proprioceptive neuromuscular facilitation，PNF）倡导一种新的治疗理念，是利用牵张、关节压缩和牵引、施加阻力等通过刺激本体感受器和应用螺旋对角线运动模式来改善和促进肌肉功能的一种方法。PNF 的原则和技巧主要建立在神经生理学、解剖学和发育学的基础之上。其特点是以正常的运动模式和运动发展为基本技术，强调整体而不是单一肌肉活动。特征是肢体和躯干的螺旋形对角线主动、被动、抗阻运动，类似于日常生活中的功能活动，主张通过手的接触、语言命令、视觉引导来影响运动模式。PNF 能提高肌肉力量、耐力和控制能力，能够有效调动人体协调的潜在功能，建立稳定与活动的平衡，改善日常生活活动能力。

PNF 的十大基本要素为：徒手接触、口令与交流、牵张、牵引和挤压、阻力、体位和身体力学、扩散和强化、顺序、视觉刺激和运动模式。

PNF 训练模式包含三组动作：屈、伸，内收、外展，以及内、外旋转。

上肢 D1：屈曲—内收—外旋和伸展—外展—内旋（"抓拉安全带"&"下插安全带"）

上肢 D2：屈曲—外展—外旋和伸展—内收—内旋（"拔剑"&"插剑"）

下肢 D1：屈曲—内收—外旋和伸展—外展—内旋（"踢球"&"足趾离地"）

下肢 D2：屈曲—外展—内旋和伸展—内收—外旋（"武术踢腿"&"芭蕾舞位"）

PNF 技术通常在康复技术中被用来提高力量和活动度。其中 PNF 力量增强技术包括：节律性动作启动、重复收缩、慢速逆转、慢速逆转—保持，节律性稳定技术。PNF 拉伸技术包括：收缩—放松、保持—放松，慢速逆转—保持—放松。

①重复收缩：单一肌肉或者肌群的重复收缩可以用来解决全身肌肉或者某块肌肉的力量不足的问题。患者在运动防护师给予的最大阻力下进行等速运动，直到出现疲劳为止，此时，在该范围内对肌肉进行拉伸，以促进更大力量的产生。所有的阻力都要根据患者的情况进行调整。由于要求患者使用最大的力进行对抗，所以这一技术对于某些损伤来说是禁忌的。

②节律性动作启动：节律性动作启动包括一整套渐进性方案，首先是被动活动，其次是主动协助性运动，最后通过原动肌来进行主动运动。节律性启动在患者受伤当天就可进行，并在接下来的几天和几周内都可以在患者可以忍受的范围内逐渐加大力度和范围。这项技术可以帮助活动受限的患者逐渐增加力量和活动度。

③稳定反转：该技术的目的是增加患者的稳定、平衡能力，还有肌力以及主动肌和拮抗肌之间的协调性。在主动肌和拮抗肌上都施加阻力来帮助其平滑并节律性地收缩。

④慢速逆转—保持：这项技术中，患者用主动肌等张移动身体部位，然后等长收缩。患者要被告知在每次等张收缩末端保持不动。这样做的主要目的是在活动度的某一点提高肌肉力量。

⑤节律性稳定技术：节律性稳定利用主动肌的等长收缩，然后是拮抗肌的等长收缩。通过反复的收缩就能达到最大力量。

⑥收缩—放松：被动移动身体部位直到感受阻力。然后告诉患者等长收缩拮抗肌。运

动防护师保持此动作 10 秒，或患者感觉疲惫，此时可以让患者休息 10 秒。休息后运动防护师再朝另一个方向进行牵引，或者朝相同方向重复三次。

⑦保持—放松：保持—放松技术与收缩—放松技术相似，均利用了等长收缩。患者主动移动身体直到感受到阻力并保持该姿势。运动防护师等长对抗 10 秒。患者休息 10 秒，然后将患者身体被动移动到新的活动范围，或者患者主动移动到新的活动范围。将此技术重复三次。

⑧慢速逆转—保持—放松：患者移动自己的身体直到感受到阻力并保持该姿势。

4. 肌肉能量技术

肌肉能量技术（muscle energy technology，MET）是利用神经生理来放松过度紧张的肌肉和 / 或拉伸慢性缩短的肌肉的手动拉伸技术，可用来治疗复杂的运动链功能失调，是 PNF 收缩—放松和保持—放松技术的分支。肌肉能量技术是由运动防护师在远端施加不同强度的阻力后让患者主动收缩的方法。

使用肌肉能量技术需注意以下五点：

①患者要主动收缩。

②肌肉收缩要保证在一个特定方向。

③患者要对收缩有一定的控制。

④由运动防护师控制关节位置。

⑤运动防护师要提供合适的阻力。

肌肉能量技术的操作是先拉伸某一紧张肌肉至关节活动度末端，该位置被称为阻力障碍点。从阻力障碍点开始，患者收缩拮抗肌（要被拉长的肌肉）10 秒。此时，患者要完全放松，然后运动防护师要将身体移动到下一个阻力障碍点。该步骤要重复 3 ~ 5 次，直到肢体活动度不再发生变化。

（四）常用的运动疗法技术

1. 肌肉力量训练

测试肌肉力量、耐力或爆发力可以使用徒手肌力检查、渐进性抗阻测试或等长收缩测试等方法。等长收缩测试通常能提供最可靠的力量变化的客观指标。

肌肉力量训练是通过主动运动或被动运动的方式，采用不同的肌肉收缩形式恢复或增强患者肌肉力量的训练。力量训练可以使人体的相对力量增加，提高肌肉的收缩速度和爆发力。肌力训练具有防治各种肌萎缩、促进神经系统损害后肌力恢复以及矫治关节畸形、维持关节稳定等重要意义，也是预防运动损伤的基础。常用的肌力训练方法分为辅助主动运动、主动运动、抗阻力主动运动和等长收缩运动等。

（1）主要的运动方式

从人体运动的力量来源可以将人体的运动分为主动运动和被动运动两种。

主动运动是人体通过主动收缩肌肉来完成的运动。根据其主动用力的程度，可分为辅助主动运动、主动运动与抗阻运动等。

被动运动则是人体运动完全通过外力作用来进行。外力包括运动防护师的手法治疗、器械作用下的运动以及人体自身带动（重力和健侧肢体带动患侧肢体运动）等。被动运动通常是肢体瘫痪、肌力在2级以下不能进行主动运动的患者所采取的运动方式，用来维持关节活动度，防止肌肉粘连和关节挛缩，保持肌肉张力和弹性，为主动运动做准备。

（2）肌肉收缩的形式

根据肌肉收缩时肌肉长度和肌肉张力的变化，可将肌肉收缩分为三种形式。应根据不同的康复治疗目的和患者的肌力情况，选用不同的肌肉收缩形式来进行练习。

①等长收缩：等长收缩是指虽有肌肉收缩且肌张力明显增加，但肌肉长度基本无变化，不产生关节运动，是仅在静止状态下产生的肌肉收缩。等长收缩是由于使肌肉拉长的外力与肌肉本身所产生的最大张力相等所致。等长收缩训练经常应用于关节制动一段时间后进行康复的早期阶段。等长收缩训练既可以增加肌肉静态力量并减少萎缩，也可以改善任何方向的力量的薄弱情况，还可以形成肌肉泵效应来消除积液和水肿从而减少肿胀。

②等张收缩：等张收缩指肌肉收缩过程中，肌张力基本不变，但肌肉长度发生变化，从而引起关节的运动。根据肌肉起止部位的活动方向，可分为向心性收缩和离心性收缩两类。

向心性收缩是指肌肉收缩时，肌肉起止点彼此靠近，肌肉长度缩短，又称为短缩性肌收缩、克制性收缩；离心性收缩是指肌肉收缩时，肌肉起止点两端彼此远离，使肌肉长度增加。向心性收缩常作用于关节，使关节产生运动，而离心性收缩常由对抗关节运动的拮抗肌产生收缩，其作用与关节运动方向相反，用于稳定关节、控制肢体动作或肢体坠落的速度等。

等张收缩适用范围较广，可在全关节活动范围内进行。等张收缩仪通常可以算出扭转力、平均力量、总功和旋转力与体重的比率，其中的每一项指标都可以被运动防护师作为诊断指标。等张收缩的值通常被用作判定运动员伤后是否能回归功能性运动训练的指标。

③等速收缩：等速收缩指在全关节运动范围内，肌肉收缩的速度保持恒定不变的运动方式，需要借助于专用设备来控制肌肉收缩速度。等速练习中肌肉的长度在收缩过程中改变而肌肉收缩的速度不变，是高效锻炼肌力的方法，具备3级以上的肌力条件才适宜进行。

理论上，在运动过程中，等速训练仪器提供的阻力是最大阻力。在整个关节活动范围内（在关节活动的各个角度）肌肉都产生最大的张力，因此，可取得更好的训练效果。

（3）常用锻炼形式分类

①开链运动：开链运动是指肢体近端固定而远端关节活动的运动，如步行时的摆动相。开链运动的特点是可单关节完成运动。通过哑铃弯举这一动作进行肱二头肌训练时，肘部固定，手握哑铃做肘关节屈伸运动。

体育运动训练中，开链运动能够孤立地训练身体的某一块肌肉，所以在运动中常选用开链运动的方式针对某块肌肉进行力量训练；开链运动时远端的运动范围大于近端，速度也快于近端，所以训练中常选用开链运动进行肌肉爆发力的训练。

肌力康复训练中，由于开链运动产生的剪切力要大于闭链运动，因此不应选择开链运动恢复功能，以免加重伤部负担。而在康复后期，当关节的功能性和本体感受通过闭链运动得到了一定的加强后，则可采用开链运动，针对关节附近的肌群进行训练。

②闭链运动：闭链运动指肢体远端（手掌或脚掌）固定而近端活动的运动，如步行时的支撑相。闭链运动的特点是需多关节协同运动。如使用杠铃进行负重蹲起训练时，足部固定，髋、膝和踝关节协同完成运动。

体育运动训练中，闭链运动参与的肌肉和关节较多，需多关节协同活动完成，更接近真实运动动作，是专业运动员首选运动训练方式。

肌力康复训练中，闭链运动是不增加关节剪切力的多关节协同运动，可刺激关节本体感受器，产生肢体的运动和保护性反射弧活动，能充分训练关节整体的协调性并促进关节本体感受器功能的恢复，从而促进关节稳定和功能康复，所以康复早期应选择闭链运动来恢复受损肢体的功能。

2. 核心稳定性训练

核心稳定性训练可以提高人体在非稳定状态下的控制能力，增强平衡能力，激活深层小肌肉群，协调大小肌群的力量输出，增强运动机能，预防损伤。

核心稳定性训练的每个练习动作中都必须严格控制身体姿势，强调神经系统的参与，关注锻炼者完成的质量，而不是完成的数量。运动防护师应指导锻炼者维持节律性呼吸，使呼吸配合动作，并随着锻炼者能力的提高逐渐加大训练的难度。

常见的核心稳定性训练有腹桥、侧桥、臀桥和"死虫子"训练，可配合瑞士球、弹力带和平衡软垫等增加训练难度。

3. 渐进性功能训练

详见第二部分第一章"体能因素"。

4. 平衡与协调训练

平衡是指人体所处的一种稳定状态，以及无论处在何种位置、何种运动状态，或受到外力作用时，都能自动地调整并维持姿势的能力。平衡功能的好坏能直接或间接地影响患者身体控制和日后的生活自理能力。协调功能是人体的自我调节，完成平滑、准确且有控制的随意运动的能力。协调功能的好坏决定了患者动作的流畅性与精确性，直接影响着患者的日常动作。平衡协调功能是人类运动的基础之一，良好的平衡协调功能可使人体维持姿态稳定，精确完成动作。

人体能在各种自身以及外环境变化的情况下保持平衡，有赖于中枢神经系统控制下的感觉系统和运动系统的参与、相互作用和整合。躯体感觉、视觉、前庭三个感觉系统在维持平衡过程中各自扮演不同的角色。维持协调功能的因素有反射、上位中枢的调节、大脑基底节、大脑皮质、感觉传入和小脑对运动的调节。

（1）平衡训练的基本原则

①支撑面积由大变小。

②从静态平衡到动态平衡。

③身体重心逐步由低到高。

④从维持平衡到平衡被破坏时的姿态维持。

⑤从注意力集中的情况下保持平衡到注意力不集中的情况下保持平衡。

⑥视觉屏蔽下的平衡。

⑦破坏前庭器官的平衡来训练保持身体的平衡。

（2）平衡训练的顺序

①根据功能体位系统进行。从坐位平衡到手膝位平衡、双膝跪位平衡，最终恢复站立位平衡。

②从易到难，渐进增加难度。从最稳定体位到最不稳定体位，从大支撑面到小支撑面，从低身体重心到高身体重心，从静态平衡训练到动态平衡训练，从睁眼训练到闭眼训练，从无头颈参与活动到有头颈参与活动。

（3）协调功能训练的要点

①一定要完成具体的练习任务。

②在完成连贯动作之前，先完成单个动作的练习。

③进行相关动作练习。

5. 水疗

水被认为是一种具有辅助性、支持性和阻力的介质，水疗主要利用水的浮力和阻力，增加关节活动度，重建正确的活动模式，提高肌肉力量、爆发力和耐力。

水的浮力可以提高关节活动度和控制能力。患者进入水中后，肢体可被水的浮力托起，患者就可以借助浮力主动增加活动范围。

对阻力的利用是水疗的另一个应用。患处要对抗水向上的力而向下。当肢体与水平面有一个正确的角度时就会产生最大的阻力。阻力技术可以通过用不同的装置来进阶难度。如要获得额外的阻力可以将漂浮物推入或者拉入水中。

除了采用特殊练习，患者可以通过最适合他们的方法，利用水的浮力和阻力来练习运动技巧。比如，可以通过练习移动或投掷技巧来重建普通动作模式。泳池是恢复功能性能力和心肺耐力的最佳场所。

6. 神经肌肉控制训练

在受伤后，休息和制动会让神经系统"忘记"如何整合肌肉和关节的机械性刺激感受器传递的冲动与皮肤、视觉和前庭的感觉。神经肌肉控制指我们有意识地去感知我们的身体的某种特定的动作。重复某个模式化动作可以逐渐使该动作变得更容易且更自如，并最终自动化。重建神经肌肉控制需要对某个动作进行大量从简到难的进阶重复性训练。

力量训练，尤其是功能性力量训练对于神经肌肉控制的恢复是十分重要的。对于运动防护师来说，重建本体感觉的位置觉和运动觉应该是首要关注点。位置觉是一种确定关节位置的能力，运动觉是能够一直检测运动的能力。我们感受到关节的所在位置的能力是由肌肉和关节中机械刺激感受器和皮肤感觉、视觉和前庭觉混合而成的。神经肌肉控制依赖中枢神经系统来翻译和整合位置觉和运动觉，并控制肌肉和关节来产生协调的运动。

恢复神经肌肉控制意味着重新获得原先就建立起的模式。中枢神经系统将某种动作的意图和结果与之前存储的该动作的信息相对比，并逐渐修正动作，直到动作完全正确。而重建神经肌肉控制的四大关键因素包括：本体感觉、动态稳定性、前馈与反馈性肌肉调节、有意识的和潜意识的功能性运动模式。

小结

1. 场外损伤评定主要包括病史、视诊、触诊、特殊检查。记录遵循 SOAP 记录模式，即主观检查（subjective）、客观检查（objective）、评定（assessment）和治疗计划（plan）。

2. 热疗的常用方法包括水凝胶包、漩涡浴、石蜡浴。冷疗主要包括冰按摩、冷水浴、冰袋、冷冻喷雾剂。电疗常包括离子导入疗法、干扰电疗法和低强度电刺激仪。电磁疗法主要包括短波热透疗法、低能级激光疗法。声疗常见超声波疗法和超声透入疗法。机械能疗法主要包括牵引和按摩。

3. 在 Maitland 分级系统中，Ⅰ、Ⅱ级松动手法用于治疗因疼痛引起的关节活动受限；Ⅲ级松动手法用于治疗疼痛并伴有活动受限；Ⅳ级松动手法用于治疗关节周围组织粘连、挛缩而引起的关节活动受限。

4. 软组织松动术能够消除疤痕组织及粘连。筋膜松解术也属于软组织松动术，常见的肌筋膜松解术包括非侵入性的手法和筋膜刀松解。

5. PNF 技术通常在康复技术中被用来提高力量和活动度。

6. 根据肌肉收缩形式可将肌肉力量训练分为等长收缩、等张收缩和等速收缩。根据肢体固定方式可将其分为开链运动和闭链运动。

7. 身体核心部位在运动中有三个主要功能：产生力量、传递力量和控制力量，因此核心稳定性训练非常重要，常包括腹桥、侧桥、臀桥等。

8. 平衡协调功能是人类运动的基础之一，良好的平衡协调功能可使人体维持姿态稳定，精确地完成动作。

9. 水疗可以通过水的浮力和阻力辅助患者进行最合适的锻炼。

10. 重建神经肌肉控制机制的四大因素包括本体感觉、动态稳定性、前馈与反馈性肌肉调节、有意识的和潜意识的功能性运动模式。

○ 复习题

1. 场外损伤评估的内容和常用的运动员损伤情况记录方法是什么？

2. 热疗的作用原理是什么？有哪些方法？

3. 什么是肌肉能量技术？

4. 运动防护师常用的运动疗法有哪些？

PART Ⅲ Common Musculoskeletal Injuries

第三部分　常见肌肉骨骼损伤

Chapter 1 Spine Injuries
第一章　脊柱损伤

○ Main Contents

1. Prevention of spine injuries.
2. Assessment of spine injuries.
3. Identification and management of common spine injuries.

○ 主要内容

1. 脊柱损伤的预防。
2. 脊柱损伤的评估。
3. 脊柱常见损伤的识别和处理。

1 Prevention of Spine Injuries

1.1 Strength Training

The muscles around the spine can limit excessive flexion, extension or rotation of different segments of the spine, so specific muscle strength training can be used to strengthen the spinal muscles. At the same time, it is necessary to strengthen the muscles that support the spine, so as to prevent spinal injuries. For example, the abdominal muscles are one of the muscles that support the spine. Enhancing the strength of the abdominal muscles will help reduce the stress on the lumbar spine. The cervical vertebrae is the weakest segment of the spine. Athletes with long neck and weak muscles have a higher risk of neck injury. Therefore, in many confrontational or contact sports, athletes responsible for interception and wrestlers should enhance neck stability to reduce injury. Manual resistance training is one of the best techniques, and isometric and isokinetic resistance training can also be chosen to improve spinal muscle strength.

1.2 Range of Motion Training

In addition to having strong muscle strength, the normal range of motion of each spinal segment should be involved in the prevention of spinal injury. The flexibility exercises can maintain the elasticity of muscles, tendons and other soft tissues, improve the function of soft tissues around the spine, reduce and prevent the injury caused by the sudden increase of the range of motion or excessive twisting in the movement. Take the cervical spine as an example, the normal range of motion of the joints should be: the lower jaw can be close to the chest when the head bends forward, the face can be parallel to the ceiling when the head extends backward, and the left and right flexion can reach a range of 45° and rotate freely. Flexibility and range of motion can be improved by static and dynamic stretching or full range of muscle strength training.

1.3 Correction of Biomechanical Abnormalities

The athletic trainer should timely observe the abnormal biomechanical performance of athletes during sports and guide them to conduct personalized training to correct the abnormal biomechanical issues. Personalized correction exercises should include not only a series of exercises that focus on strengthening the torso muscles, but also exercises that improve flexibility so that the spine is able to achieve maximum degree of flexion, rotation, and lateral flexion. The strength and flexibility training of the spinal extensor muscle group (erector spine muscle group, etc.) and the abdominal muscle group are particularly important. Strength of the spinal extensor and abdominal muscle groups is the key factor to ensure the correct posture and biomechanical performance.

1.4 Core Stability Exercises

Core stability is important to ensure the stability of the spine and the lumbar-pelvic-hip complex. Enhancing the stability of the core region can keep the mechanical posture of the pelvis and spine at an appropriate level. Core muscle training activates muscles deep in the trunk, such as the multifidus, because they are located at the center of lumbar rotation and are short in length and spiral over the spine, which can increase stability by increasing the stress between intervertebral discs with contraction. It can also reduce the impact of repeated microtrauma on the spine and pelvis by enhancing the stability and control of the whole body during exercise. In addition, core stability can help stabilize the trunk, control posture and promote the recovery of athletic injuries.

一、脊柱损伤的预防

（一）肌力训练

脊柱周围的肌肉具有限制脊柱不同节段过度屈曲、伸展或旋转的作用，因此可通过针对性的肌力训练来强化脊柱不同节段的肌肉力量。同时，还需增加支撑脊柱肌肉的力量训练，提高脊柱的稳定性，从而达到预防脊柱损伤的效果。例如，腹肌为支撑脊柱的肌肉之一，增强腹肌肌力有助于减小腰椎承受的压力。颈椎为脊柱中最薄弱的节段，若运动员颈部较长、肌力较差则会增加其颈部受伤的风险，因此在许多对抗或接触性的运动中，负责阻截的运动员和摔跤运动员等应增强颈部稳定性以减少损伤的发生。徒手肌力抗阻训练是增强脊柱肌肉力量的最佳方法之一，可有选择地使用等长和等速抗阻训练来增强脊柱部位肌肉力量。

（二）关节活动度训练

预防脊柱损伤除需要具备较强的肌肉力量外，还应保持脊柱各节段正常的关节活动度。可通过柔韧性的练习保持肌肉、肌腱等软组织的弹性，改善脊柱周围软组织的功能和伸展性，减少和预防运动中由于动作幅度突然加大或扭转过猛而导致的损伤。以颈椎为例，正常的关节活动范围应为：头部前屈时下颌能够靠近胸部、后伸时脸部可与天花板平行、左右侧屈时能够达到45°角的范围且能够自由旋转等。可通过静态、动态牵伸训练或全范围的肌力训练来提高柔韧性，增加关节活动度。

（三）纠正身体力线异常

运动防护师应及时观察运动员在运动过程中所显示出的生物力学异常表现，并指导运动员进行个性化训练以纠正异常的力线。个性化的纠正训练不仅要包括一系列侧重于增强躯干肌群力量的训练，还应包括改善柔韧性的练习，以使脊柱能够完成最大程度的屈伸、旋转和侧屈等运动。其中，脊柱伸肌肌群（竖脊肌等）和腹部肌群的力量及柔韧性训练尤为重要，脊柱伸肌肌群和腹部肌群的肌肉力量是确保正确姿势和生物力学表现的关键因素。

（四）核心稳定性训练

核心稳定性是保证脊柱、腰－骨盆－髋复合体稳定性的重要因素之一，增强核心区域稳定性可以保持骨盆和脊柱的力学姿势处于适宜的水平。通过核心肌力训练可以激活躯干深层部位的肌群，如多裂肌。因其位于腰椎的旋转中心并且长度较短、呈螺旋形覆盖于脊柱，它在收缩时可以通过增大椎间盘之间的应力来增加腰椎稳定性；还可以通过增强全身在运动过程中的稳定性和控制力，以减少反复性微小创伤对脊柱和骨盆的影响。此外，核心稳定性训练可以帮助伤者稳定躯干、姿势控制，利于运动损伤的恢复。

2 Assessment of Spine Injuries

2.1 History

The athletic trainer should first identify the cause of the injury to rule out spinal cord injury firstly.

The athletic trainer should ask the following questions:

● What happened when you got injured?

● Did the top of your head hit something else, or did it hit the ground?

● Do you have any symptoms of confusion or loss of consciousness? (If yes, it is indicating potential spinal cord injury)

● Do you have equal muscle strength in both arms? (Any sensory or motor change may indicate spinal cord injury)

● Can you move your ankles and toes?

If spinal cord injury is suspected, moving and transferring patients should be cautious.

If spinal cord injury is ruled out, the athletic trainer needs to continue to ask the injured person questions to obtain information about the nature of the injury, which can be collected by using of OPQRST, including:

O (Onset)

● When did the injury occur?

P (Palliative/Provocative)

● What do you do to cause pain? For example, standing, sitting, bending or body twisting.

● What postures or movements make the pain worse?

● What postures or movements can relieve the pain?

Q (Quality)

- Do you have numbness, tingling or burning in your shoulders, arms or hands?
- Do you have numbness or pain in your hips or the back of your thighs?

R (Radiating/Referred)

- What kind of pain is it?
- Is it radiating or referred pain? (A differential diagnosis is made by an athletic trainer.)

S (Site)

- Where do you feel the pain?
- Do you have any pain in your neck?
- Did you have any back pain before? Note that there are many causes of back pain, which may be related to the musculoskeletal or visceral systems.

T (Time)

- Did the pain happen suddenly?
- How long did the pain last?

2.2 Observation

2.2.1 Posture Analysis

The interaction and maintenance of anatomical structures such as bones, muscles and ligaments of the human body enable the human body to keep a certain posture in static and dynamic movement. Postural assessment is to determine whether there is structural or functional abnormality by observing the posture of the human body, and to analyze the reasons for its occurrence so as to correct it in time. When assessing posture, look from the front, the back, and the side. Plumb lines, posture grids and other auxiliary equipment can be selected for measurement according to different needs, so as to ensure the accuracy of posture evaluation. During postural observation, the position of important anatomical markers should be observed. When looking at the front and back, the athletic trainer should also focus on whether the anatomical markers on the left and right are symmetrical or not on the same level.

Common abnormal postures are as follows:

(1) Kyphosis

Kyphosis is defined as excessive backward projection of the thoracic segments of the spine, forward tilt of the head, and neck curvature depth of more than 5 cm. There are two types of postural (functional) kyphosis and structural kyphosis. The postural (functional) kyphosis is mostly caused by bad postural habits, and the structural kyphosis is usually caused by spinal diseases. Therefore, differential diagnosis should be done, such as Scheuermann disease which usually occurs in adolescent males and causes pain and progressive thoracic or thoracolumbar kyphosis, and could initially be mistaken for postural kyphosis.

(2) Forward Head Posture

The "head forward" position is viewed from the side, with the earlobes in front of the acromion and the lower jaw protruding forward. It can be caused by imbalance in the neck muscles. For example, after the occurrence of hunchback symptoms, the head and neck need to extend in order to maintain the horizontal vision. The neck extensor muscles contract and the flexor muscles are elongated, so that the head and neck produce compensatory changes. The forward head angle (FHA) can be used for assessment, which means using the spinous process (SP) of the 7th cervical vertebra (C7) as the reference point, a vertical line is drawn downward, and the angle between the line from the tragus to the SP of C7 and the vertical line of the SP of C7 is FHA.

(3) Swayback and Lordosis

The difference between swayback and lordosis is distinguished by the forward tilt of the pelvis, the position of the hip joints, and the imbalance of the muscles. Swayback refers to the backward extension of the hip joints and backward shift of the thoracic vertebrae caused by the forward movement of the pelvis, which is manifested as the reduced curvature of the lumbar spine, increased kyphosis angle of the thoracic vertebrae, and insufficient muscle strength of the iliopsoas muscle. Lordosis is manifested by increased lumbar curvature, pelvic forward flexion, and hip flexion, but strong iliopsoas muscle strength. The lordosis, hunchback and "head forward" posture together are known as the upper-crossed syndrome position. Lordosis can be caused by obesity, osteoporosis, lumbar spondylolisthesis, and so on.

(4) Scoliosis

Scoliosis is defined as a marked abnormal curvature on one side of a segment of the spine, and a reverse, compensatory curvature on the opposite side. It can be divided into structural scoliosis caused by defects or disorders of vertebral bone structure and functional scoliosis caused by non-spinal defects such as unequal length of lower limbs and bilateral muscle imbalance. During observation, attention should be paid to whether the shoulders are uneven, whether the spine deviates from the midline, and whether the bilateral back is in equal height when flexing forward. Differential diagnosis can also be done by flexing the trunk forward. It is functional scoliosis if scoliosis is absent, and it is structural scoliosis if scoliosis is still present.

(5) Flatback

Flatback can be caused by a decrease in lumbar curve, the posterior shifting of the pelvis, an increase in hip flexion, degenerative arthritis, spinal fusion and so on. Flatback is characterized by spinal deformity in the sagittal plane, namely, the decreasing of lumbar lordosis, which appears relatively "flat".

2.2.2 Cervical Spine Inspection

During cervical examination, the athletic trainer should focus on observing the position of the injured head, neck and shoulders as well as the ROM of head and neck, such as whether the injured head is in the center of the two shoulders, whether the two shoulders are equal in height, and whether the injured person can actively move the head and neck. When examining the cervical ROM, check the active and passive ROM, with and without resistance. In addition, observe the injured musculoskeletal condition, such as if there is deltoids atrophy (indicating axillary nerve paralysis) or head tilt (indicating sternocleidomastoid spasm).

2.2.3 Thoracic Spine Inspection

The athletic trainer should first observe the injured person for any abnormal posture in the thoracic region of the spine, such as kyphosis, scoliosis, and chest deformity. At the same time, the breathing pattern of the injured person should be observed to determine the breathing condition. For example, the patient is breathing from the abdomen or chest, and if there is pain in any part of the body while breathing (chest pain increases when the chin is placed close to the chest or when inhaling deeply, indicating possible thoracic intervertebral joint dysfunction/ disorder).

The most common cause of thoracic pain is the dysfunction of one or more thoracic segments, such as intervertebral joints. Therefore, it is necessary to assess the ROM of the neck and trunk, including flexion, extension, lateral flexion, and rotation. During neck movement, pain in the upper back may be caused by cervical disc diseases; pain in the scapula region may be caused by irritation of myofascial trigger point, long thoracic nerve or suprascapular nerve, which needs to be determined in combination with shoulder evaluation. The presence of pain during trunk activity suggests that the inferior thoracic nerve roots may be irritated.

2.2.4 Lumbar and Sacroiliac Joint Inspection

Pelvis and sacrum can maintain the normal function of the waist with the coordination of lumbar spine, once the muscle or joint capsule injury, intervertebral disc herniation or pathological changes will cause abnormal postures when standing or moving. During the inspection, the athletic trainer should observe the posture of the injured person in the standing, sitting, supine and prone positions. For example, observe whether the shoulder and pelvis on both sides are in the same level, whether the bone and soft tissue structure on both sides of the spine are in symmetry, and whether there is abnormal gait when walking.

2.3 Palpation

At the beginning of palpation, the athletic trainer should pay attention to the texture of the skin, bone, and soft tissue. Palpation should start from proximal to distal, on both sides of the spine for tenderness, percussion pain, or muscle guarding. The spinous process (SP) of the vertebral body is often taken as the anatomical reference point. The SP should be in a straight line from top to bottom normally. The SP deviation represents the rotation of a vertebral body to a certain angle, suggesting vertebral subluxation, which is commonly seen in the cervical and lumbar spine. Pressed down on the SP with a prone position could distinguish if there is central or peripheral pain. Palpate the interspinous process space to determine the presence and location of tenderness points. Tenderness indicates possible ligaments or intervertebral disc issues, and tenderness points are often in referred pain. The transverse process (TP) of the vertebral body is also a common palpation point. Pressure applied to the TP may rotate the vertebral body and increase the pain sensation. Due to the presence of paravertebral muscles, it is difficult to palpate the intervertebral joints and lamina.

When palpating the neck, it is easy to palpate the lateral and anterior anatomical markers of the cervical spine in the supine and relaxed position. When palpating the posterior cervical spine, the patient's head should be supported by both hands of the athletic trainer. When palpating the lower back, a soft pad can be placed under the hip joints of the patient for comfort. In the assessment of the lumbar spine, the athletic trainer should also palpate the abdominal muscles and the patient should perform partial sit-ups to contract the abdominal muscles to help the athletic trainer assess bilateral muscle symmetry and muscle tension. When palpating the sacroiliac joint, the presence of tenderness points should be focused. If pain involves the sacroiliac joint, pressure on the back of the sacrum may increase pain.

2.4 Special Tests

2.4.1 Cervical Special Tests
(1) Brachial Plexus Test

The patient is seated. The athletic trainer stands behind the patient and bends the patient's head to the unaffected side, with another hand on the ipsilateral shoulder to pull in the opposite direction. When the neck is flexed laterally if the pain radiates towards the shoulder and arm on the flexed side, it indicates compression injury. If the pain radiates towards the non-flexing shoulder and arm, it indicates traction injury or strain. When there is radiating pain or numbness a positive brachial plexus test can indicate nerve root injury.

(2) Cervical Compression and Foraminal Compression Tests

The cervical compression test is performed by placing the patient in a seated position with the head and neck in a neutral position, with the athletic trainer standing behind the patient and hands folded over the head of the patient. Pressure is applied downward and evenly against the cervical intervertebral joints and the cervical nerve roots to produce axial compression. Pain in different locations may indicate nerve root injury at different levels.

The foraminal compression test is performed as follows: The patient is seated, with the neck laterally flexed and slightly extended backward. The athletic trainer stands behind the patient with hands folded over the head of the patient and applies a downward, evenly compressive force. A positive result is seen if there is ipsilateral pain in the shoulder and arm on the side of the neck that is laterally flexed, which is caused by impingement of the nerve root by compression.

(3) Vertebral Artery Test

The patient is placed in the supine position. The athletic trainer extends the patient's cervical spine posteriorly and laterally and then rotates the cervical spine in the direction of lateral flexion. If the patient develops dizziness or abnormal eye movements (tremor), the test is positive and indicates compression of the vertebral artery.

(4) Shoulder Abduction Test

The patient is seated and the athletic trainer instructs the patient to abduct the ipsilateral shoulder joint by placing one hand against the ipsilateral ear. If the pain is relieved, the test is positive, suggesting possible nerve root compression due to a cervical disc herniation.

2.4.2 Lumbar Special Tests

Lumbar special tests must be done in the standing, sitting, supine, prone and side-lying positions.

(1) Tests in the Standing Position

When the patient is in a standing position, the athletic trainer should first check any abnormal postures, and then focus on gait when walking, such as walking difficulties, lameness, etc. The athletic trainer should also observe whether the body force line in the sagittal plane is normal, and whether the anatomical markers on both sides of the body are symmetrical, such as the popliteal horizontal lines and the anterior superior iliac spines.

① Flexion

The maximum forward flexion of the lumbar spine ranges from 40° to 60°. The lumbar spine flexes forward to elongate the posterior spinal ligaments. The athletic trainer should observe both sides of the posterior superior iliac spines. In normal conditions, both sides of the posterior superior iliac spines should simultaneously move during the patient's forward flexion. If the movement distance of one side of the posterior superior iliac spine is greater than that of the other side, it suggests that there may be limited movement on the farther side. If both posterior superior iliac spines do not move synchronously, it indicates that the side moving first may have limitation of motion.

② Extension

The ROM of lumbar spine extension can be 20°–35° and the patient can elongate the anterior spinal ligaments. Limitation of movement and pain during extension may indicate disc problems. The pain may also be related to spondylolysis or lumbar spondylolisthesis. Lumbar extension can be performed with a single leg support; pain in the lumbar spine or sacrum suggests possible facet injury on the supporting side, indicating vertebral spondylolisthesis.

③ Lateral Bending

A normal lumbar lateral flexion can be 15°–20° with the patient placing one hand at the side of the body as far down as possible. If the pain worsens when the patient bends to the affected side, it indicates a possible lumbar injury or sacroiliac joint dysfunction. If the symptoms are relieved by bending to the contralateral side, the lesion may originate from the joint or muscle. Patients with disc herniation usually bend to the affected side to relieve pressure on the nerves from the outside of the disc.

④ Rotation

The rotation of the lumbar spine can be 3°–18°. The patient's hands are crossed in front of the chest. The athletic trainer rotates the patient's torso to the left and right to check the symmetry of the lumbar ROM. The athletic trainer should pay attention to any pelvic and hip compensation, and the pelvis should be fixed to eliminate interference.

(2) Tests in the Seated Position

① Flexion

Flexion in the seated position is the same as the flexion in the standing position. Normally, both PSISs (posterior superior iliac spines) should move together. If one PSIS moves further, it indicates limitation of motion.

② Rotation

The rotation in the seated position is the same as the rotation in the standing position. The seated position is used to prevent hip compensation. The athletic trainer needs to check the symmetry of the rotation angles on both sides and applies more pressure on PSISs to determine any exacerbation of pain.

③ Hip Rotation

The patient is seated at the side of table with the knee flexed at 90°, and the athletic trainer places one hand on the affected knee to immobilize it and the other hand on the affected sole of the foot to internally and externally rotate the patient's affected hip. Any pain during internal rotation may indicate piriformis irritation.

④ Slump Test

The patient sits on the edge of the table with knees bent and the hips in a median position and both feet on the floor. The athletic trainer applies pressure to flex the thoracic and lumbar vertebrae. Then the patient is asked to complete the following movements in turn, and any pain generated by each movement will be assessed and recorded: flex the neck, chest and lumbar spine; straighten one knee; dorsiflex one ankle; return the cervical spine to the neutral position; straighten another knee; dorsiflex another ankle. If the patient is unable to fully extend the knee or ankle due to pain, the athletic trainer can relieve the pressure on the neck and ask the patient to actively extend the neck. This test is positive if the ROM of the knee and ankle joints improves or if symptoms decrease with cervical extension, which may help determine if there is nerve tension. If yes, it may be due to herniated disc, nerve root adhesion or spinal impingement.

Bilingual Course of Athletic Training
运动防护学双语教程

(3) Tests in the Supine Position

The athletic trainer should check any asymmetry in the legs before doing the following tests. Excessive hip external rotation indicates piriformis contracture. Iliopsoas, hip adductors and symphysis pubis should also be palpated to determine any asymmetry and tenderness.

① Straight-Leg Raising Test

The athletic trainer slowly raises the patient's one leg from 0° to 70° with the patient in the supine position, and another leg and pelvis are close to the table surface. Pain occurring at 30° suggests possible hip problem or nerve inflammation. Pain occurring at 30°–60° suggests possible involvement of the sciatic nerve. When the leg is raised to the maximum angle, an exacerbation of pain with ankle dorsiflexion suggests a possible irritation of nerve root or sciatic nerve (Lasegue sign).

② Bragard Sign

The athletic trainer raises the patient's leg with the patient in the supine position and knee straight until pain occurs or aggravates, then lowers the leg 5°–10° until the pain is relieved or disappeared. The athletic trainer holds the leg with one hand to keep the knee straight and the other hand to keep the patient's ankle dorsiflexed. Back pain on the affected side and radiating along the sciatic nerve indicates nerve root inflammation or disc herniation.

③ Kernig Test

The patient is in the supine position with knee flexion and hip flexion at 90° and without pillow. The athletic trainer slowly extends the patient's knee. The test is positive if the knee cannot be extended to 135° or there is any pain, which indicates nerve inflammation or disc herniation.

④ Brudzinski Test

The patient is in the supine position with hands behind head. The athletic trainer asks the patient to bend the neck until touching the chest, then asks the patient to flex the hip, actively straighten the knee, and stop when pain occurs. The patient then flexes the knee. The test is positive when the pain disappears, which suggests possible lumbar disc or nerve root irritation.

⑤ FABER and FADIR Tests

The flexion, abduction and external rotation (FABER) test is also called Patrick test. The patient is in the supine position. The athletic trainer instructs the patient to place the unaffected heel in front of the affected knee joint to present a "4" shape. Pain in the groin is an indication of possible hip pathology. Pain occurs when pressing on the medial side of the affected knee, suggesting sacroiliac joint pathology.

The flexion, adduction and internal rotation (FADIR) test is done with the patient in the supine position. The patient is asked to flex the hip and knee on the affected side. The athletic trainer holds contralateral PSIS, adducts and internally rotates the patient's affected hip. Increasing of pain may indicate the lumbar pathology.

· 152 ·

⑥ Sacroiliac Sway (Knee-Chest) Test

The patient is asked to bend the knee and hip in the supine position so that the knee is close to the chest. The "rolling" effect of the sacroiliac joint is achieved by hip flexion and adduction. When doing this examination, the knee should be facing to the contralateral shoulder. Pain in the posterolateral thigh when the unilateral knee is close to the chest may indicate irritation of the sacrotuberous ligament. Pain in the PSIS suggests that the sacroiliac ligament may be irritated.

⑦ Sacroiliac Distraction Test

The Sacroiliac Distraction Test is also known as the Gap Test. The patient is in the supine position and the athletic trainer places the hands crossed at the front of the iliac bone and extends outwards. Pressing on the anterior iliac bone to distract the anterior part of the sacroiliac joint is for the examination of the anterior sacroiliac ligament. If pain in the sacroiliac joint increases, it indicates a sacroiliac joint pathology.

⑧ Pelvic Tilt Test

The patient bends both knees, puts feet on the table in the supine position, raises the pelvis slowly and then returns to the starting position, causing it to tilt forward and backward, respectively. If the pain on the compressed side of the pelvis intensifies, it indicates that there may be sacroiliac joint irritation.

(4) Tests in the Prone Position

The athletic trainer should palpate the posterior spinal structures for any increased muscle tone, tenderness and asymmetry. Common palpating points include lumbar SPs, iliac crest, PSISs, sacrum, spinal erectors, gluteus maximus, gluteus medius and piriformis.

① Press-Ups

The patient lies prone with forearms on the table to support the upper body to extension. Pain radiating to the buttocks and thighs may indicate lumbar disc herniation. If it is local pain, conservative treatment is recommended. In the case of generalized pain, surgery may be required.

② Reverse Straight-Leg Raising Test

The patient is in the prone position. The athletic trainer asks the patient to extend the knees, then lifts the leg on the affected side to extend the hip. If pain is present in the front thigh, it suggests L4 nerve root irritation.

③ Spring Test

The patient is in the prone position. The athletic trainer applies a downward pressure on each SP to evaluate the A-P motion of the vertebrae. In addition, the rotation of the spine can be assessed at the transverse processes. This test is used to determine any hypermobility or hypomobility of the lumbar spine.

④ Prone Knee Flexion Test

The patient is in the prone position. The athletic trainer compares the leg length with the knee straight and with 90° flexion respectively. If the length of the lower limbs is not equal on both sides with knee extension, the posterior rotation of the sacroiliac joint on the shorter side is suggested. If the difference in the length of the lower extremity disappears with knee flexion, it suggests posterior rotation of the sacroiliac joint on the longer side.

(5) Tests in the Side-Lying Position

① Posterior Rotation Stress Test

The patient lies on one side with the contralateral knee and hip flexed to 90°, and the athletic trainer places both hands on the sacroiliac joint to rotate posteriorly. Pain around the PSISs may indicate the irritation of the sacroiliac joint. This test can only determine on which side the pain is, but not the movement direction of dysfunction.

② Iliotibial Tract Stretching Test

The patient is in the side-lying position with the leg away from the table behind another. The athletic trainer puts one hand on the ASIS of the patient, and another hand applies downward pressure on the lateral knee away from the table. Being in a lateral position can shorten the iliotibial tract and cause persistent or recurrent sacroiliac joint problems. Pain on the contralateral PSIS may indicate the sacroiliac problem.

③ Quadratus Lumborum Stretching Test

The patient lies on one side. The starting motion is the same as the iliotibial tract stretching test, but with a rolled-up pillow placed under the lumbar area to make the lumbar spine flex laterally, so that the quadratus lumborum can be palpated. Pain during the stretching indicates possible quadratus lumborum tightness.

④ Piriformis Muscle Test

The patient is in the side-lying position with hip flexed to 90°, with one leg away from the table against the resistance applied by the athletic trainer to abduct the hip. Any pain indicates the piriformis tightness or myofascial pain. This test can be done with both hip and knee flexed to 90° in the seated position. Pain may occur when the hip external rotates with resistance.

⑤ Femoral Nerve Stretching Test

The patient is in the side-lying position. The athletic trainer places one hand fixed on the pelvis and another hand on the medial side of the knee joint that is away from the table to extend hip and flex the knee to 90°. Pain in the anterior thigh with hip extension indicates the impingement of the lumbar nerve root. This test can be done in the prone position.

⑥ Sacroiliac Compression Test

The patient is in the lateral position. The athletic trainer stands on the back of the patient with hands crossed and applies downward compressive force on the back of the sacroiliac joint. Exacerbation of pain in the sacroiliac joint indicates the sacroiliac joint pathology.

2.4.3 Neurological Test

(1) Sensation Test

If neurological symptoms are present, the athletic trainer should examine the dermatome of the nerve root and the peripheral sensory distribution of the peripheral nerves. Sensation of the dermatome can be involved in partial or complete dysfunction if the nerve root is injured.

(2) Reflex Test

Deep tendon reflexes in the upper extremity include the biceps (C5 and C6), brachioradialis (C6) and triceps (C7) reflexes. Deep tendon reflexes in the lower extremity include patellar (L4) and the achilles tendon (S1) reflexes.

二、脊柱损伤的评估

（一）病史

进行脊柱损伤的评估时，首先要明确导致损伤的原因以排除脊髓损伤的可能性。

运动防护师应询问以下问题：

- 患者受伤时发生了什么？
- 患者的头部是与别的物体相撞，还是直接接触地面？
- 患者是否出现了神志不清或意识丧失的症状？（如是，提示可能存在脊髓损伤）
- 患者的两侧上肢肌力是否一样？（如感觉或运动异常，提示可能存在脊髓损伤）
- 患者是否能活动踝关节和脚趾？

在前期进行病史采集过程中如怀疑脊髓损伤，在搬运和转移患者时要非常小心。

如排除脊髓损伤，运动防护师需继续询问患者以获取有关损伤性质的信息，可采用OPQRST 方式进行采集，包括：

O（Onset）

- 患者什么时间发生的损伤？

P（Palliative/Provocative）

- 患者做什么事情会引起疼痛？例如站立、坐着、弯腰或身体扭转等。
- 患者什么姿势或动作会使疼痛加剧？
- 患者什么姿势或动作能够缓解疼痛？

Q（Quality）

- 患者的肩部、手臂或手是否出现麻木、刺痛或灼烧感？
- 患者髋部或大腿后侧是否有麻木感或疼痛感？

R（Radiating/Referred）

- 患者具体的疼痛表现形式是什么？
- 患者是放射痛还是牵涉痛？（由运动防护师来判断）

S（Site）

● 患者什么部位有疼痛感？

● 患者颈部是否有疼痛感？

● 患者以前出现过任何背部疼痛吗？注意，引起背部疼痛的原因有很多，可能是肌肉骨骼系统的原因，也可能是内脏系统的问题导致的牵涉性疼痛。

T（Time）

● 患者的疼痛是突然出现的吗？

● 患者的疼痛持续了多长时间？

（二）视诊

1. 姿势评估

人体的骨骼、肌肉、韧带等解剖结构的相互作用与维持，使得人体在静态体位和动态运动中可以保持一定的姿势。姿势评估是通过观察人体的姿势，判断其是否存在结构或功能异常，分析其产生的原因以便及时纠正。在进行姿势评估时，要分别从前面、后面和侧面进行观察。可根据需要选取垂线、姿势网格坐标等辅助设备进行测量，保证姿势评估的准确性。在进行姿势评估时，要着重观察重要解剖标志点的位置。观察前面和后面时，运动防护师还应着重观察左右两侧的解剖标志点是否对称或在同一水平线上。

常见姿势问题包括：

（1）驼背

驼背是指脊柱胸段过度向后凸、头部前倾，颈曲深度超过 5 厘米的异常姿态。其分为姿势（功能）性驼背和结构性驼背两种，其中姿势（功能）性驼背多数是因不良的姿势习惯导致的；结构性驼背通常由脊椎病变造成。因此，在诊断时需进行鉴别诊断，例如，休门氏症（Scheuermann disease）多发于青春期男性，引起疼痛和渐进性胸椎或胸腰椎后凸，初期易被误认为是姿势性驼背。

（2）"头前伸"姿势

"头前伸"姿势需从侧面进行观察，表现为耳垂位于肩峰的前方，下颌向前探出。可由颈部肌肉不均衡导致，例如，出现驼背症状后，头颈部为了保持水平视线需要伸展颈椎，颈部伸肌收缩，屈肌被拉长，使头颈部产生代偿性改变。可采用头前伸角度（forward head angle，FHA）进行评估，即以第七颈椎（C7）棘突为参照点，向下画一条垂线，耳屏到 C7 棘突的连线与 C7 棘突垂线的夹角为 FHA。

（3）"摇摆背"和脊柱前凸

要分清"摇摆背"和脊柱前凸之间的差异，需要对骨盆的前倾、髋关节的位置和肌肉失衡的情况进行区分。"摇摆背"是指骨盆前移引起的髋关节后伸、胸椎后移，表现为腰椎曲度减小，胸椎后凸角度增加，髂腰肌肌力不足。脊柱前凸表现为腰椎曲度增加、骨盆前倾及髋关节屈曲，但髂腰肌肌力较强。肥胖、骨质疏松、腰椎滑脱等都可引起脊柱前凸。脊柱前凸、驼背及"头前伸"姿势一同被称为上交叉综合征。

（4）脊柱侧弯

脊柱侧弯是指脊柱某一节段的一侧出现明显的异常弯曲，而对侧出现反向、代偿性弯曲。脊柱侧弯分为由脊椎骨性结构的缺陷或障碍引起的结构性脊柱侧弯和由下肢不等长、两侧肌肉不平衡等非脊柱缺陷引起的功能性脊柱侧弯。在视诊时应注意观察双肩是否高低不平，脊柱是否偏离中线，肩胛骨是否一高一低，前屈时双侧背部是否等高。也可通过躯干前屈来进行鉴别诊断，若脊柱侧弯消失则为功能性脊柱侧弯，若脊柱侧弯仍存在则为结构性脊柱侧弯。

（5）平背

平背的原因包括腰椎曲度减小、骨盆后倾、屈髋角度增加等，也可能由退行性关节炎或脊柱融合术等导致。平背表现为矢状面上的脊柱畸形，即腰椎曲度减小，看上去相对较"平坦"。

2. 颈椎视诊

进行颈椎视诊时，运动防护师应着重观察患者的头部、颈部、肩部姿势及头颈部活动度，例如，患者头部位置是否在两肩正中央，患者两侧肩膀是否等高，患者能否主动活动头颈部等。检查颈部活动度时，注意分别检查颈部主动、被动和抗阻、非抗阻运动时屈曲、伸展、侧屈和旋转的活动范围。还需观察患者肌肉骨骼的状况，如患者是否三角肌有萎缩（提示腋神经麻痹）或头部倾斜（提示胸锁乳突肌痉挛）。

3. 胸椎视诊

进行胸椎视诊时，运动防护师应先观察患者脊柱胸段是否存在异常姿势，如脊柱后凸、脊柱侧弯、胸部畸形；同时应观察患者的呼吸形式，来判断患者呼吸时的状况。如，患者是采用腹式呼吸还是胸式呼吸，在呼吸时是否有身体部分的疼痛（将下颌靠近胸部或深吸气时胸部疼痛增加，提示可能存在胸椎椎间关节功能障碍／紊乱）。

引起胸椎疼痛的最常见原因是一个或多个胸椎关节功能障碍，如椎间关节等。因此需要对患者进行颈部及躯干的关节活动度评估，包括屈曲、伸展、侧屈和旋转活动。在颈部运动过程中，上背部的疼痛可能是颈椎间盘病变引起的牵涉痛，肩胛骨区域的疼痛可能是肌筋膜扳机点、胸长神经或肩胛上神经受到激惹所致的，需要结合肩部评估确定。在躯干活动过程中，若出现疼痛，提示胸下部神经根可能受到激惹。

4. 腰椎和骶髂关节视诊

因腰椎与骨盆、骶骨的协调运动起到维持腰部正常功能的作用，一旦出现肌肉或关节囊损伤、椎间盘突出或病变等问题就使患者在站立或运动时产生异常姿势。在进行视诊时，运动防护师应分别观察患者在站立位、坐位、仰卧位和俯卧位时的姿势。如观察患者肩部及骨盆两侧是否处于同一水平线上，脊柱两侧的骨性和软组织结构是否对称，在行走时是否存在异常步态等。

（三）触诊

在触诊开始时，运动防护师应关注患者损伤部位的皮肤、骨骼及软组织的质感等。触诊应从近端开始，至远端结束，触诊脊柱两侧肌肉是否存在压痛、叩击痛或肌卫现象等问题。脊柱部位的触诊通常以椎体棘突作为解剖定位点，正常情况下棘突应从上到下呈直线排列。如发现棘突偏移，代表某个椎体发生了一定角度的旋转，提示可能发生了椎体错位，常见于颈椎、腰椎。触诊时患者俯卧位，向下按压棘突以鉴别中心性疼痛和周围性疼痛；触诊棘突间隙以确定压痛点的情况及位置，如有压痛，提示可能存在韧带或椎间盘相关问题，牵涉性疼痛常存在压痛点。椎体横突也是常用的触诊定位点，在横突处施加压力可使椎体产生旋转，增加痛感。由于椎旁肌肉的存在，很难触诊到椎间关节和椎板等。

触诊颈部时，在患者仰卧位及颈部肌群处于放松状态时易触及颈椎侧方与前方解剖标志点，在颈椎后方触诊时，要用双手支撑患者头部进行触诊。触诊下背部时，可在患者髋关节下方垫一软垫以增加舒适感。评估腰椎时，运动防护师应同时触诊腹部肌肉，患者应做半仰卧起坐使腹部肌群收缩，从而帮助运动防护师评估双侧肌群的对称性及肌肉紧张度。触诊骶髂关节时，应重点寻找是否存在压痛点，如疼痛累及骶髂关节，在骶骨后侧施加压力可能会增加痛感。

（四）特殊试验

1.颈椎特殊试验

（1）臂丛神经试验

患者坐位，运动防护师站在患者身后，一只手抵住患侧头部向健侧侧弯，另一只手置于患者同侧肩膀，向相反方向牵拉。当颈部侧屈时，若疼痛向屈曲侧的肩部和手臂放射，则提示压迫性损伤；若疼痛向非屈曲侧的肩部和手臂放射，则提示牵引性损伤或拉伤。当出现放射性疼痛或麻木的感觉，臂丛神经试验为阳性，可判断为神经根损伤。

（2）颈椎挤压试验和椎间孔挤压试验

颈椎挤压试验的操作过程为：患者坐位，头颈部处于中立位，运动防护师站在患者身后，双手交叠置于患者头顶，向下均匀施加压力挤压颈椎椎间关节和颈部脊神经根，产生对颈椎的轴向挤压。疼痛位置不同，可提示不同水平的神经根损伤。

椎间孔挤压试验的操作过程为：患者坐位，颈部侧屈且稍向后伸；运动防护师站在患者身后，双手交叠置于患者头顶，向下均匀施加压力挤压。如颈部侧屈一侧的肩和手臂出现疼痛，则为阳性。这是由于挤压使神经根受到撞击而引起疼痛。

（3）椎动脉试验

患者仰卧位，运动防护师使患者颈椎后伸、侧屈，然后向侧屈方向旋转颈椎。如患者出现头晕或眼球异常运动（震颤），则此试验为阳性，提示椎动脉受压。

（4）肩外展试验

患者坐位，运动防护师令患者将一侧手与同侧耳朵贴合以使同侧肩关节外展。如疼痛减轻，则此试验为阳性，提示可能存在由颈椎间盘突出导致的神经根压迫。

2.腰椎特殊试验

腰椎特殊试验应在站位、坐位、仰卧位、俯卧位和侧卧位进行。

（1）站立位腰椎特殊试验

患者处于站立位时，运动防护师首先判断其是否存在不良身体姿势，其次着重观察患者行走时的步态，如有无行走困难、跛行等。还应观察患者矢状面的身体力线是否处于正常水平，身体两侧的体表标志点是否对称，如两侧腘窝横纹、髂前上棘是否对称。

①前屈

腰椎最大的前屈角度为 40°～60°，患者腰椎前屈可拉长脊柱后侧韧带。运动防护师需观察两侧髂后上棘状态，正常情况下，患者前屈过程中两侧髂后上棘应同时产生运动。如一侧髂后上棘的移动距离大于另一侧，提示较远一侧可能存在活动受限；如两侧开始产生活动的时间不一致，提示先开始活动的一侧可能存在活动受限。

②后伸

腰椎后伸角度能够达到 20°～35°，患者腰椎后伸可拉长脊柱前侧韧带。如后伸时存在活动受限和疼痛，提示可能存在椎间盘问题。疼痛还可能与峡部裂或腰椎滑脱有关。患者可在单腿支撑条件下进行腰椎后伸，若出现腰椎或骶骨处疼痛，表明支撑侧关节突可能存在损伤，提示椎体滑脱。

③侧屈

正常腰椎侧屈角度能够达到 15°～20°，患者一侧手放于体侧并尽力向下。若患者向患侧侧屈时疼痛加剧，则提示可能存在腰椎损伤或骶髂关节功能障碍；若患者向健侧弯曲时症状改善，则病变可能源自关节或肌肉。椎间盘突出的患者通常会向患侧侧屈以缓解神经根受到的来自椎间盘外侧的压力。

④旋转

腰椎的旋转角度能够达到 3°～18°，患者双手交叉置于胸前，运动防护师令患者躯干分别向左侧和右侧旋转，检查腰椎活动度的对称性。如果患者是站立位，检查时需注意骨盆和髋关节代偿运动的影响，应通过固定骨盆排除干扰。

（2）坐位腰椎特殊试验

①前屈

坐位前屈同站立位前屈，正常情况下前屈过程中两侧髂后上棘应共同运动。如一侧髂后上棘的移动距离较远，则该侧可能存在活动受限。

②旋转

坐位旋转同站立位旋转。采取坐位是为了防止髋关节代偿运动，运动防护师需检查患者腰椎向两侧旋转角度的对称性，可同时施加较大的压力以确定疼痛是否加剧。

③髋关节旋转

患者坐于治疗床边，膝关节屈曲 90° 角，运动防护师一只手置于检查侧膝关节上并使其固定，另一只手置于检查侧足底，内旋和外旋患者髋关节。内旋时肌肉被拉伸，出现疼痛提示可能存在梨状肌激惹。

④Slump 试验

患者屈膝坐在治疗床的边缘，髋关节保持正中姿势，双脚置于地面上。运动防护师施加压力使患者胸椎和腰椎屈曲。随后令患者依次完成以下动作，评估并记录每一个动作产生的疼痛：屈曲颈、胸、腰椎；伸直一侧膝关节；一侧踝关节背屈；颈椎回到中立位；伸直另一侧膝关节；另一侧踝关节背屈。若患者因疼痛无法完全伸直膝关节或踝关节无法完全背屈，运动防护师可减轻颈部施加的压力，让患者主动做颈部后伸，此步骤后若膝关节和踝关节活动度有所改善或症状随头后伸而减轻，则此测试阳性。Slump 试验可判断是否存在神经紧张，如有，可能由于椎间盘突出、神经根粘连或脊椎间撞击导致。

（3）仰卧位腰椎特殊试验

在进行仰卧位腰椎特殊试验之前，运动防护师应首先检查患者是否存在两侧腿不对称，如一侧腿过度外旋，则提示该侧可能存在梨状肌挛缩；还应触诊髂腰肌、股内收肌和耻骨联合等以判断是否存在双侧不对称和压痛点。

①直腿抬高试验

患者仰卧位，运动防护师将患者的一条腿从 0° 位缓慢抬高至 70° 位，另一条腿和骨盆紧贴治疗床面。抬高至 30° 位时出现疼痛，提示可能存在髋关节问题或神经炎症。抬高至 30°～60° 时出现疼痛，提示可能累及坐骨神经。抬高至最大角度时，运动防护师背屈患者踝关节，若疼痛增加，提示可能神经根或坐骨神经受到激惹（Lasegue 征）。

②直腿抬高加强试验

患者仰卧位，膝关节伸直，运动防护师将患者一侧腿缓慢抬高，出现疼痛后，角度放低 5°～10° 至疼痛缓解或消失。运动防护师一只手固定住此下肢保持膝伸直，另一只手使患者踝关节背屈。若引起患侧腰部疼痛沿坐骨神经放射，则该试验为阳性，提示神经根炎症或椎间盘突出。

③ Kernig 试验

患者去枕仰卧位，屈膝、屈髋 90°。运动防护师缓慢伸直患者膝关节，若膝关节不能伸直至 135° 或出现疼痛，则此试验为阳性。其中背部疼痛可能是神经根受到激惹的表现。

④ Brudzinski 试验

患者仰卧位，且双手抱在头后。运动防护师让患者屈曲颈部直至碰到胸部，此时令患者屈髋并主动伸直膝关节，当产生疼痛感后停止。随后患者膝关节屈曲，如果疼痛感消失，则此试验为阳性，提示可能存在腰椎间盘或神经根激惹。

⑤屈曲外展外旋和屈曲内收内旋试验

屈曲外展外旋（FABER）试验又叫作 Patrick 试验。患者仰卧位，运动防护师让患者检查侧下肢足跟放在非检查侧膝关节前方，呈"4"字形状。若腹股沟处出现疼痛，则提示可能存在髋关节病变。若用手按压患者检查侧膝关节内侧时出现疼痛，则提示可能存在骶髂关节病变。

在屈曲内收内旋（FADIR）试验中，患者仰卧位，运动防护师令患者患侧屈髋屈膝，一手固定住对侧髂前上棘，随后内收、内旋患者患侧髋关节。如患者腰痛加剧，则可能存在腰椎病变。

⑥骶髂摇摆（膝-胸）试验

患者仰卧位，令患者屈膝和屈髋使膝关节靠近胸部。通过屈曲和内收髋关节来实现骶髂关节的"滚动"效果。做此项检查时，膝关节应朝向对侧的肩关节。单侧膝靠近胸部时，如大腿后外侧出现疼痛，则可能存在骶结节韧带激惹；如髂后上棘出现疼痛，则可能存在骶髂韧带激惹。

⑦骶髂关节分离试验

骶髂关节分离试验，又称间隙试验。患者仰卧位，运动防护师双手交叉分别放在髂骨前端，向外张开。检查时双手在髂骨前端处向下用力按压，以扩张骶髂关节的前端部分用于检查骶髂前韧带。如骶髂关节疼痛加剧，则提示骶髂关节病变。

⑧骨盆倾斜试验

患者仰卧，膝关节屈曲，双脚踩在治疗床上，缓慢抬起骨盆后放下，使其分别前倾和后倾，如一侧骨盆疼痛加剧，则表明可能存在骶髂关节激惹。

（4）俯卧位腰椎特殊试验

开始俯卧位腰椎特殊试验前，运动防护师应触诊患者脊柱后侧结构以判断是否存在肌张力增高、压痛点、两侧不对称等情况。通常容易触诊的体表位置包括腰椎棘突、髂嵴、髂后上棘、骶骨、竖脊肌、臀大肌、臀中肌和梨状肌等。

①俯卧撑

患者俯卧位，前臂置于治疗床上，用力支撑起上半身，使其进行一个后伸动作。如出现疼痛并放射至臀部和大腿，则表明可能存在腰椎间盘突出。如为局部性疼痛，建议保守治疗；如为广泛性疼痛，可能需要手术治疗。

②反向直腿抬高试验

患者俯卧位，运动防护师令患者膝关节保持伸直位，然后抬起测试腿使髋关节后伸。如大腿前部出现疼痛，则提示可能存在 L4 神经根激惹。

③Spring 试验

患者仰卧位，运动防护师在每节脊椎棘突处施加向下的压力以评估脊椎前后向的活动。此外，还可在横突处评估脊椎的旋转活动。本试验可用于判断腰椎是否存在过度活动或活动受限。

④俯卧屈膝试验

患者俯卧位，运动防护师以足跟为标志点，比较完全伸膝和屈膝 90° 时的下肢长度。如患者伸膝位两侧下肢不等长，则提示较短一侧骶髂关节后旋；如屈膝后两侧下肢长度差异消失，则提示较长侧骶髂关节后旋。

（5）侧卧位腰椎特殊试验

①后旋压力试验

患者侧卧位，对侧屈膝屈髋 90° 角，运动防护师双手置于骶髂关节处使其后旋。如髂后上棘附近出现疼痛，则提示骶髂关节可能受到激惹。该试验仅能确定疼痛在哪一侧，无法判定具体功能障碍的运动方向。

②髂胫束拉伸试验

患者侧卧位，远离床侧腿置于另一侧腿之后，运动防护师一只手置于患者髂前上棘处固定，另一只手置于远离床一侧腿膝关节外侧，向下按压。处于侧卧位可使髂胫束缩短以及使骶髂关节问题持续存在或复发。如对侧髂后上棘出现疼痛，则提示存在骶髂关节问题。

③腰方肌拉伸试验

患者侧卧位，其起始动作与髂胫束拉伸试验动作一致，但需在腰部下方放置一个卷起的枕头使腰椎侧屈，便于运动防护师触诊腰方肌。在牵拉过程中如出现疼痛，则提示可能存在腰方肌紧张。

④梨状肌试验

患者侧卧位，屈髋90°，远离床一侧腿对抗运动防护师施加的阻力进行髋关节外展。如出现疼痛，则提示梨状肌紧张或肌筋膜疼痛。本试验也可在坐位屈髋屈膝90°时进行，抗阻外旋髋关节也会引起损伤部位的疼痛。

⑤股神经牵拉试验

患者侧卧位，运动防护师一只手固定其骨盆，另一只手置于远离床侧膝关节内侧，使其伸髋并屈膝90°，如伸髋时大腿前侧出现疼痛，则提示腰神经根受到撞击。俯卧位时也可进行本试验。

⑥骶髂关节挤压试验

患者侧卧位，运动防护师站在患者后侧，双手交叉置于患者骶髂关节后部并向下用力按压。如骶髂关节疼痛加剧，则提示骶髂关节病变。

3. 神经检查

（1）感觉检查

如果发现神经症状，运动防护师需检查患者神经根的皮区以及外周神经的外周感觉分布。如损伤累及神经根，皮区感觉功能可能会出现部分或完全障碍。

（2）反射检查

上肢深肌腱反射包括肱二头肌（C5和C6）、肱桡肌（C6）和肱三头肌腱（C7）反射。下肢深肌腱反射包括髌腱反射（L4）和跟腱反射（S1）。

3 Identification and Management of Common Spine Injuries

3.1 Cervical Spine

3.1.1 Cervical Fracture

(1) Etiology

Most of the cervical fractures are caused by violence applied on the top of the head. The force is transmitted to the cervical spine through the skull to flex the neck, resulting in compressive fractures or dislocations of the cervical spine. In addition, fractures may also occur when the neck is subjected to sudden hyperextension violence. For example, the face is impacted by the violence from the front, causing the head and neck hyperextension and then cervical spine injury.

The incidence of cervical spine fractures is relatively low in cervical spine injuries. It may occur in gymnastics, diving, rugby and other events. Patients with cervical spine fractures will miss longer training time, and severe cases may cause spinal cord injury and paralysis, so the athletic trainer needs to be prepared to deal with cervical spine fractures.

(2) Symptoms and Signs

Symptoms and signs of the cervical fracture may include one or more of the following:

● Neck, chest and upper limb pain

● Neck tenderness, restricted mobility

● Cervical spine deformity

● Neck muscle spasm

● Trunk and/or limb numbness, weakness or paralysis

● Incontinence

(3) Management

① Neck injury combined with weakness and numbness of the lower limbs must be treated as serious neck injury before the spinal cord injury is confirmed by the medical professionals. ② Make sure the airway of the injured is unobstructed and hemorrhage is controlled, and the neck guard and spine board are used for fixation in time. Unconscious patients should not be moved before the position and fixation are corrected. Wrong handling and movement will cause unnecessary spinal cord injury. ③ It is allowed to leave the scene after the professionals have determined that the unstable fracture is unlikely to cause spinal cord injury. The handling and transfer process should be very careful to avoid secondary injuries.

3.1.2 Cervical Dislocation

(1) Etiology

Cervical dislocation is often caused by falling from a height and strong impact on the head and neck, etc. When the head is violently flexed and rotated, it is easy to cause cervical dislocation. The anatomical characteristics of the cervical spine make the probability of cervical dislocation higher than other segments. The facet joint surface of the cervical spine is flat. When the upper joint surface exceeds the normal range or the contact surface with the lower joint surface is less, it will cause cervical dislocation. The former is a complete dislocation, and the latter is an incomplete dislocation, which is relatively more common.

(2) Symptoms and Signs

Pain, numbness, muscle weakness, etc. may occur after cervical dislocation. In unilateral cervical dislocation, the neck bends to the affected side. The neck muscles on the affected side are relatively loose, and the contralateral muscles are stretched and tight. Bilateral cervical dislocation mainly causes severe head and neck pain, neck muscle spasm, movement restriction and other symptoms.

(3) Management

Cervical dislocation is very likely to cause spinal cord injury, so attention should be paid to fixing the patients head to prevent neck rotation when transferring and transporting the injured, ensure the airway is unblocked, and wait for medical staff to help.

3.1.3　Acute Cervical and Upper Back Strains

(1) Etiology

Suddenly turning back or picking up heavy objects causes the head and neck to twist suddenly, and the muscles contract and stretch strongly without any preparation, resulting in tearing or damage of the neck muscles, ligaments and other soft tissues. The most involved parts are trapezius, levator scapulae and sternocleidomastoid muscles or neck fascia and ligament tissues.

(2) Symptoms and Signs

The main symptoms are local pain and limited activity. The muscles are in a state of protective contraction. Shoulder rotates with head rotating. The damaged muscles will have obvious tenderness and local soft tissues will be slightly swollen.

(3) Management

① After injury, immediately use the POLICE principle to allow the patient to rest and relax. Wear a neck guard when necessary to reduce neck activities such as bowing, twisting, and tilting, and avoid muscle contraction and stretching. ② After the acute period, according to the actual situation, gradually start range of motion exercises, isometric contraction and isotonic contraction exercises. You can also use drugs, physiotherapy, or acupuncture for adjuvant treatment.

3.1.4　Cervical Sprain (Whiplash)

(1) Etiology

It can be seen that the car brakes suddenly when driving at high speed, and the head and neck suddenly bend forward and then extends backwards, resulting in cervical hyperflexion and hyperextension. The injury can be seen as ligament tear, intra-articular bleeding and cartilage avulsion. In severe cases, it can also cause joint dislocation, fracture and cervical spinal cord injury.

(2) Symptoms and Signs

Whiplash injuries usually last for several days, and the common symptoms are neck pain, headache, and limited cervical spine movement. It may be accompanied by stiffness, dizziness, and radicular pain. The pain sometimes radiates to the arm with numbness. After the neck sprain occurs, the muscle strength and muscle tone are weak below the injury level, and the skin sensitivity is decreased. Inflammation and restriction of movement can cause muscle-protective spasms and pain.

(3) Management

① First of all, prevent secondary damage. Secondly, a doctor should check to determine whether there is spinal cord or nerve root injury, and avoid using an excessively rigid neck brace to cause repeated cervical spine hyperextension mechanisms to aggravate the injury. ② The POLICE principle should be applied in the acute phase after injury. ③ For severely injured patients, doctors should perform neurological examinations to assess the injury (CT or MRI if necessary) to determine the severity. If there is no neurological injury, bed rest and medication can be taken to relieve pain and muscle spasms. Cryotherapy, hyperthermia, massage, traction, etc. can also have certain effects.

3.1.5 Acute Torticollis

(1) Etiology

Acute torticollis can occur due to abnormal head and neck posture during sleep, maintaining single posture for a long time, and being frightened during sleep, which can cause sudden muscle pain on the affected side, with the head and neck being restricted or tilted to the flexion or extension position. Acute torticollis is quite common. Patients usually complain that pain is on one side of the neck when waking up. This is caused by the impingement of the synovial membrane in the cervical facet joints.

(2) Symptoms and Signs

The head and neck are tilted and twisted to one side. A slight movement of the head will cause stretching pain on the neck and back. The pain can radiate to the shoulders, the neck muscles are contracture and tenderness, and there is a muscle guarding phenomenon.

(3) Management

① Mild traction, joint mobilization and acupuncture can alleviate muscle guarding, thereby reducing pain and alleviating spasms with mild problems, and the patient can return to normal in 4–5 days. ② In severe cases, it can last for several weeks without healing. It is not appropriate to receive cervical traction and massage in the acute stage. Neck rotation or oblique traction is prohibited. It is also helpful for patients to wear a soft neck guard. ③ Improving the patient's neck position during sleeping can help relieve pain. With the gradual recovery of exercise, the muscle guarding phenomenon will also be relieved.

3.1.6 Spinal Cord and Nerve Root Injury

(1) Etiology

Spinal cord and nerve root injury refer to the compression or rupture of the spinal cord caused by various external forces acting on the spine. The most common site are the junction of the middle and lower cervical vertebrae and the thoracolumbar region. The causes include laceration, hemorrhage, contusion, cervical cord neuropraxia and shock.

① Laceration. Cervical dislocation along with fracture usually causes the spinal cord laceration. The jagged edges of cervical fracture may cut or tear the spinal cord or nerve root, resulting in different degrees of paralysis below the injury level. ② Hemorrhage. Hemorrhage is caused by spinal fracture, dislocation, sprain and strain. It usually does not affect the extradural musculature and the arachnoid membrane, because blood dissipates faster than it accumulates in those structures. Hemorrhage in the spinal cord can result in irreversible severe damage. ③ Contusion. Abnormal cervical motion caused by violent force can compress the spinal cord, resulting in swelling in the spinal cord and different degrees of temporary and/or permanent spinal cord or nerve root injury. ④ Cervical Cord Neuropraxia. When the neck is severely twisted or hit, the cervical canal is narrowed, and the patient cannot move some body parts or feels numbness or tingling. After a period of time, the symptoms and signs disappear except for cervical soreness. If cervical cord neuropraxia occurs, it should be treated according to a severe neck injury. ⑤ Shock. Severe trauma to the spinal cord such as cord transection can cause spinal cord shock, resulting in function loss below the injury level. Function loss involves extremities weakness and loss of deep tendon reflexes. As the disease progresses, extremities weakness develops into muscle spasms, and loss of deep tendon reflexes develops into hyperreflexia.

(2) Symptoms and Signs

Spinal cord injury at different injury levels has different clinical manifestations, such as motor, sensory, and sphincter dysfunction below the injury level, pain at the injury site, tenderness of the vertebral body and spinous process at the fracture site, and local swelling. Spinal cord injury can be divided into complete injury and incomplete injury. Complete spinal cord injury refers to the complete loss of sacral sensory and motor function at the lowest position below the injury level. Incomplete spinal cord injury refers to part of the sensory and motor function below the injury level. In addition incomplete spinal cord injury syndromes, also includs anterior spinal cord syndrome, posterior spinal cord syndrome, central spinal cord syndrome, and Brown-Séquard Syndrome.

(3) Management

When spinal cord or nerve root injury is suspected, timely treatment is required. Early and correct treatment is related to the patient's life safety and the recovery of spinal cord function. It must be treated under the guidance of professional medical personnel to reduce the possibility of other injuries.

3.1.7 Cervical Stenosis

(1) Etiology

In addition to bony stenosis, it also includes bulging of the intervertebral disc, osteophyte formation, loosening of the ligamentum flavum, and abnormal intervertebral movement.

(2) Symptoms and Signs

The initial symptoms of cervical stenosis are numbness, allergies, or pain in the limbs.

Movement dysfunction usually appears after sensory dysfunction, manifested as pyramidal sign, weak, rigid and inflexible limbs. The symptoms above generally disappear within 10–15 minutes. When the nerve function is restored, the neck may reach to full range of joint activities.

(3) Management.

① Since the initial symptoms of cervical stenosis are relatively unobvious, it needs to be dealt with caution. Patients must undergo diagnostic examinations such as X-ray and MRI to determine the severity of damage. ② Physical therapy, immobilization and symptomatic treatment can be used for patients with mild symptoms. Most patients can be relieved by non-surgical treatment. For severe symptoms, surgical treatment should be performed as soon as possible.

3.1.8 Brachial Plexus Neuropraxia

(1) Etiology

When the brachial plexus is over-stretched or compressed, there will be temporary nerve apraxia, which is more common in cervical spine nerve injury. It usually causes a certain degree of peripheral nerve function damage, but without any degenerative changes. The brachial plexus is commonly stretched when the upper limb is pulled strongly, the head and neck are excessively bent to the opposite side or the shoulder is forced down. In addition, when the neck extends back while squeezing and rotating to one side, the ipsilateral brachial plexus may be compressed.

(2) Symptoms and Signs

Brachial plexus injury has different symptoms depending on the location and extent of the injury. Mild cases may have temporary upper limb dysfunction, which may be accompanied by upper limb tingling or burning sensation. In severe cases, upper limbs may have varying degrees of muscle paralysis or weakness, motor and sensory dysfunction, and weakened or disappeared reflexes. If the patient complains that pain and numbness radiating to all fingers, it indicates that at least the C6, C7, and C8 nerve roots are involved. If only the deltoid muscle and biceps muscle are weak, it indicates that the C5 nerve root is involved.

(3) Management

① First of all, the patient's injury should be evaluated. Patients with mild injury can be observed advanced, flexibility and strengthening exercises should be taken when the symptoms are relieved, and regular re-examination should be carried out. In severe cases, surgery may be applied. ② Athletes as rugby players can wear neck and shoulder guards to protect the brachial plexus.

3.1.9 Cervical Disc Injury

(1) Etiology

Cervical disc injury usually refers to the degenerative disease of the cervical disc, especially the nucleus pulposus, which protrudes out of the posterior spinal canal by the external force. It is commonly caused by repeated cervical spine loading due to neck trauma, long-term desk work, etc.

(2) Symptoms and Signs

The main manifestations are shoulder pain and radiating pain in the upper limbs, or varying degrees of movement and sensory dysfunction. Depending on the degree and location of the cervical disc herniation, there will be corresponding symptoms of spinal cord or nerve root compression.

(3) Management

① At the early stage of injury, rest is very important, which is helpful to the resolution of local inflammation and nerve root edema. Medication can be used to relieve symptoms. ② Most patients can relieve their symptoms through non-surgical treatments, including head and neck traction, physical therapy, and traditional Chinese medicine treatment. In severe cases, surgical treatment should be considered.

3.2 Thoracic Spine

Scheuermann's Disease

(1) Etiology

Due to various reasons, the blood supply of the epiphyseal plate is reduced. The cartilage plate becomes thinner and the anti-pressure ability is reduced. Under excessive load, the nucleus pulposus protrudes into the vertebral body at the rupture. The thoracic segments of the spine part bend backward. With the increase of age and the growth of the body, the height of the posterior (half) vertebra is higher and higher than the height of the anterior part. The vertebral bodies form a wedge shape, and several wedge-shaped vertebral bodies increase the kyphosis of the thoracic spine to form kyphosis. The currently accepted diagnostic criteria is that the wedge deformation of at least 3 adjacent vertebral bodies is greater than 5°. Scheuermann's disease is more common in adolescents and is common in gymnastics and swimming.

(2) Symptoms and Signs

The typical symptoms of Scheuermann's disease are kyphosis, round back deformity. Patients may have obvious chest and back pain, which can be aggravated by standing and intense physical activity. The disease also stops developing after growth stops. Pain symptoms in late adolescence can usually be relieved. In addition, the hamstrings of patients with Scheuermann's disease are tighter.

(3) Management

① The severity of deformity and pain must be determined in the diagnosis of Scheuermann's disease. ② The goal of treatment is to prevent progressive kyphosis. Non-surgical treatment mainly involves functional training, such as low back muscle strength training, stretching training and posture training, etc. ③ Taping, physiotherapy, bracing and anti-inflammatory drugs also have certain effects.

3.3 Lumbar Spine

3.3.1 Lumbar Fracture and Dislocation

(1) Etiology

Lumbar spine fracture is usually caused by trauma and skeletal diseases, which are more commonly seen in trauma caused by falling from heights or car accidents. Common types include compressive fractures and fractures of TPs and SPs. Compressive fractures are mainly caused by the violence from the head and feet to the spine resulting in sudden excessive flexion. Fragments of the spine protrude into the bone marrow and damage the spinal cord or cauda equina. When the back is impacted, it is easy to cause fractures of TPs and SPs. Lumbar dislocations are rare. Acute lumbar sprains can cause dislocations of the lumbar facet joints.

(2) Symptoms and Signs

The injury is manifested as local pain, tenderness, percussion pain in the back, paraspinal muscle tightness, usually accompanied by local edema and muscle protective spasm.

(3) Management

① When the lumbar spine is fractured a spinal board is needed to carry and transfer the patient to limit the movement of the fracture site. ② Those having been diagnosed as stable fractures or without nerve damage can take conservative treatments such as rest and prevent complications during rest.

3.3.2 Lumbar Muscle Strains

(1) Etiology

Lumbar muscle strain is a local acute injury caused by sudden over-stretching of lumbar muscles, fascia, ligaments and other soft tissues due to external forces, which exceeds the normal body load. Acute lumbar injuries are often caused by lifting heavy weights. In addition, abnormal postures can also cause chronic lumbar muscle strains.

(2) Symptoms and Signs

Symptoms of acute lumbar injury mainly include back pain, lumbar muscle spasm and limited mobility. For chronic lumbar strain, the symptoms are mainly slow onset and long course. Generally, there is no obvious history of acute trauma, and it often manifests as lumbar soreness, heaviness and inconvenience of the lumbar spine etc., which can be relieved after rest.

(3) Management

① After muscle strain occurs, bed rest is used to limit the stress of the waist, so as to relieve pain and facilitate the recovery of the injured muscle. ② It should be combined with icing or ice massage to relieve pain and avoid the aggravation of blood stasis and swelling, and elastic bandages for compression bandaging. ③ According to the individual situation, progressive stretching and strengthening exercises can be carried out in the early stage, focusing on the stretching of the lumbar flexor and extensor muscles and the strength training of the lumbar extensor muscles.

3.3.3 Myofascial Pain Syndrome

(1) Etiology

Myofascial pain syndrome is a common local chronic pain syndrome related to soft tissue injury or dysplasia. It is characterized by pressing or palpating the tenderness or trigger point of a muscle, causing referred pain of another site. Trigger points are tender points on muscle tension belts, which are common in the neck, upper back and lumbar region.

(2) Symptoms and Signs

There is chronic and persistent soreness or dull pain in the affected area, presenting a sense of tightness or pressure from heavy weights. It can occur in the waist, back, sacrum, buttocks, legs, knees, soles, neck, shoulders, elbows, or wrists. Ipsilateral or local muscle tension, spasm, bulge, contracture or stiffness, small nodules and string-shaped solid objects appear. The string-shaped solid objects tremble when stimulated, involving pain with touching the trigger point, and motion restriction of the muscles or adjacent joints. Palpating the trigger point of the quadratus lumborum muscle can cause sharp pain and soreness on the lateral side of the lumbar or abdominal region.

(3) Management

The key to improving myofascial pain is to make the muscles back to their resting length through stretching and strengthening exercises so as to relieve the pain caused by the trigger point, which can be combined with acupuncture and massage therapy.

3.3.4 Lumbar Sprains

(1) Etiology

Bending and lifting or moving heavy weights with lumbar rotation can easily cause acute sprains of the facet joints of the lumbar spine. The severity of chronic and repetitive lumbar sprains will gradually increase with physical activity. This injury is commonly seen in young adults, physical workers and athletes.

(2) Symptoms and Signs

Persistent and severe pain in the lumbar spine occurs immediately after the injury. Local bleeding, swelling, and lower back pain may be more serious in the next day. The lumbar movement is restricted and the back cannot be straight. The pain can be aggravated by coughing, sneezing, and urinating. In severe cases, lumbar deformities, muscle cramps, and local tenderness may occur.

(3) Management

① The POLICE principle should be utilized in the initial stage to relieve pain, and patients should wear protective gear or support belts to restrict activities. Joint mobilization can also be helpful. ② Stretching and strengthening exercises of the abdominal and lumbar extensors should be performed within a pain-free range. Patients should perform trunk stability exercises under the guidance of the athletic trainer. ③ The movements or postures that may cause lumbar sprains should be avoided.

3.3.5 Back Contusions

(1) Etiology

Most of the back contusions are caused by trauma. The incidence of back contusions is second only to strains and sprains. Certain symptoms and signs can be produced when the back is hit by a significant impact, which needs differential diagnosis with spinal fractures, and X-ray examinations can be performed if necessary.

(2) Symptoms and Signs

After the injury, the patient will feel back pain or dull pain, as well as symptoms such as local swelling, subcutaneous bruising and discoloration of the skin.

(3) Management

① In the acute phase, icing, compression and rest should be performed. It can be treated with trauma ointment. ② Ultrasound therapy can be performed when deep muscles are involved.

3.3.6 Sciatica

(1) Etiology

The lesions of the local and surrounding structures of the sciatic nerve can stimulate, compress and damage the sciatic nerve and thereby cause inflammation of the sciatic nerve, which is usually related to the following factors: ① herniated disc compresses the peripheral nerve root; ② irregular structure of the intervertebral foramina; ③ piriformis tightness.

(2) Symptoms and Signs

The patient can feel pain, numbness or burning. The pain is mainly located in the sciatic nerve distribution area, posterior thigh, posterolateral calf and the foot. Patients with severe pain can assume a unique posture with lumbar flexion, knee flexion and toe landing. Increased pain can make walking difficult.

(3) Management

① Pay attention to rest, and timely determine and eliminate the cause of the disease in the acute phase. ② Oral anti-inflammatory drugs, lumbar traction, and piriformis stretching can alleviate sciatica. Surgical treatment may be considered if it can not be relieved for a long time.

3.3.7 Lumbar Disc Herniation

(1) Etiology

Degenerative changes, tears and ruptures of the annulus fibrosus are caused by abnormal biomechanical effects, trauma or continuous, abnormal pressure effects. When the lumbar spine is abnormally flexed or rotated, the aging intervertebral disc may be herniated or bulged. That is, the nucleus pulposus protrudes into the annulus or completely penetrates the annulus. If the nucleus pulposus separates from the intervertebral disc and begins to dissociate, then a herniated disc is formed. The common reasons are repeated bending and twisting, heavy physical labor or trauma.

(2) Symptoms and Signs

Patients with lumbar disc herniation often present clinically with low back pain radiating to the buttocks, back or legs along the dermatome, numbness and weakness in the lower limbs, and may manifest symptoms such as scoliosis, decreased lumbar mobility, muscle atrophy or decreased muscle strength. Pain increases with trunk flexion and sitting, and relieves with extension of the trunk.

(3) Management

① In the initial stage, bed rest should be the main focus with the goal of relieving pain. Icing or electrical stimulation therapy can be performed, and muscle relaxation techniques should be used for manual treatment; isotonic exercise training in the back region should be avoided. ② When the pain is relieved and the posture returns to normal, the strengthening exercises of the back extensors and abdominal muscles should be started in time to improve the stability of the lumbar spine. ③ Postures that may aggravate symptoms should be avoided.

3.3.8 Spondylolysis and Spondylolisthesis

(1) Etiology

Spondylolysis refers to the bone discontinuity or bone defect in the upper and lower articular process and the transverse process transition area of the lumbar spine, with manifestation of degenerative changes in the spine. The main causes are congenital factors, and unclosed or weak isthmus during development. Acquired factors are mostly related to trauma and overuse, such as momentary violence or repeated lumbar spine vibrations, extensions and other movements and frequent stress on the lumbar isthmus. Spondylolysis is usually unilateral. One vertebral body may slip on another vertebral body if progressing to both sides, and that is spondylolisthesis, which is considered to be a complication of spondylolysis, causing excessive movement of one vertebral body. It is noted that spondylolysis is more likely to occur in male adolescents, while spondylolisthesis is more likely to occur in female adolescents.

(2) Symptoms and Signs

Many patients with spondylolysis are asymptomatic and are only diagnosed by X-ray or CT. Patients with spondylolysis mainly have pain in the lower back. The symptoms are obvious with lumbar extension, but there is no pain during physical activity. Complaints include frequent changes of posture to relieve the pain. A few patients will suffer sciatica, radiating pain to the buttocks and the posterior thighs. Those with spondylolisthesis secondary to spondylolysis will have lower back pain during walking and standing, which is relieved during bed rest and accompanied by intermittent claudication. Pain, numbness, soreness, weakness, etc., appear after standing or walking for a while. Cauda equina nerve damage can occur in severe cases.

(3) Management

① In the acute stage of lumbar pain, the patient can rest in bed for 1–3 days, and wear lumbar gear to help relieve the pain. ② The vertebral body with excessive activity should be subjected to stability or control exercises, including progressive strengthening exercises, dynamic stability exercises for core muscles, etc. ③ Electrotherapy, thermotherapy and other physical therapy on body surface can also promote recovery.

3.4 Sacroiliac Joint Dysfunction

3.4.1 Sacroiliac Joint Sprains

(1) Etiology

External torsional force by abnormal posture, imbalanced muscles and loose ligaments can cause the uneven sacroiliac joint surface to be arranged disorderly, and the gap is widened. When the joint cavity is under negative pressure, the synovial membrane is sucked into the joint space, causing severe pain. Anterior or posterior dislocation of sacroiliac joint can be caused depending on the direction of the sprain. Twisting the body while landing on both feet, violently landing on one foot, lumbar flexion while lifting weights with knee extension, running downhill, repetitive single-foot activities may cause sacroiliac joint sprains, which are commonly seen in excessive twisting when doing golf swings, pole vaulting, hurdles or gymnastics.

(2) Symptoms and Signs

A few patients may have no obvious history of trauma. In the acute stage, ipsilateral pain may occur in the low back. Most patients may have severe, radiating pain in the buttocks or groin area. Patients often take the side-lying or prone position, and the pain is aggravated when turning over. Standing or flexing the lower limbs is refused. A lame gait with dropping of gluteal sulcus is often seen when walking. There may be localized tenderness in the sacroiliac joints, limited straight leg raising on the affected side and sacral pain. During the examination by the athletic trainer, it can be found that the anterior superior iliac spine/posterior superior iliac spine on both sides are asymmetry, which may be caused by the relative anterior or posterior rotation of the pelvis on one side. Leg length discrepancy may be found.

(3) Management

The symptoms can be relieved by resting on a hard bed, physical therapy, local massage, external application of plasters and local sealing. Joint mobilization and strengthening training can be applied. For those who are accompanied by lumbar or lumbosacral joint degeneration or intervertebral disc herniation, it is necessary to treat it accordingly.

3.4.2 Coccygeal Injuries

(1) Etiology

Coccyx injuries are mainly caused by direct impact, such as touching the ground with the buttocks when falling or being subjected to violence. Coccyx injuries include sprains, subluxations and fractures. In addition, maintaining an abnormal posture for a long time can also cause overuse injury and inflammation of the tailbone.

(2) Symptoms and Signs

The injury is manifested as swelling and pain in the affected area. In the acute phase, local hemorrhage, edema and severe pain will occur. If the pain persists for a long time, X-ray examination and anal examination should be performed.

(3) Management

The use of analgesics and circular cushions can reduce the pressure on the tailbone when sitting. At the same time, it is important to rest and avoid sitting for a long time. Appropriate local hot compress can be applied. Massage and physical therapy can promote recovery.

三、脊柱常见损伤的识别和处理

（一）颈椎

1. 颈椎骨折

（1）病因

颈椎骨折多数是由于暴力作用于头顶所致，力量通过颅骨传到颈椎使之屈曲，造成颈椎前侧压缩性骨折或脱位。除此以外，颈部受到突然的过伸暴力时也可能引发骨折，如面部遭受来自正前方暴力的冲击，使头颈部向后过伸而造成颈椎损伤。

颈椎骨折的发生率在颈椎损伤中占比相对较小，在体操、跳水、橄榄球等项目中可能出现颈椎骨折。发生颈椎骨折会耽误较长训练时间，严重时可能会引起脊髓损伤从而导致瘫痪，因此运动防护师需要做好处理颈椎骨折的准备。

（2）症状和体征

颈椎骨折的症状和体征可能包括以下一种或多种：①颈胸部和上肢疼痛、颈部压痛、活动受限；②颈椎畸形；③颈部肌肉痉挛；④躯干和/或肢体麻木、无力或瘫痪；⑤大小便失禁。

（3）处理

①颈部损伤合并下肢无力、麻木，在由专业医护人员确认排除脊髓损伤之前需按照严重的颈部损伤来处理。②保证患者呼吸道通畅并控制出血，及时用护颈和脊柱板进行固定，无意识的患者在未摆正体位和固定之前不应该被移动，错误的处理和移动有可能造成不必要的脊髓损伤。③在由专业人员明确患者的不稳定骨折不可能引发脊髓损伤后，才可以允许患者从现场离开，搬运和转移的过程应十分小心，避免出现二次伤害。

2. 颈椎脱位

（1）病因

颈椎关节脱位常由高处跌落、头颈部遭到强烈撞击等原因导致，当头部受到暴力屈曲和旋转时，容易引起颈椎关节脱位。颈椎的解剖特点导致颈椎脱位的发生概率高于其他节段。颈椎的关节突关节面平坦，当上关节面的活动超出正常范围或与下关节面的接触面积极少时，就会引起颈椎脱位。前者为完全脱位，后者为不完全脱位，后者相对更常见。

（2）症状和体征

颈椎脱位发生后会出现疼痛、麻木、肌肉无力等症状状单侧颈椎脱位时，颈部会向患侧侧屈，患侧颈部肌肉相对松弛，对侧肌肉被拉长呈紧张状态。双侧颈椎脱位时，主要会出现头颈部剧痛，颈部肌肉痉挛，活动受限等症状。

（3）处理

颈椎脱位极可能引起脊髓损伤，因此在转移和搬运患者时需注意固定患者头部，防止颈部旋转，并保证呼吸道畅通，等待医护人员的救助。

3. 颈部及上背部急性拉伤

（1）病因

突然回头或扛拾重物等原因使头颈部突然扭转，肌肉无准备地受到强烈收缩和牵拉，导致颈部肌群、韧带等软组织发生撕裂或损伤。受累较多的结构包括：斜方肌、肩胛提肌及胸锁乳突肌或颈部筋膜和韧带组织等。

（2）症状和体征

主要症状为局部疼痛及活动受限，肌肉处于保护性收缩状态，转头时两肩随之转动，受损肌肉有明显压痛，局部软组织轻微肿胀。

（3）处理

①发生损伤后，立即采取 POLICE 原则，让患者休息放松，必要时佩戴护颈，减少低头、扭头、仰头等颈部活动，避免肌肉用力和牵拉肌肉。②急性期过后，根据实际情况循序渐进开始进行关节活动度练习、等长收缩和等张收缩练习，也可以通过药物、理疗、针灸等方式进行辅助治疗。

4. 挥鞭伤

（1）病因

可见于汽车高速行驶中突然急刹车，头颈部突然大幅度前屈继而后伸，致颈椎发生过屈及过伸运动，犹如鞭子挥动而造成的颈部损伤。损伤可见韧带撕裂、关节内出血及软骨撕脱。严重者亦可造成关节脱位、骨折及脊髓损伤。

（2）症状和体征

挥鞭伤通常持续数天，常见症状为颈痛、头痛及颈椎活动受限，可伴有僵硬、晕眩和神经根痛，疼痛有时放射至手臂并伴有麻木感。颈部扭伤发生后，损伤平面以下，肌力、肌张力减弱，皮肤敏感性降低。炎症反应和活动受限会引起保护性肌肉痉挛，引发疼痛感。

（3）处理

①首先应预防二次损伤。其次应由医生进行检查以确定有无脊髓或神经根损伤，同时避免使用过硬的颈托造成重复颈椎过伸从而加重损伤。②在受伤后的急性期应采取POLICE原则进行处理。③严重损伤的患者，医生应进行神经检查以评估伤势（必要时进行CT或MRI），确定严重程度，若无神经损伤，卧床休息、药物治疗可缓解疼痛和肌肉痉挛，冷冻疗法、热疗、按摩、牵引等也有一定疗效。

5. 急性斜颈

（1）病因

睡眠时头颈姿势异常、长时间保持单一姿势、睡眠时受惊等原因都可导致急性斜颈，造成突发性颈部一侧肌肉疼痛，出现头颈部被限制或屈曲位或后伸位的一侧倾斜的症状。急性斜颈较为常见，通常患者主诉睡醒时一侧颈部疼痛，这是由关节囊内滑膜在颈椎关节面关节内受到撞击引起的。

（2）症状和体征

头颈向一侧倾斜、扭转，稍活动头部即感颈背牵拉痛，疼痛可向肩部放射，颈项部肌肉挛缩压痛，存在肌卫现象。

（3）处理

①轻者通过轻度牵引、关节松动及针灸等可缓解肌卫现象，减轻疼痛及缓解痉挛，4～5日即可恢复正常。②严重者可延续至数周不愈。急性期不宜做颈椎牵引和推拿，禁用颈部旋转法或斜扳法。患者佩戴软护颈有一定帮助。③改善患者颈部睡姿可帮助缓解疼痛。随着运动的逐渐恢复，肌卫现象也会随之减轻。

6. 脊髓和神经根损伤

（1）病因

脊髓和神经根损伤指由于各种外力作用于脊柱而造成的脊髓压迫或断裂，易发部位为颈椎中下部和胸腰交界处。脊髓和神经根损伤的病因主要包括以下5种，即裂伤、出血、挫伤、颈髓神经失用症和脊髓休克。

①裂伤：颈椎脱位合并骨折常引起脊髓裂伤。颈椎骨折断端可能会切断或撕裂脊髓或神经根，导致损伤部位以下不同程度的瘫痪。②出血：脊柱骨折、脱位、扭伤和拉伤等通常会引起出血，由于硬膜外肌肉组织和蛛网膜，因为这些结构中血液吸收速度快于积聚速度，所以一般不会受到出血影响。脊髓内出血会导致不可逆的严重损害。③挫伤：颈部受到暴力作用时，颈椎的异常活动会压迫脊髓，引起脊髓内水肿，造成脊髓或神经根不同程度的暂时性或永久性损伤。④颈髓神经失用症：颈髓神经失用症是指颈部受到严重扭转或撞击后使颈椎管变得狭窄，患者会表现出脊髓损伤的症状和体征，如某个身体部位无法活动、出现麻木或刺痛感等。持续一段时间后，除颈部酸痛外，其他症状和体征消失。如出现颈髓神经失用症，需按照严重颈部损伤进行处理。⑤休克：脊髓受到严重创伤（通常为脊髓横断）后会引起脊髓休克，导致损伤平面以下功能丧失。功能丧失表现为四肢无力和深肌腱反射消失。四肢无力会随病程发展为肌肉痉挛，深肌腱反射消失会发展为反射亢进。

（2）症状和体征

不同损伤平面的脊髓损伤临床表现不同，常出现损伤平面以下运动、感觉和括约肌功能障碍，损伤部位疼痛，骨折部位椎体、棘突压痛及局部肿胀等症状。脊髓损伤分为完全性损伤和不完全性损伤。完全性脊髓损伤指损伤平面以下的最低位即骶段感觉、运动功能完全丧失；不完全性脊髓损伤指损伤平面以下仍保留有部分感觉和运动功能。此外，脊髓不完全损伤综合征包括前脊髓综合征、后脊髓综合征、中央脊髓综合征以及脊髓半切综合征。

（3）处理

怀疑脊髓或神经根损伤时，需及时治疗，早期正确治疗关乎患者生命安全及脊髓功能恢复程度。需在专业医疗人员指导下进行处理，以减少发生其他损伤的可能性。

7. 颈椎椎管狭窄

（1）病因

除骨性狭窄外，还包括由于退行性改变出现椎间盘的膨出、骨赘形成、黄韧带松弛和异常椎间活动。

（2）症状和体征

颈椎椎管狭窄症的初期症状为四肢麻木、过敏或疼痛，运动障碍多在感觉障碍之后出现，表现为椎体束征、四肢无力、僵硬不灵活。上述症状一般在 10 ~ 15 分钟内消失。当神经功能恢复后，颈部可能会达到全范围的关节活动。

（3）处理

①由于颈椎狭窄初期症状相对不明显，因此需要谨慎处理。患者必须进行 X 射线、MRI 等诊断性检查以确定损伤程度。②对症状较轻的患者可采用理疗、制动及对症处理。大多数患者的症状可以通过非手术治疗得到缓解。对症状较重者则应尽快进行手术治疗。

8. 臂丛神经失用症

（1）病因

臂丛神经受到过分牵拉或压迫时，会出现暂时性神经失用，这在颈椎神经损伤中较为常见。其通常会造成周围神经功能出现一定程度的损害，但无任何退行性改变。见于强力牵拉上肢、头颈过度向对侧弯曲或强力将肩部下压时使臂丛神经受到牵拉时。此外，当颈部后伸的同时向一侧挤压和旋转时也可能使同侧臂丛神经受到压迫。

（2）症状和体征

臂丛神经损伤因损伤部位和程度不同而症状不同。轻者出现上肢暂时性功能障碍，可伴有上肢刺痛或灼烧感；重者可出现上肢不同程度的肌肉麻痹或无力、运动和感觉功能障碍、反射减弱或消失等症状。若患者主诉疼痛和麻木感向所有手指放射，表明至少累及 C6、C7 和 C8 神经根。如只存在三角肌和肱二头肌无力，表明累及 C5 神经根。

（3）处理

①首先应评估患者受伤情况。轻者可进行观察，待症状缓解可加强颈部肌肉柔韧性和力量性功能训练，并定期复查；重者可采取手术等方式。②橄榄球等项目运动员可佩戴护

颈和护肩以保护臂丛神经。

9. 颈椎间盘损伤

（1）病因

颈椎间盘损伤通常指颈椎间盘，尤其是髓核发生退行性病变，在外力作用下脱出于后方椎管内。常见于因颈部创伤、长期伏案工作等造成的反复的颈椎负荷。

（2）症状和体征

患者主要表现为肩部疼痛以及上肢放射性疼痛，或出现不同程度的运动障碍、感觉障碍。根据颈椎间盘突出的程度与部位，会出现相应的脊髓或神经根压迫症状。

（3）处理

①损伤初期应注意休息，有利于局部炎症及神经根水肿的消退，可配合药物治疗以减轻症状。②大多数患者可通过非手术治疗缓解症状，包括头颈牵引、理疗、中医治疗等方法，严重者则需考虑手术治疗。

（二）胸椎

休门氏症

（1）病因

由于各种原因，骺板血液供应减少，软骨板变薄且抗压力降低，在过多的负荷下出现碎裂髓核在破裂处突入椎体内，脊柱胸段向后弯曲，前方骨骺的坏死影响了前半椎体高度的发育。随着年龄的增加和机体的生长，后半椎体越来越高于前半椎体，椎体形成楔形，数个楔形的椎体使胸椎的后凸加大，形成驼背。目前公认诊断标准为至少 3 个相邻椎体的楔形变均大于 5°。休门氏症多于青少年，常见于体操和游泳项目。

（2）症状和体征

休门氏症典型症状为脊柱后凸畸形，呈匀称的圆背畸形。患者可出现明显的胸背部疼痛，可因站立及激烈的体力活动而加重，生长停止后本病亦停止发展，青春期后期疼痛症状通常可以缓解。此外，休门氏症患者的腘绳肌较为紧张。

（3）处理

①对休门氏病后凸畸形诊断时须确定患者畸形、疼痛的程度。②治疗的目标是预防渐进性驼背，非手术治疗主要采取功能性训练，如腰背部肌力训练、伸展性训练和姿势训练等。③贴扎、理疗、支具和抗炎类药物治疗也有一定疗效。

（三）腰椎

1. 腰椎骨折和脱位

（1）病因

腰椎骨折通常由创伤、骨骼疾病所致，多见于外伤，如高空坠落、车祸等导致的外伤，常见类型有压缩性骨折和横突、棘突骨折。压缩性骨折主要是由于来自头、足方向的暴力传导至脊柱使其骤然过度屈曲而形成，其产生的脊椎碎片会突入骨髓，损伤脊髓或马尾神经。背部受到冲击时易造成横突、棘突骨折，而腰椎脱位较罕见，急性腰部扭伤可以引起腰椎小关节脱位。

（2）症状和体征

损伤表现为腰背部局部疼痛、压痛、叩击痛，椎旁肌紧张，通常伴随局部水肿及肌肉保护性痉挛。

（3）处理

①腰椎骨折时，需用脊柱固定板进行患者的搬运和转移，以限制骨折部位的活动。②经诊断为稳定骨折或无神经损伤者可采取保守治疗如硬板床卧床，并防止卧床期间并发症的发生。

2.腰部肌肉拉伤

（1）病因

腰部肌肉拉伤是腰部肌肉、筋膜、韧带等软组织因外力作用而发生突然的过度牵拉，由于超出正常身体负荷所引起的局部急性损伤。常因为搬重物等原因而导致急性腰部损伤，除此以外，异常姿势也会造成慢性腰部肌肉拉伤。

（2）症状和体征

急性腰部损伤的症状主要是腰痛、腰肌痉挛、腰部活动受限。而慢性腰部劳损由于发病缓慢、病程较长，一般没有明显的急性外伤史，常表现为腰部的酸胀、沉重和活动不便等，休息后可以减轻。

（3）处理

①发生腰部肌肉拉伤后，采用卧床休息来限制腰部的受力，从而缓解疼痛便于损伤肌肉的恢复。②应配合冰敷或冰按摩缓解疼痛和避免瘀血、肿胀的加重，使用弹性绷带等进行加压包扎。③根据个人情况，早期可开展渐进性拉伸和力量练习，侧重于腰部屈肌和伸肌的拉伸以及腰部伸肌的力量训练。

3.肌筋膜疼痛综合征

（1）病因

肌筋膜疼痛综合征是一种常见的与软组织损伤或发育不良有关的局部慢性疼痛综合征，其特征是当按压或触诊某块肌肉的压痛点或扳机点时，会引起另外一个部位的牵涉痛。扳机点是指肌肉紧张带上的压痛点，常见于颈部、上背部和腰部。

（2）症状和体征

患部出现慢性持续性酸胀痛或钝痛，疼痛呈紧束感或重物压迫感，腰、背、骶、臀、腿、膝、足底、颈、肩、肘或腕等部位均可发生。一侧或局部肌肉紧张、痉挛、隆起、挛缩或僵硬，出现小结节和条索状硬物，条索状硬物受刺激时出现颤动，触摸扳机点时出现牵涉痛，肌肉或邻近关节活动受限。触诊腰方肌的扳机点时会引起腰部侧面或腹部侧面锐痛和酸痛。

（3）处理

改善肌筋膜疼痛的重点是通过拉伸和力量练习将肌肉拉伸至其静息长度，以缓解因扳机点造成的疼痛，也可配合以针灸、推拿疗法。

4. 腰部扭伤

（1）病因

弯腰举起或移动重物的同时进行腰部旋转容易引起腰椎小关节面急性扭伤。慢性、反复性腰部扭伤的严重程度会随着体力活动逐渐加重。腰部扭伤常见于青壮年、体力工作者和运动员。

（2）症状和体征

受伤后立即出现腰部疼痛，呈持续性剧痛，次日会因局部出血、肿胀、腰痛更为严重，腰部活动受限，不能挺直。咳嗽、喷嚏、大小便可使疼痛加剧。严重者可出现腰部畸形、肌肉痉挛和局部压痛。

（3）处理

①初期应采取 POLICE 原则缓解疼痛，患者应佩戴护具或支持带以限制活动。关节松动术也可有一定帮助。②应在无痛范围内进行腹部和腰部伸肌的拉伸及力量练习。患者应在运动防护师的指导下进行躯干稳定性练习。③尽量避免出现引起腰部扭伤的动作或姿势。

5. 背部挫伤

（1）病因

大部分背部挫伤由外伤导致。背部挫伤的发生率仅次于拉伤和扭伤。背部受到明显撞击时可产生一定的症状和体征，需与脊柱骨折进行鉴别诊断，必要时可进行 X 射线检查。

（2）症状和体征

受伤后会感到背痛或隐痛，以及会出现局部肿胀、皮下瘀伤、皮肤变色等症状。

（3）处理

①急性期应进行冰敷、加压包扎及休息，可配合外伤膏治疗。②累及深层肌肉时，可进行超声波治疗。

6. 坐骨神经痛

（1）病因

坐骨神经局部及周围结构的病变会形成对坐骨神经的刺激、压迫与损害，从而引起坐骨神经炎症。它通常与以下因素有关：①椎间盘突出压迫外周神经根；②椎间孔内结构不规则；③梨状肌紧张。

（2）症状和体征

患者有疼痛、麻木或灼烧的感觉。疼痛主要限于坐骨神经分布区、大腿后部、小腿后外侧和足部。疼痛剧烈的患者可呈特有的姿势：腰部屈曲、屈膝、脚尖着地。疼痛加重可导致行走困难。

（3）处理

①急性期要注意休息、及时确定和消除病因等。②口服消炎药、腰椎牵引、牵拉梨状肌等可缓解坐骨神经痛，如长时间得不到缓解，可考虑手术治疗。

7. 腰椎间盘突出症

（1）病因

腰椎间盘常因异常的生物力学作用、创伤，或持续、异常的压力作用等造成纤维环的退行性变化、撕裂和破裂。当腰部异常前屈或扭转时，会引起老化的椎间盘突出或膨出，即髓核突入纤维环或完全穿过纤维环。如髓核与椎间盘分离且开始游离，则形成椎间盘突出。其突出的常见原因是反复弯腰扭转、重体力劳动或外伤。

（2）症状和体征

腰椎间盘突出症患者临床常表现为腰痛，且沿皮区向臀部、背部或腿部放射，下肢麻木、无力，可能表现出脊柱侧凸、腰椎活动度减少、肌肉萎缩或肌力下降等症状。患者躯干向前弯曲和坐位时疼痛增加，躯干后伸时疼痛减轻。

（3）处理

①初期应以卧床休息为主，以缓解疼痛为目标，可进行冰敷或电刺激疗法，手法治疗以肌肉松弛类手法为主；应避免腰背部的等张运动训练。②当疼痛缓解和姿势恢复正常后，应及时开始背部伸肌和腹肌的力量练习，改善腰椎稳定性。③避免可能加重症状的体位和姿势；减少腰背受力。

8. 峡部裂和腰椎滑脱症

（1）病因

峡部裂是指腰椎的上下关节突与横突移行区骨质不连续或骨质缺损。峡部裂是脊椎出现退行性改变的一种表现。峡部裂主要为先天性因素造成，发育过程中峡部没有闭合或薄弱，后天性因素中多与外伤及劳损有关，如突然暴力或腰椎反复做震动、后伸等动作，以及腰椎峡部频繁受到应力等，都使峡部裂发生率增加。峡部裂通常为单侧；如向两侧发展，一个椎体可能会在另一个椎体上产生滑动，即椎体滑脱，这是峡部裂的并发症。值得注意的是，峡部裂多发于男性青少年，而腰椎滑脱症多发于女性青少年。

（2）症状和体征

很多峡部裂患者并无症状，仅在 X 射线或 CT 下被发现。峡部裂患者主要表现为腰部疼痛，腰部后伸时症状明显，但进行身体活动过程中无疼痛出现。患者主诉频繁变换姿势以缓解疼痛。少部分患者会出现坐骨神经痛，疼痛向臀部及大腿后侧放射。峡部裂继发椎体滑脱者，腰部疼痛常在行走与站立时发生，卧床休息时缓解，伴有间歇跛行；站立或行走一段时间后出现疼痛、麻木、酸胀、无力等症状，严重时可产生马尾神经损伤。

（3）处理

①患者在腰部疼痛急性期可卧床休息 1 ～ 3 天，并佩戴腰部护具以减轻疼痛。②出现过度活动的椎体部位应进行稳定性或控制性练习，包括渐进性力量练习、核心肌群的动态稳定性练习等。③对体表部位进行电疗、热疗等理疗也可以促进恢复。

（四）骶髂关节功能障碍

1. 骶髂关节扭伤

（1）病因

当姿势不正、肌力失调、韧带松弛时，扭转的外力可使凸凹不平的骶髂关节面排列紊乱，间隙加宽，在关节腔负压的情况下将滑膜吸入关节间隙嵌顿，引起剧烈疼痛。根据扭伤的方向不同可引起骶髂关节前脱位或后脱位。双足着地的同时身体扭转、单足猛烈着地、搬举重物时伸直膝关节向前弯腰、下坡跑、重复的单足活动等都可能会造成骶髂关节扭伤，常见于高尔夫挥杆身体过度扭转、撑杆跳高、跨栏或体操等动作或项目中。

（2）症状和体征

少数患者可无明显外伤史。在急性发作期，腰部一侧可出现疼痛，大多较为严重，疼痛可放射至臀部或腹股沟区。患者常取侧卧位或俯卧位，翻身时疼痛加剧。应避免站立或下肢屈曲姿势。步行时，患侧常呈臀沟下垂状跛行步态。体格检查时，骶髂关节处可有局限性压痛，直腿抬高患侧受限，并有骶部疼痛。运动防护师进行检查时，可发现两侧髂前上棘／髂后上棘不对称，这可能是由于一侧骨盆相对旋前或旋后所致，运动防护师还可能发现两侧下肢不等长。

（3）处理

卧硬板床休息、理疗、局部按摩、膏药外敷及局部封闭等方法可缓解多数症状，可施以关节松动术、力量训练。对同时伴有腰椎或腰骶关节退变或椎间盘突出者，需加以相应处理。

2. 尾骨损伤

（1）病因

尾骨损伤主要由直接撞击引起，如跌倒时臀部后方接触地面、受到暴力等。尾骨损伤包括扭伤、半脱位和骨折。除此之外，长时间保持异常姿势也会引起尾骨慢性劳损及炎症。

（2）症状和体征

损伤表现为患处肿胀和疼痛，在急性期的时候会出现局部渗血以及水肿和疼痛剧烈的症状。如疼痛长期存在，则应进行 X 射线检查和肛门检查。

（3）处理

使用镇痛药和环形坐垫可以减轻坐位时尾骨的压力，同时注意休息，避免久坐。局部可进行适当热敷。按摩和理疗可促进恢复。

Summary

1. Specific training can effectively prevent spinal injury, including paraspinal muscle strengthening training, spinal range of motion training, alignment correction, and core stability training.

2. Special tests for spinal injuries are as follows:

Cervical special tests: Brachial Plexus Test, Cervical Compression and Spurling's Test, Vertebral Artery Test, Shoulder Abduction Test. Lumbar special tests: Tests in the standing position: Flexion, Extension, Lateral Bending, Rotation; Tests in the Seated Position: Flexion, Rotation, Hip Rotation, Slump Test; Tests in the supine position: Straight-Leg Raising Test, Bragard Sign, Kernig Test, Brudzinski Test, FABER and FADIR Tests, Sacroiliac Sway (Knee-Chest) Test, Sacroiliac Distraction Tests, Pelvic Tilt Test; Tests in the prone position: Press-Ups, Reverse Straight-Leg Raising Test, Spring Test, Prone Knee Flexion Test; Tests in the side-lying position: Posterior Rotation Stress Test, Iliotibial Tract Stretching Test, Quadratus Lumborum Stretching Test, Piriformis Muscle Test, Femoral Nerve Stretching Test.

Neurological Test: Sensation test, Reflex test.

3. Cervical injuries are cervical vertebra dislocation caused by falling and collision, muscle strain or ligament tear caused by sudden rotation, forward flexion or backward extension of the head and neck, herniated discs and spinal cord, nerve root injuries. There are also combined injuries to the vertebrae, disc and ligaments.

4. Most injuries of the lumbar spine are fractures and dislocations caused by trauma, skeletal diseases, degenerative changes in annulus fibrosus due to abnormal biomechanics and stress. Intervertebral discs between the 4th and 5th lumbar vertebrae are the most prone to injury, followed by intervertebral discs between the 5th lumbar vertebrae and the 1st sacrum.

⭕ Review Questions:

1. Briefly describe the main methods to prevent spinal injury.

2. Explain what OPQRST stands for in the history examination.

3. Briefly describe the common special tests of cervical spine.

4. Briefly describe the symptoms of spinal cord and nerve root injury.

5. What is a whiplash injury? Try to describe the mechanism of this injury.

小结

1. 进行针对性的训练可以有效地预防脊柱损伤，包括：脊柱周围肌肉力量训练、脊柱关节活动度训练、纠正身体力线异常、核心稳定性训练。

2. 脊柱损伤的特殊试验如下：

颈椎特殊试验：臂丛神经试验、颈椎挤压试验和椎间孔挤压试验、椎动脉试验、肩外展试验。

腰椎特殊试验：站立位腰椎特殊试验有前屈、后伸、侧屈、旋转；坐位腰椎特殊试验有前屈、旋转、髋关节旋转、Slump 试验；仰卧位特殊试验有直腿抬高试验及直腿抬高加强试验、Kernig 试验、Brudzinski 试验、屈曲外展外旋和屈曲内收内旋试验、骶髂摇摆（膝－胸）试验、骶髂关节分离试验、骨盆倾斜试验；俯卧位腰椎特殊试验有俯卧撑、反向直腿抬高试验、Spring 试验、俯卧屈膝试验；侧卧位腰椎特殊试验有后旋压力试验、髂胫束拉伸试验、腰方肌拉伸试验、梨状肌试验、股神经牵拉试验、骶髂关节挤压试验。

神经检查：感觉检查、反射检查。

3. 颈椎损伤多为跌落、碰撞导致的颈椎脱位，头颈部突然旋转、前屈、后伸导致的肌肉拉伤或韧带撕裂，椎间盘突出以及脊髓、神经根损伤，也存在椎体、椎间盘和韧带的联合损伤。

4. 腰椎损伤多为创伤、骨骼疾病所致的骨折及脱位，以及异常生物力学及压力等作用造成的纤维环退行性变化。其中，第 4 和 5 腰椎间的椎间盘最容易出现损伤，其次是第 5 腰椎和第 1 骶椎间的椎间盘。

○ 复习题

1. 简述预防脊柱损伤的主要手段。
2. 简述病史检查时 OPQRST 所代表的含义。
3. 简述颈椎特殊试验的常用方法。
4. 简述脊髓和神经根损伤症状。
5. 何为挥鞭伤？试述其损伤机制。

Chapter 2 Shoulder Injuries
第二章　肩部损伤

○ **Main Contents**

1. Prevention of shoulder injuries.
2. Assessment of shoulder injuries.
3. Identification and management of common shoulder injuries.

○ **主要内容**

1. 肩部损伤的预防。
2. 肩部损伤的评估。
3. 肩部常见损伤的识别和处理。

1 Prevention of Shoulder Injuries

1.1 Identify Risk Factors for Injury

Glenohumeral internal-rotation deficit, rotator cuff strength deficit or imbalance, and scapular dyskinesis are possible risk factors in overhead athletes. Posterior shoulder stiffness is not the most common, but this is a risk factor for shoulder impingement and labral pathology. Additionally, functional deficiencies such as incorrect biomechanics and throwing fatigue may also be risk factors.

Take the rotator cuff muscle strength as an example. Overhead athletes often exhibit sport-specific adaptation, which results in a relative decrease in the strength of the external rotators, further resulting in rotator cuff muscle imbalance. Research has found that in individuals with shoulder injuries, the isometric, eccentric, and isokinetic strength of the external rotation muscles all decrease.

1.2 Utilize Measurements with Good Reliability and Validity

Therapists need to use objective and valid assessment tools. A goniometer or inclinometer can be applied to measure the rotation ROM of the shoulder. The position of the scapula during the measurement process is important, and research recommends using the patient's supine position to abduct the shoulder joint and bend the elbow joint 90 °. The joint range of motion of horizontal adduction reflects stiffness behind the shoulder joint, and research suggests measuring horizontal adduction at 90 ° forward flexion of the shoulder joint.

Numerous testing protocols have been described to examine isokinetic and isometric rotator cuff strength. Isokinetic strength measurement is the "golden standard" for testing muscle strength, but it is too expensive and not practical for clinical use. For the isometric strength measurements, hand-held dynamometry (HHD) is a reliable and valid tool.

1.3 Modify Risk Factors by Preventive Training

If any deficits are assessed, there is a need for science-based training programs to restore normal values. Various exercises have been described to strengthen the rotator cuff muscles, including concentric, eccentric, isometric, and plyometric exercises. When training external rotation muscle strength, attention should be paid to emphasizing the training in the eccentric stage and avoiding the training in the concentric stage to better increase eccentric strength. Slow exercises should be performed to increase maximum strength, while fast exercises should be performed to increase muscle endurance and plyometric ability. If scapular dyskinesis exists, restoring muscle extension and improving muscle performance is necessary. The main goals for patients with scapular dyskinesis are: ① to restore the flexibility of the surrounding soft tissue of the scapula, in particular, pectoralis minor, levator scapulae, rhomboid, and posterior shoulder structures; ② to increase scapular muscle performance around the scapula, focusing on either muscle control and intermuscular coordination or muscle strength and balance.

In summary, in order to prevent shoulder injuries and return to exercise after injury, the athletic trainer should evaluate the potential risk factors for shoulder injuries in patients, especially the ROM of internal rotation of the shoulder joint, rotator cuff muscle strength, and scapular movement performance. If abnormalities are found, intervention should focus on improving the shoulder joint's range of motion, strengthening the rotator cuff's strength, and restoring the extensibility and muscle balance of the scapula muscle.

一、肩部损伤的预防

（一）识别损伤风险因素

过顶项目运动员中盂肱关节内旋活动度不足，肩袖肌肉力量不足或不平衡，以及肩胛骨动力障碍可能是肩部损伤的风险因素。肩关节后方僵硬并不是最常见的，但这却是肩峰下撞击和盂唇病变的风险因素。此外，功能的缺陷（如，错误的生物力学和投掷疲劳）可能是损伤的风险因素。

以肩袖肌肉力量为例，过顶项目运动员通常会表现出对运动专项的适应，出现外旋肌肉力量相对下降，造成了肩袖肌肉力量不平衡。研究发现在肩部损伤人群中外旋肌肉的等长、离心和等速力量均下降。

（二）使用具备良好信度和效度的测量工具

运动防护师需要使用客观有效的测量工具进行评估。肩关节旋转活动度的测量可以使用关节活动度尺或倾斜仪。测量过程中肩胛骨的位置很重要，研究推荐使用患者仰卧位肩关节外展、肘关节屈曲 90°。水平内收的关节活动度反映了肩关节后方僵硬，研究建议在肩关节前屈 90° 测量水平内收。

很多测试方法可以用于评价肩袖肌肉的等速和等长力量。肌肉力量测试的“金标准”是等速测试，但这种测试昂贵，在临床中使用并不现实。对于等长力量，手持测力计已经被证明有很好的信度和效度。

（三）预防性的训练改善风险因素

通过评估如果发现患者肩关节有任何缺陷，需要有科学的训练方案帮助其恢复到正常范围。肩袖肌肉力量的练习有很多方法，包括向心、离心、等长和超等长练习。在外旋肌肉力量训练时，应注意强调离心阶段的训练，避免向心阶段的练习，从而更好地增加离心力量。增加最大力量应进行慢速练习，增加肌肉耐力和超等长能力应进行快速练习。如果存在肩胛骨动力障碍，需要恢复肌肉的延展性和改善肌肉的表现。主要的目标是：①恢复肩胛骨周围软组织的延展性，特别是胸小肌、肩胛提肌、菱形肌和肩关节后方的组织；②增加肩胛周围肌肉力量，关注肌肉控制和肌肉之间的协调。

　　总之，为了做好肩部损伤的预防以及损伤后能重返运动，运动防护师应该评估患者肩部损伤的潜在风险因素，特别是肩关节内旋活动度、肩袖肌肉力量和肩胛骨的运动表现。若发现异常，干预应着重于改善肩关节活动度，加强肩袖肌力，恢复肩胛肌的延展性和肌肉平衡。

2 Assessment of Shoulder Injuries

2.1 History

The athletic trainer should ask the following questions:

● Patient's occupation. Jobs with repetitive arm movements and prolonged abduction may be related to injuries.

● The onset of pain, its location, nature, severity, duration, and aggravating and relieving factors.

● Is there referred pain? The referred pain area caused by rotator cuff muscle group or subacromial pathology is on the lateral side of the upper limb. The internal pathology of the glenohumeral joint involves the posterior of the shoulder joint. Referred pain in acromioclavicular joint lesions is usually medial to the scapula, neck, or medial to the clavicle.

● Whether the pain is constant or night pain? This indicates the presence of inflammation.

● Is there pain in other joints? This suggests the possibility of osteoarthritis or other systemic inflammations such as rheumatoid arthritis.

● Does the patient have other medical and medication history, such as lung or breast cancer?

● Does the patient receive any therapy before or at present? Does the therapy reduce pain?

2.2 Observation

Observe the entire shoulder girdle and compare it with the contralateral side during walking and standing. The examiner observes in front of, on the side of, and behind the patient, identifying any asymmetrical postures, swelling, bony/joint deformity, muscle atrophy, cramp, or protection reflexion during this process.

2.3 Palpation

Bony and soft-tissue marks are the main parts of palpation. Focal tenderness can identify areas of trauma. In the case of trauma, bone fricative indicates fracture.

2.4 Range of Motion

Glenohumeral range of motion should be evaluated in every patient with shoulder complaints. This should always be compared with the contralateral side because the shoulder range of motion can vary widely in individuals. Evaluation of both the active and passive range of motion of the shoulder will help rule out certain diagnoses. For example, a decrease in active and passive range of motion indicates adhesive osteoarthritis or glenoid humeral joint osteoarthritis; If the active range of motion decreases, but the passive one is normal, it indicates rotator cuff muscle injury or shoulder joint impingement. For patients with persistent pain, it is helpful to assess the range of motion in the supine position.

2.5 Muscle Strength

It is important to evaluate the muscle strength of the rotator cuff in patients with shoulder pathology. Ideally, check the muscle strength of both upper limbs and compare it with the injured side.

- The main function of the deltoid muscle is abduction; therefore, testing abduction resistance is performed at positions where shoulder abduction exceeds 15 °.
- Muscle strength testing of internal (subscapularis) and external rotation (infraspinatus) should be performed with the arm at the side in neutral position and the elbow flexed to 90°.
- Supraspinatus muscle strength can be tested using the Jobe test. The Jobe supraspinatus test is performed with the shoulder in 90° flexion in the scapular plane (scaption) with the elbow extended, and the examiner applies resistance to the patient's forearm. This test can be conducted simultaneously on both sides to compare the muscle strength of the injured side and the opposite side. The decrease in muscle strength indicates the presence of rotator cuff muscle tears or tendon lesions.
- The Speed test and Yergason test can be used to examine the biceps brachii, and if there is pain, it is considered positive.
- Evaluation of the pectoralis major should be part of any routine shoulder exam. Beyond a visual exam evaluating for the complete tear of the tendon, the patient's arm and elbow should be flexed to 90°, shoulder externally rotated, and then the patient should perform adductive resistance. If there is pain in the chest or in the tendon insertion of the proximal humerus, the test result is positive.

2.6 Special Tests

2.6.1 Acromioclavicular Joint

(1) O'Brien Test

The patient is in a relaxed sitting position, with the lateral shoulder joint flexed 90° and horizontally adducted 10°. The elbow joint is extended, the shoulder joint is rotated internally, and the forearm is rotated forward with the thumb pointing toward the ground. The examiner applies downward resistance at the distal end of the forearm, and the patient resists upward. Perform the same experiment when the shoulder joint is rotated outward with the palm facing upwards. It indicates acromioclavicular joint injuries if the pain is exacerbated during internal rotation and reduced during external rotation.

(2) Paxinos Test

The patient sits with their upper limbs relaxed to the side of their body. The examiner's thumb is placed below the outer side of the acromion, and the index and middle fingers are placed at the midpoint of the clavicle. During the examination, the examiner applies a forward and upward force to the acromion with the thumb and applies a downward force at the midpoint of the clavicle with the index and middle fingers. If the patient experiences pain, it indicates lesions in the acromioclavicular joint.

(3) Acromioclavicular Resisted Extension Test

The patient's arm and elbow are flexed at 90° while the shoulder is internally rotated to ensure that the forearm is parallel to the ground. The patient is then asked to horizontally abduct the arm against resistance. The test is positive if pain is present in the AC joint.

2.6.2 Rotator Cuff Tendinopathy or Tear

(1) Lift-Off Test

The patient's arm is fully internally rotated with the hand on the back. The patient is then asked to lift the wrist off the back. If the patient cannot lift the wrist off the back using the shoulder for rotation, the lift-off test is considered positive. The test is used to evaluate complete subscapularis muscle rupture but is less meaningful for partial rupture.

(2) Belly Press Test

With the patient's hand on the abdomen and the elbow just anterior to the plane of the body, the patient is then asked to press on the abdomen. If the shoulder is painful or has decreased strength compared to the opposite side, the test is positive, indicating subscapularis injuries.

(3) Bear Hug Test

The bear hug test is performed with the patient's affected open palm on the opposite superior shoulder, with the affected shoulder flexed to 90°. The patient's affected forearm resists external rotation resistance. Decreased muscle strength compared to the contralateral side indicates subscapular injuries.

(4) Empty Can Test

The patient's arm to be tested is moved into 90° of abduction in the plane of the scapula. The examiner's hands apply downward pressure on the superior aspect of the distal forearm and the patient resists. Pain indicates positive test results, which means supraspinatus injuries are possible.

(5) Drop Arm Test

The examiner stands behind the patient and supports the elbow joint to make the shoulder joint abduct 90°. Release the upper limb to let the patient's upper limb fall slowly. This test is positive if the patient's upper limbs cannot fall smoothly and controlled. This experiment is not specifically aimed at supraspinatus muscle injury but can identify rotator cuff lesions.

(6) Lag Test

The patient's shoulder is abducted at 20° and the elbow flexed at 90°. The forearm is passively externally rotated to its maximum extent and released. If the patient cannot maintain the maximum external rotation position, this test is positive, indicating a lesion in the infraspinatus muscle. This test relies on the normal range of joint motion, and if the patient has adhesive bursitis or the overall joint range of motion decreases, the test results will be affected.

(7) Hornblower Test

The patient's arm is passively abducted and externally rotated at 90°. The inability to maintain this position is a positive sign, suggesting posterior cuff and teres minor pathology. Pain with resistance at this position may indicate the teres minor muscle tendon lesion or partial tear.

2.6.3 Biceps Pathology

(1) Palpation of the Long Head of the Biceps Tendon

This test is performed by palpating the biceps tendon in the intertubercular sulcus just below the anterior acromion with the arm in 10° internal rotation. If the tenderness point moves with the full range of motion of internal and external rotation of the shoulder, the test is positive.

(2) Speed Test

With the patient's shoulder flexed at 90°, elbows extended, and forearm supinated, a downward force is applied to the arms by the examiner. Pain along the biceps tendon or within the intertubercular sulcus indicates biceps disease or upper labrum injury.

(3) Yergason's Test

The patient should sit or stand in the anatomical position, with the humerus in a neutral position, the elbow joint flexed 90°, and the forearm rotated forward. The examiner uses a wristband to apply resistance around the distal end of the forearm (above the wrist joint), requiring the patient's shoulder joint to rotate outward and the arm to rotate backward. If there is pain in the intertubercular sulcus, the test is considered positive and suspicion of biceps tendinitis or upper labrum injury.

2.6.4 Thoracic Outlet Syndromes

(1) Adson Test

This test aims to determine whether the subclavian artery is compressed when entering the channel between the anterior and middle scalenus muscles. The test can be performed with the patient in either a sitting or standing position with the elbow in full extension. The examiner palpates the radial pulse, making the patient's arm relaxed and extended, while the patient then elevates the chin, turns the face toward the extended hand, takes a deep breath, and holds it. If the pulse is depressed or stopped completely in the testing position, the result of the test is considered to be positive.

(2) Allen Test

The purpose of this experiment is to determine the compression of the subclavian artery, axillary artery, and brachial plexus nerve when passing through the pectoralis minor muscle and below the coracoid process. The patient relaxes the sitting position, abducts the upper limb shoulder joint by 90 °, and rotates outward to the maximum angle, and flexes the elbow joint by 90 °. Palpation of the radial artery during shoulder level extension and external rotation. Ask the patient to turn their head in the opposite direction of extending their hand. The test is considered positive if the radial pulse becomes diminished or absent after rotation of the head.

(3) The Military Brace Position Test

This experiment aims to determine the compression of the subclavian artery under the clavicle. The patient is standing with their shoulders contracted back in a military posture. The arm is abducted to 30° and extended, and the head is turned to the opposite shoulder. If the pulse decreases or completely stops in this position, the test is positive.

(4) Roos Test

The patient is in a sitting position, and both arms are abducted to 90° and externally rotated. The patient opens and closes the hands slowly for a 3-minute period. If the strength in the hands or sensation in the upper extremity decreases, the result of the test is considered to be positive.

2.6.5 Labral Pathology

(1) O'Brien Test

This test is performed as described earlier for the AC joint, but if the pain occurs deep inside the shoulder joint instead of at the AC joint, and there is pain in the internal rotation position and relief in the external rotation position, this is a positive test for labral pathology.

(2) Crank Test

The patient can be in a sitting, standing, or supine position. The examiner flexes the patient's elbow to 90° and elevates the patient's arm to approximately 160° in the scapular plane. In this position, the examiner applies a gentle compressive force on the glenohumeral joint along the axis of the humerus while simultaneously moving the humerus into internal and external rotation. The test is considered positive if pain is present.

(3) Anterior Slide Test

The test is performed with the patient in a sitting position with the hand resting on the hip with the thumb facing posteriorly. The examiner puts one hand on the top of the patient's shoulder, stabilizing the scapula, acromion, and clavicle. The examiner cups the other hand on the elbow/distal aspect of the humerus and exerts a superior and anterior force along the line of the humerus. The test is considered positive if the patient feels any pain.

(4) Biceps Load I Test

With the patient in the supine position, the examiner grasps the patient's wrist and elbow to abduct the arm to 90° and flex the elbow joint to 90 °with the forearm supinated. The examiner externally rotates the arm until any apprehension is felt or the patient attempts to flex the elbow. The test is positive if the apprehension remains or the pain is exacerbated during resistive flexion of the elbow.

(5) Biceps Load II Test

While the patient is in the supine position, the examiner places the patient's shoulder in 120° of abduction, the elbow in 90° of flexion, and the forearm in supination, and then externally rotates the shoulder. The test is positive if any pain is felt during resistive flexion of the elbow.

(6) Modified Dynamic Labral Shear

The examiner flexes the patient's elbow joint to 90°, abducts the shoulder joint to 120°, rotates outward to the maximum angle, and horizontally abducts the arm to the maximum angle. While maintaining maximum horizontal abduction and external rotation, the examiner lowers the patient's arm from abduction 120° to abduction 60°. A positive test occurs with pain along the posterior joint line between 120° and 90° of abduction.

(7) Labral Tension

The patient is in a supine position, with the examiner abducting their upper limbs to 120°, the forearm in a neutral position, and the shoulder joint in maximum external rotation. The examiner holds the patient's hand, and the patient's forearm resists a supinate resistance. If there is pain, it is considered positive.

(8) Resisted Supination External Rotation

The patient is lying supine on a therapeutic bed with the scapula near the edge of the bed. While the examiner supports the affected arm at the elbow and hand, the arm is placed into 90° of abduction, 70° of flexion, and the forearm in neutral position. As the shoulder is externally rotated, the patient supinates the hand against resistance with a positive test resulting from pain in the shoulder. This test can be used to distinguish the pain from apprehension or anterior instability of the shoulder.

2.6.6 Shoulder Instability

(1) Beighton Score

The components of this test include passive flexion of the small fingers beyond 90°, passive apposition of the thumbs to the volar forearm, hyperextension of the elbows greater than 10°, hyperextension of the knees beyond 10°, for the above four items, one point for single side, two points for double side. Touching the palms of the hand on the floor while flexing forward with the trunk and keeping the knees extended scores one point. The total score is nine points. At present, the threshold for diagnosing ligament laxity is different, and it is generally believed that 4-6 points indicate excessive ligament laxity.

(2) Anterior/Posterior Instability

The patient is in a supine position, and the examiner passively moves the elbow joint to 90 ° flexion and the shoulder joint to 90 ° abduction. The examiner slowly applies external rotation force to the upper limb to the maximum external rotation position of the shoulder joint while applying forward force behind the humeral head. If the patient shows fear of the test but no pain, the test is positive, indicating instability in the front of the shoulder joint. If the patient shows pain but no fear, it suggests the presence of pathological changes, such as rotator cuff impingement, rather than instability.

(3) Jobe Relocation

If the patient experiences apprehension with the anterior apprehension test, and applying a posteriorly directed force to the humeral head with the arm still in maximal abduction and external rotation will lead to relief of the patient's apprehension, it will be a positive finding for anterior instability.

(4) Anterior Drawers

The patient is in a supine position with the injured shoulder joint above the edge of the therapeutic bed. The patient's shoulder joint is completely relaxed, with the upper limb abduction reaching 80° to 120°, flexion 0° to 20°, and external rotation 0° to 30°. Place the hand on the fixed side at the scapula to ensure that the thumb and four fingers are placed on the coracoid process and scapular spine. The examiner applies a sliding force on the glenoid humeral joint by pulling the patient's upper limb forward with the other hand. The movement of the shoulder joint can be compared with that of the opposite side. If the sliding exceeds the glenoid lip or there is any fear, it indicates instability in the front of the shoulder joint.

(5) Load and Shift

With the patient supine, the humeral head is loaded in 20 degrees of abduction and flexion, to align it congruently within the glenoid fossa. The examiner places one hand on the shoulder joint and scapula to stabilize the shoulder girdle while applying a load in the anteroposterior direction to the humeral head with the other hand, paying attention to the translation distance.

If there is a significant displacement compared to the opposite side, it indicates instability in the anterior aspect of the shoulder joint.

(6) Jerk Test

With the patient sitting, the examiner holds the patient's scapula with one hand while abducting the patient's arm to 90° and internally rotating it by 90°. The other hand applies load axially at the patient's elbow while applying force in the horizontal adduction direction. Sharp pain with or without a clunk is considered positive for posterior instability.

(7) Kim Test

The patient sits in a chair with the arm abducted at 90°. The examiner holds the patient's elbow joint and lateral part of the upper arm, applies axial force, and abducts the patient obliquely upward at 45°, while pushing the upper arm inferiorly and posteriorly. Pain in the posterior shoulder with or without a clunk is a positive sign of tears of the posteroinferior labrum.

(8) Sulcus Test

The patient is in the seated position with the arm to be tested relaxed. One of the examiner's hands stabilizes the shoulder girdle on the side to be tested. Then, the examiner grasps the elbow and applies traction in an inferior direction. If there is instability, pain, or a gap between the lateral acromion and humeral head during the test, the test is positive. Type one sulcus is less than 1 cm, type two is 1–2 cm, and type three is more than 2 cm. In addition, if the Sulcus test is positive at 30 ° abduction, it indicates pathological relaxation of the rotator cuff muscles septum.

(9) Gagey Test

The examiner presses a forearm onto the patient's shoulder strap to fix it, and uses the other hand to abduct the patient's shoulder joint, maintaining a 90 ° flexion of the elbow joint. Abduction exceeding 105° is considered a positive finding for the laxity of the inferior glenohumeral ligament.

2.6.7 Scapular Dyskinesis

(1)Lateral Scapular Slide Test(LSST)

The patient should be evaluated in three different positions, including with the upper limbs hanging by the sides of the body, with the thumbs placed on the bilateral iliac crests, and with the shoulder joints rotated internally and abducted to 90 degrees. The examiner measures the distance between the bilateral subscapular angles and the corresponding height spinous processes in each position, calculates the difference in bilateral distance, and takes the absolute value. If the absolute value of the difference in distance between the two sides is bigger than 1.5 centimeters, the test is positive, indicating the presence of scapular dyskinesis.

(2)Scapular Assistance Test (SAT)

When the patient engages in abduction activities, the examiner fixes the subject's superior scapular angle with one hand and pushes the inferior scapular angle with the other hand to assist in the upward rotation of the scapula, while observing and inquiring about the patient's response. If, compared to without assistance, the patient's pain is relieved after the examiner assists in scapular rotation, this test is judged to be positive.

(3)Scapular Retraction Test (SRT)

The test is performed based on a positive result in the empty can test. The examiner applies moderate force to the inside edge of the patient's scapula with their hand and forearm, helping the patient to retract and tilt the scapula posteriorly. With the examiner's assistance, the patient consciously retracts the scapula and performs the empty can test again. If the patient's supraspinatus muscle strength increases or pain symptoms decrease during shoulder abduction with the help of the examiner, the test is considered to be positive.

2.6.8 Shoulder Impingement

(1) Neer's Test

The examiner should stabilize the patient's scapula with one hand, while the patient's upper limb is passively flexed under internal rotation. This test is positive if the patient experiences pain in the front or outside of the shoulder joint during the examination.

(2) Hawkins Kennedy Test

The examiner places the patient's arm in the test position with the shoulder joint flexed at 90° and the elbow joint flexed at 90°. Then, the patient passively moves the shoulder joint to the end of the internal rotation. If the patient reports pain, the result of the test is considered to be positive.

(3) Posterior Impingement Test

The patient is in a supine position, with the shoulder joint extended to 90°~110° and the elbow joint slightly extended. The examiner rotates the shoulder joint to maximal external rotation. The deep pain behind the shoulder joint indicates a positive test. This test has shown good sensitivity (95%) and specificity (100%) in patients with partial rotator cuff tears or partial rotator cuff tears in non-contact injury.

(4) Jobe Relocation Test

This test has been discussed in the unstable part of the shoulder joint. Research has found that this experiment can also be used to inspect internal impingement. However, unlike instability in the front of the shoulder joint, applying a posteriorly directed force can cause pain, but applying an anteriorly directed force can alleviate it.

Early literature described impingement as a pathology or a diagnosis, but today, impingement is considered to be a cluster of symptoms, rather than a pathology itself. Numerous studies have demonstrated the relationship between impingement syndrome and various potential pathological mechanisms, indicating that impingement syndrome is caused by rotator cuff pathology, scapular dyskinesis, shoulder instability, biceps pathology, SLAP lesions, and glenohumeral internal rotation deficit. Therefore, athletic trainers should identify specific impingement signs and infer potential pathological mechanisms. Research has proposed a clinical reasoning method for shoulder pain examination related to impact signs, and the special tests involved in this method have been introduced in this section.

There are many different pathologies in and around the glenohumeral joint that can cause a patient to have shoulder pain. Each test described does not need to be performed on every patient, but a therapist should possess an in-depth understanding of the physical examination of the shoulder. This section has already introduced the examination of common shoulder joint injuries in clinical practice, helping exercise protectors make the most accurate diagnosis in a limited time. An appropriate shoulder examination helps the therapist focus on further diagnostic strategies and treatment options.

二、肩部损伤的评估

（一）病史

运动防护师应询问以下问题：

● 患者的职业。这可能与损伤相关，尤其是涉及重复上肢运动和长时间外展的工作。

● 疼痛什么时候出现，疼痛的位置、性质、严重程度、持续的时间，以及加重和缓解的因素。

● 是否存在牵涉痛？肩袖肌群或肩峰下的病变引起的牵涉痛区域在上肢外侧；盂肱关节内部的病变牵涉至肩关节后方；肩锁关节病变的牵涉痛通常在肩胛骨内侧、颈部或锁骨内侧。

● 疼痛是否持续存在？是否存在夜间痛？这提示存在炎症。

● 其他关节是否存在疼痛？这提示可能存在骨关节炎或其他系统炎症，如类风湿关节炎。

● 是否有其他病史和用药史，如肺癌或乳腺癌。

● 目前或之前是否接受过其他治疗？治疗能否缓解疼痛？

（二）视诊

在患者站立位和步行时进行整体的观察，并与对侧做对比。检查者分别在患者前方、侧方和后方进行观察，在这个过程中识别任何不对称的姿势、肿胀、骨或关节畸形、肌肉萎缩、痉挛程度或保护反射等。

（三）触诊

触诊主要检查肩部骨性和软组织标志。局部压痛可以确定损伤区域。若患者存在创伤史，则必须要识别摩擦音，这可能提示存在骨折。

（四）关节活动度

每一个存在肩部不适的患者都必须进行盂肱关节活动度的检查。由于每个人的关节活动度有很大的差别，因此检查结果应与对侧进行对比。评价主动和被动的关节活动度有助于排除某些疾病。比如，主动和被动活动度下降提示粘连性关节囊炎或盂肱关节骨关节炎；若主动关节活动下降但被动关节正常，则提示肩袖肌肉损伤或肩关节撞击。对于存在持续性疼痛的患者，关节活动度的评估可以在仰卧位进行。

（五）肌肉力量

存在肩关节病变的患者需要进行肩袖肌肉力量的评估，理想情况下检查双侧上肢肌力并与损伤侧进行对比。

- 三角肌主要功能是外展，因此测试在肩关节外展超过 15° 的位置进行的外展抗阻。
- 内旋肌（肩胛下肌）和外旋肌（冈下肌）力量测试在上肢中立位肘关节屈曲 90° 下进行。
- 冈上肌肌肉力量可以采取 Jobe 测试，在肩胛平面肩关节屈曲 90° 肘关节伸展的体位下进行，检查者在患者前臂施加阻力。此测试可以双侧同时进行，比较损伤侧与对侧的肌肉力量；肌肉力量的下降提示存在肩袖肌肉撕裂或肌腱病变。
- 肱二头肌检查可以通过 Speed 试验和 Yergason 试验，若出现疼痛则为阳性。
- 胸大肌的检查也是肩关节常规检查的一部分。除了视诊评价肌腱完全断裂，还需要在患者上肢和肘关节屈曲 90° 且肩关节外旋位进行检查。检查者要求患者内收抗阻，若前胸疼痛不适或沿肱骨近端肌腱止点疼痛则为阳性。

（六）特殊试验

1. 肩锁关节

（1）O'Brien 试验

患者处于放松坐位，测试侧肩关节屈曲 90°，水平内收 10°，（肘关节伸直），肩关节内旋，前臂旋前将拇指指向地面。检查者在前臂远端施加向下的阻力并且患者向上对抗。在肩关节外旋手掌向上时进行相同的试验。如果内旋肩锁疼痛加重、外旋减轻，提示肩锁关节病理改变。

（2）Paxinos 试验

患者坐位，上肢放松于身体侧方。检查者拇指放于肩峰后外侧的下方，食指和中指放于锁骨中点处。检查时用拇指对肩峰施加向前上方的力，用食指和中指在锁骨中点处施加向下的力。患者出现疼痛，提示肩锁关节病变。

（3）肩锁关节抗阻伸展试验

患者上肢和肘关节屈曲 90°，同时肩关节内旋，保证前臂与地面平行。患者水平外展抗阻，如果肩锁关节存在疼痛，则为阳性。

2. 肩袖肌群病变或撕裂

（1）抬离试验

患者肩关节充分内旋使手放于背部，要求患者腕部抬离背部；如果患者不能通过肩关节旋转使腕部抬离背部则为阳性。该试验用于评价肩胛下肌完全断裂，但对于部分断裂的诊断意义较低。

（2）压腹试验

患者手放于腹部，肘关节在身体平面前方，要求患者手压腹部。如果引起肩部疼痛或相比于对侧肌力下降，则该试验为阳性，提示肩胛下肌病变。

（3）熊抱试验

患者将损伤一侧手掌放于对侧肩上部，损伤侧肩关节屈曲90°。要求患者用该前臂抵抗检查者施加的外旋阻力，与对侧相比存在肌力下降则提示肩胛下肌病变。

（4）空罐试验

患者上肢在肩胛骨平面外展90°，检查者在患者前臂远端施加压力，患者进行抵抗。如果患者在检查中出现疼痛，则此试验为阳性，提示冈上肌病变。

（5）落臂试验

检查者站于患者后方，支撑患者肘关节以使其肩关节外展90°。释放上肢让患者的上肢缓慢落下。如果患者上肢不能平滑、有控制地落下，此试验为阳性。此试验不单独针对冈上肌损伤，但可以识别肩袖病变。

（6）滞后试验

患者肩关节外展20°，肘关节屈曲90°。前臂被动外旋至最大然后释放。若患者不能维持最大外旋位则此试验阳性，提示冈下肌病变。此测试依赖于正常的关节活动范围，如果患者存在粘连性滑囊炎或整体关节活动度下降，试验结果将会受到影响。

（7）霍恩布洛尔试验

患者肩部被动外展外旋至90°：若患者无法维持此位置则该试验为阳性，提示肩袖后部和小圆肌病变；若在此位置抗阻时出现疼痛，则提示小圆肌肌腱病变或部分撕裂。

3. 肱二头肌病变

（1）肱二头肌长头腱触诊

患者肩关节内旋10°，触诊肩峰前方结节间沟中的肱二头肌肌腱。压痛点随着肩关节全范围的内旋和外旋移动，则该试验为阳性。

（2）Speed 试验

患者肩关节屈曲90°，肘关节伸展，前臂旋后，检查者在前臂施加向下的力，若二头肌肌腱或结节间沟存在疼痛，该测试为阳性，提示肱二头肌病变或上盂唇损伤。

（3）Yergason 试验

患者应按解剖位坐或站，肱骨为中立位，肘关节屈曲90°，前臂旋前位。检查者用手环绕前臂远端（手腕关节上方）施加阻力，要求患者肩关节向外旋转、手臂旋后。若结节间沟处出现疼痛，则试验被认为是阳性，怀疑有肱二头肌肌腱炎或上盂唇损伤。

4.胸廓出口综合征

（1）Adson 试验

本试验的目的是确定锁骨下动脉是否在进入前、中斜角肌之间的通道时被挤压。患者采取坐位或站立位，肘关节伸展。检查者触诊桡动脉，使前臂放松然后后伸，患者抬起下颌，将头转向伸出手的一边，深吸一口气，屏住呼吸。如果在这个姿势下脉搏降低或完全停止，则该测试为阳性。

（2）Allen 试验

本试验的目的是确定锁骨下动脉、腋动脉和臂丛神经穿过胸小肌和喙突下方时受压。患者放松坐位，上肢肩关节外展 90°并外旋至最大角度，肘关节屈曲 90°。肩部水平后伸外旋时触诊桡动脉。要求患者将头转向手伸出的相反方向。如果在这个姿势下脉搏降低或完全停止，则该测试为阳性。

（3）军姿姿势试验

本试验的目的是确定锁骨下动脉在锁骨下受压。患者站立位，肩部向后收缩像军姿姿势，上肢外展 30°并后伸，头转向对侧肩关节。如果在这个姿势下脉搏降低或完全停止，该测试为阳性。

（4）Roos 试验

患者坐位，双上肢外旋并且外展 90°。患者交替张开和握紧手指 3 分钟。手的力量下降或上肢感觉丧失，则该试验为阳性。

5.盂唇病变

（1）O'Brien 试验

此试验已经在肩锁关节病变部分讨论过，但如果疼痛在肩关节内而不是在肩锁关节且位置较深，并且内旋位出现疼痛而外旋位缓解，则该试验为阳性，提示盂唇病变。

（2）曲柄试验

此试验一般在坐位进行，也可以在站立位或仰卧位进行。检查者屈曲患者肘关节至90°，在肩胛平面外展上肢大约至 160°。在这个体位下，检查者沿肱骨长轴施加一个力挤压盂肱关节，同时移动肱骨使之内外旋。若患者出现疼痛则提示该测试为阳性。

（3）前向滑动试验

患者坐位，手放于髋部，拇指向后。检查者一只手放于患者肩部后方，固定肩胛骨、肩峰和锁骨；另一只手放于患者肘关节或肱骨远端，沿肱骨长轴施加向前上方的力。如果患者感到疼痛，则认为该试验是阳性。

（4）肱二头肌载荷 I 试验

患者仰卧位，检查者握住患者腕和肘部，肩关节外展至 90°，肘关节屈曲 90°，前臂旋后；检查者外旋肩关节直到患者出现任何恐惧或试图屈曲肘关节时停止。若肘关节屈曲抗阻时，恐惧没有改变或疼痛加重，则该试验为阳性。

（5）肱二头肌载荷 II 试验

患者仰卧，检查者握住患者腕和肘部，肩关节外展至 120°，肘关节屈曲 90°，前臂旋后，肩关节外旋。患者肘关节屈曲抗阻出现疼痛，则该试验为阳性。

（6）改良动态盂唇剪切试验

检查者屈曲患者肘关节至 90°，肩关节外展至 120°，外旋至最大角度，同时水平外展至最大角度。在保持最大水平外展、外旋的状态下，检查者将患者手臂从外展 120° 降低至外展 60°，若后关节线在外展 90 ~ 120° 时出现疼痛，则该试验为阳性。

（7）盂唇张力试验

患者仰卧位，检查者外展患者上肢至 120°，前臂中立位，肩关节最大外旋。检查者握住患者的手，患者前臂旋后抗阻，若存在疼痛，则该试验为阳性。

（8）旋前外旋抗阻试验

患者仰卧于治疗床，肩胛骨靠近治疗床边缘。检查者外展患者损伤侧肩关节至 90°，肘关节屈曲至 70°，前臂中立位。当患者肩关节外旋时，前臂抗阻旋后肩关节出现疼痛，则试验为阳性。此试验对于区分疼痛是来自于恐惧还是来自于肩关节前方不稳很重要。

6. 肩关节不稳

（1）贝顿评分

此测试包括小指被动背屈超过 90°；拇指被动触碰到前臂；肘关节过伸超过 10°；膝关节过伸超过 10°；以上 4 项，单侧计 1 分，双侧计 2 分。膝关节伸直时，躯干屈曲手掌可以触碰到地面，计 1 分。总分为 9 分。目前诊断韧带松弛的阈值不同，一般认为 4 ~ 6 分即存在韧带过度松弛。

（2）前方恐惧试验

患者仰卧位，检查者被动运动肘关节至屈曲 90°，肩关节外展至 90°。检查者缓慢地在上肢施加外旋力至最大肩关节外旋位，同时在肱骨头后方施加向前的力。如果患者表现出对测试恐惧但没有疼痛，则测试为阳性，提示肩关节前方不稳；如果患者表现出疼痛但没有恐惧，则提示存在病理学改变，如肩袖后部撞击而不是不稳。

（3）Jobe 复位

如果前方恐惧试验为阳性，在患者肩关节最大外展外旋位下，检查者在肱骨头前方施加一个向后的力，患者恐惧消失，则测试为阳性，提示肩关节前方不稳。

（4）前抽屉试验

患者仰卧位，损伤侧肩关节在治疗床边缘上方。患者肩关节完全放松，上肢外展至 80° ~ 120°，前屈 0° ~ 20°，外旋 0° ~ 30°。固定侧的手放于肩胛骨处保证拇指和四指放于喙突和肩胛冈。检查者另一只手将患者的上肢向前拉，施加一个盂肱关节滑动的力。肩关节的运动可与对侧进行对比，若滑动超过关节盂唇或有任何的恐惧，则提示肩关节前方不稳。

（5）载荷移动试验

患者仰卧位，肩关节外展前屈 20°，保证肱骨头在关节盂窝内的中间。检查者将一只手放在肩关节和肩胛骨上以稳定肩带，同时用另一只手在肱骨头施加前后方向的载荷，注意平移的距离，若与对侧相比有较大的位移则提示肩关节前方不稳。

（6）Jerk 试验

患者坐位，检查者一只手固定患者肩胛骨，同时将患者上肢外展至 90°，内旋 90°；另一只手在患者肘部轴向施加载荷，同时向水平内收方向施加力。若伴有或不伴有撞击声的剧烈疼痛，则被认为是后侧不稳定的阳性表现。

（7）Kim 试验

患者坐位，肩关节外展 90°。检查者一只手握住患者肘关节和上臂外侧，施加轴向力并斜向上 45° 外展，同时另一只手向后下方推上肢。若伴有或不伴有撞击声的肩后方疼痛被认为是后下方盂唇撕裂的阳性表现。

（8）Sulcus 试验

患者坐位，上肢处于放松状态。检查者一只手固定测试侧肩带，然后在肘关节处施加向下方的拉力。若测试中出现不稳、疼痛或在肩峰外侧与肱骨头之间出现间隙，则试验为阳性。1 型间隙小于 1 厘米，2 型间隙为 1 ~ 2 厘米，3 型间隙大于 2 厘米。此外，Sulcus 试验在外展 30° 下呈阳性，提示肩袖肌间隔病理性松弛。

（9）Gagey 试验

检查者一只手前臂压于患者肩带固定，用另一只手外展患者的肩关节，保持肘关节屈曲 90°。若外展大于 105° 则此试验为阳性，提示下盂肱韧带松弛。

7. 肩胛骨动力障碍的检查

（1）肩胛骨侧方移位试验

患者分别在上肢垂于身体两侧，双手拇指朝后放于双侧髂嵴上，以及肩关节内旋、外展 90° 三种测试位置进行评估。检查者分别在每一个体位下测量双侧肩胛下角与对应高度棘突之间的距离，计算双侧距离的差值，取绝对值。若两侧距离差值的绝对值大于 1.5 厘米，则试验为阳性，提示存在肩胛骨动力障碍。

（2）肩胛骨辅助试验

患者进行外展活动时，检查者一手固定受试者的肩胛上角，另一手推动肩胛下角，辅助肩胛骨做上回旋运动，同时观察和询问患者的反应。若与不辅助时相比，检查者帮助肩胛骨上回旋之后，患者疼痛缓解，则判断此试验为阳性。

（3）肩胛骨后缩试验

该试验是在空罐试验阳性的基础上进行的。检查者的手和前臂在患者肩胛骨内侧缘施加中度的力，帮助患者肩胛骨后缩以及后倾。在检查者的帮助下，患者有意识后缩肩胛骨后再次进行空罐试验，若此时患者肩关节上抬时冈上肌力量增加或疼痛症状减轻，则判断此试验为阳性。

8. 肩峰下撞击综合征的检查

（1）Neer 试验

检查者一只手固定患者肩胛骨，同时患者上肢在内旋下被动屈曲。如果在检查中患者肩关节前方或外侧出现疼痛，则此试验为阳性。

（2）Hawkins 试验

检查者将患者上肢置于肩关节屈曲 90°、肘关节屈曲 90° 的测试位置。患者被动活动肩关节到内旋活动度末端。如果患者在检查中出现疼痛，则此试验为阳性。

（3）后方撞击试验

患者仰卧位，肩关节外展至 90°～110°，肘关节轻度伸展，检查者最大限度地外旋肩关节。肩关节后方深部疼痛，则表示此试验为阳性。该试验已经被证明在诊断后盂唇撕裂和非接触性损伤患者部分肩袖撕裂中有很好的敏感性（95%）和特异性（100%）。

（4）Jobe 复位试验

此试验已经在肩关节不稳部分讨论过。研究发现此试验也可以用于检查内部撞击。但与肩关节前方不稳不一致的是，施加后方的力会引起疼痛但施加前方的力会缓解疼痛。

早期的研究将撞击征作为一种病理或诊断，但如今撞击征被作为一系列的症状而不是病理本身。大量研究证明撞击综合征和各种潜在病理机制的关系，结果表明肩袖肌肉病变、肩胛骨动力障碍、肩关节不稳、肱二头肌病变、SLAP 损伤和盂肱关节内旋不足都可能引起撞击征。因此运动防护师应该明确特定的撞击征，并且推断出潜在的病理机制。研究已经提出撞击征相关的肩痛检查临床推理方法，此方法中涉及的特殊试验已经在本节中进行了介绍。

盂肱关节周围大量不同的病理改变引起患者肩关节疼痛。本章介绍的每一种测试不需要给每一个患者使用，但运动防护师应深刻了解肩关节的每一个检查以帮助进行诊断。本节已经介绍了临床中常见肩关节损伤的检查，帮助运动防护师在有限的时间内做出最准确的诊断。恰当的肩关节检查有助于防护师关注进一步的诊断策略和治疗选择。

3 Identification and Management of Common Shoulder Injuries

3.1 Shoulder Impingement

3.1.1 Etiology

Studies have found multiple types of impingements with the advancement of basic science research in the areas of anatomy and biomechanics of the human shoulder. Knowledge regarding this may help develop a specific treatment approach.

Primary impingement is a direct result of compression of the rotator cuff tendons between the humeral head and the overlying anterior third of the acromion, the coracoacromial ligament, and the coracoid or acromial clavicular joint. The main reason is a decrease in physiological space between the rotator cuff tendon's upper surface and the shoulder peak's lower surface.

Secondary impingement is due to the instability of the glenohumeral joint. Attenuation of the static stabilizers of the glenohumeral joint, such as the capsular ligaments and labrum, from the excessive demands incurred in throwing or overhead activities can lead to anterior instability of the glenohumeral joint. The instability of the humeral head can cause impingements between the biceps tendon and the rotator cuff tendon. At the same time, progressive joint instability can also lead to a decrease in the dynamic functional stability of rotator cuff muscles.

3.1.2 Symptoms and Signs

The patient complains of diffuse pain at night, exacerbated by overhead activities. The pain is typically localized to the anterolateral acromion and frequently radiates to the lateral humerus. A complete shoulder examination is essential to confirm impingement. ROM and strength should be evaluated first. Usually, the active and passive shoulder joint ROM of patients is normal. The test of strength of rotator cuff muscle strength uses different examination methods, and generally, patients have weakened muscle strength. Special tests such as Neer test, Hawkins test, empty pot test and falling arm test can be used, and the results are usually positive. It should be noted that although the Neer test and Hawkins test have good sensitivity but poor specificity.

3.1.3 Management

Specific goals should be based on the information obtained from a thorough assessment. The final goal is to restore normal biomechanics to the shoulder joint to maintain the normal subacromial space during overhead activity.

The initial management of shoulder impingement should include physical therapy, nonsteroidal anti-inflammatory drugs (NSAIDs), and corticosteroid injections. Physical therapy is frequently employed to relieve pain and improve function. The commonly used physical therapy mainly includes manual therapy, stretching to relieve joint capsule tension, ROM exercises, and rotator cuff muscle strength exercises to improve muscle balance and coordination. In addition to these interventions, activity and workplace modifications must be considered. Patients should reduce or avoid overhead activities until symptoms are relieved. When conservative management fails to relieve the symptoms or a complete cuff rupture is seen on MRI, operative intervention should be recommended.

3.2 Scapular Dyskinesis

3.2.1 Etiology

Altered scapular motion and position have been termed scapular dyskinesis (SD). The definition of dyskinesis is the alteration of normal scapular kinematics.

Multiple factors may cause dyskinesis: ① neurological factors, including injuries to the long thoracic nerve, accessory spinal nerve, and dorsal scapular nerve; ② joint position factors, including upper lip injury, instability of the shoulder, separation of sternoclavicular joint; ③ bone factors, including clavicle and scapular fractures; ④ insufficient soft tissue extension, including tension in the rotator muscle of the shoulder (limited internal rotation of the shoulder) and tension in the pectoralis minor muscle; ⑤ muscle factors, including weak strength of the lower trapezius and serratus anterior muscles, and excessive activation of the upper trapezius muscles; ⑥ kinetic chain, including weak lower limbs and core strength.

SD is usually classified into four types. Type I inferior angle, Type II medial border, Type III superior border, Type IV symmetric scapulohumeral.

Type I: The characteristic of type I is that in the non-moving state of the shoulder joint, the boundary of the subscapular angle is far from the chest wall and protrudes towards the dorsal side. During shoulder joint movement, the scapula is excessively tilted forward, which is mainly an abnormality in movement around the horizontal axis.

Type II: The characteristic of type II is that in the non-moving state of the shoulder joint, the medial edge of the scapula protrudes towards the dorsal side. During shoulder joint movement, the scapula undergoes excessive internal rotation, which is mainly caused by abnormal movement around the vertical axis.

Type III: The characteristic of type III is the upward movement of the entire scapula and the protrusion of the superior scapular angle in the non-moving state of the shoulder joint. During shoulder joint movements, the scapula does not have sufficient upward rotation movement but instead lifts upwards, indicating a noticeable shrug of the patient's shoulders.

Type IV: Type IV refers to the condition where the bilateral scapula does not have excessive displacement and is symmetrical when the shoulder joint is not in motion. During shoulder joint activity, the symmetry of the bilateral scapula is sufficient and rotates upwards.

3.2.2 Symptoms and Signs

The affected side of the patient is lower than the other side. The lower medial margin of the scapula protrudes dorsalis, especially in the preparation of the throwing motion. This is due to tension in the pectoralis major and minor muscles and weakness in the lower trapezius and serratus anterior muscles. During the overhead motion, the scapula is tilted backwards, which narrows the subacromial functional gap and causes painful abduction and external rotation. When the scapula is at rest, the entire medial margin of the scapula is raised dorsalward, and the medial margin of the scapula leaves the chest wall to form the winged scapula when the upper limb is raised. If a lateral scapular slide test is conducted, the difference between the two sides may be greater than 1.5 centimeters. If there are symptoms of pain, the scapular assist and retraction test may be positive.

3.2.3 Management

The best rehabilitation method for scapular dyskinesis is to address all possible causes, balance muscle strength, and maintain the scapula in a normal position and movement. The rehabilitation program should consist of stretching the posterior shoulder capsule, the pectoralis minor and short head of the biceps, and strengthening the scapular stabilizers. Throwing athletes should return to training when there is some evidence of improvement in scapular positioning.

3.3 Subacromial Bursitis

3.3.1 Etiology

Acute or chronic inflammation in the subacromial bursal, called subacromial bursitis, can occur in isolation or in association with other rotator cuff injuries. There are many mechanisms leading to this injury, such as external factors: acute trauma to the shoulder joint or chronic micro-trauma in the subacromial space; internal factors: inflammation–rheumatoid arthritis and gout, calcific bursitis, adhesive capsulitis, or rotator cuff tendinopathy and tear. The pathological process involves the progression from a persistent inflammatory state to fibrosis and the production of fluid accumulation.

3.3.2 Symptoms and Signs

The patient complains of pain under the acromion, weakness and stiffness of the upper limbs, and swelling of the shoulder joints. Physical examination finds subacromial tenderness, and impingement tests may be positive. If accompanied by infection, a fever reaction may occur.

3.3.3 Management

The goal of treatment for subacromial bursitis is to reduce inflammation, relieve pain, and address potential risk factors. Reduce inflammation through non-steroidal anti-inflammatory drugs, physical therapy, and local physical therapy. Subacromial steroid injections can also be employed. If impingement is the primary mechanism , the idea and method of treating the subacromial impingement sign should be adopted to treat this injury.

3.4 Bicipital Tendinopathy

3.4.1 Etiology

Although considerable studies have explored the anatomy of the long head of the biceps tendon (LHB) and the pathological conditions that affect it, there are still controversies about the function of LHB and its management after injury. The causes of LHB tendinopathy may include a series of pathological changes, such as inflammation, degenerative changes, overuse, and traumatic injury. Pathological changes may be secondary to repeated traction, friction, and rotation of the glenoid humeral joint, resulting in the application of shear force at the tendon, causing the tendon and synovial sheath to be stimulated and injured when passing through the intertubercular sulcus transverse ligament.

3.4.2 Symptoms and Signs

Due to chronic repetitive changes, most patients complain of progressive pain and functional decline in the anterior shoulder joint. Patients usually complain of pain in the anterior medial shoulder joint and the intertubercular sulcus, which radiates to the biceps muscle belly.

The most common feature on physical examination is palpation tenderness of LHB in the intertubercular sulcus. Due to inflammation, there may be some swelling, increased skin temperature, and crepitus. The special tests introduced previously, such as the Yergason and Speed tests may be positive. Imaging examinations may help identify LHB tendon lesions and related pathologies. Magnetic resonance imaging can display lesions in the biceps tendon, intertubercular sulcus, osteophyte, and edema, while also helping to identify other related pathologies, but the consistency between MRI and arthroscopic examination results is poor. Ultrasound has cost-effectiveness and accuracy in the pathological diagnosis of shoulder joints, but this method is highly dependent on the operator's level.

3.4.3 Management

LHB tendinopathy is usually treated non-surgically initially, using similar treatment techniques as other tendinopathies. This includes several days of complete rest and the use of non-steroidal anti-inflammatory drugs. Physical therapy is to correct potential scapular rhythm abnormalities and other shoulder disorders, and to perform progressive strength and stretch training. If the initial treatment proves to be unsuccessful, corticosteroid injections can be used. Conservative treatment is the first choice for LHB tendinopathy and generally has a good prognosis.

3.5 Biceps Rupture

3.5.1 Etiology

Biceps strain often occurs during muscle contraction, especially during eccentric contraction. Risk factors for injury include previous biceps injury, age, weak adductor muscle strength, muscle fatigue, and decreased joint mobility. Ruptures of the proximal biceps muscle account for 90%–97% of all ruptures, and almost all involve the long head of the biceps.

3.5.2 Symptoms and Signs

The patient can hear a breaking sound and feel sudden and intense pain in the injured area. Athletic trainers can observe protrusions in the middle of the biceps brachii, and the patients will feel weakness and pain during active resistance and passive stretching of the biceps brachii. According to the examination results, the injuries can be divided into three degrees:

First degree–Severe muscle pain during injury, the same pain when muscle contraction occurs. During rest, muscle pain is usually minimal, and there is no significant decrease in ROM and function.

Second degree–Partial rupture. Muscle strength decreases due to pain.

Third degree–Complete rupture. Muscles cannot contract and lose strength. Muscle belly can feel gaps, muscle can "rise" to form local swelling.

3.5.3 Management

The therapists treat the patient based on the examination results. If the injury is of the first degree, the POLICE should be used immediately, and rehabilitation training should be carried out after the acute phase. If the pain is severe and is a second-degree or third-degree injury, after emergency managements are taken, place the patient's upper limbs in a shoulder sling and make a referral to doctors for imaging examination and subsequent rehabilitation as soon as possible. In most cases, patients with biceps brachii rupture require surgical repair.

3.6 Adhesive Capsulitis (Frozen Shoulder)

3.6.1 Etiology

Adhesive capsulitis, or frozen shoulder, is a common condition involving scapulohumeral pain and decreased joint mobility. It is currently widely believed that it is a condition of uncertain etiology characterized by significant restriction of both active and passive shoulder motion that occurs in the absence of a known intrinsic shoulder disorder. Basic studies attempting to find out the pathogenesis of frozen shoulder are limited, but some biomechanical factors, kinetics factors and neovascularization, have been proven. Most information stems from arthroscopic and open treatment. Persistent inflammation causes pain during active and passive movement, so the individual gradually decreases activity due to pain, leading to shoulder stiffness or freezing.

3.6.2 Symptoms and Signs

Most patients with frozen shoulder seek medical help only weeks to months after the onset of pain and stiffness. Because the onset is gradual, patients only go to the clinic when there is severe life function limitation.

The patient's pain is generally insidious, night pain, which leads to the reduction of the passive range of motion of the shoulder. Usually, palpation of the deltoid insertion and the anterior and posterior of the joint capsule causes tenderness. Active movement and passive movement of the shoulder joint in all directions decrease.

3.6.3 Management

Conservative treatment is the preferred treatment for adhesive arthritis, while surgical treatment is required for stubborn injuries.

Conservative treatment usually uses physical factor therapy, acupuncture and NSAIDs to relieve pain. Use joint mobilization, traction, and active movement to restore normal ROM. Strengthen the muscles around the shoulder and stabilize the glenohumeral joint within the range of pain. Regardless of the conservative treatment method chosen, at least 6 months of conservative treatment should be performed before considering surgical treatment.

3.7 Shoulder Dislocations

3.7.1 Etiology

The anatomical architecture of the glenohumeral joint is often likened to that of a golf ball and tee. This geometry provides a functional benefit by allowing for a large ROM, but it also potentially leads to the risk of instability and potential dislocation of the shoulder joint. A study has found that shoulder joint dislocation caused by trauma accounts for 1.7% of the general population. The anterior dislocation of the shoulder accounts for 90% of all dislocations. Shoulder dislocation is more common in young adults, with a majority in males.

The glenohumeral joint relies on static and dynamic structures that aid in stabilizing the joint. Factors providing static stability to the glenohumeral joint include the congruency of the humeral head and the articular glenoid, the periarticular glenohumeral ligaments, and the negative intra-articular pressure. Dynamic stabilizers are primarily muscular and include the rotator cuff, the long head of the biceps, and scapular muscles.

The instability of the glenohumeral joint can be classified based on the direction of instability, the time of injury, and the cause. Understanding the pathophysiology and etiology related to the patient's glenohumeral instability may aid in determining the risk of recurrence and ultimately guide management. The most common injury mechanism is abduction, external rotation, and extension under external force, which causes the humeral head to detach from the joint cavity and result in anterior, posterior, or inferior dislocation, with anterior dislocation being more common. Some patients may experience spontaneous dislocation. Other injuries accompanying dislocation may involve tearing of the labrum and ligament tissue, tearing of the rotator cuff muscle or long head tendon of the biceps brachii, damage to the brachial plexus nerve, and significant bleeding. In anterior shoulder dislocation, the damage to the inferior glenohumeral ligament and anterior labrum is called Bankart injury. The injury that occurs in the anterior and posterior parts of the upper labrum is SLAP injury. The labrum injury that occurs on the posterior side of the humeral head is called HillSachs injury.

3.7.2 Symptoms and Signs

A thorough history and physical examination are essential. Athletic trainers should pay attention to the patient's age, activity level, participation in exercise, and dominant hand. If the injury history is related to the patient's symptoms, attention should be paid to the position of the patient's upper limbs during the event. The therapist should ask about any related symptoms, including neurological deficits and functional limitations. Patients generally complain of severe pain and limited mobility in the shoulder joint, feeling that the shoulder joint is about to protrude from the glenoid cavity. If accompanied by labrum injury, there may sometimes be nighttime pain.

Both shoulder joints should be evaluated during physical examination, with the healthy side as the control. The athletic trainer can see the flattened contour of the deltoid muscle on the injured shoulder joint. Palpation may cause tenderness, and there may be pain and restricted movement during active movement. Patients with anterior dislocation usually have mild abduction and external rotation of the affected upper limb and cannot touch the opposite shoulder with the affected hand. Patients with posterior dislocation usually maintain adduction and internal rotation of the upper limbs, with the humeral head visible from behind. For patients with dislocation, labrum examinations such as the O'Brien test, crank test, and forward sliding test should be performed to avoid missed diagnosis. At the same time, further imaging examinations can be used to confirm and differentiate between shoulder dislocation and labrum injury.

3.7.3 Management

Initial management of the shoulder dislocation requires immediate immobilization, using a shoulder sling to fix the upper limb patient in a comfortable position and refer to the doctor for examination and reduction. Generally, for anterior dislocation, braces need to be worn for 3-6 weeks after reduction, fixed in the relaxed position of adduction and internal rotation. For posterior dislocation, mild external rotation and external rotation should be fixed for 6-8 weeks.

After shoulder joint reduction, non-steroidal anti-inflammatory drugs and physical factors such as heat therapy, ice compress, and percutaneous nerve electrical stimulation can be used to alleviate pain and swelling. Exercise therapy should be started as soon as possible after immobilization. During the immobilization stage, patients can perform isometric muscle strength exercises, gradually increase ROM (avoiding abduction and external rotation for 6 weeks in patients with anterior dislocation), and gradually advance to centripetal, eccentric, and plyometrics training. The criteria for the patient's return to exercise is that the internal and external rotation force is 20% of the patient's body weight.

Surgical treatment is generally not recommended for patients with dislocation for the first time. If dislocation is accompanied by severe ligament and labrum injuries, non-steroidal anti-inflammatory drugs can be used to alleviate symptoms, while rehabilitation training for rotator cuff muscle strength can be carried out. If conservative treatment is ineffective, surgical treatment will be used. The surgical plan should be determined based on the direction of dislocation, the severity of injury, and the extent of bone loss.

3.8 Recurrent Instabilities of the Shoulder

3.8.1 Etiology

Shoulder instability is common among young people. Recurrent shoulder instability occurs in anterior, posterior, inferior, or multidirectional. Multidirectional instability most commonly occurs in combinations of front and bottom or back and bottom, but may also involve three directions. In recurrent shoulder instability, there are several risk factors that must be paid special attention to. The first is the time of the first injury because this is an important indicator of the prognosis. Studies have found that the recurrence rate of shoulder dislocation among patients younger than 20 years old is 90%. While the rate for patients older than 40 years old is only 10%; they are more prone to rotator cuff injury. Patients who participate in high-level and contact sports also have an increased risk of recurrence if they receive non-surgical treatment after their first dislocation.

The instability of the shoulder joint may be caused by trauma, overuse, congenital instability (joint capsule laxity), or insufficient neuromuscular control. The instability of the surrounding static and dynamic structures is an important cause of recurrent instability.

3.8.2 Symptoms and Signs

One should enquire about the condition and frequency of previous subluxation or dislocation of the shoulder joint. Determine all previous treatment information, including whether there is a fixed or physical treatment time, as well as surgical interventions. Usually, patients complain of pain and clicking during activity, as well as pain around the shoulder joint.

During the physical examination, both shoulders should be evaluated, with the healthy shoulder as the reference. On inspection, atrophy of the rotator cuff, deltoid, and periscapular muscles was seen. Palpation of the anterior and posterior sides of the glenohumeral joint to identify potential tender points. Comparison of contralateral and injured shoulder ROM and strength usually showed a decrease in internal rotation range of motion and muscle strength. In patients with recurrent dislocations, tests for ligament laxity, such as drawer and load mobility tests, are needed. Other tests for shoulder instability, such as anterior fear and Jobe reduction tests, may be positive. In patients with multidirectional instability, any symptoms and signs associated with recurrent anterior and posterior instability will be present. Similar to shoulder dislocation, recurrent shoulder instability may also be associated with labrum or ligament damage, which requires relevant examination to identify.

3.8.3 Management

Recurrent instabilities may use either conservative or surgical treatment. The initial choice is almost always conservative. Early treatment can use non-steroidal anti-inflammatory drugs, Ice compress, and ultrasound to relieve symptoms. If there is dislocation accompanying such as tendinopathy or bursitis, a steroid injection can be used. Regardless of the type of recurrent instability, joint mobilization and flexibility exercises should be avoided, and various types of shoulder straps can be used to limit shoulder movement.

The key to conservative treatment of recurrent instability is to increase the stability of the shoulder joint. Different methods of strength training can enhance the muscles around the glenoid humeral joint and the muscles acting on the scapula. For different types of instability, the focus on muscles is also slightly different. Attention should be paid to strengthening the strength of the pronator muscle and the long head muscles of the biceps brachii. Pay attention to strengthening the strength of the external rotation muscles when the rear is unstable. Multi-directional instability should enhance the strength of the internal and external rotation muscles, as well as the long head of the biceps brachii muscle. If conservative treatment cannot improve the function of the shoulder joint, surgical intervention is required. Doctors can choose various surgical techniques or methods to enhance shoulder stability.

3.9 Clavicular Fractures

3.9.1 Etiology

The clavicle fracture is the most common injury in sports, accounting for about 4% of adult fractures and 35% of shoulder fractures. Fractures are generally due to external stress such as a fall or impact. According to the site of injury, clavicle fractures were divided into mid-segment fractures and lateral one-third fractures. Compared with middle clavicle fractures, lateral clavicle fractures generally have a poor prognosis and most of them require surgical treatment, accounting for 10%-15% of all clavicle fractures. In adolescent patients, this type of damage is also called greenstick fracture.

3.9.2 Symptoms and Signs

Most patients complain of local pain above the shoulder joint and have a clear history of injury. If it is a high-energy external force, attention should be paid to the examination of surrounding tissues. The inspection can reveal a deformity similar to acromioclavicular joint dislocation, but it is difficult to observe the deformity due to swelling. If there is significant dislocation, there will be tension in the skin. Ecchymosis and abrasion are commonly seen. Palpation of pain on the inner side of the clavicle or there is pain during shoulder joint activity. Further confirm the diagnosis by imaging examinations such as X-ray film, CT, MRI, or ultrasound.

3.9.3 Management

Clavicle fractures should be treated immediately with a sling and swathe bandage. In most cases, midshaft fractures can generally be treated conservatively, and almost all cases can heal gradually and fully restore function. Due to the good prognosis, non-surgical treatment is the first choice for almost all midshaft fractures. For lateral fractures, if displaced, surgery has long been an option, with the goal of reducing and fixing the fracture to restore the integrity and function of the acromioclavicular joint.

3.10 Fractures of the Humerus

3.10.1 Etiology

The etiology of humeral fractures varies according to different types of injuries. Fractures can occur in the shaft of the humerus, the proximal humerus, and the distal humerus. In this section, we mainly introduce proximal humeral fractures. Fractures of the proximal humerus account for 4% to 5% of all fractures and are one of the most common fractures in musculoskeletal trauma. This type of injury is also common in the elderly after a fall. The cause of injury is generally due to external stress and can result in fractures of various parts of the proximal humerus, such as the anatomical neck, the intertubercular sulcus, and the surgical neck.

Humeral shaft fractures rarely occur and are generally caused by external stress or falling on the limb. It is usually a comminuted or transverse fracture, and often produces deformities. Sometimes, fragments from fractures can affect the radial nerve, causing paralysis, wrist-drop deformity, and the inability to rotate the forearm backward.

3.10.2 Symptoms and Signs

Knowledge of the patient's injury history is important for accurate assessment. Usually through inquiry, you can know whether there is a potential for humeral fracture. For example, during the interrogation, an elderly person has a history of falls, and the presence of a fracture should be considered.

Patients generally complain of pain and inability to move the upper limbs. Swelling and changes in skin color can be observed. There is tenderness on palpation and percussion pain along the long axis of the humerus. Because it is close to the proximal of the humerus with the axillary blood vessels and brachial plexus, the fracture may cause severe hemorrhaging or paralysis. If the patient is suspected of having a fracture, he/she should be immediately fixed and referred to a doctor for imaging and further treatment.

3.10.3 Management

The goal of treatment should be to maximize the function and minimize the possibility of treatment failure. All treatments should be carried out within the patient's expectations. For most fractures, conservative treatment can lead to fracture healing and improve function. As a sports protection specialist, if a patient is found to have a fracture, they should be immediately fixed with shoulder straps and bandages and referred to a doctor for treatment before starting rehabilitation treatment. Generally, patients with humeral shaft fractures take 3–4 months to return to activities, and the proximal humerus fracture takes 2–6 months.

3.11 Thoracic Outlet Syndrome

3.11.1 Etiology

Thoracic outlet syndrome (TOS) is one of the most controversial clinical diseases. Although it is generally accepted that TOS is caused by compression of the brachial plexus, subclavian artery, and subclavian vein in the neck and shoulder, clinicians have significant differences in their diagnostic criteria and optimal treatment methods. Some doctors even suspect the existence of TOS. This is because there is no objective diagnostic test for TOS, and its true incidence rate is also very different. TOS is more common in women, and symptoms usually appear between the ages of 20 and 50. According to the position of compression, TOS is divided into three types:

① Brachial plexus compression is called neurogenic TOS;

② Compression of subclavian vessels is called vascular TOS;

③ Non-specific TOS manifests chronic pain syndrome.

A patient may have both blood vessel and nerve compressions.

In addition, the location of the compression is very helpful for understanding the underlying causes.

① Compression occurs between the first rib and the clavicle;

② Compression occurs between the anterior and the middle scalene muscle;

③ Compression appears in the pectoralis minor muscle.

3.11.2 Symptoms and Signs

The clinical manifestations of many diseases may be similar to TOS, and in many cases, exclusion diagnosis is necessary. When the brachial plexus, subclavian artery, and subclavian vein are subjected to abnormal pressure, various symptoms occur, including sensory abnormalities, pain, cold sensation, terminal blood circulation disorders, muscle weakness, muscle atrophy, and radial nerve paralysis. Adson test, Allen test, the military brace position test and Roos test may be positive.

3.11.3 Management

For most TOS patients, conservative interventions are usually employed, such as avoiding induced activities and formulating individually tailored physical therapy programs. Studies have found that 50%–90% of patients can be improved after conservative treatment. Urgent surgery is only necessary in rare cases.

Regarding physical therapy, soft tissue stretching, manual therapy, breathing pattern adjustment, and nerve mobilization can be used to improve soft tissue function. Scapula stability training improves muscle imbalance while optimizing patient habits and posture. If conservative treatment fails, surgery may be required to loosen the anterior scalene muscle or remove the first rib.

3.12 Peripheral Nerve Injuries

3.12.1 Etiology

Shoulder injuries can cause serious nerve injuries, usually due to trauma or strain. When the patient participates in a lot of overhead exercises or heavy physical work, it will also cause damage to the peripheral nerves.

3.12.2 Symptoms and Signs

The clinical symptoms and signs depend on the part of nerve compression. Usually, peripheral nerve injuries can lead to the innervated muscle weakness. Many patients may have no symptoms after peripheral nerve injury, as compensation can be achieved through other muscles with similar functions.

Patients usually complain of pain during upper extremity activities, inability to perform upper extremity functional activities, or decline in functional activity level. Physical examination can reveal muscle atrophy, tenderness on palpation at nerve compression points, and decreased muscle strength. Other auxiliary examinations can use electromyography.

3.12.3 Management

If the injury is caused by contusion, POLICE should be applied immediately. In many cases, muscle weakness is temporary and can quickly restore normal function. If it results from long-term physical activity, peripheral nerve injuries can be treated by stretching, neurodynamics, and posture correction. If muscle weakness persists or if there is any muscle wasting or conservative treatment fails, it is essential to refer to a physician.

三、肩部常见损伤的识别和处理

（一）肩峰下撞击综合征

1. 病因

随着对人体肩关节的解剖学和生物力学的研究进展，已经发现了多种类型的肩关节撞击。了解撞击的原因对于制订特定的治疗方案有很大的帮助。

原发性的撞击征直接源于肩袖肌腱在肱骨头和肩峰前 1/3 处、喙肩韧带、喙突或肩锁关节处的挤压。其原因主要是肩袖肌腱上表面与肩峰下表面之间的生理空间减少。

继发性的撞击是源于盂肱关节的不稳定。大量的过顶运动和投掷运动，都会导致如关节韧带和盂唇等盂肱关节的静态稳定结构能力下降，从而进一步造成盂肱关节前方不稳。肱骨头的不稳定会引起肱二头肌肌腱与肩袖肌腱撞击。同时，渐进性的关节不稳也会造成肩袖肌群动态功能稳定能力下降。

2. 症状和体征

患者通常主诉夜间疼痛，做过顶运动时疼痛加重。疼痛通常局限在肩峰的外侧，并经常向肱骨外侧放射。全面的肩部检查对于确诊撞击是十分必要的。首先进行关节活动度（ROM）与肌肉力量的检查。通常患者的主动与被动肩关节 ROM 正常。肩袖肌肉力量检查分别使用不同的检查手段，并且一般患者存在肌肉力量减弱的情况。同时可以使用特殊试验检查如 Neer 试验、Hawkins 试验、空罐试验和落臂试验，通常检查结果呈现为阳性，但需要注意的是，Neer 试验与 Hawkins 试验虽然有很好的敏感性，但特异性较差。

3. 处理

康复计划的具体目标应基于全面评估的结果。最终目标是恢复正常肩关节的生物力学结构，以维持过顶活动时正常的肩峰下间隙。

传统上，肩峰下撞击的首选治疗包括物理治疗、非甾体抗炎药和皮质类固醇注射。物理治疗用于缓解患者疼痛和功能的改善。常用的物理治疗主要包括手法治疗、牵拉松解紧张的关节囊、ROM 练习和肩袖肌肉力量练习，以改善肌肉之间的平衡与协调。除了以上这些干预，必须考虑对患者的日常活动和工作场所进行调整。患者应减少或避免过顶运动，直到症状缓解。当针对撞击的保守治疗失败或肩袖肌群在 MRI 中出现断裂，应该推荐手术治疗。

（二）肩胛骨动力障碍

1. 病因

肩胛骨运动和位置的改变被定义为肩胛骨动力障碍（Scapular Dyskinesis，SD），对于障碍的定义为正常肩胛骨动力学的改变。

引起肩胛骨动力障碍的原因有很多，主要包括以下几个方面：①神经因素，包括胸长神经、副脊神经和肩胛背神经损伤；②关节位置因素，包括上盂唇损伤、盂肱关节不稳、胸锁关节分离；③骨的因素，包括锁骨和肩胛骨骨折；④软组织延展性不够，包括肩关节旋转肌紧张（盂肱关节内旋受限）和胸小肌紧张；⑤肌肉因素，包括下斜方肌和前锯肌力弱和上斜方肌过度激活；⑥动力链因素，包括下肢和核心力弱等。

一般将肩胛骨动力障碍分为 4 型：Ⅰ型肩胛下角、Ⅱ型肩胛骨内侧缘、Ⅲ型肩胛骨上缘和Ⅳ型对称的肩胛骨。

Ⅰ型的特征为在肩关节非运动状态下，肩胛下角边界远离胸壁，突向背侧；在肩关节运动时，肩胛骨过度前倾，这主要是围绕水平轴运动出现的异常。

Ⅱ型的特征为在肩关节非运动状态下，肩胛内侧缘突向背侧；在肩关节运动时，肩胛骨过度内旋，这主要是围绕垂直轴运动出现的异常。

Ⅲ型的特征为在肩关节非运动状态下，整个肩胛骨上移以及肩胛上角突出；在肩关节运动时，肩胛骨没有足够的上回旋运动，而是以上提代替，可以看到患者有明显的耸肩。

Ⅳ型为在肩关节非运动状态下，双侧肩胛骨无过度位移且对称；在肩关节活动时，双侧肩胛骨对称性充分且向上回旋。

2. 症状和体征

患者受影响侧肩部比另一侧低，肩胛骨的下内侧缘向背侧突出，特别是在投掷运动的准备阶段。这是由于胸大肌和胸小肌紧张，下斜方肌和前锯肌无力造成的。在做过顶动作期间，肩胛骨向后倾斜，使得肩峰下功能间隙变窄，导致外展和外旋疼痛。肩胛骨静止时，整个内侧缘向背侧抬起，在上肢抬起时肩胛骨的内侧缘离开胸壁，形成翼状肩胛。如进行肩胛骨外侧方移位试验，双侧差异可能会大于 1.5 厘米；若存在疼痛症状，则肩胛骨辅助和后缩试验可能呈阳性。

3. 处理

肩胛骨动力障碍的最佳的康复方法是消除所有能够引起障碍的因素，平衡肌肉力量，使得肩胛骨在一个正常的位置并维持正常的运动。康复计划应该包括牵拉后关节囊、胸小肌和肱二头肌短头；加强肩胛稳定肌。对于投掷运动员，应在肩胛骨的位置有所改善后再回到训练中。

（三）肩峰下滑囊炎

1. 病因

肩峰下滑囊出现急性或慢性炎症，称为肩峰下滑囊炎，可以单独出现或伴随其他肩袖损伤同时出现。导致这种损伤的机制有很多，比如外部因素有急性肩关节的创伤或肩峰下空间内慢性微小的损伤；内部因素有炎症反应——类风湿关节炎和痛风、钙化性滑囊炎、粘连性关节囊炎或肩袖肌腱病变与撕裂。病理过程涉及从持续的炎症状态发展到纤维化和产生积液。

2. 症状和体征

患者主诉肩峰下疼痛，上肢无力与僵硬，肩关节肿胀。体格检查表现为肩峰下压痛，撞击征特殊试验可能呈阳性。如果伴有感染，可能出现发热反应。

3. 处理

肩峰下滑囊炎的处理目标是减少炎症反应，缓解疼痛，并且解决潜在的风险因素。通过非甾体抗炎药、物理治疗和局部的理疗降低炎症反应，也可以采取肩峰下类固醇注射。如果撞击是引起滑囊炎的主要机制，应采取治疗肩峰下撞击征的思路和方法来治疗这种损伤。

（四）肱二头肌腱病变

1. 病因

虽然大量研究对于肱二头肌长头腱（long head of the biceps tendon，LHB）的解剖结构和影响它的病理条件进行了探索，但关于 LHB 的功能和损伤后的管理仍然存在争议。LHB 肌腱病变的原因可能包含了一系列的病理变化，如炎症、退行性改变、过度使用和创伤性损伤。病理的变化可能继发于重复的牵引、摩擦和盂肱关节的旋转，从而在肌腱处施加剪切力，导致肌腱和滑膜鞘在穿过结节间沟横韧带时受到刺激，发生损伤。

2. 症状和体征

由于慢性重复性的改变，大多数患者主诉渐进性的肩关节前方疼痛和功能下降。通常患者主诉肩关节前内侧和结节间沟处出现疼痛，并且向肱二头肌肌腹放射。

临床检查中最常见的特征是 LHB 在肩关节结节沟处的触诊压痛。由于炎症反应，可能有一些肿胀、皮温升高和捻发音。之前介绍的肩关节结节间沟处特殊试验（如 Yergason 试验和 Speed 试验），结果可能呈现阳性。

影像学检查可能有助于识别 LHB 肌腱病变和相关的病理。核磁共振成像可以显示肱二头肌肌腱病变、结节间沟、骨赘和水肿，同时有助于识别其他相关病理，但 MRI 与关节镜检查的结果一致性较差。超声在肩关节病理诊断中具有成本效益和准确性，但是这种方法高度依赖于操作者的水平。

3. 处理

LHB 肌腱病变最初通常通过非手术治疗，使用与其他肌腱病变类似的治疗技术。这其中包括完全休息数天以及使用非甾体抗炎药。物理治疗是为了纠正潜在的肩胛骨节律异常和其他肩部紊乱，进行渐进性的力量和牵拉训练。如果最初的治疗被证明是不成功的，可以尝试皮质类固醇注射。保守治疗是 LHB 肌腱病变的首要选择，并且一般预后良好。

（五）肱二头肌腱断裂

1. 病因

肱二头肌损伤经常发生于肌肉收缩过程中，尤其是在离心收缩阶段。损伤的风险因素包括了之前的肱二头肌损伤、年龄、内收肌力量弱、肌肉疲劳和关节活动度下降等。肱二头肌近端肌肉断裂占所有断裂的 90% ~ 97%，并且几乎全部涉及肱二头肌长头。

2. 症状和体征

患者可听到断裂声，在受伤处感到突然和剧烈的疼痛。运动防护师可观察到肱二头肌中间处出现隆起，肱二头肌主动抗阻与被动拉长时出现无力和疼痛。根据检查结果，可将其分为三个程度的损伤：

Ⅰ度——损伤时肌肉剧烈疼痛，肌肉收缩时会出现同样的疼痛；在休息时，肌肉疼痛通常很轻，活动度和功能没有显著的下降。

Ⅱ度——部分断裂，由于疼痛肌肉力量下降。

Ⅲ度——完全断裂，肌肉无法进行收缩，失去力量，肌腹可以感觉到间隙，肌肉可以"向上"形成局部肿胀。

3. 处理

运动防护师根据检查结果对患者进行处理。若为Ⅰ度损伤，应立即按照 POLICE 原则，在急性期之后进行康复性的训练。若疼痛剧烈，为Ⅱ度或Ⅲ度损伤，在紧急措施处理之后，将患者上肢放于肩吊带中，尽快送医进行影像学检查以及后期的康复治疗。在大多数情况下，肱二头肌断裂患者需要手术修复。

（六）粘连性关节囊炎（冻结肩）

1. 病因

粘连性关节囊炎也称为冻结肩，是一种常见的肩关节损伤，经常涉及肩胛骨与肱骨疼痛，并且关节活动度下降。目前普遍认为这种疾病的病因不明，其特征是在没有确定的肩关节疾病情况下，肩关节的主动和被动活动均受到严重限制。冻结肩病因的基础研究有限，但是一些生物力学因素改变、动力学因素改变和新生血管的生成已经被证明与其相关，这些病因的信息主要来源于关节镜与开放性的手术治疗。持久的炎症引起患者主动和被动运动时疼痛，因此个体由于疼痛逐渐减少活动，导致肩部僵硬或冻结。

2. 症状和体征

大多数冻结肩患者在疼痛和僵硬发作数周至数月后才寻求医疗帮助。由于发病是渐进性的，患者在出现严重的生活功能受限时才去就诊。

患者的疼痛一般是隐匿性的夜间痛，疼痛会导致被动盂肱关节活动范围减小。通常触诊三角肌止点、关节囊前方和后方会产生压痛。肩关节在所有方向的主动运动和被动运动活动度下降。

3. 处理

粘连性关节囊炎的治疗方案首选保守治疗，对于顽固性的损伤需要使用手术治疗。

保守治疗通常使用物理因子治疗、针灸和非甾体抗炎药缓解疼痛，使用关节松动术、牵拉与主动运动恢复正常的 ROM；在疼痛范围内，加强肩周肌肉力量，稳定盂肱关节。无论选择何种保守治疗的方法，在考虑手术治疗前，应至少进行 6 个月的保守治疗。

（七）肩关节脱位

1. 病因

盂肱关节的解剖结构可以看作高尔夫球与球座，这种结构可在功能上为肩关节提供很好的关节活动范围，但也具有肩关节不稳定与脱位的潜在风险。有研究发现在大众人群中，创伤导致的肩关节脱位占 1.7%。盂肱关节前方的脱位占据所有脱位的 90%。肩关节脱位多发于青壮年中，男性居多。

盂肱关节的稳定依赖于静态与动态稳定结构。为盂肱关节提供静态稳定的因素主要有：肱骨头与关节盂的一致性、关节周围的盂肱韧带和关节内的负压。由于在关节活动范围内只有 1/4 的肱骨头与盂唇接触，盂唇与韧带结构对于盂肱关节的稳定十分重要。动态稳定结构主要包括肩袖肌肉、肱二头长头肌和肩胛骨周围肌肉。

盂肱关节不稳可根据不稳定的方向、损伤的时间和病因进行分类。了解与患者盂肱关节不稳相关的病理生理学和病因学有助于确定其复发风险，并最终指导治疗。最常见的损伤机制是外力下的外展、外旋和伸展，这种外力使肱骨头脱离关节腔，发生前方、后方或下方的脱位，通常前脱位更常见。有些患者可能出现自发性的脱位。伴随脱位的其他损伤，可能涉及盂唇和韧带组织的撕裂、肩袖肌肉或肱二头肌长头腱的撕裂、臂丛神经损伤和大量出血。在肩关节前脱位中，下盂肱关节韧带与盂唇前方的损伤称为 Bankart 损伤；发生在上盂唇前后部的损伤为 SLAP 损伤；发生在肱骨头后侧面的盂唇损伤，称为 HillSachs 损伤。

2. 症状和体征

全面的病史和体格检查是必不可少的。应注意患者的年龄、活动水平、参与运动和优势手。如果损伤史与患者的症状有关，则应注意损伤发生时患者上肢的位置。运动防护师应询问患者相关的症状，包括神经功能缺陷和功能限制。患者一般主诉肩关节严重的疼痛和活动受限，感觉肩关节要从关节盂内脱出。若伴有盂唇损伤，则有时可能存在夜间痛。

体格检查时应对双侧肩关节都进行评估，将健康侧作为对照。运动防护师可见损伤侧肩关节扁平的三角肌轮廓。触诊可能存在压痛，主动活动时存在疼痛与活动受限。前脱位患者患侧上肢通常可轻度外展和外旋，不能用患侧手触摸对侧的肩部；后脱位患者上肢通常保持内收和内旋位，肱骨头可以在后面看到。对于脱位的患者，需要进行盂唇的检查如 O'Brien 试验、曲柄试验和向前滑动试验，避免漏诊。同时可以通过进一步的影像学检查确认与鉴别肩关节脱位与盂唇损伤。

3. 处理

肩关节脱位后，运动防护师应使用肩吊带将患者上肢固定于舒适的位置，转诊给医生进行检查和复位。一般前脱位在复位后需要佩戴支具 3 ~ 6 周，固定于内收和内旋的放松位，后脱位在轻度外旋和外展位固定 6 ~ 8 周。

肩关节复位后，可以使用非甾体抗炎药与物理因子（如热疗、冰敷、经皮神经电刺激）缓解疼痛与肿胀。运动疗法在固定后应尽快开始，在固定阶段患者可以进行等长肌肉力量练习，逐渐增加 ROM（前脱位患者 6 周内避免外展外旋），逐渐进阶到向心、离心与超等长的训练。患者重返运动的标准是：内旋和外旋力量为患者体重的 20%。

对于初次发生脱位的患者一般不建议使用手术治疗。若脱位伴随严重的韧带与关节盂唇的损伤，可以先使用非甾体抗炎药缓解症状，同时进行肩袖肌肉力量的康复训练。若保守治疗无效，将会采用手术治疗。手术的方案要具体根据脱位的方向、损伤的严重程度与骨量丢失的情况决定。

（八）复发性肩关节不稳

1. 病因

肩关节不稳在年轻人群中很常见，复发性肩关节不稳包括了前方、后方、下方或多个方向的不稳。多方向不稳最常发生在前下方或后下方的组合，但也可能涉及三个方向。在复发性肩关节不稳中，有几个风险因素一定要特别注意。首先是第一次损伤的时间，因为这对于预后是一个重要的指标。研究指出，小于 20 岁的肩关节脱位患者复发率为 90%，而大于 40 岁的患者复发率仅为 10%，但其更容易发生肩袖损伤。参加高水平和接触性运动的患者，在首次脱位后，如果接受非手术治疗，复发的风险也会增加。

肩关节不稳的原因可能是创伤、过度使用、先天性不稳（关节囊松弛）或神经肌肉控制不足。盂肱关周围的静态与动态结构的失稳是导致复发性不稳的重要原因。

2. 症状和体征

运动防护师询问患者既往肩关节半脱位或脱位的情况和出现的频率。确定之前的所有治疗信息，包括有无进行固定、物理治疗的情况，以及是否进行手术干预。通常患者主诉活动时有疼痛与咔哒声，肩关节周围存在疼痛。

体格检查时应当对双侧肩关节都进行评估，将健康侧作为参照。视诊可见肩袖、三角肌和肩胛骨周围肌肉萎缩。触诊盂肱关节前方与后方，寻找潜在的压痛点。将对侧与损伤侧肩关节 ROM 与力量进行对比，通常表现出内旋活动度和肌肉力量的下降。对于反复脱位的患者，需要对韧带松弛度进行测试，如抽屉和载荷移动试验。其他肩关节不稳的测试如恐惧试验、Jobe 复位等试验可能呈阳性。对于多方向不稳的患者，与前方和后方复发性不稳相关的任何症状和体征都会出现。与肩关节脱位相似，复发性肩关节不稳也可能会伴随盂唇或韧带的损伤，需要通过相关的检查进行鉴别。

3. 处理

复发性不稳可以进行保守治疗或手术治疗，保守治疗通常是首选的方法。早期的治疗可以使用非甾体抗炎药、冰敷和超声波来缓解症状。如果存在脱位并伴随其他损伤如肌腱病变或滑囊炎，可以使用类固醇药物治疗。不管复发性不稳是哪种类型，都应避免关节松动术和灵活性的练习，可以使用各种类型的肩带限制肩部运动。

复发性不稳保守治疗的关键在于增加肩关节的稳定性，可以通过不同方式的力量训练增强盂肱关节周围的肌肉，以及作用于肩胛骨的肌肉。对于不同的不稳，关注的肌肉也略有不同。前方不稳注重加强内旋肌肉和肱二头肌长头肌的力量；后方不稳注重加强外旋肌肉的力量；多方向不稳应加强内旋、外旋肌肉和肱二头肌长头肌的力量。如果保守治疗不能改善肩关节的功能，则需要手术治疗的介入。医生可以选择各种外科技术或方法以增强肩部稳定性。

〔九〕锁骨骨折

1. 病因

锁骨骨折是运动中最常见的损伤，大约占成年人骨折的 4%，肩关节骨折的 35%。损伤一般是由外部的应力如摔倒或撞击造成的。根据损伤部位的不同，将锁骨骨折分为中段骨折和外侧三分之一骨折。相比于中段骨折，锁骨外侧的骨折一般预后较差，多数需要手术治疗，占所有锁骨骨折的 10% ~ 15%。在青年患者中，这类损伤也称为青枝骨折。

2. 症状和体征

多数患者主诉在肩关节上方局部疼痛，有明确的损伤史，如果是高能量的外力应注意对周围组织的排查。视诊可发现类似于肩锁关节脱位的畸形，但是由于肿胀，畸形的观察比较困难。如果有明显的脱位，皮肤会存在张力；可见明显的瘀斑和擦伤。触诊锁骨内侧存在疼痛、肩关节活动时存在疼痛，可进一步通过影像学检查如 X 射线、CT、MRI 或超声进行确诊。

3. 处理

锁骨骨折应立即用肩吊带和包扎进行处理。多数情况下，中段骨折一般可以采取保守治疗的方式，几乎所有病例都能顺利愈合并且完全恢复功能。由于良好的预后，非手术治疗是几乎所有中段骨折的首选治疗方法。存在移位的外侧锁骨骨折，则需要手术治疗，目的是复位和固定骨折，以恢复肩锁关节的完整性和功能。

〔十〕肱骨骨折

1. 病因

肱骨骨折的病因根据不同类型的损伤而不同，骨折可能发生在肱骨干、肱骨近端和肱骨远端。本节中我们主要介绍肱骨近端骨折。肱骨近端骨折占所有骨折的 4% ~ 5%，是肌肉骨骼创伤中最常见的骨折之一。在老年人摔倒之后，这种损伤也很常见。损伤的原因一般是由于外界应力导致，可以造成肱骨近端各个部位骨折，比如解剖颈、结节间沟和外科颈等部位的骨折。

肱骨干骨折很少发生，一般是由于外界应力或摔倒落于肢体上造成的。通常是粉碎性或横向的骨折，并且经常产生畸形。有时由于骨折脱落的碎片对桡神经产生影响，导致桡神经麻痹、垂腕畸形和前臂不能旋后。

2. 症状和体征

了解患者的损伤史，对于准确的评估十分重要。通常通过问诊，可以了解到是否有潜在发生肱骨骨折的可能性。比如在询问过程中，一位老人有跌倒史，应该考虑存在骨折的可能。

患者一般主诉疼痛和上肢无法运动。视诊可观察到肿胀与肤色改变。触诊有压痛以及沿肱骨长轴的叩击痛。由于腋窝处血管和臂丛神经接近肱骨上端，骨折后可能导致严重的出血或麻痹。如果怀疑患者存在骨折，应立即固定后转诊给医生，进行影像学检查和进一步的治疗。

3. 处理

治疗的目标应该是最大限度地发挥肩关节功能，最大限度地减少治疗失败的可能，所有的治疗都应在患者的期望范围内进行。对于多数的骨折，保守治疗可使骨折愈合并改善功能。作为运动防护师，如果发现患者存在骨折，应立即用肩吊带和绷带固定并转诊给医生，医生处理后才可以开始进行康复治疗。一般肱骨干骨折的患者需要 3 ~ 4 个月才能重返运动，肱骨近端骨折需要 2 ~ 6 个月。

（十一）胸廓出口综合征

1. 病因

胸廓出口综合征（TOS）在医学诊断中是具有争议性的一种疾病。尽管临床工作者和学者们认为 TOS 是由臂丛神经、锁骨下动脉或锁骨下静脉在颈部和肩部受到压迫导致，但临床医生对其诊断标准和最佳治疗方法存在很大分歧。一些医生甚至怀疑 TOS 的存在，这是由于 TOS 没有客观的确诊试验，同时其真实发病率也存在很大的分歧。TOS 在女性中更常见，症状通常在 20 ~ 50 岁出现。根据卡压的位置，TOS 可分为三种：①臂丛神经卡压称为神经性 TOS；②锁骨下血管的卡压称为血管性的 TOS；③非特异性的 TOS 通常表现出慢性疼痛综合征。通常一名患者可能同时出现血管和神经卡压。

此外，卡压的位置对于了解潜在的病因有很大的帮助。

①卡压出现在第一肋骨和锁骨之间；②卡压出现在前斜角肌和中斜角肌之间；③卡压出现在胸小肌。

2. 症状和体征

许多疾病的临床表现都会与 TOS 相似，在许多情况下，需要进行排除性诊断。臂丛神经、锁骨下动脉和锁骨下静脉受到异常压力时产生多种症状，包括感觉异常、疼痛、感觉寒冷、末端血液循环障碍、肌肉无力、肌肉萎缩和桡神经麻痹等。Adson 试验、Allen 试验、军姿姿势、Roos 试验可能呈阳性。

3. 处理

对多数 TOS 患者通常使用保守的干预方式，比如避免诱发性的活动和制订个性化的物理治疗方案，研究发现 50% ~ 90% 的患者在保守治疗后可以改善。只有在很少情况下需要进行紧急的手术治疗。

关于物理治疗，可以使用软组织牵拉、肌肉松解、呼吸模式调整和神经松动术改善软组织功能；肩胛肌稳定性训练改善肌肉失衡问题，同时优化患者的习惯与姿势。如果保守治疗失败，可能需要手术松解前斜角肌或移除第一肋骨。

（十二）周围神经损伤

1. 病因

肩关节损伤可以引起严重的神经损伤，通常由挫伤和拉伤引起。同时，当患者参与过多的过顶运动或重体力工作时，也会导致周围神经出现损伤。

2. 症状和体征

临床症状与体征取决于神经卡压的部分，通常神经支配的肌肉表现出无力。许多患者发生周围神经损伤后可能没有症状，因为可以通过其他功能相似的肌肉进行代偿。

通常患者主诉上肢活动时疼痛，无法进行上肢功能活动或功能活动水平下降。体格检查可以发现肌肉萎缩、神经卡压处触诊有压痛和肌肉力量下降。其他辅助检查可以使用肌电图。

3. 处理

如果损伤是由挫伤引起的，应立即应用 POLICE 原则。在许多情况下，肌肉无力只是暂时的，能够很快恢复正常功能。如果是长时间体力活动导致的周围神经损伤，可以通过肌肉牵拉、神经松动、姿势的纠正和物理因子进行治疗。如果肌肉无力持续存在或者保守治疗无效，应转诊给医生。

Summary

1. Shoulder is one of the most commonly injured areas in sports. The prevention should be taken from the following aspects: identification of risk factors; measurement tools with acceptable reliability and validity; preventive training.

2. Special tests of shoulder injuries include tests for scapular dyskinesis (lateral scapular slide test, scapular assistance test, scapular retraction test), tests for shoulder impingement (Neer test, Hawkins test, posterior impingement test).

3. Shoulder impingement is due to a decrease in space under the coracoacromial arch, leading to aseptic inflammation caused by repetitive pressure of supraspinatus tendon, gliding acromial bursa, and long head tendon of biceps brachii.

4. The best rehabilitation method for scapular dyskinesis is to address all possible causes, balance muscle strength, and maintain the scapula in a normal position and movement.

5. The reasons for shoulder instabilities may be traumatic (major trauma), atraumatic, micro-

traumatic (repeated use), congenital, or neuromuscular. Traumatic episodes lead to complete or partial joint displacement.

6. The fracture of the clavicle occurs in the middle and outer one-third of the clavicle. After confirming the fracture, shoulder straps and bandages should be immediately applied for treatment. Surgery may be required if the fracture is at the lateral end of the clavicle, which may puncture the skin.

7. Shoulder injuries can cause serious nerve injuries, which commonly stem from blunt trauma or a stretch type of injury. Nerve injury must be considered when there is constant pain, muscle weakness, paralysis, or muscle atrophy.

Review Questions

1. What are the steps for shoulder injury prevention?
2. What are the special tests for shoulder impingement?
3. What are the types of scapular dyskinesis?
4. What is the cause of thoracic outlet syndrome?

小结

1. 肩部是运动中最常见的损伤部位之一。肩部损伤的预防应从以下几个方面进行：识别损伤与再次损伤的风险因素；使用具备良好信度和效度的测量工具；预防性的训练改善风险因素。

2. 肩部特殊试验检查中肩胛骨动力障碍的检查包括肩胛骨侧方移位试验、肩胛骨辅助试验、肩胛骨后缩试验；肩峰下撞击综合征的检查包括 Neer 试验、Hawkins 试验、后方撞击试验。

3. 肩关节撞击是由于喙肩弓下空间结构减小，下方的冈上肌腱、肩峰下滑囊和肱二头肌长头肌腱受到反复的压力最终发生的无菌性炎症。

4. 肩胛骨动力障碍的最佳康复方法是解决所有能够引起障碍的原因，平衡肌肉力量，使得肩胛骨维持在一个正常的位置。

5. 肩关节不稳可能是由于创伤（大的创伤）、非创伤、微创伤（重复使用）、先天性或神经肌肉等原因造成的，创伤可能导致完全或部分的脱位。

6. 锁骨骨折处常位于锁骨中、外侧三分之一段。确认骨折后，应立即应用肩吊带和包扎进行处理，如骨折位于锁骨外侧末端并可能刺破皮肤时，需要进行手术治疗。

7. 肩部损伤可以引起严重的神经损伤。它通常由挫伤和拉伤造成。当有持续的疼痛、肌肉无力、瘫痪或肌肉萎缩时，必须考虑神经损伤。

○ 复习题

1. 肩关节损伤预防的步骤是什么？
2. 肩关节撞击征的特殊试验检查有哪些？
3. 肩胛骨动力障碍分为哪些类型？
4. 胸廓出口综合征的原因是什么？

Chapter 3 Elbow Injuries
第三章　肘部损伤

O **Main Contents**

1. Prevention of elbow injuries.

2. Assessment of elbow injuries.

3. Identification and management of common elbow injuries.

O **主要内容**

1. 肘部损伤的预防。

2. 肘部损伤的评估。

3. 肘部常见损伤的识别和处理。

1 Prevention of Elbow Injuries

Elbow injuries can be classified into two categories: acute and chronic. Acute injuries are common in contact and impingement sports such as American football, hockey, ice hockey, and martial arts, which can result from a direct or indirect impact on the elbow joint. Chronic elbow injuries always occur in gymnastics, boxing, weight lifting, and other sports, usually due to overuse.

Most acute injuries are difficult to prevent. Guiding athletes to deal with falls correctly and use protective equipment rationally can reduce the risk of elbow injuries. Athletes should also cultivate a sense of self-protection consciously. To reduce the incidence of the elbow injury, athletes should carry out strength training to maintain the strength and endurance of the muscles around the elbow joint at an appropriate level. At the same time, the muscles around the elbow, forearm, and wrist should also be stretched regularly. If an athlete already has chronic overuse injuries, the training intensity should be adjusted, appropriate treatment should be given to alleviate pain or stiffness symptoms, and promote injury recovery. In addition, athletes who have been injured should gradually undergo recovery training before returning to the competition to reduce the risk of re-injury.

一、肘部损伤的预防

肘部损伤可分为急性与慢性两类。急性损伤在接触性与撞击性运动中较为常见，如美式橄榄球、曲棍球、冰球以及武术等，通常由肘关节的直接或间接撞击造成。慢性损伤通常由过度使用导致，常发生在体操、拳击、举重等运动项目中。

多数急性损伤难以预防。指导运动员正确应对跌倒状况并合理运用护具可以降低肘部损伤的风险。运动员也要自觉培养预防意识。为了避免肘部损伤的发生，运动员应该进行主动训练以使肘部、前臂与手腕周围的肌肉力量与肌耐力保持在适当的水平，并定期牵拉肘部、前臂与手腕肌肉。若运动员已经存在慢性过度使用性损伤，则应调整训练强度，进行适当的治疗，减轻疼痛或僵硬症状，促进损伤恢复。除此之外，损伤后的运动员在重返赛场前应循序渐进地进行恢复训练，降低再次损伤的风险。

2 Assessment of Elbow Injuries

2.1 History

The athletic trainer should ask the following questions:

- What happened when you got injured? Is it due to direct or indirect injury?
- How long did the symptoms last?
- What's the location, extent, and nature of the pain? Does it get worse during the night?
- Is there any pain reduction or worsening?
- If so, what are the activities that aggravate or reduce the pain?
- Is there a feeling of locking or click when the elbow brings up a movement?
- Has the elbow injury been diagnosed or treated previously?

2.2 Observation

The patient's bilateral elbow joints should be extended with the palm side forward. First of all, the shape of the elbow joint should be observed to determine whether there is obvious joint swelling or deformity. An abnormal increase of the carrying angle indicates the existence of cubitus valgus, and the abnormal reduction indicates the cubitus varus. Secondly, the range of motion of both sides should be assessed and compared. Finally, determine whether there is an isosceles triangle made up of the medial and lateral condyle of the humerus and olecranon process on posterior observation when the elbow is flexed at 90°.

2.3 Palpation

The bony and soft-tissue landmarks should be palpated by the athletic trainer. Look for the tenderness, abnormal state, temperature or texture changes, or masses in the affected area, and pay attention to bilateral contrast during the examination.

2.4 Special Tests

2.4.1 Tests for Capsular Injury

The elbow should be flexed to 45° when testing the capsular pain after hyperextension. And then make the wrist flex and extend as much as possible. If the pain is severe during the test, a moderate to severe capsular sprain or fracture should be suspected. Chronic injuries may also cause capsule pain.

2.4.2 Varus and Valgus Stress Tests

The varus stress test is for lateral collateral ligament and the valgus stress test examines the injury of the medial collateral ligament. The athletic trainer holds the patient's wrist in one hand to keep the arm in an extended position, and places the other hand on the medial or lateral condyle. Using the hand above the condyle as a fulcrum, the other hand pushes the forearm. By applying varus or valgus stress, the athletic trainer should observe whether the lateral or medial collateral ligaments relax or not. In the above test, if there is pain on the lateral or medial of the elbow joint that affects the forearm movement, although the elbow lateral and medial collateral ligaments have not reached the degree of rupture, the injury of this part should also be considered.

2.4.3 Lateral Epicondylitis Test

(1) Cozen's Test

The athletic trainer places the thumb on the lateral epicondyle of the patient to fix the elbow. The patient turns his/her forearm into pronation with the fist clenched and makes his/her wrist radially deviated. Then the patient extends his/her wrist against the athletic trainer. A sudden pain around the lateral epicondyle of the humerus indicates positive symptoms of the test, and palpation can determine the pain point.

(2) Mill's Test

The athletic trainer places the thumb on the lateral epicondyle of the patient to fix the elbow. Then the athletic trainer passively rotates the forearm of the patient with complete wrist flexion and elbow extension. The positive symptoms include pain that appears around the lateral condyle. This action will also pull the radial nerve. The patients with radial nerve compression will have similar positive symptoms.

The athletic trainer can also put resistance on the middle finger of the patient, and the patient does finger extension exercises against the resistance. The positive symptom includes pain appearing on the lateral epicondyle of the humerus.

(3) Medial Epicondylitis Test

The athletic trainer palpates the patient's medial epicondyle, and then makes the patient's forearm supinate with the wrist flexed and elbow extended passively. Pain arising from the medial humeral epicondyle indicates a positive result of the test. The athletic trainer can also place the patient's forearm on the thigh or on the examination table. Then flex the elbow joint at about 50°, and fully flex the wrist joint. The athletic trainer straightens the patient's flexed wrist joint. Pain at the medial epicondyle of the humerus is positive.

2.4.4 Test of Neurological Dysfunction

(1) Tinel's Sign

The patient's forearm is flexed at 90° and the athletic trainer taps the sulcus for ulnar nerve between the olecranon and the medial epicondyle. The pain, electrical feeling, numbness, or abnormal perception in the ulnar nerve distribution area (ring finger and little finger) indicates the positive results. However, it should also be noted that excessive force during knocking may lead to false positive signs. The test can also be used to detect the degree of nerve fiber regeneration. The farthest end with abnormal sensation is the boundary of nerve regeneration.

(2) Pinch Grip Test

The patient is instructed to pinch the tips of the thumb and index finger together. Using the finger pulp instead of fingertip pinching to compensate for this movement indicates the median nerve branch–anterior interosseous nerve compression.

(3) Pronator Teres Syndrome Test

The patient is seated with elbows flexed at 90°. The athletic trainer applies certain resistance to restrict the forearm to pronation. If the pain in the proximal of the pronator teres is aggravated, it is positive.

(4) Elbow Flexion Test

The athletic trainer instructs the patient to make the elbow flexed completely with the wrist extension and shoulders depression and abduction. Hold for 3–5 minutes. If it causes tingling or an abnormal feeling in the ulnar nerve distribution area of the forearm and hand, it is positive, indicating the patient has cubital tunnel syndrome.

二、肘部损伤的评估

（一）病史

运动防护师应询问以下问题：
- 患者损伤机制是什么？是直接损伤还是间接损伤？
- 患者症状持续了多长时间？
- 患者疼痛的位置、范围以及性质是什么？是否在夜间加剧？
- 患者是否存在疼痛减轻或加重的情况？
- 患者若存在肘部损伤，加重或减轻疼痛的活动是什么？
- 患者运动过程中肘关节是否有绞锁感或弹响声？
- 患者之前是否发生过肘部损伤？是否接受过治疗？

（二）视诊

患者双侧肘关节伸展，掌侧向前。首先对肘关节形态进行观察，判断患者是否存在明显的关节肿胀或畸形。肘外翻时提携角增大，肘内翻时提携角减小（枪托畸形）。其次，对患者的关节活动度进行评价，并进行双侧对比。最后在屈肘90°的体位下从后方观察肘后三角，判断肱骨内、外侧髁与尺骨鹰嘴是否可以构成一个等腰三角形。

（三）触诊

运动防护师应触诊主要骨性和软组织标志。寻找患处是否存在压痛、异常状态、温度或质感的变化或不正常的肿块，检查时注意双侧对比。

（四）特殊试验

1. 关节囊损伤的检查

检查因肘关节过伸而产生的关节囊疼痛时，患者肘关节应屈曲45°，腕关节先尽可能地屈曲，然后再尽量伸展。若测试过程中关节疼痛剧烈，则怀疑有中度或重度的关节囊扭伤或撕裂。除此之外，慢性损伤也可能造成关节囊疼痛。

2. 内翻和外翻应力试验

内翻应力试验用于检查外侧副韧带的损伤；外翻应力试验用于检查内侧副韧带的损伤。患者仰卧位或站立位，运动防护师一只手握住患者的手腕使手臂处于伸展的位置，并将另一只手放在内侧髁或外侧髁上。以髁上方的手为支点，另一只手推动前臂。通过施加内翻或外翻应力观察外、内侧副韧带有无松弛的现象。进行以上试验时，若出现肘关节外侧或内侧疼痛而影响前臂活动的情况，虽然肘外、内侧副韧带未达到断裂的程度，也要考虑该部位的损伤。

3. 肱骨外上髁炎的检查

（1）Cozen 检查

运动防护师将拇指放在患者外上髁部来固定患者肘部。患者握拳，前臂旋前，腕关节桡偏，与运动防护师做对抗伸腕运动，若肱骨外上髁部突然出现剧烈疼痛则为阳性体征，触诊可以确定痛点。

（2）Mill 检查

运动防护师将拇指放在患者的肱骨外上髁来固定肘部，而后使患者的肘关节伸直、前臂被动旋前并完全屈腕。若肱骨外上髁部有疼痛症状即为阳性。此动作也会同时拉扯到桡神经，因此患者若存在桡神经压迫也会出现类似的阳性症状。

运动防护师也可在患者中指的远端施压，使患者对抗阻力做伸指运动，若肱骨外上髁出现疼痛即为阳性。

（3）肱骨内上髁炎的检查

运动防护师触诊患者的内上髁，被动旋后患者的前臂并完全伸腕伸肘，若肱骨内上髁出现疼痛即为阳性；或令患者前臂置于大腿上或检查台上，肘关节屈曲约50°，腕关节完全屈曲，运动防护师用力将患者屈曲的腕关节伸直，若肱骨内上髁部位产生疼痛即为阳性。

4. 神经功能障碍的检查

（1）肘部 Tinel 征

患者前臂屈曲90°，运动防护师轻敲在鹰嘴和肱骨内上髁之间的尺神经沟，若引起尺神经分布区域（环指和小指）疼痛、电击感、麻木或知觉异常即为阳性。但应注意检查时过度用力敲击也可能会导致假阳性结果的产生。该测试也可以用来检测神经纤维再生的程度，有异常感觉的最远端即为神经再生的边界。

（2）捏握检查

嘱患者拇指和食指的指尖相捏。若患者无法做到指尖与指尖相接触，而是用拇指指腹与食指腹捏紧替代，则为阳性，说明正中神经的分支——骨间前神经存在卡压。

（3）旋前圆肌综合征试验

患者坐位，肘关节屈曲 90°。在患者做肘关节伸展的动作时，运动防护师给予前臂旋前动作一个较强的阻力。若旋前圆肌近端疼痛症状加剧则为阳性。

（4）肘部屈曲试验

运动防护师指导患者肘关节完全屈曲、腕关节伸展、同时肩关节下沉并外展，保持此姿势 3 ~ 5 分钟，若前臂和手部的尺神经支配区域有针刺感或感觉异常，则为阳性，表示患者可能患有肘管综合征。

3 Identification and Management of Common Elbow Injuries

3.1 Contusions

3.1.1 Etiology

Because there are fewer ligaments and muscles around the elbow to protect itself, the elbow often becomes contused.

3.1.2 Symptoms and Signs

A contusion may swell rapidly after irritation of the olecranon bursa or the synovial membrane.

3.1.3 Management

① POLICE treatment should be taken immediately after the injury. Cold therapy and compression should last for at least 24 hours. ② An X-ray examination should be conducted to determine whether there is a fracture when the injury is serious.

3.2 Olecranon Bursitis

3.2.1 Etiology

The olecranon bursa is lying between the end of the olecranon process and the skin. Its superficial location makes it prone to the impact of external forces, leading to the occurrence of acute or chronic injuries.

3.2.2 Symptoms and Signs

As with other inflammatory signs, olecranon bursitis produces pain, swelling, and point tenderness near the bursa.

3.2.3 Management

① If the condition is acute, a cold compress should be applied for at least 1 hour. ② In the case of chronic olecranon bursitis, the surface skin should be treated and compressed. If the swelling fails to resolve or remains serious, aspiration can be used for treatment. ③ The elbow protection brace should be used when the patient needs to participate in the competition.

3.3 Strains

3.3.1 Etiology

Acute injury to the muscles around the elbow is usually associated with excessive resistance movement, such as a fall on the outstretched hand with the elbow in extension, which forces the joint into hyperextension, resulting in muscle strain. This often appears in the distal biceps brachii at its radial attachment.

3.3.2 Symptoms and Signs

The injured area is swollen and the range of motion will decrease. Patients experience pain during active and resistance exercises. When the athletic trainer stretches the joint, the pain will also appear.

3.3.3 Management

① Acute stage: apply POLICE treatment. ② Recovery stage: continue to use cold therapy. And ultrasound or other modalities methods can be used to relieve pain and inflammation and reduce swelling. In addition, exercise therapy should also be used as an intervention. ③ Functional stage: do resistance band exercises and the appropriate neuromuscular facilitation exercise.

3.4 Ulnar Collateral Ligament Injuries

3.4.1 Etiology

Ulnar collateral ligament injuries often occur in throwing sports and movements that require repeated arm swings, usually related to overuse. It can be caused by falling on the hand and with the dislocation of the elbow joint sometimes. Injury can result in contracture of the elbow joint and joint instability.

3.4.2 Symptoms and Signs

Pain and tenderness appear on the medial of the elbow. In the case of an acute injury, swelling and bruising may occur on the medial side of the elbow and top of the forearm. The elbow is stiff and the patient cannot extend it. If combined with ulnar nerve injury, the patient may experience numbness and tingling in the little finger and ring finger. The athletic trainer performing the valgus stress test shows the ulnar collateral ligament laxity.

3.4.3 Management

① Acute stage: apply splint fixation, adopt the POLICE principle, use NSAIDs drugs and analgesics as needed, and use protective equipment. ② Recovery stage: modalities including heat therapy, transcutaneous electrical nerve stimulation (TENS), and ultrasound. Exercise therapy includes elbow joint range of motion exercise, strengthening exercise to elbow flexors, and wrist muscles. ③ Functional stage: resistance exercises, PNF stretching, etc. ④ Surgical treatment, such as ligament reconstruction, should be implemented if conservative treatment is failed.

3.5 Lateral Epicondylitis (Tennis Elbow)

3.5.1 Etiology

Overuse syndrome at the insertion of the extensor group of the forearm, is also known as tennis elbow. It is related to the repeated extension of the wrist joint and the forearm supination.

3.5.2 Symptoms and Signs

The patient complains of a palpation related to tenderness in the lateral epicondyle of the humerus and the pain near the lateral epicondyle of the humerus during and after movement. And the pain is increased in resisting the wrist extension and completing the elbow extension. The elbow range of motion is reduced.

3.5.3 Management

① NSAIDs and analgesics are given as needed, and local injections are used to block treatment. ② Apply protective bracing. ③ Manual treatment: massage and joint mobilization. ④ Modalities: heat therapy, electrotherapy, and extracorporeal shock wave. ⑤ Exercise therapy: do more eccentric strength exercise of the wrist extensor, stretching exercise, and sports-specific exercise. ⑥ Surgical treatment: for patients who have failed conservative treatment.

3.6 Medial Epicondylitis

3.6.1 Etiology

Medial epicondylitis may involve the pronator teres, flexor carpi radialis, and ulnaris, as well as the palmaris longus tendons. Repeated forceful flexions of the wrist and extreme valgus torques of the elbow can lead to the occurrence of medial epicondylitis. Medial epicondylitis often occurs in golf, racquetball, and javelin athletes.

3.6.2 Symptoms and Signs

The symptoms and signs of medial epicondylitis are similar to lateral epicondylitis. The patient complains of palpation-related tenderness in the medial epicondyle of the humerus with mild swelling. Pain around the medial epicondyle of the humerus can be produced during wrist flexion or extension resistance. Pain can sometimes radiate to the forearm and wrist.

3.6.3 Management

① POLICE treatment, NSAIDs and analgesics should be given as needed. The protective brace should be used for protection. ② For the severe case, splint fixation and rest are needed. After symptom relief, the patient should perform exercise therapy and the PNF stretching.

3.7 Elbow Osteochondritis Dissecans

3.7.1 Etiology

Elbow osteochondritis dissecans are seen in young patients between the ages of 10 and 15 who are frequently involved in throwing or striking sports. Repeated stress on the capitellum is the main cause of injury.

3.7.2 Symptoms and Signs

Children or adolescent patients often complain of sudden pain and locking of the elbow joint. Palpation reveals tenderness points around the radio humeral joints. The range of motion is decreased. Swelling, pain and click may also occur. X-ray examination shows a flattening of the capitellum, a crater in the capitellum, and loose bodies.

3.7.3 Management

① Patients whose osteoepiphysis is still not closed should stop throwing movements and limb weight bearing. Then have a rest. ② Modalities: cold therapy, transcutaneous nerve electrical stimulation (TENS), ultrasound. ③ Exercise therapy: the range of motion exercises, muscle strength, rotator cuff muscle group and core muscle group should be carried out within the painless range. The above exercises should follow the progressive principle. ④ Surgical treatment: in the case of loose bodies or repeated joint locking, surgery should be performed to remove the fragments.

3.8 Little League Elbow

3.8.1 Etiology

Little League elbow is an overloading injury to the medial of the elbow caused by repeated throwing, often involving young players. Little League elbow is an age-related injury and may cause different injuries at different ages. Children: medial epiphysitis; Early adolescence: avulsion fracture of the medial epicondyle associated with increased muscle strength; Late adolescence to young adults: medial epicondylitis and ulnar collateral ligament injuries.

3.8.2 Symptoms and Signs

There is progressive pain and weakness in the medial of the elbow joint. The patient complains of locking and the extension range of motion has decreased.

3.8.3 Management

① POLICE, NSAIDs, and analgesics should be given as needed. The key to early injury is rest and throwing is prohibited. ② Modalities: ice compress, transcutaneous electrical nerve stimulation (TENS), ultrasound. ③ Exercise therapy: muscle strengthening exercises for the muscle groups around the elbow joint. Initially, isometric muscle strength exercises are performed on the scapula and the muscle groups around the shoulder joint, and then dynamic exercises and core muscle exercises. The above exercises should follow the progressive principle. ④ Surgical treatment: in some cases, surgery may be required to remove the loose bodies.

3.9 Cubital Tunnel Syndrome

3.9.1 Etiology

Cubital tunnel syndrome is often caused by injury to the ulnar nerve. The ulnar nerve can become impinged by the arcuate ligament during flexion activities. The ulnar nerve is vulnerable to injury or compression due to swelling (such as injury, pregnancy), hyperostosis, arthritis, injury, or repetitive loading. Ulnar nerve injuries are common in sports such as baseball, tennis, racquetball, and javelin. There are four common causes of cubital tunnel syndrome: (1) injury due to valgus stress traction, (2) irregularities within the tunnel, (3) subluxation of the ulnar nerve because of ligament laxity, and (4) compression of the ligament on the nerve.

3.9.2 Symptoms and Signs

The patient complains of pain on the medial aspect of the elbow, which sometimes radiates toward the proximal and distal ends of the joint. There is tenderness at the palpation of the cubital tunnel and intermittent burning and tingling of the fourth and fifth fingers.

3.9.3 Management

① Rest and immobilization should be performed for 2 weeks after the occurrence of injury, and NSAIDs should be used at the same time. ② If there is subluxation of the ulnar nerve, use a splint and perform surgical decompression or reduction. Patients should be careful to avoid excessive elbow flexion and valgus activities.

3.10 Dislocation of the Elbow

3.10.1 Etiology

Dislocation of the elbow most often occurs either by a fall on the outstretched hand with the elbow in a position of hyperextension or by a severe twist while the elbow is in a flexed position. The ulna and radius may be dislocated anteriorly, posteriorly, and laterally. Anterior dislocation usually results in joint deformities, while posterior dislocation is the most common type.

3.10.2 Symptoms and signs

Elbow dislocations involve rupturing and tearing of the surrounding stabilizing ligaments with profuse hemorrhage and swelling, even accompanied by severe pain and dysfunction. The ulnar nerve, median nerve, or neurovascular unit in the area of the brachial artery may be injured. Elbow dislocation is usually accompanied by a radial head fracture.

3.10.3 Management

① After the injury, the POLICE principle should be used immediately. And the patient should be referred to the clinician for surgical reduction. Neurovascular status and range of motion are assessed before and after reduction. The range of motion exercise should be performed

2-3 days after immobilization to avoid prolonged fixation. NSAIDs and analgesics are given on demand. ② Active and active assist range of motion exercises can be started on the third day after surgery. Start strengthening exercises in the third week. ③ Patients should pay attention to avoiding manual massage and intense joint movement before complete healing to avoid the occurrence of myositis ossificans.

3.11 Elbow Fracture

3.11.1 Etiology

An elbow fracture is usually caused by a fall on the outstretched hand or a direct hit by external force when the elbow is bent and supported on the ground. A fall on the outstretched hand often causes fractures of the humerus above the condyles, the condyles proper, or the area between the condyles. Fractures of the medial and lateral condyle of the humerus can result in a gunstock deformity, which means the forearm is extended at an angle to the upper arm and becomes a gunstock shaped relative to the long axis of the upper arm. Ulna and radius may also be injured when stress is applied directly to the olecranon or transferred to the head of the radius.

3.11.2 Symptoms and Signs

It often results in hemorrhage, swelling, and muscle spasms in the injured area. Elbow fractures may or may not be accompanied by significant fracture deformities.

3.11.3 Management

① After the injury, the patient should be treated immediately by the POLICE. In case of stable fracture, surgery is not required and splint can be used for 6–8 weeks. If the fracture is unstable, surgical fixation is required. ② Modalities: cold therapy, heat therapy, transcutaneous nerve electrical stimulation (TENS), ultrasound. ③ Range of motion exercises can be practiced in the early period after the injury, and joint load should be avoided within the first 3 months.

3.12 Volkmann's Contracture

3.12.1 Etiology

Volkmann's contracture, usually associated with supracondylar fractures of the humerus, is an ischemic contracture of the forearm caused by injury to the brachial artery. Typical symptoms are median nerve injury, which may result in loss of motor and sensory function. Contracture occurs as a result of insufficient arterial perfusion and venous stasis followed by ischemic degeneration of the muscles. Irreversible muscle necrosis begins after 4 to 6 hours, and the resulting edema can damage the circulatory system. Regular monitoring of the brachial or radial pulse is necessary for patients with severe elbow injuries to detect the presence or absence of Volkmann's contracture.

3.12.2 Symptoms and Signs

Early signs of tissue compression include pain, cutaneous temperature reduction, and decreased motion. Stretching patients' fingers passively, the pain in the forearm is exacerbated and the brachial and radial artery pulses disappear. Contractures may persist.

3.12.3 Management

Treatment involves removing elastic bandages or casts and elevating the injury part. The patient must be closely monitored.

3.13 Pronator Teres Syndrome

3.13.1 Etiology

Pronator teres syndrome is mainly caused by entrapment of the median nerve. The median nerve may be compressed above the elbow or in the pronator teres muscle itself where the median nerve passes between the superficial and deep heads of the muscle. When edema or swelling occurs in the pronator teres, the median nerve can also be compressed, causing symptoms.

3.13.2 Symptoms and Signs

The sensory and motor functions of the flexor side of the forearm are affected. Numbness, tingling, and/or pins appear in the thumb, index finger, middle finger, and half the ring finger. Motor dysfunction includes the loss of flexion, and opposition of the thumb and fingers is also involved. If the entrapment position is above the pronator teres, the pronation function will be reduced. Symptoms are reproduced by gripping tightly with resisted pronation of the arm from the elbow to full extension.

3.13.3 Management

① Rest and immobilization. NSAIDs drugs are applied. Improve the daily living activities of patients. The splint can be used for immobilization if necessary. ② Modalities: transcutaneous electrical nerve stimulation (TENS), ultrasound. ③ Nerve mobilization. ④ Surgical treatment: if the conservative treatment is failed, the patient can take the method of surgical decompression.

三、肘部常见损伤的识别和处理

（一）挫伤

1. 病因
由于肘关节周围的韧带和肌肉较少，缺乏足够的保护，肘部经常会发生挫伤。

2. 症状和体征
当鹰嘴滑囊或滑膜受到损伤性应力刺激后会迅速发生肘关节肿胀。

3. 处理

①伤后应立即采取 POLICE 原则进行处理，冷敷和加压包扎应至少持续 24 小时。②对于损伤较为严重的患者应进行 X 射线检查以确定是否存在骨折。

（二）鹰嘴滑囊炎

1. 病因

鹰嘴滑囊位于鹰嘴和皮肤之间，因它所处的位置接近表皮，所以易受到外力撞击导致急性或慢性损伤。

2. 症状和体征

与其他炎性体征相同，患者鹰嘴滑囊炎会产生疼痛和肿胀，并且在鹰嘴滑囊附近有压痛点。

3. 处理

①若是急性损伤，应至少冷敷 1 小时。②若是慢性损伤，应先对表层皮肤进行处理并进行加压包扎。若肿胀未得到有效缓解或较为严重，可进行穿刺抽吸处理。③当患者需要参加比赛时，应使用护肘充分保护肘关节。

（三）拉伤

1. 病因

肘关节周围肌肉的急性损伤通常与过度的抗阻运动有关。摔倒时手撑地迫使肘关节过伸是导致肌肉拉伤的常见动作，损伤常位于肱二头肌远端桡骨附着处。

2. 症状和体征

患者损伤部位出现肿胀与压痛，关节活动度下降。患侧在进行主动和抗阻运动时产生疼痛，运动防护师对患肢进行牵拉时也会出现疼痛。

3. 处理

①急性期：按照 POLICE 原则进行处理。②恢复期：继续使用冷疗，可采用超声波等理疗方法消炎止痛，减轻肿胀。除此之外还应同时采用运动疗法进行干预。③功能期：进行弹力带抗阻肌力练习、PNF 练习。

（四）尺侧副韧带损伤

1. 病因

尺侧副韧带损伤常发生在投掷运动以及需要反复挥臂上举的运动中，通常与尺侧副韧带的过度使用有关。跌倒时的手撑地动作也可能造成尺侧副韧带的损伤，甚至伴随肘关节脱位的发生。尺侧副韧带损伤的患者可能会出现肘关节屈曲挛缩以及关节不稳等症状。

2. 症状和体征

患者有肘关节内侧疼痛和压痛。若为急性损伤，肘关节和前臂上部内侧会出现肿胀、淤青。肘关节僵硬，患者无法伸直肘关节。若合并尺神经损伤，患者小指和无名指会有麻木、刺痛感。运动防护师进行外翻应力试验可见尺侧副韧带有松弛的表现。

3. 处理

①急性期：用夹板固定，采用 POLICE 原则，按需给予非甾体抗炎药（NSAID）及镇痛药，穿戴护具。②恢复期：理疗，包括热疗、经皮神经电刺激（TENS）、超声波。运动治疗包括肘关节活动度练习、腕屈肌群肌力练习。③恢复期：抗阻训练、PNF 牵拉等。④若保守治疗无效，需进行手术治疗，即韧带重建。

（五）肱骨外上髁炎（网球肘）

1. 病因

肱骨外上髁炎是前臂伸肌群肌腱起点的过度使用综合征，也称为"网球肘"，与工作和体育活动中反复伸展腕关节、前臂旋后有关。

2. 症状和体征

患者肱骨外上髁压痛，并在活动时和活动后出现疼痛。肘关节活动范围减小，抗阻伸腕和完全伸肘时疼痛。

3. 处理

①按需给非甾体抗炎药及镇痛药，并局部注射进行封闭治疗。②应用保护性支具。③手法治疗：按摩和关节松动术。④理疗：热疗、电疗及体外冲击波。⑤运动疗法：加强腕伸肌离心力量练习、牵拉练习、运动专项练习。⑥手术治疗：用于保守治疗无效的患者。

（六）肱骨内上髁炎

1. 病因

肱骨内上髁炎是一种涉及旋前圆肌、桡侧腕屈肌、尺侧腕屈肌以及掌长肌肌腱的炎症，常因反复的腕关节屈曲以及过度的肘外翻运动导致。常发生于高尔夫球、壁球及标枪运动员中。

2. 症状和体征

肱骨内上髁炎的症状和体征与外上髁炎相似。患者肱骨内上髁处存在压痛点，伴随轻度肿胀。在进行抗阻屈腕及被动伸腕时在肱骨内上髁周围会产生疼痛，有时疼痛可向前臂及腕部放射。

3. 处理

①按 POLICE 原则进行处理，按需给予非甾体抗炎药及镇痛药。应用支具进行保护。②对于症状较重的患者，可使用夹板固定并适度休息。待症状缓解后可进行运动疗法和PNF 牵拉等。

（七）肘关节剥脱性骨软骨炎

1. 病因

肘关节剥脱性骨软骨炎常发生于 10 ~ 15 岁且经常参与投掷类运动或击打类运动的年

轻人群。反复施加在肱骨小头上的应力是损伤发生的主要病因。

2. **症状和体征**

儿童或青少年患者会突然出现疼痛和肘关节绞锁，触诊可在肱桡关节附近发现压痛点。患者关节活动度减小，可能伴发肿胀、疼痛和关节弹响的出现。X射线检查显示肱骨小头变平，在肱骨小头上形成坑洞或者出现关节游离体。

3. **处理**

①对于骨骺未闭合的患者，应停止其投掷运动及肢体负重，多休息。②理疗：冷疗、经皮神经电刺激（TENS）、超声波。③运动疗法：在无痛范围内进行关节活动度练习、肌力练习、肩袖肌群和核心肌群肌力练习，上述练习均应遵循渐进性原则。④手术治疗：若有关节游离体或重复的关节锁定现象，应采取手术将碎片取出。

（八）棒球肘

1. **病因**

"棒球肘"是一种肘关节内侧的超负荷损伤，通常由于反复投掷运动所致，多发于年轻运动员。"棒球肘"的发生与运动员年龄相关，在不同年龄阶段可能会导致不同的损伤。儿童时期：内侧骨骺炎；青少年早期：与肌力增加相关的内上髁撕脱骨折；青少年晚期至年轻成人：内上髁炎和尺侧副韧带损伤。

2. **症状和体征**

患者肘关节内侧进行性疼痛与无力，患者主诉存在肘关节绞锁感，肘关节伸展活动范围减小。

3. **处理**

①采用POLICE原则，按需给予NSAIDs和镇痛药。损伤早期的关键在于休息，禁止进行投掷运动。②理疗：冰敷、经皮神经电刺激（TENS）、超声波。③运动疗法：肘关节周围的肌群肌力练习。最初对肩胛骨及肩关节周围肌群进行等长肌力练习，逐步进阶至轻度的动力性练习、核心肌群练习。上述练习均应遵循渐进性原则进行。④手术治疗：有些情况可能需要手术移除关节内游离体。

（九）肘管综合征

1. **病因**

肘管综合征通常是由尺神经受损导致的。尺神经在屈曲活动时可能会受到肘管弓状韧带的撞击，从而出现损伤。除此之外，肿胀（例如损伤、怀孕）、骨质增生、关节炎或重复负荷也会使尺神经受到损伤或卡压，出现肘管综合征。尺神经损伤常发生在棒球、网球、壁球以及标枪等运动项目中。造成肘管综合征的原因通常有4种：①外翻应力牵拉；②肘管的不规则性；③韧带松弛造成的尺神经半脱位以及④韧带对神经的压迫。

2. **症状和体征**

患者主诉肘关节内侧疼痛，有时会向关节的近端和远端放射。触诊肘管处有压痛，第四和第五手指有间歇性的灼烧感和刺痛感。

3. 处理

①损伤发生后应休息和固定 2 周，同时配合使用非甾体抗炎药。②若存在尺神经半脱位，应使用夹板固定并进行手术减压或复位。患者应当注意避免进行肘关节过度屈曲和外翻活动。

（十）肘关节脱位

1. 病因

肘关节脱位常发生于手撑地跌倒伴随肘关节过伸时，或发生于肘关节屈曲伴严重的扭转时。尺桡骨可向前、后和外侧脱位，前脱位的患者通常会出现关节畸形，后脱位则是最常见的一种。

2. 症状和体征

肘关节脱位时，周围起稳定作用的韧带组织会发生撕裂或断裂，同时伴随大量出血和肿胀，甚至出现剧烈的疼痛和功能障碍。可能伴有尺神经、正中神经或肱动脉分布区的神经血管受损。肘关节脱位通常伴有桡骨小头骨折的发生。

3. 处理

①损伤后立即采取 POLICE 原则进行处理，并将患者转诊至临床医生处进行手术复位。在复位之前和之后都需要对神经血管状况和关节活动度进行评估。固定 2 ~ 3 天后开始关节活动度练习，避免长时间固定。按需给予非甾体抗炎药及镇痛药。②术后第 3 天可开始主动和辅助关节活动度练习。第 3 周开始增强肌力练习。③患者应注意在完全愈合之前应避免手法按摩和剧烈的关节活动，以免发生骨化性肌炎。

（十一）肘关节骨折

1. 病因

肘关节骨折的主要原因是跌倒时手撑地伴随肘关节过伸，或屈肘手撑地时肘部受到外力的直接打击。若跌倒时肘关节处于伸直位，则易造成肱骨髁上方、内外侧髁或髁间的骨折。肱骨内外侧髁骨折可导致"枪托状畸形"，即前臂伸展时与上臂形成一个角度，前臂相对上臂长轴形成枪托状。当应力直接作用到尺骨鹰嘴上或传递到桡骨头时，尺骨和桡骨也可能受到损伤。

2. 症状和体征

损伤通常会导致出血、肿胀和受伤部位肌肉痉挛的发生。肘关节骨折可伴或不伴明显的骨折畸形。

3. 处理

①伤后立即采取 POLICE 原则处理，若是稳定性骨折，可不需要手术治疗，使用夹板固定 6 ~ 8 周即可。若是不稳定性骨折，则需采用外科手术固定。②理疗：冷疗、热疗、经皮神经电刺激（TENS）、超声波。③伤后早期便可进行关节活动度练习，最初 3 个月

内应避免关节负荷。

（十二）福尔克曼挛缩

1. 病因

福尔克曼挛缩是指由于肱动脉损伤造成的前臂缺血性挛缩，通常与肱骨髁上骨折有关。典型症状为正中神经损伤，可能会造成运动和感觉功能的丧失。动脉灌注不足和静脉淤滞都会导致挛缩的产生，随后肌肉出现缺血性变性，并在4~6小时后发生不可逆的坏死。由此形成的水肿会损害循环系统，所以对于肘关节严重损伤的患者，一定要定期监测肱动脉或桡动脉的脉搏，观察有无挛缩情况的发生。

2. 症状和体征

组织受压早期症状包括疼痛、皮温下降、活动减少。被动伸展患者手指会使其前臂疼痛症状加剧，并且肱动脉和桡动脉的搏动消失。挛缩可能会持续存在。

3. 处理

移除弹性绷带或石膏，同时抬高患肢，密切监测患者情况。

（十三）旋前圆肌综合征

1. 病因

正中神经容易在肘部上方或通过旋前圆肌浅层和深层肌肉之间时受到卡压，从而导致旋前圆肌综合征的产生。当旋前圆肌发生水肿或肿胀时，正中神经也会受到卡压从而引起相关症状的发生。

2. 症状和体征

患者前臂屈肌侧的感觉和运动功能均会受到影响。拇指、食指、中指和无名指的一半有麻木、刺痛感和/或针刺感。屈曲功能丧失，拇指对掌和手指的功能障碍。若卡压部位在旋前圆肌以上，旋前功能也会下降。肘关节在伸展过程中进行抗阻旋前活动可诱发出症状。

3. 处理

①休息和制动，应用非甾体抗炎药，改善患者日常生活活动，必要情况下可应用夹板进行固定。②理疗：经皮神经电刺激（TENS）、超声波。③神经松动术。④手术治疗：若保守治疗无效，可采取手术减压的方法。

Summary

1. In order to reduce the incidence of the elbow injury, athletes should carry out strength training and regularly stretch the muscles of the elbow, forearm, and wrist. Additionally, athletes should use equipment to prevent injury.

2. Special tests include: tests for capsular injury, varus and valgus stress tests, lateral

epicondylitis test (Cozen's test, Mill's test), medial epicondylitis test, and tests of neurological dysfunction (Tinel's sign, pinch grip test, pronator teres syndrome test, elbow flexion test).

3. The ulnar collateral ligament injury may be caused by valgus stress caused by repetitive overhead throwing.

4. Lateral epicondylitis or tennis elbow is often caused by extensor tendon injury in the forearm caused by repeated wrist extension.

5. Medial epicondylitis, also known as throwing elbow, racquetball elbow, golfer's elbow, and javelin throwing elbow, occurs because of repetitive forced flexion of the wrist.

6. Osteochondritis dissecans is often associated with loose bodies in the joint.

7. Elbow dislocations result from elbow hyperextension. A typical injury is an extension of the arm during a fall, causing the radial and ulnar bones to dislocate backward.

8. Fractures of the elbow may be caused by a direct strike or hand support when falling. Fractures can be immobilized by casting or by surgical reduction and fixation.

O Review Questions

1. You received a patient who sustained a serious injury to the left elbow. What tests and basic examinations should be performed to determine the nature of this injury?

2. A tennis player complains of an aching pain around the lateral epicondyle. She indicates that the pain seems to be worse when she tries to hit a backhand shot. What is likely the cause of her pain, and how should the athletic trainer treat this problem according to the content you learned in this chapter?

3. Li Hua is a newly selected pitcher from the school baseball team. As an athletic trainer, what measures do you plan to take to avoid injury to his elbow?

小结

1. 为减少肘关节损伤的发生，运动员应进行力量训练，并定期牵拉肘部、前臂和手腕的肌肉。此外，运动员也要通过合理应用护具来预防运动损伤的发生。

2. 特殊试验包括以下内容：关节囊损伤的检查，内翻和外翻应力试验，肱骨外上髁炎的检查（Cozen 检查、Mill 检查），肱骨内上髁炎的检查，神经功能障碍的检查（肘部 Tinel 征、捏握检查、旋前圆肌综合征试验、肘部屈曲试验）。

3. 尺侧副韧带损伤可能是由于受到重复性过顶投掷产生的外翻应力造成的。

4. 肱骨外上髁炎或网球肘常因重复的伸腕动作导致前臂伸肌腱损伤引起。

5. 肱骨内上髁炎也称为投手肘、壁球肘、高尔夫球肘和标枪投掷肘，是由于手腕反复负重屈曲而引起的。

6. 肘关节剥脱性骨软骨炎常与关节中的游离体有关。

7. 肘关节脱位常由肘关节过伸引起。如跌倒时手撑地，肘关节过伸，造成桡骨和尺骨向后脱位。

8. 肘部的骨折可能由于直接打击或跌倒时手撑地造成。骨折可通过石膏固定或手术复位再进行固定。

○ 复习题

1. 你接诊了一位左肘严重受伤的患者，应该进行哪些检查和基本检查程序来确定损伤的性质？

2. 一名网球运动员的肱骨外上髁周围疼痛，当进行反手击球动作时，疼痛加重。根据本章所学的内容，这名运动员疼痛的原因可能是什么？运动防护师应该如何处理这个问题？

3. 李华是学校棒球队新选拔出来的一名投手。作为棒球队的运动防护师，你打算采取哪些方法来避免他的肘关节在运动中受到损伤？

Chapter 4 Forearm, Wrist and Hand Injuries
第四章　前臂、腕和手部损伤

○ Main contents

1. Prevention of forearm, wrist and hand injuries.
2. Assessment of forearm, wrist and hand injuries.
3. Identification and management of common forearm, wrist and hand injuries.

○ 主要内容

1. 前臂、腕和手部损伤的预防。
2. 前臂、腕和手部损伤的评估。
3. 前臂、腕和手部常见损伤的识别和处理。

1 Prevention of Forearm, Wrist and Hand Injuries

In the discussion of upper limb injuries, FOOSH is often mentioned. FOOSH is a sort of acronym and stands for a "fall onto an outstretched hand". FOOSH injuries are mostly caused by the impact of the ground while accidentally slipping and falling and could affect the upper extremities, including the hand, wrist, forearm, elbow, upper arm, and shoulder. They can happen to anyone, though they are more likely to happen in older adults and the adults that engage in high-impact sports. Proper identification and treatment of these injuries are important for better prognosis in patients.

The key of forearm, wrist and hand injuries prevention is to avoid acute injuries resulting from falling and chronic overuse injuries resulting from technical errors. Therefore, the athletic trainer should help athletes learn proper fall landing techniques to avoid injuries caused by hand support when falling. In addition, the athletic trainer should help correct incorrect technical movements that can lead to injuries during training, such as wrist hyperextension, excessive ulnar deviation, or radial deviation.

In addition, the athletic trainers need to reasonably control exercise load, reduce weekly load variation, and balance training and rest time. If any previous injuries or discomfort in the arm are found, the examination and treatment should be carried out as soon as possible. Kinesio taping, wrist bracer, and compression belt can be applied.

一、前臂、腕和手部损伤的预防

在讨论前臂、腕和手部损伤时，常常会提到"FOOSH"这个术语，这是一个首字母缩略词，意思是"倒在伸出的手上"（fall onto an outstretched hand）。FOOSH 损伤是指由于滑倒时手撑地，地面对上肢的冲击导致手、手腕、前臂、肘部、上臂和肩部出现的各种损伤。这种损伤可能发生在任何人身上，尤其容易发生在老年人和从事高强度运动的成年人身上。正确地识别和治疗这些损伤对患者良好的预后是重要的。

对前臂、腕和手部损伤预防的重点在于避免摔倒产生的急性损伤和因技术动作错误导致的慢性过用性损伤。因此，运动防护师应教授运动员学习正确的摔倒落地技术，避免摔倒时手撑地产生的损伤。另外，应该帮助纠正运动员在训练中可能导致损伤的错误技术动作，例如腕关节过伸、过度的尺偏或桡偏。

此外，运动防护师要负责合理管控运动负荷，减少每周的负荷变化，权衡训练和休息的时间。如果发现运动员存在陈旧性损伤或手臂不适，应尽早进行相应检查和治疗。同时，也可以合理使用肌贴、护腕、加压带等防护用品。

2　Assessment of Forearm, Wrist and Hand Injuries

2.1　History

The athletic trainer should ask the following questions:

- What happened when you got injured?
- What were the symptoms after injury?
- Is there any redness or swelling in the injured region or any changes of skin color?
- Did the injured part lose function immediately?
- How is the injured region feeling now?
- Have you had similar injuries before?
- What are the factors that aggravate or relieve pain?
- What treatment measures have been taken?

2.2　Observation

The athletic trainer should pay attention to the following questions:

- Are there obvious deformities, edema, or skin ulcers on the forearms, wrists, and hands?
- Are the patient's forearms and hands symmetrical?
- Are there any wrong postures?
- Have protective measures been taken?

2.3　Palpation

Bony and soft-tissue landmarks are important in palpation. The test results of pain, edema, skin temperature and pseudo joints should be recorded. The palpation should be gentle.

2.4　Range of Motion

During the functional examination, the range of motion of the forearm, wrists and fingers should be recorded. The steps are as follows: Forearm (pronation and supination); Wrist (flexion, extension, radial deviation, and ulnar deviation); Metacarpophalangeal joint (flexion and extension); Proximal and distal interphalangeal joints (flexion and extension); Fingers (abduction and adduction); Metacarpophalangeal joints, proximal and distal interphalangeal joint of thumb (flexion and extension); Thumb (abduction, adduction, and opposite finger movement); Pinkie (finger-to-finger movement).

2.5 Muscle Strength

Athletic trainer need to conduct passive, active, and resistance motion tests on patients' wrists and hands, and monitor and record their movement quality and range of motion.

2.6 Special Tests

2.6.1 Finkelstein's Test

Finkelstein's test is the classic provocative test for diagnosis of De Quervain tenosynovitis. The athletic trainer instructs patient to make a fist with the thumb tucked inside and then the deviate the wrist into ulnar flexion. Severe pain indicates stenosing tenosynovitis.

2.6.2 Tinel's Sign

This test is a special test for carpal tunnel syndrome. The athletic trainer knocks on the transverse carpal ligament above the carpal tunnel. Tingling and numbness occur on the thumb, index finger, middle finger, and the radial side of the ring finger, indicating carpal tunnel syndrome.

2.6.3 Phalen's Test

This is a special test for carpal tunnel syndrome. During the examination, the patient should fold both wrists as much as possible and squeeze each other, and then maintain this posture for 1 minute. If there is any pain in the carpal tunnel area, the test is considered positive.

2.6.4 Varus/Valgus and Slide Test

This series of experiments can check the integrity of the ligaments of wrist, hand and interfinger joints. The varus/valgus and slide test can be used to determine whether there are sprains in several ligaments connecting the carpus. Varus/valgus stresses exert tension on the collateral ligaments between the phalanges, while sliding forward and backward imposes tension on the joint capsule. If there is pain aggravation or instability, it indicates ligament sprain.

2.6.5 Lunatriquetral Ballottement Test

The Lunotriquetral Ballottement test, also called the Reagan test, is used to evaluate the integrity of the lunotriquetral ligament of the wrist joint. The athletic trainer holds the lunate bone with his thumb and index finger while sliding it forward and backward to examine any signs of laxity, pain, and crepitus. The positive results indicate the instability of the lunar triangle joint, which often results in lunate dislocation.

2.6.6 Allen's Test

Allen's test aims to examine the radial and ulnar arteries that supply blood to the hand. The patient clenches and opens the fist three or four times, the athletic trainer presses both the radial and ulnar arteries at the last clench, and then the patient opens the palm. The normal palm should immediately return to blood color when releasing the pressure of one of the blood vessels. Repeat and examine the other artery in the same way.

After the above examination, the sensory changes of the hand should be examined, especially in cases of suspecting tunnel impingement. The athletic trainers should evaluate nerve involvements of patients by observing their active and resistant movements.

2.6.7 TFCC Compression Test

The test is used to examine damage to the triangular fibrocartilage complex (TFCC). The patient maintains the flexed elbow position on a flat surface. The athletic trainer places one hand on the distal radius and ulna to provide stabilization, with the other hand holding the patient's hand (looking like a handshake). The athletic trainer will then ulnar deviate the patient's hand and maneuver the wrist back and rotate from supination to pronation. If click or pain during rotation occurs, the compression test is considered positive.

二、前臂、腕和手部损伤的评估

（一）病史

运动防护师应询问以下问题：
- 什么引起了患者的损伤？
- 患者损伤后出现了什么症状？
- 患者受伤部位是否有红肿或皮肤颜色改变？
- 患者损伤部位是否即刻丧失功能？
- 患者损伤部位现在感觉如何？
- 患者以前有过类似的损伤吗？
- 患者疼痛加重和缓解的因素是什么？
- 患者采取了哪些治疗措施？

（二）视诊

运动防护师在视诊时，应该注意：
- 患者前臂、腕和手是否有明显畸形、水肿或皮肤破溃？
- 患者的前臂和手是否对称？
- 患者有没有错误姿势出现？
- 患者的受伤部位是否采取了保护措施？

（三）触诊．触诊检查患者主要的骨性和软组织标志，检查是否有疼痛、水肿、皮温异常和假关节等。注意触诊时动作要轻柔。

（四）关节活动度

在检查前臂、腕和手指的活动时，要记录关节活动范围，检查内容如下：前臂（旋前和旋后）；腕关节（屈曲、伸展、桡偏和尺偏）；掌指关节（屈曲和伸展）；近、远端指骨间关节（屈曲和伸展）；手指（外展和内收）；拇指的掌指关节、近端和远端指骨间关节（屈曲和伸展）；拇指（外展、内收和对掌运动）；小指（对指运动）。

（五）肌肉力量

运动防护师需要对患者的腕部及手部进行被动运动、主动运动和抗阻运动测试，并监测和记录其运动质量和运动范围的大小。

（六）特殊试验

1. 握拳屈拇尺偏试验（Finkelstein 试验）

握拳屈拇尺偏试验是检查桡骨茎突狭窄性腱鞘炎的经典激惹试验。检查时，患者用四指握住拇指后握拳尺偏，出现剧烈的疼痛提示有狭窄性腱鞘炎。

2. 神经叩击试验（Tinel 征）

神经叩击试验是检查腕管综合征的特殊试验。检查时，敲击腕管上方的腕横韧带，如果肢体远端拇指、食指、中指和无名指的桡侧出现刺痛麻木，则提示出现腕管综合征。

3. 屈腕加压试验（Phalen 试验）

屈腕加压试验是检查腕管综合征的特殊试验。检查时，患者在运动防护师指导下尽可能屈曲双腕，相互挤压，保持该姿势 1 分钟。如果腕管区域出现疼痛，则该试验结果是阳性。

4. 内外翻及滑移试验

这一系列的试验可以检查腕关节、手关节和手指间关节韧带结构的完整性。运用内外翻应力试验和向前与向后滑动，共同判断连接腕骨的众多韧带是否有扭伤。内外翻应力会给手指指骨间的侧副韧带施加拉伸力，而向前和向后滑动会给关节囊施加拉伸力。在任意试验中出现疼痛加重或者活动中出现不稳定的情况，通常提示有韧带拉伤的情况。

5. 月三角关节稳定性试验

月三角关节稳定性试验也称为 Reagan 试验，这是检查月三角骨间韧带完整性的特殊试验。试验中运动防护师用一只手的拇指和食指按住月骨，向前和向后滑动，看是否有松弛、疼痛和捻发音的出现。阳性结果则提示月三角关节不稳，月三角关节不稳经常导致月骨错位。

6. Allen 试验

Allen 试验用于检查供应手部血液的桡动脉和尺动脉。患者在运动防护师的指示下握紧拳头，接着完全打开三或四次。当患者最后一次握拳时，运动防护师同时向桡动脉和尺动脉施加压力，接着患者在指示下打开手掌，手掌颜色应该变白。松开其中一条血管的压迫，正常情况下，手掌会立即恢复血色。再重复一遍，以同样的方法检查另一条动脉。

在做完上述检查后，检查手部感觉的变化，尤其是在怀疑有腕管挤压的情况时，要在之后做主动运动和抗阻运动，进一步评估神经受累情况。

7. TFCC（triangular fibrocartilage complex）挤压试验

TFCC 挤压试验是用来检查三角纤维软骨盘复合体（TFCC）损伤的。患者在平面上保持屈肘姿势。运动防护师将一只手放在患者的桡骨和尺骨远端以提供稳定，另一只手握住患者的手（看起来像握手）。然后运动防护师将患者的手尺侧偏移，从旋后到旋前来回旋转手腕。如果在旋转过程中发生弹响或疼痛，则认为试验结果为阳性。

3 Identification and Management of Common Forearm, Wrist and Hand Injuries

3.1 Forearm Injuries (Contusion)

3.1.1 Etiology

Forearm bruises often occur in contact sports. Since the ulnar side of the forearm bears most of the impact, it is more likely to cause contusion injury.

3.1.2 Symptoms and Signs

The forearm has different degrees of pain, swelling or hematoma. Hematoma may develop into severe fibrosis. Repetitive blows to the forearm can cause chronic contusion, resulting in continuous pain.

3.1.3 Management

① The POLICE principle should be followed during the acute phase, and cold compress can be carried out the next day. ② Prevention is very important. For example, arm guards can be used for athletes whose forearms are vulnerable to impact.

3.2 Forearm Splints

3.2.1 Etiology

The deep lacuna of the forearm contains the flexor digitorum profundus, flexor pollicis longus and pronator quadratus. This area is the most susceptible to nerve and muscle ischemic changes. Excessive use of forearm muscles can cause forearm splints, which often occurs before and after the competition season.

3.2.2 Symptoms and Signs

The main symptoms are dull pain in the extensor muscle group on the dorsum forearm. When the muscles contract, there will be weakness and severe pain. Palpation can induce pain in the interosseous membrane and the surrounding tissue.

3.2.3 Management

Treatment of forearm stress syndrome should be based on symptoms. If symptoms continue to appear, the management should include rest and cold therapy or heat therapy, and wearing supportive wrap during exercise. Patients should increase forearm strength through resistance exercises.

3.3 Forearm Fracture

3.3.1 Etiology

Fractures of the forearm are common in children and young people and are often caused by violent blows or by stretching their hands when they fall. The fracture of radius or ulna alone is less common than that of both. A direct blow to the forearm often results in fractures of the ulnar shaft.

3.3.2 Symptoms and Signs

The characteristics of forearm bone fracture are in line with that of long bone fracture: pain, edema, deformity, and pseudarthrosis. The patient can hear the sound of bone fracture, followed by moderate to severe pain, edema, and loss of forearm function. There may be tenderness, edema, hematoma, and bony crepitus in the fracture site.

3.3.3 Management

Start with the POLICE principle, followed by splinting. Refer the patient to the hospital after the condition is stabilized.

3.4 Colles' Fracture

3.4.1 Etiology

Colles' fracture refers to the fracture of the lower radius, which is the most common forearm fracture. It often occurs when the hand falls to the ground and the wrist stretches back, which makes the radius subject to upward and outward violence (wrist hyperextension). The pressure is concentrated on the cancellous bone of the distal radius, easily leading to fractures. Because the wrist is in the hyperextension position when damaged, the distal end of the fracture often combines with shifts to the dorsal and radial sides.

3.4.2 Symptoms and Signs

Anterior dislocation of radius leads to an obvious deformity of wrist joint, which is commonly called "fork hand" deformity. Bleeding is profuse in this area, and extravasated fluids can cause further swelling of the wrist and even the forearms and fingers. The ligaments of forearm and finger are less likely to be damaged, but the tendons may be torn, and the median nerve may be injured.

3.4.3 Management

Cold compression and splint fixation with a simple sling can be applied. The patient can be referred to the surgeon for X-ray examination and manual reduction.

3.5 Wrist Sprain

3.5.1 Etiology

The wrist sprain is often caused by hyperextension in a fall, but external force flexing and twisting of the wrist can also tear the surrounding supporting structures. Since the wrist is supported by the palmar and dorsal ligaments that transport the major nutrient vessels to the carpal bones and stabilize the joints, repetitive wrist sprains may disrupt blood supply and even eventually cut off blood circulation around the wrist bone.

3.5.2 Symptoms and Signs

The main symptoms include pain, swelling, and wrist dysfunction. Tenderness, swelling, and limited mobility may occur during the examination. All patients with severe sprains should be referred to the surgeon for an X-ray examination to further determine the potential fractures. Misdiagnosis of wrist sprains includes, but is not limited to, scaphoid fractures, hook of hamate fractures, distal radial fractures, nerve entrapment, tendinous subluxation, and triangular fibrocartilage complex (TFCC) tears.

3.5.3 Management

① POLICE principle should be followed in the acute stage of mild and moderate wrist sprains, and splint fixation and analgesic can also be applied. ② Start the hand strength training in the early stage of injury. ③ Taping technique can strengthen wrist stability which is beneficial to recovery and prevention.

3.6 Triangular Fibrocartilage Complex Injury (TFCC Injury)

3.6.1 Etiology

TFCC is the main structure to stabilize the ligaments between the distal radioulnar joint and the wrist joint. It provides a mechanism for the radiocarpal joint to rotate stably around the ulnar axis, and can reduce the pressure transmitted from the ulnar carpal axis. TFCC is prone to be damaged, causing cartilage tears, wrist pain and the impact feeling. When the players swing and hit the ball, the excessive twists can cause damage to the triangular fibrocartilage plate. Hyperextension by external force can also cause damage to the triangular fibrocartilage. For example, when the hand is stretched out too much during a fall, the triangular fibrocartilage disc is squeezed between the distal ulnar joint and the carpal bone. In addition, TFCC injury often occurs with ulnar collateral ligament sprain.

3.6.2 Symptoms and Signs

The pain usually occurs on the ulnar side of the wrist. The patient feels hard to complete wrist extension or has pain during extension, especially on the ulnar side of the wrist. When moving the wrist joint, there will be a click or impact. The wrist may have various severity of swelling. The result of TFCC compression test is positive.

3.6.3 Management

The wrist joints should be fixed by splints for 2–4 weeks, and then the mobility training and functional training can be carried out. If conservative treatment fails, surgery should be performed.

3.7 Nerve Compression

3.7.1 Etiology

Some nerves pass from the wrist to the hand through the narrow tubes, and it is easy to cause nerve compression and entrapment when the wrist is damaged or compressed for a long time. The median nerve, which passes through the carpal tunnel, and the ulnar nerve, which passes through the ulnar tunnel, are most likely to be compressed.

3.7.2 Symptoms and Signs

Nerve compression can cause sharp, burning pain with skin hypersensitivity, feeling loss, or paresthesia. Claw hand deformity, a common deformity of the hand, which is caused by hypothenar muscles, ring finger and little finger inside muscle atrophy due to injury to the ulnar nerve. The paralysis of the radial nerve can lead to wrist-drop deformity, because the extensor muscle group paralysis causes the wrist and fingers to be unable to extend. The median nerve paralysis causes ape's hand deformity, in which the thumb is on the same level as the four fingers, the palms cannot touch each other, and the other four fingers are overextended.

3.7.3 Management

Irreversible nerve damage may occur if nerve compression cannot be relieved. If conservative treatment fails, then decompression surgery should be performed.

3.8 Carpal Tunnel Syndrome

3.8.1 Etiology

The carpal canal is located at the front of the carpal joint and is formed by the carpal bone at the bottom and the transverse carpal ligament covering it. Eight finger flexor tendons with their synovial sheath and median nerve pass through this narrow area. Carpal tunnel syndrome is caused by increased pressure in the tunnel, resulting in compression of the median nerve. Although direct damage to the front of the wrist can also cause carpal tunnel syndrome, repeated wrist flexion movement is the main cause.

3.8.2 Symptoms and Signs

The main symptoms include a loss of sensation and movement. Sensory changes involving tingling and numbness could occur in the middle-innervated area of the thumb, index finger, middle finger, and palm. The patient may experience definite finger sensation loss, decreased strength, and atrophy of the thenar muscles, reducing thumb flexibility and the strength of pinching, and even failing to do finger-to-finger movement.

3.8.3 Management

Conservative treatment is recommended at the early stage, including rest, immobilization, and non-steroidal anti-inflammatory drugs. Cortisol can be injected if symptoms are not resolved. Decompression of the transverse carpal ligament should be performed if conservative treatment fails.

3.9 De Quervain's Syndrome

3.9.1 Etiology

The frequent movements of the wrist and thumb cause the extensor pollicis brevis and the extensor pollicis longus tendon to rub against each other, leading to aseptic inflammation, edema fibrosis, and thickening tendon sheath. Ultimately, it leads to obstruction of tendon sliding within the tendon sheath, resulting in clinical symptoms.

3.9.2 Symptoms and Signs

The main symptom is an aching pain in the hands and forearms. There is tenderness in the processes radial styloid, and the stiff nodus may be palpated. Wrist movements will aggravate the pain and the Finklestein's test is positive. Thumb abduction and extension can also cause pain and weakness. There is pain and swelling near the base of the thumb, and there is a feeling of "stuck" when the thumb moves.

3.9.3 Management

① POLICE principle should be followed in the acute phase, including rest, analgesics, and thumb splint. After the acute stage, ultrasound and other physiotherapy can be carried out. Joint mobilization is used to maintain the ROM. If necessary, corticosteroid injections can be used. ② Patients with persistent symptoms after conservative treatment may undergo tendon decompression.

3.10 Dislocation of the Lunate Bone

3.10.1 Etiology

Lunate bone dislocation is uncommon, but lunate bone is the most likely carpal bone to get dislocated. Lunate bone dislocation is mostly caused by external force wrist over extension, such as during a fall, which increases the gap between the distal and proximal ends of the wrist bones, pulling the lunate bone forward.

3.10.2 Symptoms and Signs

The main symptoms are pain, swelling, and difficulty with wrist flexion. Compression of the median nerve due to lunate dislocation may lead to numbness and even paralysis of the flexors.

3.10.3 Management

The patient should be initially treated according to the POLICE principle and referred to the surgeon for repositioning. If the lunate dislocation is not detected early enough, the bone can be further damaged and surgical removal is required.

3.11 Scaphoid Fracture

3.11.1 Etiology

Scaphoid fracture is the most frequent fracture of wrist bone. When the wrist is overextended during a fall, the impact and pressure from the ground compact the scaphoid, which is located between the radius and the distal carpal bone, resulting in a scaphoid fracture. The disease is prone to be misdiagnosed as a severe sprain, resulting in incomplete immobilization of the wrist. Scaphoid fracture, without proper splinting, cannot heal well due to the lack of adequate blood supply, and thus can develop into degeneration and necrosis.

3.11.2 Symptoms and Signs

① Signs of scaphoid fracture include swelling of the wrist bone and severe pain in the nasopharyngeal fossa. Applying pressure in the nasopharyngeal fossa is the best way to distinguish a wrist sprain from a scaphoid fracture. ② Applying pressure along the long axis of the thumb, radial deviation and ulnar deviation can irritate pain.

3.11.3 Management

① The POLICE procedure should be followed; the injured region should be splinted and the patient should be referred to the surgeon for X-ray examination and plaster fixation. ② In most cases, after about 6–8 weeks of cast immobilization, strength training can be started under the protection of taping. Prolonged immobilization is not conducive to scaphoid rehabilitation. ③ If conservative treatment is ineffective, surgical treatment can be chosen to avoid causing bone nonunion and delaying rehabilitation treatment.

3.12 Wrist Ganglion

3.12.1 Etiology

The ganglion cyst of the wrist is a common synovial cyst in sports. It is a cystic mass in the sheath of the wrist joint. It is often caused by the degeneration of connective tissue in joint capsules, ligaments, and tendon sheaths. The capsules contain colorless, transparent, orange, or light yellow thick mucus. A round mass can be seen in the affected area with a slight soreness. The etiology is not yet clear, and may be related to chronic trauma or overwork.

3.12.2 Symptoms and Signs

The main symptoms include wrist swelling and intermittent pain or no pain. The pain increases during wrist movement. The cystic structure can be soft, tough or very hard on palpation.

3.12.3 Management

① The swelling can be reduced by finger pressure, and then the pressure pad can be applied. ② Puncture extraction and drug injection, continuous pressure, or pressure pad can be used. ③ If none of the above methods can effectively prevent recurrence, surgical removal is the most radical treatment.

3.13 Contusions and Bruises on Hands and Fingers

3.13.1 Etiology

The metacarpal and phalangeal bones play an important role in fine motor activity with little protective fat and muscle padding, so it is easy to be damaged by external impact or extrusion.

3.13.2 Symptoms and Signs

This injury can be distinguished from the history of injury, pain, and soft tissue swelling.

3.13.3 Management

① After hemostasis, pressure and a cold compress should be applied immediately, followed by gradual hyperthermia of the area after the acute phase. ② The contusion of the distal phalanx can lead to a sub-fingernail hematoma, causing accumulated blood under the nails and severe pain. Before hemostasis, patients should soak their hands in ice water to reduce the blood flow.

3.14 Trigger Finger

3.14.1 Etiology

The trigger finger is stenosed tenosynovitis, most commonly seen in the shared tendon sheath of the flexor tendon and other tendons. It is often caused by hand overuse. It may lead to a thickening tendon and sheath, which can limit the tendon slip.

3.14.2 Symptoms and Signs

① The patient complains of a sense of stretching resistance and a sound of clicking when the fingers and thumb are flexed. ② During palpation, there will be pain in the fingers and a lump at the end of the flexor tendon sheath.

3.14.3 Management

① The initial treatment is the same as the treatment of De Quervain's syndrome. But if the treatment is failed, steroids can be injected to relieve the pain. Splint should be used to fix the tendon when the above methods fail. ② In the later stage, maintaining the ROM through exercise can prevent tendon adhesion and contracture. Surgical treatment can be carried out when the conservative treatment fails.

3.15 Extensor Tendon Avulsion (Mallet Finger)

3.15.1 Etiology

The mallet finger is also called "baseball finger" or "basketball finger", which is caused by external force blowing to the fingertips, resulting in stuck and torn at the insertion of finger extensor tendons, and even avulsion fractures.

3.15.2 Symptoms and Signs

The main symptom is pain in the distal interphalangeal joint. X-ray examination reveals a possible bony avulsion of the dorsal proximal phalanx. The fingers cannot be fully extended and only remain in flexion position at about 30°. Tenderness points occur in the affected finger, and the avulsed bone can be touched by palpation. There may also be edema or even hematoma.

3.15.3 Management

The pain and swelling should be addressed according to the POLICE principle. The distal phalanx should be held in the extension position with a splint for 6–8 weeks if there is no fracture. If the patient is unable to recover or intolerant to splint treatment, surgical intervention is required.

3.16 Buttonhole Deformity

3.16.1 Etiology

Buttonhole deformity is caused by the rupture of the dorsal extensor tendon of the middle phalanx. The injury occurs at the end of the proximal interphalangeal joint (PIP joint). The torn extensor muscles on the PIP joint and the ruptured tendon slid bilaterally beyond the transverse axis of the proximal interphalangeal joint, resulting in the distal interphalangeal joint (DIP joint) in the extended position but the PIP joint in the flexed position. As the disease progresses, the PIP joint passes through the torn extensor tendon, just like a button passes through the buttonhole.

3.16.2 Symptoms and Signs

The main symptoms include severe pain and weakness in the DIP joint. There are tenderness points, swelling, and obvious deformities.

3.16.3 Management

① Ice compress is applied in the initial phase, followed by the fixation of the PIP joint anchorage in the extended position. Note: The buttonhole deformity may be permanent without adequate fixation of a splint. ② Splint fixation should last for 5–8 weeks. Flexion of the distal phalanx should be encouraged during the fixation. ③ After conservative treatment, if the patient is still unable to passively extend the proximal interphalangeal joint, surgical intervention can be considered.

3.17 Gamekeeper's Thumb

3.17.1 Etiology

The injury mechanism is usually an acute sprain of the ulnar collateral ligament of the first metacarpophalangeal (MCP) joint caused by violent extension and abduction of the proximal phalangeal bone of the thumb. It is most commonly seen in skiers and rugby players.

3.17.2 Symptoms and Signs

The patient complains of pain in the ulnar collateral ligament, weakness of the finger-to-finger movement, with aggravated symptoms during thumb extension and abduction. Pain and swelling can be found in the middle part of the thumb. Tenderness occurs in the thumb root during palpation. The chronic patient's joint presents laxity.

3.17.3 Management

① Due to the severe damage to finger-to-finger ability, appropriate treatment should be given promptly. ② If joint instability occurs, refer patients to orthopedists immediately. If the joint is stable, an X-ray should be performed to determine if there is a fracture. ③ Splint the thumb for 3 weeks until the pain subsides. The thumb brace should be from the wrist to the end of the thumb, with the thumb in a neutral position. ④ After the splint is removed, the taping should be used in activities. ⑤ If the ligament is completely torn, a surgical repair is needed to resume the function of the thumb.

3.18 Sprains of the Interphalangeal Joints of the Fingers

3.18.1 Etiology

Interphalangeal joint sprains include proximal and distal interphalangeal joint injuries. Injuries range from minor collateral ligament damage to a complete tear. Sprain of the lateral collateral ligament of the interphalangeal joint is common in sports such as basketball, volleyball, and football, usually due to excessive axial forces and the pressure of valgus or varus acting on the interphalangeal joint.

3.18.2 Symptoms and Signs

The main symptoms include joint pain and swelling. There is tenderness at the joint, especially in the collateral ligament. The joint is unstable in the lateral and axial direction when it is at 150° flexion. The damage to collateral ligament can be evaluated by the varus and valgus stress test.

3.18.3 Management

① POLICE, X-ray, and splint fixation should be applied in the acute phase. The PIP joint is usually fixed at 30°–40° for about 10 days. ② If the distal interphalangeal joint is injured, it should be splinted in the extended position for a few days. ③ If it is a mild sprain, the injured finger and the undamaged finger should be fixed together to provide protective support. Later, the checkrein taping can be used to protect the fingers.

3.19 PIP Dislocation, MCP Dislocation

3.19.1 Etiology

The incidence of phalangeal dislocation is high, including dorsal dislocation of the PIP joint, palmar dislocation of the PIP joint, and MCP dislocation. The PIP or MCP joint dislocation is caused by the twisting of the finger in a different direction.

3.19.2 Symptoms and Signs

The main symptoms include pain and swelling in the PIP joints. The PIP and MCP joint will have obvious deformity and loss of function.

3.19.3 Management

The POLICE principle should be followed in the acute stage, followed by splint fixation. Manual reduction is performed by doctors. Splint the finger for 3–4 weeks in PIP joint after reduction, and tape it after removing the splint.

3.20 Metacarpal Fracture

3.20.1 Etiology

Metacarpal fractures are usually caused by direct axial impact or stress. The fifth metacarpal fracture is more common in boxing and martial arts and is also called a boxer's fracture.

3.20.2 Symptoms and Signs

The main symptoms include pain, swelling, and angular or rotational deformity of the fingers.

3.20.3 Management

Apply the POLICE principle and analgesics in the acute phase, followed by an X-ray examination. After manual reduction and splinting for 4 weeks, range of motion exercises are initiated.

三、前臂、腕和手部常见损伤的识别和处理

（一）前臂损伤（挫伤）

1. 病因

在一些身体接触类型的运动中，经常会发生前臂挫伤。由于前臂的尺骨侧承受了大部分的撞击，因此更容易造成挫伤。

2. 症状和体征

前臂一般会有不同程度的疼痛、肿胀或血肿。若血肿严重可能会发展成为骨化性肌炎。当前臂受到重复性打击时可引起慢性挫伤，从而出现持续的疼痛。

3. 处理

①对前臂挫伤的急性期处理应遵循 POLICE 原则，可在第二天进行冷敷疗法。②预防非常重要。例如，对于前臂易受到撞击的运动员，可以利用护臂进行防护。

（二）前臂应力综合征

1. 病因

前臂深层腔隙包含指深屈肌、拇长屈肌和旋前方肌，此区域最容易受到神经和肌肉缺血变化影响。前臂肌肉的过度使用会导致前臂应力综合征，常出现在赛季前和赛季后。

2. 症状和体征

主要症状是前臂背部伸肌肌群钝性疼痛。肌肉收缩时，会有无力感和剧烈疼痛。触诊骨间膜和周围组织会引起疼痛。

3. 处理

对前臂应力综合征应对症治疗。如果症状持续出现，那么治疗重心应放在休息和冷、热疗等治疗上，同时在运动过程中佩戴支持性绑带。患者应该通过抗阻练习增加前臂力量。

（三）前臂骨折

1. 病因

前臂骨折高发于儿童和年轻人，常由暴力打击或是摔倒时伸出手撑地引起。一般来说，单独的桡骨或尺骨骨折比桡骨、尺骨同时骨折更为少见。对前臂直接的打击经常造成尺骨干骨折。

2. 症状和体征

前臂的骨折符合长骨骨折的特点：疼痛、水肿、畸形和假关节。患者能听到骨断裂的声音，接下来会出现中度或剧烈疼痛、水肿和前臂功能丧失。骨折部位局部有可能出现压痛、水肿、血肿和骨擦音。

3. 处理

损伤后及时按照 POLICE 原则进行处理，随后迅速进行夹板固定，待伤情稳定后及时转运至医院进行临床处理。

（四）柯莱斯（Colles）骨折

1. 病因

Colles 骨折是指桡骨远端骨折，是前臂骨折中最常见的一种类型。损伤机制通常是跌倒时手掌着地，使桡骨远端受到向上和向外的暴力（腕过伸），此时压力集中于桡骨远端松质骨处从而引起骨折。由于受损时处于腕过伸位置，骨折远端多出现向背端及桡侧的移位。

2. 症状和体征

从外形上，桡骨向前脱位导致腕关节出现明显的畸形，被称为"餐叉手"畸形。该区域出血量大，而渗出的液体会导致腕部甚至是前臂和手指进一步的肿胀。前臂与手指的韧带组织通常不容易损伤，但肌腱可能出现撕裂，并且可能存在正中神经的损伤。

3. 处理

主要的处理手段为加压冷敷、夹板固定腕关节和患肢悬挂吊带。将患者转诊到外科医生处做 X 射线检查和手法复位。

（五）腕部扭伤

1. 病因

腕部扭伤常见原因是摔倒时腕过伸，但外界暴力的屈曲动作和扭转也会撕裂周围的支持结构。因为腕部主要的支持结构来源于掌侧和背侧韧带，它们将主要的营养血管输送到腕骨并稳定关节，所以重复性腕扭伤可能会阻断血液供应甚至最终切断腕骨周围的血液循环。

2. 症状和体征

患者主诉疼痛、肿胀及手腕功能障碍。在检查过程中，会有压痛、肿胀和活动度受限的情况。所有出现严重扭伤情况的患者应该转诊给外科医生进行 X 射线检查，以进一步判断是否有骨折的可能。腕部扭伤容易误诊的常见情况包括但不限于手舟骨骨折、钩骨骨折、桡骨远端骨折、神经卡压、肌腱半脱位和三角纤维软骨复合体（TFCC）撕裂。

3. 处理

①轻度和中度的腕部扭伤急性期应该以 POLICE 原则处理，使用夹板固定和止痛剂镇痛。②在损伤后早期可以开始进行手部力量练习。③贴扎技术能够加强腕部稳定，有利于损伤的修复和预防进一步的损伤。

（六）三角纤维软骨盘复合体损伤（TFCC 损伤）

1. 病因

三角纤维软骨盘复合体是稳定远端桡尺关节和腕关节之间韧带的主要结构。它使桡腕关节可以灵活地绕尺骨轴旋转，并且能够减小来自尺腕轴上传递的压力。三角纤维软骨盘很容易受到损伤，造成软骨撕裂，引起腕部疼痛和撞击感。一些暴力扭转动作可造成运动员三角纤维软骨盘发生损伤，例如挥击球拍。暴力的过伸动作也会引起三角纤维软骨盘的损伤。例如当跌倒时手过伸着地，会挤压远端桡尺关节和腕骨间的三角纤维软骨盘，从而导致损伤。此外，三角纤维软骨盘的损伤经常合并尺侧副韧带的扭伤。

2. 症状和体征

疼痛一般发生在腕关节尺侧。患者很难完成伸腕动作或者伸腕时有疼痛，尤其腕尺侧疼痛会更为明显。在活动腕关节时会有弹响声或撞击感。腕关节会有一定程度的肿胀。TFCC 挤压试验结果为阳性。

3. 处理

腕关节需使用护具固定 2 ~ 4 周，在制动后可以进行活动能力训练和功能性训练。如果保守治疗无效，应该进行外科手术治疗。

（七）神经卡压

1. 病因

从腕到手的神经要经过狭窄的管道，当腕部受损或长时间受挤压时会导致这些管道狭窄，从而引起神经压迫和卡压。其中，从腕管经过的正中神经和从腕尺管通道经过的尺神经最易受压。

2. 症状和体征

神经压迫会造成刺痛和灼烧痛并伴发皮肤感觉过敏、感觉减退或感觉异常。"爪形手畸形"是一种常见的手部畸形，是尺神经损伤引起的小鱼际肌、环指和小指内在肌萎缩所致。桡神经麻痹会导致"垂腕畸形"，是由于伸肌肌群麻痹使腕部和手指不能正常伸展。正中神经麻痹引起"猿手畸形"，主要表现为拇指与四指平齐，不能对掌，其余四指过伸。

3. 处理

如果持续慢性神经卡压不能缓解，将会导致不可逆的神经损伤。如果保守治疗无效，那么应该进行减压手术治疗。

（八）腕管综合征

1. 病因

腕管位于腕关节前部，由底部的腕骨和覆盖在上面的腕横韧带构成。有很多解剖结构通过这一狭窄区域，包括 8 条手指屈肌肌腱及其滑膜鞘和正中神经。腕管综合征的出现是由于管内的内容物增加或腕管容积减小导致管内压力增高，进而导致正中神经受压。尽管腕前部的直接损伤也可以造成腕管综合征，但是腕部重复屈曲的运动是导致出现腕管综合征的主要原因。

2. 症状和体征

正中神经的压迫通常引起感觉和运动功能共同缺失。感觉变化会逐渐发展为正中神经支配区的拇指、食指、中指和手掌的刺痛、麻木。患者可出现明显的手指感觉减退或丧失以及大鱼际和支配的肌肉力量的下降和萎缩，从而导致拇指的灵活度降低，与其他手指对捏的力量下降，甚至不能完成对指动作。

3. 处理

初期进行保守治疗，包括休息、固定、使用非甾体抗炎药。若症状还未消除，可以注射皮质醇。若保守治疗无效，可考虑进行腕横韧带解压术。

（九）桡骨茎突狭窄性腱鞘炎

1. 病因

桡骨茎突狭窄性腱鞘炎是由于拇指或腕部活动频繁，使拇短伸肌和拇长展肌的肌腱在桡骨茎突部的腱鞘内长期相互摩擦，导致该处肌腱与腱鞘产生无菌性炎症反应，局部出现水肿和纤维化，鞘管壁变厚，肌腱局部增粗造成肌腱在腱鞘内的滑动受阻而引起的临床症状。

2. 症状和体征

最主要的症状是手和前臂的酸痛，桡骨茎突明显压痛，有时可触及硬结节。手腕的活动会加重疼痛，Finklestein 试验呈阳性。拇指外展和伸展也会有疼痛和无力的症状。拇指根部附近疼痛与肿胀，移动时有"卡住"的感觉。

3. 处理

①急性期按照 POLICE 原则进行处理，包括休息、使用镇痛药和拇指夹板。急性期后可进行超声波等理疗技术进行治疗。使用关节松动术，维持关节活动范围。必要时可进行皮质类固醇注射治疗。②保守治疗后仍有持续症状的患者可以进行腱鞘减压术。

（十）月骨脱位

1. 病因

在腕部损伤中，月骨脱位虽然不是很常见，但是月骨是所有腕骨中最容易脱位的。大部分月骨脱位是由暴力性腕关节过伸造成的。比如摔倒时手过伸导致腕骨远端和近端间隙增大，牵拉月骨向前（掌侧）脱位。

2. 症状和体征

主要症状是腕部疼痛、肿胀和手腕屈曲困难。当月骨脱位导致正中神经压迫时，可导致屈肌麻木，甚至瘫痪。

3. 处理

首先按急性期 POLICE 原则进行处理，并且将患者转诊给外科医生进行复位。如果月骨脱位没有尽早发现，损伤会被进一步恶化，这时则需要外科手术移除。

（十一）手舟骨骨折

1. 病因

手舟骨是腕骨骨折最频发的部位。摔倒时，当腕关节处于过伸位，地面的冲击力挤压位于桡骨和远端腕骨之间的舟状骨，导致手舟骨骨折。此病容易误诊为严重扭伤，导致未对手腕进行完全的固定。如果没有合适的夹板进行固定，手舟骨常会由于缺乏足够的血液供应而恢复不良，因此发展为退行性病变和坏死。

2. 症状和体征

手舟骨骨折征象包括腕骨肿胀和鼻烟窝处剧烈疼痛。在鼻烟窝加压是鉴别腕扭伤和手舟骨骨折的最佳办法。沿拇指长轴施加压力，桡偏和尺偏都会激惹手舟骨的疼痛。

3. 处理

①按 POLICE 原则处理，用夹板固定，转诊到外科医生处进行 X 射线检查和石膏固定。②大部分情况下，石膏固定 6 ~ 8 周后，在贴扎保护下可以开始力量训练，过久的固定不利于手舟骨康复。③若保守治疗无效，可选择手术治疗，以免造成骨不连，延误康复治疗的时间。

（十二）腕部腱鞘囊肿

1. 病因

腕部腱鞘囊肿是运动中常见的一种滑膜囊肿，是发生于腕部关节腱鞘内的囊性肿物，常由关节囊、韧带、腱鞘中的结缔组织退变所致。囊内含有无色透明或橙色、淡黄色的浓稠黏液，发病部位可见一圆形肿块，有轻微酸痛感。病因尚不清楚，可能与慢性外伤或过度劳损有一定关系。

2. 症状和体征

患者主诉腕部肿胀、间发性疼痛或不痛，腕活动过程中可出现疼痛加剧。触诊时囊状结构可以是柔软的、坚韧的或者是非常坚硬的。

3. 处理

①可通过指压法消除肿胀，再贴上压力垫来进行治疗。②可采取穿刺抽取加药物注射治疗，并持续加压或者使用压力垫进行治疗。③若上述方法都不能有效防止腕部腱鞘囊肿复发，手术移除是最彻底的治疗方法。

（十三）手和手指的挫伤和压伤

1. 病因

掌骨和指骨都是进行精细活动的重要组成部分，但其周围只有很少的脂肪垫和肌肉垫来保护，因此受外力撞击或挤压时容易形成损伤。

2. 症状和体征

这类损伤可以从损伤既往史、疼痛史和软组织肿胀鉴别出来。

3. 处理

①在止血后，应该立即加压和冷敷。急性期之后再逐渐对损伤部位进行热疗。②远节指骨的挫伤会导致指甲下的血肿，造成指甲下积血并导致严重的疼痛。在止血前，患者应该将手置于冰水中浸泡，减缓该处血流。

（十四）扳机指

1. 病因

扳机指即狭窄性腱鞘炎，最常出现在屈肌肌腱和其他肌腱共同的腱鞘中，常由手的过度使用导致。扳机指可能会出现肌腱和腱鞘增厚，导致肌腱滑移受限。

2. 症状和体征

患者主诉当手指和拇指屈曲时，有软组织的抵抗感，还会有关节弹响声。触诊过程中，手指会有疼痛，可在指屈肌腱腱鞘末端触及肿块。

3. 处理

①早期治疗与桡骨茎突腱鞘炎的处理方法相同。但如果治疗效果不显著，可以注射类固醇缓解疼痛。当上述方法均未见效，应当使用支具固定肌腱。②中后期通过运动疗法保持关节活动度以防止肌腱粘连和痉挛也非常重要。保守治疗失败后，可进行手术松解。

（十五）伸肌腱撕裂（锤状指）

1. 病因

锤状指也叫作"棒球手"或者"篮球手"，是由于手指尖受到暴力打击导致手指伸肌肌腱在止点处卡顿与撕裂，严重时会造成撕脱性骨折。

2. 症状和体征

患者主诉远端指间关节疼痛。X 射线片可能显示有近节指骨背侧的撕脱性骨折；患者不能完全伸直手指，只能保持在屈曲位 30° 左右；患侧手指存在压痛点，撕脱的部分可以通过触诊触及。可能出现肿胀甚至血肿。

3. 处理

运用 POLICE 原则处理手指的疼痛和肿胀。如果没有骨折问题，远节指骨应该用支具固定在伸展位，保持 6 ~ 8 周。若患者未能恢复或不耐受夹板治疗，则需要进行手术干预。

（十六）纽孔畸形

1. 病因

纽孔畸形是由中节指骨背侧伸肌肌腱断裂引起的损伤。损伤发生在近端指间关节的末端。近端指骨间关节上的伸指肌撕裂，并且断裂的肌腱向近端指骨间关节两侧滑移到横轴，导致远端指骨间关节处于伸展位，而近端指骨间关节处于屈曲位。随着病情的发展，近端指间关节穿过撕裂的伸肌肌腱，就像纽扣穿过纽扣眼一样。

2. 症状和体征

患者主诉远端指骨间关节有严重疼痛和伸展无力感。有压痛点、肿胀和明显的畸形。

3. 处理

①在开始阶段进行冰敷，紧接着使用支具将近端指骨间关节固定于伸展位。注意：如果没用夹板充分的固定，那么纽孔畸形可能会永久存在。②夹板固定应该持续 5 ~ 8 周。手指被夹板固定时，应当鼓励患者屈曲远节指骨。③保守治疗后，如果患者仍然不能被动伸展近端指间关节，也可考虑手术干预。

（十七）猎场看护人拇指

1. 病因

猎场看护人拇指损伤机制通常是拇指近节指骨的暴力性伸展和外展导致的第一掌指关节尺侧副韧带的急性扭伤，多见于滑雪运动员和橄榄球运动员。

2. 症状和体征

患者主诉尺侧副韧带疼痛并且对指无力，拇指伸展和外展时症状加重。检查可发现拇指中段疼痛和肿胀。触诊拇指根部时会引起触痛。慢性症状患者会出现关节松弛。

3. 处理

①由于对指功能受损严重，应该及时进行合适的治疗。②如果出现关节失稳，应该立即咨询医生。如果关节稳定，应进行 X 射线检查以确定是否有骨折。③拇指夹板持续固定3 周，直到拇指疼痛症状消失。拇指支具的长度应该从腕部到拇指末端，并把拇指固定在中立位。④拆除支具后，参与运动时应该采用人字贴扎。⑤如果韧带完全撕裂，需要进行手术修复，使拇指恢复正常功能。

（十八）手指指骨间关节扭伤

1. 病因

手指指骨间关节扭伤包括近端指骨间关节和远端指骨间关节损伤。损伤程度从侧副韧带微细损伤到完全撕裂不等。手指指骨间关节侧副韧带扭伤在篮球、排球、足球这些运动中很常见，通常是由过大的轴向力、外翻或内翻的压力作用于指间关节所致。

2. 症状和体征

患者主诉受累关节疼痛和肿胀。在关节处有压痛，尤其是侧副韧带区域。在屈曲 150°时，关节可能会侧向和轴向失稳。侧副韧带的损伤能够通过内外翻应力试验进行评估。

3. 处理

①急性期运用 POLICE 原则、X 射线检查和夹板固定。近端指骨间关节一般固定在屈曲 30°～ 40°，固定 10 天左右。②如果损伤发生在远端指骨间关节，为了尽早恢复，用夹板固定在伸展位，固定数天。③如果是轻微扭伤，应当将损伤手指和其他手指一同固定，以提供保护性支持。之后，可以运用保护性马镫贴扎法对拇指和四指提供保护。

（十九）近端指骨间关节脱位，掌指关节脱位

1. 病因

指骨脱位的发生率很高，包括近端指骨间关节向背侧脱位、近端指骨间关节向掌侧脱位和掌指关节脱位。近端指骨间关节和掌指间关节脱位机制是由手指受到不同方向的扭转造成的。

2. 症状和体征

患者主诉近端指骨间关节出现疼痛和肿胀。近端指骨间关节会有很明显的撕裂畸形和

功能丧失。

3. 处理

急性期运用 POLICE 原则进行处理，并用夹板固定，由医生进行手法复位。复位后手指用夹板固定 3 ~ 4 周。去除夹板后，可用贴扎进行保护。

（二十）掌骨骨折

1. 病因

掌骨骨折一般是受到轴向直接暴力或者压力所致。第五掌骨骨折在拳击和武术项目中比较常见，因此第五掌骨骨折也叫作拳击手骨折。

2. 症状和体征

患者主诉疼痛和肿胀，手指成角畸形或旋转畸形。

3. 处理

急性期运用 POLICE 原则和镇痛药，进行 X 射线检查。手法复位后，用夹板固定 4 周，然后开始活动度练习。

Summary

1. To reduce the incidence of forearm, wrist, hand, and finger joint injuries, athletes should improve their understanding of injury prevention, get regular physical examinations, reasonably control exercise loads, and appropriately utilize protective equipment.

2. The special tests include: Finkelstein's test, Tinel's sign, Phalen's test, varus/valgus and slide test, lunotriquetral ballotment test, Allen's test, and TFCC compression test.

3. The forearm consists of ulna, radius, and connecting soft tissue. Sports injuries in this area include contusions, acute sprains, chronic stress syndrome of the forearm, and fractures. Colles' fractures in distal radius and ulna are the most common forearm fractures.

4. "Fallen onto an outstretched hand" or repetitive fatigue movements are the main causes of wrist injuries. Common injuries include sprain, lunate dislocationand scaphoid fractures.

5. Common hand injuries are caused by contusions and chronic compression. Nerve compression and nerve paralysis can lead to hand deformities such as claw hand deformity, wrist-drop deformity, or ape's hand deformity.

○ Review Questions

1. List the movements that may cause injuries to wrist and hand.

2. Describe the operation of the Finkelstein test.

3. Describe the symptoms of carpal tunnel syndrome.

4. Li Ming is a ski enthusiast. He fell during a ski trip. When Li Ming fell, his right wrist propped up on the ground. Suddenly, he had severe pain on the ulnar side of his wrist joint, limiting its movement, and he was not daring to stretch. As an athletic trainer, please briefly describe the evaluation and general treatments that need to be carried out.

小结

1. 为减少前臂、腕、手、手指关节损伤的发生，运动员应该增强防伤认识，定期进行身体检查，合理管控运动负荷，并合理使用护具。

2. 常用的特殊试验包括：握拳尺偏试验、神经叩击试验、屈腕加压试验、内外翻应力及滑移试验、月三角关节稳定性试验、Allen 试验和 TFCC 挤压试验。

3. 前臂由两块骨组成：尺骨、桡骨，以及相连的软组织。此区域的运动损伤包括：挫伤、急性扭伤、前臂慢性应力综合征和骨折。桡骨和尺骨远端的 Colles 骨折是最常见的前臂骨折。

4. 摔倒时的手撑地动作或重复性的疲劳运动是引起腕部损伤的常见原因。常见损伤包括扭伤、月骨脱位、手舟骨骨折。

5. 常见手部损伤是由挫伤和慢性压迫引起的。神经压迫和神经麻痹会导致手部出现畸形，如：爪形手畸形、垂腕畸形或者猿手畸形。

○ 复习题

1. 列举容易导致腕与手部损伤的动作。

2. 简述 Finkelstein 试验的操作方法。

3. 简述腕管综合症的症状。

4. 李明是一名滑雪爱好者，在一次滑雪中摔倒。李明摔倒时右手手掌撑地，顿时腕关节尺侧剧痛，活动受限，不敢伸展。请作为运动防护师的你简述需要进行的评估和简易处理。

Chapter 5 Injuries Around the Thighs and Pelvis

第五章　大腿和骨盆周围损伤

○ Main Contents

1. Prevention of injuries around the thighs and pelvis.

2. Assessment of injuries around the thighs and pelvis.

3. Identification and management of common injuries around the thighs and pelvis.

○ 主要内容

1. 大腿和骨盆周围损伤的预防。

2. 大腿和骨盆周围损伤的评估。

3. 大腿和骨盆周围常见损伤的识别和处理。

1　Prevention of Injuries Around the Thighs and Pelvis

The sacrum, two pelvic bones and the symphysis pubis form the pelvis. The sacroiliac joints on both sides can make the force acting on the trunk evenly transmitted to the lower limbs, and make the entire pelvis has a certain degree of elasticity, thus acting as a buffer for external forces. There are some strong ligaments and powerful muscles surrounding the hip, making it the largest and most stable joint in the body. The muscle groups around the hip joint play an important role in normal running and jumping. The pelvis, which is connected by ligaments and capsule, and the muscles around the hip joint work together to provide good stability for the functional activities of the limbs.

Therefore, this motion segment should not only ensure sufficient power transmission, but also play a stable role, resulting in the region of the muscles, joints and ligaments being vulnerable to injury. Developing the strength and flexibility of the thigh, hip and pelvic muscles is a fundamental way to avoid or minimize injury. The individual should focus on stretching the quadriceps, hamstring and inguinal muscles. The presence of a muscle strain in any muscle group can have a long-term effect on injury healing and cause dysfunction. Muscle strengthening programs should include squats, deadlifts, leg press and a variety of core strength strengthening exercises. A core stabilization training program is designed to help an individual gain strength, neuromuscular control, power and muscular endurance in the lumbo-pelvic-hip complex, thus facilitating a balanced muscular functioning of the entire kinetic chain. The goal of core stabilization should be to develop optimal levels of functional strength and dynamic stability and reduce injuries.

一、大腿和骨盆周围损伤的预防

骨盆由骶骨、两块髋骨及尾骨构成。骶髂关节连接骶骨和髂骨，两侧的骶髂关节能使作用在躯干上的力向双下肢均匀地传导，还能使整个骨盆环具有一定的弹性，从而起到缓冲外力的作用。尽管髋关节周围强韧的韧带，以及有力的肌群使其成为全身最大且稳定性较高的关节，但其依旧会发生许多损伤。髋关节周围肌群对于身体进行正常的跑步和跳跃等运动发挥着重要作用。由韧带、关节囊连接着的骨盆和髋关节周围的肌肉共同作用，为四肢进行功能活动提供了良好的稳定性。

因此，此运动环节既要保证足够的动力传导，同时也要发挥稳定的作用，否则此区域的肌肉、关节和韧带极易损伤。强化大腿、髋关节与骨盆周围肌群的力量和柔韧性是避免大腿和骨盆周围损伤或使其发生率最小化的基本方法。因此应注重对股四头肌、腘绳肌以及腹股沟区域的肌肉牵伸。在任何肌肉群中存在肌肉拉伤情况都会对损伤的愈合有着长期的影响并造成功能障碍。肌力增强训练方案应包括深蹲、硬拉、腿推举及各种核心力量增强的训练内容。核心稳定性训练的目的在于帮助运动员增强腰椎－骨盆－髋关节复合体的肌力、神经肌肉控制、爆发力和肌耐力，以此促进肌肉的功能平衡。核心稳定性的目标是使运动员获得理想的功能性力量和增强动态稳定性，减少损伤的发生。

2 Assessment of the Injuries Around the Thighs and Pelvis

2.1 History

The athletic trainer should ask the following questions:

- What happened when you got injured?
- What is the location of the pain? Is there radiating pain?
- What's the duration and nature of pain?
- What's the patient's habitual working posture or body motion?
- Is there any loss of lower limb strength?
- Is there any numbness/hypoesthesia or hypersensitivity?
- Does the patient have difficulty urinating?
- Are the patient's symptoms improving or getting worse, or remaining unchanged?
- What movement can relieve or aggravate the symptoms?
- Whether the patient has other medical conditions (such as rheumatoid arthritis, ankylosing spondylitis, etc.)?

2.2 Observation

The athletic trainer should pay attention to the following questions:

- Position. The athletic trainer should be aware of pelvic tilt, such as unequal leg length, unbalanced muscle contraction or scoliosis.
- Whether the patient is able or willing to stand on two legs.
- Balance.
- Whether the body posture is identical and symmetrical.
- Any significant shortening of the lower limb.
- Skin texture and color.
- Whether there is a scar.
- Ambulation. Observe the patient's walking and sitting posture.

2.3 Palpation

The bony landmarks, including the anterior superior iliac spine, anterior inferior iliac spine, greater trochanter, and symphysis pubis, need to be palpated. The soft-tissue sites of major concern are in the regions of the thighs, the groin, femoral triangle, sciatic nerve and major muscles.

2.4 Range of Motion and Muscle Strength

The patient is asked to perform both passive and active movements, to evaluate the range of motion and active and resistive strength. Activities include hip abduction, hip adduction, hip flexion and extension, hip internal and external rotation, and knee flexion and extension.

2.5 Special Tests

2.5.1 Thomas Test

The Thomas test is used to evaluate hip flexion contracture. The patient is in the supine position, and the athletic trainer checks for excessive lordosis, which is often associated with the tension in the hip flexor muscles. The athletic trainer flexed on thigh against the chest to test the opposite hip and knee, and ensures that the back is attached to the bed and the pelvis is in a neutral position. The patient maintains hip flexion. If there is no flexion contracture, the tested side hip is still on the examination bed. In the presence of contractures, the patient's lower extremities of the subject side will be elevated and there will be traction in the muscle. If the lower limb of the subject is pressed on the bed, the patient presents with increased lumbar lordosis, which also suggests a positive test result.

2.5.2 Patrick (Faber) Test

The patient is in the supine position and the athletic trainer places the tested foot on the knee of the other side, then slowly presses down on the knee joint of the tested side. If there is pain in the hip or the sacroiliac joint, the test result is positive, indicating the possible involvement of the homolateral hip joint, as well as possible psoas spasm or sacroiliac joint involvement.

2.5.3 Trendelenburg's Sign

The test assesses the stability of the hip joint and the stabilization of the pelvis by the hip abductor. The patient stands on one leg, and normally, the contralateral pelvis should rise. If the contralateral pelvis drops, the test result is positive, indicating poor gluteus medius muscle strength or unstable hip joint (such as dislocation of hip joint).

2.5.4 Ober's Test

The Ober's test is used to evaluate the contracture of the tensor fasciae latae (iliotibial tract). The patient lies on the unaffected side, and the balance is maintained by flexing the hip and knee joints of the unaffected side. The athletic trainer abducts and extends the thigh of the affected side and keeps the knee straight. After stabilizing the pelvis, the athletic trainer releases the abducted leg and allows it to drop into the adduction position with the knee straight. A contracted tensor fasciae latae or iliotibial tract will keep the thigh in an abducted position instead of falling into adduction.

2.5.5 Nobel's Test

The test is used to determine the presence of iliotibial tract friction syndrome around the knee joint. The patient is in the supine position with knees bent at 90° and hips flexed. The athletic trainer places pressure with his/her thumb on the lateral femoral epicondyle. The patient is asked to slowly extend the knee joint, and when extended to about 30° of flexion, a positive test result is indicated if there is severe pain in the lateral femoral epicondyle.

2.5.6 Ely's Test

The patient is in the prone position, and the athletic trainer passively flexes the patient's knee joint. If the patient's homolateral hip flexes while flexing the knee, the rectus femoris is tense and the test is considered positive.

2.5.7 Piriformis Test

The patient is in the lateral position, with the tested lower limb on the upper side. The patient flexes the hip to 60°, then flexes the knee. The athletic trainer stabilizes the hip with one hand while pressing down on the knee. If the piriformis muscle is tense, pain may occur. If the piriformis muscle compresses the sciatic nerve, pain in the buttocks and sciatica will occur.

2.5.8 Gaenslen's Test

The patient lies prone at the edge of the table with the contralateral hip and knee flexed. The ipsilateral hip is partially off the table surface so that the sacroiliac joint is on the edge of the table. The athletic trainer stands on the patient's side and gently presses the knee of the patient's tested side down. If there is pain in the sacroiliac joint, it indicates the presence of sacroiliac joint dysfunction.

2.5.9 Femoral Nerve Stretching Test

The patient lies prone on the examination table with the knees flexed, and the athletic trainer extends the hip of the patient's test side and maintains knee flexion. If there is pain or numbness in the front of the thigh and the back, there is a lesion in the femoral nerve and/or lumbar nerve roots.

2.5.10 Straight Leg Raise Test

The patient lies supine and flexes the hip with the knee joint in extension. In general, hip flexion can be achieved up to 70° with no pain. Some athletes with good flexibility, such as gymnasts, may not experience pain until the angle of flexion reaches 120°. Therefore, it is more important to observe the angle at which pain occurs than the pain as a symptom. If the sciatic nerve is compressed, the patient may feel pain radiating from the hip down to the knee joint. If the pain is confined to the back of the thigh, the hamstring could be the source of the problem.

2.5.11 Active Straight Leg Raise Test

The patient lies supine and is required to lift one leg about 20 cm off the bed with the knee straight. Ask the patient which leg is more difficult to lift or if sacroiliac joint pain is present.

How difficult it is to perform the test is an indicator of the severity of the condition.

2.5.12 Gillet (Sacral Fixation) Test

This test is also known as the ipsilateral supination test. The patient is in a standing position. The athletic trainer stands behind the patient with one thumb placed on the posterior superior iliac spine and the other thumb parallel to the sacrum. Ask the patient to stand on one leg with the other flexed as far as possible towards the chest, so that both hip and sacrum on the same side are rotated backward. Compare bilateral examination. If there is less movement of the sacroiliac joint in knee flexion (ipsilateral), it indicates a decrease in the range of motion of the sacroiliac joint.

2.5.13 Contracture Test of Rectus Femoris

The patient lies supine, with the shank lowered to the edge of the examination bed. When the patient flexes one knee to the chest, the angle of the knee on the subject side should be kept at 90°. If this is not possible (such as mild extension of the knee on the test side), the test is positive, indicating possible rectus femoris contracture.

2.5.14 Pelvic Falling Test

The patient should stand on a 20 cm high stool or pedal on one leg, and then slowly lower the non-weight-bearing lower limbs to the ground. The normal performance should be placing the arms on both sides of the trunk, maintaining the trunk upright, and no adduction or internal rotation of the hip. If the torso tilts forward and backward, the hip rotates inward and adducts, and the upper limb abducts in the process of lowering the leg, it indicates that the hip joint is unstable or the external rotation muscle is weak.

2.6 Leg-Length Measurement

2.6.1 Anatomical Discrepancy

The patient lies supine and the pelvis is in a neutral position. Measurement is taken between the medial malleolus and the anterior superior iliac spine of each leg.

2.6.2 Functional Discrepancy

The patient lies supine and the pelvis is in a neutral position. Measurement is taken between the navel and the medial malleolus of both lower limbs. If the anatomical length of the lower limbs is normal but the distance from the navel to the medial malleolus is different, it is suggested that the functional length of the lower limbs is unequal.

二、大腿和骨盆周围损伤的评估

（一）病史

运动防护师应询问以下问题：

- 患者的损伤是怎么造成的？
- 患者的疼痛位置在哪里？是否存在放射痛？
- 患者的疼痛的持续时间和性质是什么？
- 患者惯常的姿势或身体动作是什么？
- 患者是否存在下肢力量减退的情况？
- 患者是否有麻木感 / 感觉减退、感觉过敏？
- 患者是否存在排尿困难的情况？
- 患者的症状是改善、加重还是不变？
- 患者做什么动作会激惹或者缓解症状？
- 患者是否有其他疾病，如类风湿关节炎、强直性脊柱炎等？

（二）视诊

运动防护师应视诊以下问题：

- **姿势**。运动防护师应注意患者是否存在骨盆倾斜，例如双下肢不等长，肌肉收缩不平衡或脊柱侧弯。
- 患者是否能够或者愿意双腿站立。
- 患者的平衡性。
- 患者的肢体姿势是否相同和对称。
- 患者有无任何明显的下肢短缩。
- 患者皮肤的纹理和颜色。
- 患者是否有瘢痕。
- 患者的移动情况。观察患者走和坐时的姿势。

（三）触诊

应触诊患者的髂前上棘、髂前下棘、大转子及耻骨联合等主要的骨性标志。软组织触诊主要关注大腿、腹股沟区域、股三角、坐骨神经和主要的肌肉。

（四）关节活动度和肌肉力量

可让患者进行被动和主动活动，以评估其活动度和主动、抗阻肌力。活动包括：髋外展、髋内收、髋屈伸、髋内外旋及膝屈伸。

（五）特殊试验

1. 托马斯试验

托马斯试验用于评估髋关节是否存在屈曲挛缩。患者仰卧位，运动防护师检查是否存在过度腰椎前凸，此表现常伴随有屈髋肌群紧张。运动防护师屈曲患者一侧大腿紧贴胸部，测试对侧髋关节和膝关节，保证背部贴在床面且骨盆处于中立位，患者保持该姿势。若没有屈曲挛缩，则受试侧髋部仍位于检查床上；若存在挛缩，则患者受试侧下肢将抬高，且屈肌有牵拉感。若受试侧下肢被压在床上，则患者可呈现腰椎前凸增加，此表现也提示试验结果呈阳性。

2. 髋外旋外展试验 /Patrick 试验 /Faber 试验 /4 字试验

患者仰卧位，运动防护师将被检查侧下肢的足部置于另一侧下肢的膝关节上。运动防护师缓缓向下压被检查侧下肢的膝关节。若在髋或骶髂关节处感到疼痛，试验结果为阳性，提示同侧髋关节可能受累，以及可能存在腰肌痉挛或骶髂关节受累。

3. 单足站立试验 /Trendelenburg 征

Trendelenburg 征评估髋关节的稳定性和髋外展肌对骨盆的稳定能力。患者单腿站立，正常情况下对侧骨盆应上升。若对侧骨盆下降，则试验结果为阳性，提示臀中肌力量较差或髋关节不稳（如髋关节脱位）。

4. Ober's 试验

Ober's 试验用于评价阔筋膜张肌（髂胫束）挛缩。患者健侧卧位，健侧下肢屈髋屈膝保持平衡。运动防护师外展、后伸患侧大腿并保证膝关节伸直，稳定骨盆后，松开外展的大腿并允许其在伸直情况下下落至内收位。阔筋膜张肌或髂胫束短缩将使大腿保持外展位而不下落至内收位。

5. Nobel 试验

Nobel 试验用于确定膝关节周围是否存在髂胫束摩擦综合征。患者仰卧位，屈膝 90° 角，同时屈髋。运动防护师用拇指在股骨外上髁处施压。嘱患者缓慢伸展膝关节，当伸展至大约 30° 角时，若股骨外上髁出现严重的疼痛，提示试验结果为阳性。

6. 提踵试验

患者俯卧位，运动防护师屈曲患者膝部。屈膝时，患者同侧髋部同时屈曲，提示股直肌紧张，试验结果为阳性。

7. 梨状肌试验

患者侧卧位，受试侧下肢位于上方。患者屈髋 60° 并屈膝。运动防护师一只手稳定髋部，同时下压膝部。若梨状肌紧张，则会出现疼痛；若梨状肌压迫坐骨神经，则出现臀部疼痛和坐骨神经痛。

8. 盖氏试验（床边试验）

患者俯卧于检查台边缘，对侧髋关节和膝关节屈曲。同侧臀部一部分离开检查台台面，使骶髂关节位于检查台边缘。运动防护师站在患者一侧，轻轻将患者被测试侧膝部向下压，若骶髂关节出现疼痛，提示存在骶髂关节功能障碍。

9. 股神经牵拉试验

患者俯卧于检查台上，膝关节屈曲。运动防护师伸展患者被测试侧髋部，并维持膝关节屈曲。若大腿前方和背部疼痛或麻木，则股神经和 / 或腰椎神经根存在病变。

10. 直腿抬高试验

患者仰卧位，在膝关节伸直的状态下屈曲髋关节。正常情况下，可屈曲达到 70° 而不出现疼痛症状，某些如体操运动员等柔韧性较好的运动员在屈曲角度达到 120° 之前可能都不会出现疼痛症状。因此，观察疼痛出现的角度比观察疼痛这种症状本身更为重要。若坐骨神经受到压迫，患者会感到从臀部放射到膝关节以下的疼痛。如果仅大腿后部出现疼痛，则问题可能来源于腘绳肌。

11. 主动直腿抬高试验

患者仰卧，单腿抬离台面约 20 厘米，膝盖伸直。运动防护师询问患者抬起哪条腿更困难，或是否出现骶髂关节疼痛。执行这项测试的困难程度是判定病情严重程度的一个指标。

12. 骶骨固定试验

该试验也称为同侧后旋试验。患者站立位，运动防护师位于患者身后，一只手拇指放于髂后上棘，另一只手拇指平行放于骶骨上。嘱患者单腿站立，使另一侧下肢尽量屈向胸部，使得同侧髋和骶骨均向后旋转。双侧检查进行比较。若膝关节屈曲（同侧）骶髂关节移动得很少，则表示骶髂关节活动度减小。

13. 股直肌挛缩试验

患者仰卧，小腿下垂至检查床边缘。患者屈曲一侧膝关节至胸前时，受试侧膝关节角度应保持在 90°。若不能（如受试侧膝关节轻度伸展），则试验结果为阳性，提示可能存在股直肌挛缩。

14. 骨盆降落试验

患者单腿站于 20 厘米高的凳子或踏板上，然后缓慢放下非负重侧下肢至地面上。正常表现应该双臂置于躯干两侧，躯干直立，髋部无内收和内旋。若在放下腿的过程中出现躯干前后倾、髋部内旋内收、上肢外展等动作，则提示髋关节不稳定或外旋肌无力。

（六）下肢长度检查

1. 结构性不等长

患者仰卧位，骨盆处于中立位，分别测量双侧髂前上棘至内踝的距离。

2. 功能性不等长

患者仰卧位，骨盆处于中立位，分别测量肚脐至双侧下肢内踝的距离。若结构性下肢长度正常但肚脐至内踝的距离有差异，则表示存在功能性下肢不等长。

3 Identification and Management of Common Injuries Around the Thighs and Pelvis

3.1 Quadriceps Contusions

3.1.1 Etiology

It is usually caused by a direct impact to the anterior, medial or lateral of the thigh. The rectus femoris is the most frequently injured muscle because of its position.

3.1.2 Symptoms and Signs

Pain, weakness, a transitory loss of function, and immediate capillary bleeding usually occur at the instant of trauma. Palpation may reveal a circumscribed swollen area that is painful to the touch. Grade 1 contusion was accompanied by mild pain, swelling, increased muscle tone, and knee flexion at more than 90°. Grade 2 contusion was accompanied by moderate pain and swelling, knee flexion is limited to 45° to 90°, and limp occurs when walking. Grade 3 contusion may result in loss of function, tear of fascia and development of muscular herniation, deep muscle bleeding with spread into the septum, severe pain, swelling and hematoma, knee flexion less than 45°, and limp.

3.1.3 Management

① After the quadriceps contusions, the knee should be placed passively in a flexion position and treated according to the POLICE principle; NSAIDs and acesodyne are considerable. To avoid myositis ossificans, hot compress, massage and ultrasonic treatment should not be adopted in the acute stage of injury. ② For the patient with grade 2–3 contusions, crutches are available. ③ If there is more bleeding in the anterior thigh, it should be managed in time. ④ Follow-up rehabilitation program consists of range of motion (ROM) exercises and progressive resistance exercises (PRE) within a pain-free limitation. ⑤ Treatments such as heat therapy can be used after the acute phase of injury. An elastic bandage should be used to provide constant pressure and mild support to the quadriceps area. Exercise should be carried out progressively within a pain-free condition.

3.2 Heterotopic Ossification (Myositis Ossificans)

3.2.1 Etiology

Severe or repeated impacts to the thigh usually result in bleeding or hematoma within the quadriceps muscle, which can lead to myositis ossificans or heterotopic ossification. The inflamed tissue produces calcification similar to bone or cartilage, which can be shown on radiographs 4 to 6 weeks after injury.

3.2.2 Symptoms and Signs

Symptoms of Myositis ossificans include pain in the muscle, particularly during exercise. The athlete will have a restricted range of motion in the leg and a hard lump may be felt in the deep muscle. An X-ray can confirm the diagnosis and show the calcification.

3.2.3 Management

① Modalities: ultrashort wave, kerotherapy, magnetic therapy, millimeter wave and ice compress. ② If there is pain and limited mobility, surgical treatment should be used to remove the calcification area. ③ To avoid the development of myositis ossificans, initial bleeding should be controlled and early inappropriate treatments such as massage should be avoided.

3.3 Quadriceps Muscle Strain

3.3.1 Etiology

A quadriceps strain usually occurs when the hip joint is in an extended position. When the hip and knee flex suddenly, a powerful contraction of the muscle can cause a quadriceps strain. Most strains occur at the junction of the muscle and tendon, in which the rectus femoris strain is more common and severe.

3.3.2 Symptoms and Signs

Patients often experience severe pain, swelling, and inability of knee flexion.

Patients with grade 1 quadriceps femoris strain may complain of tension in the anterior part of the thigh, which may or may not be accompanied by swelling, and have a normal gait, but they usually experience mild discomfort on palpation.

Patients with a grade 2 quadriceps strain may have an abnormal gait. The patient may have felt a sudden twinge and pain down along the rectus femoris during activity. Swelling may be noticeable, and palpation and resistant knee extension may produce pain.

Patients with grade 3 quadriceps femoris strain have severely limited functional mobility and severe pain. The patient is often intolerant to palpation; swelling develops immediately after injury, and the patient is unable to complete active or resistant knee extension activities.

3.3.3 Management

① Patients with grade 1 quadriceps femoris strain should be immediately treated according to the POLICE principle, and the active range of motion exercise and quadriceps femoris isometric muscle strength training should be conducted within the painless range. Pain-free quadriceps progressive resistive strengthening exercises may be performed within 2 days. Compression with a protection equipment should be used at all times until the patient is free of pain and no longer complaining of tightness. ② Patients with grade 2 quadriceps femoris strain should be treated with ice compress and pressurized bandage, and be on crutches for 3–5 days after injury. On the third day after the injury, patients can receive quadriceps isometric training and active range of motion training within the painless range. Ice compress combined with active range of motion training can help patients recover their range of motion and enhance muscle strength in a painless range. ③ Patients with grade 3 quadriceps strain should use crutches for 7–14 days or longer to help return to normal gait. After the injury, we should immediately take a pressure bandage and ice compress treatment to avoid quadriceps muscle stretching activities. In the absence of pain, the patient may begin quadriceps isometric training and a small range of active range of motion training, with load gradually increasing after 2 weeks according to the patient's condition.

3.4 Hamstring Muscle Strains

3.4.1 Etiology

Acute/severe trauma: associated with traction and eccentric loading, seen in sports that require deceleration and change of direction.

Chronic/minor trauma: seen in repeated activities (e.g., long-distance running), may be associated with muscle weakness, fatigue, and biomechanical abnormalities.

3.4.2 Symptoms and Signs

Hamstring strain can involve the muscle belly or bony attachment. The extent of injury can vary from the pulling apart of a few muscle fibers to a complete rupture or an avulsion fracture. Capillary hemorrhage, pain, and immediate loss of function vary according to the degree of trauma. Grade 1 hamstring strain usually is evidenced by muscle soreness during movement, accompanied by point tenderness. The soreness of the mild hamstring strain in most instances can be attributed to muscle spasm rather than to the tearing of tissue. Fewer than 20 percent of fibers are torn in a grade 1 hamstring strain. Grade 2 hamstring strain represents a partial tearing of muscle fibers, identified by a sudden snap or tear of the muscle accompanied by severe pain and a loss of function during knee flexion. Fewer than 70 percent of fibers are torn in a grade 2 hamstring tear. Grade 3 hamstring strain has a tendon or muscle rupture, with severe bleeding and dysfunction. There is severe edema, muscle tension, loss of function, ecchymosis, palpable mass or intermuscular depression. Grade 3 muscle strain has more than 70% of muscle fiber tears.

3.4.3 Management

① Initially, POLICE, NSAIDs and analgesics are given as needed. The patient should not be allowed to resume full activity until the complete function of the injured part is restored. ② POLICE should be used for 24 to 48 hours in patients with grade 2 strains and for 48 to 72 hours in patients with grade 3 strains. ③ After the injury's inflammatory phase, a treatment regimen of isometric exercise, cold therapy, and ultrasound may be beneficial. In later stages of healing, gentle stretching within tolerable pain limits, jogging, and ergometer cycling may be used. After the pain has gone away, the athlete can begin to stretch and flex the knee. In the process of muscle rehabilitation after injury, eccentric exercise should be emphasized.

3.5 Femoral Fractures

3.5.1 Etiology

Femoral fractures are more common in middle-aged patients and elderly individuals with osteoporosis. Risk factors for fracture of the femur include wrong training methods, such as suddenly increasing the intensity or volume of training; gender; internal factors including poor alignment of the lower extremity, decreased bone mass, and metabolic diseases. The prognosis of the fracture is dependent on the specific location of the injury and the degree to which the blood supply is compromised.

3.5.2 Symptoms and Signs

The patient complains of severe pain and the inability to stand or walk. The patient's muscles are contracted tonically due to protective effects and they are unable to move.

3.5.3 Management

① The patient must be immediately immobilized and transported for medical care. The physician will perform either an open or a closed reduction with some type of rigid internal fixation. ② After surgery, the athlete must be immobilized with a hinged brace. Rehabilitation requires a slow progression over approximately a 4-month period.

3.6 Adductor/Hip Flexor Strain (Groin Strain)

3.6.1 Etiology

The musculature of the groin includes the iliopsoas, the rectus femoris and the adductor group (the pectineus, gracilis adductor brevis, adductor longus and adductor magnus). Muscle strains in this region may present as acute injury or an overuse syndrome that occurs at the muscle-tendon junction. The injury mechanism usually involves a sudden pull due to the external rotation of the abduction leg, or inflammation of the muscles and tendons.

3.6.2 Symptoms and Signs

The strain can be felt as a sudden twinge or a feeling of tearing during an active movement, or the patient may notice it after the activity. Like most tears, the adductor/hip flexor strain produces pain, weakness and internal hemorrhage.

3.6.3 Management

① The strain should be treated by POLICE, NSAIDs and analgesics as needed for 48 to 72 hours. Passive, active and resistive muscle tests should be given to ascertain the exact muscle or muscles that are involved. ② Maintain resting and immobilization. Take daily whirlpool therapy or cryotherapy to relieve the pain. Exercise should be delayed until the groin area is pain-free. In the exercise rehabilitation process, gradual stretching and restoration of the normal range of motion should be emphasized. Until normal flexibility and strength are restored, bandages or protective devices should be applied. ③ Perform trunk stability training in functional activity pattern, and balance training in an unstable plane, emphasizing proprioception input. The patient should pay attention to the hip adductor group of eccentric strength exercises. ④ Modalities: ice compress, hyperthermia, massage, ultrasound, TENS and shock wave, etc.

3.7 Trochanteric Bursitis

3.7.1 Etiology

Trochanteric bursitis is a relatively common condition of the greater trochanter of the femur. Although commonly called bursitis, the condition can also be inflammation at the site where the gluteus medius muscle inserts or the iliotibial tract passes over the trochanter. Injuries are most common from overuse and in people with pelvic or gait abnormalities.

3.7.2 Symptoms and Signs

Pain in the lateral hip, located just above the great trochanter or above the posterior surface of the greater trochanter, may extend from the lateral thigh to the knee joint and may be worsened after physical activity and relieved after rest.

3.7.3 Management

① Apply POLICE, NSAIDs and analgesics as needed. ② Correct mechanical problems, such as unequal length of lower limbs or abnormal mechanism of the lumbar spine. ③ If it is caused by overuse, the training plan should be changed. ④ Adopting exercise therapy: hip internal and external rotation muscle stretching exercises, hip muscle stretching exercises. ⑤ Modalities: cold therapy, shallow hyperthermia, electrical stimulation, ultrasound.

3.8 Sprains of the Hip Joint

3.8.1 Etiology

Hip sprain usually results from tearing of the tissue around the hip due to excessive movement beyond the normal range of motion.

3.8.2 Symptoms and Signs

The patients cannot circumvent the thigh. Symptoms are similar to a stress fracture. There is significant pain in the hip region, which can be increased by hip rotation.

3.8.3 Management

① Take further imaging examinations to exclude fracture. ② POLICE, NSAIDs and analgesics should be given as needed. ③ Weight bearing should be limited according to the grade of sprain. ④ Patients with grade 2 or 3 sprains should walk on crutches. ROM and PRE exercises should be delayed until the hip is pain-free.

3.9 Hip Joint Dislocation

3.9.1 Etiology

The hip joint is a ball-and-socket joint and it is stable, because it is surrounded by tough ligaments and protected by strong muscles. Dislocation through the weak area between the ligaments can occur only with indirect violence. Most of the injured people are young and middle-aged, who suffer from the impact of strong violence in labor or car accidents. Torsion, lever or conduction of violence can be the causes. A hip dislocation causes serious pathology by tearing capsular and ligamentous tissue. A fracture is often associated with this injury, accompanied by possible damage to the sciatic nerve.

3.9.2 Symptoms and Signs

Posterior dislocation of the hip is more common. Posterior dislocation of the hip presents with a flexed, adducted and internally rotated thigh. Palpation will reveal that the head of the femur has moved to a position posterior to the acetabulum.

3.9.3 Management

① Medical attention must be ensured immediately after displacement, or muscle contractures may complicate the reduction. Patients often require 2 weeks of bed rest and crutches for 1 month or more. ② Adopting exercise therapy: A. Quadriceps muscle isometric contraction exercise, gradually developed to isometric resistance and isotonic contraction exercise. B. Muscle strength exercise of the trunk and undamaged lower limbs. C. Gluteal muscle strength exercises. ③ Position guidance: the affected limb should be placed in a neutral position with the abduction of 10°–15°and ankle dorsiflexion of 90°.

3.10 Femoral Head Avascular Necrosis

3.10.1 Etiology

It is a common clinical disease, due to a variety of different etiology, such as fracture, dislocation or medical diseases destroying the blood supply of the femoral head, leading to femoral head ischemia, necrosis and collapse, often resulting in severe hip joint dysfunction. Certain other risk factors, such as the use of some medications (e.g., steroids), blood coagulation disorders, or excessive alcohol use, create increased pressure within the bone, causing the blood vessels to narrow and making it hard for the vessels to deliver enough blood to the bone cells.

3.10.2 Symptoms and Signs

There is pain around the hip or knee, which gets worse during walking or weight training, dysfunction of the hip joint, and decreased bone mass of the affected hip joint. The patient may have a history of corticosteroid use and hip trauma.

3.10.3 Management

① Use analgesics and non-steroidal anti-inflammatory drugs. ② Use two crutches when walking. ③ Adopting exercise therapy: range of motion exercise within the pain-free range of the affected hip joint, hip muscle stretching, hip and gluteal muscle strength exercise, hydrotherapy, fixed cycling. ④ Modalities: cold therapy, hyperthermia, transcutaneous electrical nerve stimulation (TENS).

3.11 Hip Labral Tear

3.11.1 Etiology

A hip labral tear most often results from repetitive movements, such as running or rotation of the hip, that cause degeneration and damage to the labrum. It may also be caused by an acute injury, such as a dislocation.

3.11.2 Symptoms and Signs

There is hip-around pain, catching and locking. The pain is aggravated when the hip joint rotates during walking. The pain is more obvious at night. The hip function is limited.

3.11.3 Management

① Rest. ② Modalities: heat therapy, cold therapy, ultrasound. ③ Treatment for a hip labral tear may consist of exercises to maximize hip range of motion, hip strengthening and stability exercises, and avoid movements that place stress on the hip joint. ④ Analgesic and corticosteroids. ⑤ If pain persists for more than 4 weeks, surgery may be indicated, either to remove a piece of the torn labrum or to repair the tear.

3.12 Sciatica/Piriformis Syndrome

3.12.1 Etiology

Sciatica is a term used to describe any pain produced by irritation of the sciatic nerve. The sciatic nerve can be irritated by an intervertebral disk problem in the lower back, direct trauma, or trauma from surrounding structures such as the piriformis muscle, in which case sciatic nerve irritation is also called piriformis syndrome. Lesions of the piriformis muscle itself, such as myofascial pain, muscle hypertrophy, trauma or sacroiliac joint dysfunction, can lead to sciatic nerve pain.

3.12.2 Symptoms and Signs

The athlete trainer should differentiate low back problems (intervertebral disk disease) from piriformis syndrome as the cause of sciatica. In the case of piriformis syndrome, the patient might report a deep pain in the buttock, without low back pain, and possibly radiating pain in the back of the thigh, lateral calf and foot, also indicating sciatica. Palpation in the sciatic notch also produces pain. It is possible that pain is associated with an active myofascial trigger point in the piriformis.

3.12.3 Management

① NSAIDs, muscle relaxants and analgesics should be given as needed. ② Adopting exercise therapy: stretching piriformis muscle in hip flexion, adduction and internal rotation position; hip abductor, external rotation and other core muscle strength exercises, lumbar and back stability exercises. ③ Modalities: hyperthermia, ultrasound.

3.13 Slipped Capital Femoral Epiphysis

3.13.1 Etiology

Slipped capital femoral epiphysis is more common in teenage males. 25 percent of cases are caused by trauma. X-ray examination may show femoral head slippage posteriorly and inferiorly.

3.13.2 Symptoms and Signs

A slipped capital femoral epiphysis causes groin pain. In the early stages of this condition, signs may be minimal. In the final stage of its development, however, there is hip and knee pain during passive and active motion, limitations of abduction, flexion and medial rotation, and a limp.

3.13.3 Management

In minor slippage, rest and non-weight bearing may prevent further slipping. Noticeable displacement usually requires corrective surgery.

3.14 Snapping Hip

3.14.1 Etiology

Snapping hip refers to the audible or felt sound of the hip joint during active flexion and walking. Extra-articular popping is common. The main reason is that the posterior edge of the iliotibial tract or the anterior edge of the gluteus maximus tendon is thickened. When the hip joint is flexed, adducted and rotated, the thickened tissue slides back and forth in the greater trochanter and gives out a snap. There is no such phenomenon during passive movement, which is more common in young adults and bilateral. The sound is often spontaneous and can develop to the severity of one step one sound. But there is generally no pain. If there is pain, it is often complicated by bursitis of the greater trochanter. Other causes are anatomical structures that can predispose an individual to a snapping hip, including a narrow pelvis, abnormal increases in abduction range of motion, and lack of range of motion into external rotation or tight internal rotators. Intraarticular causes are loose bodies, acetabulum labral tears and subluxation of the hip joint itself.

3.14.2 Symptoms and Signs

The hip becomes unstable, and the patient may complain of a snapping, possibly accompanied by severe pain and disability with each snap. Ober's test result may be positive.

3.14.3 Management

① Ice compress, NSAIDs and physiotherapy are often used in the treatment to reduce inflammation and relieve pain. ② Adopting rehabilitation measures: After the pain symptoms are relieved, stretching exercises and muscle strengthening exercises can be applied.

3.15 Pelvic Contusion (Hip Pointer)

3.15.1 Etiology

Contusion of iliac crest and abdominal musculature contusion, commonly known as a hip pointer, mostly occurs in contact sports.

3.15.2 Symptoms and Signs

A hip pointer produces immediate pain, spasms and transitory paralysis of the soft structures. As a result, the patient is unable to rotate the trunk or flex the thigh without pain.

3.15.3 Management.

① Treatment should follow the POLICE principle immediately after injury and keep it intermittently for at least 48 hours. ② In severe cases, bed rest should be performed for 1 to 2 days and the X-ray examination should be performed. ③ Massage and ultrasound after the ice therapy. ④ Steroids injection. ⑤ Oral anti-inflammatory drugs. The recovery period lasts from 1 to 3 weeks.

3.16 Athletic Pubalgia (Sports Hernia)

3.16.1 Etiology

Athletic pubalgia may be caused by repetitive stress to the symphysis pubis, such as movements in soccer and ice hockey. Forceful hip adduction from a hyperextended position creates shear forces that are transmitted through the symphysis pubis to the common insertion of the rectus abdominis, the hip adductors and the conjoined tendon at the pubic tubercle. These forces may result in micro tears of the transversalis fascia or the aponeurosis of the internal and external obliques abdominal.

3.16.2 Symptoms and Signs

Chronic pain often occurs only during exertion and may persist for several months. Sharp, burning pain localizes to the lower abdominal and inguinal region initially and later radiates to the adductors and testicles. There is point tenderness at the pubic tubercle. Pain is increased with resisted hip flexion, internal rotation and abdominal muscle contraction. Pain also occurs with resisted hip adduction, although the adductors are not tender, which differentiates this condition from an adductor strain.

3.16.3 Management

① Conservative treatment should be adopted after the injury. ② After a week, stretching of the hip flexors, adductors and rotators, hamstrings and low back muscles can be incorporated. ③ After 2 weeks, strengthening of the abdominals and hip adductors and flexors should be started. ④ At 3 to 4 weeks, running can be started and subsequent jumping and kicking exercises can be started within the pain tolerance range. ⑤ If conservative treatment fails, surgery is required.

3.17 Pelvic Floor Dysfunction

3.17.1 Etiology

Pelvic floor dysfunction is common for females of all ages. Pelvic floor dysfunction mostly occurs in athletes engaging in sports involving high-impact activities such as gymnastics, track and field, or sports that involve jumping.

3.17.2 Symptoms and Signs

In female athletes, pelvic floor dysfunction is most likely to result in urinary incontinence, prolapse of the pelvic organs, or complaints of chronic pelvic pain.

3.17.3 Management

① NSAIDs and analgesics should be given as needed. ② Pelvic floor muscle strength training. ③ Modalities: electrical stimulation of pelvic floor muscles. ④ If there is a trigger point in the relevant muscle, it should be released to relieve the pain.

3.18 Sacroiliac Joint Dysfunction

3.18.1 Etiology

Sacroiliac joint dysfunction and pain is a subtype of posterior pelvic (lower back) pain. There are many causes, such as trauma, repeated hip flexion and rotation, bending and other activities.

3.18.2 Symptoms and Signs

The pain is located in the posterior sacral sulcus or posterior superior iliac spine of the pelvis and radiates distally to the buttocks and sometimes to the lower limbs. In some patients, pain can radiate around the hip joint and into the groin. In the lower limb activities, there will be clicking and locking. Running will aggravate the pain. Gaenslen test result is positive.

3.18.3 Management

① Manual manipulation can be highly effective. ② NSAIDs and analgesics were administered as needed. ③ Adopting exercise therapy: lumbar and pelvic range of motion training, pelvic floor muscle and core muscle strength exercise, core stability exercise, joint mobilization. ④ Using kinesio tape. ⑤ Proceeding physical therapy: heat therapy, cold therapy.

3.19 Femoroacetabular Impingement Syndrome

3.19.1 Etiology

It refers to abnormal contact or collision between the proximal femur and the edge of the acetabulum at the end of the hip joint movement due to the abnormal anatomical morphology of the femur and the acetabulum, resulting in cartilage damage of the labrum and the edge of the acetabulum. It's called a syndrome because the impact can cause a series of joint injuries. Hip impingement syndrome = abnormal bone friction impingement + labrum injury + cartilage injury. It can be divided into two categories: ① Cam type: It often occurs in men who love sports, mainly because of the abnormal protrusion of the femoral head and neck joint, making it a cam-like non-spherical body. During strenuous activities, especially when the hip joint is flexed, the protruding part squeezes, collides and shear acetabulum cartilage and acetabulum labrum, thus causing pain and other symptoms. ② Pincer type: It usually occurs in middle-aged women who enjoy activities and is mainly caused by acetabular abnormalities. It is found in patients with backward acetabular tilt or too deep acetabulum.

3.19.2 Symptoms and Signs

Pain in the groin region, hip or greater trochanter (c-sign) is intermittent and may worsen after physical activity, prolonged walking or prolonged sitting. During an examination, patients usually present with limited hip movement, especially in flexion, adduction and internal rotation.

3.19.3 Management

① Conservative treatment: including changes in the hip joint movement pattern, that is, to avoid excessive flexion of the hip joint and reduce the amount of exercise to reduce the occurrence of collisions, as well as the use of NSAIDs to relieve symptoms. However, conservative treatment provides only temporary relief of pain symptoms and does not eliminate the cause of impingement and therefore does not prevent the progression of joint degeneration. ② Surgical treatment.

3.20 Stress Fractures

3.20.1 Etiology

Stress fractures in the pelvic area are seen mostly in distance runners. Repetitive periodic forces created by ground counterforces can produce stress fractures in the pelvis and the proximal femur. The most common sites are the inferior pubic ramus, the femoral neck and the subtrochanteric area of the femur.

3.20.2 Symptoms and Signs

Commonly, the patient complains of groin pain along with an aching sensation in the thigh that increases with activity and decreases with rest. Standing on one leg may be impossible for the patient. Deep palpation will cause severe point tenderness.

3.20.3 Management

① Rest. ② Proper weight-bearing. ③ Adopting exercise therapy: painless range of motion exercise and static exercise, concentric exercise. Gradually restore the full range of motion exercise. The eccentric exercise can be started until pain disappeared. ④ Modalities: heat therapy, cold therapy, transcutaneous electrical nerve stimulation (TENS). ⑤ Surgical surgery.

三、大腿和骨盆周围常见损伤的识别和处理

（一）股四头肌挫伤

1. 病因

股四头肌挫伤常由大腿前侧、内侧或外侧受到直接撞击导致。由于股直肌位于最前方，因此股直肌是最常损伤的肌肉。

2. 症状和体征

创伤发生后立刻出现疼痛、无力、短暂的功能丧失以及出血。局部触诊有肿胀和压痛。1级挫伤伴有轻度疼痛、肿胀、触诊肌肉紧张，患者屈膝角度大于90°；2级挫伤伴有中度疼痛、肿胀，屈膝角度局限于45°～90°，行走时会出现跛行；3级挫伤可导致功能丧失，筋膜撕裂以及肌疝发生，深层肌肉出血并向肌间隔扩散，伴有严重疼痛、肿胀以及血肿，屈膝角度小于45°并有跛行症状。

3. 处理

①股四头肌挫伤后应将膝关节被动放置在屈曲位，并根据POLICE原则进行处理；可给予非甾体抗炎药及镇痛药。损伤急性期不可采取热敷、按摩及超声波等处理，以避免发生骨化性肌炎。②2、3级挫伤的患者，可拄拐。③大腿前侧如果有较多出血，应及时处理。④后续康复包括在疼痛可忍受范围内进行关节活动度和渐进性抗阻训练。⑤在损伤急性期之后可采取热敷等处理。使用弹性绷带给股四头肌提供持续的压力和支撑。训练应在无痛情况下循序渐进。

（二）异位骨化（骨化性肌炎）

1. 病因

大腿部受到严重的撞击或受到反复撞击，通常会引起股四头肌内出血或血肿，长此以往会导致骨化性肌炎或异位骨化的发生。发炎的组织会产生类似于骨或软骨的钙化，在损伤4～6周后可通过X射线显示钙化区。

2. 症状和体征

骨化性肌炎的症状包括肌肉疼痛，特别是在运动时。腿部活动范围会受到限制，肌肉深处可能会有硬块。影像学可以确诊并显示钙化。

3. 处理

①物理治疗：超短波、蜡疗、磁疗、毫米波及冰敷。②若有疼痛并存在活动度受限，应采取手术治疗，移除钙化区域。③为了避免骨化性肌炎的发生，应尽可能控制最初的出血量和避免早期采取按摩等不合适的治疗方法。

（三）股四头肌拉伤

1. 病因

当髋关节处于伸展位，如果突然屈髋屈膝，使肌肉产生强有力的收缩，就会造成股四头肌拉伤。大多数拉伤发生在肌肉和肌腱结合部，其中股直肌拉伤较为常见且严重。

2. 症状和体征

患者常表现为剧烈疼痛、肿胀以及无法屈膝。1级股四头肌拉伤的患者可能主诉感觉大腿前侧紧张，可伴或不伴有肿胀，步态正常，但触诊时患者通常会有轻微不适感。2级股四头肌拉伤的患者可能存在步态异常的表现。患者在活动中会感到沿股直肌向下的突然刺痛和疼痛。可见肿胀，触诊和抗阻伸膝会引起疼痛。3级股四头肌拉伤的患者功能活动严重受限，且有严重的疼痛。患者通常无法耐受触诊检查，伤后立刻出现肿胀，不能完成主动或抗阻伸膝活动。

3. 处理

①1级股四头肌拉伤后立即按照POLICE原则进行处理，并在无痛范围内进行主动关节活动度训练和股四头肌等长肌力训练。伤后2天内可进行无痛的股四头肌渐进性抗阻训练。应持续使用护具加压保护，直到患者疼痛症状消失且不再感到大腿前部紧张。②2级股四头肌拉伤的患者伤后应及时冰敷和加压包扎，并在伤后3~5天拄拐。伤后第3天，患者可在无痛范围内进行股四头肌等长练习和主动关节活动度训练。冰敷结合主动关节活动度训练可帮助患者在无痛范围内恢复关节活动度以及增强肌力。③3级股四头肌拉伤的患者应该使用拐杖7~14天或更久，以帮助恢复正常的步态。伤后应立即采取加压包扎和冰敷等处理，避免进行股四头肌拉伸活动。在无痛情况下，患者可以开始股四头肌等长训练和小范围的股四头肌主动关节活动度训练，2周后根据患者情况逐渐增加负荷。

（四）腘绳肌拉伤

1. 病因

急性/重大创伤：与牵拉、离心负荷相关，见于需要减速和变换方向的运动。慢性/轻微创伤：见于反复活动（如长跑），可能与肌肉无力、疲劳和生物力学异常有关。

2. 症状和体征

腘绳肌拉伤可能发生在肌腹或者肌腱附着点。轻度损伤为少量肌纤维断裂，严重的肌纤维可能完全断裂，或是撕脱性骨折。根据损伤的程度不同，可能出现毛细血管出血、疼痛、即刻丧失功能。1级腘绳肌拉伤通常依据运动时是否有酸痛和压痛点来判断。轻度腘绳肌拉伤后的酸痛多是因为肌肉痉挛而不是组织撕裂。1级拉伤的肌纤维撕裂比例少于20%。2级腘绳肌拉伤有部分肌纤维撕裂，诊断依据是肌肉被突然拉断或者撕裂，伴有严重的疼痛和屈膝功能丧失。2级拉伤的肌纤维撕裂比例少于70%。3级腘绳肌拉伤有肌腱或肌肉断裂，伴随严重出血和功能障碍，有严重的水肿、肌紧张、功能丧失、瘀斑、可触诊到的肿块或肌间凹陷。3级肌肉拉伤的肌纤维撕裂比例超过70%。

3. 处理

①损伤初期根据 POLICE 原则进行处理，服用非甾体抗炎药及镇痛药。患者应在损伤部位完全恢复后再进行全身性活动。②2 级拉伤时，POLICE 原则应实施 24 ~ 48 小时，3 级拉伤时，POLICE 原则应实施 48 ~ 72 小时。③在损伤的急性炎症期后，可采用静力训练、冷疗和超声波进行治疗。之后的恢复期可以进行在疼痛可耐受范围内的牵拉练习、慢跑和功率车等练习。在疼痛症状消失后，患者可开始进行伸展和屈膝练习。损伤之后的肌肉康复应强调肌肉的离心运动。

（五）股骨骨折

1. 病因

股骨骨折多见于中年人和患有骨质疏松的老年人。导致股骨发生骨折的危险因素包括：错误训练，如突然增加训练强度或训练量；性别；内在因素，如下肢力线排列不良、骨量降低以及代谢性疾病等。骨折的预后取决于损伤的位置和血供受损的程度。

2. 症状和体征

患者主诉疼痛剧烈，无法站立或行走。由于保护作用，患者的肌肉发生强直性收缩，无法活动。

3. 处理

①应立即将患者制动并送往医院。外科医生会实施切开或闭合复位术以及内固定。②手术之后，患者必须使用铰链式支具制动。康复过程较长，需历时约 4 个月。

（六）内收肌 / 髋屈肌拉伤（腹股沟拉伤）

1. 病因

腹股沟区域的肌组织包括髂腰肌、股直肌和内收肌群（耻骨肌、股薄肌、短收肌、长收肌和大收肌）。此区域内肌肉拉伤可表现为急性损伤或者发生在肌肉、肌腱交界处的过度使用综合征。损伤机制通常涉及外展腿部时用力外旋所致的突然牵拉，或者肌肉肌腱存在炎症。

2. 症状和体征

拉伤时患者通常感觉腹股沟区域突然刺痛或有撕裂的感觉，患者也可能运动结束后才有所感觉。和大多数撕裂伤一样，内收肌 / 髋屈肌拉伤会引发疼痛、无力和内出血。

3. 处理

①伤后应根据 POLICE 原则进行处理，采用非甾体抗炎药和按需给予镇痛药 48 ~ 72 小时。应进行被动、主动和抗阻肌力测试以确定受累肌群。②保持休息和制动，每日采用旋涡疗法或冷冻疗法以减缓疼痛。在疼痛症状消失之前都不应进行运动。运动康复过程中应注重渐进的牵拉和恢复正常关节活动范围的练习。可使用绷带或护具在活动时进行保护。③进行功能活动模式下的躯干稳定性训练；在不稳定平面进行平衡训练，强调本体感觉输入；应注重髋内收肌群的离心力量练习。④进行理疗：冰敷、热疗、按摩、超声、经皮神

经电刺激和冲击波等。

（七）大转子滑囊炎

1. 病因

大转子滑囊炎是相对常见的股骨大转子病症。尽管一般被称为滑囊炎，这种病症也可能是臀中肌止点或髂胫束跨过大转子处的炎症。损伤常由过度使用所致，常见于骨盆或步态异常的人群。

2. 症状和体征

髋部外侧疼痛，疼痛位于大转子上方或后表面的上方，疼痛可从大腿外侧向远端牵涉至膝关节，并且在体力活动后症状加重，休息后缓解。

3. 处理

①根据 POLICE 原则进行处理，采用非甾体抗炎药以及按需给予镇痛药。②矫正力学问题，例如下肢不等长或腰椎力学机制异常。③若是过度使用所致，则应改变训练计划。④采用运动疗法：髋关节内、外旋肌肉牵伸练习，髋部及臀部肌肉肌力练习。⑤进行理疗：冷疗、浅层热疗、电刺激、超声波。

（八）髋关节扭伤

1. 病因

髋关节扭伤常因超过正常活动范围的过度运动导致髋部周围组织撕裂而发生。

2. 症状和体征

患者无法完成大腿环转动作。症状与应力性骨折相似，髋关节区有剧烈疼痛，进行旋转活动将加重疼痛。

3. 处理

①进行进一步的影像学检查以排除骨折。②根据 POLICE 原则进行处理，采用非甾体抗炎药，按需给予镇痛药。③应限制负重。④2 级或 3 级扭伤患者应拄拐步行。在疼痛症状消失后再进行活动度练习和渐进性抗阻练习。

（九）髋关节脱位

1. 病因

髋关节为球窝关节，周围有坚韧的韧带以及强大的肌肉保护，因而十分稳定。只有在间接暴力的作用下，才会通过韧带之间的薄弱区脱位。损伤人群多为青壮年，在劳动中或车祸时遭受强大暴力的冲击而致伤。扭转、杠杆或传导暴力均可引起。髋关节脱位会造成关节囊和韧带结构撕裂。此损伤常连带骨折，还有可能损伤坐骨神经。

2. 症状和体征

一般髋关节后脱位最为常见。髋关节后脱位表现为大腿屈曲、内收和内旋。触诊可发现股骨头移位到髋臼后方。

3. 处理

①伤后应立即进行医疗护理，以免肌肉挛缩使复位变得困难。患者常需 2 周卧床制动并使用拐杖行走 1 个月或更久。②运动疗法：a）股四头肌等长收缩练习，逐步进展到等长抗阻及等张收缩练习。b）躯干及健侧下肢的肌力练习。c）臀肌肌力练习。③体位指导：患肢置于外展 10°~15° 中立位，踝关节背屈 90°。

（十）股骨头缺血性坏死

1. 病因

股骨头缺血性坏死是临床常见疾病，有各种不同的病因，如骨折、脱位或内科疾病等破坏了股骨头的血供导致股骨头缺血、坏死、塌陷，常导致严重的髋关节功能障碍。其他风险因素例如使用某些药物（如类固醇）、凝血障碍、酒精过量摄入等，使骨内压力增加，造成血管径变窄，从而增加了为骨细胞供血的难度。

2. 症状和体征

髋周或膝关节疼痛；步行过程或负重训练时疼痛加重；髋关节功能活动障碍；患侧髋关节骨量减少；患者可能有皮质类固醇用药史、髋部创伤史。

3. 处理

①使用镇痛药和非甾体抗炎药。②步行时使用双拐。③采用运动疗法：患侧髋关节无痛范围内活动度练习，髋部肌肉牵伸，髋周及臀部肌肉肌力练习，水中运动练习，骑固定自行车。④进行理疗：冷疗，热疗，经皮神经电刺激（TENS）。

（十一）髋关节盂唇撕裂

1. 病因

髋关节盂唇撕裂常由重复性动作引起，例如跑步或髋的旋转导致盂唇的退行性变和破坏，也可能由急性损伤引起，例如脱位。

2. 症状和体征

髋周疼痛、绞锁感；步行中，髋关节旋转活动时疼痛加重；夜间痛较明显；髋关节功能活动受限。

3. 处理

①休息制动。②理疗：热疗，冷疗，超声波。③最大范围地扩大髋关节活动度，进行力量和稳定性练习，避免进行对髋关节产生压力的活动。④使用镇痛药和皮质类固醇激素。⑤如果疼痛症状持续超过 4 周，需进行手术，移除撕裂的部分盂唇或进行缝合修复。

（十二）坐骨神经 / 梨状肌综合征

1. 病因

任何因坐骨神经受刺激而引起的疼痛统称坐骨神经痛。坐骨神经可受腰部椎间盘疾病、直接创伤或周围组织（如梨状肌）创伤刺激，也称为梨状肌综合征。如梨状肌本身存在病变，如肌筋膜痛、肌肉肥大、创伤或骶髂关节功能障碍等，都可导致坐骨神经疼痛。

2. 症状和体征

要辨别坐骨神经痛的原因是腰部问题（椎间盘疾病）还是梨状肌综合征。若患者患有梨状肌综合征，主诉臀部深层的疼痛，无腰痛症状，有向大腿后、小腿和足的放射痛，则同样表明有坐骨神经痛。触诊坐骨切迹也产生疼痛。疼痛有可能与存在梨状肌肌筋膜扳机点有关。

3. 处理

①按需给予非甾体抗炎药、肌肉松弛药和镇痛药。②采用运动疗法：髋关节屈曲、内收、内旋体位下牵伸梨状肌，进行髋外展、外旋肌和其他核心肌群肌力练习，进行腰背部稳定性练习。③进行理疗：热疗、超声波。

（十三）股骨骺滑脱症

1. 病因

股骨骺滑脱症的问题多见于青少年男性。创伤所致的占病例的 25%。X 射线检查可能显示股骨头向后和向下方滑脱。

2. 症状和体征

腹股沟区疼痛。在此病的早期阶段可能几乎无症状。而在其发展的最终阶段，出现髋和膝主动和被动活动时的疼痛，外展、屈曲和内旋受限，跛行。

3. 处理

轻微滑脱时，制动休息和避免负重的方法可阻止其进一步滑脱。明显的滑脱常需进行矫正手术治疗。

（十四）弹响髋

1. 病因

弹响髋是指髋关节在主动伸屈活动和行走时，出现听得见或感觉得到的响声。关节外弹响较常见。发生的主要原因是髂胫束的后缘或臀大肌肌腱部的前缘增厚，在髋关节做屈曲、内收、内旋活动时，增厚的组织在大转子前后滑动而发出弹响。被动运动时无此现象，多见于青壮年，常为双侧性。这种弹响往往是自发地出现，可以发展到走一步响一声的严重程度。但一般无疼痛，如出现疼痛，则常是并发大转子滑囊炎的结果。其他原因包括骨盆狭窄、外展活动度异常增加、外旋活动度过小或内旋肌紧张。关节内因包括存在游离体、髋臼盂唇撕裂和关节本身半脱位。

2. 症状和体征

髋关节不稳，患者主诉有弹响，且每次弹响伴随着剧烈疼痛和功能障碍。Ober's 试验结果可能出现阳性。

3. 处理

①治疗方法常采用冰敷，应用非甾体抗炎药以及理疗等措施，减轻炎症，缓解疼痛。

②康复措施：患者在疼痛症状减轻后可开始牵拉练习以及肌力增强练习。

（十五）骨盆挫伤（髋骨隆凸挫伤）

1. 病因

髂嵴挫伤和腹部肌肉挫伤，俗称髋骨隆凸挫伤，常发生于接触性的运动项目中。

2. 症状和体征

髋骨隆凸挫伤将立即引起疼痛、痉挛和暂时性软组织麻痹。患者无法无痛地扭转躯干或屈曲大腿。

3. 处理

①损伤后立即采取 POLICE 原则处理，并且间歇性地保持至少 48 小时。②对于病情严重的案例，应进行 1 ~ 2 天的卧床制动，并进行 X 射线检查。③冰敷后进行按摩和超声治疗。④注射类固醇激素。⑤口服消炎药。康复期为 1 ~ 3 周。

（十六）运动疝

1. 病因

运动疝可能由耻骨联合受反复应力导致，常见于足球和冰球运动。髋关节于过度伸展位置突然做内收动作，剪切力由耻骨联合传导至腹直肌、髋内收肌和联合腱位于耻骨结节处的共同止点，可导致腹横筋膜或腹内外斜肌筋膜的损伤。

2. 症状和体征

慢性疼痛常只在用力时发生，持续数月。锐痛、烧灼痛起初只局限于下腹部和腹股沟区，之后开始向内收肌和睾丸区域放射。触诊耻骨结节有压痛。在髋抗阻屈曲、内旋和腹部肌肉收缩时疼痛加剧。疼痛也在髋抗阻内收时出现，内收肌无压痛症状，此表现可与内收肌拉伤相鉴别。

3. 处理

①伤后采取保守治疗方法处理。②1 周后，可加入髋屈肌、内收肌、旋转肌、腘绳肌和腰部肌群的牵拉练习。③2 周后，可开始腹部肌群、髋内收肌和屈肌的力量练习。④3 ~ 4 周可以开始跑步，后续开始在疼痛可忍受范围内进行跳跃和踢腿运动。⑤若保守治疗失败，则需进行手术治疗。

（十七）盆底功能障碍

1. 病因

盆底功能障碍常见于全年龄段女性患者群体。盆底功能障碍常发生于体操、田径运动员，或涉及跳跃等高冲击强度运动项目的运动员中。

2. 症状和体征

在女性运动员中，盆底功能障碍可能导致尿失禁、盆腔器官脱垂或骨盆慢性疼痛症状的出现。

3. 处理

①按需给予非甾体抗炎药和镇痛药。②进行盆底肌肌力训练。③采用理疗：电刺激盆底肌。④若相关肌肉存在扳机点，则应进行松解来缓解疼痛。

（十八）骶髂关节功能障碍

1. 病因

骶髂关节功能障碍和疼痛是骨盆后侧（腰部）疼痛的一个亚型。病因较多，如创伤、反复的髋关节屈曲和旋转、弯腰等活动都可导致。

2. 症状和体征

疼痛位于骨盆后侧骶骨沟或髂后上棘，向远端放射至臀部，有时放射至下肢。某些患者的疼痛可放射至髋关节周围和腹股沟。在进行下肢活动时，会出现弹响及卡顿，跑步时疼痛加重。盖氏试验结果呈阳性。

3. 处理

①手法治疗是最直接有效的方法。②按需给予非甾体抗炎药及镇痛药。③采用运动疗法：腰椎—骨盆活动度训练，盆底肌及核心肌群肌力练习，核心稳定性练习，关节松动术。④进行肌内效贴。⑤进行理疗：热疗、冷疗。

（十九）髋关节撞击综合征

1. 病因

髋关节撞击综合征是指由于股骨和髋臼的解剖形态异常，在髋关节运动终末期股骨近端和髋臼边缘发生异常的接触或碰撞，引起盂唇和髋臼边缘的软骨损伤。之所以称为综合征，是因为撞击可能引发一系列关节损伤。髋关节撞击综合征 = 异常的骨摩擦碰撞 + 盂唇损伤 + 软骨损伤。可分为两类：①凸轮撞击（Cam type）：常发生于爱好运动的男性，主要是股骨头颈结合处存在异常突起，使其成为凸轮样的非球体，在剧烈活动尤其是髋关节屈曲时，突出的部分挤压、碰撞并剪切髋臼软骨及髋臼盂唇，从而引起疼痛等症状。②钳夹撞击（Pincer type）：常发生于喜欢运动的中年女性，主要是髋臼异常所致，见于髋臼后倾或髋臼过深的患者。

2. 症状和体征

腹股沟区、臀部或大转子处疼痛（C 字征），疼痛呈间歇性，在进行体育运动、长时间行走或长时间保持坐位后疼痛可加重。检查时患者通常表现为髋关节活动受限，特别是屈曲、内收内旋受限。

3. 处理

①保守治疗：包括改变髋关节的运动方式，即避免过度屈曲髋关节和减少运动量来减少撞击的发生，以及应用非甾体抗炎药来缓解症状等。但保守治疗只能暂时缓解疼痛症状，并不能消除产生撞击的因素，因此不能阻止关节退变。②手术治疗。

（二十）应力性骨折

1. 病因

骨盆区的应力性骨折常见于长跑运动者。地面反作用力产生的反复周期性力可造成骨盆和股骨近端的应力性骨折。常见发病部位是耻骨下支和股骨颈以及股骨转子下区。

2. 症状和体征

患者主诉腹股沟疼痛，并在活动时加重，休息时减轻。患者不能单脚站立。触诊时按压可导致剧烈压痛。

3. 处理

①休息制动。②适当负重。③采用运动疗法：无痛范围内关节活动度练习以及静力性练习，向心运动练习，逐渐恢复全关节活动度练习，疼痛症状消失后可进行离心运动练习。④理疗：热疗，冷疗，经皮神经电刺激（TENS）。⑤外科手术。

Summary

1. The injuries around pelvis mainly include lesions in thigh, hip, groin and pelvis. Prevention involves developing strength and flexibility of the thigh, hip, groin and pelvis muscles. Strength training includes squats, dead lift, core strength exercises, etc.; flexibility training includes stretching of quadriceps, hamstring and inguinal muscles.

2. Special tests include the Thomas test, Patrick (Faber) test, Trendelenburg's test, Ober test, Nobel's test, Ely test, Piriformis test, Gaenslen test, femoral nerve stretching test, straight leg raise test, active straight leg raise test, Gillet (sacral fixation) test, rectus femoris contracture test and pelvic falling test.

3. The structure of the thigh consists of the femur, muscle tissue, nerves, blood vessels and the fascia that encloses the soft tissue. Quadriceps contusion and hamstring strain are the most common sports injuries in the thigh. The incidence of quadriceps femoris contusion is the highest. Early detection and prevention of internal bleeding are very crucial in acute thigh contusions.

4. Jumping or falling on a bent knee can strain the quadriceps muscle and hamstring muscle. The strain occurs most often to the short head of the biceps femoris muscle.

5. Acute femoral fractures often occur in the femoral shaft, usually from a direct impact. Femoral stress fractures are most common in the femoral neck.

6. Groin strain can occur in any muscle located in this region. Running, jumping, or twisting can produce a groin strain.

○ Review Questions

1. Describe the symptoms and signs of dislocation of hip joint, as well as the rehabilitation measures.

2. Describe the rehabilitation treatment measures for the hamstring strain.

3. Describe the symptoms and signs, rehabilitation measures of grade 2 quadriceps femoris strain.

4. A track and field athlete complained of pain in the deep buttocks, with no symptoms of low back pain, but to the back of the thigh, lower leg and foot radiating pain. Palpation of ischial notch also produces pain. Describe what additional tests should be performed to complete the assessment and make a diagnosis.

5. Patients completed the lower limb strength training 3 days before, and pain presented when the right lower limb single leg landing support. Pain area is in the butt. Special test shows Patrick test (+), Gaenslen test (+). Pelvic extrusion test (+). The pain worsens in patients with unilateral lower limb weight bearing and activities. No abnormalities in the lumbar spine, hip and knee joints. Try to give a diagnosis opinion and elaborate on rehabilitation treatment measures.

小结

1. 骨盆周围损伤主要包括大腿、髋关节、腹股沟和骨盆处的损伤。此部位损伤的预防主要包括增加大腿、髋关节和骨盆周围肌群的力量和柔韧性。力量训练包括深蹲、硬拉、核心力量练习等；柔韧性训练包括股四头肌、腘绳肌及腹股沟处肌肉的牵拉。

2. 特殊试验包括托马斯试验、Patrick 试验（Faber 试验）、Trendelenburg 征、Ober's 试验、Nobel 试验、提踵试验、梨状肌试验、盖氏试验、股神经牵拉试验、直腿抬高试验、主动直腿抬高实验、骶骨固定试验、股直肌挛缩试验、骨盆降落试验。

3. 大腿的结构包括股骨、肌肉组织、神经、血管和包裹软组织的筋膜。股四头肌挫伤和腘绳肌拉伤是大腿常发生的运动损伤；其中股四头肌挫伤的发生率较高。及早发现和防止内出血在大腿急性挫伤时十分关键。

4. 屈膝起跳或落地可导致股四头肌拉伤或腘绳肌拉伤，拉伤常发生于股二头肌的短头。

5. 急性股骨骨折常发生于股骨干，常是直接撞击所致。股骨应力性骨折常发生在股骨颈。

6. 腹股沟拉伤可累及此区域的任何一块肌肉。跑、跳或扭转活动皆可导致腹股沟拉伤。

◯ 复习题

1. 简述髋关节脱位的症状体征以及康复治疗措施。

2. 简述腘绳肌拉伤的康复治疗措施。

3. 简述2级股四头肌拉伤的症状体征及康复措施。

4. 1名田径运动员，主诉臀部深层的疼痛，无腰痛症状，有向大腿后、小腿和足的放射痛，触诊坐骨切迹也产生疼痛。试述为完成评估并给出诊断意见应补充何检查。

5. 患者于3日前进行下肢力量训练，右侧下肢单腿跳跃落地支撑时出现疼痛。疼痛位于臀部，特殊试验检查结果显示 Patrick 试验结果阳性，盖氏试验结果阳性，骨盆挤压试验结果阳性。患者单侧下肢负重及活动时疼痛加重，腰椎、髋关节及膝关节排查无异常。试给出诊断意见，并详细阐述康复治疗措施。

Chapter 6 Knee Injuries
第六章　膝部损伤

○ Main Contents

1. Prevention of knee injuries.

2. Assessment of knee injuries.

3. Identification and management of common knee injuries.

○ 主要内容

1.膝部损伤的预防。

2.膝部损伤的评估。

3.膝部常见损伤的识别和处理。

1 Prevention of Knee Injuries

The knee joint is a segment in the lower limb kinetic chain, so the condition of the joint and surrounding soft tissues forming the kinetic chain must also be considered as risk factors for knee injuries. The strength of the muscle groups around the knee joint must be strong and muscles should keep appropriate flexibility.

1.1 Strength Training

Noncontact knee injuries are associated with muscle function. Therefore, generic exercises for all tibiofemoral joint injuries should include strength training for the trunk lateral flexors, gluteus maximus and gluteus medius.

Strength training for athletes with knee injuries usually follows a progression from isometric exercises to isotonic exercises, then to isokinetic exercises, and finally to plyometric exercises.

1.2 Knee Braces

Knee braces are generally divided into two types: prophylactic braces and functional braces. Prophylactic knee braces were recommended to athletes to prevent anterior cruciate ligament (ACL) and medial collateral ligament (MCL) injuries or to reduce the severity of injuries. Functional knee braces are most commonly used in rehabilitation measures to provide stability for knees after ACL reconstruction. There are many other knee braces used to provide support for the knee ligaments, but the effectiveness of these braces in preventing injury remains controversial.

一、膝部损伤的预防

膝关节是下肢运动链的一个环节，此运动链的关节和周围软组织的状况都可能成为膝关节损伤的危险因素。膝关节周围肌群肌力应该强大，并且具有适当的柔韧性。

（一）肌力训练

非接触性膝关节损伤与肌肉功能相关。因此，所有胫股关节损伤的常规训练应该包括躯干外侧屈肌、臀大肌和臀中肌的力量训练。

膝部有损伤的运动员的力量训练通常遵循从等长收缩练习到等张收缩练习，再到等速练习，最后进展到增强式训练的原则。

（二）护具的使用

膝关节护具一般分为预防性和功能性两种。预防性膝关节护具通常用于预防或降低前交叉韧带和内侧副韧带的损伤或降低损伤的严重程度，功能性膝关节护具最常用于保护手术重建的前交叉韧带，目的是为术后的膝关节提供稳定。其他的一些膝关节护具通过防止内翻或外翻增加对膝关节韧带的支撑，但目前对于这些护具预防损伤的效果仍存在争议。

2 Assessment of Knee Injuries

2.1 History

The athletic trainer should ask the following questions.

For patients with acute injuries:

- What happened when you got injured?
- Where is the area of your pain? Is it local or widespread?
- How severe is the pain?
- What does the pain feel like?
- Does it hurt when you move the limbs? Does your knee feel unstable?
- What was your body posture when you got injured?
- Have you ever heard any noise or felt a tear, such as a crack or crunch during an injury? (A crack or a "popping" sensation in the knee could indicate an ACL tear; a crunch may indicate a torn meniscus; and a tearing sensation may indicate a capsular tear).
- Could you move the knee joint immediately after the injury? If not, was it locked in a bent or extended position?
- Is there any swelling? (Rapid swelling may indicate a rupture of the cruciate ligament or fracture of the tibia, whereas later swelling may indicate capsular bursa or meniscus tear.)
- Does the knee lock at any angle?
- Which treatment was applied immediately?
- Is there a history of knee injuries?

For patients with chronic injuries:

- What is the subjective complaint?
- When did you first notice this problem?
- Where was the area of pain initially?
- How long has the pain been present?
- Is there any recurrent swelling?
- Is the pain present in daily activities?
- Is there joint locking in the knee joint? Is the locking recurrent? (If so, it may be a torn meniscus or a loose body in the knee joint.)
- Do you feel any friction or grinding?

- Do you feel knee pain during weight bearing activity?

- How do you feel when you go up and down stairs?

- What treatment have you received? (Surgery or physical therapy, etc.)

2.2 Observation

The patient should be observed in a variety of situations: walking, half-squat, and going up and down stairs. At the same time, athletic trainers should check the alignment of the lower limbs and whether the lower limbs are symmetrical.

- Does the patient walk with a limp, or can he/she walk easily? Is the patient able to fully extend the knee during heel strike?

- Can the lower leg of the affected side be fully loaded?

- Can the patient go up and down stairs easily?

- Can the patient achieve full range of motion?

2.2.1 Alignment of Lower Limb

Abnormal alignment of lower limb may be a potential factor leading to injury. The alignment of the lower limb should be evaluated from anterior and lateral view. Anterior view: exam whether the patient has genu valgum and genu varum and observe the position of the patella. Lateral view: evaluate whether the patient has knee hyperextension or protective flexion.

2.2.2 Abnormal Alignment of Lower Limb

Common abnormal alignment of lower limbs include: improper alignment of the patella, genu valgum (knock-knees), genu varum (bowlegs) and genu recurvatum (hyperextended knees).

2.2.3 Patellar Malalignment

In patients with patella alta, the erect position of the patella is higher than normal, while the patella baja is lower than normal. Patellar malalignment may be caused by complicated factors, such as knee hyperextension, genu varum, genu valgum, internal rotation of the hip, and the increase of femoral neck-shaft angle. In addition, the femoral anteversion angle too large or too small is considered to be an important factor affecting lower limb alignment.

2.2.4 Genu Valgum and Genu Varum

When heels are close together, if the distance between two knees is beyond 1.5 cm, it indicates a positive sign of genu varum; if the knees can touch each other but the distance between two heels is beyond 1.5 cm, it means that the patient is diagnosed as genu valgum.

2.2.5 Hyperextended Knees

Hyperextended knee is also called genu recurvatum. It is usually a compensatory pattern that occurs due to lordosis or swayback.

2.2.6 Knee Symmetry

The patients are observed to determine whether the bilateral knee joints are symmetrical, and whether there is swelling and muscular atrophy.

2.2.7 Leg-Length Discrepancy

There are many reasons for discrepancies in leg length, including structural or functional reasons. The structural length of the limb is measured from the anterior superior iliac spine (ASIS) to the medial malleolus and the functional leg length is measured from the navel to the medial malleolus. Structural differences in the length of the lower limbs can cause problems in load-bearing joints. Functional differences in the length of the lower limbs can be caused by pelvic rotation or poor spinal alignment.

2.3 Palpation

Palpation can be done to determine the presence of pain or deformity caused by fractures and dislocations as well as changes in soft tissues. Palpation of joint effusion and associated swelling pattern are important in the evaluation of knee joint injury. Swelling can occur both inside and outside the capsule. Swelling in the capsule of the joint is also called joint effusion.

2.4 Special Tests

2.4.1 Floating Patella Test

The patient is in the supine position, with the knee joint of the affected side fully extended and the quadriceps femoris muscle relaxed. The athletic trainer squeezes the suprapatellar capsule with one hand so that the joint fluid accumulates behind the patella, and the other hand lightly presses the patella with the index finger. If there is a floating sensation or feeling that the patella is hitting the femoral condyle, the test is positive, indicating excessive fluid accumulation in the joint.

2.4.2 Effusion Induction Test

The patient is in the supine position with the quadriceps femoris muscle relaxed. The athletic trainer, with one hand on the medial side of the affected knee joint, pushes the effusion upward from the bottom to the suprapatellar capsule and the lateral side of the knee joint, and the other hand on the lateral side of the knee joint pushes the effusion from top to bottom to the medial side of the knee joint. The test will be positive if there is filling or bulging on the medial side of the knee joint.

2.4.3 Valgus Stress Test

The valgus stress test is used to assess the integrity of the medial collateral ligament (MCL) of the knee. The athletic trainer applies a valgus stress on the knee with one hand, while the other hand holds the patient's foot and stabilizes it in a slightly external rotated position. The knee is tested in a fully extended position, followed by a slight bend (30° flexion). A positive test occurs when medial joint gapping or pain is noted with this test in full knee extension or 30° of flexion.

2.4.4 Varus Stress Test

The athletic trainer applies a varus stress (pushing the knee out) on the knee with one hand, while the other hand holds the patient's foot in place at full extension of the knee and then at a slight bend (30° flexion). If the tibia is too far away from the femur, it is considered a positive sign.

2.4.5 Lachman Test

This test shows good reliability and validity for the examination of ACL, especially for the posterolateral bundle of ACL. The patient is in the supine position, while the athletic trainer fixes the involved lower extremity in the position of 30° flexion, stabilizes the femur with one hand, and pulls the proximal part of the tibia forward with the other hand. If there is no or only soft end-feel, the test result is positive, indicating that the ACL (especially the posterolateral bundle) might be damaged.

2.4.6 Anterior Drawer Test

The patient is positioned supine, with the knee flexed at 90°. The athletic trainer sits on the patient's foot for fixation with hands around the shin below the knee, making sure that the hamstring is in a relaxed state, and then pulls the tibia forward relative to the femur. If the displacement is more than 0.5 cm, it indicates that the anterior cruciate ligament (especially the anteromedial bundle) is possibly damaged.

2.4.7 Axial Pivot Shift Test

The patient is positioned supine with legs relaxed. The athletic trainer grasps the heel of the involved leg with the examiner's opposite hand placed laterally on the proximal tibia just distal to the knee. The athletic trainer then applies valgus stress and an axial load while internally rotating the tibia as the knee is moved into flexion from a fully extended position. A positive test is indicated by subluxation of the tibia while the femur rotates externally followed by a restoration of the tibia at 30°–40° of flexion, indicating anterior cruciate ligament rupture.

2.4.8 Posterior Drawer Test

The patient is in the supine position, with the knee to be tested flexed to approximately 90°. The athletic trainer then sits on the foot of the tested extremity to help stabilize it. The athletic trainer grasps the proximal lower leg, approximately at the tibial plateau or joint line with the thumbs placed on the tibial tuberosity. Then the athletic trainer attempts to push the lower leg posteriorly. The test is considered positive if there is a lack of end feel or excessive posterior shift, indicating posterior cruciate ligament injury.

2.4.9 Godfrey's Test

The patient is in the supine position, and the athletic trainers lift the patient's legs and maintain the hip and knee flexion to 90°. If the patient's knee joint is not stable enough to the rear, the tibia can be observed to be concave into the rear. If the backward force is applied, the displacement of the tibia can be increased. It is suggested that the posterior cruciate ligament and posterior oblique ligament may be damaged.

2.4.10 Tests for Meniscal Injuries

Since there is no blood supply or innervation to the medial two-thirds of the meniscus, meniscus injury can lead to mild or no pain and swelling, making the diagnosis particularly difficult. The diagnosis of meniscus injury should be based on the patient's medical history and imaging examination.

2.4.11 McMurray's Test

McMurray's Test is mainly aimed at the injury of the posterior horn of meniscus. The patient is in a supine position, and the knee joints are fully flexed (the heels touch the buttocks). The athletic trainer rotates the patient's tibia internally and extends the knee. If there are fragments of a torn meniscus in the joint cavity, the whole movement will produce a snap and pain. Test the medial meniscus in the opposite way.

2.4.12 Apley's Compression Test

When performing the Apley compression test, the patient should be positioned prone. The athletic trainer will place the patient's knee into 90° of flexion and apply a firm grasp at the patient's heel. While applying a downward axial force, the athletic trainer will rotate the leg medially and laterally. A positive test occurs when pain or popping is noted with rotation, indicating damage to the meniscus.

2.4.13 Thessaly Test

The patient stands on one leg while the athletic trainer extends both hands to support the patient. The patient then flexes the knee to 5° and rotates the femur on the tibia medially and laterally three times, while maintaining the 5° flexion. The test is then repeated at 20° flexion. The test is considered positive for a meniscus tear if the patient experiences medial or lateral joint line discomfort or a sense of locking/catching in the knee. Pay attention to the contrast between the unaffected side and the affected side.

2.4.14 Patella Assessment

Assessment of the knee should generally include examination of the patella, it mainly includes the following three items.

(1) Q Angle

The Q angle is formed when lines are drawn from the middle of patella to the ASIS and from the tubercle of the tibia through the center of patella. The knee should be measured at full extension and 30° flexion. Normal Q angles are 10° for men and 15° for women. If the Q angle is greater than 20°, it is considered to be too large, which may cause pathological symptoms related to abnormal movement of patella in the trochlear notch of femur.

(2) Patella Compression Test

The purpose of this test is to detect the presence of patellofemoral joint disorder. The patient is in the supine position with the knee flexed at 20°. The athletic trainer pressures patella towards intertrochanteric fossa of femur and moves it up and down. If the patient feels pain, the test is considered positive.

(3) Patella Grinding Test

The purpose of this test is to detect the presence of patellofemoral joint disorder. This test is also known as Clarke's Test. The patient is in the supine position with the knee extended. The athletic trainer lightly presses the proximal end and upper pole of the patella with the first web space of hand, and asks the patient to contract quadriceps. If there is pain and the patient is unable to keep the contraction, the test is considered positive.

2.4.15 Quadriceps Pull Test

The patient is in the supine position with the knee extended, and then contracts the quadriceps. The patella should move toward the proximal end with slight lateral displacement. If the patella moves obviously toward lateral, it indicates the mal-tracking and potential instability.

2.4.16 Apprehension Test

This test is used to evaluate patella dislocation. The patient is in the supine position, relaxes the quadriceps and bends the knees at 30°. At the same time, the athletic trainer carefully pushes the patella outward. If the patient feels that the patella will dislocate, he/she will contract the quadriceps muscle to pull the patella back into place with a frightened expression, the test is considered positive.

二、膝部损伤的评估

（一）病史

运动防护师应询问以下问题：

①对急性膝痛的患者：

- 损伤是怎么发生的？
- 疼痛的位置在哪里？是局部的还是广泛的？
- 疼痛有多严重？
- 疼痛的性质是怎样的？
- 当你移动肢体时会痛吗？感觉膝关节不稳定吗？
- 受伤时你的身体处于什么姿势？
- 在损伤发生时有没有听到弹响声或"砰""啪"的声音，或感到撕裂？（"啪"的一声提示前交叉韧带断裂，弹响声可能提示半月板损伤，撕裂感可能提示关节囊的撕裂。）

● 损伤后膝关节是否可以立即活动？如果不能，是在屈曲还是伸直的体位下不能动？

● 是否有肿胀产生？（伤后肿胀快速出现可能提示交叉韧带断裂或胫骨骨折，而迟发的肿胀可能由关节囊、滑囊或半月板撕裂造成。）

● 膝关节有卡住的情况吗？

● 立即进行了什么治疗？

● 之前有过膝关节损伤史吗？

②对慢性损伤的患者：

● 患者的主诉是什么？

● 第一次注意到这种情况是什么时候？

● 最初的疼痛在哪里？

● 疼痛出现多久了？

● 是否发生反复肿胀？

● 日常活动中疼痛是否存在？

● 膝关节是否有关节绞锁？绞锁是否反复发生？（如果有，可能提示半月板撕裂，撕裂的游离体可以引起反复性绞锁。）

● 膝关节运动时是否有任何摩擦感或研磨感？

● 负重活动时是否感觉膝关节疼痛？

● 上下楼梯时有无异常感觉？

● 为此曾接受过什么治疗？（手术、物理治疗等）

（二）视诊

可在多种情况下对患者进行观察：步行、半蹲、上下楼梯。同时运动防护师应检查下肢力线排列以及双侧下肢是否对称。

● 患者走路是否存在跛行？足跟着地时膝关节能否伸直？

● 患侧下肢足部能够完全负重吗？

● 患者能轻松完成上下楼梯吗？

● 患者能完成全关节活动范围的活动吗？

1. 下肢力线评估

下肢力线排列异常可能是导致损伤发生的一个潜在因素。评估可以从前方和侧面进行。前面观：检查患者有无膝外翻、膝内翻并观察髌骨的位置。侧面观：检查患者有无膝过伸或保护性屈曲的情况。

2. 异常下肢力线排列

常见的异常下肢力线排列包括：髌骨对线不良、膝外翻（X型腿）、膝内翻（O型腿）和膝反张（膝过伸）。

3. 髌骨对线不良

存在高位髌骨的患者，其站立位时髌骨位置比正常偏高，而低位髌骨则比正常偏低。

PART III Common Musculoskeletal Injuries

第三部分　常见肌肉骨骼损伤

髌骨对线不良可能由一系列复杂的因素所导致，比如膝过伸、膝内翻、膝外翻、髋关节内旋以及股骨颈干角增大等。此外，股骨前倾角过大或过小被认为是影响下肢力线的一个重要因素。

4. 膝外翻（X 型腿）与膝内翻（O 型腿）

当足跟并拢时，若两侧膝关节之间距离超过 1.5 厘米，表示该患者有膝内翻畸形，如果两侧膝关节可以相互接触但脚踝无法相互接触，则表示存在膝外翻现象。

5. 膝过伸

也称膝反张，是一种通常因脊柱前凸增加或摇摆背而出现的代偿模式。

6. 膝对称性

通过观察确定患者双侧膝关节是否对称，是否有肿胀及肌萎缩存在。

7. 下肢不等长

造成腿部长度差异的原因有很多，包括结构或功能方面的原因。肢体结构长度从髂前上棘（ASIS）至内踝处测量，肢体功能长度从脐至内踝处测量。下肢长度上的结构差异会导致承重关节出现问题。下肢长度的功能差异可能是由骨盆旋转或脊柱对齐不良引起的。

（三）触诊

通过触诊确定是否有因骨折、脱位以及软组织改变所造成的疼痛或畸形。在评估膝关节损伤时，触诊关节积液及相关的肿胀具有重要意义。肿胀在关节囊内和关节囊外都有可能发生，关节囊内肿胀也称为关节积液。

（四）特殊试验

1. 浮髌试验

患者仰卧位，患侧膝关节伸直并放松股四头肌。运动防护师一只手挤压患者髌上囊，使关节液积聚于髌骨后方，另一只手食指轻压髌骨。如果有浮动的感觉或能感到髌骨碰撞股骨髁的碰击声，则试验结果为阳性，提示关节内积液过多。

2. 积液诱发试验

患者仰卧位，放松股四头肌。运动防护师一只手掌根位于患侧膝关节内侧，由下向上滑推，将积液推至髌上囊及膝关节外侧，另一只手位于膝关节外侧，由上向下将积液挤向内侧，若在膝关节内侧出现充盈饱满或膨出现象，则试验结果为阳性。

3. 外翻应力试验

外翻应力试验用于检查内侧副韧带的完整性。运动防护师一只手施加一个外翻应力在膝部，另一只手固定患者的足部，并把足部稳定在轻微的外旋姿势下。先在患者的膝关节完全伸直位测试，然后在轻微弯曲（30°屈曲）下测试。如果发现患者有疼痛或内侧关节间隙增大，则试验结果为阳性。

4. 内翻应力试验

运动防护师一只手施加一个内翻应力（把膝关节推向外）在膝部，另一只手固定患者的足部。先在患者膝关节完全伸直位测试，然后在轻微弯曲（30°屈曲）下测试。若胫骨过度远离股骨，则试验结果为阳性。

5. Lachman 试验

Lachman 试验在检查前交叉韧带方面具有良好的信度和效度，尤其是对前交叉韧带的后外侧束的检查。患者仰卧位，运动防护师将检查侧下肢固定在30°屈曲位置，一只手固定患者股骨，另一只手将胫骨的近端向前拉动。若感到没有或是只有轻微的末端感觉，则试验结果为阳性，提示前交叉韧带（尤其是后外侧束）可能存在损伤。

6. 前抽屉试验

患者仰卧位，膝关节屈曲90°，运动防护师坐在患者足部以固定，两手位于患者膝关节下方胫骨周围，确定腘绳肌腱处于放松状态，然后将胫骨相对于股骨往前拉动。若位移超过0.5厘米，提示前交叉韧带（尤其是前内侧束）可能存在损伤。

7. 轴移试验

患者仰卧位，双腿放松。运动防护师一只手握住患腿的足跟，另一只手侧向放在胫骨近端。当患者膝关节从完全伸展的位置移动到屈曲时，运动防护师在胫骨内旋转时施加外翻应力和轴向载荷。当患者股骨向外旋转时，胫骨发生半脱位，随后当胫骨屈曲30°～40°时出现复位，则试验结果为阳性，提示前交叉韧带断裂。

8. 后抽屉试验

患者仰卧位，待测膝关节屈曲约90°。运动防护师坐在被测试肢体的足部以固定。运动防护师抓住患者小腿近端，大约在胫骨平台或关节线上，拇指放在胫骨粗隆。然后运动防护师尝试将患者小腿向后平移。如果无末端感觉或向后平移过度，则试验结果为阳性，提示后交叉韧带可能存在损伤。

9. 重力试验

患者仰卧位，运动防护师抬起患者双腿并将患者的髋关节和膝关节维持在屈曲90°的位置，若患者膝关节向后的稳定性不足，可观察到胫骨向后凹陷；若运动防护师徒手施加向后的力，患者胫骨向后的位移可能会增加，提示后交叉韧带和后斜韧带可能存在损伤。

10. 半月板损伤的检查

因为半月板内侧2/3没有血供和神经支配，所以半月板的损伤可能导致轻微疼痛或没有疼痛以及肿胀，使得诊断尤为困难。半月板损伤的诊断需要结合患者的病史及影像学检查来进行判断。

11. 半月板回旋挤压试验（麦氏征）

麦氏征主要针对半月板后角的损伤。患者仰卧位，膝关节完全屈曲（足跟接触臀部）。运动防护师将患者胫骨内旋并伸膝，若关节腔有外侧半月板撕裂碎片，整个过程中产生弹响和疼痛，试验结果为阳性。反之则检查内侧半月板。

12. Apley 挤压试验

进行 Apley 挤压试验时，患者应处于俯卧位。运动防护师将病人的膝关节弯曲90°，并紧紧抓住患者的脚后跟。当施加一个向下的轴向载荷时，运动防护师将向内侧和外侧旋转患者腿。当旋转时患者出现疼痛或爆裂感时，试验结果呈阳性，提示半月板存在损伤。

13. Thessaly 试验

患者单腿站立，运动防护师伸出双手支撑患者。然后患者屈曲膝关节至约 5°，并在保持约 5° 屈曲的同时，向内侧和外侧旋转胫骨上方的股骨 3 次，然后以膝关节 20° 屈曲重复这个测试。如果患者出现内侧或外侧关节线不适或膝关节锁定 / 夹住感，则认为半月板撕裂试验结果呈阳性。注意健患侧对比。

14. 髌骨的检查

对膝关节的评估一般均应包括对髌骨的情况进行检查，主要包括以下 3 种检查。

（1）Q 角

Q 角为髌骨中点至髂前上棘的连线与胫骨粗隆至髌骨中点的连线相交形成的夹角。应在膝关节完全伸直位和屈曲 30° 位进行测量。男性正常 Q 角为 10°，女性为 15°。Q 角大于 20° 则考虑为偏大，可能导致与髌骨在股骨滑车切迹内运动轨迹不正常相关的病理症状。

（2）髌骨挤压试验

髌骨挤压试验的目的是检测髌股关节紊乱。患者仰卧位，膝关节保持屈曲约 20°，向下将髌骨压向股骨滑车切迹方向，然后将其上下移动。若患者感觉疼痛，则试验结果为阳性。

（3）髌骨研磨试验

髌骨研磨试验的目的是检测髌股关节紊乱。这个试验也被称为 Clarke 测试。患者仰卧位，伸直膝关节。运动防护师用手掌虎口部轻压髌骨近端和上部，并嘱患者收缩股四头肌，若出现疼痛并使患者不能保持收缩，则试验结果为阳性。

15. 股四头肌牵拉试验

患者仰卧位，伸直膝关节。患者收缩股四头肌，髌骨受牵拉后主要向近端移位，正常情况可有轻度向外侧移位。若髌骨显著向外侧移位，则可认为髌骨轨迹异常及有潜在的不稳定性。

16. 恐惧试验

恐惧试验用于检查髌骨半脱位。患者仰卧，放松股四头肌，屈膝 30°，同时运动防护师小心地向外推髌骨。若患者感到髌骨将要脱位，会收缩股四头肌将髌骨拉回原位并伴有惊恐的表情，则试验结果为阳性。

3 Identification and Management of Common Knee Injuries

3.1 Ligament injury

3.1.1 Medial Collateral Ligament Sprain

(1) Etiology

The mechanism of medial collateral ligament (MCL) sprain primarily involves a direct impact (valgus stress) from the lateral side or the lateral rotation of the tibia, which often occurs in skiing and other cutting and pivoting sports, such as basketball and soccer. The flexion and extension angle of the knee joint is an important factor in determining the degree of vulnerability. But the knee joint can be injured in any position as long as the external force is sufficient. Medial sprain causes more damage than the lateral sprain because the medial collateral ligament is more closely related to the capsule and the medial meniscus.

A severe injury to the medial collateral ligament may result in O'Donoghue's Triad, also known as Terrible Triad, which refers to a knee injury involving multiple ligaments and cartilage within the knee. The medial collateral ligament (MCL), anterior cruciate ligament (ACL) and medial meniscus are all damaged. Meniscus tears often occur when the collateral ligament becomes loose after repeated damage and fails to maintain stability.

Medial collateral ligament sprain can be divided into three grades of injury according to the injured degree:

Grade I sprain: mild injury, with minimally torn fibers and no loss of MCL integrity.

Grade II sprain: moderate injury, with an incomplete tear and increased laxity of the MCL.

Grade III sprain: severe injury, with a complete tear and gross laxity of the MCL

(2) Symptoms and Signs

Most of the patients with grade I sprain feel pain when we apply force on the lateral of a slightly bent knee, but there are no other symptoms. Patients with grade II sprain complain about pain and significant tenderness on the medial of the knee, and moderate laxity in the joint is observed. Patients with grade III sprain have significant pain and swelling over the MCL. Most of the time, they have difficulty in bending their knees. The result of the valgus stress test is positive. Grade II and III sprain can be distinguished clinically on valgus stress test; Grade II is lax in 30° of knee flexion but solid in full extension, whereas Grade III is lax in both of these positions.

(3) Management

The management of an MCL injury is dependent on the grade of injury. Grade I sprain: POLICE, physiotherapy and NSAIDs. Conduct appropriate strength rehabilitation training. Grade II and III sprain: Except for the same content as grade I sprain, the protective braces or crutches can be used, and weight bearing and strength training should be carried out within the tolerance range. Avulsion fracture or combined with other ligament ruptures need to be operated on.

3.1.2 Lateral Collateral Ligament Sprain

(1) Etiology

The lateral collateral ligament (LCL) sprain is the least common of all knee ligament sprains. An isolated LCL injury is almost always the result of a varus stress applied to the knee.

(2) Symptoms and Signs

There is pain and tenderness around LCL, which can be palpated with the knees bending and internal rotating. There is swelling and effusion around the injured LCL. The pain is most severe in Grade I and II. With a Grade III sprain, the pain is intense at first and then becomes dull.

(3) Management

Management of the LCL injury is similar to that of medial collateral ligament injury. In the case of a grade III, the LCL sprain that involves multiple ligamentous injuries with associated instability needs to be surgically repaired or reconstructed, and the patient should be placed in a postoperative brace with partial weight bearing for 4 to 6 weeks.

3.1.3 Anterior Cruciate Ligament Sprain

(1) Etiology

An anterior cruciate ligament (ACL) sprain is often considered the most serious knee ligament injury. The exact mechanism that causes ACL injuries is still controversial.

ACL injury more commonly occurs as a noncontact injury. In a noncontact injury, injuries to the ACL usually occur as a result of twisting stress in the knee when landing after a jump. In a contact injury, a direct impact to the lateral of the knee causes it to buckle inwards. This stress causes excessive movement of the tibia resulting in damage to other structures within the knee, as well as a torn ACL.

(2) Symptoms and Signs

The patient might complain of knee pain, swelling and knee instability. When an ACL sprain occurs, the patient will often feel a "snap", then be unable to move and complain of the knee sliding. ACL tears cause rapid swelling at the joint line. The hematoma of the joint can form within 6 hours. The results of the anterior drawer test and the Lachman test would be positive in patients with simple ACL tears. The results of the pivot shift test may be positive, too. An accurate diagnosis can be made through MRI or arthroscopy.

(3) Management

① In the case of acute injury, emergency treatment should be carried out according to the POLICE principle. ② After swelling has decreased, the patient can be fitted with a knee brace to help control knee instability. ③ The patient can begin immediately after injury with quadriceps isometric contraction training and straight leg-raising to regain motor control and minimize atrophy. ④ The treatment after a complete ACL tear is controversial. However, it is generally accepted that ACL rupture, if not treated effectively, will eventually lead to severe joint degeneration. Therefore, ACL reconstruction can be performed to enhance the stability of the knee joint.

3.1.4 Posterior Cruciate Ligament Sprain

(1) Etiology

The posterior cruciate ligament (PCL), one of the most important ligaments in the knee joint, restricts excessive posterior displacement of the tibia. PCL injury most often occurs when landing with 90° knee flexion or when the knee is strongly impacted from the front.

(2) Symptoms and Signs

The symptoms of PCL injuries include acute pain, swelling and difficulty in walking. Patients may complain of laxity of the knee joint with a sensation of the knee giving away. Patients with chronic PCL tears may present with only mild knee pain and instability. Imaging tests are used to help diagnose.

(3) Management

① Isolated PCL tears can be treated with conservative management. POLICE principle shall be adopted for treatment immediately after damage. The patient can begin immediately after injury with quadriceps sets and straight leg raising to regain motor control and minimize atrophy. Conduct early exercises in pain-free range-of-motion (EPFRM). ② The patient can be fitted with a knee brace to help control knee instability, and physical therapy can be performed in the mid to late stages, with a focus on strengthening the quadriceps femoris. As pain subsides and ROM improves, isotonic open-chain extension exercises may be incorporated. ③ Surgical intervention is recommended for severe PCL tears.

3.2 Meniscus Injury

3.2.1 Etiology

The most common mechanism of meniscus injury is weight bearing combined with internal or external rotation while extending or flexing the knee. A large number of medial meniscus lesions are caused by the sudden and intense internal rotation of the femur. It appears that most lateral meniscus injuries are traumatic, whereas most medial meniscus injuries are degenerative. Risk factors for meniscus injury include physical activity involving twisting and stopping; acute or chronic ACL tear; acute ACL tear and medial collateral ligament tear; instability of any knee ligament.

3.2.2 Symptoms and Signs

① After a meniscus injury, the patient needs to be examined as soon as possible. Muscle spasm and swelling after injury will influence the examination. Increased exudation and swelling will present within 48 to 72 hours, combined with joint space pain and loss of movement. The knee joint has the locking and giving way. Pain occurs when the patient squats. ② Chronic meniscus injuries may also show repeated swelling and significant atrophy of the muscles around the knee joint, inability to squat fully and pain during rapid changes of direction. MRI can help diagnose.

3.2.3 Management

① The acute stage is treated according to the POLICE principle. Anti-inflammatory medications (NSAIDs) can be used to control pain and swelling. If the knee discomfort, dysfunction and locking continue to occur, arthroscopic surgery is required. ② Displaced meniscal tears can eventually lead to serious articular degeneration with major impairment and disability. Such injuries usually warrant surgical intervention.

3.3 Osteochondral Fracture of Knee

3.3.1 Etiology

This injury most frequently occurs during a violent twist of the knee, especially when weight is applied. The twist may occur from direct trauma such as impact or a fall.

3.3.2 Symptoms and Signs

The athlete will feel immediate pain at the time of injury with rapid swelling. The pain will get worse when weight is applied and the knee joint may lock or feel unstable.

3.3.3 Management

Treatment depends on the severity of the injury. Common injuries are treated with physical therapy and rehabilitation. More severe injuries usually require arthroscopic surgery to remove or repair the damaged fragment.

3.4 Bursitis

3.4.1 Etiology

Bursitis in the knee can be acute, chronic or recurrent. Anterior prepatellar, deep infrapatellar and suprapatellar bursae have the highest incidence of irritation in sports. The inflammation of the prepatellar bursa is often caused by the pressure on the knee in the kneeling position or repetitive crawling or kneeling on the knee, while the inflammation of the deep infrapatellar bursa is often caused by the overuse of the patellar tendon. Injuries to the ligaments of the knee and fractures of the patella may occur along with acute prepatellar bursitis.

3.4.2 Symptoms and Signs

Prepatellar bursitis may cause local swelling of the knee joint and tenderness during palpation. There may be localized redness and increased skin temperature.

3.4.3 Management

Acute prepatellar bursitis should be treated conservatively, and rehabilitation should begin with ice, compression, anti-inflammatory medication, and possibly a brief period of immobilization by a knee splint. When bursitis has progressed to chronic or recurrent, a steroid injection can be used. If the treatment fails, surgery is needed.

3.5 Patellar Fracture

3.5.1 Etiology

Patellar fractures may be caused by direct or indirect trauma. Most patellar fractures are caused by indirect trauma. When the knee joint is in a semi-flexion position, the patella bears great pressure from the quadriceps tendon and the patellar ligament, resulting in the injury.

3.5.2 Symptoms and Signs

Symptoms for patellar fractures typically include: pain and swelling in the front of the knee; bruising; inability to straighten the knee or keep it extended in a straight leg raise; inability to walk.

3.5.3 Management

Treatment is determined by the amount of displacement of the fracture and whether the extensor mechanism of the knee is intact. For patients with a nondisplaced or minimally displaced fracture and intact extensor mechanisms, nonoperative treatment may be suitable. It usually includes a knee splint for 4–6 weeks. The patient is usually allowed to bear weight in the splint during this period. In the case of displaced fracture or disrupted extensor mechanism, surgical management is usually required.

3.6 Patellar Subluxation or Dislocation

3.6.1 Etiology

When the patella slides completely out of position, it is called patella dislocation. When the patella slides partially out of position, it is called a patella subluxation. They are usually caused by a noncontact twisting injury to the knee, or direct contact with the medial aspect of the patella.

3.6.2 Symptoms and Signs

Acute patella dislocation often leads to swelling and hematoma in the joints. Patellar subluxation often presents with recurrent episodes of mild swelling. During the examination, the patella position is abnormal and knee joint functional activity disorder can be found.

3.6.3 Management

① After restoration, the knee should be kept in the extension position and immobilized for 4 weeks or more, while the patient is instructed to walk with crutches. ② Strength training of the muscles around the hip joint, thigh and knee joint is needed. ③ Shoe orthotic devices may be used to reduce foot pronation and tibial internal rotation, and subsequently to reduce stress on the patellofemoral joint. Postural malalignments must be corrected as much as possible. ④ Rehabilitation for a patella subluxation should focus on regaining a balance in strength of all musculature associated with the knee joint.

3.7 Infrapatellar Fat Pad Injury

3.7.1 Etiology

The infrapatellar fat pad (IFP) injury, also known as a syndrome of infrapatellar fat pad impingement, is mostly caused by trauma, deformity, strain and pressure stimulation. Fat pads are risk of impingement between the femur and tibia during exercises that require constant repetition of maximal extension of the knee, causing edema and hypertrophy of fat pad.

3.7.2 Symptoms and Signs

It is characterized by the tenderness of the fat pad and tenderness during palpation along the edge of the patellar tendon. The patient always complains that there is pain and discomfort under the patellar ligament. If the irritation persists, scarring and calcification may appear. When the knee joint is extended, the knee joint may present giving away, mild swelling and stiffness. Sagittal MRI is the most common imaging technique used to assess IFP pathology.

3.7.3 Management

① Rest and appropriate exercise. In the early avoid stage, patients with infrapatellar fat pad syndrome should avoid strenuous exercise, especially avoid those activities that are easy to trigger pain symptoms, such as continuous running, squatting with load, going up and down stairs, and jumping, etc. Proper rest can effectively relieve the pressure in the cavity of the knee joint, and reduce the pressure and friction of the fat pad under the patella, so as to relieve related symptoms. The closed chain quadriceps exercises can improve lower limb control. Training of the gluteus medius and stretching the anterior hip may help decrease internal rotation of the hip and valgus force at the knee. ② Medication and injection, such as Voltaren or Chinese herbs for external use, injection of the anesthesia, etc. ③ If the conservative treatment is not complete and the symptoms are recurrent, arthroscopic surgery can be considered.

3.8 Patellofemoral Pain Syndrome (PFPS)

3.8.1 Etiology

At present, the specific pathogenesis of PFPS is still unknown, but most scholars support that abnormal patella motion track is an important cause of PFPS. The causes of abnormal patella motion track include anatomical structure abnormality (such as increased Q Angle, patella structure abnormality), the decrease of muscle strength around or near the knee joint, the tension of soft tissue around the knee joint, overload and trauma.

3.8.2 Symptoms and Signs

Patients may experience pain in the front of the knee while walking, running, driving, going up and down stairs, or squatting, recurrent swelling around the patella, and grinding of the knee during flexion and extension. The results of the patella compression test and the patellar grind test may be positive.

3.8.3 Management

Avoid stimulating exercises such as climbing stairs, squatting, etc. Foot orthoses are recommended to relieve pain if lower limb alignment is abnormal.

Perform isometric exercises of quadriceps and hamstring in a painless range, neuromuscular training and taping.

3.9 Patellar Tendinitis (Jumper's Knee)

3.9.1 Etiology

Patellar tendinitis is a common overuse injury, caused by repeated stress on the patellar tendon. Patellar tendinitis weakens the knee extensor significantly and is one of the common sports injuries among athletes.

3.9.2 Symptoms and Signs

The patient complains of pain and tenderness behind the lower pole of the patella. There are three stages of pain:

- Stage 1 — post-exercise pain.
- Stage 2 — pain during and after exercise.
- Stage 3 — long periods of pain during and after exercise.

3.9.3 Management

Jumper's knee involves chronic inflammation and the treatments include rest, anti-inflammatory medication, ice compress, and ultrasound. Shockwave is a common treatment for enthesopathy, such as patellar tendinitis. Eccentric training should be primarily used in functional training. The use of a tenodesis strap or brace has also been recommended for patellar tendinitis.

3.10 Patellar Tendon Rupture

3.10.1 Etiology

The incidence of the patellar tendon rupture increases with age. Sudden forceful contraction of the quadriceps may result in patellar tendon rupture. Patellar tendon rupture usually occurs in the area of the knee extensor with chronic inflammation. So tendon ruptures rarely occur in the middle of the tendon, usually at the upper and lower pole of the patella.

3.10.2 Symptoms and Signs

The patella will move up toward the thigh, where the defect can be felt by palpation and the patient cannot extend the knee. There will be obvious swelling and pain at first.

3.10.3 Management

Patellar tendon rupture usually requires surgical repair. If the patient has patellar tendinitis, conservative treatment can effectively reduce the occurrence of patellar tendon rupture. However, repeated steroid injections can lead to deformation of tendon fibers and increase the risk of patellar tendon rupture.

3.11 Iliotibial Tract Friction Syndrome (Runner's Knee)

3.11.1 Etiology

Iliotibial tract friction syndrome is a common cause of lateral knee pain. Repetitive flexion and extension of the knee result in excessive friction of the iliotibial tract against the lateral femoral condyle and subsequent inflammatory change within the iliotibial tract. It may result in cysts or bursitis. Iliotibial tract friction syndrome is an overuse injury that often occurs in runners and cyclists and is accompanied by knee varus and foot varus.

3.11.2 Symptoms and Signs

The patient experiences pain at the lateral aspect of the knee that may radiate inferiorly along the iliotibial tract insertion. The patient has tenderness, crepitus, and swelling around the lateral condyle. Ober's test will induce pain in the involved area.

3.11.3 Management

① POLICE principle shall be adopted. Treatments include stretching the iliotibial tract and physiotherapy which can reduce inflammation. ② Rehabilitation should focus on correcting the underlying biomechanical factors that may cause the problem.

3.12 Pes Anserinus Bursitis

3.12.1 Etiology

Pes anserinus bursitis (PAB) refers to a disorder that is one of the most frequent soft tissue pain syndromes affecting the knee. It is inflammation of the pes anserine bursa located at the medial side of the knee inferior to the joint line. The pes anserinus is where the sartorius, gracilis and semitendinosus converge and terminate at the tibia. Osteoarthritis, excessive anteversion at the hip, genu valgum deformities, vastus medialis weakness and excessive pronation of the foot can lead to inflammation of the bursa. PAB often occurs together with knee osteoarthritis and may lead to increased pain. Predisposing factors for this syndrome include incorrect training techniques, excessive tightness of the hamstring muscles, valgus alignment of the knee, and excessive external rotation of the lower leg.

3.12.2 Symptoms and Signs

The hallmark of this condition is tenderness when palpating over the pes anserine bursa. Patients may experience pain when walking down the stairs and may not be able to walk with the heel. Patients will experience increased pain with passive valgus and external rotation of the knee. Resisted flexion at the knee will elicit pain, and sudden release of resistance will produce a significant increase in pain. This area is often swollen but rarely inflamed.

3.12.3 Management

The most important thing to temper the pain caused by bursitis is rest. And pay attention to avoid walking stairs, climbing, or other irritating activities. NSAID can be taken to alleviate the pain. An ice massage of 15 minutes every 4–7 hours will reduce the inflammation. An elastic bandage can be wrapped around the knee to reduce any swelling or to prevent swelling from occurring. Rehabilitation exercises include leg muscle stretching and strength training.

三、膝部常见损伤的识别和处理

（一）韧带损伤

1. 内侧副韧带扭伤

（1）病因

内侧副韧带（medial collateral ligament，MCL）扭伤较常见的原因是由外侧面向内侧方向的直接撞击（外翻力）或胫骨外旋。这种情况经常发生在滑雪和其他有削切和旋转动作的运动中，如篮球和足球。膝关节的屈伸角度是其易受损伤的重要因素。但是如果外力过大，膝关节在任何位置都可能造成损伤。内侧扭伤所造成的损伤比外侧扭伤更严重，因为MCL与关节囊和内侧半月板的联系更紧密。

严重的 MCL 损伤可出现 O'Donoghue 三联征，也被称为恐怖三联征，指的是 MCL、前交叉韧带（anterior cruciate ligament，ACL）和内侧半月板均受损。半月板撕裂的发生常常是由于侧副韧带反复损伤后变得松弛，不能维持稳定性。

MCL 扭伤按照损伤程度可分为三度损伤：

I 度扭伤：轻度损伤，纤维轻微撕裂，MCL 完整性未丧失。II 度扭伤：中度损伤，不完全撕裂，MCL 松弛增加。III 度扭伤：严重损伤，完全撕裂，MCL 明显松弛。

（2）症状和体征

大多数 I 度扭伤患者会在膝关节轻微弯曲或受外翻应力时感到疼痛，但没有其他症状。II 度扭伤患者主诉膝关节内侧疼痛和明显压痛，可观察到关节有中度松弛。III 度扭伤患者 MCL 明显疼痛和肿胀，膝关节屈曲受限。外翻应力试验结果为阳性。该试验可区分 II 度和 III 度扭伤。II 度扭伤在膝关节屈曲 30° 时是松弛的，但在完全伸展时是紧张的，而 III 度扭伤在这两个位置都是松弛的。

（3）处理

MCL 损伤的处理取决于损伤的程度。

I 度损伤：应用 POLICE 原则进行处理，使用理疗和非甾体抗炎药等。进行适当的康复力量训练。II、III 度损伤：除与 I 度损伤相同的处理内容外，膝关节可使用护具或拐杖，负重和力量训练需在耐受范围内进行。有撕脱骨折或合并有其他韧带的断裂需要进行手术。

2. 外侧副韧带扭伤

（1）病因

外侧副韧带（lateral collateral ligament，LCL）扭伤是所有膝关节韧带扭伤中最不常见的。单纯的 LCL 损伤是内翻应力作用于膝关节的结果。

（2）症状和体征

膝屈曲和内旋时可触诊到 LCL 周围疼痛和压痛。损伤 LCL 周围肿胀和炎症渗出。Ⅰ度和Ⅱ度扭伤疼痛最严重；Ⅲ度扭伤时，疼痛一开始剧烈然后变为钝痛。

（3）处理

LCL 损伤的处理步骤与 MCL 损伤的处理步骤相似。如果是Ⅲ度 LCL 扭伤，涉及多处韧带损伤并伴有不稳定性，需要手术修复或重建，患者应使用术后支具，部分负重 4～6 周。

3. 前交叉韧带扭伤

（1）病因

前交叉韧带（anterior cruciate ligament，ACL）扭伤通常被认为是最严重的膝关节韧带损伤。但对于造成 ACL 损伤的确切机制目前仍存在争议。

ACL 损伤最常见的是非接触性损伤。在非接触性损伤中，通常由跳跃后着地时膝关节的扭转应力造成 ACL 损伤。在接触性损伤中，对膝外侧的直接打击会导致它向内弯曲。这种压力使胫骨产生过度移动，可导致包括 ACL 在内的其他结构撕裂。

（2）症状和体征

患者主诉膝关节疼痛、肿胀和膝关节不稳定。当 ACL 撕裂发生时，患者通常会感到"啪"的断裂感，之后便出现无法行动的情况，患者感觉膝关节有滑动感。ACL 撕裂会引起关节间隙处迅速肿胀，在 6 小时内形成明显的关节血肿。单纯性 ACL 撕裂的患者前抽屉试验和 Lachman 试验结果呈阳性，轴移试验结果也可能呈阳性。可通过磁共振成像或关节镜检查做出准确诊断。

（3）处理

①急性损伤时按 POLICE 原则进行紧急处理。②肿胀消退后，患者可以佩戴膝关节支具，以控制膝关节不稳定。③可以在受伤后立即开始股四头肌等长收缩训练和直腿抬高训练，以恢复运动控制并最大限度地减少肌肉萎缩。④ACL 完全撕裂后的治疗存在一定争议。但目前普遍共识是，ACL 断裂若不能得到良好有效的治疗，最终将导致严重的关节退变。故可进行 ACL 的重建以增强膝关节稳定性。

4. 后交叉韧带扭伤

（1）病因

后交叉韧带（posterior cruciate ligament，PCL）能够限制胫骨向后过度移位，是膝关节中最重要的韧带之一。后交叉韧带损伤最常发生在膝关节屈曲 90° 位着地或受到来自前方的大力撞击时。

（2）症状和体征

PCL 损伤的症状表现为急性疼痛、肿胀和行走困难。患者主诉膝关节松弛，有打软腿的感觉。慢性 PCL 撕裂患者可能仅表现为轻度膝关节疼痛和不稳定。影像学检查可辅助诊断。

（3）处理

①单纯性 PCL 撕裂可采用保守治疗，损伤后立即采取 POLICE 原则进行处理。患者可

以立即开始股四头肌训练和直腿抬高训练，以恢复运动控制并最大限度地减少肌肉萎缩。早期进行无痛关节活动范围内的锻炼。②使用护具帮助防止膝关节不稳，中后期可进行物理治疗，重点是加强股四头肌训练。随着疼痛的减轻和关节活动度的改善，患者可以进行等张开链练习。③严重的 PCL 损伤推荐手术治疗。

（二）半月板损伤

1.病因

半月板损伤最常见的机制是在伸直或屈曲膝关节时负重并结合内旋或外旋。很多内侧半月板损伤是股骨突然且强烈的内旋造成的。大多数外侧半月板损伤是创伤性的，而大多数内侧半月板损伤是退行性的。导致半月板损伤的危险因素包括：涉及扭转和急停的体育运动；急性或慢性 ACL 撕裂；MCL 撕裂；任何膝关节韧带的不稳定。

2.症状和体征

①半月板损伤后，运动防护师应尽早进行检查，伤后出现的肌痉挛和肿胀会影响检查。48 ~ 72 小时内炎症渗出物增多，肿胀明显，关节间隙疼痛和活动能力丧失，膝关节有绞锁感和打软腿；患者下蹲时出现疼痛。②慢性半月板损伤也可能表现出反复肿胀和膝关节周围肌肉明显萎缩，不能完全下蹲以及在快速变向时有疼痛感。可结合磁共振成像帮助诊断。

3.处理

①急性期按 POLICE 原则进行处理。可使用非甾体抗炎药控制疼痛和肿胀。若膝部不适感、功能障碍和绞锁持续发生，需要进行关节镜手术处理。②移位的半月板撕裂最终会导致严重的关节退化，造成严重的损伤和残疾，这种损伤通常需要手术干预。

（三）膝关节骨软骨骨折

1.病因

这种损伤最常发生在膝关节剧烈扭曲，特别是负重时。扭转可能发生于直接的创伤，如撞击或跌倒。

2.症状和体征

运动员在受伤时会立即感到疼痛和迅速肿胀。在负重时疼痛会加重，膝关节可能会有绞锁感或不稳定感。

3.处理

治疗措施取决于患者受伤的严重程度。普通损伤采用物理治疗和康复治疗。更严重的损伤通常需要采用关节镜手术来移除或修复损坏的碎片。

（四）滑囊炎

1.病因

膝关节滑囊炎可以是急性的、慢性的或复发性的。在运动中，髌前囊、髌下深囊和髌上囊的刺激发生率最高。髌前囊的炎症常由跪姿或爬行对膝前方受到压力导致，而髌下深囊的炎症常因髌腱的过度使用导致。膝关节韧带的损伤以及髌骨的骨折可能与急性髌前滑囊炎同时发生。

2. 症状和体征

髌前囊炎可导致膝关节局部肿胀，触诊时有触痛，局部皮肤可能有发红和温度升高的现象。

3. 处理

急性髌前滑囊炎应保守治疗，康复应从冰敷、加压、抗炎药治疗开始，可使用膝关节支具短暂固定。当滑囊炎已发展为慢性或复发性时，可使用封闭治疗。如果封闭治疗失败，应考虑手术治疗。

（五）髌骨骨折

1. 病因

髌骨骨折可能由直接或间接创伤导致。绝大多数髌骨骨折是间接创伤所致，当膝关节位于半屈曲状态时，髌腱会对股骨产生巨大的拉力，进而使髌骨承受来自股四头肌腱和髌韧带的巨大压力，从而造成损伤。

2. 症状和体征

髌骨骨折最常见的症状是膝关节前部疼痛和肿胀；局部瘀伤；不能伸直膝关节或在直腿抬高时不能保持膝关节伸直；无法行走。

3. 处理

治疗取决于骨折移位的程度以及膝关节伸肌机制是否完整。对于非移位性或轻度移位性骨折和伸肌机制完整的患者，可以进行保守治疗，膝关节夹板固定 4～6 周。在此期间，通常允许患者在佩戴夹板时承重。在移位骨折或伸肌断裂的情况下，通常需要手术治疗。

（六）髌骨脱位和半脱位

1. 病因

当髌骨完全移位时，称为髌骨脱位；当髌骨部分移位时，称为髌骨半脱位。两者通常是由膝关节非接触性扭转损伤或直接接触髌骨内侧造成的。

2. 症状和体征

急性髌骨脱位常会导致肿胀以及关节积血；髌骨半脱位常会有轻度肿胀反复发作的表现。在检查中会发现患者髌骨位置异常且膝关节功能活动障碍。

3. 处理

①复位后膝关节保持伸展位，制动 4 周或以上，同时指导患者拄拐行走。②加强髋关节、大腿及膝关节周围肌群的肌力训练。③鞋矫正装置可用于减少足内旋和胫骨内旋，从而减少髌股关节的应力。姿势不良必须尽可能地纠正。④慢性髌骨半脱位的康复应该集中于恢复与膝关节相关的所有肌肉组织的力量平衡。

（七）髌下脂肪垫损伤

1. 病因

髌下脂肪垫损伤，又称髌下脂肪垫撞击综合征，多由外伤、畸形、劳损和压力的刺激等引起。在需要不断重复膝关节最大伸展的运动中，脂肪垫面临股骨和胫骨之间撞击的风险，造成脂肪垫水肿和肥厚。

2. 症状和体征

髌下脂肪垫损伤特征是脂肪垫的接触压痛和沿髌腱边缘触诊时的压痛。患者主诉髌韧带下方有疼痛和不适感。若刺激持续存在，可能出现瘢痕和钙化。在膝关节伸展时，膝关节可能会有无力、轻度肿胀和僵硬的表现。矢状面磁共振成像是评估髌下脂肪垫损伤常用的影像学技术。

3. 处理

①休息及合理运动。髌下脂肪垫损伤的患者早期应避免剧烈运动，尤其是避免容易激发疼痛症状的活动，如持续跑步、负重下蹲、上下楼梯、大幅度跳跃等。适当休息可有效缓解膝关节腔内压力，减少髌下脂肪垫所受的压迫和摩擦，从而缓解相关症状。股四头肌闭链训练可改善下肢控制等。训练臀中肌和拉伸髋关节前侧肌肉可能有助于减少髋内旋和膝外翻。②外用药涂抹及局部注射，如扶他林或中药外用、封闭注射等。③在保守治疗不彻底，症状反复时，可以考虑关节镜下手术治疗。

（八）髌股疼痛综合征

1. 病因

目前髌股疼痛综合征的具体发病机制仍不清楚，但大多数学者认为髌骨运动轨迹的异常是引起髌股疼痛综合征的重要病因。引起髌骨运动轨迹异常的原因有：解剖结构异常（如Q角加大、髌骨结构异常）、膝关节周围或邻近关节肌肉力量的下降、膝关节周围软组织紧张、超负荷及创伤等。

2. 症状和体征

患者可能在步行、跑步、驾车、上下楼梯或下蹲时感到膝前方疼痛，其髌骨周围可能反复出现肿胀，并且膝关节在屈伸活动时有研磨感。髌骨挤压试验或髌骨研磨试验结果可能呈阳性。

3. 处理

避免进行刺激性的活动如爬楼梯、下蹲等。如果存在下肢力线异常，建议使用足部矫形器减轻疼痛。也可以在无痛范围内进行股四头肌和腘绳肌的等长收缩练习、神经肌肉训练以及贴扎等。

（九）髌腱炎（跳跃膝）

1. 病因

髌腱炎是一种常见的过度使用损伤，由髌腱的反复受力引起。髌腱炎使伸膝装置功能明显减弱，是运动员常见的运动损伤之一。

2. 症状和体征

患者主诉髌骨下极点后方疼痛和压痛。髌腱炎有三个疼痛阶段：

- 阶段 1——运动后疼痛。
- 阶段 2——运动中和运动后疼痛。
- 阶段 3——运动中和结束后长时间疼痛。

3. 处理

髌腱炎是慢性炎症，治疗方法包括休息、服用抗炎药、冰敷和超声波治疗。此外，冲击波是髌腱炎等末端病的常用治疗方法。在功能训练中，以离心训练为主。对于髌腱炎，也推荐使用肌腱带或护具。

（十）髌腱断裂

1. 病因

髌腱断裂的发生率会随着年龄的增长而增加。股四头肌的突然强力收缩可能会导致髌腱断裂。髌腱断裂一般发生在存在慢性炎症的伸膝肌肌腱区域。因此，髌腱断裂很少发生在腱的中段，一般发生在髌骨上极处，或在髌骨下极处。

2. 症状和体征

髌腱断裂后髌骨会向上移动至大腿，触诊时可摸到缺损，患者无法伸膝。一开始会有明显的肿胀和疼痛。

3. 处理

髌腱断裂通常需要手术修复。若患者有髌腱炎症状，对髌腱炎进行保守治疗可以有效降低髌腱断裂的发生。但多次封闭治疗可导致腱纤维变形，增加髌腱断裂的风险。

（十一）髂胫束摩擦综合征（跑步膝）

1. 病因

髂胫束摩擦综合征是指膝关节的重复屈曲和伸展导致髂胫束对股骨外侧髁的过度摩擦，并引起髂胫束内的炎症变化，导致膝外侧囊肿或滑囊炎。髂胫束摩擦综合征常见于跑步者和骑自行车的人，并伴有膝内翻和足内翻情况的过劳损伤。

2. 症状和体征

患者在膝关节外侧感到疼痛，疼痛可能沿着髂胫束插入部位向下放射。触诊有压痛、捻发音和外侧髁肿胀。Ober's 试验将诱发问题部位的疼痛。

3. 处理

①应用 POLICE 原则进行处理，治疗方法包括对髂胫束的牵拉和消除炎症的理疗方法。②康复应该着重于纠正可能导致问题的潜在生物力学因素。

（十二）鹅足滑囊炎

1. 病因

鹅足滑囊炎是一种影响膝关节的最常见的软组织疼痛综合征之一，是位于膝关节内侧关节线以下的鹅足滑囊的炎症。鹅足肌腱由缝匠肌、股薄肌和半腱肌交汇止于胫骨的部分组成。骨关节炎、髋关节过度前倾、膝外翻畸形、股内侧肌无力和脚过度内旋会导致炎症的发生。鹅足滑囊炎通常与膝骨关节炎一起发生，并可能导致疼痛加重。诱发因素包括不正确的训练技术、腘绳肌过度紧绷、膝关节外翻以及小腿过度外旋。

2. 症状和体征

触诊鹅足滑囊时的触痛为鹅足滑囊炎症的标志。患者在下楼梯时可能会感到疼痛，并且可能无法用脚后跟行走。患者会因被动外翻和膝关节外旋而增加疼痛。膝关节处的抗阻屈曲会引起疼痛，突然释放阻力会导致疼痛明显加剧。该区域经常肿胀，但炎症很少。

3. 处理

缓解鹅足滑囊炎引起的疼痛，重要的是休息。避免爬楼梯、攀爬或其他刺激性活动，可以服用非甾体抗炎药来缓解疼痛。每 4 ~ 7 小时进行一次 15 分钟的冰敷按摩可以减轻炎症。可以在膝关节周围缠上弹性绷带，以减少肿胀或防止肿胀的发生。康复训练包括腿部肌肉的牵伸和力量训练。

Summary

1. To avoid knee injuries, the athletes can wear functional or protective knee braces during sports.

2. The most common mechanism of meniscus injury is weight bearing combined with internal or external rotation while extending or flexing the knee. It appears that most lateral meniscus injuries are traumatic, whereas most medial meniscus injuries are degenerative.

3. ACL injury more commonly occurs as a noncontact injury and the results of the anterior drawer test and the Lachman test would be positive in patients with simple ACL tears.

4. MCL, LCL and PCL injuries are generally treated nonoperatively. In the case of a grade 3 sprain that involves multiple ligamentous injuries with associated instability, surgical repair or reconstruction is commonly adopted.

5. A severe injury to the medial collateral ligament may result in O'Donoghue's Triad, also known as the Terrible Triad. The medial collateral ligament (MCL), anterior cruciate ligament (ACL) and medial meniscus are all damaged.

6. Patellar fractures may be caused by direct or indirect trauma. Most patellar fractures are caused by indirect trauma.

7. Pes anserinus bursitis refers to a disorder that is one of the most frequent soft tissue pain syndromes.

○ Review Questions

1. How to prevent knee joint injury?

2. Try to describe the treatment of medial collateral ligament.

3. What is the injury mechanism of patellar fracture?

4. What is the cause of "runner's knee"? How to deal with it?

5. Discuss the difference between contact and noncontact ACL injury, and describe the symptoms and management of ACL injury.

小结

1. 为避免运动中膝关节发生损伤，运动员在运动中也可佩戴功能性或防护性膝护具。

2. 半月板损伤最常见的机制是在伸直或屈曲膝关节时负重并结合内旋或外旋转造成。大多数外侧半月板损伤是创伤性的，而大多数内侧半月板损伤是退行性的。

3. ACL 损伤更常见的是非接触性损伤，单纯性 ACL 撕裂的患者将表现出前抽屉试验结果呈阳性和 Lachman 试验结果呈阳性。

4. MCL、LCL 和 PCL 损伤通常采用非手术治疗。如果是 3 级扭伤，涉及多处韧带损伤并伴有不稳定性，需要手术修复或重建。

5. 严重的 MCL 的损伤可出现 O'Donoghue 三联征，也被称为恐怖三联征。MCL、ACL 和内侧半月板均受损。

6. 髌骨骨折可能由直接或间接创伤导致。绝大多数髌骨骨折是间接创伤所致。

7. 鹅足滑囊炎是一种影响膝关节的最常见的软组织疼痛综合征之一。

○ 复习题

1. 如何预防膝关节的损伤？

2. 试述 MCL 扭伤的处理方式。

3. 髌骨骨折的损伤机制是什么？

4. 引起"跑步膝"的原因是什么？怎么处理？

5. 讨论 ACL 接触性损伤和非接触性损伤的不同，并描述其症状和处理方式。

Chapter 7 Ankle and Lower Leg Injuries
第七章　踝和小腿损伤

Main Contents

1. Prevention of ankle and lower leg injuries.
2. Assessment of ankle and lower leg injuries.
3. Identification and management of common ankle and lower leg injuries.

主要内容

1. 踝和小腿损伤的预防。
2. 踝和小腿损伤的评估。
3. 踝和小腿常见损伤的识别和处理。

1 Prevention of Ankle and Lower Leg Injuries

The lower leg consists of two bones: the tibia and fibula. The ankle joint or talocrural joint bony structure includes the distal tibia, the distal fibula, and the talus. The four muscular compartments of the leg are the superficial posterior compartment, the deep posterior compartment, the lateral compartment, and the anterior compartment: anterior chamber muscles for ankle dorsiflexion; lateral chamber muscles for ankle valgus; posterior superficial chamber muscles for ankle plantar flexion; and posterior deep chamber muscles for ankle varus. The ligaments around the ankle include the tibiofibular ligaments, lateral collateral ligament [anterior talofibular ligament (ATFL), calcaneofibular ligament (CFL), the posterior talofibular ligament (PTFL)], and the medial ligament. There are some interventions to prevent the injuries of the ankle and lower leg: achilles tendon stretching, muscle strength training, neuromuscular control exercise, using taping and bracing, etc.

1.1 Muscle Strength Training

Muscle strength training aims to develop the balance of muscle strength around the ankle joint. Isometric exercise should be performed on the four major ankle motion planes. The exercise can be combined with isometric plantar flexion and dorsiflexion exercises early in the rehabilitation stage. As the rehabilitation progresses and the range of motion increases, the patient can begin strength training in all motion planes. Athletic trainers should take care to avoid tibial rotation as a compensatory exercise during inversion and eversion exercises.

1.2 Neuromuscular Control Exercise

Specific exercise performed on an unstable support surface can help improve the range of motion and neuromuscular control. A significant decrease in joint position sense and kinesthesia in individuals with chronic ankle instability can increase the risk of an ankle sprain. For patients with chronic ankle instability, strengthening and regaining balance control is most important for preventing and rehabilitating ankle injury. Balance training can be applied by standing on two feet with their eyes closed and progressing to standing on one leg. Then, they can train on BAPS board, BOSU ball, or balance board. Other closed kinetic chain exercises may also help establish a good balance and proprioception, such as mini-squats exercises and exercises with resistance bands.

1.3 Taping and Bracing

Ankle taping does improve the effect of ankle joint instability to a certain extent. The choice of ankle braces is mainly to improve functional stability, proprioception, posture stability, balance, neuromuscular control, and functional performance. The wearing of the brace can attract the patient's attention to the movement of the ankle joint to reduce the occurrence of injury.

一、踝和小腿损伤的预防

小腿由胫骨和腓骨两块骨组成。踝关节（又称距上关节）的骨性结构包括胫骨远端、腓骨远端和距骨。小腿肌肉被筋膜分为四个室：前室肌肉使踝背屈；外侧室肌肉使踝外翻；后侧浅室肌肉使踝跖屈；后侧深室肌肉使踝内翻。踝关节的韧带支持包括了胫腓韧带、外侧副韧带（距腓前韧带、跟腓韧带、距腓后韧带）和内侧副韧带。踝和小腿损伤的预防可以采取以下措施：跟腱拉伸、肌力训练、神经肌肉控制训练以及使用贴扎和护具等。

（一）肌力训练

肌力训练应着重于实现踝关节周围肌群肌力的平衡。等长肌力练习应在踝关节活动的四个主要平面内完成，可在康复阶段早期结合等张跖屈和背屈练习。随着康复过程的进展以及活动度的增加，患者可开始所有活动平面内的力量训练。内翻和外翻练习时必须特别小心，以避免胫骨旋转的代偿运动。

（二）神经肌肉控制训练

在不稳定支撑面上进行练习有利于改善关节活动范围并改善神经肌肉控制。慢性踝关节不稳的患者，其关节位置觉和运动觉明显减退，会增加踝关节扭伤的风险。强化和重获对平衡的控制是踝关节损伤预防和康复的关键所在，这对于慢性踝关节不稳的患者尤其重要。患者可通过闭眼双脚站立进阶至单脚站立的方法来恢复平衡能力。此后可在 BAPS 板、BOSU 平衡训练器或平衡板上站立并保持平衡。其他闭链运动可能对于建立良好的平衡能力和本体感觉也有帮助，如浅蹲练习以及弹力带抗阻练习。

（三）贴扎和护具

踝关节贴扎能够在一定程度上改善踝关节不稳。踝部支具主要可以提高功能稳定性、本体感觉、姿态稳定性、平衡性、神经肌肉控制和功能表现。支具的佩戴可引起患者对踝关节运动的注意，以此可减少损伤发生。

2 Assessment of Ankle and Lower Leg Injuries

2.1 History

The athletic trainer should ask the patients with acute pain the following questions:
● What happened when you got injured?

- What did you hear when the injury occurred—a crack, snap, or pop?
- Point to the location of your pain or abnormal feelings.
- Was there immediate swelling or bruise? Did the swelling occur immediately or later (or not at all)?
- Any muscle weakness while walking?
- Have you had a similar injury before?

Ask the patients with chronic pain:

- Occupation.
- What are your regular activities or recreational activities?
- What injuries or pain have you had in your ankle?
- How severe and where is the pain?
- When does pain get worse—with weight, after exercise, or in the morning?
- What emergency management and treatment measures were taken for injuries?

2.2 Observation

When assessing the ankle joint, the athletic trainer should record the information of the following points:

- Any postural abnormalities?
- Any difficulties in walking?
- Any obvious deformity or swelling of the ankle joint?
- Is the bony profile of the ankle joint normal and symmetrical?
- Are the skin colour and texture normal?
- Is there any redness, swelling, or heat at present?
- Is the range of motion of the ankle normal?
- If the patient can walk, is their gait normal?
- What are the characteristics of the shoes' abrasion?

2.3 Palpation

Palpate the area of injury to identify obvious structural deformities, areas of swelling, and points of tenderness.

2.4 Special Tests

2.4.1 Lower Leg Alignment Tests

Poor lower limb alignment could exert more stress on feet, ankles, calves, knees, and hips, thus affecting the whole body's function. Tibial torsion, the twist of tibia and fibula in the transverse plane, is often implicated in the predisposition of the lower extremity to injury.

Common poor calf alignment includes internal/external rotation of the tibia. In the case of external rotation of the tibia, the tibial trochanter leans laterally. In the case of tibial internal rotation, the tibial trochanter deflects medially.

2.4.2 Lower Leg Compression Test

The patient lies supine. The athletic trainer grasps the lower leg at the midcalf and squeezes the tibia and fibula together before releasing. If pain is present, it may indicate a fracture, contusion, and ventricular septal syndrome, requiring further X-ray examination.

2.4.3 Thompson Test

The patient lies prone with his or her feet out of the bed. The athletic trainer grasps and squeezes the calf muscles. When the muscles are squeezed, if there is no plantar flexion, the result is positive, and the achilles tendon is ruptured.

2.4.4 Homan's Sign

Homan's sign test is a physical examination procedure used to test for Deep Vein Thrombosis (DVT). The patient's knee is extended, and the foot is in passive dorsiflexion. The gastrocnemius muscle pain is a positive sign, and it may represent deep venous thrombophlebitis. There will be pain symptoms during gastrocnemius palpation. In addition, the athletic trainer may also find paleness and edema in the lower legs and the absence of a dorsal foot artery pulse.

2.4.5 Anterior Drawer Test

This test is used to evaluate injuries to the anterior talofibular ligament and ligamentous instability. The patient lies supine with the foot relaxed. The athletic trainer stabilizes the tibia and fibula, holds the patient's foot in 20° of plantar flexion and draws the talus forward in the ankle mortise. Excessive anterior displacement is the positive sign. Sometimes, a dimple may appear over the area of the anterior talofibular ligament on anterior translation if pain and muscle spasm are minimal.

2.4.6 Talar Tilt Test

This test is used to examine the ankle for injury of the anterior talofibular ligament and the calcaneofibular ligament. The patient is seated with foot and ankle unsupported. The foot is positioned in 10°–20° of plantar flexion. The distal lower leg is stabilized by the athletic trainer with one hand, and the hindfoot is inverted with the other hand. The lateral aspect of the talus is palpated to determine if tilting occurs. The laxity is compared to the contralateral side.

2.4.7 Kleiger's Test

With the patient sitting with the knee flexed at 90° over the bed's edge, the athletic trainer stabilizes the patient's lower leg, slightly dorsiflexes the ankle, and externally rotates the foot. Pain along the anterior inferior tibiofibular ligament or posterior tibiofibular and interosseous membrane indicates a syndesmotic sprain.

Medial ankle pain and a palpable subluxation of the talus within the ankle mortise indicates that the medial ligament is injured. The athletic trainer should compare this result to the other side.

2.4.8 Functional Tests

Functional tests are essential in evaluating ankle injuries. The athletic trainer often performs these tests on individuals with ankle sprains to decide if an athlete is ready for return to play (RTP). However, such tests are not appropriate when the patient is unable to bear the load. The following functional tests are commonly used:

- Single-limb stance with eyes open/closed
- The star excursion balance test/Y-Balance test
- Lateral and forward hop test
- Heel rocker test
- Single limb triple cross-over hop
- Single-leg vertical jump
- Limited time 6-meter single-leg hop

二、踝和小腿损伤的评估

（一）病史

①运动防护师应询问急性疼痛期的患者以下问题：

- 损伤是如何发生的？
- 损伤发生时听到什么响声——咔嚓、嘣、啪？
- 请指出疼痛或感觉异常的位置。
- 有无发生肿胀或淤伤？如有，是立即发生还是之后发生的？
- 行走时是否有任何肌无力或行走困难的感觉？
- 之前有过类似损伤吗？

②应询问慢性疼痛的患者以下问题：

- 患者的职业。
- 经常进行的活动或者娱乐是什么？
- 踝关节有无受伤史或疼痛史？
- 疼痛程度和位置。
- 什么情况下疼痛会加重——负重、运动后、晨起时？
- 针对损伤采取了什么处理和治疗措施？

（二）视诊

在检查踝关节时，运动防护师应检查以下几点：

- 患者有无任何姿势异常？
- 患者步行是否有障碍？
- 患者相关部位是否存在明显畸形或肿胀？
- 患者踝关节的骨性轮廓是否正常及对称？
- 患者踝关节皮肤颜色和状态正常吗？
- 患者踝关节是否存在红、肿、热？
- 患者踝关节活动范围正常吗？
- 若患者可以行走，其步态是否正常？
- 患者鞋子磨损的特点是什么？

（三）触诊

通过触诊可以确认明显的结构畸形、肿胀和压痛点等问题。

（四）特殊试验

1. 下肢力线检查

下肢力线不良可能导致足、踝、小腿、膝关节和髋关节受力异常，进而影响全身的功能。胫骨扭转，即胫骨和腓骨在水平面的扭转，常与下肢损伤易感性相关。常见的小腿力线不良包括胫骨内 / 外旋。胫骨外旋的情况下，胫骨粗隆偏向外侧；胫骨内旋的情况下，胫骨粗隆偏向内侧。

2. 小腿挤压试验

患者仰卧位，运动防护师握住小腿中段，并将胫骨与腓骨向一起挤压并放开。如果有疼痛出现，则提示可能存在骨折、挫伤和室间隔综合征，需进一步进行 X 射线检查。

3. 汤普森试验

患者俯卧位，足伸出床面。运动防护师在患者放松的情况下捏住患者小腿后侧肌肉。当肌肉被挤压时，足部没有出现跖屈的动作，代表试验结果为阳性，跟腱存在断裂的情况。

4. 霍曼氏征

该试验用来检查下肢深静脉血栓。患者膝关节伸直，足部被动做背屈动作。若腓肠肌出现疼痛症状为阳性体征，代表可能有深层静脉血栓性静脉炎。同时在触诊腓肠肌时，也会有疼痛的症状。除此之外，运动防护师还可以发现小腿有苍白、肿胀以及足背动脉脉搏消失的情形。

5. 前抽屉试验

该测试用于评估距腓前韧带的损伤和韧带不稳定性。病人仰卧，足部放松。运动防护师固定胫骨和腓骨，保持患者足跖屈 20°，并在踝穴处向前拉距骨。距骨出现过度的前移是阳性表现。如果疼痛和肌肉痉挛轻微，在向前移动时，距腓骨前韧带区域会出现凹陷。

6. 距骨倾斜试验

该试验用于检查踝关节距腓前韧带和跟腓韧带的损伤情况。患者坐位，足部和踝关节悬空。足处于跖屈 10° ~ 20° 的位置。运动防护师用一只手固定远端小腿，另一只手将后足内翻。触诊距骨外侧以确定是否发生倾斜。与对侧比较松弛程度。

7. 克雷格氏试验

患者坐位，膝关节屈曲 90° 并下垂于检查床边。运动防护师一只手固定患者足部，另一只手使其足呈解剖位置（90°），在背屈末端对其施以一向外侧旋转的压力。若患者在胫腓前韧带或胫腓后韧带以及骨间膜有疼痛症状出现，则表示有韧带联合损伤；若患者有足内侧疼痛，并且运动防护师也感觉到距骨相对于内踝有移位或脱位的情况，则代表足内侧韧带存在损伤。注意与另一侧比较。

8. 功能性测试

功能性测试是评估踝关节损伤的重要内容。运动防护师在决定患者是否能重返运动时需要对踝关节扭伤的患者进行这类测试。但是，如果不能负重则不能进行此类测试。常见功能性测试如下：

- 睁眼 / 闭眼下单足站立
- 星型偏移平衡测试 / "Y" 平衡测试
- 向前 / 侧单足跳
- 足跟摇摆测试
- 单足连续变向跳
- 单足纵跳
- 限时六米单足跳

3 Identification and Management of Common Ankle and Lower Leg Injuries

3.1 Inversion Ankle Sprains

Most ankle sprains involve the lateral ligaments. The anterior talofibular ligament (ATFL) is the most commonly sprained lateral ankle ligament, followed by the calcaneofibular ligament (CFL). Infrequently, the posterior talofibular ligament (PTFL) is affected. Sometimes, an inversion force is strong enough to cause a portion of the bone to be avulsed from the lateral malleolus, an avulsion fracture of the lateral malleolus and medial malleolus fracture, which is called bimalleolar fracture (Pott's fracture). The athletic trainer can determine whether an X-ray is necessary to confirm the presence of a fracture according to the Ottawa Ankle Guidelines.

Etiology: The severity of the ligament sprain should be graded. In every case of ligament sprain, the foot is forced to inversion, causing the injury, such as when a basketball player jumps up and down on another player's foot, or one walks or runs on uneven ground.

3.1.1 Grade I Ligament Sprain

It's mild ligament sprain without laxity. Ligament returns to resting length, but there is micro-lesion in some fibers.

(1) Symptoms and Signs

There is mild pain and functional impairment, mild weight-bearing disorder, and tenderness and swelling of the ligaments. There is no presence of joint instability.

(2) Management

① The POLICE principle is used for 30 to 60 minutes every 2 hours for 1 to 2 days. ② Patients are advised to limit weight-bearing activities for one to two days. Anterior and posterior mobilization of the talus should be applied as soon as possible after injury within the tolerable range of pain. Early rehabilitation methods for ankle include range of motion training, isometric exercise and isotonic exercise, In the mid-term of rehabilitation, proprioception training and specific exercise can help athletes return to performance as soon as possible. ③ Taping can provide additional protection. Usually, a patient can return to activity in 7 to 10 days.

3.1.2 Grade II Ligament Sprain

It's partial ligamentous rupture resulting in mild instability.

(1) Symptoms and Signs

The patient often complains of a pop or snap on the lateral of the ankle. There is moderate pain and dysfunction, difficulty in weight bearing, tenderness, hematoma in the joints, possible ecchymosis, and a positive talus tilt test. The front drawer test shows a positive result. This injury can lead to persistent ankle instability, recurrent sprain, and the development of traumatic arthritis in the long run.

(2) Management

① Apply the POLICE principle intermittently for at least 48 hours. ② X-ray examination should be performed for grade II ligament sprain. The anterior to posterior mobilization of the talus should be completed within a tolerable range as soon as possible after injury. ③ Patients should be on crutches for 5 to 10 days, during which time the partial load is gradually progressing to full load. Patients should wear protective braces for 1 to 2 weeks. ④ Exercise for plantar flexion and dorsiflexion in the painless range should begin 48 hours after injury. Early movement helps maintain the range of motion and proper proprioception. PNF has good effects on increasing muscle strength, maintaining range of motion, and improving proprioception. In addition, treatment should include 4 weeks of isometric contraction exercise with the ankle immobilized, range of motion exercise, progressive resistance exercise, and balance training. Taping using a closed basket weave technique may protect the patient during the early stages of walking. ⑤ Avoid walking or running on uneven ground for 2 to 3 weeks from the start of load-bearing. ⑥ The long-term effects of grade II ligament sprain may include chronic ankle instability, recurrence of the injury, joint degeneration, and osteoarthritis.

3.1.3 Grade III Ligament Sprain

It's a complete tear with accompanying joint instability.

(1) Symptoms and Signs

The patient complains of severe pain in the lateral malleolus area and cannot walk with weight because of severe swelling. Tenderness is obvious and subcutaneous bleeding appears within about 12 hours. The results of the talus tilt test and front drawer test are positive.

(2) Management

The POLICE principle should be applied intermittently for at least 3 days. During joint fixation, isometric muscle strength exercises should be performed, and range of motion training, progressive resistance, and balance training should be completed later. Some conditions also allow surgery to restore stability to the athlete's ankle.

3.2 Eversion Ankle Sprains

3.2.1 Etiology

Eversion ankle sprains account for only about 5% to 10% of all ankle sprains. Eversion ankle sprains are less common than inversion sprains, mainly due to the anatomical structure of bone and ligaments. Although eversion sprains are relatively rare, they are more severe and take longer to heal than inversion injuries. Excessive pronation of the foot or flatfoot is more prone to eversion ankle sprain.

3.2.2 Symptoms and Signs

Depending on the extent of the injury, patients often complain of foot and calf pain. The affected limb cannot withstand weight-bearing activities. Adduction and abduction can cause pain, but pressing directly upward against the bottom of the foot does not cause pain.

3.2.3 Management

① X-ray examination is often necessary to screen for fractures. ② At the initial stage of injury, POLICE treatment is recommended, and the affected limb is not weight-bearing. NSAIDs and analgesics are given as needed. ③ The treatment procedure of eversion sprain is the same as inversion sprain. The patient needs to conduct progressive resistance and balance training for the posteromedial ankle muscles and wear shoes with built-in wedge heel pads.

3.3 Syndesmotic Sprain

3.3.1 Etiology

A syndesmotic sprain (high ankle sprain) is an injury to the distal tibiofibular syndesmosis with possible disruption of the distal tibiofibular ligaments and interosseous membrane. Forced external rotation or dorsiflexion is the generally accepted mechanism of injury, which is often combined with severe sprains of the medial and lateral collateral ligaments. In the neutral position of the ankle, excessive external rotation of the talus can cause the fibula to deviate from the tibia, resulting in damage to the tibiofibular ligament and even rupture of the deltoid ligament.

3.3.2 Symptoms and Signs

Acute (< 4 weeks) stage: anterolateral ankle pain; mild swelling; ecchymosis; reduced ability to bear total weight on the affected foot; antalgic gait. Patients may require a wheelchair or an assistive device for ambulation until full weight-bearing (FWB) is permitted.

Chronic (> 3 months) stage: ankle pain and instability; gait deficits; impaired strength (e.g., inability to perform a single-heel raise) and reduced balance (e.g., poor single-leg stand ability).

3.3.3 Management

Sprains of the syndesmotic ligaments are extremely hard to treat and often take months to recover. The treatment of this disease is the same as the treatment of medial or lateral sprains, with the difference being an extended period of immobilization. Restoration of functional activity may take longer than inversion or eversion sprains. The patient with partial syndesmotic ligament sprains can use ankle braces and do early functional exercise; the surgical repair should be performed in the case of a total tear of the ligaments.

3.4 Chronic Ankle Instability

3.4.1 Etiology

Chronic ankle instability is a condition characterized by a recurrent giving way of the lateral side of the ankle. This condition often develops after repeated ankle sprains. About one-third of acute ankle sprains develop chronic ankle instability. Many studies suggest that mechanical and neuromuscular factors contribute to this instability. In general, chronic ankle instability is further classified as mechanical instability and functional instability. Mechanical instability is a condition in which the joint laxity is too much to allow the ankle to move beyond its physiological limits. Functional instability is the subjective feeling that repeated ankle sprains cause instability of the ankle. Functional instability is attributed to decreased proprioception and/or neuromuscular control. These declines harm posture control and further affect the ability to stabilize and balance.

3.4.2 Management

The rehabilitation of chronic ankle instability should focus on strengthening ankle muscles and combining with neuromuscular control training to improve proprioceptive function and the stability of the ankle joint. The combination of mechanical instability and functional instability indicates the need for surgery.

3.5 Ankle Fracture/Dislocation

3.5.1 Etiology

When the foot is subjected to passive stress and abduction forces, it can lead to transverse fractures of the distal tibia and fibula. In contrast, a foot fixed in combination with a forced internal rotation of the leg can produce a fracture to the distal and posterior tibia.

3.5.2 Symptoms and Signs

In most fractures, the pain and swelling are severe. X-ray shows bone damage and apparent displacement.

3.5.3 Management

Bleeding and swelling should be controlled immediately after injury. The fractures should be fixed on-site and transferred to the hospital for further treatment. After the reduction of the fracture, a walking cast or brace can be used for protection. Immobilization usually lasts at least 7 to 9 weeks. Surgery is needed to restore joint stability if there is displacement.

3.6 Achilles Tendon Strain

3.6.1 Etiology

Achilles tendon strain is common in sports and most often occurs with ankle sprains and sudden excessive dorsiflexion of the ankle. Achilles tendon strain is a complex injury; poor flexibility, muscle strength, and fatigue are risk factors.

3.6.2 Symptoms and Signs

The patient can experience severe pain and weakness in plantar flexion. The severe injury is a partial or complete tear or rupture of the achilles tendon.

3.6.3 Management

POLICE principle should be applied in the early treatment of injuries. Apply sustained pressure with an elastic bandage when bleeding abates. Considering the tendency of acute tendon injury to develop into a chronic injury, timely and appropriate conservative treatment is necessary. Patients should begin stretching and strengthening the tendon as early as possible. Use a heel pad to ease the tension on the achilles tendon, thereby reducing some of the stress that can lead to chronic inflammation.

3.7 Achilles Tendinopathy

3.7.1 Etiology

Achilles tendinopathies may involve tendonitis, tenosynovitis, or tendinosis. Achilles tendinitis is an inflammatory condition that affects the achilles tendon and/or the tendon sheath. It is called achilles tenosynovitis when occurs in the tendon sheath. Achilles tendonitis or tenosynovitis can cause fibrosis and scar tissue, limiting the tendon's movement within the tendon sheath. Tendonitis or tenosynovitis of the achilles tendon may accompany or cause achilles tendinosis. Most people with achilles tendon pain have achilles tendinosis. In the case of achilles tendinosis, there is no sign of inflammation. The injured area of the tendon loses its normal appearance. The collagen fibers cells that make up the tendon are disorganized, scarred, and degenerated.

3.7.2 Symptoms and Signs

Patients often complain of pain and stiffness in the achilles tendon area and decreased flexibility of the gastrocnemius and soleus muscles.

Muscle strength tests can show weakness in raising the heel. Initially, patients experience discomfort when they begin to move, and as the activity progresses, the symptoms disappear. The symptoms may gradually develop into morning stiffness and discomfort following prolonged sitting. Palpating tendinous tissue may present with fever and pain. During active plantar flexion and dorsiflexion the sense of crepitation can be palpated, and pain can be caused by passive traction. Chronic inflammation of the achilles tendon can cause the affected tendon to thicken relatively to the healthy side.

3.7.3 Management

① It is essential to establish an appropriate healing environment, such as reducing the stress load on the achilles tendon. Patients should wear proper shoes and foot orthotics and perform achilles tendon stretch and eccentric resistance training. ② Physical therapy, such as ice compress, can help reduce early symptoms of pain and inflammation, and ultrasound and shockwave therapy can improve blood circulation around the achilles tendon. ③ Cross-friction massage techniques can be used to release adhesion that may form during the healing stage and further improve the ability of the paratenon to slide.

3.8 Achilles Tendon Rupture

3.8.1 Etiology

Achilles tendon ruptures are common in athletes over the age of 30. It often occurs in individuals with chronic inflammatory and microscopic tears that lead to degenerative changes in the achilles tendon. Young athletes often get injured under sudden and large loads, such as kicking off or starting fast, due to the combination of acceleration and deceleration. The initial injury is usually the result of a sudden pushing-off action of the forefoot followed by full passive extension of the knee.

3.8.2 Symptoms and Signs

When the rupture occurs, the patient complains of a sudden feeling of tissue tearing and something kicking them in the calf. The pain occurs immediately but decreases rapidly, often accompanied by tenderness, swelling, and abnormal skin color. The patient is unable to complete the heel raising and would fail to perform plantar flexion as usual. Thompson's test is positive.

3.8.3 Management

A complete rupture of the achilles tendon is often repaired surgically. The other treatments include POLICE, NSAIDs, and analgesic, as well as 6 weeks of non-weight-bearing cast fixation followed by 2 weeks of lower limb walking exercise with brace. The rehabilitation period lasts for about 6 months, including a range of motion exercise, progressive resistance exercise, etc.

3.9 Tibial Contusion

3.9.1 Etiology

The anterolateral tibia lies just under the skin, so it is exceedingly vulnerable and sensitive to blows and bumps. Without the protection of muscle and fat pads, the periosteum bears the impact force from the calf's front.

3.9.2 Symptoms and Signs

The patient complains of severe pain in the shin, the rapid development of a hematoma. And there are the possibility of co-existence of fascia compartment syndrome and the potential risk of tibial fracture.

3.9.3 Management

Treatments include POLICE, NSAIDs, and analgesic. It is essential to keep pressure on the hematoma area. In some cases, the hematoma may need to be extracted. Patients need movement and progressive resistance exercise within the tolerable range of pain. Proper protective braces should be used in sports, such as soccer and football, where the lower leg is very vulnerable to injury.

Without proper treatment, periosteum injury may develop into osteomyelitis, leading to the destruction and deterioration of bone.

3.10 Leg Cramps and Spasms

3.10.1 Etiology

The exact cause of muscle cramps is unclear. Some of the reasons are excessive fluid loss due to fatigue, sweating, and unbalance of antagonistic muscle coordination. The gastrocnemius muscle is particularly vulnerable to this condition.

3.10.2 Symptoms and Signs

The patient had considerable muscle colic and pain with gastrocnemius tetanus. You can even see the gastrocnemius twitching under the skin, and the muscle feels stiff by palpation.

3.10.3 Management

① Gentle and progressive stretch will relieve most of the spasm. ② Cramps can also be relieved with ice compress or gentle ice massage. ③ Avoid excessive fatigue or fluid loss for athletes who have recurrent cramps.

3.11 Gastrocnemius Strain (Tennis Leg)

3.11.1 Etiology

The medial gastrocnemius is especially prone to strain at the musculotendinous junction. The lateral gastrocnemius, soleus, plantaris, and flexor hallucis longus muscles may also be involved. Usually, injury occurs when excessive stress is applied to the medial head of the gastrocnemius muscle during activities requiring a quick start and stop or sudden jump. Gastrocnemius strain is often accompanied by rupture of the plantar tendon.

3.11.2 Symptoms and Signs

Depending on the extent of the injury, there can be varying degrees of pain, swelling, and muscle weakness. The patient may have complained the feeling of being hit by a stick in the back of the calf. The examination will reveal signs of edema, tenderness, and loss of functional muscle strength. Resistant muscle contraction test is positive with increased pain or a broken depression. The patient in severe condition may have the sensation of tearing, swelling and subcutaneous ecchymosis or muscle rupture, which needs an MRI to confirm.

3.11.3 Management

After the injury, POLICE, NSAIDs, and analgesics should be given as needed. For mild gastrocnemius strain, cold compresses are applied to the muscle followed by gentle, progressive stretching. During the rehabilitation phase, weight-bearing exercises should be applied within the patient's tolerance. Heel pads can help reduce tension on the gastrocnemius during walking. An appropriate elastic tape may protect the muscles during exercise. At the same time, patients should begin to carry out progressive functional training. The ruptured plantaris tendon requires no special treatment.

3.12 Acute Lower Leg Fractures

3.12.1 Etiology

Fibula fractures occur most frequently among all lower limb fractures. It mainly occurs in the middle 1/3 segment, while tibial fractures occur in the lower 1/3 segment. Fractures of the shaft of the tibia and fibula are caused by direct or indirect trauma.

3.12.2 Symptoms and Signs

This injury causes soft tissue damage and bleeding. The patient complained of severe pain and dysfunction. A bang sound is heard when bones break. Deformed appearance, stiffness, and swelling may appear in the lower limbs.

3.12.3 Management

The athletic trainer should carry out on-site fixation and transfer the patient to the hospital in time for further examination. In most cases, fracture reduction and immobilization with a cast are approximately 6 weeks, depending on the severity of the injury and the presence of other complications.

3.13 Medial Tibial Stress Syndrome

3.13.1 Etiology

Medial tibial stress syndrome (MTSS) is the pain in the lower 2/3 of the anterior tibia. Stress fractures, muscle strains, and chronic compartment syndromes are collectively manifested as pain in the tibia. MTSS can be caused by high-intensity activities, which lead to increased stress and overload in the lower limbs. Then the calf muscles become too exhausted to absorb the impact energy, which is absorbed by the tibia. Factors that lead to MTSS include the imbalance of lower limb muscle strength, inappropriate footwear, and improper training (e.g., running on hard surfaces, overtraining). Problems with poor alignment such as tensed achilles tendon and excessive foot pronation or supination can also cause MTSS.

3.13.2 Symptoms and Signs

The pain caused by medial tibial stress syndrome can be classified into four grades: Grade 1 pain occurs after exercise; Grade 2 pain occurs before and after exercise but does not affect performance; Grade 3 pain occurs before, during, and after exercise and affects performance. Grade 4 pain is too intense to move.

3.13.3 Management

① Management of this injury is difficult because many factors can contribute to the development of medial tibial stress syndrome. Referral to a physician is recommended for a bone scan and X-ray to rule out a stress fracture. ② Conservative treatment: POLICE and ice massage can help relieve pain and inflammation. NSAIDs can be used if the pain is too severe. When the pain is reduced, the calf and gluteal muscles need to be strengthened, and the flexibility of the calf also needs to be trained. Also, shoes and foot orthotics can be used to correct abnormal pronation during walking and running. ③ Surgery is needed if the conservative treatment fails. ④ Perform warm-up and stretching before high-impact activities to prevent tibia pain.

3.14 Compartment Syndrome

3.14.1 Etiology

Compartment syndrome is a condition in which the muscle and neurovascular tissue in any of the four fascial cavities of the lower leg are compressed due to increased pressure. Compartment syndrome is mainly caused by severe trauma or excessive exercise.

Compartment syndrome can be divided into acute compartment syndrome, acute exertional compartment syndrome, and chronic compartment syndrome. Acute compartment syndrome is a complication following fractures, soft tissue trauma, and reperfusion after acute arterial obstruction. Acute exertional compartment syndrome occurs without any induced trauma, and mild to moderate activity can be performed after injury. Chronic compartment syndrome is associated with movement, primarily in running and jumping sports, and symptoms appear at specific stages of action rather than consistently.

3.14.2 Symptoms and Signs

Because compartment syndrome is associated with increased intra-compartmental pressure, the patient complains of deep, aching pain, tightness and swelling in the affected area, and pain in the affected muscles when passively stretched. An examination of the foot may detect circulation obstruction and sensory changes. Intra-compartmental pressure measurements could be taken to determine the severity of symptoms further.

3.14.3 Management

① Emergency management of acute compartment syndrome should include ice compress and elevation of the affected limb. NSAIDs can be prescribed when the pain is severe. However, the elastic bandage should not be used to control edema, as there is already a problem with increased compartment pressure. The use of an elastic bandage will only increase the pressure further. ② In acute compartment syndrome and acute exertional compartment syndrome, the surgical incision is necessary to relieve the intraluminal pressure. Surgery should be performed as early as possible to avoid permanent damage. ③ The initial stage of the treatment of chronic compartment syndrome is the conservative approach, with movement adjustment, icing, and the stretching exercise of anterior compartment musculature and achilles tendon. If conservative treatment fails, fasciotomy in the affected area will effectively restore regular functional activity as early as possible.

3.15 Stress Fracture of the Tibia or Fibula

3.15.1 Etiology

A stress fracture of the tibia or fibula is a common overuse injury, especially among runners. Stress fractures of the lower leg, like other overuse injuries, are more likely to occur in individuals with structural deformities of the lower limb. Individuals with excessive pronation feet were more likely to have fibular stress fractures, while individuals with pes cavus were more likely to have tibial stress fractures. Stress fractures often occur in the lower 1/3 of the lower leg in runners; in the middle 1/3 in ballet dancers. They are generally caused by activity-related biomechanical, and metabolic factors, etc. Activity-related factors include ill-fitting shoes and uneven floors. Biomechanical factors include stiffness or weakness of the calf muscles, unequal lower limbs, flat feet, or high arch, etc. Metabolic factors include bone loss due to specific disease states and hormonal or nutritional imbalances. These factors tend to increase the loading and bending forces on the bones or impair the ability of the bones to deal with such forces.

3.15.2 Symptoms and Signs

The patient complains of more intense leg pain during and after exercise with tenderness, but it is difficult to distinguish between bone and soft tissue pain. It distinguishes bone pain from mild tissue pain by percussion. X-ray examination may help confirm the occurrence of a stress fracture.

3.15.3 Management

① Patients should stop running and other stressful activities for at least 14 days. When the pain is severe, the patient should use crutches or wear braces while walking. After the pain is relieved, the patient can resume weight-bearing activities. After no pain symptoms for at least 2 consecutive weeks, patients can gradually continue running exercise or using foot orthotics to correct the foot biomechanical abnormalities. ② Protective and progressive exercise is needed in the later stages of rehabilitation to heal the bones fully. Furthermore, pain or persistent swelling indicates the patient needs more rest before activities. ③ Surgery is needed to remove the sclerosing bone nonunion.

三、踝和小腿常见损伤的识别和处理

（一）踝内翻扭伤

大多数踝关节扭伤会累及外侧副韧带，尤其以距腓前韧带（anterior talofibular ligament，ATFL）损伤较为常见，其次是跟腓韧带（calcaneofibular ligament，CFL），有时会伤及距腓后韧带（posterior talofibular ligament，PTFL）。有时内翻应力足以造成外踝部分骨性撕脱的发生，也可造成外踝撕脱性骨折及内踝骨折，这种损伤称为双踝骨折（Pott's骨折）。运动防护师可依据"渥太华踝关节准则"判断是否需要 X 射线检查来确定患者患处是否存在骨折。

病因：应根据韧带扭伤的严重程度进行分级。在每一例韧带扭伤病例中，足部都是被强制内翻进而导致损伤的发生，如打篮球时跳起下落踩到别人脚上，或在不平整的地面行走或跑步。

1. Ⅰ度韧带扭伤

Ⅰ度韧带损伤为轻度扭伤，无松弛现象。韧带恢复到原长度，但一些纤维中存在微裂纹。

（1）症状和体征

出现轻度疼痛和功能障碍，负重轻度障碍，韧带压痛和肿胀，没有关节不稳的表现。

（2）处理

①在损伤发生的第 1 ~ 2 天，每隔 2 小时进行 30 ~ 60 分钟的保护、制动、冰敷、加压包扎和抬高患肢（POLICE 原则）处理。②建议患者先限制负重活动 1 ~ 2 天。距骨前后向的松动手法应在伤后疼痛可忍受的范围内尽早进行。踝的早期功能康复应包括关节活动度训练和等长、等张肌力训练。在康复中期，加入渐进本体感觉训练，随后应重点对患者进行运动专项训练，以帮助其尽早重返赛场。③患者进行负重训练时，应用贴扎可以提

供额外的保护。通常经过 7 ~ 10 天的康复治疗，患者就可恢复活动。

2. Ⅱ度韧带扭伤

Ⅱ度韧带损伤为中度扭伤，侧副韧带有部分撕裂，轻度关节不稳。

（1）症状和体征

患者常主诉踝关节外侧有"啵"或"啪"的弹响。有中度疼痛和功能障碍，负重困难，关节有压痛和血肿，可能存在瘀斑，距骨倾斜试验结果可呈阳性。前抽屉试验结果可呈阳性。此损伤可导致持续性的踝关节不稳，扭伤的反复发生，长此以往会发展为创伤性关节炎。

（2）处理

①在至少 48 小时内间歇应用 POLICE 原则进行处理。②Ⅱ度韧带扭伤应做 X 射线检查。适度的距骨前后向的松动手法应在伤后尽早进行。③患者应拄拐 5 ~ 10 天，在此期间从部分负重渐进至全负重。患者需穿戴保护性支具 1 ~ 2 周。④伤后 48 小时可在无痛范围内进行跖屈和背屈练习。早期活动有助于维持关节活动范围和正常的本体感觉。本体感觉神经肌肉促进疗法有助于增强力量，保持关节活动度及增强本体感觉。此外，治疗措施还应包括持续 4 周的踝制动下的等长收缩训练、活动度训练、渐进性抗阻训练和平衡训练。早期行走阶段可给予患者闭锁编篮式技术贴扎保护。⑤告知患者在负重开始的 2 ~ 3 周应避免在不平整的地面上行走或跑动。⑥Ⅱ度韧带扭伤的长期影响可能导致慢性踝关节不稳和损伤的反复发生。这种不稳定可导致关节发生退行性变和骨性关节炎。

3. Ⅲ度韧带扭伤

Ⅲ度韧带损伤为重度扭伤，侧副韧带完全撕裂伴关节不稳。

（1）症状和体征

患者主诉外踝区域有剧烈疼痛，且因为严重肿胀而不能负重行走。伤处有明显压痛，约 12 小时内出现皮下淤血。距骨倾斜试验呈阳性，前抽屉试验结果呈阳性。

（2）处理

应至少持续 3 天间歇应用 POLICE 原则进行处理。在关节固定时应进行等长肌力练习，后期进行关节活动度训练、渐进抗阻训练和平衡训练。如有必要可通过手术治疗来恢复运动员踝关节的稳定性。

（二）踝关节外翻扭伤

1. 病因

踝关节外翻扭伤只占所有踝扭伤的 5% ~ 10%。踝外翻扭伤不如内翻扭伤常见，这很大程度上归因于骨性和韧带的解剖结构。尽管外翻扭伤相对少见，但其严重程度相较于内翻损伤更为严重且需要更长的愈合时间。足过度旋前或扁平足更易发生外翻损伤。

2. 症状和体征

根据受伤的程度，患者主诉通常存在足和小腿的疼痛。患肢不能负重，进行内收及外展都会引起疼痛，但垂直向上挤压足底却不会引起疼痛。

3. 处理

①X 射线检查排查是否存在骨折问题。②损伤早期，建议按照 POLICE 原则进行处理且患肢不负重；按需给予非甾体抗炎药和镇痛药。③外翻扭伤的处理程序与内翻扭伤一样，患者需进行踝关节后内侧肌肉的渐进性抗阻训练、平衡训练，患者需穿内置楔形跟垫的鞋等。

（三）胫腓联合韧带扭伤

1. 病因

胫腓联合韧带扭伤或高踝关节扭伤是指远端胫腓联合损伤，并可能破坏远端胫腓韧带和骨间膜。胫腓韧带受到过度外旋或强制背屈的应力会发生撕裂，常与内侧和外侧副韧带的严重扭伤合并发生。在踝关节中立位的情况下，距骨的过度外旋会导致腓骨偏离胫骨，从而损伤胫腓韧带，甚至会合并三角韧带断裂。

2. 症状和体征

急性期（< 4 周）：踝关节前外侧疼痛；轻微的肿胀；瘀斑；患足承重能力下降；避痛步态。患者可能需要轮椅或辅助设备来移动，直到能够完全负重。

慢性期（> 3 个月）：踝关节疼痛和不稳；步态不良；力量受损（如不能进行单足提踵）和平衡能力下降（如单腿站立能力差）。

3. 处理

联合韧带扭伤的治疗较困难，扭伤恢复时间较长。处理方法与内、外翻扭伤的处理基本一致，区别在于患者的制动时间更长，恢复功能活动可能需要比内、外翻扭伤更长的时间。对于部分胫腓联合韧带撕裂，可指导患者使用踝关节支具并进行早期功能性治疗；而对于胫腓联合韧带全部撕裂的患者，应进行手术修复。

（四）慢性踝关节不稳

1. 病因

慢性踝关节不稳指踝关节外侧反复出现不稳定的状况。这种情况通常发生在踝关节反复扭伤之后。约 1/3 的急性踝扭伤会发展为慢性踝关节不稳。许多研究认为是力学和神经肌肉因素导致了这一不稳定现象的产生。通常慢性踝关节不稳被进一步分类为机械性不稳和功能性不稳。机械性不稳的本质是关节松弛度过大从而允许踝关节活动超过生理限制范围。功能性不稳是由反复踝扭伤导致的主观感觉上的踝关节不稳，归因于本体感觉或神经肌肉控制能力下降，这些功能的下降会对姿势控制产生消极影响并进一步影响稳定和平衡的能力。

2. 处理

慢性踝关节不稳的康复应着重于增强踝部肌力练习，并结合神经肌肉控制训练来改善本体感觉功能，从而提高踝关节的稳定性。若出现机械性和功能性的联合不稳，则可能需要手术治疗。

（五）踝关节骨折／脱位

1. 病因

当足部受到被动的应力使其外展可导致胫骨和腓骨远端横形骨折。相反，足部保持稳定而小腿受外力内旋可导致胫骨远端和后侧骨折。

2. 症状和体征

在绝大多数骨折中，疼痛和肿胀的症状都很严重。X 射线显示骨损伤，有时有明显的移位。

3. 处理

损伤后应立即控制出血和肿胀，现场进行固定并转运到医院进行处理。复位后可以使用石膏或支具保护。固定通常至少持续 7 ~ 9 周。若骨折发生移位，一般需要通过手术来恢复关节稳定性。

（六）跟腱拉伤

1. 病因

跟腱拉伤常见于运动中，最常发生于踝关节扭伤和踝突然过度背屈时。跟腱拉伤是一种复杂的损伤，可能由柔韧性不足、肌力不足、疲劳等多种因素引起。

2. 症状和体征

损伤发生后，患者会出现剧烈疼痛和跖屈无力的症状。较严重的损伤是部分或完全的跟腱撕裂或断裂。

3. 处理

损伤的早期处理应用 POLICE 原则进行处理。当出血减轻后用弹性绷带给予持续的压力。急性跟腱损伤有发展为慢性损伤的趋势，因此需及时进行相应的保守治疗。患者应尽早开始牵拉和强化跟腱。用足跟垫来减轻对跟腱的拉力，从而减轻一些导致慢性炎症产生的压力。

（七）跟腱病

1. 病因

跟腱病（包括跟腱炎、腱鞘炎或跟腱变性）是一类炎性病症，涉及跟腱、腱鞘，当发生在腱鞘时称为跟腱腱鞘炎。跟腱炎、腱鞘炎会形成纤维化及瘢痕组织，限制跟腱在腱鞘内的活动。跟腱炎、腱鞘炎可伴发或导致跟腱变性。有跟腱疼痛的大多数人都存在跟腱变性的情况。对于跟腱变性来说，没有炎症迹象，跟腱的损伤区域失去了原有的形态，构成跟腱的胶原纤维细胞排列紊乱，组织形成瘢痕并发生退变。

2. 症状和体征

患者常主诉跟腱区域存在疼痛并有僵硬的症状，并且腓肠肌和比目鱼肌的柔韧性也会下降。

肌力测试可显示患者提踵无力。最初患者在开始活动时会有不适感，随着活动的进行症状会消失。症状可能逐渐发展为晨僵及久坐之后有不适感。触诊腱组织可能有发热及疼痛症状。主动跖屈和背屈时可触诊到捻发感，被动牵拉引起疼痛。跟腱慢性炎症可导致患侧跟腱相对健侧增厚。

3. 处理

①建立良好的促进愈合的环境，如减少跟腱所承受的应力负荷非常重要。患者应穿合适的鞋及足矫形器，还应进行跟腱的牵拉和离心抗阻训练。②冰敷能减轻早期的疼痛和炎症症状，超声波和冲击波治疗可改善跟腱周围的血液循环。③应用横向摩擦按摩技术可能解决在愈合阶段形成的粘连并进一步改善腱旁组织的滑动能力。

（八）跟腱断裂

1. 病因

跟腱断裂在30岁以上的运动员中非常常见。跟腱断裂通常基于慢性炎症和细微撕裂，导致跟腱发生退行性病变。年轻运动员多在突然而强力的动作中，如蹬地、跳跃或快速启动时受伤。首次受伤通常是脚掌突然蹬伸伴膝被动完全伸直的情况下。

2. 症状和体征

当断裂发生时，患者主诉突然感到组织有断裂的感觉且像有东西踢在他的小腿上。疼痛立即产生但迅速减轻，常伴有压痛、肿胀和皮肤颜色异常的表现，患者无法完成提踵动作且跖屈功能受损。汤普森试验结果呈阳性。

3. 处理

跟腱完全断裂采取手术修复的方法进行治疗。其他治疗包括采取 POLICE 进行处理，按需给予非甾体抗炎药和镇痛药治疗，以及6周无负重石膏固定加上随后2周的支具保护下的步行训练。运动康复阶段约6个月，内容包括关节活动度练习、渐进性抗阻训练等。

（九）胫骨挫伤

1. 病因

胫骨前外侧表面仅有一层皮肤，对于外部打击和撞击非常敏感且易受到伤害。此外，由于没有肌肉和脂肪垫保护，骨膜承受着来自小腿前方的撞击力。

2. 症状和体征

患者主诉小腿骨挫伤处剧痛，血肿迅速产生，也可能合并存在筋膜间隔区综合征，还可能存在胫骨骨折的风险。

3. 处理

处理方法包括采用 POLICE 原则进行处理，按需给予非甾体抗炎药和镇痛药。保持血肿区的加压很重要。如果血肿明显，需要抽出血肿。患者需要在疼痛可忍受范围内进行活动度和渐进性抗阻训练。在橄榄球和足球等小腿十分易受损伤的运动项目中，需适当使用保护性护具。

处理不当的骨膜损伤可能发展为骨髓炎，导致骨破坏及退行性病变等严重情况的发生。

（十）腿部绞痛和痉挛

1. 病因

肌肉绞痛的具体原因通常不明确。疲劳和出汗导致体液流失过多、拮抗肌协调失衡是个体易发生强直性肌痉挛的部分原因。腓肠肌尤其易发生这种情况。

2. 症状和体征

患者有相当明显的肌肉绞痛和疼痛，伴腓肠肌强直收缩。甚至可以见到腓肠肌在皮肤下抽搐，触诊感觉肌肉僵硬。

3. 处理

①轻柔地、渐进式地牵伸痉挛的肌肉能缓解大部分痉挛症状。②冰敷或轻柔的冰敷按摩也可有效缓解痉挛症状。③面对痉挛反复发作的患者，运动防护师应确保避免其出现过度疲劳或体液流失过多。

（十一）腓肠肌拉伤（网球腿）

1. 病因

腓肠肌内侧头在肌腹肌腱交界处尤其容易拉伤。腓肠肌外侧肌、比目肌、跖肌和拇长屈肌也可累及。在需要快速启动和停下或突然跳起的活动中，过度的应力施于腓肠肌内侧头从而导致损伤。腓肠肌的拉伤常伴有跖腱断裂。

2. 症状和体征

不同程度的损伤会有不同程度的疼痛、肿胀和肌肉无力的症状。患者可能主诉曾有"小腿后侧有被棒子击打"的感觉。进行检查会发现有水肿、压痛和功能性肌力丧失的表现。肌肉收缩抗阻试验结果呈阳性，疼痛加剧或有断裂的凹陷出现。严重者可有撕裂样感，肿胀明显及皮下淤血严重，可能有肌肉断裂，需进一步进行磁共振成像确定。

3. 处理

损伤后采取 POLICE 原则处理，按需给予非甾体抗炎药和镇痛药治疗。针对轻度腓肠肌拉伤，冷敷肌肉后进行轻柔的、渐进式的牵拉。康复阶段在患者可忍受范围内开始负重训练。足跟垫的使用可协助减少行走时腓肠肌上的牵拉力。适宜的弹性贴扎可在运动时保护肌肉。同时患者需开始渐进性功能训练。跖腱断裂不用特殊处理。

（十二）急性小腿骨折

1. 病因

在所有下肢骨折中，腓骨骨折的发生率最高，主要发生在中 1/3 段，而胫骨骨折基本发生在下 1/3 段。胫骨和腓骨骨干的骨折皆是由直接或间接创伤所致。

2. 症状和体征

此损伤导致软组织受损和出血。患者主诉有严重疼痛和功能障碍。发生骨折时可听到

"嘣"的声响。下肢可出现畸形、僵硬和肿胀。

3. 处理

运动防护师要现场进行固定并将患者及时转运到医院进行进一步检查。大多数情况下，骨折复位后使用石膏固定制动约 6 周，制动时间取决于损伤的严重程度及有无其他并发症。

（十三）胫骨内侧应力综合征

1. 病因

胫骨内侧应力综合征一般指胫骨前内侧下 2/3 的疼痛。应力性骨折、肌肉拉伤和慢性间隔室综合征都可以表现为胫部疼痛。胫骨内侧应力综合征由高强度活动引起，这些活动导致下肢压力增加和超负荷，使得小腿肌肉疲劳过快，无法吸收冲击能量，从而导致胫骨吸收冲击。导致胫骨内侧应力综合征发生的因素包括下肢肌力较弱、鞋不合适以及训练不当（如在较硬的地面跑步、过度训练）等。力线排列不良的问题如跟腱紧张、足部过度旋前或旋后也能引起胫骨内侧应力综合征。

2. 症状和体征

胫骨内侧应力综合征所引起的疼痛可分为四级：一级疼痛发生在运动后；二级疼痛发生在运动前和后，但不影响运动表现；三级疼痛发生在运动前、中、后并影响运动表现；四级疼痛剧烈，无法运动。

3. 处理

①对此损伤的处理较为困难，因为众多因素可共同导致胫骨内侧应力综合征的出现。建议转诊至医生处利用骨扫描和 X 射线检查排除应力性骨折的可能性。②保守治疗：采取POLICE 原则处理并冰敷按摩此区域，可缓解疼痛症状和炎症反应。若疼痛难忍，可以使用非甾体抗炎药，当疼痛减轻时，重点强化小腿和臀部肌肉训练，同时应注意训练小腿后侧肌群的柔韧性。另外，可以使用鞋垫或矫形器纠正走和跑时异常的旋前活动。③若保守治疗失败，则可以进行手术干预。④建议在剧烈活动之前拉伸下肢肌肉并进行充分的热身，以帮助预防胫骨疼痛。

（十四）筋膜间隔区综合征

1. 病因

筋膜间隔区综合征是指小腿四个筋膜腔中，其中任何一个内压力增加造成腔内肌肉和神经血管组织受压而引起相应症状的病症。筋膜室综合征主要由严重的创伤或过度运动引起。

筋膜间隔区综合征可分为三种类型：急性筋膜间隔区综合征、急性疲劳性筋膜间隔区综合征和慢性筋膜间隔区综合征。急性筋膜间隔区综合征是骨折、软组织创伤和急性动脉阻塞后再灌注的并发症。它是由封闭的、非弹性的肌腔室出血或水肿引起的。急性疲劳性筋膜间隔区综合征发生时不伴任何诱发性创伤，损伤后可进行轻至中度活动。慢性筋膜间隔区综合征与运动相关，常在跑跳类运动项目中发生，症状在运动的特定阶段出现而不是持续出现。

2. 症状和体征

筋膜间隔区综合征伴有筋膜腔内压力增加，因此患者主诉存在一种深层的酸痛，受累区域紧张和肿胀，受累肌肉被动牵拉时疼痛。足部检查可发现循环受阻和感觉改变。可通过筋膜腔内压力测量以进一步明确症状的严重程度。

3. 处理

①急性筋膜间隔区综合征的紧急处理包括冰敷和抬高患肢，疼痛严重时给予患者非甾体抗炎药。但是，在这种情况下不应使用弹性绷带来控制水肿，因为已经存在筋膜腔内压力增高的问题，使用弹性绷带只会进一步增加压力。②在急性筋膜间隔区综合征和急性疲劳性筋膜间隔区综合征这两种损伤中，采用手术切开的方法解除腔内压力十分必要。手术应尽早进行，以防筋膜室内的肌肉和其他软组织产生永久的损伤。③慢性筋膜间隔区综合征治疗的起始阶段采取保守治疗的方法，辅以活动调整、冰敷和前室肌组织及跟腱的牵拉练习。若保守治疗失败，在受累部位进行筋膜切开术对于患者尽早恢复正常的功能活动有着良好效果。

（十五）胫骨或腓骨应力性骨折

1. 病因

胫骨或腓骨应力性骨折是一种常见的过劳损伤，尤其见于长跑。下肢结构存在异常的患者更容易出现胫骨或腓骨应力性骨折。例如，足过度旋前的患者更易发生腓骨应力性骨折，而有着高弓足的人更易发生胫骨应力性骨折。跑步运动员常在小腿下 1/3 段出现应力性骨折；芭蕾舞者常在小腿中 1/3 段发生应力性骨折。一般是由活动相关性、生物力学性和代谢性的因素等引起的。活动相关性因素包括鞋子不合适和地面不平整等；生物力学性因素包括小腿肌肉僵化或无力、下肢不等长、扁平足或高弓足等；代谢性因素包括特定疾病状态和激素或营养失衡所致骨质流失。这些因素都会增加施加在骨骼上的负荷力和弯曲力，或削弱骨骼承受此类应力的能力。

2. 症状和体征

患者主诉在运动时和运动后腿部疼痛加重，常有压痛，但难以区分是骨性疼痛还是软组织疼痛。叩诊可区分骨性疼痛和软组织疼痛。X 射线检查可帮助确诊应力性骨折是否发生。

3. 处理

①患者应至少停止跑步和进行其他应力性活动 14 天。当疼痛严重时，患者需在步行时使用拐杖或穿戴支具。在疼痛减轻后，患者可恢复负重活动。在至少连续 2 周无疼痛症状后，患者可逐渐恢复跑步运动，也可采用矫形器辅助运动。②后期康复的关键原则是进行有保护、渐进性的锻炼，以使骨骼充分愈合。另外，疼痛或持续性肿胀表明骨骼还需要更久的休息才能开始积极的康复活动。③硬化型骨不连应采用手术处理。

Summary

1. Interventions that can prevent ankle and calf problems include stretch and strength training, neuromuscular training, taping, and braces.

2. Ankle sprains are the most common injuries among athletes. Ankle sprains include inversion, eversion, or syndesmotic damages. Sometimes ankle fractures occur with ankle sprains.

3. The achilles tendon is prone to acute strain, developing into chronic tendonitis and achilles tendinopathy. Achilles tendon ruptures are common in older athletes.

4. Compartment syndrome is a condition in which the muscle and neurovascular tissue in any of the four fascial cavities of the lower leg are compressed due to increased pressure. Compartment syndrome is mainly caused by severe trauma or excessive exercise.

5. Other acute injuries in the lower leg are shin contusions, muscle cramps, gastrocnemius strains, tibia, or fibula fractures.

⭕ Review Questions

1. Describe the method of the Thompson test.
2. List the factors that could induce medial tibial stress syndrome (MTSS).
3. Describe the categories and symptoms of compartment syndromes.
4. Sun, 32-year-old, is a programmer. He went to work out in the gym 2 days ago. During the box jump training, he got a leg injury. He recalled there was a feeling of "being kicked" in the lower part of the leg. Immediately, he could not jump, but he could walk. After 2 days of ice compress and rest under the personal trainer's arrangement, he found that he was getting better but still had pain during exerting force. Please give the possible further examination and diagnosis according to the description.

小结

1. 预防踝和小腿损伤的措施包括：牵拉、肌力训练、神经肌肉控制训练、合理使用贴扎和护具。

2. 踝扭伤是运动员中最常见的损伤。踝扭伤分为内翻、外翻和韧带联合损伤。有时踝骨折伴踝扭伤发生。

3. 跟腱易发生急性拉伤，可发展为慢性肌腱炎和跟腱病。跟腱断裂是高龄运动员的常见损伤。

4. 筋膜间隔区综合征是指小腿四个筋膜腔中，其中任何一个内压力增加造成腔内肌肉和神经血管组织受压所引起相应症状的病症。筋膜间隔区综合征主要由严重的创伤或过度运动引起。

5.小腿骨挫伤、肌肉痉挛、腓肠肌拉伤、胫骨或腓骨骨折都是小腿可能发生的急性损伤。

○ 复习题

1. 简述汤普森试验的操作方法。

2. 列举可能导致胫骨内侧应力综合征的因素。

3. 简述筋膜间隔区综合征的分型和症状。

4. 32 岁的孙某是一名程序员。2 天前到健身房锻炼，结果在一次跳箱训练中小腿发生损伤。他回忆起跳瞬间小腿后下部有"被踢了一脚"的感觉，当即无法跳跃，但仍能行走。在私人教练安排下进行了冰敷并且休息了 2 天，2 天后他发觉有所好转但发力时仍有疼痛。请根据描述给出所需要的检查及可能的诊断。

Chapter 8 Foot Injuries
第八章 足部损伤

O Main Contents

1. Prevention of foot injuries.

2. Assessment of foot injuries.

3. Identification and management of common foot injuries.

O 主要内容

1.足部损伤的预防。

2.足部损伤的评估。

3.足部常见损伤的识别和处理。

1 Prevention of Foot Injuries

Repeated stresses and strains during exercise are the risk factors of acute injury and overuse injury. Suitable shoes and orthopedic insoles, and foot hygiene and care can effectively prevent foot injuries.

1.1 Suitable Shoes or Orthopedic Insoles

Choosing the right shoes is one of the most important steps to prevent foot injuries. Before choosing a pair of shoes, an athletic trainer needs to assess the patient's structural deformities such as forefoot valgus or varus and rearfoot varus. The choice of shoes should correspond to the existing structural deformity.

Customized orthopedic insoles play a positive role in preventing foot injuries and other injuries that occur as a result of force line problems caused by structural abnormalities in the foot. For the correction of structural forefoot varus deformity (excessive pronation of the foot), the orthotic should be the rigid type and should have a medial wedge under the head of the first metatarsal. It is also advisable to add a small wedge under the medial calcaneus to make the orthotic more comfortable. For the correction of structural forefoot valgus deformity (excessive supination of the foot), the orthotics should be semirigid and have a lateral wedge under the head of the fifth metatarsal. Similarly, a small wedge is placed below the lateral of the calcaneus to make the orthotic more suitable for the foot. For the correction of structural hindfoot varus deformity, a semirigid orthotic should be used, including a wedge under the medial calcaneus and a small wedge under the head of the first metatarsal.

1.2 Foot Hygiene and Care

Regular foot care can help reduce the occurrence of foot injuries. For example, trim your toenails in time, scrape off the local keratin, keep your feet clean, wear clean and suitable socks, and keep your feet as dry as possible to prevent tinea of foot.

一、足部损伤的预防

运动时足反复受到的应力和应变刺激是急性损伤和过度使用损伤的易发因素。挑选合适的鞋或矫形鞋垫，注意足部卫生和护理可有效预防足部损伤的发生。

（一）合适的鞋或矫形鞋垫

选择合适的鞋是预防足损伤最重要的措施之一。在选鞋之前，运动防护师需要评估患者的足是否存在结构性缺陷，例如前足内、外翻和后足内翻，鞋的选择应该与存在的结构性缺陷相对应。

　　定制的矫形鞋垫在预防足部损伤，以及预防因为足部结构异常导致身体力线问题而出现的其他部位损伤方面有着积极的作用。针对结构性前足内翻畸形（足过度旋前）的矫正，可使用硬质矫形器，并在第 1 跖骨头下方放置内侧楔形垫，同时也可在跟骨内侧下方放置小楔形垫以使矫形器更加适合足部。针对结构性前足外翻畸形（足过度旋后）的矫正，可使用半硬质的矫形器，并在第 5 跖骨头下方放置外侧楔形垫。同理，在跟骨外侧下放置小楔形垫可使矫形器更加适合足部。针对结构性后足内翻畸形的矫正，可使用半硬质的矫形器，在跟骨内侧下放置楔形垫和在第 1 跖骨头下放置小楔形垫。

（二）注重足部卫生

　　运动员进行常规的日常足部保养有助于减少足部损伤的发生。例如，及时修剪脚趾甲，刮除局部增生的角质，保持双脚清洁，穿干净、合适的袜子，尽可能保持足部干燥从而预防足癣的发生。

2 Assessment of Foot Injuries

2.1 History

When an athletic trainer assesses the foot, a detailed and complete medical history is important. The athletic trainer should ask the following questions:

- What happened when you got injured?
- Is the process acute or chronic?
- What is the injury process?
- Are there any short-term or persistent deformities when the foot is injured?
- What is the location and range of pain or abnormal sensation?
- What type of pain does the patient experience?
- Can the patient point to the exact site of the pain?
- When does the pain or other symptoms get worse or relieved?
- What shoes do you wear for training?
- Have the ankles been injured, sick or operated before?

2.2 Observation

The athletic trainer should observe the patients to determine the following problems:

- Compare the posture of the feet with and without weight.
- The patient's willingness and ability to use the feet.

- Are the contours of the bones and soft tissues of the foot normal? Is the color normal?
- Is the foot well structured? Does it maintain its shape during weight-bearing?
- Is there a flat foot (pes planus) or a high arch (pes cavus)?
- Are there any deformities in the toes?

2.3 Structural Deformities

The patient should be in a prone position with the distal 1/3 of the leg protruding out of the bed. A bisector line is drawn from the beginning of the musculotendinous junction of the gastrocnemius to the distal end of the calcaneus. The patient was kept in the prone position, and the athletic trainer should palpate the talus while the forefoot is inverted and everted. One hand is placed in front of the fibula, and the other hand palpates the talus in the anterior segment of the medial malleolus.

First, place the subtalar joint in a neutral position. Starting from the neutral position, the athletic trainer should make the foot slightly dorsiflexed and observe the relationship between the metatarsal heads and the plantar surface of the calcaneus. Forefoot varus is a bony deformity of medial metatarsal heads with respect to the plane of the calcaneus and can be caused by tibialis anterior muscle tension combined with malposition of the calcaneocuboid joint. Forefoot valgus is a bony deformity of the lateral metatarsal relative to the rearfoot. In a rearfoot varus deformity, when the foot is in the neutral position of the subtalar joint and under the condition of non-weight bearing, the position of the medial metatarsal heads is elevated.

Several Structural Deformities

- Flatfoot is a condition in which the longitudinal arch of the foot is lost. It also involves the abduction of the forefoot and valgus deformity of the hind foot. In flexible flatfoot, the arch is present during non-weight bearing but is lost during weight bearing. In rigid flatfoot, the arch is absent in weight-bearing and non-weight-bearing positions.

- High arch foot is a foot with an abnormally high plantar longitudinal arch. People who have this condition will place too much weight and stress on the sole and heel of the foot while standing and/or walking.

- An equinus foot is characterized by restricted dorsiflexion of the ankle joint (less than 10°), usually due to contractures of the gastrocnemius tendon, soleus tendon, or achilles tendon. It may also be caused by talar deformity, trauma or inflammation. This deformity can cause increased pressure on the forefoot and excessive pronation of the subtalar joint.

- Morton's phalangeal pain refers to the formation of interdigital neuroma due to toe nerve injury. Generally, the toe nerve between the third and fourth toes is the most common. Put the two phalanges together during the examination, the pain will be induced by the compression of the toe nerves.

2.4 Shoe Wear Patterns

The athletic trainer must carefully check the inside and outside of the patient's shoes, so that the weight-bearing condition of the foot and the form of wear of the shoes can be found. Most people tend to wear out the outside edges of the heel. Just before the heel strike, the tibialis anterior muscle contracts to prevent the foot drop. The anterior tibialis contraction makes the foot dorsiflex and slightly invert, so wear often occurs in the heel outside. Individuals with excessive pronation often wear out the front of the running shoes under the second metatarsal; individuals with excessive supination have wear-out on the outside side of the shoes.

2.5 Palpation

In addition to identifying pain scales, swelling, and deformities, palpation is also used to assess circulation in the foot.

2.6. Special Tests

2.6.1 Movement Assessment

As with other joint examinations, the athletic trainer must compare the two sides to see if there is any symmetry, because the situation differs between people.

Examining the extrinsic and the intrinsic foot muscles for pain and range of motion under active, passive, and resistive isometric contraction.

2.6.2 Morton's Test

The patient is in the supine position, and the athletic trainer grabs the patient's foot at the head of the metatarsals and pinches the five metatarsals heads together. If there is pain, the test result is positive, indicating a stress fracture or a neuroma.

2.6.3 Neurological Assessment

The athletic trainer needs to distinguish between the sensory distribution of the peripheral nerves and the sensory nerve distribution of the dermis. Although the sensory distribution of the dermis varies from person to person, the distribution of peripheral nerves is relatively consistent. Reflexes and cutaneous distribution should be tested and any alteration in skin sensation should be recorded.

2.6.4 Tinel Sign (Ankle)

Tinel sign can be induced in two places around the ankle. One is the anterior branch of the deep peroneal nerve, which is tapped in front of the ankle. The other is the posterior tibial nerve, which can be tapped behind the medial malleolus. If there are pricking and abnormal skin sensation during tapping, the test result is considered positive.

二、足部损伤的评估

进行足部评估时，采集患者详细、完整的病史非常重要。

（一）病史

运动防护师应询问患者以下问题：

- 损伤是怎样产生的？
- 损伤是急性的还是慢性的？
- 损伤过程是什么？
- 足部受伤时是否有短暂或持续的畸形？
- 疼痛或感觉不适的位置在何处，范围有多大？
- 患者的疼痛是哪种类型？
- 患者能指出痛点吗？
- 疼痛或其他症状何时加重或缓解？
- 训练时穿着什么鞋？
- 以前踝部是否有过受伤、患病或动过手术的情况？

（二）视诊

运动防护师通过观察患者以确定下列问题：

- 比较承重时和未承重时足的姿势。
- 患者使用足的意愿和能力。
- 足的骨及软组织的外形和颜色是否正常？
- 足的结构如何？负重时外形是否保持不变？
- 是否有扁平足或高足弓的情况？
- 足趾是否有任何异常？

（三）检查结构缺陷

患者处于俯卧位并将腿远端 1/3 伸出床面，从腓肠肌肌腱连接处到跟骨远端画一条平分线。患者保持俯卧位。运动防护师内翻、外翻患者的前足，一只手位于腓骨前方，另一只手在内踝前部，分别触诊距骨。

首先将患者足距下关节置于中立位。从中立位开始，足部轻度被动背屈，同时观察距骨头与跟骨底的关系。前足内翻是指内侧距骨头相对于跟骨平面内翻的骨性畸形，可由胫骨前肌紧张合并跟骰关节错位导致。前足外翻是指距骨外侧相对于后足外翻的骨性畸形。后足内翻畸形是指当足处于距下关节中立位和无负重情况下，内侧距骨头位置升高，跟骨处于内翻位的情况。

常见结构性缺陷：

● 扁平足，是一种足弓纵向丧失的足部结构异常。它还包括前足外展和后足外翻畸形。在柔性平足中，足弓在非承重时存在，但在承重时消失。在刚性平足中，承重和非承重位置均不存在足弓。

● 高足弓，是指足底纵向弓异常高的足。患有这种疾病的人在站立或行走时，足底和足跟会承受过多的重量和压力。

● 马蹄足，畸形的特征为踝关节的背屈活动受限（少于10°），通常由腓肠肌肌腱、比目鱼肌腱或足跟腱的挛缩引起，也可能由距骨畸形、外伤或炎症引起。该畸形会导致前足压力增加和距下关节过度旋前。

● 莫顿趾骨疼痛，指趾神经受伤导致趾间神经瘤的形成。一般第三和第四趾之间的趾神经痛最常见。检查时挤压两根趾骨，疼痛会因为趾神经受到压迫而被诱发。

（四）鞋的磨损模式

运动防护师要检查患者的鞋子以发现足承重的情况和鞋子磨损的形式。大多数人都易磨损鞋跟后外侧，因为足跟着地前，胫骨前肌收缩防止足下垂。胫骨前肌收缩不仅会使足背屈还会使足轻度内翻，所以磨损常发生在鞋跟外侧。过度旋前的人常磨损跑鞋的前端内侧，即第二跖骨下方的位置。足过度旋后的人的鞋外侧边磨损严重。

（五）触诊

除了确定痛点、肿胀和畸形，触诊也可应用于检查足部的血液循环情况。

（六）特殊检查

1. 运动检查

如同其他关节检查，检查者一定要比较双侧，观察是否对称，因为每个人之间的情况也会有所不同。

在主动、被动、抗阻等长收缩下检查足外在肌和内在肌的疼痛和活动度情况。

2. 莫顿氏试验

患者仰卧位，运动防护师在跖骨头处抓握患者的足部，并将五个跖骨头捏在一起。若出现疼痛，则试验结果为阳性，表示存在应力性骨折或神经瘤。

3. 神经学检查

运动防护师需要分辨周围感觉神经分布与皮节感觉神经分布的差异。虽然皮节感觉神经分布在个体间会有所差异，但周围感觉神经分布在个体间是较为一致的。需要检查反射和体表分布，任何皮肤感觉改变都应被记录。

4. 神经叩击试验（蒂内尔征）

在踝部周围有两处可诱发蒂内尔征现象。一处为腓深神经的胫前分支，在踝关节前方加以叩击；另一处是胫后神经，可在内踝后方叩击到。若叩击时出现刺痛和皮肤感觉异常，则试验结果为阳性。

3 Identification and Management of Common Foot Injuries

3.1 Fractures of the Talus

3.1.1 Etiology

Talus fractures occur laterally or medially. Lateral fractures are caused by severe inversion and dorsiflexion forces. When the foot is forced into a dorsiflexion position, the front part of the tibia collides with the neck of the talus, causing a fracture. The medial fractures are caused by the inversion and plantar flexion forces combined with external rotation of the tibia relative to the talus.

3.1.2 Symptoms and Signs

Patients often have a history of repeated ankle injuries, accompanied by obvious swelling and pain from the ankle to the subtalar joint. The swelling may obscure the surface marks of the ankle joint. If the fracture is displaced or the ankle joint is dislocated, the skin contour of the joint may become inconspicuous or deformed.

Patients experience pain with weight-bearing and complain of clicking or intermittent swelling. Patients with talus fractures usually present with tenderness on palpation of the ankle joint and below, which can be localized and extensive. X-ray and CT examination should be used to assist diagnosis.

3.1.3 Management

① Simple, non-displaced fracture is suitable for conservative treatment, including symptom-based, non-weight bearing, protective immobilization, progressing to full weight bearing. ② Rehabilitation training can help restore range of motion, muscle strength and proprioception. ③ If the conservative treatment fails, the symptoms are not reduced, or there is a displaced of osteochondral fracture, the loose bodies must be removed by arthroscopic surgery.

3.2 Calcaneus Fracture

3.2.1 Etiology

Axial stress on the foot after a fall or jump can lead to a calcaneal contusion or severe calcaneal fracture. Avulsion fractures may also occur at the anterior part of the attachment of the calcaneonavicular ligament to the sustentaculum tali or the posterior part of the attachment of the talocalcaneal ligament.

3.2.2 Symptoms and Signs

There is often immediate swelling and pain. The pain is often quite severe, and the affected limb cannot bear weight. Swelling and tenderness are usually more pronounced and can be severe. The heel may be noticeably deformed. X-ray and CT examination should be used to assist diagnosis.

3.2.3 Management

POLICE should be used immediately to relieve the pain and swelling. For nondisplaced fractures, immobilization and early range of motion exercises within the range of pain tolerance are recommended.

3.3 Calcaneal Stress Fracture

3.3.1 Etiology

Calcaneal stress fractures are caused by repeated calcaneal impingement and are most common in long-distance runners. This kind of fracture is characterized by a sudden onset of persistent pain in the area of the plantar-calcaneal.

3.3.2 Symptoms and Signs

There is heel pain when walking the first few steps after getting up, similar to plantar fasciitis. However, unlike plantar fasciitis, calcaneus stress fractures usually show tenderness on both sides of the calcaneus. The pain increases during weight-bearing activities, especially when the heel strikes in running. The patients usually complain of persistent pain after training. Imaging tests can help confirm the diagnosis.

3.3.3 Management

① For patients with mild symptoms, restricting activities and using heel pads may be sufficient. For patients with severe symptoms, crutches and no weight bearing are recommended until the symptoms subside. ② For patients who want to maintain cardiorespiratory fitness during fracture healing, it is recommended that they perform non-weight-bearing exercises, such as swimming and running in the pool. When the pain and tenderness disappear, the patient can gradually resume activities.

3.4 Calcaneal Apophysitis

3.4.1 Etiology

Calcaneal apophysitis, or Sever's disease, is an overwork injury that occurs in young athletes aged 8–15. Sever's disease is a traction injury at the apophysis of the calcaneus where the achilles tendon attaches.

3.4.2 Symptoms and Signs

At the posterior heel below the attachment of the achilles tendon, there will be activity-related pain, which may be unilateral or bilateral. Tenderness is confined to the calcaneal bone process, usually 1–2 cm distal to the achilles tendon attachment point. It often occurs during strenuous exercise and disappears at rest.

3.4.3 Management

① Take rest, icing, stretching (achilles tendon), shock wave and anti-inflammatory drugs and other measures for treatment. ② The heel pad can reduce the pressure on the apophysis. Conservative treatment usually relieves pain in 3–6 weeks.

3.5 Retrocalcaneal Bursitis

3.5.1 Etiology

Retrocalcaneal bursitis is an inflammation of the bursa between the achilles tendon and the calcaneus, which is caused by shoe compression and is confined to the inflammation of the bursae located between the skin and the achilles tendon at the top of the heel.

3.5.2 Symptoms and Signs

Palpation of the bursa above and anterior to the insertion of the achilles tendon can trigger pain. There may be swelling on both sides of the achilles tendon. If the stimulus is present, a bony callus may form. The early symptoms may only be redness and pain, and the skin temperature is high. Subsequently, the surface skin is eroded. After a few months or longer, fluctuating, tender cystic nodules with a diameter of 1 to 3 cm appear. It may be red or skin-colored. In chronic patients, fibrosis and calcification of the bursa can occur. This condition is a chronic disease that develops gradually over a long period of time and takes a longer time for patients to recover.

3.5.3 Management

① Early treatment after injury, including POLICE, NSAIDs and analgesic, should be used as needed. ② Ultrasound treatment can relieve inflammation. Stretching the achilles tendon and thickening the sole of the shoes to reduce stress on the tendon.

3.6 Cuboid Subluxation

3.6.1 Etiology

Excessive foot pronation and trauma are thought to be the main factors leading to the occurrence of cuboid subluxation. It is often caused by acute ankle varus injury or overuse syndrome. The subluxation of the cuboid bone may be caused by small damage to the calcaneocuboid ligament, which allows the cuboid bone to slide out of its normal anatomical position.

3.6.2 Symptoms and Signs

The results of imaging examinations are usually normal, and the diagnosis is based on clinical manifestations. There is often local tenderness of the cuboid bone. Similar to the sprain of the lateral foot ligament, pain and tenderness of the cuboid and proximal calcaneal joints, the displacement of the cuboid causes pain along the fourth and fifth metatarsals as well as over the cuboid. Patients often complain of mid-foot sprain with pain on the dorsum of the foot and/

or over the anterior/lateral ankle frequently after an inversion mechanism. The pain is increased when the patient stands after a prolonged non-weight-bearing period. Obvious swelling or tenderness indicates a more serious injury.

3.6.3 Management

① The manipulative reduction of cuboid has a good therapeutic effect. If the manipulation is appropriate, the patient's symptoms can often be quickly relieved. ② After the manipulative reduction of the cuboid, orthotics are often used to maintain it in a normal position. Patients should also wear volume-fitted orthotics during training and competition to reduce the possibility of recurrence.

3.7 Tarsal Tunnel Syndrome

3.7.1 Etiology

Tarsal tunnel syndrome refers to a series of symptoms caused by compression of the tibial nerve in the ankle under the transverse tarsal ligament. Below the retinaculum (or flexor retinaculum), there is a tube that contains the flexor digitorum longus and flexor longus foot tendon, vascular bundle, tibial nerve and inner and outer plantar nerves. The most common cause of tarsal tunnel syndrome is a fracture or dislocation involving the talus, calcaneus or medial malleolus.

3.7.2 Symptoms and Signs

Typical manifestations are pain, burning, numbness and tingling sensations involving the soles, distal feet, toes and heels. The pain can radiate upwards to the calf or higher. The discomfort is often the most severe at night. On physical examination, the nerves behind the medial malleolus show a positive Tinel sign, accompanied by loss of sensation on the toe surface, but do not extend to the dorsum of the foot.

3.7.3 Management

① For patients with symptoms of tarsal tunnel syndrome but no history of trauma, conservative treatment includes using NSAIDs and footwear adjustments. Apply appropriate orthotics to correct excessive pronation. ② If the symptoms recurred periodically, surgical treatment should be considered.

3.8 Plantar Fasciitis

3.8.1 Etiology

Plantar Fasciitis (PF) is one of the most common causes of foot pain in adults. Possible risk factors for plantar fasciitis include obesity, prolonged standing or jumping, flat foot, and decreased ankle dorsiflexion. The higher incidence among runners indicates that plantar fasciitis can be caused by injuries caused by repeated small traumas. In addition, for sports enthusiasts, there are also the following risk factors, including overtraining, poor running shoes, running on hard ground, flat foot, limited ankle dorsiflexion, high arches, and walking or standing on hard ground for a long time.

3.8.2 Symptoms and Signs

The patients usually complain of pain on the anterior and medial side of the calcaneus, usually in the areas where the plantar fascia joins the calcaneus. The examiner dorsiflexes the toes of the patient with one hand to tighten the plantar fascia, and then uses the thumb or index finger of the other hand to palpate from the heel to the forefoot along the fascia to find scattered tender points.

3.8.3 Management

There are three stages of treatment:

Stage one: acute injury phase. Use POLICE and NSAIDs to reduce inflammation and pain, and may also use injection therapy including trigger point closure injection. Exercise therapy methods include walking with crutches, stretching the achilles tendon and using the foam roller to relax the plantar fascia.

Stage two: tissue repair stage. Treatments include the use of ultrasound, cross-friction massage technology, arch taping and so on. Exercise therapy methods include continuous stretching of the achilles tendon and foam roller exercises to stretch the plantar fascia. Begin progressive weight-bearing exercises when pain subsides and begin strengthening the flexor plantar muscles.

Stage three: functional remodeling period. The exercise therapies include stretching the achilles tendon and plantar fascia, strengthening the plantar flexors, performing the general exercises to the lower leg and gradually starting running within the painless range.

3.9 Metatarsal Stress Fractures

3.9.1 Etiology

Metatarsal stress fractures often occur in recruits and are referred to as "marching fractures". When the first metatarsal bone is larger than the other metatarsals, stress fractures are more likely to occur. If the individual has anatomical structural defects, such as hallux valgus or the first metatarsal is shorter, the second metatarsal is longer than the first metatarsal. The stress on the second metatarsal bone will increase, resulting in a high incidence of stress fractures in the second metatarsal bone.

3.9.2 Symptoms and Signs

The patients usually complain of pain during and after activities. Tender points may exist. At first, the pain is intermittent when the affected metatarsal bone is affected. If the patient continues the activity that caused the stress fracture, the injury may progress, leading to more extensive swelling and severe pain even during normal activities.

3.9.3 Management

Metatarsal stress fracture treatment methods include basic analgesia and rest to facilitate fracture healing. There is usually no need for the patient to immobilize or bear no weight. Patients usually return at 2–3 weeks to determine whether the initial treatment has improved the pain. It is recommended to follow up on x-rays at 4–8 weeks to confirm healing. After 4–8 weeks, if the patient can perform daily activities without pain, he can gradually resume more impactful activities.

3.10 Hallux Valgus Deformities (Bunions)

3.10.1 Etiology

Hallux valgus is a structural deformity of the hallux that deviates more than 15° laterally relative to the first metatarsal bone. There are many risk factors for bunions. In general, bunions are related to structural forefoot varus. Bunions are often caused by wearing shoes with high heels and narrow toe boxes. However, the shoe is likely to aggravate the mechanical abnormality, rather than the cause of the abnormality.

3.10.2 Symptoms and Signs

There is a noticeable deformity and prominence on the medial side of the MTP joint. Pain may get worse after wearing shoes. ROM of the great toe is restricted. Improper footwear can aggravate irritation and pain.

3.10.3 Management

① NSAIDs can be used to relieve pain and inflammation. ② Wearing wide-toed shoes is necessary. Wearing orthotics to correct the structural forefoot varus deformity. ③ Stretching and mobilization can be used to maintain range of motion. ④ Once conservative management fails, surgery may be an option.

3.11 Metatarsalgia

3.11.1 Etiology

Generally, metatarsalgia refers to pain on the distal metatarsal surface of the second and third metatarsal bones. The pain usually results from intense training, poor gait pattern, abnormal foot anatomy (a high arch), ill-fitting shoes, etc.

3.11.2 Symptoms and Signs

The patient complains of sharp pain in the plantar surface of the distal metatarsal bones. The pain is often described as like stepping on stones. The second and third metatarsal heads are the most common pain sites. Sitting down can relieve pain, and shoes with forefoot support can also occasionally relieve pain.

3.11.3 Management

① Conservative measures (such as minimizing the volume and intensity of training, resting, changing shoes or using a metatarsal pad) are the preferred choice. ② When conservative measures don't relieve the pain and metatarsalgia is complicated by foot conditions such as mallet toe deformity, surgery to realign the metatarsal bones might be an option.

3.12 Hammer toe, Mallet Toe, and Claw Toe

3.12.1 Etiology

Hammer toe is a Z-shaped deformity caused by flexion contracture of the proximal interphalangeal joint (PIP) and the extension of the distal toe joint. Mallet toe is caused by flexion contracture of the distal interphalangeal joint (DIP). A claw-shaped toe is also called supine toe deformity, which is caused by flexion contracture of the distal interphalangeal joint and overextension of the metatarsophalangeal joint (MP).

3.12.2 Symptoms and Signs

Patients complain of stiffness, blisters, swelling, pain, and frequent infections in their feet.

3.12.3 Management

Wear loose-toed shoes, toe pads, and braces, or use them in combination. If conservative methods are ineffective, the surgical correction could be an option. If it is accompanied by metatarsal pain, using over-the-counter or prescription orthotics with metatarsal pads and cushions may help relieve the pain.

3.13 Blood Under the Toenail (Subungual Hematoma)

3.13.1 Etiology

When the toe is stepped on, dropping an object on the toe, or kicking another object, blood will quickly gather under the nail. Repeated stresses on the toes, as seen in long-distance runners, can cause nail bed bleeding. In many cases, blood that accumulates in a confined space underneath the nail can cause severe pain. Because blood separates the nail plate from the nail bed, the nail usually falls off after a few weeks. New nail armor will regenerate under the remnant, and replace the old armor when all of them grow out.

3.13.2 Symptoms and Signs

The area under the toenail appears as a purple-black spot on all or part of the nail, with severe pain, and gentle pressure on the nail can greatly exacerbate the pain.

3.13.3 Management

Use ice packs immediately after injury to reduce bleeding. In the next 12 to 24 hours, it can release blood and relieve pain by piercing the nail plate.

三、足部常见损伤的识别和处理

（一）距骨骨折

1. 病因

距骨骨折可发生在外侧或内侧。外侧骨折由严重的内翻和背屈方向的力导致，当足部被迫进入背屈位置时，胫骨前部与距骨颈部发生碰撞则可能导致骨折。内侧骨折则由内翻和跖屈方向的力合并胫骨相对距骨外旋导致。

2. 症状和体征

患者常有反复的踝关节损伤史，伴随着从脚踝到距下关节的明显肿胀和疼痛。肿胀可能使踝关节的体表标志变得模糊，如果骨折移位或踝关节脱位，关节的皮肤轮廓可能变得不明显或变形。

患者负重时感到疼痛，有弹响或间歇性肿胀。距骨骨折患者通常表现为踝关节及其下方触诊压痛，可为局限性或广泛性的疼痛。可采用 X 射线、CT 扫描协助诊断。

3. 处理

①单纯性、无移位的骨折适合采用保守治疗，处理方法包括基于症状的无负重的石膏保护性制动，渐进至全体重负重。②康复训练帮助其恢复活动范围、肌力和本体感觉。③若保守治疗失败、症状不减或者出现骨软骨骨折移位，则必须采用关节镜手术摘除游离体。

（二）跟骨骨折

1. 病因

通常人从高处坠落或跳跃时后足部受到的轴向应力，可导致跟骨挫伤或严重的跟骨骨折。撕脱性骨折可发生于跟舟韧带与载距突结合部位的前部或者距跟韧带止点的后部。

2. 症状和体征

患者一般表现为立刻肿胀并疼痛，疼痛往往相当剧烈，患肢不能负重。肿胀和压痛通常较明显且可能较严重。足跟可能会明显变形。可采用 X 射线、CT 扫描协助诊断。

3. 处理

立即应用 POLICE 原则处理以减轻疼痛和肿胀。对于无移位骨折，建议制动和在疼痛可忍受范围内进行早期活动度训练。

（三）跟骨应力性骨折

1. 病因

跟骨应力性骨折由跟骨反复受撞击所致，常见于长距离跑者，特征是突然开始的跟骨底区域的持续性疼痛。

2. 症状和体征

起床后行走前几步时出现足跟部疼痛，类似于足底筋膜炎。然而，与足底筋膜炎不同的是，跟骨的应力性骨折通常表现出跟骨两侧的压痛。患者负重活动时足跟部疼痛加重，尤其是在跑步足跟着地时。主诉训练结束后疼痛持续存在。可通过影像学检查帮助确诊。

3. 处理

①对于症状轻微的患者，限制活动并配合使用足跟垫即可。对于症状严重的患者，推荐使用拐杖且不负重，直至症状消退。②对于在骨折愈合过程中想保持心肺功能的患者，建议其进行非负重运动，如游泳和池中跑步。当疼痛和压痛消失，患者可逐渐恢复活动。

（四）跟骨骨突炎

1. 病因

跟骨骨突炎，或称塞弗氏病，是一种常见于 8 ～ 15 岁年轻运动员的过劳性损伤。塞弗氏病是跟腱止点 - 跟骨骨突处的拉伸性损伤。

2. 症状和体征

患者的足跟后侧、跟腱止点下方会出现活动相关疼痛，可能为单侧或双侧。压痛局限于跟骨骨突，通常在跟腱附着点远端 1 ～ 2 cm 处。疼痛常发生于剧烈运动时，休息时消失。

3. 处理

①采取休息、冰敷、牵伸（跟腱）、冲击波和抗炎药等措施进行处理。②足跟垫可以减少施加在骨突上的压力。保守治疗 3 ～ 6 周通常即可缓解症状。

（五）跟骨后滑囊炎

1. 病因

跟骨后滑囊炎是发生于跟腱与跟骨之间滑囊的炎症，指位于鞋后跟皮肤和跟腱之间的滑囊炎症，由鞋压迫造成。

2. 症状和体征

从跟腱止点上方和前方触诊滑囊可激发疼痛，跟腱两侧可能伴有肿胀。若刺激源始终存在，则可能已形成一个骨性结节。早期症状可能仅为发红和疼痛，皮温高。随后，表面皮肤被侵蚀。几个月或更长时间后，出现波动性的、触痛的囊性结节，直径 1 ～ 3 cm，可能是红色的或肤色的。在慢性病人中，滑囊会发生纤维化和钙化，这种情况的形成和恢复都需要相当长一段时间。

3. 处理

①损伤后早期处理包括采用 POLICE 原则处理，根据需要合理应用非甾体抗炎药和镇痛药。②可进行超声波治疗缓解炎症。牵拉跟腱，垫高鞋底以减少施加在跟腱上的应力。

（六）骰骨半脱位

1. 病因

足部过度旋前以及创伤是导致骰骨半脱位发生的主要因素。经常由急性踝关节内翻损伤或过度使用综合征引起。骰骨半脱位原因可能是跟骰韧带出现损伤，使骰骨从正常解剖位置滑出。

2. 症状和体征

影像学检查结果通常正常，诊断依据为临床表现。常有骰骨局部压痛。类似于足外侧韧带扭伤，即骰骨及近端跟骨关节疼痛和压痛，受累部位也导致第4、5跖骨和骰骨区疼痛。患者通常主诉足中段扭伤伴足背疼痛或经常在内翻活动后出现踝前/外侧疼痛。长时间从非负重状态下站起时患足疼痛可加重。明显的肿胀或压痛提示有更严重的损伤。

3. 处理

①骰骨半脱位的手法复位具有良好的治疗效果。若手法操作得当，患者的疼痛症状常能得到迅速缓解。②骰骨复位后，可应用矫形器使其保持在正常位置。患者还应在训练和比赛中穿戴量体适配的矫形器以减小复发的可能。

（七）跗管综合征

1. 病因

跗管综合征是指胫神经在踝部行经跗横韧带下方时受到压迫而产生的一系列症状。在此支持带（或屈肌支持带）下方有一个管道，该管道中包含趾长屈肌和足拇长屈肌肌腱、血管束、胫神经和足底内、外侧神经。跗管综合征常见的原因是累及距骨、跟骨或内踝的骨折或脱位。

2. 症状和体征

典型表现为累及足底、足远端、足趾和足跟的疼痛以及烧灼、麻木和刺痛感。疼痛可向上放射到腓肠肌或更高部位。严重的不适感经常在夜间出现。查体可见内踝后方的神经有明显的蒂内尔征阳性，并伴有足趾表面的感觉丧失，但未向足背延伸。

3. 处理

①有跗管综合征症状但没有创伤史的患者应进行保守治疗，包括使用非甾体抗炎药、调整鞋的松紧等。佩戴矫形器可纠正足过度旋前。②若症状周期性复发则考虑采取手术治疗。

（八）足底筋膜炎

1. 病因

足底筋膜炎是成人足痛常见的病因之一。引发足底筋膜炎的可能危险因素包括肥胖、长时间站立或跳跃、平足和踝关节背屈减少。跑步者的发病率较高，说明足底筋膜炎可由反复微小创伤造成的损伤导致。此外，对于运动爱好者而言，还有以下危险因素：过度训练、跑步鞋质量差、在坚硬的地面上跑步、平足、踝关节背屈受限、高足弓、长时间行走或站立在坚硬的地面上。

2. 症状和体征

患者主诉跟骨前内侧疼痛，通常在足底筋膜与跟骨的结合部位，疼痛逐渐转移至筋膜中部。运动防护师一只手使患者足趾背屈从而绷紧足底筋膜，然后用另一只手的拇指或食指沿筋膜从足跟向前足触诊，可以找到分散的压痛点。

3. 处理

治疗可分为三个阶段。

阶段一：急性损伤期，可以应用 POLICE 原则处理，用和非甾体抗炎药来减轻炎症反应和疼痛，也可以进行扳机点封闭注射等，还可以通过拄拐行走、足底筋膜和腓肠肌牵伸、使用泡沫轴来放松足底筋膜。

阶段二：组织修复期，治疗方法包括超声波、横向摩擦按摩技术、足弓贴扎等。牵伸跟腱和滚轴练习以拉伸足底筋膜。开始无痛范围内的渐进性负重练习，并开始足底屈肌的力量练习。

阶段三：功能重塑期，继续牵拉跟腱和足底筋膜，进行足底屈肌群的力量练习、小腿的常规性锻炼，并逐渐开始在无痛范围内跑步。

（九）跖骨应力性骨折

1. 病因

跖骨应力性骨折因常发生于入伍新兵而被称为"行军性骨折"。当第 1 跖骨大于其他跖骨时，发生应力性骨折的可能性更大。若个体存在解剖学结构缺陷，如拇外翻或第 1 跖骨较短，第 2 跖骨长于第 1 跖骨，则第 2 跖骨所承受的应力会变大，从而导致第 2 跖骨应力性骨折的发生率增大。

2. 症状和体征

患者主诉活动中和活动后疼痛，可能存在压痛点。起初是间歇性疼痛，只有在使用受累跖骨时才会出现。如果患者继续进行可能造成应力性骨折的活动，则损伤可发展为更广泛的肿胀并在日常活动中也会出现严重疼痛。

3. 处理

跖骨应力性骨折的处理方法包括基础镇痛和休息，以便骨折愈合。通常没有必要制动和让患者不负重。患者通常在 2 ~ 3 周时复诊，以确定初始治疗是否使疼痛得到改善。建议在 4 ~ 8 周时随访 X 射线平片，以证实骨折处是否愈合。4 ~ 8 周后，若患者能进行日常活动且无疼痛，则可逐渐开始恢复冲击性更高的活动。

（十）拇外翻畸形（拇囊炎）

1. 病因

拇外翻畸形是指拇趾相对于第 1 跖骨向外侧偏移 15° 以上的结构性畸形。拇外翻畸形的风险因素很多，一般情况下，拇外翻畸形与结构性前足内翻有关，常因穿前端过尖、过窄的鞋所导致，但通常鞋只是加重了这种机械性异常，不是导致异常的根源。

2. 症状和体征

患者跖趾关节内侧有明显的畸形和突出，穿鞋后疼痛加重，大脚趾活动度受限。若穿不合适的鞋则会加重刺激和疼痛。

3. 处理

①可以使用非甾体抗炎药缓解疼痛和炎症。②选择宽头、低跟鞋；用矫形器改善足的支撑和力线。③用拉伸和关节松动手法保持关节活动度。④若保守治疗失败可选择手术。

（十一）跖痛症

1. 病因

一般指第 2 和第 3 跖骨骨干远端跖骨表面疼痛。疼痛通常源于过度训练、不良步态、足部解剖异常（高足弓）及不合脚的鞋等。

2. 症状和体征

患者主诉远端跖骨区域的跖面锐痛，疼痛感像踩在石头上。第 2 和第 3 跖骨是常见的疼痛部位。坐下可减轻疼痛，具有前足支撑的鞋也能偶尔缓解疼痛。

3. 处理

①首先选择保守治疗，比如减少训练量、休息、换鞋或使用跖骨垫等。②当保守措施不能缓解疼痛，而跖骨痛又因足部疾病（如槌状趾）而复杂化时，可选择手术治疗。

（十二）锤状趾、槌状趾、爪状趾

1. 病因

锤状趾是一种 Z 形畸形，是由近端趾间关节屈曲挛缩、远端趾关节伸直所致。槌状趾是远端趾间关节屈曲挛缩所致。爪状趾又称仰趾畸形，是远端趾间关节发生屈曲挛缩所致，伴跖趾关节过伸。

2. 症状和体征

患者足部存在僵硬，伴有水泡、肿胀、疼痛和反复感染。

3. 处理

穿宽松的鞋、趾垫、支具，或联合使用。如果保守方法都没有效果，手术矫形通常可以缓解症状。如果伴有跖痛，使用带有跖骨垫的非处方矫正器或处方矫正器可能有助于缓解疼痛。

（十三）足趾甲下出血（趾甲下血肿）

1. 病因

当脚趾被踩到、砸到，或脚趾踢到某物时可造成趾甲下出血，受伤后血液快速聚集在甲下。足趾受到反复的应力，常见于长跑运动员，可造成甲床出血。趾甲下局部积血可产生剧烈疼痛，由于血液使甲板与甲床分离，通常几周后甲会脱落。在残甲下会有新甲再生，当全部长出后取代旧甲。

2. 症状和体征

趾甲下区域表现为全部或部分甲下的紫黑色点，有剧痛，轻微按压足趾会加剧疼痛。

3. 处理

伤后立即使用冰袋冷敷，抬高患足以减少出血。在之后的 12 ~ 24 小时，可通过穿刺甲板以释放血液和缓解疼痛。

Summary

1. Foot injuries can be prevented by selecting appropriate footwear, correcting biomechanical structural deformities through the use of appropriate orthotics, and appropriate foot hygiene and care.

2. The assessment of foot injury includes medical history, palpation of bone structure and soft tissue. Observation should include the examination of the presence of structural malformations; special movement assessments should include examining the extrinsic and the intrinsic foot muscles for pain and range of motion under active, passive, and resistive isometric contraction. Besides, the neurological assessment of the foot is also necessary.

3. Common injuries to the feet include: fractures of the talus; calcaneus fracture; calcaneal stress fracture; apophysitis of the calcaneus (Sever's disease); retrocalcaneal bursitis; cuboid subluxation; tarsal tunnel syndrome; plantar fasciitis; metatarsal stress fractures; hallux valgus deformities (bunions); metatarsalgia; hammer toe, mallet toe and claw toe; blood under the toenail, etc.

⭕ Review Questions:

1. When an athletic trainer is assessing foot injuries, what questions should the athletic trainer focus on?

2. What are the special tests for foot injuries and what should be paid attention to?

3. List several common injuries of the feet, and briefly describe their etiology, symptoms and signs, and management.

小结

1. 足部损伤预防的内容包括：挑选合适的鞋，应用矫形器矫正足部存在的结构畸形和力学异常，并注意足部卫生。

2.足损伤的评估包括询问病史、触诊骨性结构和软组织；视诊应包括检查存在的结构畸形；特殊检查包括在主动、被动、抗阻等长收缩下检查外在和内在肌的疼痛和活动度。此外还有对足部的神经反射检查。

3.足部的常见损伤包括：距骨骨折、跟骨骨折、跟骨应力性骨折、跟骨骨突炎、跟骨后滑囊炎、骰骨半脱位、跗管综合征、足底筋膜炎、跖骨应力性骨折、拇外翻畸形（拇囊炎）、跖痛症、锤状趾、槌状趾、爪状趾及足趾甲下出血等。

○ 复习题

1.运动防护师在评估足部损伤时，应该重点询问患者哪些问题？

2.足部损伤的特殊检查包括哪些检查，应该注意什么？

3.列举几个常见的足部损伤，并简述它们的病因、症状和体征及处理方法。

Chapter 9 Other Common Injuries
第九章　其他常见损伤

○ Main Contents

1. Identification and management of craniocerebral injuries.
2. Identification and management of maxillofacial and dental injuries.
3. Identification and management of eyes, ears, nose and throat injuries or diseases.

○ 主要内容

1. 常见颅脑部损伤的识别和处理。
2. 常见颌面、牙齿损伤的识别和处理。
3. 常见眼、耳、鼻、喉部伤病的识别和处理。

1 Identification and Management of Craniocerebral Injuries

1.1 Skull Fractures

1.1.1 Etiology

A skull fracture occurs when there is a significant force against the head. Skull fracture, accounting for 15% to 20% of cerebral injuries, occurs most often from blunt trauma, such as a baseball hitting the head or a fall from a height causing the head to hit the ground. Skull fracture types include sunken, linear, compound and penetrating. Any skull fracture is serious and requires the immediate attention of a physician.

1.1.2 Symptoms and Signs

The patient complains of severe headache and nausea, and may also be unconscious. There may be blood in the ear canal, middle ear, through the nose, ecchymosis around the eyes (raccoon eyes) or ecchymosis behind the ear (Battle's sign). Cerebrospinal fluid (straw-colored fluid) may appear in the ear canal and nose.

1.1.3 Management

Skull fractures are not life-threatening themselves, but their complications can be fatal and require urgent treatment. Its complications include cerebral hemorrhage, bone fragments and (severe or lethal) infections in the brain, and the patient should be hospitalized immediately and transferred to the Neurosurgery department.

1.2 Concussion

1.2.1 Etiology

A concussion is a temporary impairment of brain function caused by an impact on the head. The most common injuries include motor vehicle accidents, falls and sports-related concussions. Concussions can be caused by direct external forces on the head, face and neck. It can also be caused by impacts from other parts of the body being transmitted to the head, which can cause coup injury and contrecoup injury.

1.2.2 Symptoms and Signs

Concussion can be classified into mild, moderate, and severe. In mild concussion with unconscious loss, the patient's symptoms (such as dizziness) or functional abnormalities (such as loss of balance) will disappear in less than 15 minutes. Moderate concussion does not cause loss of consciousness, but the patient's symptoms and abnormalities may last for more than 15 minutes. If an athlete experiences any degree of coma, it is considered a severe concussion.

1.2.3 Management

① The first part of assessing a player with a head injury during sports is to check the airway, breathing, and circulation, and then to stabilize the cervical spine. If there is an unusual condition, including lack of response, a deteriorating condition, loss of consciousness, or concern about a spine or neck injury, emergency care should be sought immediately. Cervical spine injuries should be suspected in athletes who lost consciousness. Cervical spine should be smoothly immobilized, followed by an assessment of motor and sensory function of the extremities. ② If an athlete is not unconscious or has regained consciousness quickly, he or she may be evaluated on the sidelines every 5 to 10 minutes. The evaluation includes speech, memory, attention, behavior, mental status, and balance (e. g., Romberg test, BESS test). It can also be assessed using the Sports Concussion Assessment Tool (SCAT5). ③ The patient needs continuing observation of changes in pupils, consciousness, vital signs, and physical activities for a period of time after injury. Pay attention to bed rest, psychological adjustment and treatment, and avoid external adverse stimuli. ④ Generally, players are not allowed to return to play after the first concussion until there are no residual signs or symptoms, such as headache, nausea, dizziness or forgetfulness, complete recovery of coordination and blood pressure.

1.3 Post-Concussion Syndrome

1.3.1 Etiology

Post-concussion syndrome is a chronic sequelae that lasts for at least 3 months after a concussion. It may occur in cases of mild head injury without losing consciousness, in cases of severe concussions, or in patients with secondary injury.

1.3.2 Symptoms and Signs

Symptoms include persistent headaches, memory disorders, lack of concentration, anxiety, irritability, dizziness, fatigue, depression and visual disturbances. Common visual deficits are blurriness and photosensitivity. About 70% of patients will experience headaches, which are the most common symptom of post-concussion syndrome. The severity and duration of symptoms depend on the severity of the concussion.

1.3.3 Management

Physical exercise, vestibular rehabilitation and cognitive behavioral therapy are effective interventions. Physical therapy, massage and acupuncture are also complementary treatments. Patients should return to competition or training after all symptoms are eliminated. If the headache becomes severe, or if the athlete is experiencing vomiting or a decline in mental status, the athlete should be taken to an emergency room immediately to check for subdural hematoma or intracranial bleeding. Both conditions can be life-threatening.

1.4 Second Impact Syndrome

1.4.1 Etiology

Second impact syndrome, or SIS, happens when the brain swells rapidly after a person suffers a second concussion before symptoms from an earlier concussion have subsided. The mechanism is that trigeminal dysfunction following the first impact leads to an increase in vascular congestion. The stress from the first impact can affect the parasympathetic activity and contribute to the vasodilation.

1.4.2 Symptoms and Signs

The patient's condition degenerates rapidly within 15 seconds to several minutes, with loss of eye movement, dilated pupils, loss of consciousness leading to coma, and respiratory failure. The mortality rate of the second impact syndrome is around 50%.

1.4.3 Management

The patient with second impact syndrome must be saved within 5 minutes. The patient must be transferred to the nearest emergency center immediately to have a CT scan of the head that evaluates for swelling and/or bleeding in the brain. The best way to manage the secondary impact syndrome is to avoid it. Whether the patient can return to the game must be determined after the symptoms of concussion syndrome disappear.

1.5 Epidural Hematoma

1.5.1 Etiology

An epidural hematoma is bleeding between the outer membrane of the brain (dura) and the skull. An impact on the head or a skull fracture can cause a tear of the meningeal arteries in the bony depression of the skull. Blood accumulation and hematoma can occur within minutes to a few hours due to the influence of arterial blood pressure.

1.5.2 Symptoms and Signs

In most cases, an epidural hematoma can lead to loss of consciousness, but clear thinking after recovery, and almost no symptoms of severe head injury occur. But then, the intracranial pressure starts to rise, and the symptoms gradually appear and worsen. Late-stage characteristics of epidural hematoma include a stiff neck, unconsciousness, decreased pulse and respiratory rate, and convulsions.

Signs of elevated intracranial pressure include: headache, nausea, vomiting, unequal pupils, orientation disturbances, progressive or sudden-onset consciousness impairment, gradual increase in blood pressure, and declining pulse rate.

1.5.3 Management

A CT scan can be used to diagnose epidural hematoma. The pressure of an epidural hematoma must be surgically relieved immediately to avoid death or permanent disability.

1.6 Subdural Hematoma

1.6.1 Etiology

A subdural hematoma is bleeding between the outer layer (dura) and middle layer (arachnoid) of the membrane covering the brain. Subdural and epidural hematomas are caused by a direct blow to the head and occur primarily in contact sports. Acute subdural hematoma is the most common cause of death in athletes. The acceleration/deceleration force tears the blood vessels between the dura mater and the brain, causing subdural hematoma.

1.6.2 Symptoms and Signs

The symptoms include headache, dizziness, nausea or insomnia. Patients with simple subdural hematomas are usually conscious, and patients with complex subdural hematomas are usually unconscious. Vomiting, seizure activity, and hemiparesis may be evident, and the patient will have enlarged pupils on the same side of the lesion.

1.6.3 Management

The athletes with symptoms of either an epidural or subdural hematoma should be immediately removed from the game and transported to the emergency room. A CT scan or MRI diagnosis can determine the location and extent of the bleeding. For patients with acute subdural hematoma, removal of hematoma within 6 hours after the injury can lower the fatality rate and promote functional recovery. Because symptoms vary so much depending on the degree of the injury, there is no set standard for recovery of subdural and epidural hematomas. Each case must be evaluated individually. Current guidelines recommend that any athletes with an intracranial bleed or lesion should be out of game for a minimum of one year, or retire completely from contact sports.

一、常见颅脑部损伤的识别和处理

（一）颅骨骨折

1. 病因

头部受到很大的压力，可导致颅骨骨折。该损伤大多数由钝挫伤引起，约占颅脑损伤总数的15%～20%。例如棒球击中头部或从高处跌落致使头部着地。颅骨骨折类型包括凹陷型、线型、复合型和穿透型。任何颅骨骨折都是严重的，需要立即接受医生的治疗。

2. 症状和体征

患者有严重头痛和恶心，还可处于意识丧失状态。此外，还包括耳道出血、中耳出血、流鼻血、眼周瘀斑（浣熊眼）或耳后瘀血斑（Battle征）。脑脊液（淡黄色液体）可进入耳道和鼻腔。

3. 处理

颅骨骨折本身并不危及生命，但是其并发症却是致命的，需要紧急处理。其并发症包括脑出血、脑中有骨碎片、感染（可能致命），运动防护师应该立即将患者转送到医院神经外科处理。

（二）脑震荡

1. 病因

脑震荡是由头部受到外力打击后，即刻发生的暂时性脑功能损伤。常见的损伤原因包括机动车事故、跌倒和运动中的冲撞。脑震荡既可由作用于头面颈部的直接外力所致，也可能是身体其他部位的冲击力传递至头部所致，可造成冲击伤和对冲伤。

2. 症状和体征

脑震荡可分为轻度、中度和重度。轻度脑震荡无意识丧失，患者的症状（如头晕）或功能异常（如失去平衡）在不到15分钟内就会消失。中度脑震荡不会导致意识丧失，但患者的症状和异常持续时间会超过15分钟。如果运动员出现任何程度的昏迷，就属于重度脑震荡。

3. 处理

①在运动中如果头部受伤，首先要检查气道、呼吸和循环，然后稳定颈椎。如果出现异常行为、反应缺乏、病情恶化、意识丧失，或担心脊柱或颈部受伤，应立即进行紧急救护。失去意识的患者要考虑是否有颈椎损伤。若有损伤，颈椎应该平稳固定，然后对所有四肢的运动和感觉功能进行评估。②如果患者没有昏迷或很快恢复知觉，则需要将其移至场边接受评估。每5~10分钟应该进行一次评估，包括对言语、记忆力、注意力、行为、精神状态和平衡能力（例如Romberg测试、BESS测试）的评估，也可使用运动脑震荡评估工具（SCAT5）进行评估。③患者伤后在一定时间内需要进行持续观察，密切注意瞳孔、意识、生命体征和肢体活动的变化。注意卧床休息，进行心理调节和治疗，避免外界不良刺激。④患者在第1次脑震荡后直到没有残留的体征或症状，比如头痛、恶心、眩晕或健忘，并且完全恢复协调性和正常的血压的情况下才能允许其重返赛场。

（三）脑震荡后综合征

1. 病因

脑震荡后综合征是脑震荡后持续至少3个月的一种慢性后遗症，可在未丧失意识的轻度头部损伤或严重脑震荡的患者中发生，在二次受伤的患者中也可能出现。

2. 症状和体征

脑震荡后综合征的症状包括持续性头痛、记忆障碍、专注度缺乏、焦虑、易怒、眩晕、疲劳、抑郁和视觉紊乱等。常见的视觉紊乱是模糊和光敏。大约70%的患者会出现头痛，头痛是脑震荡后综合征最常见的症状。症状的严重程度和持续时间取决于脑震荡的严重程度。

3. 处理

体育运动、前庭康复、认知行为疗法等都是治疗脑震荡后综合征的有效方法，另外还可以运用物理、按摩、针灸等治疗方法。患者应在所有症状消除后再恢复比赛或训练。如果头痛变得严重，或者患者开始呕吐或精神状态下降，应立即将其送往急诊室，以便排除硬膜下血肿或颅内出血。这两种情况都可能危及生命。

（四）二次撞击综合征

1. 病因

二次撞击综合征，是指患者在早期脑震荡的症状消退之前，遭受再次脑震荡后不久，大脑出现迅速肿胀的症状。主要原因是首次撞击后的三叉神经功能障碍导致血管充血增加，来自首次撞击的压力也会影响副交感神经活动，从而促进血管扩张。

2. 症状和体征

患者状况可在 15 秒至数分钟内快速恶化，表现为眼球运动消失、瞳孔放大、意识丧失导致昏迷以及呼吸衰竭。二次撞击综合征死亡率约为 50%。

3. 处理

必须在 5 分钟内采取措施挽救患者生命。须将患者尽快送至急救中心对其头部进行CT 扫描，以评估是否有脑肿胀和 / 或出血。二次撞击综合征的最佳处理方法是避免其发生，一定要在脑震荡综合征症状消失之后再决定患者能否继续比赛。

（五）硬脑膜外血肿

1. 病因

硬脑膜外血肿是大脑外膜（硬脑膜）和颅骨之间的出血。头部受到撞击或颅骨骨折会造成颅骨内骨性凹陷处的脑膜动脉撕裂。由于动脉血压的影响，血液积聚和血肿通常在数分钟至数小时内快速产生。

2. 症状和体征

硬脑膜外血肿在多数情况下会导致患者意识丧失，患者在恢复意识后思维清晰，几乎没有严重头部损伤的症状出现。但随后，颅内压开始升高，症状逐渐出现并加重。硬脑膜外血肿后期的特征为颈部僵直、意识不清、脉搏和呼吸频率降低以及抽搐。

提示颅内压升高的情况包括：头痛、恶心呕吐、瞳孔不等大、定向障碍、渐进性或突发性的意识障碍、血压逐渐升高和脉搏下降等。

3. 处理

CT 扫描可诊断硬脑膜外血肿。若患者为硬脑膜外血肿，应立即进行手术以消除硬脑膜外血肿产生的压力，避免死亡或产生永久性残疾。

（六）硬脑膜下血肿

1. 病因

硬脑膜下血肿是脑膜外层（硬脑膜）和中间层（蛛网膜）之间的出血。硬脑膜下和硬脑膜外血肿是由头部受到直接打击引起的，主要发生在接触性运动中。急性硬脑膜下血肿是导致运动员死亡的最常见原因。加速 / 减速的作用力使硬脑膜和脑部中间的血管撕裂，从而引发硬脑膜下血肿。

2. 症状和体征

患者呈现出头痛、头晕、恶心或失眠的症状。单纯硬脑膜下血肿患者通常意识清醒，复杂的硬脑膜下血肿患者通常无意识。患者可能会出现呕吐、癫痫发作和偏瘫，损伤部位同侧的瞳孔放大。

3. 处理

出现硬脑膜外或硬脑膜下血肿症状的运动员应立即退出比赛，并送往医院急诊室。CT 扫描或磁共振成像诊断可以确定出血部位和程度。对于急性硬脑膜下血肿，伤后 6 小时内手术清除血肿可降低病死率，提高功能恢复率。由于症状因损伤程度而异，硬脑膜下和硬脑膜外血肿的恢复没有固定的标准。目前的指导方针建议任何有颅内出血或损伤的运动员至少退出运动 1 年，或者永久退出接触性运动。

2 Identification and Management of Maxillofacial and Dental Injuries

2.1 Maxillofacial Injuries

With any type of injury to the face, the athletic trainer should always suspect the possibility of an associated head injury.

2.1.1 Mandible Fracture

(1) Etiology

Fractures of the lower jaw or mandible occur most often in contact sports and are the second most common type of facial fracture. Due to the relatively small amount of tissue surrounding the mandible and the relatively sharp skeletal contours, the mandible or the front of the ear are susceptible to damage when directly impacted.

(2) Symptoms and Signs

The general symptoms include pain, swelling, loss of normal tooth occlusion and difficulty in opening the mouth. There might be significant facial distortions. Blunt trauma in contact sports can also result in other oral traumas, such as when lips and gums are forcefully compressed against teeth, bleeding around the teeth and numbness of the lower lip.

(3) Management

Mandibular fractures need to be temporarily fixed with an elastic bandage and then repositioned and fixed by a doctor. The recovery time is 4–6 weeks, and physical activities can be resumed after 2-3 months. Wearing a special orthodontic appliance and a custom tooth articulator is necessary. Surgery will be needed if fractures and dislocations occur. Once the jaw is healed, the athletes should wear a mouth guard to prevent recurrent injuries.

2.1.2 Mandibular Luxation

(1) Etiology

Because of the greater mobility of the temporomandibular joint (TMJ), the different sizes of the mandibular condyles and the temporal fossa, dislocation is prone to occur in the mandible. The most common type is anterior dislocation. When the patient suffers a lateral blow with the mouth open, the mandibular condyle can prolapse from the temporal fossa forward, causing dislocation (complete dislocation) or malposition (partial dislocation). Complications of jaw luxation are recurrent dislocation, TMJ dysfunction and malocclusion.

(2) Symptoms and Signs

There is pain or tenderness in one or both of the temporomandibular joints, and difficulty in chewing or chewing with pain. Locking of the joint makes it difficult to open or close the mouth.

(3) Management

Apply ice compress and bandage fixation at the beginning of treatment. Manipulative reduction is the first choice for acute treatment. Later, the patient needs to eat soft food, and take non-steroidal anti-inflammatory drugs (NSAIDs) and other pain medication if necessary.

2.1.3 Temporomandibular Joint Disorder

(1) Etiology

It is a condition that limits the movement of jaws and is often associated with pain. Common causes of TMJ disorders include mental factors, a history of trauma, and occlusal disorders that disrupt the balance of function in the joint's internal structures. TMJ disorders can also be caused by the muscles around the joint, dental diseases and loss of articular cartilage from trauma or overuse, as well as systemic diseases such as rheumatoid arthritis.

(2) Symptoms and Signs

The most common clinical manifestations of TMJ disorders are local pain, joint clicking sounds and mandibular movement disorders. It can cause headaches, vertigo, tinnitus, inflammation, and neck pain that is associated with trigger points and muscle stiffness.

(3) Management

Conservative treatment with relaxation techniques should be used to avoid unnecessary pressure on the temporomandibular joint. Physical therapy, such as hot compresses, can also be used to help relax the surrounding muscles. Short-term NSAIDs or a mixture of steroids and local anesthetics can be used for patients to relieve symptoms. If the above methods are ineffective, the patient will need to be referred to the dentist for treatment.

2.1.4 Zygomatic Complex Fracture

(1) Etiology

The zygomatic complex fracture is the third most common facial fracture, often caused by a direct blow. Furthermore, common causes of zygomatic fractures include violence, accidents, and sport-related injuries. Fractures are more common in men than in women.

(2) Symptoms and Signs

An obvious deformity occurs in the cheek region, or a bony discrepancy can be felt during palpation. It is usually accompanied by epistaxis, restrictive mouth opening and malocclusion. The patient commonly complains of diplopia, restricted eye movements and enophthalmos. There is also numbness, tenderness and swelling in the cheekbones.

(3) Management

Apply ice to control bleeding and quickly refer to a doctor. If the X-ray shows an inward compression of the broken zygomatic bone, surgery will be needed. The recovery takes 6–8 weeks, and appropriate protective gear is needed when returning to training or game.

2.1.5 Maxillary Fracture

(1) Etiology

A severe blow to the upper jaw can produce a fracture of the maxilla, such as in football or baseball games. This type of injury is the fourth most common type of facial fracture.

(2) Symptoms and Signs

After a severe blow to the upper jaw, the patient complains of pain while chewing, malocclusion, nosebleed, double vision, and numbness in the lip and cheek region.

(3) Management

Because of the large amount of bleeding in the maxillary fracture, it is necessary to ensure that the airway is not obstructed. The patient should be immediately transported to the hospital, and conscious patients should remain upright and forward-leaning during transportation. Specific treatments are fracture reduction, fixation and immobilization. It takes 6–8 weeks to cure after surgery.

2.2 Dental Injuries

Most sports-related dental injuries are preventable, especially for players in contact and collision sports such as basketball, football, and soccer. The use of properly fitted athletic mouth guard, such as a fitted mouthguard, could absorb and distribute the traumatic forces of impact, thereby reducing (but not eliminating) the incidence of dental injuries. Individuals should practice good dental hygiene which includes regular brushing, rinsing, and flossing. Everyone should have at least one dental check every year to prevent dental caries.

2.2.1 Tooth Fracture

(1) Etiology

A tooth fracture is a break or crack in the hard shell of the tooth. The outer shell of the tooth is called enamel. It protects the softer inner pulp of the tooth, which contains nerves and blood vessels. Any impacts or direct trauma to the upper or lower jaw can cause a broken tooth.

(2) Symptoms and Signs

Enamel-only fractures are mild and often appear as roughness along the incisal edge of the tooth crown, but there is no bleeding from the fracture and the pulp chamber is not exposed. In an enamel-dentin fracture, there is bleeding from the fracture, and the pulp chamber is exposed. Enamel-dentin fractures will elicit painful sensations when the exposed dentin is subjected to air, cold drinks, or when touched. Enamel-dentin-pulp fractures are the most complex of tooth fractures. The athlete may report acute pain. Any impact that can cause a broken tooth can also lead to a mandibular fracture or even a concussion.

(3) Management

Simply save the broken portion into a plastic bag with physiological saline or skim milk. The athlete should wear protective trays to continue the competition and require a dental department within 24 hours after the game. If bleeding, cover with gauze at the break. Do not push the teeth, as this will aggravate injury.

2.2.2 Tooth Luxation and Tooth Avulsion

(1) Etiology

Any impact on teeth can cause loose teeth. Loosening of teeth can result in subluxation, luxation or avulsion. Tooth luxation: The tooth is dislocated within its socket but maintains some attachment. Tooth avulsion: The tooth is disarticulated, and the entire periodontal ligament is severed as the vascular and neural supply to the pulp of the tooth is cut off.

(2) Symptoms and Signs

When luxated, the tooth is not broken but is very loose and can move forward or backward. When the tooth is avulsed, the entire tooth is knocked out of the mouth.

(3) Management

When a tooth is luxated, no special treatment is required on-site. The patient needs to stabilize the tooth by gently biting on a towel or wet paper tissue and be transferred to a dentist for treatment as soon as possible. For an avulsed tooth, the athletic trainer should grasp the crown with the finger to rinse it (it cannot be scraped or scrubbed) and try to reimplant the tooth. If the tooth can no longer be implanted, it should be placed in a tooth preservation box containing skim milk or saline to avoid tooth dryness. The patient should be transferred to a dentist as soon as possible.

二、常见颌面、牙齿损伤的识别和处理

（一）颌面损伤

面对任何面部损伤，运动防护师都应考虑到存在头部损伤的可能性。

1. 下颌骨骨折

（1）病因

下颌骨骨折常发生在接触性运动中，是面部骨折中的第二常见类型。由于下颌骨周围组织相对较少、骨骼轮廓相对较锋利，下颌骨或耳前方在受到直接打击时易受损伤。

（2）症状和体征

下颌骨骨折症状包括下颌疼痛、肿胀，咬合紊乱，张口受限。可能会有明显的面部畸形。接触性运动中的钝性创伤也会导致其他口腔创伤，例如嘴唇和牙龈与牙齿间发生挤压伤，导致牙齿周围出血以及下唇麻木。

（3）处理

下颌骨骨折需要用弹性绷带暂时固定后由医生进行复位和固定。康复时间为 4～6 周，2～3 月后才能进行体育运动，应佩戴特殊的牙齿矫正器和定制的牙齿咬合器。如果发生骨折移位，则需要进行手术治疗。一旦颌骨愈合，患者应该佩戴护口器以防止反复受伤。

2. 下颌脱臼

（1）病因

由于颞下颌关节活动度较大、下颌髁突和颞窝大小不一，下颌处易发生脱位。其中，前脱位较为常见。脱位的损伤机制通常为患者在张嘴时受到侧向打击，使下颌髁突从颞窝处向前脱出，可造成脱臼（完全脱位）或错位（部分脱位）。下颌脱臼的并发症包括反复性脱位、颞下颌关节紊乱和咬合不正。

（2）症状和体征

单侧或双侧颞下颌关节疼痛或压痛，咀嚼困难或咀嚼时疼痛。由于关节被卡住导致口开合受限。

（3）处理

可进行冰敷并用绷带固定。手法复位是急症治疗的首选方法。后期需要摄入软食，服用非甾体抗炎药。

3. 颞下颌关节紊乱

（1）病因

颞下颌关节紊乱是一种下颌活动受限的疾病，常伴有疼痛。常见病因有精神因素、创伤史以及咬合紊乱破坏了关节内部结构间功能的平衡。关节周围的肌肉、牙科疾病和由创伤或过度使用造成的关节软骨丧失，以及类风湿关节炎等系统性疾病等也会导致颞下颌关节紊乱。

（2）症状和体征

颞下颌关节紊乱最主要的临床表现有关节局部疼痛、关节弹响和下颌运动障碍，能引起头痛、眩晕、耳鸣、炎症以及与扳机点和肌肉僵硬相关的颈痛。

（3）处理

采用放松技术保守治疗，避免对颞下颌关节造成不必要的压力；也可使用物理治疗如热敷，其有助于放松周围的肌肉。若患者症状严重，可使用短期非甾体抗炎药或类固醇和局麻药混合物来缓解症状。如果上述矫正方法都无效，患者需转诊至牙医处进行治疗。

4. 颧骨复合体骨折

（1）病因

颧骨复合体骨折是面部骨折的第三大常见类型。直接打击可造成颧骨复合体骨折。此外，常见的原因还包括暴力、意外事故以及运动相关损伤。颧骨复合体骨折在男性中比在女性中更常见。

（2）症状和体征

颧骨处明显变平或凹陷，或可触及骨性差异。通常伴有鼻衄、口开合受限和咬合不正。患者常主诉出现复视、眼球运动受限和眼球内陷。此外还有颧骨处麻木、压痛和肿胀。

（3）处理

对患者进行冰敷以控制出血并快速转诊送至医生处。如果 X 射线检查显示骨折的颧骨向内压迫，应进行手术治疗。康复需要 6 ~ 8 周，当患者重新训练或比赛时需要佩戴适宜的护具。

5. 上颌骨骨折

（1）病因

上颌受到严重打击时会产生上颌骨骨折，常发生在橄榄球或棒球运动中。这种损伤属于面部骨折的第四大常见类型。

（2）症状和体征

上颌受到严重打击后，患者主诉咀嚼时疼痛，咬合不正，鼻出血，复视，以及唇、脸颊区域麻木。

（3）处理

由于上颌骨骨折出血量通常较大，需要确保患者气道畅通。需立即运送患者至医院，有意识的患者在运送过程中应保持直立前倾的姿势。具体的治疗方法为骨折复位、固定和制动。若手术治疗，一般在 6 ~ 8 周即可愈合。

（二）牙齿损伤

大多数运动相关的牙齿损伤是可以预防的，特别是接触性和碰撞性的项目（如篮球、橄榄球、足球）的运动员。通过使用合适的运动口腔防护器，如护齿套，可以吸收和分散创伤的冲击力，因此能减少（但不能消除）牙齿损伤的发生率。在平时应该注意保持牙齿卫生和清洁，包括常规的刷牙、漱口和牙线清洁。每个人每年都应该进行至少一次牙科检查以预防龋齿。

1. 牙齿断裂

（1）病因

牙齿断裂是牙齿坚硬的外壳破裂或开裂。牙齿的外层叫作牙釉质，它保护牙齿柔软的内髓，里面有神经和血管。任何对上颌或下颌的撞击或直接外伤都能引起断牙。

（2）症状和体征

单纯釉质断裂症状轻微，通常表现为牙冠边缘粗糙，断裂处没有出血，牙髓没有暴露。牙釉质－牙本质断裂有出血情况，牙髓被暴露。当暴露的牙本质接触到空气、冷饮，或被触摸时，会引起疼痛的感觉。牙釉质－牙本质－牙髓断裂是牙齿断裂中最复杂的，运动员会有急性疼痛。任何能引起牙齿断裂的撞击力也可导致下颌骨骨折甚至脑震荡。

（3）处理

先将断牙在装有生理盐水或脱脂牛奶的塑料袋中保存；运动员可佩戴防护牙托继续比赛，并在赛后 24 小时内到牙科进行处理。如果断牙处出血，将纱布覆盖在断裂处。不要随意推动损伤的牙齿，因为这样做会加剧断裂。

2. 牙齿脱臼与牙齿撕脱

（1）病因

任何对牙的撞击都可引起牙齿松动，牙齿松动能导致错位、脱位或撕脱。牙齿脱位是牙齿仍在牙槽内，仍有一些附着。牙齿撕脱是牙齿脱出，整个牙周韧带被切断，牙髓的血管和神经供应被切断。

（2）症状和体征

牙齿脱位时，牙齿虽没有断裂但松动明显，可向前或向后活动。牙齿撕脱时，牙齿完全从口腔中脱出。

（3）处理

牙齿脱位时，现场不用特殊处理，患者在口中轻轻咬合毛巾或湿纸巾以固定脱位的牙齿，然后尽快转诊至牙科进行处理。对于撕脱的牙齿，运动防护师可手捏牙冠冲洗撕脱牙根上的污垢，但不能刮或擦洗，再尝试植入撕脱的牙齿；如果无法再植入牙齿，可将牙齿保存在脱脂牛奶或生理盐水中（避免牙齿干燥），并尽快转诊至牙科进行处理。

3 Identification and Management of Eyes, Ears, Nose and Throat Injuries or Diseases

3.1 Eyes Injuries or Diseases

3.1.1 Eye Injuries

Eye injuries account for approximately 2% of all sports injuries. The incidence of eye damage in basketball, baseball, boxing, football, swimming and racket games is high. In sports such as ice hockey, rugby, hockey and squash, the athletes need to wear masks and helmets and goggles for training and competition.

3.1.2 Orbital Fractures

(1) Etiology

Strikes on the eyes or the area above the eyes may cause fractures at the top of the orbital cavity. The force acting on the eyeball causes it to move backwards, squeezing the fat inside the orbit until the bottom of the orbit bursts or fractures, resulting in orbital fractures around the eye. Boxing injuries and car accidents are common pathogenic factors for orbital fractures.

(2) Symptoms and Signs

Patients with orbital fractures usually have diplopia, downward displacement of the eyes, restricted eye movement, and pain with soft tissue swelling and bleeding. Patients may experience symptoms of pain, headache, and concussion.

(3) Management

Doctors need to use antibiotics preventively to reduce the likelihood of infection in patients. Conservative treatment can be used for patients with fractures which are minor or discontinued through CT. However, most orbital fractures require surgery.

3.1.3 Corneal Abrasions and Lacerations

(1) Etiology

Cornea is the most commonly injured part in the eyes. Patients often try to rub their eyes to remove objects entering the eye, which may cause corneal abrasion and lacerations by fingernails, foreign bodies and contact lenses. Most corneal abrasions are caused by mechanical injuries affecting the superficial epithelial layer.

(2) Symptoms and Signs

The patient complains of severe pain and grit-feeling, especially in bright light and when blinking, as well as watering of the eye, photophobia, and spasms of the orbicular muscle of the eyelid.

(3) Management

Clinical management of membrane abrasion includes the exclusion of penetrating wounds and intraocular foreign bodies, and then application of antibiotic ointment to the closed eyelid and semi-pressure dressing. An eye patch can be applied and the patient should be transported to the doctor in time.

3.1.4 Hyphema

(1) Etiology

A blunt impact to the front of the eye can cause anterior chamber bleeding, which is the accumulation of blood in the anterior chamber. Patients with a hyphema may suffer permanent damage, blindness or cataracts.

(2) Symptoms and Signs

After the injury, the anterior chamber of the eye turns red first, then the blood accumulates within 2 hours or fills the entire eye chamber, and the blood can change to pale green. Vision may be partially or completely lost. Iris loss may occur.

(3) Management

The patient with mild symptoms doesn't need emergency treatment and should rest and then consult the ophthalmologist within several days. However, the patient with severe vision loss and/or severe trauma should be referred to the doctor immediately. Routine treatment includes hospitalization, bed rest in a 30°–40° head elevation position, bandages on both eyes to control additional bleeding, sedation and medication to reduce anterior chamber pressure. Be aware that complications such as glaucoma may impair vision.

3.1.5 Acute Bacterial Conjunctivitis (Pink Eye)

(1) Etiology

Acute bacterial conjunctivitis is usually caused by different bacteria or allergens. Initially, the conjunctiva can be irritated by wind, dust, smoke or air pollution. It is also related to a common cold or other upper respiratory conditions.

(2) Symptoms and Signs

The patient complained of eyelid swelling, a burning sensation, sometimes purulent discharge, red and itchy eyes, scabby corners and eyelids, and blurred vision.

(3) Management

Acute bacterial conjunctivitis is highly infectious and must be isolated and prevented. Saline can be used to clean the eyes to remove the secretions, and then antibiotic eye drops can be applied, and there is no need to bandage. Prevention is important, including eye hygiene and avoiding rubbing eyes with hands.

3.1.6 Hordeolum and Blepharitis

(1) Etiology

A hordeolum is a swollen sebaceous gland at the edge of the eyelid. Blepharitis is an infection of an eyelash follicle. Infections are usually caused by Staphylococcus aureus invasion of the eyelash root sebaceous or meibomian glands, which spreads through friction or dust particles. Children and teenagers are susceptible to hordeolum, which could be recurrent.

(2) Symptoms and Signs

Patients with hordeolum will present with a swollen mass at or above the margin of the eyelid. The lesions can also be significantly edematous and may occasionally blur the patients' vision. The eyelid skin appears to have limited redness, swelling, heat, pain, and adjacent bulbar conjunctiva edema. The main manifestations include induration and dense yellow spots. The symptoms start with erythema on the eye and develop into pustules within a few days.

(3) Management

Most hordeolum will resolve spontaneously in less than 4 weeks. Treatment consists of the application of hot, moist compresses. Antibiotics and ointments are not necessary unless the entire lid becomes inflamed or infected. Surgery is needed if the regular treatment is ineffective.

3.2 Ear Injuries or Diseases

Athletes should wear ear muffs during training and competitions, and some ointment, such as Vaseline, can be applied to the ears of athletes who are prone to auricular hematoma. The best way to prevent ear infections is to dry the ears with a soft towel and use ear drops containing weak acid (3% boric acid) and alcohol solution before and after each swim to avoid the occurrence of ear infections.

3.2.1 Auricular Hematoma (Cauliflower Ear)

(1) Etiology

Hematoma of the auricle, also called cauliflower ear, usually causes subcutaneous hemorrhage to auricular cartilage after compression and shear injury in the auricle and ear cartilage ischemia necrosis. Necrotic tissue gradually becomes connective tissue, and fibrous connective tissue is prone to shrink, causing the auricle to gradually thicken and wrinkle, inducing a mass of prominences in various shapes. There will be gaps between the prominences, which makes the auricle like a cauliflower, and therefore, the auricular hematoma is also called cauliflower ear, which is common in boxing and wrestling.

(2) Symptoms and Signs

The symptom of auricular hematoma is the presence of many irregular raised scar tumors on the ear's surface, with folds and gaps in the middle resembling cauliflower, hard to touch, and often tender. The keloid often forms in the region of the helix fossa or concha. The keloid can only be removed through surgery once it occurs.

(3) Management

If the ears become red due to excessive rubbing or twisting, bleeding can be reduced by applying ice immediately. Once the ears become swollen, put the ice pack on the ears for at least 20 minutes with an elastic bandage. If the swelling is still present after the use of the ice pack, fluid extraction by a physician is needed.

3.2.2 Otitis Externa (Swimmer's Ear)

(1) Etiology

Otitis externa is an ear infection caused by Gram-negative bacteria and Pesudomonas pyocyaneum, which usually occurs in people engaged in aquatic activities. The main causes include local damage and dampness in ear canal.

(2) Symptoms and Signs

Symptoms include otalgia, itching, or fullness, with or without hearing loss. Signs include tenderness of the outer ear or diffuse ear-canal edema or erythema with or without otorrhea, regional lymphadenopathy, tympanic membrane erythema, or surrounding cellulitis.

(3) Management

Patients should be referred to a hospital immediately if they exhibit symptoms of external ear inflammation. The mainstays of treatment for otitis externa include pain control, treatment of infection, and avoiding precipitating factors. These goals are most often accomplished with an aural test, a topical antibiotic and topical steroid, and over-the-counter oral pain medication if needed. The addition of topical steroids can reduce ear canal edema and otorrhea and speed up pain relief.

3.2.3 Otitis Media (Middle Ear Infection)

(1) Etiology

Otitis media is the accumulation of fluid in the middle ear caused by local or systemic inflammation and infection. It is an inflammatory lesion involving all or parts of the middle ear (including the auditory tube, tympanum, tympanic sinus, and mastoid air chamber). Common pathogens are mainly pneumococcus, Haemophilus influenza, and so on.

(2) Symptoms and Signs

It is usually painful in the ear, with fluid flowing out of the ear canal, and temporary hearing loss. In addition, systemic infections can cause headaches, irritability, fever, anorexia, and nausea. The problem generally begins to resolve within 24 hours, although pain may last for 72 hours.

(3) Management

Analgesics can be used to relieve pain. The doctor can draw liquid from the middle ear to determine the most appropriate antibiotic therapy. Before application, boric acid or alcohol should be used to clean the external auditory canal and the pus in the middle ear cavity. Prevention of acute otitis media (AOM) recurrence is important to limit complications.

3.3 Nose Injuries or Diseases

3.3.1 Nasal Fractures

(1) Etiology

Nasal bone fracture is a common facial fracture. Due to the anatomical characteristics of protruding nasal bones on the body surface, they are more susceptible to external injuries. Blunt injuries such as traffic accidents, sports activities, disputes, and beatings are the leading causes of nasal bone fractures. Both frontal and lateral impacts can lead to nose injuries, while lateral impacts are more likely to lead to nose deformations.

(2) Symptoms and Signs

The nasal fracture appears frequently as a separation of the frontal processes of the maxilla, a separation of the lateral cartilages, or both of the above conditions. Due to the tear of the nasal mucosa, a large amount of bleeding may occur when the nasal bone is fractured, and edema will occur immediately. If the nose is hit from the side, deformity may occur. Abnormal movements and crepitus can be felt by shallow palpation. In severe cases, headache and loss of consciousness may occur, suggesting the possibility of intracranial injury.

(3) Management

Apply ice packs to the nose, but avoid pressing hard. If combined with nasal bleeding, pinch both sides of the nose while lowering patient's head to prevent blood from flowing to the pharynx. The patient should be then transferred to a doctor for X-ray examination and fracture reduction.

A simple fracture of the nasal bone does not pose a danger to the patient, and the game can resume after a few days. An important aspect of the nasal bone fracture treatment is the management of the nasal septum fracture regardless of whether the surgery involves a closed or an open reduction. Patients who suffer from nasal fractures require early diagnosis and treatment to prevent complications such as respiratory obstruction. Be careful to avoid collisions with the nose to prevent further injury. The nose clip can prevent the nose from being hit.

3.3.2 Epistaxis (Nosebleed)

(1) Etiology

Epistaxis (Nosebleed) is usually the result of a direct blow to the nose, causing varying degrees of nasal septal vibration. Significant epistaxis can also result from nasal or septal trauma and can be associated with underlying nasal bone fractures. Epistaxis can be divided into anterior or posterior epistaxis. The anterior epistaxis is more common. The causes of epistaxis include allergies, infection, high humidity, intranasal foreign body or other serious damage to the face or head.

(2) Symptoms and Signs

Nosebleeds have different manifestations due to different etiologies. Most nosebleeds are unilateral or bilateral, intermittent bleeding or continuous bleeding. The amount of bleeding varies. Light-headedness, chest pain, syncope and polypnea are the signs of severe blood loss.

(3) Management

Patients with acute nosebleeds should maintain an upright sitting position, lean forward, and press the bleeding side nasal wing towards the nasal septum for 5 minutes. In addition, a gauze roll should be placed between the upper lip and gums to press on the arteries at the nasal mucosa.

When the bleeding stops, the patient can resume exercise, but he should be reminded not to blow his nose for at least 2 hours after bleeding.

3.4 Throat Injuries (Contusions)

3.4.1 Etiology

Throat injuries do not occur frequently in sports, but occasionally an athlete suffers a blow to the throat. One type of trauma is known as "clothesline", in which a runner is hit in the throat by an opponent's outstretched arm while running.

3.4.2 Symptoms and Signs

The patient may experience severe pain, hoarseness, and spasmodic cough immediately and complain of difficulty in swallowing and breathing. Laryngeal cartilage fractures are rare, but if there is blood in the sputum or the patient can not breathe, a laryngeal cartilage fracture may occur.

3.4.3 Management

The airway of patients with laryngeal contusion should be kept open, and patients with difficulty breathing should be immediately taken to an emergency department. The primary issue is to ensure airway patency. In most cases, intermittent ice compress should be applied to control surface bleeding and swelling, and hot compresses should be performed after the acute phase. For most neck contusions, it is best to use a neck brace. For severe cases, surgeries are necessary.

三、常见眼、耳、鼻、喉部伤病的识别和处理

（一）眼部伤病

1. 眼部损伤

眼部损伤约占所有运动损伤的 2%。篮球、棒球、拳击、足球、游泳和持拍类运动中发生眼部损伤的概率较高。很多运动项目，如冰球、橄榄球、曲棍球和壁球等运动员需要佩戴头盔、面罩或护目镜进行训练和比赛。

2. 眼眶骨折

（1）病因

对眼睛或眼睛上方区域的打击可能会导致眼眶顶部骨折。眼球受到的作用力使眼球向后移动，挤压眼眶内脂肪直至眼眶底部爆裂或断裂，从而导致眼睛周围的眼眶骨折。拳击伤和车祸是眼眶骨折的常见致病因素。

（2）症状和体征

眼眶骨折患者通常发生复视、眼球下移、眼动受限以及疼痛，并伴有软组织肿胀和出血，患者会出现眼眶疼痛、头痛以及脑震荡的症状。

（3）处理

医生需要预防性地使用抗生素以降低患者感染的可能性。对于 CT 显示轻微裂隙或骨折不连续者，保守治疗即可。大多数眼眶骨折需要手术治疗。

3. 角膜擦伤和撕裂伤

（1）病因

常见的眼部损伤部位是角膜，患者经常试图以揉搓眼睛来清除眼中异物，有可能因指甲、眼中异物或接触性隐形眼镜使角膜擦伤或轻微撕裂。大多数角膜擦伤是由影响表层上皮的机械损伤引起的。

（2）症状和体征

患者主诉严重的疼痛和沙砾感，尤其是在明亮的光线下及眨眼时。症状还包括泪液分泌、畏光、眼睑轮匝肌痉挛。

（3）处理

角膜擦伤的临床处理包括首先排除穿透性伤口和眼内异物，然后用抗生素药膏涂抹至闭合的眼睑处并进行半压力包扎。可以使用眼罩，要及时将患者送至医生处。

4. 眼前房出血

（1）病因

钝性撞击眼前部可导致眼前房出血，即血液积聚在前房。眼前房积血的患者可能遭受眼部永久性损伤、失明或患白内障。

（2）症状和体征

损伤后眼前房处先变为红色，随后在 2 小时内血液向后积聚，或可充满整个眼房，血液可变为淡绿色。视力部分或完全消失，有时可能会发生虹膜脱落。

（3）处理

如果只有轻微症状，没有必要急诊治疗，伤者应当休息并在几天之内咨询眼科医生。大多数出血伴有严重视力下降或严重创伤者，应立即被转诊至医生处。常规治疗包括住院、以头部抬高至 30°～40° 体位卧床休息、双眼使用绷带控制额外的出血、保持镇静、服药以降低眼前房压力。注意，并发症如青光眼可能会损伤视力。

5. 急性细菌性结膜炎（红眼病）

（1）病因

急性细菌性结膜炎可由多种细菌或过敏原引起。初期可因风、灰尘、烟或空气污染刺激结膜引起，还与普通感冒或其他上呼吸道病症有关。

（2）症状和体征

患者主诉眼睑肿胀，有灼烧感，有时出现脓性分泌物，眼睛发红、瘙痒，眼角和眼睑结痂，视力模糊。

（3）处理

急性细菌性结膜炎具有高传染性，必须做好隔离和预防。处理原则一般为使用生理盐水对眼部进行清洁，使眼部的分泌物去除，再利用抗生素眼药水进行治疗，无须包扎。预防方面主要注意用眼卫生，不可使用手部揉眼。

6. 睑腺炎和睑缘炎

（1）病因

睑腺炎是眼睑边缘的皮脂腺肿胀。睑缘炎是睫毛毛囊的感染。感染通常是由金黄色葡萄球菌入侵睫毛根部皮脂腺或睑板腺引起的急性化脓性炎症，葡萄球菌通过摩擦或尘埃颗粒扩散。多发于青少年及儿童，较易反复。

（2）症状和体征

睑腺炎患者会在眼睑边缘或上方出现肿物。病变也可明显水肿，偶尔可使患者的视力模糊。眼睑皮肤局限性红、肿、热、痛，邻近球结膜水肿。出现硬结及黄色致密斑点为主要临床表现。病症以眼部红斑开始，在数天内发展成脓疱。

（3）处理

大多数睑腺炎在四周内自行消退。治疗方法为湿热敷。通常不需要使用抗生素和涂抹药膏，除非整个眼睑发炎或感染。对于常规治疗无效者，需手术切除。

（二）耳部伤病

运动员应该在训练和比赛时佩戴耳罩，可在易发生耳廓血肿的耳部涂抹一些润滑剂，如凡士林。预防耳部感染的最佳方法是使用软毛巾擦干耳朵，在每次游泳前后使用含弱酸（3%硼酸）和酒精溶液的滴耳剂，避免耳部感染。

1.耳廓血肿（菜花耳）

（1）病因

耳廓血肿也称为菜花耳。耳廓受到挤压剪切力损伤后引起皮下出血至耳廓软骨，导致耳廓软骨缺血坏死，坏死组织逐渐机化成为结缔组织，纤维结缔组织易发生收缩，致使耳廓逐渐变厚而且皱缩，表面出现许多不规则形态的突起，突起间又有深浅不等的皱缩间隙，形如菜花，因而称之为菜花耳畸形。耳廓血肿常见于拳击和摔跤项目中。

（2）症状和体征

耳廓血肿的症状为在耳部表面有很多不规则的突起的瘢痕瘤，中间是皱褶缝隙，状似菜花，触之坚硬，常有压痛。瘢痕瘤通常在耳轮窝或耳甲处形成，一旦形成，只能通过手术矫正。

（3）处理

如果耳朵由于过度摩擦或扭曲而发红，立即冰敷可缓解出血。一旦耳部出现肿胀，应马上用弹性绷带将冰袋置于耳朵上至少20分钟。如果在冰敷后仍有肿胀，需由医生进行抽液治疗。

2.外耳炎（游泳耳）

（1）病因

外耳炎是由革兰氏阴性细菌和绿脓杆菌引起的耳部感染，多发于从事水中项目的人群。主要病因是局部损伤和潮湿的耳道环境。

（2）症状和体征

外耳炎症状包括耳痛、瘙痒或饱胀，伴有或不伴有听力损失。体征包括外耳压痛或弥漫性耳道水肿，可能伴耳漏的红斑、局部淋巴结病、鼓膜红斑或周围蜂窝织炎。

（3）处理

当患者表现出外耳炎症状时，应立即转诊至医院。外耳炎治疗的核心包括疼痛控制、感染治疗和避免诱发因素。这些通常是通过听觉测试、局部抗生素和局部类固醇以及非处方口服镇痛药来实现的。添加局部类固醇可减少耳道水肿和耳漏，并加速疼痛缓解。

3. 中耳炎（中耳感染）

（1）病因

中耳炎是由局部或系统性炎症和感染引起的液体在中耳处积聚，累及中耳（包括咽鼓管、鼓室、鼓窦及乳突气房）全部或部分结构的炎性病变。常见的致病菌主要是肺炎球菌、流感嗜血杆菌等。

（2）症状和体征

中耳炎症状一般为耳痛，耳道有液体流出，短暂性听力减弱。此外，系统性感染可导致头痛、易怒、发烧、厌食和恶心。中耳炎一般在 24 小时内开始发作至消退，但疼痛可能会持续 72 小时。

（3）处理

可使用镇痛药缓解疼痛，医生可从中耳处取液来选择最适宜的抗生素进行治疗，用药前需要先用硼酸或酒精清除外耳道以及中耳腔内的脓液。预防急性中耳炎复发对于限制并发症非常重要。

（三）鼻部损伤

1. 鼻骨骨折

（1）病因

鼻骨骨折是常见的面部骨折。由于鼻骨突出体表的解剖特点使其较易受到外力伤害。交通事故、体育运动、纠纷殴打等钝性创伤是鼻骨骨折的主要原因。正面和侧面的撞击均可引起鼻部受伤，且侧面撞击引起的变形程度大于正面。

（2）症状和体征

鼻骨骨折常表现为上颌骨额突偏曲、外软骨偏曲或同时有上述两种情况。由于鼻黏膜撕裂，鼻骨骨折时可大量出血，立即产生水肿。如鼻部受到侧向打击，可使鼻部变形。浅触诊能感觉到活动异常且有捻发音。严重时出现头痛和意识丧失，提示有颅内损伤的可能。

（3）处理

用冰袋等对鼻背部冷敷，但尽量避免用力按压。若合并鼻腔出血，可捏住双侧鼻翼，同时低头，以防止血液流向咽部。随后将患者转诊至医生处进行 X 射线检查和骨折复位。

单纯鼻骨骨折不会对患者造成危险，患者在数天后可恢复训练或比赛。无论手术是闭合复位还是开放复位，鼻骨骨折治疗的一个重要干预措施是鼻中隔损伤的处理。患者需要早期的诊断和治疗以防止并发症，如呼吸阻塞。注意避免鼻部的碰撞，防止再次受伤。使用鼻夹有一定的保护作用。

2. 鼻衄（鼻出血）

（1）病因

鼻衄通常为鼻部受到直接打击的结果，引起不同程度的鼻中隔震动。鼻腔或鼻中隔损伤导致严重鼻出血，并可能与潜在的鼻骨骨折有关。鼻衄可分为前侧或后侧，前侧鼻衄更为常见。鼻出血的原因还涉及许多其他因素，包括过敏、感染、湿度大、鼻内异物或其他面部或头部严重损伤。

（2）症状和体征

鼻出血由于原因不同所以表现各异，多数鼻出血为单侧，也可为双侧；可间歇性反复出血，也可持续性出血，出血量多少不一。失血严重时，出现头晕、胸痛、晕厥和呼吸急促。

（3）处理

急性鼻出血患者应保持直立坐位，身体前倾，将出血侧鼻翼压向鼻中隔5分钟，另外应将纱布卷置于上唇和牙龈之间，以按压住鼻黏膜处的动脉。

出血停止后，患者可恢复运动，但应提醒患者在出血后至少2小时内都不要擤鼻涕。

（四）喉部损伤（挫伤）

1. 病因

在体育运动中，喉部损伤的概率并不高，但偶尔有运动员喉部被击中的情况。其中有一种外伤称作"伸臂抱颈阻截"，即运动员在跑动中，喉部被对手伸出的胳膊击中。

2. 症状和体征

受伤后，患者会立即感到剧痛，声音嘶哑，痉挛性咳嗽以及主诉吞咽困难甚至出现呼吸困难。喉软骨骨折较少见，但如出现无法呼吸以及痰中带血则表明喉软骨有骨折的可能。

3. 处理

喉部挫伤应保持呼吸道通畅，呼吸困难的患者应被立即送往急救机构。首要的问题是要确保气道的通畅性，应进行间歇性冰敷以控制表面出血和肿胀，急性期过后进行热敷。针对大多数颈部挫伤，最好使用颈托固定。严重者需要进行手术治疗。

Summary

1. Concussion may be caused either by a direct blow to the head, face, neck, or elsewhere on the body with an "impulsive" force transmitted to the head. In addition, care should be taken to prevent secondary collisions.

2. Injuries to the face could involve fractures of the mandible, maxilla, or zygoma, dislocations of the mandible and temporomandibular dysfunction. These injuries often occur in contact sports, and protective face masks can be worn, which can greatly reduce the incidence of facial injuries.

3. Any impacts or direct trauma to the upper or lower jaw can cause broken teeth. Protective braces should be worn in all sports to prevent tooth damage, particularly those in contact/collision sports (e.g. basketball, rugby and football).

4. Nasal bone fractures are the most common facial fractures due to the prominent anatomic characteristics of nasal bone. Nasal bone is easy to be injured by external forces. Patients who have nasal fractures require early diagnosis and treatment to prevent complications such as

respiratory obstruction.

5. Ear injuries are uncommon in sports, but repeated blows or pressure on the ear, such as in boxing and wrestling can cause bleeding. If untreated, it can lead to cauliflower ears. Cauliflower ear (auricular hematoma) is common in wrestlers and usually causes subcutaneous hemorrhage to auricular cartilage after compression. It can be treated with aspiration and ice compress.

6. Eye injuries are common in baseball, basketball, boxing, and racquets. Athletes may experience vision loss, blurry vision, double vision, or corneal deformation. Some non-urgent eye conditions are corneal abrasions. Other emergent eye conditions include hyphema, orbital wall fractures.

7. In sports, the probability of throat injury is not high, but it occasionally occurs. The airway of patients with laryngeal contusion should be kept open. Patients with difficulty breathing should be immediately taken to an emergency facility.

⭕ Review Questions

1. What inspections should we do on the football player who has a concussion?

2. How to prevent head facial injury effectively?

3. A volleyball player slipped in the locker room and broke a tooth. He brought the broken tooth to you. What should you do as an athletic trainer?

4. What is cauliflower ear? What's the cause?

小结

1. 脑震荡可能是由头部、面部、颈部或身体其他部位受到直接打击，并向头部传递"冲击力"引起的。此外，需要注意预防二次撞击。

2. 面部受伤可能包括下颌骨、上颌骨或颧骨骨折，下颌脱臼，颞下颌关节功能障碍。这些损伤经常发生于接触性运动。可佩戴保护性的面罩，其可以很大程度上减少面部损伤。

3. 任何对上颌或下颌的撞击或直接外伤都能引起断牙。所有运动项目中都应佩戴防护牙托以预防牙齿损伤，特别是在具有接触性和碰撞性的项目（如篮球、橄榄球、足球）中。

4. 鼻骨骨折是常见的面部骨折。由于鼻骨突出体表的解剖特点使其较易受到外力伤害。患者需要早期的诊断和治疗。以防止并发症，如呼吸阻塞。

5. 耳部的损伤在运动中并不常见，但重复地击打或压迫耳部，如拳击和摔跤等，可导致出血，如果不治疗可导致耳廓血肿。耳廓血肿在摔跤运动员中很常见，通常是由于耳廓受到挤压损伤后引起的。它可以通过冰敷和抽液来治疗。

6. 眼部损伤在棒球、篮球、拳击和持拍类运动中很常见，运动员可能会出现视力下降、视力模糊、复视、角膜变形等。一些较轻微的眼部损伤是角膜擦伤。严重的眼部情况包括眼前房积血、眼眶骨折。

7. 在体育运动中，喉部损伤的概率并不高，但偶有发生。喉部挫伤应保持呼吸道通畅，呼吸困难的患者应被立即送往急救机构。

○ 复习题

1. 对足球赛场上发生脑震荡的运动员应该做哪些检查？

2. 如何有效预防头部、面部损伤？

3. 一名排球运动员在更衣室滑倒导致一颗牙齿断裂，他将断掉的牙齿拿给你，作为运动防护师，你该怎么做？

4. 什么是耳廓血肿？产生的原因是什么？

PART IV Athletic Training in Traditional Chinese Medicine

第四部分　中医运动防护

Chapter 1 The Basic Theories of Athletic Training in Traditional Chinese Medicine
第一章　中医运动防护理论基础

○ Main Contents

1. Outline of traditional Chinese medicine basic theory.
2. Outline of acupoints, meridians and collaterals.

○ 主要内容

1. 中医基础理论概要。
2. 经络腧穴概要。

1 Outline of Traditional Chinese Medicine Basic Theory

The theories and methods of Traditional Chinese Medicine (TCM) are widely used in the field of competitive sports in China, in which acupuncture, tuina, traditional Chinese exercise, Chinese herbs and other therapeutic techniques are applied in the prevention and rehabilitation of various acute and chronic sports injuries/diseases, which have made outstanding contributions to the competitive sports in China. The technique of athletic training in TCM is based on the basic theories of TCM, with holism running through it, and to prevent and treat sports injuries and diseases from the perspective of syndrome differentiation.

1.1 The Basic Characteristics of Traditional Chinese Medicine

1.1.1 Holism

Holism is a unified, integrated and interrelated view. TCM theory holds that the human body is an organic entirety, which is closely related to nature and is influenced by society. This view on the human body as well as the spirit and the unity of the internal and external environment is called the holism concept.

The unity of the human body is based on the concept of the unity of the five *zang* organs and the six *fu* organs as the center through the meridian system. The meridians belong to the internal organs, and are connected to the extremities. Five *zang* organs constitute five systems of the body, through the meridian system to link the whole body organically, and form a complete unity of up and down communication, close coordination and mutual cooperation, realizing the integrity of the functional activities of the body's *qi*, blood and body fluids.

1.1.2 Treatment Based on Syndrome Differentiation

In TCM, treatment based on syndrome differentiation is the basic method to diagnose and treat diseases. It is a clinical characteristic and one of the basic characteristics.

The key to differentiation is "discrimination". "Discrimination" means to distinguish, determine, and to analyze other elements. The so-called "syndrome", including "symptom" and "signs", is a total sum of disease pathology of the body in a certain stage of the disease development. Differentiation is to collect data regarding signs and symptoms of the disease by four diagnostic methods (inspection, olfaction and auscultation, inquiry and palpation), then under the guidance of TCM theory, by comparison, analysis and synthesis, to discern the reasons, nature, location, stage of development and relationship between health and pathogenic of the disease, in the end to summarize and judge as a syndrome. Therefore, the whole process of differentiation is applied by comprehensive analysis, reasoning, judgment and diagnosis.

On the basis of differentiation, treatment is to select the appropriate treatment and establish the corresponding treatment principles and methods. Differentiation is the premise and basis of treatment, while treatment refers to means and methods to cure diseases. They are both closely connected.

1.2 The Foundation of Chinese Philosophy of Traditional Chinese Medicine

1.2.1 Yin-Yang

Yin-yang theory holds that the natural world is made up of material, and the material world is generated, developed and constantly changed under the interaction of yin and yang.

The original meanings of yin and yang are simple and specific, mainly referring to the sides in the opposite or same direction to the sunlight. That is to say that anything that is exposed to the sun belongs to yang while that unexposed to the sun belongs to yin. Later, yin and yang symbolize two opposite and related sides in the natural world, such as cold and heat, downside and upside, day and night, darkness and brightness, water and fire, motionless and motion, etc. In a word, anything that is warm, bright, positive, exterior and upward belongs to yang, whereas anything freezing, dark, static, interior and downward belongs to yin.

Yin-yang theory is an abstract theory describing the opposition of two antithetical elements in the natural world. Yin and yang represent either two things in opposition or two opposite sides of a single entity. Based on the different characteristics of yin and yang, all things in the universe can be classified as one or the other. However, the yin-yang nature of things is relative, not absolute, and anything in the universe that is classified as yin or yang can be further divided into another pair of yin and yang infinitely.

The contents of yin-yang theory include opposition of yin and yang, mutual rooting of yin and yang, waning and waxing of yin and yang, and mutual convertibility of yin-yang.

It is believed in TCM that all the tissues and organs in the body are organically related to each other and these tissues and organs can also be signified by yin or yang. Generally speaking, the upper part of the body pertains to yang while the lower to yin; the body surface belongs to yang while the interior to yin; the back pertains to yang while the abdomen to yin; the lateral sides of the four limbs pertain to yang while the medial sides to yin.

The theory of yin-yang holds that human life activity is the outcome of keeping coordination between the two sides of yin-yang.

The material and functions that can promote, warm and excite the body pertain to yang, such as qi, while those which nourish and moisten the body pertain to yin, such as blood.

1.2.2 Five Phases

Five phases refer to five categories of things in the natural world, namely wood, fire, earth, metal, and water, and their movements, transformations and interrelationships.

The theory of the five phases holds that all things in the natural world can be classified by wood, fire, earth, metal and water and maintain a harmonious balance (Table 1-1).

Table 1-1 Five Phases Classification

Five phases	Five zang	six fu	Five orifices	Body	Five emotions
wood	liver	Gallbladder	eye	tendon	anger
fire	heart	small intestine	tongue	vessels	joy
earth	spleen	stomach	mouth	meat	contemplation
metal	lung	large intestine	nose	skin	grief
water	kidney	bladder	ear	bone	fear

一、中医基础理论概要

中国传统医学的理论和方法广泛应用于我国竞技体育领域中，其中针灸、推拿、传统功法、中药等治疗技术在各种急慢性运动创伤及运动性疾病的预防和康复中的应用，为我国竞技体育事业做出了突出贡献。中医运动防护技术以中医基础理论为根本，以整体观贯穿始终，以辨证论治的观点进行运动伤病的预防和治疗。

（一）中医学的基本特点

1. 整体观

整体观是统一的、完整的和相互关联的观点。中医理论认为，人体是一个有机的整体，它和自然界紧密地相关联并受到社会条件的影响，这种认为形与神以及内外环境相统一的观点称为整体观念。

人体的整体统一性，是以五脏为中心，配以六腑，通过经络系统"内属于脏腑、外络于肢节"的联系作用而实现的。人体以五脏为中心，通过经络系统的联系成为有机的整体，形成一个上下沟通、密切协调、相互协作的完整的统一体，实现了人体气、血、津液的功能活动的完整性。

2. 辨证论治

辨证论治，是中医诊断和治病的基本方法，它是中医学的临床特点和基本特征之一。

辨证的关键是"辨"。"辨"是区分、判定以及对其他要素的辨析。所谓"证"，包含"症状"和"证据"，即在疾病发展过程中某一阶段人体的疾病病理的总和。辨证就是将四诊（望、闻、问、切）所收集的有关疾病的所有资料，运用中医学理论进行分析、综合，辨清疾病的原因、性质、部位及发展趋向，然后概括、判断为某种性质的证候的过程。因此，辨证就是综合分析、推理、判断和诊断疾病的全过程。

论治，是在辨证的基础上选择适当的治疗方式，确立相应的治疗原则和方法。辨证是论治的前提和基础，而论治是治疗疾病的方法，它们都是紧密联系的。

（二）中医学的中华哲学基础

1. 阴阳

阴阳学说认为自然世界是物质的，而物质世界的产生、发展和不断变化是阴阳双方相互作用的结果。

阴和阳的原义是简单而具体的，主要是面对阳光的反正方向。也就是说，任何面向阳光的一面属于阳而背向阳光的一面属于阴。随后阴阳的含义发展为象征着在自然世界中两个相反的相关方，如冷和热、下行和上行、黑夜和白天、黑暗与光明、水和火、静与动等。总之，如果事物是温暖的、明亮的、积极的、外部的、向上的就属于阳；反之，冰冷的、黑暗的、静态的、内部的和向下的就属阴。

阴阳是描述自然世界中两个对立方的抽象理论。阴和阳既可以代表两个对立的事物也可以代表一个事物内部相反的两个方面。宇宙中所有的事物均可以划分为一阴或一阳，而事物的阴阳属性是相对的，不是绝对的，且任何事物分为阴或阳之后，又可再进一步分为另一对阴阳。

阴阳学说的基本内容包括阴阳对立、阴阳相成、阴阳消长、阴阳转化。

中医学认为人体的所有组织和器官之间保持着有机的相互联系，人体的组织和器官同样也可以划分为阴或阳。通常位于身体上部的属于阳，下部属于阴；体表属阳，体内属阴；背属阳，腹属阴；四肢外侧属阳，内侧属阴。

阴阳学说认为，人的生命活动是由阴阳双方保持协调的结果。

相互促进的物质和功能中具有温暖、兴奋作用的属阳，如气；反之，具有营养、滋润作用的属阴，如血。

2. 五行

五行指的是自然世界中的五类事物，即木、火、土、金、水，以及它们的运动、变化及相互关系。

五行学说认为，自然界的一切事物都可以用木、火、土、金、水进行分类并维持平衡。

2 Outline of Meridians and Acupoints

This section mainly introduces the abstract of meridians and acupoints. The meridian system is an important part of the human body structure, which runs the qi and blood of the whole body, connects the *zang-fu*, body and organs, communicates with the inside and outside, and conducts information. Acupoints are special parts of the body where the qi and blood from the zang-fu organs and meridians are infused into the body surface. They are not only the reaction sites of the disease but also the stimulation sites of TCM treatment. In the overview of meridians and acupoints, the concept and composition of meridians are introduced as a whole, and the definition and classification of acupoints are explained. TCM believes that by stimulating the relevant acupoints of the body and generating stimulation, this stimulation can be transmitted along the meridians to the organs to play the role of acupoint therapy. The meridian theory is the key point of TCM and the focus of integration of traditional Chinese and Western medicine. It also has a wide range of applications for TCM athletic training.

2.1 General Introduction of Meridians

2.1.1 Concept of Meridians

The meridians are the pathways that transport *qi* and blood, and connect the internal *zang-fu* organs with the surface and other parts of the body, which are also called "*Jing*" and "*Luo*" in Chinese. "Jing" originally means "pathways", which are the main components of the meridian system and travel at a relatively deeper level in an upward-downward fashion. "*Luo*" means "network", which is translated as branches of the meridian system and runs superficially and transversely all over the body like a net.

The meridian system is composed of the system of the channels, which includes twelve regular channels, the eight extra channels and the twelve divergent meridians, the twelve muscle regions, and the twelve cutaneous regions attached to the twelve regular channels, and the system of the collaterals, which includes the fifteen collaterals, the superficial collaterals and tertiary collaterals.

2.1.2 Composition of Twelve Regular Channels

The twelve main Channels are associated with the *zang-fu* organs, which include the three yin Channels of the hand (the lung Channel of hand-*taiyin*, the heart Channel of hand-*shaoyin* and the pericardium Channel of hand-*jueyin*), the three yang Channels of the hand (the large intestine Channel of hand-*yangming*, the small intestine Channel of hand-*taiyang* and the triple energizer Channel of hand-*shaoyang*), the three yang Channels of the foot (the stomach Channel of foot-*yangming*, the bladder Channel of foot-*taiyang* and the gallbladder Channel of foot-*shaoyang*), the three yin Channels of the foot (the spleen Channel of foot-*taiyin*, the kidney Channel of foot-*shaoyin* and the liver Channel of foot-*jueyin*).

2.2 General Introduction of Acupoints

2.2.1 Concept of Acupoints

"Shu Xue" are places for acupuncture and moxibustion, also known as points, acupoints or acupuncture points. They are specific sites where the qi and blood of *zang-fu* organs and meridians transport to the body's surface. There is a close relationship among points, *zang-fu* organs and meridians. A meridian point is distributed along the course of a meridian and the meridian links with certain *zang-fu* organs, so there exists a close link between the points and internal *zang-fu* organs. Acupoints are not only the reflecting places of disorders but also the sites to receive stimulation by TCM.

2.2.2 Classification of Acupoints

Meridian points are short for "points of the fourteen meridians", which are affiliated to twelve regular meridians plus governor vessel and conception vessel and distribute along the fourteen meridian roads. A meridian point has a definite name, fixed location and specific indication . There are 362 meridian points still used today.

"Acupoint beyond meridians'' or "extra points'' for short are points that have definite locations but have not been recognized as points of the fourteen meridians. Extra points have specific names and effective indications.

An Ashi-Point refers to the site which is neither a point of the fourteen meridians nor an extra point, but merely the tender spot instead. Ashi-Points are usually seen around the lesion or far from the lesion. Those points are the tender spots or other reflecting spots functioning as acupoints. This kind of points have neither definite names nor fixed locations.

二、经络与腧穴概要

本节主要介绍了经络和腧穴的概要。经络是运行全身气血、联络脏腑形体官窍、沟通上下内外、感应传导信息的通路系统，是人体结构的重要组成部分。腧穴是人体脏腑经络之气血输注于体表的特殊部位，既是疾病的反应处，也是中医治病的刺激部位。在经络腧穴概述中，从整体上介绍了经络的概念和组成，阐释了腧穴的定义和分类。传统中医学认为是通过对机体相关穴位产生刺激，并使这种刺激沿着经络向所属脏器传递来发挥经穴治疗的作用。经络学说是中医学的灵魂，也是中西医结合的焦点，在中医运动防护中有着广泛的应用。

（一）经络概述

1. 经络的概念

经络是经脉和络脉的简称，是运行气血、联络脏腑、沟通内外的通道。"经"，有"路径"的含义，以上下纵行为主，为经络体系的主体部分；"络"，有"网络"的含义，从经脉中分出侧行，为经络体系的分支部分。

经络系统由经脉系统和络脉系统组成，其中经脉系统包括十二经脉、奇经八脉，以及附属于十二经脉的十二经别、十二经筋、十二皮部；络脉系统包括十五络脉、浮络及孙络等。

2. 十二经脉的组成

十二经脉是指脏腑所属的经脉，包括手三阴经（手太阴肺经、手少阴心经、手厥阴心包经），手三阳经（手阳明大肠经、手太阳小肠经、手少阳三焦经），足三阳经（足阳明胃经、足太阳膀胱经、足少阳胆经），以及足三阴经（足太阴脾经、足少阴肾经、足厥阴肝经）。

（二）腧穴概述

1.腧穴的概念

腧穴是人体脏腑经络之气血输注于体表的特殊部位。腧穴与脏腑、经络有密切关系，由于经穴属于经脉，经脉又联络脏腑，所以经穴与脏腑有密切关系。腧穴既是疾病的反应处，也是中医治病的刺激部位。

2.腧穴的分类

经穴，即"十四经穴"的简称，是指归属于十二经脉和任、督二脉的腧穴。经穴有具体的穴名，分布在十四经循行路线上，有明确的定位和主治症。经穴总数为362个。

"经外奇穴"简称"奇穴"，是指未归入十四经穴范围而有具体的位置和名称的腧穴。

阿是穴，是指该处既不是经穴，也不是奇穴，只是以压痛点取穴。阿是穴多见于病变附近，也可在与其距离较远处，以压痛或其他反应点作为刺灸的部位。这类穴既无具体名称，也无固定位置。

Summary

1. The technique of athletic training in TCM is based on the basic theories of TCM, with a holism running through it, and preventing and treating sports injuries and diseases based on the perspective of syndrome differentiation.

2. The meridian system is an important part of the human body structure, which runs the *qi* and blood of the whole body, connects the *zang-fu*, body and organs, communicates with the inside and outside, and conducts information.

3. Acupoints are special parts of the body where the qi and blood from the internal organs and meridians are infused into the body surface. They are not only the reaction site of the disease but also the stimulation site of TCM treatment.

○ Review Question

1. What are the main characteristics of the theoretical system of TCM?

2. What are the meanings and basic contents of yin-yang?

3. What is the composition of the meridian system?

4. What are the basic concepts of acupoints and their classification?

小结

1. 中医运动防护技术以中医基础理论为根本，以整体观贯穿始终，以辨证论治的观点进行运动伤病的预防和治疗。

2. 经络是运行全身气血，联络脏腑形体官窍，沟通上下内外，感应、传导信息的通路系统，是人体结构的重要组成部分。

3. 腧穴是人体脏腑经络之气血输注于体表的特殊部位，既是疾病的反应处，也是中医治病的刺激部位。

复习题

1. 中医理论体系的主要特点包括哪些内容？

2. 阴阳的含义及其基本内容有哪些？

3. 经络系统由什么组成？

4. 腧穴的基本概念及其分类分别是什么？

Chapter 2 Techniques of Athletic Training in Traditional Chinese Medicine

第二章　中医运动防护技术

○ Main Contents

1. *Cupping* therapy.
2. *Guasha* therapy.
3. *Tuina* therapy.
4. *Daoyin* therapy.

○ 主要内容

1. 拔罐。
2. 刮痧。
3. 推拿手法。
4. 导引疗法。

In the prevention and management of sports injuries/diseases, the commonly used protection and rehabilitation techniques guided by the theory of TCM include clinical treatment techniques such as *cupping*, *Guasha*, *Tuina* and acupuncture, and exercise therapy techniques such as *daoyin*, Tai Chi and Chinese Medical *Qigong*. In the field of competitive sports and national fitness in China, these technologies have been widely used, providing valuable resources for professional athletes and fitness enthusiasts in sports injury prevention and rehabilitation, health promotion and other aspects. It is necessary for Chinese athletic trainers to understand and learn the experience and achievements of TCM in this field.

在运动伤病预防和治疗中，以中医理论为指导的常用防护和康复手段不仅包括了拔罐、刮痧、推拿、毫针针刺等临床治疗技术，也包括了以太极拳以及健身气功等经典导引功法为代表的运动治疗技术。在我国竞技体育和全民健身领域，这些技术都有着广泛的运用，在运动伤病预防和康复、健康促进等方面为专业运动员、健身爱好者提供了宝贵的保障资源。在我国开展运动防护工作，有必要了解和学习中医在这方面的经验成果。

1 *Cupping* Therapy

Cupping therapy is to exhaust the air inside the cup to cause negative pressure, so that it adsorbs on the body's acupoints or the surface of a specific part, causing local skin congestion and stasis to produce stimulation, promote local blood vessel expansion, accelerate metabolism, improve tissue microcirculation, in order to achieve the effect of blood circulation and pain relief. When the muscles and muscular fasciae are under tension, local blood circulation is blocked and the tissue is ischemic. *Cupping*, especially moving *cupping*, can stretch muscles and fascia, increase blood perfusion, so that muscles can be relaxed, and fatigue can be relieved, and it plays a similar role to massage. *Cupping* can significantly increase the local pain threshold and tolerance threshold of *cupping*, significantly reduce the pain intensity, and significantly improve the dysfunction caused by pain. At the same time, when *cupping*, oxygen and hemoglobin content of the local tissue are increased, which can reduce delayed muscle soreness, and thus achieve athletic training.

Three types that are most commonly used are bamboo cups, glass cups, and suction cups. According to practical demands, choosing cups of different sizes (Figure 2-1).

1.1 *Cupping* Methods

Ignite a 95% alcohol-soaked cotton ball held with tweezers, put the flame into the cup and circle the flame inside it 2 to 3 times. Remove the flame and place the cup onto the skin very quickly. This is a safe and commonly used method (Figure 2-2, 2-3).

Figure 2-1

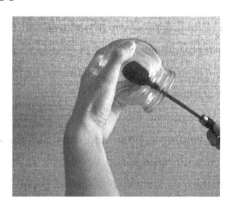

Figure 2-2   Figure 2-3

1.2 Moving *Cupping* Therapy

It is also known as "sliding *cupping*". A lubricant should be applied to the skin over the treatment area before using this method. Once suction has been created, the cup is held and slid across the skin until it becomes rosy and congested, or even blood stagnation is seen. It's suitable for treating large, thickly-muscled areas such as the back, lumbar region and the thighs.

1.3 Quick *Cupping* Therapy

This method is done by rapidly placing and removing the cup repeatedly over the same place until the skin turns red. The method does for the situations where it is inadvisable to use retention *cupping*, such as with kids and on the cheeks of young ladies.

1.4 Removing the Cup

When removing a cup, it should be held in one hand, while the index finger and thumb of the opposite hand press the skin around the mouth of the cup to break the seal created by the suction. In this way, the air is let in and the cup is released. If the strength of suction is too strong, do not forcibly lift or rotate the cup.

1.5 The Function and Indications of *Cupping*

Cupping therapy has the action of activating meridians and collaterals, invigorating qi and blood circulation, relieving blood stagnation, alleviating pain and swelling and dispelling dampness and cold. With this extensive range of indications, it's commonly applied for rheumatic pain, soft tissue damage, colds, coughs, asthma, indigestion, epigastric pain, dizziness, abdominal pain, dysmenorrhea, headaches and other diseases.

1.6 Precautions of *Cupping*

① When *cupping*, it is important to choose an appropriate position and a muscular area. Improper posture, uneven bones, and areas with abundant hair are not suitable.

② The sizes of cups is determined by the *cupping* location. The operation must be done rapidly to make the cups tight.

③ Precautions should be taken to avoid scalding the skin.

④ *Cupping* is contraindicated in patients with skin allergies, ulcers, edema and places supplied with large blood vessels. It is also contraindicated for those that have high fevers accompanied by convulsions, and on the abdominal and sacral areas of pregnant women.

一、拔罐

拔罐疗法是排尽罐内空气造成负压，使罐吸附于人体腧穴或某一特定部位的表面，造成局部皮肤充血瘀血而产生刺激，促进局部血管扩张，加快新陈代谢，改善组织微循环，以达到活血止痛的作用的疗法。当肌肉处于紧张状态时，局部血液循环受阻，组织缺血。拔罐，特别是走罐能拉伸肌肉和筋膜，增加血液灌流量，从而使肌肉得到放松，疲劳得到缓解，起到类似推拿的作用。拔罐能使拔罐局部痛阈、耐痛阈显著升高，使患者的疼痛强度明显降低，由疼痛引起的功能障碍明显改善。同时，当拔罐时，局部组织氧和血红蛋白含量增高，可以降低延迟性肌肉酸痛，达到运动防护的作用。

火罐的类型主要有三种：竹罐、玻璃罐和抽气罐。根据实际需要选择不同大小的罐。罐又有不同的大小（图 2-1）。

（一）拔罐的方法

用镊子夹浓度为 95% 的酒精棉球，点燃后在罐内绕 2～3 圈再抽出，并迅速将罐子扣在应拔的部位上。这种方法是常用的拔罐方法，比较安全（图 2-2、图 2-3）。

（二）走罐

在罐口或拔罐部位涂一些油膏等润滑剂，再将罐拔住，然后用右手握住罐子，上下往返推移，直到所拔皮肤潮红、充血或瘀血时，将罐取下。一般用于面积较大、肌肉丰厚的部位，如腰背部、大腿部等。

（三）闪罐

此法是将罐拔住后，又立即取下，再迅速拔住，如此反复多次地拔上起下，起下再拔，至皮肤潮红为止。适用于不宜留罐的患者，如小儿、年轻女性的面部。

（四）起罐

起罐时一般用左手夹住火罐，右手拇指或食指在罐口旁边按压一下，使空气进入罐内，即可将罐取下。罐吸附力过强时，切不可强行上提或旋转提拔，以轻缓为宜。

（五）拔罐的作用和适用症

拔罐法具有通经活络、行气活血、消肿止痛、祛风散寒等作用，其适应范围较为广泛，适用于风湿痹痛、软组织损伤、感冒、咳嗽、哮喘、消化不良、胃脘痛、眩晕、腹痛、痛经、头痛等病症。

（六）拔罐的注意事项

①拔罐时要选择适当体位和肌肉丰满的部位。体位不当或骨骼凹凸不平、毛发较多的部位均不适宜。

②根据所拔部位的面积大小来选择大小适宜的罐。操作时必须动作迅速才能使罐拔紧，吸附有力。

③用火罐时应注意勿灼伤或烫伤皮肤。

④皮肤有过敏、溃疡、水肿和大血管分布部位，不宜拔罐，高热抽搐者和孕妇的腹部、腰骶部，亦不宜拔罐。

2 *Guasha* Therapy

Guasha is an external treatment method under the guidance of the theory of meridian acupoints in TCM, and a special device is used to scrape the surface of the body. Flushing of skin, red multiform, or purplish red or dark red blood spots and blood bubbles appear for promoting blood circulation, preventing and curing diseases. *Guasha* has the effects of clearing the channels and activating collaterals, promoting blood circulation and removing blood stasis, improving microcirculation, and regulating pain. After the injury, the pain causes muscle tension and limited movement, which causes adhesions and scars. *Guasha* therapy can interrupt the pain cycle, which eliminates muscle tension and pain. Modern medicine has proven that after a certain amount of *guasha* treatment, the swelling of the injured area can be reduced and the metabolism of local pain substances can be accelerated. Scraping a certain part of the athlete will increase the skin temperature in the local and remote areas, which can promote blood circulation and improve hypoxia. It can accelerate local tissue metabolism and reduce the accumulation of pain factors to achieve the purpose of relaxing muscles and alleviating delayed muscle soreness.

2.1 *Guasha* Tools

2.1.1 *Guasha* Board

Guasha board is the main *guasha* apparatus. Nowadays, there are *guasha* boards in different shapes and *Guasha* combs with many functions. Normally, there are buffalo horn ware and jade ware. Generally speaking, the *Guasha* board is shaped in a rectangle with smooth edges and cambered corners. For the two long edges of the *Guasha* board, one is thicker while the other is thinner. The thinner edge is for the flat parts of the body, the thicker edge is for healthcare, and the corners are for hollow parts of the body.

2.1.2 Lubricant

The lubricant should have the function of pharmacologic therapy with good permeability and lubricity but without toxic side effects. The actions of the lubricant mainly include heat-clearing and toxicity relieving, blood activating and stasis resolving, inflammation diminishing and pain relieving. Those actions can help dredge meridians, smooth qi and blood, activate blood and resolve stasis. And the lubricant can moisten the skin and protect it. Using the lubricant not only relieves pain and accelerates disease recovery but also protects the skin, prevents infection and makes the *Guasha* safe and effective.

2.2 Operation Methods of *Guasha*

During the treatment, single or combined use of the following methods can be applied according to the different states of illness and the areas to be treated.

2.2.1 Corner Stimulating

Stimulate the points with one of the *gua sha* board's corners perpendicularly. The stimuli should get stronger gradually. End the stimulation after a brief space of time. And then repeat the above-mentioned steps several times. This method is feasible for regions of soft tissue such as Shènyú (BL23), Shénmén (HT7) (Figure 2-4).

2.2.2 Corner Rubbing

Rub the area around the point from upper to lower with one of the *guasha* board's corners at the angle of 45°. This method is always applied at Jiānyú (LI15), Dànzhōng (RN17) (Figure 2-5).

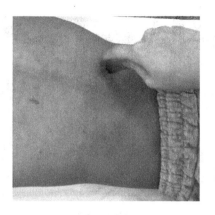
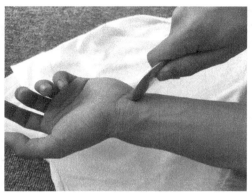

Figure 2-4

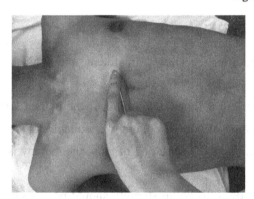
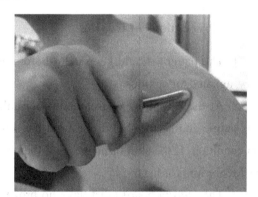

Figure 2-5

2.2.3 Surface Rubbing

When applying this method, 1/3 of the *guasha* board is needed. Form an angle of 30° to 60° between the edge of the board and the skin. The 45° angle is the best option. Apply unidirectional rubbing on the skin by wrist strength. The direction of rubbing is the same as the inclination direction of the board. This method is suitable for the flat parts of the body (Figure 2-6).

2.2.4 Unblocking Meridian

Rub along the meridian trend with the *guasha* board. Long-way rubbing is advisable. Generally, the rubbing starts at the elbow joint (or the knee joint) to the fingertip (or the toe tip). When applying this method, the strength should be well-distributed, mild and sustained. This method is always applied after the *Guasha* treatment is finished or when healthcare is needed to harmonize the meridians to relax the muscles and banish fatigue (Figure 2-7).

The *sha* will appear at the treated area in different colors and shapes due to the different conditions of the patients. The *sha* can be bright red, dark red, purple, patchy or blister in shape and appear dense or dispersed. A sensation of generating heat will occur in the treated area. The *sha* will disappear in 5 to 7 days later.

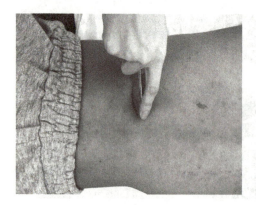

| Figure 2-6 | Figure 2-7 |

2.3 Precautions of *Guasha*

① The patient should keep calm before and after the *guasha* treatment, and avoid being angry, agitated, or anxious.

② At the beginning of treatment, normally 3 to 5 times of rubbing, if the patient's skin turns purple and he (or she) doesn't get the sensation of pain, the therapy is suitable for his (or her) condition. If the skin turns red, and the patient gets the sensation of pain, the therapy is not feasible for him (or her).

③ The *guasha* board must have no broken edges. Rubbing strength should be proper, and the rubbing should be from top to bottom, from middle to side. Lubricant is needed to protect the skin from getting hurt.

④ Ventilation should be kept at the duration of the treatment. Chill should be avoided.

⑤ Posture is determined by the patient's comfort. Generally speaking, there are supine posture, prostrate posture, back-prone posture and prone-torso posture.

⑥ Wipe the lubricant away after the treatment, and apply a little pain-relieving aromatic method (qū fēng yóu) on the purple area. And then let the patient have a rest. If the patient feels depressed or feverish in the chest, then scrape one layer on each side of the third and fourth rib spaces in front of the patient's chest.

二、刮痧

刮痧是在中医经络腧穴理论指导下，用特制的器具，在体表进行相应的手法刮拭，出现皮肤潮红，或红色粟粒状，或紫红色或暗红色的血斑、血泡等出痧变化，达到活血透痧、防治疾病等的一种外治法。刮痧具有疏经活络、活血化瘀、改善微循环、缓解疼痛等作用。运动损伤后由于疼痛导致肌肉紧张活动受限，进而造成粘连、瘢痕。采用刮痧疗法，能够打断疼痛循环，即消除肌肉紧张和疼痛。现代医学证明，损伤局部经一定的刮痧治疗后，能够消肿，加快局部致痛物质的代谢。对运动员某一部位实施刮痧，其局部及远隔部位皮肤温度都有升高，能够促进血液循环，改善缺氧状况。刮痧能够加速局部组织代谢，减少致痛因子的堆积，从而达到放松肌肉、缓解延迟性肌肉酸痛的目的。

（一）刮痧工具

1. 刮痧板

刮痧板是刮痧的主要工具。目前各种形状的刮痧板、集多种功能的刮痧梳相继问世，有水牛角制品，也有玉制品。刮痧板一般加工为长方形，边缘光滑，四角钝圆。刮板的两长边，一边稍厚，一边稍薄。薄面用于人体平坦部位的治疗刮痧，凹陷的厚面适合于按摩保健刮痧，刮板的角适合于人体凹陷部位刮拭。

2. 润滑剂

刮痧治疗的润滑剂应为有药物治疗作用的润滑剂，这种润滑剂应由具有清热解毒、活血化瘀、消炎镇痛作用，同时又没有毒副作用的药物及渗透性强、润滑性好的植物油加工而成。药物的治疗作用有助于疏通经络，宣通气血，活血化瘀。植物油有滋润、保护皮肤的作用。刮痧时涂以润滑剂不但能够减轻疼痛，加速病邪外排，还可保护皮肤，预防感染，使刮痧安全有效。

（二）刮痧的操作方法

在治疗过程中，根据病情和刮拭部位，以下几种刮拭方法可结合起来灵活运用。

1. 点刺法

用刮板角垂直逐渐加力点刺穴位，每次点刺片刻后迅速抬起，多次重复，手法连贯。这种手法适用于无骨骼的软组织处和骨骼凹陷部位，如肾俞穴、神门穴（图 2-4）。

2. 角刮法

使刮板角与穴位呈 45° 角，自上而下刮拭皮肤。这种刮法多用于肩髃穴、膻中穴（图 2-5）。

3. 面刮法

用刮板的三分之一边缘并与皮肤呈 30° ~ 60° 角接触皮肤，以 45° 应用最佳，利用腕力多次向刮板倾斜的同一方向刮拭。这种手法适用于身体比较平坦的部位（图 2-6）。

4. 疏通经络法

依据经络循行走向，用刮板循经刮拭，一次刮拭面宜长，一般从肘/膝关节部位刮至指/趾尖。用力均匀，和缓平稳不间断。常用于治疗刮痧结束后或保健刮痧时对经络进行整体调理，以松弛肌肉，消除疲劳（图 2-7）。

刮痧治疗，由于病情不同，治疗局部可出现不同颜色、不同形态的痧。皮肤表面可出现鲜红色、暗红色、紫色及青黑色的痧，其形态可以是斑块状或水疱状，呈现密集或分散，局部皮肤可有明显发热的感觉。刮出的痧一般 5 至 7 天即可消退。

（三）刮痧的注意事项

①刮痧前后患者不宜发怒、烦躁或忧思焦虑，应保持情绪平静。

②初刮时尝试 3 ~ 5 下即见皮肤青紫而患者并不觉痛者，为本疗法适应证。如见皮肤发红且患者呼痛，则非本法适应证。

③工具必须边缘没有破损，要掌握手法轻重，由上而下、从中至侧顺刮，并时时蘸植物油或水保持润滑，不能干刮，以免刮伤皮肤。

④治疗时，室内要保持空气流通，注意避免受风寒。

⑤刮痧疗法的体位可根据需要以及患者的舒适程度选择，一般有仰卧、俯卧、仰靠、俯靠等。

⑥刮完后应擦干油或水渍，并在青紫处抹少量驱风油，让患者休息片刻。如患者自觉胸中郁闷、心里发热等，再在患者胸前两侧第三、四肋间隙处各刮一道即可。

3 *Tuina* Therapy

When pressure is applied to the human body, stress stimulation will be generated. This stimulation stimulates or suppresses the nervous system through afferent nerve fibers in local muscles, tendons, and deep tissues. Utilizing the neurohumoral regulation mechanism and meridian sensing can alleviate muscle soreness after exercise, accelerate lactic acid metabolism in the muscles, eliminate fatigue, and improve physical function.

3.1 Overview of *Tuina*

3.1.1 Definition of *Tuina*

Tuina, also known as "Anmo" or "Anqiao", guided by the theory of TCM, is a therapeutic method performed by using a manual technique on certain regions or acupoints of the patient. It is one of the most important physical therapeutic methods used in TCM.

3.1.2 Effect of Manipulations in *Tuina*

By stimulating sensitive meridians, different manipulations in Tuina can cause different effects on patients, all of which contribute to activating meridians and collaterals, promoting qi and blood circulation, smoothing joints, and regulating viscera. Excellent Tuina manipulations are the key to achieving clinical efficacy.

3.1.3 Basic Demands of Manipulation in *Tuina*

There are the most crucial requirements: the manipulation should be performed evenly, forcefully, softly, continuously and thoroughly. First, the practitioner should make sure that the movements have a steady and even rhythm to keep pressure in a certain range. Second, during the whole therapeutic process, it is significant to continue powerful force as long as possible.

However, considering different body conditions, injured areas, or the severity of the trauma, individuals deserve various adjustments to their treatments. Besides, manipulation should be performed gently without any rough movements. Only when it is performed gently and lasts a long time can the manipulations enhance the effect into deeper muscles and body structures. The key to success is emphasizing mildness and patience.

3.1.4 Categories of Manipulations in *Tuina*

Manipulations are divided into basic and compound types. With the diversified stimulation, intensity and time, there are various types of basic manipulations, such as pressing manipulation, pushing manipulation, etc. Among the varied categories, the basic manipulations can be separated into the types of swaying, vibrating, percussion, pressing, rubbing and joint movement. Two or more basic techniques with similar kinematic characteristics or the same part of action are combined to form a compound massage technique, such as holding and kneading.

3.2 Commonly Used Basic *Tuina* Techniques

3.2.1 Rolling Manipulation

(1) Definition

Rolling manipulation is to use the back of the hand on the ulnar side as the contact surface, the swing of the forearm drives the flexion and extension of the wrist joint and rolls on the surgical site on the body surface.

(2) Methods for Performing Manipulations

The therapist naturally straightens their thumb, holds an empty fist, and attaches the small finger side of the back of their palm to the treated area while actively swinging their forearm. The synergistic motion of driving significant wrist flexion and extension, as well as forearm rotation, causes the ulnar side of the back of the hand to continuously roll back and forth on the treated area, with a swing frequency of about 120 times per minute (Figure 2-8).

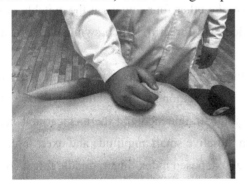 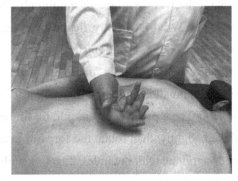

Figure 2-8

3.2.2 Kneading Manipulation

(1) Definition

As one of the commonly-used manipulations, kneading manipulation is to fix the body surface with a certain part of the finger or palm, then knead in circles to rotate the subcutaneous tissues slowly and softly. According to different touching areas, it can be divided into palm-based kneading manipulation, major thenar kneading manipulation, and finger kneading manipulation.

(2) Methods for Performing Manipulations

① Major thenar kneading manipulation: the practitioner should exert force with major thenar and flex the elbow joint slightly to 120°–140°, then use the elbow joint as a pivot and sway the forearm initiatively about 120–160 times per minute with major thenar and make it sway on the affected area (Figure 2-9).

② Palm-based kneading manipulation: the practitioner should flex the fingers naturally and stretch the wrist joint slightly backward to exert force with palm base, and then use the elbow joint as a pivot and sway the forearm initiatively 120–160 times per minute to knead with the palm base on the affected area (Figure 2-10).

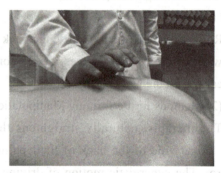

Figure 2-9	Figure 2-10

③ Thumb kneading manipulation: the practitioner should exert force 120–160 times per minute with the whorl surface of the thumb while the other four fingers in the suitable position (Figure 2-11). Wrist is slightly flexed or extended, and forearm, which swings slightly, drives thumb to rotate on the operation site.

④ Index finger kneading manipulation and three fingers kneading manipulation: index finger kneading manipulation and three fingers kneading manipulation means that the practitioner should use the elbow as a pivot with the middle finger joint straightened and the metacarpophalangeal joint flexed slightly, then rotate the forearm in an initiative small amplitude and exert force 120–160 times a minute with the index finger or with a juxtaposed index finger, middle finger and ring finger (Figure 2-12).

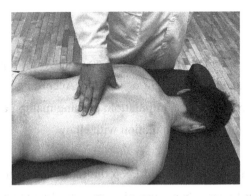

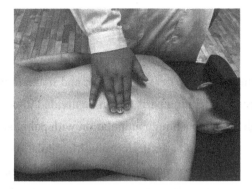

Figure 2-11   Figure 2-12

3.2.3 To-and-Fro Rubbing Manipulation

(1) Definition

To-and-fro rubbing manipulation is to exert force on the affected area with the major thenar, palm base, or minor thenar to perform straight to-and-fro rubbing movement, and penetrate the warm into the deep layer through the body surface. It can be divided into to-and-fro rubbing manipulation with palm, to-and-fro rubbing manipulation with major thenar, and to-and-fro rubbing manipulation with minor thenar.

(2) Methods for Performing Manipulations

Take to-and-fro rubbing manipulation with palm as an example.

To-and-fro rubbing manipulation with palm: the practitioner should keep the palm close to the skin while straightening the wrist joint, then take the shoulder joint as the pivot, and move the upper arm initiatively with the palm rubbing on the body surface to-and-fro along a straight line 100–120 times per minute. It is often applied to the chest, hypochondriac regions and abdomen (Figure 2-13).

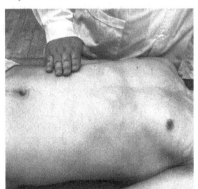

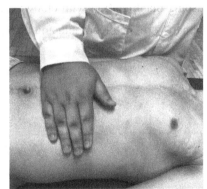

Figure 2-13

3.2.4 Pushing Manipulation

(1) Definition

Pushing manipulation is to exert force on the affected area or certain acupoint with fingers, palms or other parts of the body, and make movement in a straight or arc line. According to the different operating parts, it can be divided into three kinds of manipulation: pushing manipulation with thumb, pushing manipulation with palm, and pushing manipulation with elbow.

(2) Methods for Performing Manipulations

① Pushing manipulation with thumb: the practitioner should keep the thumb close to the body surface, which is supported by the other four fingers, then flex and extend the elbow to bring the thumb to push slowly in a one-way direction along the meridian or along the direction of the muscular fiber. Repeat the manipulation 5 to 15 times continuously (Figure 2-14).

Figure 2-14

② Pushing manipulation with palm: the practitioner should press on the body surface with palm and exert force with the palm base (or the whole palm), then flex and extend the elbow to push the palm slowly along a certain direction. Repeat the manipulation 5 to 15 times continuously (Figure 2-15).

③ Pushing manipulation with elbow: the practitioner should flex the elbow and exert force on a certain part with the olecranon, and then push slowly along the direction of muscular fiber in a straight line.

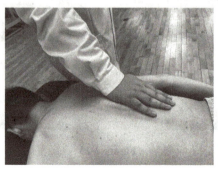

Figure 2-15

3.2.5 Pressing Manipulation

(1) Definition

Pressing Manipulation is to press a certain acupoint or part of the body surface with a finger or palm and press down and release rhythmically.

(2) Methods for Performing Manipulations

When performing palm pressing manipulation, the practitioner should straighten the palm. If the force of one palm is not enough, the other palm can be overlapped on it and pressed (Figure 2-16).

3.2.6 Point-pressing Manipulation

(1) Definition

Point-pressing manipulation is to press a certain point or site at the point of the finger end or joint protrusion, which can be divided into point-pressing manipulation with a finger and point-pressing manipulation with elbow.

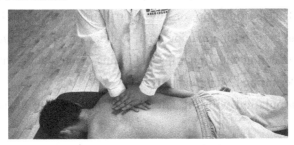

Figure 2-16

(2) Methods for Performing Manipulations

① When performing point-pressing manipulation with the finger, the practitioners should make a hollow fist, straighten the thumb and make it close to the middle interphalangeal joint of the index finger, the distal segment of the index finger overlaps with the middle finger to assist, and then exert a steady force from light to heavy on a certain acupoint or part of the body with the tip of the thumb (Figure 2- 17).

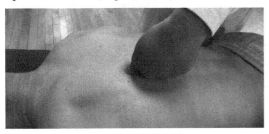

Figure 2-17

Figure 2-18

② When performing point-pressing manipulation with the elbow, the practitioner bends the elbow, applies force to the ulnar eminence, leans forward slightly, transfers the weight of the upper body through the shoulder joint and upper arm to the elbow, and continues to point pressure. (Figure 2-18).

3.2.7 Grasping Manipulation

(1) Definition

Grasping manipulation is to exert force symmetrically with the thumb and the other four fingers to lift and pinch the extremities or the muscle and tendons.

(2) Methods for Performing Manipulations

First, the performer needs to relax the wrist joint and clamp the operated part tightly with the thumb and the whorl surface of the other four fingers. Then pinch the muscle and tendon and perform alternating light and heavy continuous lifting and pinching movements (Figure 2-19).

3.2.8 Hitting Manipulation

(1) Definition

Hitting manipulation is to hit the operated part rhythmically with the palm base, the minor thenar, the back of a fist, the fingertip, or a mulberry stick, which can be divided into hitting manipulation with palm base, hitting manipulation with lateral side of palm, hitting manipulation with a fist, hitting manipulation with fingertips and hitting manipulation with a stick.

(2) Methods for Performing Manipulations

Take hitting manipulation with the lateral side of palm and hitting manipulation with fingertips as examples.

① Hitting manipulation with the lateral side of palm: when performing the manipulation, the practitioner should stretch the fingers naturally and the wrist joint slightly backward, and then hit the body surface with the minor thenar of one or both palms alternately (Figure 2-20).

② Hitting manipulation with fingertips: when performing the manipulation, the practitioner should hit the treated part with the tips of the fingers which are closing up like a plum blossom or an open claw (Figure 2-21).

| Figure 2-19 | Figure 2-20 |

Figure 2-21

3.2.9 Rotating Manipulation

(1) Definition

It is a passive movement performed within the range of the joint, called rotating manipulation. It is a commonly used manipulation, and there are different methods to perform it on different parts.

(2) Methods for Performing Manipulations

Shoulder-rotating manipulation by supporting the elbow: the patient takes a sitting position and relaxes his shoulders and flexes his elbow. When performing this manipulation, the athletic trainer should stand by the side of the patient, with the upper body inclining forward slightly, then fix the upper part of the patient's shoulder blade with one hand, and hold the affected elbow with the other hand, rotating clockwise or counterclockwise for several times (Figure 2-22).

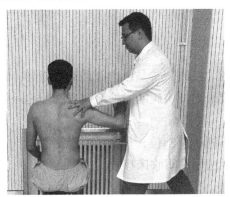

Figure 2-22

3.2.10 Pulling-extending Manipulation

(1) Definition

Pulling-extending manipulation or traction manipulation means to fixate one end of a joint or an extremity, pull and extend the other to enlarge the joint space with constant force, which can be applied to different joints.

(2) Methods for performing manipulations

Pulling-extending manipulation of the neck in a supine position: the patient takes a supine position. When performing this manipulation, the athletic trainer sits in front of the patient's head with one hand holding the patient's occiput and the other holding the patient's chin, then the athletic trainer should pull and extend the neck along the direction of a longitudinal axis of the cervical vertebrae with both hands simultaneously (Figure 2-23).

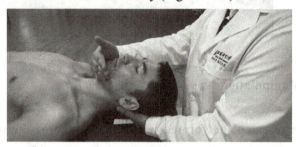

Figure 2-23

三、推拿手法

推拿使力作用于人体，产生压力刺激，这种刺激通过局部肌肉、肌腱和深层组织的感受器传入神经纤维活动，对神经系统起兴奋或抑制作用，并且通过神经—体液调节机制和经络的传感，减轻运动后肌肉酸痛，加速肌肉中的乳酸代谢，消除疲劳，提高身体机能。

（一）推拿概述

1. 推拿的定义

推拿，又称"按摩"或"按跷"，是以中医理论为指导，治疗师运用推拿手法作用于患者体表的特定部位或穴位来治疗疾病的一种治疗方法，是一种重要的中医疗法。

2. 推拿治疗的作用

推拿手法刺激机体的不同敏感部位，具有疏通经络、行气活血、滑利关节、调节脏腑功能等作用。良好的推拿手法是取得临床疗效的关键。

3. 推拿手法的基本要求

均匀、有力、柔和、持久、深透是推拿手法的基本要求。所谓"均匀"，是要求手法动作有节奏性，速度、压力在一定范围内维持恒定；"有力"，是要求手法必须具有恰当的力量，力量的大小应根据病人的体质、病情和治疗部位的不同进行调整，切忌使用拙力、暴力；"柔和"，是要求手法轻柔缓和，不能生硬粗暴；"持久"，是要求手法操作能持续一定的时间，且动作规范不变形；"深透"，是指手法作用达到组织深层。只有符合持久、有力、均匀、柔和要求的手法才能深透。成功的手法应以柔为先、和为贵。

4. 推拿手法的分类

推拿手法分为基本手法和复式手法。由于刺激方式、强度、时间的不同，形成了许多操作方法不同的基本手法，如按法、推法等。根据手法动作形态推拿基本手法可分为摆动类、振动类、叩击类、按压类、摩擦类、活动关节类。两个或两个以上运动学特征相近或作用部位相同的基本手法结合起来操作，构成复式推拿手法，如拿揉法。

（二）常用推拿基本手法

1. 滚法

（1）定义

以尺侧手背为接触面，前臂摆动带动腕关节屈伸，在体表施术部位滚动，称为滚法。

（2）操作方法

治疗师拇指自然伸直，手握空拳，以手掌背部小指侧部分贴附于治疗部位上，前臂主动摆动，带动腕关节较大幅度的屈伸和前臂旋转的协同运动，使手背尺侧在治疗部位上持续不断地来回滚动，频率为每分钟 120 次左右（图 2-8）。

2. 揉法

（1）定义

以指、掌的某一部位着力吸定于体表上，带动该处的皮下组织做轻柔缓和的环旋揉动，称为揉法，是推拿常用手法之一。根据操作时接触面的不同可分为大鱼际揉法、掌根揉法和指揉法。

（2）操作方法

①大鱼际揉法：治疗师以手掌大鱼际部着力，肘关节微屈 120°～140°，以肘关节为支点，前臂主动摆动，带动大鱼际在治疗部位揉动频率为每分钟 120～160 次（图 2-9）。

②掌根揉法：治疗师以掌根部分着力，腕关节略背伸，肘关节微屈作为支点，前臂主动摆动，带动掌根在治疗部位揉动，频率为每分钟 120～160 次（图 2-10）。

③拇指揉法：以拇指罗纹面着力，其余手指扶持于合适部位（图 2-11），腕关节微屈或伸直，前臂做小幅度摆动，带动拇指在施术部位上做环转运动，频率为每分钟 120～160 次。

④食指揉法和三指揉法：以食指或食指、中指、无名指并拢做指揉法称为食指揉法或三指揉法以食指或食指、中指、无名指罗纹面着力，指间关节伸直。掌指关节微屈，以肘关节为支点，前臂做小幅度主动运动，带动食指或食指、中指、无名指罗纹面在施术部位做环转运动，频率为每分钟 120～160 次（图 2-12）。

3. 擦法

（1）定义

治疗师以手掌的大鱼际、掌根或小鱼际着力于施术部位，做直线往返摩擦运动，使摩擦产生的热量透过体表渗透至深层，称为擦法。可分为掌擦法、大鱼际擦法和小鱼际擦法。

（2）操作方法

以掌擦法为例说明。

掌擦法：治疗师以手掌掌面紧贴皮肤，腕关节平直，以肩关节为支点，上臂做主动运动，使手掌掌面在体表做直线往返的摩擦运动。频率为每分钟 100～120 次，多用于胸胁及腹部（图2-13）。

4. 推法

（1）定义

用指掌或其他部位着力于人体一定部位或穴位上，做单方向直线或弧线移动，则称为推法。推法根据着力部位的不同，有拇指推法、掌推法和肘推法等。

（2）操作方法

①拇指推法：治疗师用拇指面着力紧贴体表，其余四指分开助力，肘关节屈伸带动拇指按经络循行或肌纤维平行方向作单方向沉缓推动，连续操作5～15遍（图2-14）。

②掌推法：治疗师用手掌按于体表，以掌根部（或全掌）为着力点，肘关节屈伸带动手掌向一定方向沉缓推动，连续操作5～15遍（图2-15）。

③肘推法：治疗师屈肘，以肘尖尺骨鹰嘴部着力于一定部位，沿肌纤维走行方向做直线缓慢的推动。

5. 按法

（1）定义

用手指或手掌面着力于体表特定的穴位或部位上，有节奏地一起一落按下，称为按法。

（2）操作方法

掌按法用手掌面按压体表，单手力量不足时，可用双手掌重叠按压（图2-16）。

6. 点法

（1）定义

以指端或关节突起部点压一定的穴位或部位，称为点法，临床上可分为指点法和肘点法。

（2）操作方法

①指点法：治疗师手握空拳，拇指伸直并靠近食指中节，以拇指端着力，食指末节叠压于中指助力，由轻而重，平稳施力，按压一定的穴位或部位（图2-17）。

②肘点法：治疗师屈肘，以尺骨鹰嘴突起部着力，身体略前倾，将身体上半身的重量通过肩关节、上臂传递至肘部，持续点压（图2-18）。

7. 拿法

（1）定义

用拇指与其他四指相对用力，提捏肢体或肌筋，称之为拿法。

（2）操作方法

治疗师腕关节放松，以拇指与食、中指或其余手指的罗纹面相对用力夹紧治疗部位，将肌筋捏起，并做轻重交替而连续的提捏动作（图2-19）。

8. 击法

（1）定义

用掌根、掌侧小鱼际、拳背、指尖或桑枝棒等有节奏地击打治疗部位，称为击法。分掌根击法、侧击法、拳击法、指尖击法和棒击法。

（2）操作方法

以侧击法、指尖击法为例说明。

①侧击法：手指自然伸直，腕关节略背伸，以手掌小鱼际部击打体表，可双手交替操作（图2-20）。

②指尖击法：五指指端合拢呈梅花状或散开呈爪状，轻快敲击治疗部位（图2-21）。

9. 摇法

（1）定义

在关节的生理活动范围内做关节的被动环形运动的手法，称为摇法。摇法是推拿常用手法之一，用于不同部位的摇法有着不同的操作方法。

（2）操作方法

托肘摇肩法：患者坐位，肩部放松，屈肘，治疗师站于侧方，取弓步势，上身略前屈，用一只手扶住患者肩胛骨上部，使其固定，另一只手托起患肢肘部，顺时针或逆时针方向各环转数次（图2-22）。

10. 拔伸法

（1）定义

固定肢体或关节的一端，持续用力地牵拉肢体或关节的另一端，使关节的间隙拉开，称为拔伸法，又称牵引法，可用于不同的关节部位。

（2）操作方法

颈部仰卧位拔伸法：患者取仰卧位，治疗师坐凳于其头前端，一只手置头颈下扶托头枕后部，另一只手掌托下颏部，两手协调用力，沿颈椎纵轴方向拔伸（图2-23）。

4 *Daoyin* Therapy

Dynamic stretching and functional training play an important role in athletic training. The knowledge in this field also has the rich theory and the long-standing practice application in Chinese traditional athletic training, this is the *daoyin* therapy of Chinese traditional sports.

Daoyin is a kind of exercise therapy, through the adjustment of breathing to make the viscera and meridian of the respiratory smooth, as well as body movement more flexible and soft as a result of body movement. *Daoyin* therapy focuses on the movement of the body, supplemented by the combination of respiration and mind, to achieve the effect of adjusting body posture, adjusting respiration, and adjusting mind.

Among the techniques of modern athletic training, many training techniques can be applied to enhance muscle strength, flexibility and neuromuscular control ability in sports protection and injury rehabilitation. In TCM, classical *daoyin* therapy also has the same effect. Taking the dynamic stretching for instance. Dynamic stretching is one of the main contents of preparation activities before exercise, which can activate the ability to stabilize the small muscle groups of joints, enhance the stability of joints during exercise, and prevent sports injuries. *Daoyin* therapy and dynamic stretching have the same effect. Its movements are slow and soft, and continuous stretching achieves the effect of "stretching the muscles and fascia and enhancing bone density", and can increase the temperature of the tissue, maintain excitability of the nervous system, and increase the expressive power of the athletic sports.

四、导引疗法

动态牵拉和功能训练在运动防护中占有重要的地位。该领域的知识在我国传统的运动防护中也有丰富的理论和悠久的实践应用，这就是我国民族传统体育运动中的导引疗法。

导引即"导气令和""引体令柔"，是运动疗法的一种，即通过调整呼吸使脏腑经络之气和顺，通过肢体运动使人体动作灵活柔和。导引是以自身肢体运动为主，并辅以呼吸、意念，三者相结合的运动形式，来达到调身、调息、调心的作用。

在现代运动防护的技术中，通过主动运动增强肌肉力量、柔韧性及神经肌肉控制能力是运动防护和损伤康复的重要内容。在中医运动防护技术中，经典的导引疗法也有同样的作用。如动态拉伸是运动之前准备活动的主要内容之一，可以激活关节周围小肌群，以增强运动过程中各关节的稳定性，预防运动损伤。导引疗法与动态拉伸有异曲同工之效，其动作缓慢柔和，持续牵拉以达到"抻筋拔骨"的作用，并且可以提高肌肉组织的温度，保持神经系统兴奋性，提高运动表现力。

Summary

1. TCM therapies are widely used in the prevention and treatment of sports fatigue and sports injuries.

2. *Cupping* allows the negative pressure inside the cup to be adsorbed on the surface of the body or the acupoints to the skin congestion or congestion, and adjust the body function to prevent disease.

3. *Guasha* in the treatment of bone and joint diseases or the acute phase can stimulate qi and blood circulation, and make qi and blood run smoothly to achieve the effect of spasm and pain relief.

4. Before exercise, *Tuina* can reduce the stickiness between muscle tissues by rolling manipulation, kneading manipulation, to-and-fro rubbing manipulation, and pushing manipulation, etc. And after exercise, relax the muscles by grasping manipulation, pressing manipulation and hitting manipulation, etc. to prevent sports injuries.

5. *Daoyin* therapy is a classic dynamic stretch and functional training.

Review Questions

1. What are the functions and indications of *cupping*?

2. What are the precautions for *Guasha*?

3. What are the categories of manipulations in *Tuina*?

4. Briefly describe the definition, operation method, essentials for performing manipulations, and precautions of Pressing Manipulation.

小结

1. 中医传统治疗技术被广泛应用于预防和治疗运动性疲劳、运动损伤防护等领域。

2. 拔罐使罐内产生负压，使之吸附于体表或腧穴上，使局部皮肤充血或淤血，从而调整机体功能以防治疾病。

3. 刮痧在骨关节疾病或急性期的治疗中可以激发经气、行气活血，使气血运行通畅来达到解痉止痛的作用。

4. 在运动之前可以通过滚、揉、擦、推等推拿手法减少肌肉组织之间的粘滞性，在运动后通过拿、按、击等手法对肌肉进行放松以此来预防运动损伤的产生。

5. 中国传统导引疗法是经典的动态牵拉和功能训练的方法。

复习题

1. 拔罐的作用和适应症有哪些?

2. 刮痧的注意事项有哪些?

3. 推拿手法的分类有哪些?

4. 简述按法的定义、操作方法、动作要领以及注意事项。

References
参考文献

[1] ANDERSON K. Evaluation and treatment of distal clavicle fractures [J]. Clinics in sports medicine, 2003, 22(2): 319-326.

[2] ANDERSON M, BARNUM M. Foundations of athletic training: prevention, assessment, and management [M]. Baltimore: Lippincott Williams & Wilkins, 2021.

[3] ANTOSH I J, TOKISH J M, OWENS B D. Posterior shoulder instability: current surgical management [J]. Sports health, 2016, 8(6): 520-526.

[4] ARTUS M, HOLT T A, REES J. The painful shoulder: an update on assessment, treatment, and referral [J]. British journal of general practice, 2014, 64(626): e593-e595.

[5] CARPINTERO P, CAEIRO J R, CARPINTERO R, et al. Complications of hip fractures: a review [J]. World journal of orthopedics, 2014, 5(4): 402.

[6] CARTWRIGHT L, PITNEY W. Fundamentals of athletic training [M]. 3rd ed. Illionois: Human Kinetics, 2011.

[7] CHARLTON P C, DREW M K, MENTIPLAY B F, et al. Exercise interventions for the prevention and treatment of groin pain and injury in athletes: a critical and systematic review [J]. Sports medicine, 2017, 47(10): 2011-2026.

[8] CHARALAMBOUS C P. The shoulder made easy[M]. Cham: Springer, 2019.

[9] CHRISTIANSEN D H, MQLLER A D, VESTERGAARD J M, et al. The scapular dyskinesis test: reliability, agreement, and predictive value in patients with subacromial impingement syndrome [J]. Journal of hand therapy, 2017, 30(2): 208-213.

[10] CUTTS S, PREMPEH M, DREW S. Anterior shoulder dislocation [J]. The annals of the Royal College of Surgeons of England, 2009, 91(1): 2-7.

[11] DAVID J. MAGEE. 骨骼检查评估 [M]. 4 版 . 罗卓荆译 . 北京：人民军医出版社, 2007.

[12] DENG S, CHEN K, MA Y, et al. The influence of test positions on clinical assessment for scapular dyskinesis [J]. American journal of physical medicine and rehabilitation, 2017,

9(8): 761-766.

[13] DESSUREAULT-DOBER I, BRONCHTI G, BUSSIERES A. Diagnostic accuracy of clinical tests for neurogenic and vascular thoracic outlet syndrome: a systematic review [J]. Journal of manipulative and physiological therapeutics, 2018, 41(9): 789-799.

[14] DUMONT G D, RUSSELL R D, ROBERTSON W J. Anterior shoulder instability: a review of pathoanatomy, diagnosis and treatment [J]. Current reviews in musculoskeletal medicine, 2011, 4(4): 200-207.

[15] ELLENBECKER T S, COOLS A. Rehabilitation of shoulder impingement syndrome and rotator cuff injuries: an evidence-based review [J]. British journal of sports medicine, 2010, 44(5): 319-327.

[16] ESTEVE E, RATHLEFF M S, BAGUR-CALAFAT C, et al. Prevention of groin injuries in sports: a systematic review with meta-analysis of randomised controlled trials [J]. British journal of sports medicine, 2015, 49(12): 785-791.

[17] FERRANTE M A. The thoracic outlet syndromes [J]. Muscle and nerve, 2012, 45(6): 780-795.

[18] HIXSON K M, HORRIS H B, MCLEOD T C V, et al. The diagnostic accuracy of clinical diagnostic tests for thoracic outlet syndrome [J]. Journal of sport rehabilitation, 2017, 26(5): 459-465.

[19] HSU J E, ANAKWENZE O A, WARRENDER W J, et al. Current review of adhesive capsulitis [J]. Journal of shoulder and elbow surgery, 2011, 20(3): 502-514.

[20] HUANG J H, ZAGER E L. Thoracic outlet syndrome [J]. Neurosurgery, 2004, 55(4): 897-903.

[21] HUGHES P C, TAYLOR N F, GREEN R A. Most clinical tests cannot accurately diagnose rotator cuff pathology: a systematic review [J]. Australian journal of physiotherapy, 2008, 54(3): 159-170.

[22] HURSCHLER C, WÜLKER N, WINDHAGEN H, et al. Evaluation of the lag sign tests for external rotator function of the shoulder [J]. Journal of shoulder and elbow surgery, 2004, 13(3): 298-304.

[23] JO M J, GARDNER M J. Proximal humerus fractures [J]. Current reviews in Musculoskeletal Medicine, 2012, 5(3): 192-198.

[24] JONES M R, PRABHAKAR A, VISWANATH O, et al. Thoracic outlet syndrome: a comprehensive review of pathophysiology, diagnosis, and treatment [J]. Pain and therapy, 2019, 8(1): 5-18.

[25] KIBLER W B, LUDEWIG P M, MCCLURE P W, et al. Clinical implications of scapular dyskinesis in shoulder injury: the 2013 consensus statement from the 'Scapular Summit' [J]. British journal of sports medicine, 2013, 47(14): 877-885.

［26］KIBLER W B, MCMULLEN J, UHL T I M. Shoulder rehabilitation strategies, guidelines, and practice [J]. Orthopedic clinics, 2001, 32(3): 527-538.

［27］KING J J, WRIGHT T W. Physical examination of the shoulder [J]. The journal of hand surgery, 2014, 39(10): 2103-2112.

［28］KOESTER M C, GEORGE M S, KUHN J E. Shoulder impingement syndrome [J]. The American journal of medicine, 2005, 118(5): 452-455.

［29］LANGE T, STRUYF F, SCHMITT J, et al. The reliability of physical examination tests for the clinical assessment of scapular dyskinesis in subjects with shoulder complaints: a systematic review [J]. Physical therapy in sport, 2017, 26: 64-89.

［30］LARSSON S. Clavicula fractures: considerations when plating [J]. Injury, 2018, 49: S24-S28.

［31］MACDONALD P B, CLARK P, SUTHERLAND K. An analysis of the diagnostic accuracy of the Hawkins and Neer subacromial impingement signs [J]. Journal of shoulder and elbow surgery, 2000, 9(4): 299-301.

［32］MACHOTKA Z, KUMAR S, PERRATON L G. A systematic review of the literature on the effectiveness of exercise therapy for groin pain in athletes [J]. BMC Sports Science, medicine and rehabilitation, 2009, 1(1): 1-10.

［33］MICHEO W. 康复医学速查丛书：肌肉骨骼 [M]. 周谋望，陈仲强，刘楠，译. 济南：山东科学技术出版社，2014.

［34］MAFFEY L, EMERY C. What are the risk factors for groin strain injury in sport? [J]. Sports medicine, 2007, 37(10): 881-894.

［35］PRENTICE W E, ARNHEIM D. Principles of athletic training: a competency-based approach [M]. New York: McGraw-Hill, 2011.

［36］PROVENCHER C D R M T, BHATIA S, GHODADRA N S, et al. Recurrent shoulder instability: current concepts for evaluation and management of glenoid bone loss [J]. The journal of bone and joint surgery, 2010, 92(Supplement 2): 133-151.

［37］RIVARA F P, GROSSMAN D C, CUMMINGS P. Injury prevention [J]. New England journal of Medicine, 1997, 337(9): 613-618.

［38］RUBIN B D, KIBLER W B. Fundamental principles of shoulder rehabilitation: conservative to postoperative management [J]. Arthroscopy, 2002, 18(9): 29-39.

［39］SEDAGHATI P, ALIZADEH M H, SHIRZAD E, et al. Review of sport-induced groin injuries [J]. Trauma monthly, 2013, 18(3): 107.

［40］SHORT S M, MACDONALD C W, STRACK D. Hip and groin injury prevention in elite athletes and team sport–current challenges and opportunities [J]. International journal of sports physiotherapy, 2021, 16(1): 270.

［41］SKELTON D A, BEYER N. Exercise and injury prevention in older people [J].

Scandinavian journal of medicine and science in sports, 2003, 13(1): 77-85.

[42] SLOBOGEAN G P, JOHAL H, LEFAIVRE K A, et al. A scoping review of the proximal humerus fracture literature [J]. BMC musculoskeletal disorders, 2015, 16(1): 1-10.

[43] SOMERVILLE L E, WILLITS K, JOHNSON A M, et al. Clinical assessment of physical examination maneuvers for rotator cuff lesions [J]. The American journal of sports Medicine, 2014, 42(8): 1911-1919.

[44] STRUYF F, NIJS J, MOTTRAM S, et al. Clinical assessment of the scapula: a review of the literature [J]. British journal of sports medicine, 2014, 48(11): 883-890.

[45] UHL T L, KIBLER W B, GECEWICH B, et al. Evaluation of clinical assessment methods for scapular dyskinesis [J]. Arthroscopy, 2009, 25(11): 1240-1248.

[46] VEMURI C, MCLAUGHLIN L N, ABUIRQEBA A A, et al. Clinical presentation and management of arterial thoracic outlet syndrome [J]. Journal of vascular surgery, 2017, 65(5): 1429-1439.

[47] WALCH G, BOULAHIA A, CALDERONE S, et al. The 'dropping' and 'hornblower's' signs in evaluation of rotator-cuff tears [J]. Journal of bone and joint surgery (British volume), 1998, 80(4): 624-628.

[48] WHITTAKER J L, SMALL C, MAFFEY L, et al. Risk factors for groin injury in sport: an updated systematic review [J]. British journal of sports medicine, 2015, 49(12): 803-809.

[49] WRIGHT A A, WASSINGER C A, FRANK M, et al. Diagnostic accuracy of scapular physical examination tests for shoulder disorders: a systematic review [J]. British journal of sports medicine, 2013, 47(14): 886-892.

[50] 蔡亚飞, 洪毅, 王方永, 等. 挥鞭样损伤的研究进展 [J]. 中国康复理论与实践, 2019, 25(3): 324-329.

[51] 贾连顺. 对过伸性颈脊髓损伤的再认识 [J]. 中华外科杂志, 2007, 45(6): 363-365.

[52] 李卫国, 邱勇. 休门氏病自然史及治疗研究进展 [J]. 中国骨肿瘤骨病, 2008(2): 111-115.

[53] 罗阿尔·贝尔, 斯韦内. 迈赫伦. 运动损伤临床指南 [M]. 高崇玄, 译. 北京: 人民体育出版社, 2007.

[54] 周天健, 李建军. 脊柱脊髓损伤现代康复与治疗 [M]. 北京: 人民卫生出版社, 2006.